# WHISKY
## *Magazine*

# TASTINGS

## The First 10 Years

# PARAGRAPH PUBLISHING

Published by

**Paragraph Publishing Ltd**
St Faiths House, Mountergate, Norwich, NR1 1PY
www.paragraphpublishing.com

© Paragraph Publishing Ltd

ISBN: 978-1-903872-23-9

A catalogue record for this book is available from the British Library.

Printed in India on behalf JFDI Print Services Ltd

*Acknowledgements:* The tasters and whisky producers
*Publisher:* Damian Riley-Smith
*Editor:* Rob Allanson
*Design:* Paul Beevis
*Publishing Consultant:* Navigator Guides (www.navigatorguides.com)
*Typeset:* Anthony Rowe Ltd

# TASTINGS

## The First 10 Years

## Contents

# Introduction

All great ideas have to have a starting point, a genesis, the moment of conception. Whether this is written on the back of a piece of paper during a discussion in a bar and considered coolly in the light of all the pertinent facts, there is always such a point in time.

*Whisky Magazine* started with the former. A discussion between its founders 10 years ago with the notion to create a magazine that celebrated the wide world of whiskies. Now published in four languages, English, French, Japanese and Spanish, *Whisky Magazine* has established itself as the magazine to turn to for information, education and above all authority.

Many readers have asked us to bring the tastings together in the ultimate tastings book, so here it is. The book forms part of the 10th anniversary of *Whisky Magazine*. In that time the rise of the single malt, blended malt and blends phenomenon has been something no one could have predicted. Aficionados and beginners alike have proved hungry for knowledge and experiences to bring them closer to their favourite drinks, and *Whisky Magazine* has been at the forefront of this.

Similarly no one, other than those championing the cause, would have seen the meteoric rise of bourbon and indeed Japanese whisky, which are now taking the world by storm.

Entwined in this increased interest in everything whisky, the cocktail scene has seen some innovative uses of spirits as the distilling world has become smaller.

Out of *Whisky Magazine* evolved the tastings pages, which review all the latest releases and put them under the scrutiny of some of the best noses in the business. In 10 years we have featured some of the best tasters in the business. Normally there are three tasters in each magazine.

Over the years the pages have featured some of the best whiskies available in the market place reviewed by some of the giants of whisky writing. Some of these whiskies are no longer available, the demand on stock has increased running some barrels dry, but what has lasted is the tasters' opinions.

It is this unbiased, independent stand point, not being afraid to pull the punches if needs be, that has made the tastings pages some of the most influential and widely read pages.

*Whisky Magazine* has constantly supported the independent bottling sector, allowing readers to explore different

# Introduction

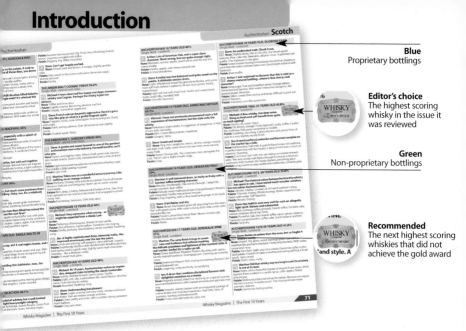

**Blue**
Proprietary bottlings

**Editor's choice**
The highest scoring whisky in the issue it was reviewed

**Green**
Non-proprietary bottlings

**Recommended**
The next highest scoring whiskies that did not achieve the gold award

bottlings from their favourite distilleries. To this end you will find nearly every tasting ever published in the last 10 years, uncut and organised in a manner where you can find what you want when you want it.

Where the same whisky has been reviewed more than twice over time by the same tasters we have removed the earliest tasting. Where they have been tasted by different tasters, we have left them all in. Occasionally there are notes where just one taster has tasted the whisky.

One of the most interesting parts of the book is looking at how distilleries, particularly in Scotland, and the various whisky categories have gone through several changes in the time *Whisky Magazine* has been bringing readers all the best bottlings from the industry.

Looking back you can see how some distilleries have risen to prominence, while others have been closed, and how some styles have experienced a resurgence, for instance rye and Irish whiskey.

The tastings book is laid out in easy to navigate sections with each geographical area containing whiskies according to its style, all sorted alphabetically.

Whiskies that appear with blue headings are proprietary bottlings whereas those in green represent offerings from the independent bottling companies.

Every year we also hold a competition involving all the world whiskies. This has been done under several titles but is now the World Whiskies Awards and selects the best whisky in the world from all those on the market.

Some of the peated whiskes were tasted together to look at the effect of peat and how it develops over the years. As a result they were scored differently to the usual tastings, but were included for posterity. Our tasters are listed below, and we hope you enjoy their findings as much as they enjoyed writing them.

## TASTERS

| | |
|---|---|
| Owen Barstow | Peter Mulryan |
| Dave Broom | Jim Murray |
| Ian Buxton | Martine Nouet |
| Michael Jackson | Paul Pacult |
| Charles MacLean | David Robertson |
| Doug McIvor | Dominic Roskrow |
| Marcin Miller | Gavin D. Smith |
| Arthur Motley | Ian Wisniewski |

**Clockwize from top left:** Cadenhead's boxes; The picturesque Strathisla; The view from Ben More on Mull across to Ulva; A Maker's Mark fermenter; Inside a bourbon warehouse

# American

## America

Looking through the tastings for American whiskey it is easy to see that the American spirit has been born again.

One of the pleasing things to see is that rye whiskey is experiencing a resurgence; brands such as Thomas Handy, Sazerac, Van Winkle Family Reserve and Rittenhouse have become the darling of bartenders, and smaller brands such as Michter's and Templeton's Rye have spearheaded a rekindling of joy in this category.

Whiskey came to the American continent with Irish and Scottish immigrants. As the groups settled, they were forced to adapt in many ways including the use of new raw materials in their surroundings such as corn and rye.

Today there are few similarities between American whiskey and its cousins the Scotch and Irish whiskies.

For example, no smoke is used to dry the corn, rye or wheat, which are used in American whiskey. Also mashbills in the US feature a higher percentage of corn and rye than other whiskies and distillers use backset from the previous distillation in the next mash – hence sour mashing.

It must also be remembered that most American whiskies come off the still at a low distillate strength and are then put into new charred barrels to mature.

Because of this, American whiskey often has a fuller, stronger and sweeter taste than most of its European counterparts.

Kentucky is still the heartland of bourbon, with all the big names, Brown Forman, Buffalo Trace, Heaven Hill, Beam, Wild Turkey and Woodford Reserve having a distillery there.

Because of this fact many people believe bourbon can only be made in Kentucky, but in fact bourbon may be produced in any state. The only prerequisites are that it must be made in the US, contain at least 51 per cent corn and that it must be matured for a minimum of two years in new, charred oak barrels.

South of Kentucky, the behemoth of Jack Daniel's holds its sway across the globe and the smaller distillery of George Dickel sits a few miles away.

Across the other side of the country, the Anchor Distilling Company embodies America's new found joy of small craft distillers. The company produces bourbon and rye in very small batches. Now small outfits are following suit and springing up across the States making quality spirit, such as Clear Creek in Oregon, the West Virginia Distilling Company and Stranahan's Colorado Whiskey.

As with the Scotch industry many of the US distillers are expanding to meet the demand of a world which is waking up to the delights of American whiskey.

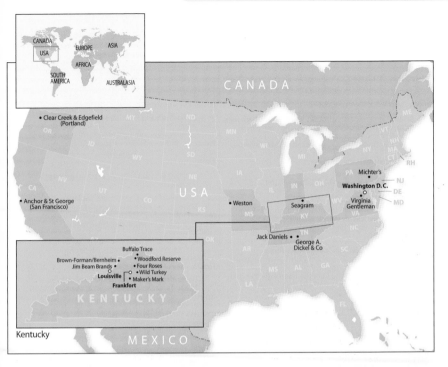

Kentucky

**Clockwise from top left:** The George Dickel homestead; Inside a Maker's Mark rickhouse; Honouring Booker Noe at the Jim Beam Distillery; Barrels lined up at Woodford Reserve

## DID YOU KNOW...

- Maker's Mark, est. 1805 is America's oldest working distillery on the same site
- Jim Beam is the biggest selling bourbon
- Early distilling techniques can be seen at Mount Vernon distillery once owned by George Washington and lovingly recreated in 2003
- Buffalo Trace distillery is named after an ancient buffalo crossing
- Four Roses is the only company that uses five different yeasts and two mashbills

## 80 STRONG KENTUCKY STRAIGHT BOURBON 40%
Bourbon - Kentucky

**7½ Dave:** All very light and clean and highly quaffable, but just lacks a little mid-palate depth.
**Nose:** Aromatic, with a bruised mint/peppermint note. Musky, heading towards camphor. Rose petals and, with water, a toasty/sawdust note.
**Palate:** A hint of soapiness, then comes vanilla and spices. Water softens things but it retains a sparkling sweet zestiness. Clean and fragrant.
**Finish:** Sweet wood sugars. Raspberry.

**7½ Arthur:** Demanded ice, a hot day and a sizzling barbecue.
**Nose:** Vanilla, iced gems, wet clay, parma violets. Then a Radox pine character.
**Palate:** Banana chews, vanilla in waves and a grainy, popcorn character.
**Finish:** Astringent and bitter, drying oak.

## AMERICAN BIKER SOUR MASH BOURBON, 6 YEARS OLD 43%
Bourbon - Kentucky

**7 Michael:** The bourbon counterpart to long-neck Bud?
**Nose:** A bit flat. Lightly fruity and nutty.
**Palate:** Thin. Brown sugar. Hint of raisins.
**Finish:** Dryish. Quick.

**6 Dave:** No easy rider this, more a Hell's Angel.
**Nose:** Cooked vegetables, wood, with musty/damp earth over hard spirit.
**Palate:** Strange. Confected and honeyed. Has weight, but little breadth.
**Finish:** Hot, short and metallic.

## BAKER'S 7 YEARS OLD 53.5%
Bourbon - Kentucky

**8½ Michael:** Good flavour development. Well balanced.
**Nose:** Sappy. Garden mint. Flowery.
**Palate:** Fresh oak. Vanilla. Fudge. Peanut brittle. Sweetish.
**Finish:** Gingery. Drier.

**8½ Jim:** A chocoholic's bourbon with a bigger rye firmness. Tasty stuff.
**Nose:** Excellent rye bite to firm and sweet nose. Fruity: mature plums and over ripe banana star.
**Palate:** Rye kicks off early and allows bitter and prickly, softly spiced, middle to ensure a characterful, multi-layered bourbon.
**Finish:** Massively complex follow through with quite enormous and beautiful chocolate notes.

## BAKER'S 7 YEARS OLD 53.5%
Bourbon - Kentucky

**8½ Michael:** With dessert, or after dinner. A lovely, soothing, whiskey.
**Nose:** Fresh oak or even cedar. Box of chocolates.
**Palate:** Smooth. Sweet but not cloying. Impeccably clean, but full of flavour. Fudge. White chocolate. Deep. Long.
**Finish:** Crisp. Brandy-snaps. Ginger cookies.

**7¾ Dave:** Big soft and gentle, but too sweet for me.
**Nose:** Big and honeyed. Bitter chocolate, wet leather, walnut cold tea, tobacco, maple syrup.
**Palate:** Sweetly robust: baked banana, overripe honeyed fruit with a praline/hickory crunch.
**Finish:** Long and thick.

## BASIL HAYDEN'S SMALL BATCH, 8 YEARS OLD 40%
Bourbon - Kentucky

**8½ Michael:** Complex, delicate, feminine.
**Nose:** Fresh. Rose-like. Not just one blossom: a hedgerow. Fresh wood. Earthy.
**Palate:** Light but soft. Berry fruits. Cream. Vanilla. Trifle sponge fingers.
**Finish:** Scented.

**8 Dave:** A sassy little glass: the charmer to Booker's bruiser. A midday Old Fashioned.
**Nose:** Clean and delicate with light and spicy rye to the fore. Lemongrass.
**Palate:** Light and delicate. Lots of rye but floats across the palate.
**Finish:** Clean. Medium length. Good balance.

## BASIL HAYDEN'S 8 YEARS OLD 40%
Bourbon - Kentucky

**7½ Martine:** Has an aromatic profile close to a rye whiskey. Quite charming. Too bad it has been emasculated by an excessive dilution. A handsome eunuch?
**Nose:** Tickly. Floral. Bergamot. Earl grey tea. Pear drop. Caramel. Develops on sour fruit (green apple, orange juice). An enticing perfumy display.
**Palate:** Mellow, but a bit soft and watery on midpalate. Develops on hot spices (tabasco).
**Finish:** Dry and hot.

**7¼ Dave:** Clean and fresh. Mid-morning.
**Nose:** Clean and quite aromatic: herbs, eucalyptus, green almond, white asparagus behind some sandalwood. High rye.
**Palate:** Light, fresh and clean. A scented (furniture polish) quality to it. Turkish Delight. Slick and soft.
**Finish:** Dry. Rye flour.

## BERNHEIM ORIGINAL STRAIGHT WHEAT WHISKEY 45%
Wheat - Kentucky

*WHISKY Magazine Editor's choice*

**8¾ Michael:** At an 'all you can eat' buffet in Chicago, a woman piling her plate said to me: "isn't this sinful?" This is temptation in a bottle.
**Nose:** Warm, welcoming, appetising. The bakery aromas of Sunday brunch.
**Palate:** Pancakes. Cornbread. Buttered corn. Peach cobbler. Pecan pie. Pints of vanilla ice cream with butterscotch sauce, garnished with sprigs of fresh mint.
**Finish:** A hint of soft, leafy, balancing dryness.

**9 Dave:** A stunning glass, gentle yet exotic.
**Nose:** The first impression is butter, then fresh baking, toasted crumpet followed by light red fruit (cherry) and allspice. Gentle, with a tricksy quality, lemon meringue lifted by a subtle spiciness. Very clean and well defined.
**Palate:** Gentle then a tingle of fresh planed oak. Reminiscent of melted rock candy with a hint of toffee and a menthol note. Very fine.
**Finish:** Long, spicy.

## BLANTON'S ORIGINAL BOURBON 49.5%
Bourbon - Kentucky

*WHISKY Magazine Recommended*

**7¾ Michael:** A bourbon with dessert.
**Nose:** Corn pudding.
**Palate:** Firm, sharp, spicy. Turkish delight. Dates. Cedar.
**Finish:** Sweet mint tea, laced with alcohol.

**9½ Martine:** What a treat this fabulous bourbon is. Absolutely everything in proportion.
**Nose:** Big toffee start and gets deeper still. Old leather armchairs and sweet pipesmoke.
**Palate:** Enormous from the off but beautifully shaped by shafts of honey and vanilla.
**Finish:** Now comes into its own, with spice and caramel interweaving.

## BLANTON'S 46.5%
Bourbon - Kentucky

*WHISKY Magazine Recommended*

**8¾ Martine:** A complex, rich and interesting character. Water cuts the edges and adds creaminess. A real delight.
**Nose:** Assertive, ethereal. Orange blossom. Cooked fruit. Lime marmalade. An earth after rain scent slowly covers up the fruit, releasing a hint of distant smoke. Spice dust.
**Palate:** Velvety, sensually mouthcoating. Does not abandon its assertiveness though.
**Finish:** Dry, oaky. Bitter orange peel.

**8¼ Dave:** Excellent balance. Recommended.
**Nose:** Fat. Aniseed twists, cake dough, allspice, millionaire's shortcake, seaside rock with spicy burnt orange overtones. In time plenty of vanilla.
**Palate:** Ripe and full-bodied. Very sweet with a cocoa powder density before a fizzing lift of spice.
**Finish:** Good length becoming sweeter.

## BOOKER'S BOURBON 63.4%
Bourbon - Kentucky

**7½ Martine:** An enticing nose but quite a rough palate. Water does not seem to tame the firewater much as it enhances spices. And don't say it is too virile for a female palate. It is NOT that!

**Nose:** Buoyant, pleasantly tangy. Floral and spicy. Carnation, black pepper. Dried flowers, hayloft. An indistinct meaty aroma (chicken broth?). Cedar.
**Palate:** Smooth and sweet in spite of the strength. Then a spicy outburst. Hot chilli. Sherbety.
**Finish:** Hot, prickly, spicy, almondy

**7¾ Dave: Broad-shouldered and old-fashioned. A true memorial to a real giant.**
**Nose:** Huge and soft. Baked fruits with thick honey (almost treacle) tropical fruits and black banana. A deep, powerful, zesty bourbon.
**Palate:** Very sweet, almost liqueur like. High, chest-hurting, alcohol burn. Blackberry and burnt sugar. Slightly nutty.
**Finish:** Long mix of wood and a ring of fire.

## BOOKER'S 6 YEARS OLD 63.25%
Bourbon - Kentucky

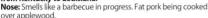

**9 Michael: Wonderfully expansive. Seems to embrace the tastes of the south, all the way from Kentucky to Louisiana.**
**Nose:** Smells like a barbecue in progress. Fat pork being cooked over applewood.
**Palate:** Rich but supple. Mature. Winey. Sherry-like.
**Finish:** Spicy. Did someone slip some Herbsaint in here?

**8¼ Dave: A huge old-style mouthful but the high-strength masks much of the subtle complexities in what is a big-boned bourbon.**
**Nose:** Huge and ripe: barley sugar/spun sugar, apricot, lashings of vanilla, orange crème brûlée – but the alcohol gives your nose a right belt.
**Palate:** Perfumed with a floral lift. Imagine flowers encased in orange blossom honey. Hickory wood.
**Finish:** Treacle, but the alcohol blurs things.

## BOOKER'S 6 TO 8 YEARS OLD 62.5%
Bourbon - Kentucky

**9 Michael: Every time I taste small batch bourbon, this one comes out on top.**
**Nose:** Soft, sweet, fresh, enticing.
**Palate:** Very big. Fat but supple and rich. Mature. Elusive flavours. Vanilla. Cigar-smoke.
**Finish:** Sweet, soothing, tongue-coating. Astonishingly long.

**8 Jim: A rich bourbon that varies in style from batch to batch. This one has a better than average middle, but is let down in the final stages.**
**Nose:** Light and quite malty: almost dank Hessian amid some growing rye.
**Palate:** Corn much more prominent and then a hugely satisfying surge of honey and spice. Delicious.
**Finish:** Slightly fat. A disappointment compared to excellent build up. Some decent rye lingers.

## BUFFALO TRACE AMERICAN STRAIGHT BOURBON 45%
Bourbon - Kentucky

**7 Michael: Some very interesting flavours, but lacks roundness and length.**
**Nose:** Rich, rummy. Figs, almond, aniseed.
**Palate:** Smooth, creamy. Faintly smoky and tobacco-like.
**Finish:** Surprisingly restrained. Pruney.

**9 Jim: Big, moody, uncompromising and complex beyond belief. One of the world's great whiskeys.**
**Nose:** Outstanding aroma, kicked off by a spicy prickle that any Bourbon lover will immediately recognise as the hallmark of the old Ancient Age distillery. Satisfyingly deep, gently vanilla-ed and molassed with even a sprig of sweet mint.
**Palate:** A rip-roaring waxy sweetness checked by a big build up of vanilla-rich oak. Corn is chewy and rye offers a rich-textured background.
**Finish:** Dries at last as the oak takes command, but rye offers extra depth and a layer of bitterness as does a lingering liquorice.

## BUFFALO TRACE EXPERIMENTAL COLLECTION CHARDONNAY, 6 YEARS OLD 45%
Bourbon - Kentucky

**6¾ Dave: The wood is simply too aggressive for the spirit.**
**Nose:** More lifted than the last one with dried lemon peel, dried mint, lavender and chocolate. Oak and orange blossom.
**Palate:** A let down on the palate. Flour sacks and some fragrance overwhelmed by a bitter oaky edge (accentuated by water). While it has energy and sweetness the tannins bite deep and bite hard.
**Finish:** Bitter.

**8½ Martine: A better balance than the preceding one. A beautiful after dinner dram.**
**Nose:** Very fruity and perfumy. Vetiver. Apricot and almond tart. An appetising sourness. Kumquat, pink grapefruit. Layered. Becomes creamier. Hint of pecan pie.
**Palate:** Like in the previous sample, wood overwhelms fruit at start. Green tea. Cigar box, blackcurrant jelly.
**Finish:** Rich, lingering, fruity.

## BUFFALO TRACE EXPERIMENTAL COLLECTION 6 YEARS OLD ZINFANDEL AGED 45%
Bourbon - Kentucky

**7½ Dave: Has blunt charm rather than complexity. A dancing bear, but don't give it any water.**
**Nose:** Deep and quite autumnal. Plenty of dark chocolate and bramble like fruit. Orange peel and thick toffee. This dominates the nose making it the sweetest so far.
**Palate:** Maraschino along with some anise. Concentrated mid-palate showing a lightly bitter edge but balanced by the huge. Cooked black fruits. Water though exposes the oak.
**Finish:** Chocolate.

**7 Dominic: A traffic light whiskey: rampant red nose, cautious amber body, and green foregone on the finish.**
**Nose:** Tangerine, traces of cocoa powder.
**Palate:** Acerbic. Lots of oak, a touch of cocoa. Softens quickly.
**Finish:** Moves on rapidly leaving a trace of fruit.

## BUFFALO TRACE EXPERIMENTAL COLLECTION CHARDONNAY, 10 YEARS OLD 45%
Bourbon - Kentucky

**6¾ Dave: The nose is great, the palate a huge let down. I'm all for experiments but this hasn't worked.**
**Nose:** Maraschino, anise, caraway, Earl Grey tea leaves, dried rose petal and toffee. Aromatic.
**Palate:** Bang! It hits the tongue with a plank of wood. Crystallised orange, 100% cocoa chocolate, matchsticks. Astringent to the point of bitterness. Water increases the tanninc hit.
**Finish:** Bitter.

**8 Martine: Not as balanced on the palate as on the nose but really enticing.**
**Nose:** Rich, intense. Damson jam. Treacle. Stewed prunes. Wood and fruit are lusciously combined. Overcooked marmalade. Demerara sugar caramel like in a rich rum.
**Palate:** Wood is dominating. Bitter start then the rich cooked fruit shine through with added spiciness. Prunes and plums. Nutmeg.
**Finish:** Lingering, fruity and spicy.

## BUFFALO TRACE EXPERIMENTAL COLLECTION 10 YEARS OLD ZINFANDEL AGED 45%
Bourbon - Kentucky

**7½ Dave: A finer structured example but the Zinfandel element seems a little bolted on.**
**Nose:** Seems to have more rye lift giving a dustier edge. Mint and coconut. Rose petals and plum jam. In the hickory smoked camp.
**Palate:** More straight down the line than the last one. Seems to have age, wet leather, canvas, coriander powder. The maraschino note is there again, fennel.
**Finish:** Surprisingly fruity and jammy.

**8 Dominic: Get past the dryness and this one's a grower.**
**Nose:** Perfumey, with vanilla, honey and beeswax traces.
**Palate:** Sharp and dry, with oak dominant.
**Finish:** Vacuum-like dryness sucks the cheeks.

## BULLEIT ORIGINAL BOURBON 45%
Bourbon - Kentucky

**7½ Michael: Cowboy allusions on the neck-label suggest a rough, frontier whisky. Maybe this soothing spirit is just for urban cowboys. It has more blacktop than Badlands.**
**Nose:** Leather saddlery, tobacco.
**Palate:** Firm. Smooth. Rich. Very pronounced vanilla, and honey (promised on the neck label, I discover). Some Madeira-like wineyness, too.
**Finish:** Late tar-like smokyness. Gunsmoke?

**8 Dave: Old-style, teeth-sucking stuff. If this was a singer it would be Merle Haggard. A great cocktail base.**
**Nose:** Feisty and intense with some citrus oil, Seville orange, banana, maple syrup, smoke and sagebrush lime.
**Palate:** Perfumed start: a whiff of dried lavender, singed orange peel, dusty spice cupboards.
**Finish:** A whipcracking lash.

### CADENHEAD'S 10 YEARS OLD, BOURBON 45%
Bourbon - Kentucky

**9 Michael: I especially like bourbons when they are big and robust. This is both hearty and complex. A wonderful winter warmer.**
**Nose:** Clean, rich, rummy. Later flowery dryness (rose petals, rosewood, violets?).
**Palate:** Juicy. Raisiny. Spicy (nutmeg?). Hard toffee. Vanilla, of course. Tobacco-like. Complex.
**Finish:** Firm. Smooth. Endless echoes of flavour. Hugely warming.

**9 Doug: A ripe age for bourbon but this one shows great balance as the wood has not dominated.**
**Nose:** Heady, beeswaxy, polished oak, rich vanilla and a trace of lavender.
**Palate:** Bursting with prickling peppery spice. Toffeeish and salty intensities infuse the grains.
**Finish:** Lingering with sweet, raisiny, smoky and salty outcrops.

### CADENHEAD'S 13 YEARS OLD, BOURBON 65.9%
Bourbon - Kentucky

**6¾ Michael: Despite this being older, it is less astringently woody than the similar five-year-old.**
**Nose:** Violets. Nutmeg. cigar smoke. Slightly woody.
**Palate:** Malty, toffeeish, juicy, lemony, spicy, minty.
**Finish:** Spicy, gingery, warming.

**9 Dave: Who said bourbon can't age?**
**Nose:** Mahogany. Lovely, fragrant, but huge nose mixing old roses, molasses, vanilla, burnt orange, cinnamon and toffee apple.
**Palate:** Ripe and sweet with an almost immediate zap of rye which gives way to sweet fruit.
**Finish:** Long, rich with caramelised fruit and well integrated oak.

### CADENHEADS AMERICA BOURBON 62.2%
Bourbon - Kentucky

**8 Dave: Has an extra dimension. Recommended.**
**Nose:** Round and plump with sweet syrupy aromas coming through. Chocolate and menthol. Red fruits, coconut cream. Millionaire's shortbread. Has complexity.
**Palate:** Big impact. Immediate classic spiciness: allspice, ginger, then becomes gentler. Honeyed deep and liquorous in the centre. An extra lift.
**Finish:** Long and smooth.

**7¾ Dominic: Impressive and bullish bourbon.**
**Nose:** Tobacco, baked apple, pears, spice, a waft of smoke.
**Palate:** Spearmint, rye, peppery spice, green banana skin.
**Finish:** Bold and sharp, aniseed balls.

### CADENHEAD'S BOURBON 5 YEARS OLD 63%
Bourbon - Kentucky

**6½ Michael: Just too woody for me, though a good splash of water brings out the other flavours.**
**Nose:** Vanilla. Charcoal. Woody.
**Palate:** Sweet, sugary, malty, chewy, creamy.
**Finish:** Gingery and hot. Woody.

**7 Dave: A little woody and young.**
**Nose:** Dark amber. Quite dry and woody with hints of hickory, candied fruit and some lemony rye zestiness.
**Palate:** Sweet smouldering hickory notes to start. Some burnt sugar/treacle mid-palate before a bite of rye freshens it up-fairly high wood.
**Finish:** Ripe, full with some smoked tea. Wood.

### EAGLE RARE 10 YEARS OLD, SINGLE BARREL 50.5%
Bourbon - Kentucky

**7¾ Michael: More delicate and restrained than I expect from Eagle Rare...distinctly the sweeter of the Bourbons.**
**Nose:** Soft, clean.
**Palate:** Lightly toffeeish. Sweet. Orangey. Some minty rye notes.
**Finish:** Gentle. Slight citrus zest.

**8 Dave: Big and sweet. Scale down the sweet vermouth when making your Manhattan.**
**Nose:** Full-on, rich sweet nose: candy, caramelised oak.
**Palate:** Big, chewy and sweet with a fresh oily zap on the back palate stopping it from becoming too cloying.
**Finish:** Long, slightly hot.

### EAGLE RARE 10 YEARS OLD 45%
Bourbon - Kentucky

**7¾ Michael: Slightly less sweet than the last bottling I tasted.**
**Nose:** Creamy. Spicy.
**Palate:** Smooth. Vanilla. Condensed milk. Coconut. Orange. Tropical fruits.
**Finish:** Gingery finish. Warming.

**7¼ Dave: Quite a mouthful which takes no prisoners.**
**Nose:** Perfumed, lemon cooked fruits. Fairly lean with (in time) cocoa/coffee cake, winey notes. Whiff of cigar smoke as well.
**Palate:** Attractive if slightly (surprisingly) austere. The mid-palate has lovely concentrated jammy fruits alongside good spicy rye.
**Finish:** Softens and begins to mellow.

### EAGLE RARE 17 YEARS OLD 45%
Bourbon - Kentucky

**7¼ Michael: Some interesting flavours, with lots of dimensions, but no balance or structure. I'm not wild about Angel Delight.**
**Nose:** Aromatic. Cedary. Orange zest. Intensely fruity. Slightly sharp at the back of the nose.
**Palate:** Orange Angel Delight. Caramel. Toffee. Wafers. Dry oiliness.
**Finish:** Orange peels. Bitter orange. Ginger marmalade. Late, lively, surge of spiciness.

**8 Dave: Big and sweet. Scale down the sweet vermouth when making your Manhattan.**
**Nose:** Full-on, rich sweet nose: candy, caramelised oak, cinnamon cooked in butter, hot cross buns and honey cakes.
**Palate:** Big, chewy and sweet with a fresh oily zap on the back palate stopping it from becoming too cloying.
**Finish:** Long, slightly hot.

### EAGLE RARE 17 YEARS OLD, SINGLE BARREL 45%
Bourbon - Kentucky

**7¾ Michael: A clean, easily drinkable, well-made Bourbon. Straight-ahead, rather than quirky. A certain mature restraint, but is that sufficient pay-off?**
**Nose:** Honeydew melons, piled up in a store.
**Palate:** Smooth. Sweet. Toffeeish. Juicy.
**Finish:** Clean, crisp, slightly toasty peppery, dryness.

**8½ Jim: Nose is great; taste is marginally less so.**
**Nose:** A fabulous combination of roasted almonds and pecan pie.
**Palate:** Light, clean with rich, leathery, liquorice, slightly phenolic oak notes.
**Finish:** Demerara sweetness and a drying vanilla.

### EAGLE RARE 17 YEARS OLD 45%
Bourbon - Kentucky

**7¼ Michael: The nose suggested an astringent palate, but there is some balancing sweetness.**
**Nose:** Burnt sugar. Molasses. Phenol.
**Palate:** Chewy malt loaf. Raisins. Burnt toast.
**Finish:** Not so much fiery as tingling.

**7½ Dave: All that candy floss, toffee apple and wood reminded me of fairgrounds.**
**Nose:** Dark, with great waves of oakiness: cherry stone, old leather, treacle toffee, vanilla pod. Given a lift with sugary notes and a sprig of mint.
**Palate:** Tannic. Marmalade, sweet fruits masked by the oak. Water calms it, but the oak is assertive.
**Finish:** Dry and oaky.

### EARLY TIMES KENTUCKY WHISKY 40%
Bourbon - Kentucky

**7 Michael: Pleasant. Easy drinking for a pre-bourbon novice. Perhaps a little unfair to judge it in this company.**
**Nose:** Marzipan.
**Palate:** Lightly smooth. Sweetish, but well balanced. Almondy. Clean.
**Finish:** Rounded.

**7 Dave: All very pleasant, but a pretty one-dimensional experience. No-one could be offended by this, but no-one will be excited either.**
**Nose:** Fragrant and soft with vanilla/custard notes and spicy wood.
**Palate:** Soft. Flows nicely across the palate.
**Finish:** A little prickle, but far too mild-mannered to annoy.

## ELIJAH CRAIG 12 YEARS OLD 47%
Bourbon - Kentucky

**7¾ Michael: Less structured than might be expected in a 12 Years Old, but a perilously drinkable, appetising bourbon.**
**Nose:** Real bourbon vanilla, with a touch of candy-store sweetness.
**Palate:** Firm, malty, sweet. Some malty fruitiness (apricot?). A suggestion of cilantro.
**Finish:** Liquorice. Rooty.

**9½ Jim: This (along with Evan Williams 12) is the finest whisky from the house of Heaven Hill.**
**Nose:** Just about nudging perfection: salty but balanced infused with delicate fruity notes.
**Palate:** Rye hits every corner of the mouth: light oils and myriad oaky, complex notes to the roof.
**Finish:** Slow build up of slightly molassed sweetness and vanilla leaves a lingering, smoky, phenolic finale.

## ELIJAH CRAIG 12 YEARS OLD 47%
Bourbon - Kentucky

**7½ Martine: Oak (and age) has lessened the creaminess and sweetness of the spirit. Would probably tune in with a cigar, but too oaky for me.**
**Nose:** Tangy. Nutty. Sweet and sour. Candy floss. Unsweetened apples. A distinct pepperiness. In the back, a cereal and grassy note.
**Palate:** Sweeter and less creamy than expected. Gently flowing. Develops on drier oaky notes. Liquorice. Nutmeg.
**Finish:** Dry, liquoriced. Inclining to bitterness.

**7½ Dave: Another from the big-boned camp.**
**Nose:** Sweet and dense. Apricot jam, stewed fruits, charred oak. A cooperage smell of charring casks and oil. Custard, cedar and a little tobacco leaf.
**Palate:** Rounded. A very sweet start, liquorice, slight dip in the centre before spiced apple takes over on the finish.
**Finish:** Sweet. Candy. Oak.

## ELIJAH CRAIG 18 YEARS OLD 45%
Bourbon - Kentucky

**8¼ Michael: Very urbane.**
**Nose:** Subtle. Nutty. Almonds.
**Palate:** Light-bodied for this distillery. Firm, smooth, almost slippery. Lots of flavour development. Sweet then fragrantly smoky.
**Finish:** Rounded. Appetising.

**8 Jim: A solid and charming bourbon.**
**Nose:** A weighty nose with a depth of honey where there had once been fruit. Perplexing coastal feel for something distilled 1,000 miles inland!
**Palate:** Lighter bodied than the 12, with a more simplistic oakiness. Honey and rye cling together.
**Finish:** Toasty with a residual rye oiliness and a soft vanilla sweetness.

## ELMER T. LEE 45%
Bourbon - Kentucky

**8 Martine: A superbly balanced giant. More on the sweet side than the spicy one. Should marry so well with my pecan pie! Avoid water.**
**Nose:** Perfumy. Bakery shop. Gingerbread. Crème brûlée. Caramelised pecan nuts. Dried apricots. Wet leaves. Hint of mushrooms.
**Palate:** Mellow and sweet. Beautiful balance between oak and fruit. Creamy.
**Finish:** Drying out on spices. Oak gives more length without any show off.

**8¾ Dave: Lulls you into a gentle world then zaps you in the middle of the mouth. A symphony in two movements. Highly recommended.**
**Nose:** Lifted, sweet and spicy. Nutmeg, banana, amaretto, coconut and some hickory. Dusty oak. Almost Cognac-like. Real complexity.
**Palate:** Soft, gentle. Quite honeyed, then a zap of lemon zest over the top of the dense fruit. Classy.
**Finish:** Tingling. Long.

## ELMER T. LEE KENTUCKY BOURBON 45%
Bourbon - Kentucky

**7¼ Michael: Light in both flavour and body for a small batch bourbon. Clean, crisp, enjoyable.**
**Nose:** Light, fruity, rummy.
**Palate:** Sweet. Raisins. Vanilla.
**Finish:** Crisp, dry.

**9 Jim: Perhaps the lightest Elmer T Lee of the dozens I have savoured.**
**Nose:** Usually fruity and a little minty, floral character, citrus lingers with the vanilla, rye and sandalwood.
**Palate:** The flavours unravel in slow motion: soft rye then a slight malty character and then fuller corn.
**Finish:** Cocoa enriches the final moments that have been sweetened by a light molasses.

## ELMER T. LEE SINGLE BARREL 45%
Bourbon - Kentucky

**8¼ Michael: The fruitiest of the Bourbons. After dinner?**
**Nose:** Aromatic. Berry-fruits. Cherries. Raisins, quite emphatically so.
**Palate:** Smooth, clean, entrance. Becoming almondy, with suggestions of bitter chocolate and rum.
**Finish:** Soothing, warming, long.

**8 Dave: A gorgeous refreshing summery glass.**
**Nose:** Assertive maltiness with cooked apple, sweet hay and an intense fragrant/perfumed lift and then a dry sugared almond nuttiness. Delicate but seductive.
**Palate:** A sweet, perfumed start then that dry malt/nut cuts through to balance well. Some smoke.
**Finish:** Dry, hay like. Crisp malt.

## ELMER T. LEE SINGLE BARREL 45%
Bourbon - Kentucky

**8½ Michael: Delicious. Dangerously drinkable. Bigger and richer than I remember.**
**Nose:** Sliced toasted almonds.
**Palate:** Butterscotch pie. A hint of sweet lemons.
**Finish:** Gently balancing dryness.

**7¼ Dave: Good, but just leaves you wanting a bit more.**
**Nose:** Sappy, pine resin. Almost sandy notes. Quite delicate and lightly honeyed along with basil leaf and toffee. Light.
**Palate:** Scented with an almost waxy feel. Oak is firm but there's some finesse. Very precise.
**Finish:** Becoming oaky.

## EVAN WILLIAMS 1990, SINGLE BARREL 43.3%
Bourbon - Kentucky

**8½ Michael: Very different in style. Liqueurish.**
**Nose:** Sweet, fresh. Spearmint. Allspice.
**Palate:** Very clean malty sweetness. Soft, light, syrupy. Clean citrus flavour. Seems at first like candied fruits, then becomes more ethereal. Orange flower water?
**Finish:** Delicately dry. Slightly sharp.

**9¼ Jim: Celebrates the part the rye and malt notes can play against the more neutral background of corn. Almost too complex to be true.**
**Nose:** A stunning herbal start blossoms into a ginger-honey sweetness.
**Palate:** A fresh and clean start allows the corn to develop beautifully before the rye takes hold.
**Finish:** Medium length only, quality outstanding with fresh rye bringing the curtain down.

## EVAN WILLIAMS 1991, SINGLE BARREL 43.3%
Bourbon - Kentucky

**8½ Michael: Where did she go? Will she return?**
**Nose:** Fragrant and slightly smoky. Orange-blossom. Potpourri. Acacia honey. Dryish.
**Palate:** Elegant. Silky. Flirtatious. Scenty (mandarin orange and mint). Feminine.
**Finish:** Disarmingly quick. A peck on the cheek. Slightly dizzying.

**8¼ Dave: One for rye fans.**
**Nose:** Resinous, zesty and citric. Hickory, planed wood.
**Palate:** That same oily/zesty rye impact leathers the palate: lemon balm, citrus and excellent balance. In time opens to show chocolate, coconut, nutty fruit treacle.
**Finish:** Round and long.

# American Evan - George

## EVAN WILLIAMS 1993, SINGLE BARREL 43.3%
Bourbon - Kentucky

**8½ Michael:** The big, malty, chocolately style that I associate with Evan Williams. A lovely, voluptuous, afterdinner bourbon. Gains from a splash of water.
**Nose:** Scenty. Dates. Turkish delight. Caramel.
**Palate:** Buttery fudge. Cocoa. Bitter chocolate.
**Finish:** Hint of citrus. Cedary, sappy. A good heavy char in the oak? Contrives to be soothing and appetising.

**8½ Dave:** I like this different, less overt, single barrel style. Yet another surprise in what is a hugely diverse and high quality range of whiskies.
**Nose:** Quite delicate, with tingling spices, orange peel, dusty rye notes, lemon, anis. More biscuity with water.
**Palate:** A gentle start, a salvo of spices, then the rye appears. Refined.
**Finish:** Spicy oak.

## EVAN WILLIAMS 23 YEARS OLD KENTUCKY STRAIGHT BOURBON WHISKEY 53.5%
Bourbon - Kentucky

**8 Michael:** A lovely bourbon, but I prefer it younger.
**Nose:** A box of dark chocolates, the lid newly opened.
**Palate:** Dark chocolate. Rum. Oak.
**Finish:** Long, warming. Some woody astringency.

**8½ Dave:** In a battle between grippy oak and the powerful sweet spirit the latter wins – just. One ice cube is enough. Great for its age.
**Nose:** Dark and chewy. Chocolate cherries. Turkish coffee, sweet spices, maple syrup, pine.
**Palate:** Sweet and fragrant. weight of wood and sweet spirit. Sweet and balanced. A big whiskey.
**Finish:** Long, syrupy.

## EVAN WILLIAMS BLACK 43%
Bourbon - Kentucky

**8 Martine:** Reminiscent of an old calvados at first. Palate is less creamy than the nose. For those who like it spicy. Water tames spices a little though.
**Nose:** Sweet and sour. First restrained then blossoming up. Cider apple, close to cider. A light floral touch (freesia). Coffee drops.
**Palate:** Thick, syrupy. Floral. Parma violet, liquorice. Somewhat austere. Oak stands fast. Nutmeg. Brazil nut.
**Finish:** Dry, oaky. Spicy outburst.

**7¾ Dave:** Not the biggest, but a versatile balanced bourbon.
**Nose:** Light, with orange notes. Tingling spices. Citrus oils, a dusting of cocoa. Crisp and quite lean. Young and fresh with a hint of apple.
**Palate:** A fresh dried tangerine quality. Balances relative lightness with a soft gentle mid-palate and a zesty finish.
**Finish:** Long, soft, citric.

## EVAN WILLIAMS SINGLE BARREL BOURBON, 1994 45%
Bourbon - Kentucky

**8¾ Michael:** Another great vintage from Heaven Hill.
**Nose:** Coconut. Vanilla. Red berry fruits. Emphatic mint toffee.
**Palate:** Powerful, smooth. Malty, nutty. Orange peels. Mint leaves. Tightly combined flavours.
**Finish:** Peach cobbler. Toasted almonds. Slight burned bitterness.

**8¼ Dave:** A class act.
**Nose:** Perfumed. Hickory. Barbecue, dusty rye notes. Spiced and elegant. Real finesse.
**Palate:** Mulled notes: sandalwood, ripe apple, allspice, coconut. Succulent weight. Great balance.
**Finish:** Cherry stone. Rye flour.

## FOUR ROSES BARREL STRENGTH LIMITED EDITION SINGLE BARREL BOURBON, 15 YEARS OLD 52.1%
Bourbon - Kentucky

**8¼ Dave:** Sugar and spice and all things nice.
**Nose:** A candy floss sweetness with some green plum, lemon balm, eucalyptus and oak. Water brings out a cinnamon note and garrigue like herbs. Good balance.
**Palate:** Perfumed, silky and sweet in the centre with fizzing spices. Good succulent flow which balances the perfumed notes with spice and toffee apple. Better with water. Great balance.

---

**Finish:** Tight and spicy, some cherry.

**7½ Martine:** A teasing nose but a dour profile on the palate. Too old? Bad wood? Water enhances the spices and masks the sourness.
**Nose:** Spicy and fruity. All spice, pepper, touch of caraway. Date chutney. A rich dried fruit sweetness tones down the wood grip.
**Palate:** Deceiving. The sweetness promised by the nose is not here. Very sour. Like old cider.
**Finish:** Much nicer than midpalate.

## FOUR ROSES BOURBON 40%
Bourbon - Kentucky

**7¼ Michael:** Even the colour is pale. This is a very gentle introduction to bourbon, but with all the elements.
**Nose:** Gentle, but quite evocative. Dessert apples. Raisin cookies. Sweet but appetising.
**Palate:** Light in body and flavour, but with some delicacy and complexity. Vanilla. Honey. Spicy.
**Finish:** Fruity flavours reminiscent of orange flower water. Drying somewhat with a hint of char.

**8 Dave:** Very well-balanced. The uptown sophisticate, a discreetly charming member of the bourgeoisie.
**Nose:** High-toned, crisp and citric: lemon, lime and tangerine peel with a hint of mintiness.
**Palate:** Zesty. Lemon, honey and spice. Nice rye balance towards the finish.
**Finish:** Touch of light woodiness getting oily as rye shows its hand.

## FOUR ROSES SINGLE BARREL 43%
Bourbon - Kentucky

**7¼ Michael:** Lacking in dimension for a single barrel. Saved by the finish.
**Nose:** Lightly nutty. Lightly winey. Some appetising sweetness.
**Palate:** Light. Very winey. Falls away in the middle.
**Finish:** Very sweet. Treacle toffee. Nice and lingering.

**9 Jim:** Unquestionably the best bottles sample from this distillery I've tasted yet.
**Nose:** Small grains to the fore with a lovely malt-rye interplay. Fittingly delicate and floral.
**Palate:** Much denser on the palate, surprisingly heavy. Roasty, burnt raisins a hint of coffee and burnt fudge. Unbelievably chewy.
**Finish:** More of the same, though the fade out is slow and tantalising.

## GEORGE A. DICKEL'S TENNESSEE WHISKY NO. 12 45%
Tennessee - Tennessee

**7¾ Michael:** Not as smoky and char-like as I remember. Very enjoyable, but less obviously Tennessean.
**Nose:** Flowering currant. Herbal. Briar-like.
**Palate:** Smooth. Starts sweet and buttery. Crème brûlée? Then lemon zest. Lemon pith dryness.
**Finish:** Slightly clovey, warming. Soothing. Long and buttery.

**8½ Dave:** A Doc Watson of a whiskey, mild-mannered but full of tricks. Please UDV, start pushing it!
**Nose:** Spicy yet soft, like apple pie, lemon cakes, honey with cloves, geraniums. Light twang of rye.
**Palate:** Mid-weight. As the nose suggests a spicy, complex, chewy number that's fragrant/floral with apple, lime blossom, ginger/cinnamon, tobacco.
**Finish:** Very clean with a nice touch of apple pie crust.

## GEORGE T. STAGG 65.9%
Bourbon - Kentucky

**6½ Martine:** Where is the pleasure? Even with water, one feels the burn, which covers the flavours. I am no masochist, thank you.
**Nose:** Spirity. A bowl of cereal. Honeyed popcorn. Grassy. Green tea. Touch of angelica. Crème caramel. Lots of vanilla.
**Palate:** Crisp, neat. Orange marmalade. Very astringent. Oak and high strength give a burning kick to the tastebuds.
**Finish:** Dry, rather short, astringent.

**7¼ Dave:** A no-holds barred glass, but doesn't have the class of the best on show.
**Nose:** The deepest and sweetest on show. Ridiculous levels of honey and caramel and char. Black honey, coffee. Liqueur like.
**Palate:** Big and fat and slightly lacking in definition and grip. Heart-burning alcohol levels. Fruits slightly sour. Not balanced.
**Finish:** Floppy.

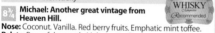

## GEORGE T. STAGG 71.35%
Bourbon - Kentucky

WHISKY *Magazine* Recommended

**8 Michael: Ideal for Thanksgiving or Christmas. If you don't like your in-laws or the television, knock yourself out after dinner.**
**Nose:** Mint toffee. Fudge.
**Palate:** Mint toffees again. Dark fudge. Candied prunes.
**Finish:** Some astringency. Lots of alcohol. The two seem to round each other into one big punch (of the pugilistic type).

**8 Dave: A sweet mother for ya!**
**Nose:** Enormous! Darker, sweeter and richer than all the others put together. Marmalade, sugar candy, orange liqueur chocolates. Sultry.
**Palate:** Sufficient spiciness and structure to balance the huge waves of sweetness. Orange again. Shows complexity.
**Finish:** Long and sweet. Lingering.

## HANCOCK'S PRESIDENT'S RESERVE 44.45%
Bourbon - Kentucky

**7½ Michael: Liked that spicy-lemon rye character, but lacking in complexity and roundness.**
**Nose:** Fresh. Lemon. Vanilla. Hint tobacco.
**Palate:** Light. Lemons. Roses. Sweetish.
**Finish:** Lemon curd.

**9 Jim: Brilliantly balanced throughout with just the correct amount of sweetness.**
**Nose:** Massive corn mingles with intense oak and a spicy buzz of rye; lashings of sweet toffee.
**Palate:** Fat and full with a quick explosion of lively rye and demarara sugar followed by sweet corn.
**Finish:** Drier towards the finale with a long oaky follow through.

## HEAVEN HILL 15 YEARS OLD, CADENHEAD'S 62.4%
Bourbon - Kentucky

**8 Michael: Fifteen years is quite old for a bourbon, but this is complex, rounded and a good example of Heaven Hill's style. Keeps the sweet notes dominant.**
**Nose:** Very malty for a bourbon.
**Palate:** Malty, then buttery. Lots of flavour development. Vanilla. Liquorice.
**Finish:** Nice balance of oaky dryness. This level of woodiness is acceptable in a bourbon.

**7¾ Martine: A tough guy exposing his complexity a bit too conspicuously. After dinner, with a cigar.**
**Nose:** Rich and heady. Plum jam, vanilla. Hint of mushroom and damp cellar. Peppery.
**Palate:** Both sweet and tangy. Spices and dark chocolate (chocolate-coated brandy cherries). Too aggressive undiluted. Cedar resin, balsamic notes.
**Finish:** Large, robust and lingering.

## HENRY MCKENNA SINGLE BARREL KENTUCKY STRAIGHT BOURBON WHISKEY 50%
Bourbon - Kentucky

**7½ Michael: Shy. Diffident. But with its own delicacy.**
**Nose:** Restrained. Fruity. Strawberries.
**Palate:** Custard. Crème anglais. Vanilla. Cream toffee.
**Finish:** Light. Dusty. Cinnamon. Balancing dryness.

**8¼ Dave: Go easy on the bitters when making an old fashioned. A good solid package.**
**Nose:** Toasted, caramelised. Black banana, spices. Rich, soft and liquorous. Candied fruits and a hint of fresh mushroom. Delicious.
**Palate:** Good balance between sweet, spicy and bitter (cherry) notes. Menthol/basil/anise.
**Finish:** Banana chips. Cocoa.

## JACK DANIEL'S GENTLEMAN JACK 40%
Tennessee - Tennessee

**7½ Michael: A slightly richer and more restrained interpretation of Jack Daniel's.**
**Nose:** Soft but insistent. Sweet then dry. Burnt brown sugar and charcoal. Slightly less overt charcoal-phenol than the regular Jack Daniel's.
**Palate:** Smooth. Very toasty. Dryish start, but becoming surprisingly sweet. Spicy. Syrupy background.
**Finish:** Cinnamon. Lemons.

**8 Jim: Gentleman by name and nature, it lacks the usual JD firepower but retains house character.**
**Nose:** A tell-tale roasty JD nose, but all gently done and laid back.
**Palate:** A dry kick off, swiftly develops a lovely, clingy sweetness, and that ever-present liquorice.
**Finish:** Remarkably demure for a JD but the rising sweetness gives way to a drier slightly burnt-sugary character.

## JACK DANIEL'S SINGLE BARREL 45%
Tennessee - Tennessee

**8 Michael: An interesting interplay of Jack Daniel's house character and a more luxurious oakiness.**
**Nose:** Oakier than a typical Jack Daniel's.
**Palate:** Noticably rounder. Polished oak. New leather.
**Finish:** Lemon. Maple syrup.

**8½ Jim: Always an interesting brand.**
**Nose:** Almost stiffly phenolic: you can cut through the sweet roasty, oaky intensity.
**Palate:** You less taste than eat this stuff...lovely oily middle with plenty of trademark burnt liquorice.
**Finish:** The small grains bravely fight their way through, first rye then malt. But the rye returns with the liquorice for the surprisingly refined finale.

## JEFFERSON'S RESERVE 15 YEARS OLD 45.1%
Bourbon - Kentucky

**8¼ Michael: Stylish and disarming, but not to be taken lightly. Reminds me of Kentucky's greatest boxer.**
**Nose:** Appetising. Fresh, smooth, spicy.
**Palate:** Smooth. Sweet. Flavours dance on the tongue.
**Finish:** Just when I had this tagged as being delicate, a big punch with a fist of oak concluded the proceedings.

**7¾ Dave: A good sipper, but too woody for me.**
**Nose:** Serious, 'aged' nose with velvety peach, vanilla, wild herb notes.
**Palate:** Very soft to start: cinnamon, butter, honey, then dries.
**Finish:** Woody.

## JIM BEAM STRAIGHT RYE 40%
Rye - Kentucky

**8 Michael: I have always had a sneaking admiration for this whiskey, and have long wondered why it is not more widely available. It is as though the Jim Beam family quietly accommodates its crazy cousin.**
**Nose:** Oily. Hemp-like, very aromatic.
**Palate:** Again, very oily. Minty. Moving to orange. Becomes very fruity and succulent. Expressive. Flavoursome.
**Finish:** Sweet. Lingering. Teasing.

**7½ Dave: A decent mid-weight introduction. Drink mixed.**
**Nose:** Light and perfumed though a little dusty with a whiff of acetone. White peppercorns, lemon myrtle, wood, pencil shavings.
**Palate:** Soft and lemony to start, with some perfumed honey. Decent hit of rye; the sourness balances nicely with the Iced Gem sweetness.
**Finish:** Dry and spicy.

## JTS BROWN 40%
Bourbon - Kentucky

**7¾ Martine: A pleasant balance between oaky and creamy notes. The finish is surprisingly long for the alcoholic strength. The mid palate is a bit watery.**
**Nose:** Sweet, delicate but intense. Touch of hyacinth. Caramelised apples, pine nuts. Chestnut purée. Coffee beans. A varnish hint. Becomes creamier and fudgier as it gets aerated.
**Palate:** Very smooth and round. Oily. Fudgy. Oak and spices slightly overtake the fruitiness.
**Finish:** Long. Drying on nutty notes. Black pepper.

**7 Dave: The lightest of the lot. Almost fragile.**
**Nose:** Very lean and slightly sappy. Hazelnut, cinnamon and almond paste. A lot of oak.
**Palate:** Sweet and citric. Dry, sandy.
**Finish:** Light lemon.

## KNOB CREEK 9 YEARS OLD 50%
Bourbon - Kentucky

**7¾ Michael: Easily drinkable, appetising.**
**Nose:** Hint of char. Spicy rye.
**Palate:** Surprisingly light start. Marshmallow maltiness. Develops smooth, satisfying, nutty, flavours. Hazelnuts.
**Finish:** Surge of fruity, apple-like flavours. Some tannin.

**9 Jim: By far the best aroma from this small batch selection, and taste and finish: classic top of the range bourbon.**
**Nose:** Marmalade on toast: beautiful, sweet fruit, dash of soft rye and edge of saltiness.
**Palate:** Spicy, busy start: early arrival of cocoa but a playfully biting, taste-bud nipping character stars.
**Finish:** Loads of cocoa balances out vanilla. A dry, slightly oily but magnificently long finish.

## KNOB CREEK 9 YEARS OLD 50%
Bourbon - Kentucky

**8 Michael: Teasing interplay of sweetness and dryness, with the latter eventually winning.**
**Nose:** Aromatic. Maple syrup.
**Palate:** Light-bodied. Very firm. Chewy. Rooty. Emphatic liquorice sweets.
**Finish:** Winey. Faintly cidery. Tannic. A hint of char. Distinctly dry.

**8¼ Dave: Less thick than Baker's and better balanced. Another great cocktail bourbon. Big and rich.**
**Nose:** Perfumed. Soft and fruity. Blackberry, treacle toffee. A big smoky bear of a drink.
**Palate:** Soft and powerful, caramelised sugars, fruit and spices: cumin/sandalwood.
**Finish:** Chocolate and honey.

## MAKER'S MARK KENTUCKY STRAIGHT BOURBON 45%
Bourbon - Kentucky

**8 Michael: Beautifully structured. Tightly combined flavours. Every bit as smooth as it claims to be.**
**Nose:** Wheaty, nutty. Bananas?
**Palate:** Buttered toast. Molasses. Maple syrup.
**Finish:** Clean, dryish, flapjack.

**8½ Jim: An old faithful of a bourbon. Never lets you down and being from the wheaty school always shows good oak balance. Nose is to die for.**
**Nose:** Aroma with delightful strands of exotic fruit and honey. Fruit cake. Oak adds to feeling of class.
**Palate:** Lush, pleasingly deep and malty. A firm nuttiness adds extra oily, chewability to the toffee.
**Finish:** Drier than of old. Caramel toffee with the oak guarantees a bittersweet edge.

## MAKER'S MARK KENTUCKY STRAIGHT BOURBON 45%
Bourbon - Kentucky

**8 Michael: This famously smooth whisky seems slightly less sweet than I remember, especially in the nose and finish. Better balanced, but fractionally less distinctive.**
**Nose:** Slightly smoky. Toasty. Maple syrup.
**Palate:** Creamy. Nutty. flapjack. Dryish. Clean. Smooth.
**Finish:** Slightly fruity, winey (Muscat). Some acidity.

**8¼ Dave: Chewy and mellow. Great balance and elegance. Still a classic.**
**Nose:** Elegant, harmonious and soft. Runny honey, cherry, peach/ apricot, butter icing/cream and fresh wild herbs.
**Palate:** Ripe, soft, creamy and fruit-filled: cherries and peaches in honey syrup with a dusting of nutmeg and cinnamon.
**Finish:** Soft then crisps up.

## MCCARTHY'S SINGLE MALT 40%
Single Malt - Oregon

**6¾ Michael: In a young whisky, I would have expected more freshness of flavour, but the elements are there, and the product shows promise.**
**Nose:** Peat. Grass. Fruit. Musty.
**Palate:** Syrupy but firm. Medium-bodied. Robust. Peaty.
**Finish:** Mustardy, scenty, dry.

**6¼ Dave: Young, maybe time in wood will mellow the rubbery nose.**
**Nose:** Smoky, dry, heathery (and leathery). There's a grappa-like earthiness, barbecue smoke then, as it opens, an overpowering rubbery/feinty note.

**Palate:** Pretty sweet with some soft fruit and that heathery smoke on the sides of the tongue.
**Finish:** Clean. Short.

## OLD CHARTER PROPRIETOR'S RESERVE 45%
Bourbon - Kentucky

**8 Michael: Finally made it to lunch.**
**Nose:** Jam. Fruit. An apricot danish. Still at breakfast?
**Palate:** Vanilla. Cream. Bread pudding. Gentle flavours, but delivered in an intense concentration.
**Finish:** Sappy. Fresh. Oak. Bittersweet.

**7¾ Dave: Old fashioned in every sense and none the worse for that.**
**Nose:** Lean and sappy. Quite intense: white pepper, powdered ginger/coriander. Softens slightly into toffee apple, toasted tea cake, cigar box.
**Palate:** Soft, syrupy feel within a pretty firm, dry structure. Serious.
**Finish:** Spices and oak.

## OLD CHARTER 12 YEARS OLD 45%
Bourbon - Kentucky

**7¾ Michael: A good, substantial bourbon.**
**Nose:** Very emphatic rich, deep, cocoa aroma.
**Palate:** Firm. Slippery-smooth. Very toffeeish. Hard toffee. Nut toffee. Peanut brittle. A suggestion of blueberries, perhaps even passion-fruit. Slight spicy-sour rye character.
**Finish:** Rye-grain. Crisp and spicy.

**7½ Dave: Outdoor/restorative stuff. Stick a bottle in your pocket and do a John Muir.**
**Nose:** Quite lean, dry and rye-accented. Appetising with light honey richness.
**Palate:** Feisty with good peppery attack. High-toned. Vibrant. Mellows slightly in the mouth with honey, red fruits.
**Finish:** Vivacious, crisp and peppery.

## OLD CHARTER THE CLASSIC 90, 12 YEARS OLD 45%
Bourbon - Kentucky

**7¾ Michael: Biscuits and gravy and a shot of Charter 12. The breakfast of champions.**
**Nose:** Restrained. Sweet. Nutty. Smoky.
**Palate:** Almond essence. Vanilla. Corn muffins.
**Finish:** Toasty. Crisp.

**7¾ Dave: A well-made, serious bourbon. One for cigars.**
**Nose:** Cooked fruits, bitter orange/orange pulp, rum and raisin. Almost leathery notes. Pipe smoke, allspice.
**Palate:** Sweet and deep, but with very pure flavours. Grilled nut. Old-fashioned rose. Ripe.
**Finish:** Begins to dry. Shows some good maturity.

## OLD FITZGERALD 12 YEARS OLD 45%
Bourbon - Kentucky

**7¾ Michael: Characterful, but not an easy whisky on the basis of this bottling. Bitterness seems to have gained a notch at the expense of the fudge flavours. Water brings it back, but not all the way.**
**Nose:** A wintery night. A leather armchair in front of a log fire. Molasses cookies?
**Palate:** Firm, heavy body. Viscous. Molasses. Medicinal. Peppery.
**Finish:** Bittersweet.

**8¾ Dave: A deep earthy affair. One to sip with a good cigar. Gene Clark.**
**Nose:** Smoky, charred nose. Complex earth tones with liquorice, cigar smoke, leather, walnut cake.
**Palate:** A deep brooding bourbon with butterscotch/vanilla underpinnings showing lovely interplay between honey and chocolate. Wood has a presence, but nuttily so.
**Finish:** Oak, but lovely balance.

## OLD FITZGERALD VERY SPECIAL 45%
Bourbon - Kentucky

**8 Martine: Surprising. Subdued at first, then shines through when oxygenated.**
**Nose:** Restrained at first. Creamy and fruity. Stewed apricots in vanilla and spices. Milk chocolate. Slowly reveals its complexity.
**Palate:** Round, unctuous at start, then becoming sherbety, somewhat fizzy. Lots of dried fruit. Liquorice. A kentuckied cognac?
**Finish:** Long, drying, spicy (coriander, ginger) with a slight astringence. Touch of passion fruit.

**8½ Dave: The softest and least in-yer-face. Just a slow steady flow of flavour. Recommended.**
**Nose:** Soft and very gentle. Peanut brittle, sloe berry. Orange Pekoe tea, privet blossom, dry spices, caramelised orange. Subtle and balanced.
**Palate:** A slow soft start. Sweet tobacco. Ripe black fruits. Orange peel. Long and generous.
**Finish:** Long and sweet.

## OLD FORESTER 86 PROOF KENTUCKY BOURBON 43%
Bourbon - Kentucky

**7½ Michael: Easy drinking, but worth more than a moment's thought.**
**Nose:** Very aromatic. Flowery. Nuts. Marzipan.
**Palate:** Light-bodied but very fruity indeed. Reminiscent of fruitcake with candied orange peels.
**Finish:** Light, clean. Vanilla pods.

**8¼ Dave: A great old-style sippin' bourbon and a great base for an Old Fashioned.**
**Nose:** Rich and deep. Leather armchairs, walnut, dark fruit and tobacco. Oaky as it opens.
**Palate:** Big and thick. Starts sweetly with a gingery lift. Great balance between old scuffed leather, nutty toffee and spicy rye.
**Finish:** Long if a little woody.

## OLD FORESTER BIRTHDAY BOURBON 13 YEARS OLD 1994 47%
Bourbon - Kentucky

**7¾ Dave: Assertive but balanced.**
**Nose:** Touch of freshly varnished wood. Dried cherry, cumin seed and some hickory with underlying sweetness. It becomes jammy and almost damson like, but always a deep scented oak. Water brings out caraway seed.
**Palate:** The perfumed note carries on. Lemon balm and zesty spiciness. Quite high tannins. Cigar smoke and drywood. Water lightens and smoothes.
**Finish:** Hints of bitter cherry stone.

**7½ Dominic: Classic old fashioned style bourbon and nothing wrong with that.**
**Nose:** Beeswax polish; tinned peach, spice.
**Palate:** Classic sweet candy then swings left with a hit of oak and rye.
**Finish:** Sharp but nice sugar and spice balance and a dash of anisette for good measure.

## OLD OVERHOLT CANADIAN RYE 40%
Rye - U.S.A.

**7¾ Michael: Originally from Pennsylvania. For years, the only reasonably accessible rye. I would have liked it to be more extrovert, to say: "I'm a rye, whether you like me or not, and I'm coming out of the closet."**
**Nose:** Oil of peppermint. Exotic fruits.
**Palate:** Well rounded. Tightly combined flavours. Plenty of substance. Gingery. Rooty. Cedary. Some rye bitterness gradually emerging.
**Finish:** Firm, long, appetising.

**8 Dave: A real bargain. Beginners start here.**
**Nose:** Soft yet lean. Fruity, yet floral and peppery: there's menthol, red peppercorn/allspice/nutmeg, rye bread, bourbon biscuits and fermenting red wine.
**Palate:** Soft, full and chewy then builds in intensity with a powerful rye attack giving flavours of bitter chocolate, spices and a slight floury (not flowery) quality. Lovely weight and energy.
**Finish:** Dry, crackling. Hint of sweetness.

## OLD POGUE 9 YEARS OLD, MASTER'S SELECT 45.5%
Bourbon - Kentucky

**7½ Michael: The body is well rounded, the flavours less so.**
**Nose:** Maple syrup. Pancakes. Brown sugar.
**Palate:** Light to medium. Rounded. Garden mint. Herbal. Leafy. Grass especially. Remarkably so.
**Finish:** Very sweet, but refreshing.

**7 Dave: Like sitting in a bar next to a gent who has overdone the aftershave.**
**Nose:** Opens with a rye flour note. On the spicy side of the fence. Water brings a fragrant note into play: rose petals.
**Palate:** Very perfumed, almost artificially so. Roses and violets. Intense and slightly overwhelming.
**Finish:** Vanilla.

## OLD POTRERO 62.1%
Single Malt - California

**8½ Michael: Despite the 'Old', a new rye. The idea was to get closer to what the first American ryes might have been. Wins points for all-rye character and assertiveness.**
**Nose:** Very fresh vanilla. Syrupy. Spearmint. Anis.
**Palate:** Soft, smooth, texture. Very fruity indeed. Begins very sweet, like tropical fruits in custard, then becomes drier and rooty.
**Finish:** Big, robust.

**7¾ Dave: Too immaculate for today's palate? Well-made, it's evident complexity needs more time to emerge fully. Bartenders love it, but is that down to its scarcity and price?**
**Nose:** Aggressively young and feisty with high-toned, perfumed notes of lemon, new make, nut and honey.
**Palate:** Though intense, young and lean it sits nicely in the mouth thanks to the high proof. The rye fizzes like space dust.
**Finish:** Bone dry. Young.

## OLD RIP VAN WINKLE'S 15 YEARS OLD, FAMILY RESERVE 53.5%
Bourbon - Kentucky

WHISKY
*Magazine*
Editor's choice

**8 Michael: Big . Rich. Hearty. Robust.**
**Nose:** Rich toffee. Creamy. Slightly smoky.
**Palate:** Creamy, becoming cedary. Dry.
**Finish:** Bittersweet. Lively.

**8½ Dave: Has a different level of depth and complexity. Sip and savour.**
**Nose:** Showing good maturity, mixing sweetness (apricot, plum, vanilla) with dry notes (green peppercorn, cold tea, biscuit). Elegant.
**Palate:** Big. Layers of flavour and deep fruitiness. Old leather, oaky tannins just picking up. Complex.
**Finish:** Dusty spices.

## PAPPY VAN WINKLE 15 YEARS OLD, FAMILY RESERVE 53.5%
Bourbon - Kentucky

WHISKY
*Magazine*
Recommended

**7¾ Martine: A big guy. On a frosty Christmas Eve maybe, waiting for Santa Claus by the fireplace. No risk of falling asleep with this fellow!**
**Nose:** Intense. Woody. Tickley. Rhubarb pie. Corn syrup. Exotic fruit. Pineapple juice. Hint of mango. Wood gradually withdrawing, letting fruit in.
**Palate:** Velvety but crisp. Oaky grip. A wave of liquorice (aniseed flavours and bitter root). Wild chervil. Spicy (tabasco, hint of caraway).
**Finish:** Everlasting and spicy. Liquorice.

**8½ Dave: An elegant old gentleman. Great balance. Highly recommended.**
**Nose:** Mature. Inside of an old wardrobe. Leather. Date, chocolate, coffee, black cherry, cigar. Good caramelisation and a tingle of sweet spices.
**Palate:** As nose suggests, in the bigger camp. Rich and precise. Bitter chocolate into raisin. Great balance.
**Finish:** Long powerful.

## PAPPY VAN WINKLE 20 YEARS OLD, FAMILY RESERVE 45.2%
Bourbon - Kentucky

WHISKY
*Magazine*
Recommended

**8¼ Michael: Showing its age, but I like its big, earthy, old-fashioned American flavours.**
**Nose:** Deep. Dried fruits. Raisins. Prunes. 'Country store' aromas. Slightly dusty.
**Palate:** Rich, buttery. Maple syrup. Slightly burnt pancakes.
**Finish:** Long. Warming. Slightly drying. Some char.

**9 Dave: A subtle sipper to be taken neat and definitely without ice!**
**Nose:** Deep, powerful and concentrated. This has moved into almost rancio territory: eucalypt/laurel, spice, burnt orange peel, apple, pear, biscuity wood.
**Palate:** Soft and surprisingly delicate given the age. A charred note adds to the complexity. Gentle and elegant: cigar box, prune, molasses, soot.
**Finish:** Long. In fact it's very, very long and complex.

## PAPPY VAN WINKLE 20 YEARS OLD, FAMILY RESERVE 45.2%
Bourbon - Kentucky

**8** **Michael: The family propensity to fall asleep seems to have struck in the bottle; given a chance to breathe and a drink of water, it comes back to life.**
**Nose:** Cocoa powder. Black chocolate. Parma violets.
**Palate:** Toasty. Slightly flat.
**Finish:** Creamy. Toffeeish. Very late spicy lift.

**7** **Dave: The elegance of youth obliterated by the oak.**
**Nose:** Dry and mature, but slightly austere. Oak shavings, coffee bean, walnut whip, marzipan. Woody.
**Palate:** Complex spirit that's been clamped in an oaky grip. Tannic and gripping.
**Finish:** Dry, splintery. Hint of sweetness behind.

## PAPPY VAN WINKLE FAMILY RESERVE, 23 YEARS OLD 47.8%
Bourbon - Kentucky

**8¼** **Michael: Big and robust but very drinkable and soothing.**
**Nose:** Polished oak.
**Palate:** Rich madeira cake.
**Finish:** Spicy. Vanilla pod. Toffee.

**7½** **Dave: Bigger and therefore better balanced than the 20 Years Old. Still grippy though.**
**Nose:** Into cooked/caramelised fruits, coffee grounds, hard toffee, aromatic. Rich and velvety. Oaky but with layers of sweetness underneath.
**Palate:** Powerful. Rich with cocoa solids, liquorice, chestnut (honey) and firm oak. Drier than the nose.
**Finish:** Long. Caramelised oak.

## PARKER HERITAGE COLLECTION 1996 CASK STRENGTH SMALL BATCH BOURBON 61.3%
Bourbon - Kentucky

**8½** **Dave: Copes with high alcohol well. Great balance, poise and sophistication.**
**Nose:** Rich with cedar and a sweet perfumed lift. Dusty with some dried flower. Has real poise and elegance disguising the strength. Water layers the aromas well bringing out some char as well as scented Chinese tea.
**Palate:** Sweet and concentrated with strawberry and cherry. Sweet juicy fruits then toffee, sandalwood and even incense. Big and thick on the palate. Balanced.
**Finish:** Spicy great length.

**8** **Dominic: A fine and full bourbon all-rounder.**
**Nose:** Glazed cherries, cedarwood, dusty polished leather.
**Palate:** Dark chocolate dipped cherries, spearmint and spice.
**Finish:** Long and warming.

## PENDLETON 10 YEARS OLD 40%
Blended - U.S.A.

**7¾** **Michael: Very drinkable, but does it have sufficient complexity to retain the drinker's interest?**
**Nose:** Spicy, minty.
**Palate:** Creamy. Grainy. Some rye spiciness. Créme caramel. Or even tiramisu?
**Finish:** Gentle surge of gingery spiciness to provide a balancing dryness. Gently warming.

**7** **Marcin: Good nose but doesn't really deliver.**
**Nose:** Pedro Ximinez or old fashioned Oloroso? Mincemeat.
**Palate:** Freshly baked pastry. Honey and nuts too. Pecan Danish.
**Finish:** Short but nicely integrated.

## PIKESVILLE SUPREME STRAIGHT RYE 40%
Rye - Kentucky

**7¾** **Michael: An old classic, originally from Maryland. Emphatically a rye, though in this instance that grain is in fruity mood, rather than being overtly spicy.**
**Nose:** Gentlemen's clubs. Leather armchairs. Tobacco.
**Palate:** Very smooth indeed. Opulent, but not a great deal of complexity. Luxurious. Cherries in brandy. Candied plums. Vanilla.
**Finish:** Sweetish. Delicious.

**8** **Dave: A cracking, edgy drink and alongside the fuller Overholt a real bargain. Great for barmen and beginners alike.**
**Nose:** Lean and young with medium intensity. Freshly ground cumin seed, green peppercorn, mint, bitter orange, hazelnut, peanut brittle. Touch of the hay-loft.

**Palate:** Quite silky and light to start, then the rye kicks in like a mule. Sherbet, ginger and spice.
**Finish:** Medium length, intense, dry with a lovely sour edge.

## RITTENHOUSE STRAIGHT RYE 100 PROOF 50%
Rye - Kentucky

**8** **Michael: A hundred American proof makes for a powerful whisky, but this is big and bold in flavour, too. I don't remember it being such a sensuous whiskey. A reborn giant?**
**Nose:** Rich dried fruits. Chocolate. Sweet peppers.
**Palate:** Clean, rich. Cocoa. Candied orange peels. Cinnamon. Nutmeg. Very spicy. Soothing.
**Finish:** Lingering dry spiciness.

**7¼** **Dave: The higher alcohol helps but there's still a lack of rye's full-on intensity.**
**Nose:** Fat and sweet: caramel, toffee apple, Caramac bars, cocoa powder, toast, but no discernible rye...
**Palate:** ...though this appears on the initially thick, dried fruit palate.
**Finish:** Sour though, almost metallic. Like chewing a coin.

## RITTENHOUSE RYE 21 YEARS OLD 50%
Rye - Kentucky

**8½** **Dave: Rye is a love or hate thing. I happen to love it. I usually prefer my ryes young, this works.**
**Nose:** A teasing mix of sweet/sour oils. Camphor, varnish, rich oak. Hugely spicy. With water there's nuts, shaved wood and flamed orange peel.
**Palate:** Intensely spicy, a firm grip and mouthtightening tannins overtake surprising sweetness. Scented lemon, dried rose petal.
**Finish:** Long wonderfully bitter. Rye!

**6¾** **Arthur: Way, way too much maturation for me.**
**Nose:** Vibrant explosion of vanilla, turpentine, banana, pot pourri. Behind these top notes there is an autumn leaf and fermenting grass character.
**Palate:** Parma violets, burnt lavender, and oak.
**Finish:** A woody bitterness and burnt rosemary.

## ROCK HILL FARM SINGLE CASK BOURBON 50%
Bourbon - Kentucky

**8¼** **Michael: The flavours may sound similar but it is the interplay of their subtleties that make this such an interesting whiskey. Try it with a double chocolate-chip cookie. Or a rocky road icecream.**
**Nose:** Raisins. Boxes of dates. Oak.
**Palate:** Black chocolate. Milk chocolate. White chocolate.
**Finish:** Balancing nutty dryness.

**9½** **Jim: Enticingly sophisticated.**
**Nose:** A dazzling array of oaky tones, but a drier, fruitier rye presence adds perfect balance. A softening sprig of mint compounds the complexity.
**Palate:** Opens evenly over the mouth: beautifully bitter sweet with the rye, toffee-cream oak.
**Finish:** Long, restrained age and some late rye and liquorice chewability. Unbelievably balanced and about as good as any bourbon gets.

## SAM HOUSTON VERY SMALL BATCH 10 YEARS OLD 45%
Bourbon - Kentucky

**7¾** **Michael: An attractive, tawny, colour and a good, straight-ahead, whiskey. Could be more complex at ten years. Ideal with a Texas barbecue?**
**Nose:** Cleanly oaky. Dessert apples. Toast. A hint of char.
**Palate:** Big, smooth, sweet.
**Finish:** Crisp.

**7¾** **Dave: Well made and pretty punchy, but maybe just a little too dry.**
**Nose:** Attractive, soft nose. Nutty (hazelnut, peanut brittle) with some oak tones. In time, liquorice, cream toffee, walnut, coffee bean, smoke/soot.
**Palate:** Soft fruits: peaches in cream with a little wood towards the back.
**Finish:** A little short and dry.

## SAZERAC 18 YEARS OLD STRAIGHT RYE 45%
Rye - Kentucky

**8½** **Michael: A trifle sophisticated for my tastes, but a very fine rye whiskey.**

**Nose:** Fragrant. Fruity. Leafy. Herbal. Peppery. Charred oak.
**Palate:** Nutty. Lightly toffeeish. Minty. Spicey. Dried fruits. Melon dusted with ginger.
**Finish:** Lively, refreshing.

**8¼ Dave: Robust, extra mature stuff but maybe the wood has the upper hand.**
**Nose:** Mature and rich: caramel, dried fruit, maraschino, vin santo, coffee grounds, tobacco with allspice, cinnamon and lemon. A little woody?
**Palate:** Round and rich to start, then spicy rye takes over. Muscular stuff, though a little tannic, making it slightly bitter rather than sour.
**Finish:** Earth, red fruit, coconut.

## ST GEORGE SINGLE MALT 43%
Single Malt - California

**6 Michael: Knowing that this distillery began with eau-de-vie, I hope I am not being suggestible, but I find the fruitiness of this whisky overwhelming.**
**Nose:** Concentrated sweet fruits.
**Palate:** Creamy. Intense berry-fruits. Predominantly blackcurrant. Also suggestions of flowering currant and passion fruit.
**Finish:** Light, dry.

**6 Dave: A dessert spirit, more muscat than malt.**
**Nose:** Incredibly sweetly fruity: a cross between a fruit eau de vie and a (moscato-based) dessert wine, all jasmine and light citrus. Water softens down the intensity but still loads of boiled sweeties, orange blossom water and dry malty notes.
**Palate:** Drier than the nose suggests. A light ethereal palate with those aromatics all the way.
**Finish:** Sweet.

## TWO BOBS KENTUCKY BOURBON 1994 CASK NO. 64 64%
Bourbon - Kentucky

**7½ Dave: Out on its own. More finesse but less power.**
**Nose:** Candy floss and baked banana. Quite scented. Lighter than most here. Slightly distant.
**Palate:** Tannins a plenty. Firm grip and big alcohol. The lighter flavours takes it into Cognac like territory of grilled nuts and spice with some tomato leaf underneath.
**Finish:** Becomes richer, sweeter and riper.

**7¾ Dominic: Hold its own in strong company.**
**Nose:** Grape, raisin, marmalade. Restrained.
**Palate:** Honey and orange, sweet spice, and then wood.
**Finish:** Long and tangy.

## TWO BOBS KENTUCKY BOURBON 1994 CASK NO. 65 63.7%
Bourbon - Kentucky

**8¼ Dave: In line with cask No. 66, but with greater complexity. One for a cigar.**
WHISKY *Editor's choice*
**Nose:** Leathery with stewed fruits. Light cardamom lift. Deep and forest-like. Rich layered and robust. On the bigger side of things. Damson, chestnut honey.
**Palate:** Concentrated. Seems to have some age. Cherry throat sweets (Tunes)/elderberry. Deep in the centre with layers of oak and nuts giving structure to the dense weight.
**Finish:** Long and slightly drying.

**8½ Dominic: Another big whiskey with plenty to offer.**
**Nose:** Honeyed vanilla, stewed fruits, plum.
**Palate:** Sharp, pinewood, mint and resin.
**Finish:** A long dash of fruit and wood.

## TWO BOBS KENTUCKY BOURBON 1994 CASK NO. 66 63.7%
Bourbon - Kentucky

**7¾ Dave: Not exactly subtle, but has a certain bruising charm.**
WHISKY *Recommended*
**Nose:** Big, upfront with masses of vanilla overlaying the inevitable spiciness. Huge, sweet and powerful. Picks up an almost dried fruit depth in time. With water a scented dustiness gives it a lift.
**Palate:** Grainy texture. Heat and oaky grip. Cherryade but the aromatic edge carries through well. Zesty.
**Finish:** Good length. Oaky.

**8½ Dominic: Not for the fainthearted. For the Kill Bill, vindaloo and extreme wrestling person in your life.**
**Nose:** Rich, deep, Christmas cake, wood polish, sandalwood.

**Palate:** Big hit of oak and spice, prunes, dark chocolate and oak. Then more wood.
**Finish:** Long, dry and spicy. Oh, and did I mention the oak?

## VAN WINKLE 12 YEARS OLD, LOT B 45.2%
Bourbon - Kentucky

**8 Michael: This should obviously be an ingredient of all self-respecting desserts. An accompaniment to them, too. And an after dinner drink. You are in a dry county? So what?**
**Nose:** Rich, creamy, flowery, fruity.
**Palate:** Chocolate pralines filled with fudgy toffee and orange cream.
**Finish:** Crunchy cookies, slightly burnt at the edges. A suggestion of char.

**8 Dave: Gentle but rich. Somehow the reverse of the Weller, smells spicy and becomes honeyed in the mouth.**
**Nose:** Takes time to open, then rich, polished oak tones alongside pepper, cumin, nutmeg. Turkish Delight.
**Palate:** Big soft and creamy, ripe berries and honey. Powerful.
**Finish:** Gentle honeyed/buttery.

## VAN WINKLE 13 YEARS OLD, FAMILY RESERVE RYE 47.8%
Rye - Kentucky

**8¼ Michael: Showing its age. It seems to have lost a little liveliness but, if you were as rich as this, would you care?**
WHISKY *Editor's choice*
**Nose:** Distinctly rich. Mint toffee. Raisin toffee.
**Palate:** Viscous. So smooth as to be almost slippery, but with the flavours of fruitcake. Very sweet.
**Finish:** Warm. Relaxing. Lots of vanilla. Bourbon-like.

**8½ Dave: A typical but a wonderful drink to sip on its own. The more I drink it the more I love it.**
**Nose:** Intense, oily and full bodied. Initially sweet: roses, lavender, black cherry, orange, chocolate and toffee, then a blast of menthol that clears the sinuses.
**Palate:** Big and sweet. The rye grabs you mid-palate then cooked fruit/cherry/treacle come back, before the sour rye gives a final bite. Lovely balance.
**Finish:** Soft, then cherry stone.

## VAN WINKLE 23 YEARS OLD 47.8%
Bourbon - Kentucky

**8¼ Michael: Even more age to handle, but it has wistful, nostalgic charm.**
**Nose:** Rich. Polished oak. A little underlying charred-oak character.
**Palate:** Raisins. Madeira cake. Vanilla.
**Finish:** Hard toffee. Drying into slight charcoal.

**7 Jim: Actually a massive improvement on the legendary 20 Years Old.**
**Nose:** A macho oaky, orangey nose hardly for the fainthearted. Honey and tannin combine effectively but over leathery and aged.
**Palate:** An enormous eruption of oak takes an uncompromising grip.
**Finish:** Bitter and dry though a thread of burnt honey comb and chocolate.

## VAN WINKLE FAMILY RESERVE KENTUCKY STRAIGHT BOURBON, 18 YEARS OLD 52.6%
Bourbon - Kentucky

**8½ Michael: The wisdom of the ages is locked in there somewhere, but it is hard to penetrate the wood.**
**Nose:** Woody. Dusty. Dried bananas. Brown crystal sugar.
**Palate:** Dense. Drying. Bitter chocolate fudge cake.
**Finish:** Aromatic. Cedary. Woody.

**7½ Dave: The wood just a little obtrusive.**
**Nose:** Huge. Concentrated and almost meaty. Pipe smoke, black cherry. Sweetness in the middle.
**Palate:** Perfume changes to rosemary and thyme. Deep and rich. Tannic.
**Finish:** Slightly bitter.

### VAN WINKLE FAMILY RESERVE, 13 YEARS OLD 47.8%
Bourbon - Kentucky

**8½ Michael: Certainly showing its age, but full of character.**
**Nose:** Good mint-toffee, rye aroma.
**Palate:** Good viscosity. Sweetish. Spicy. Cinnamon. Nutmeg. Rich fruitcake.
**Finish:** Cigar smoke. Very late soothing warmth.

**8¼ Jim: A charming rye.**
**Nose:** One of the sweetest expressions of any rye; not as, literally, hard nosed as others, attractively perfumed with a hint of malt too.
**Palate:** Firmer on the palate than nose with the arrival of the rye delayed until the middle is neared.
**Finish:** Delicious sweet coating counterbalances the more bitter rye. Rumbling oak and liquorice are pleasantly muted.

### VAN WINKLE SPECIAL RESERVE, 12 YEARS OLD 45.2%
Bourbon - Kentucky

**7¼ Michael: Well balanced. Easy to drink. Not especially complex.**
**Nose:** Vanilla. Creamy. Fruit dessert topping. Mandarin?
**Palate:** Lightly malty. Lingering. Citrus. Tangerine peels.
**Finish:** Slightly bitter, balancing dryness. Tangerine zest.

**8 Dave: Though lighter than most, is balanced and harmonious.**
**Nose:** Light and almost dusty. Dried mango, cocoa, parma violet, fruit, spiced peach, (Fry's) Turkish Delight. Light but elegant.
**Palate:** Almost Cognac-like. Light grip, touch of honey, spicy oak, light tobacco leaf. Slick with good flow and feel. Balanced.
**Finish:** Dry, tingling.

### VERY OLD BARTON 6 YEARS OLD 43%
Bourbon - Kentucky

**7½ Michael: I remember this whiskey being more flowery and dry – and thinner.**
**Nose:** Rich aroma. Pancakes with lemon.
**Palate:** Big bodied. Sweet.
**Finish:** Gingery.

**7¾ Dave: Good old style punchy bourbon. Hank Williams.**
**Nose:** Syrup candy and spice. Ripe.
**Palate:** Soft, fruity and mellow with a spicy bite.
**Finish:** Intense and crackling.

### VIRGINIA GENTLEMAN 90 PROOF SMALL BATCH BOURBON 45%
Bourbon - Kentucky

**7½ Michael: Less characterful than the Virginia Gentleman I remember, but still quite distinctive.**
**Nose:** Very light. Decidedly sweet, honeyish, spiciness.
**Palate:** Smooth. Quite rich. Malty. Brown sugar. Spicy. Cinnamon. American-style apple pie.
**Finish:** Lightly gingery. Crisp.

**7¾ Dave: Subtle and well-made.**
**Nose:** At the higher, scented end of the spectrum: lemon balm, sweet candy, caramelised fruit, fig, dry spices, vanilla.
**Palate:** Spicy. Nutmeg, apple sponge, red berry fruits, light syrup.
**Finish:** Soft, then a space dust barrage of spices.

### W.L. WELLER 60.95%
Bourbon - Kentucky

**8 Arthur: Remarkably drinkable at full strength; I didn't enjoy it as much once diluted. Impressive: but you must like 'em woody.**
**Nose:** Refresher sweeties, turpentine and eucalyptus. Rye in evidence.
**Palate:** Parma violets, vanilla and sawdust.
**Finish:** An intense progression of pine, sap and wood. A good chewin' whiskey.

**9 Dave: A phenomenal whiskey. Stephen Camisa we salute you.**
**Nose:** Great intensity of aroma. A huge, old, but gentle bourbon. Cinnamon bark, cedar, high char, heavy perfumed rose, sweet vermouth, spice. It's a ready-made Manhattan!
**Palate:** Benylin, cherry menthol then allspice. Great length. Water brings out grippy oak.
**Finish:** Long, slightly grippy.

### W.L. WELLER 12 YEARS OLD 45%
Bourbon - Kentucky

WHISKY Magazine Recommended

**8¼ Michael: Would I take a bath in this? Well, perhaps a shower.**
**Nose:** Perfumy. Almond bath soap.
**Palate:** Dry. Herbal.
**Finish:** Cleansing. Refreshing. Some orangey acidity.

**7¾ Dave: Not the most complex but has perfect balance and gentle Southern charm.**
**Nose:** Silky and soft: lemon, lint, coffee and cream, chocolate, lightly nutty. Has subtle, gentle depth.
**Palate:** Sexy and sweet, moving into pine honey. Firm mid-palate, cooked fruits, damson, coconut.
**Finish:** Sweet and soft.

### W.L. WELLER 12 YEARS OLD 45%
Bourbon - Kentucky

**7½ Martine: The nose delivers more than the palate. Once more, oak overwhelms fruit and bitterly dries the finish.**
**Nose:** Spirity. Prickly. Herbal. Jasmine tea. Cider apple. Dessert-like aromas. Ginger biscuit. Trifle. Maraschino cherry. Shortcrust pastry.
**Palate:** Firm, crisp. Good feel. Creamy. Coffee toffee. Bitter orange marmalade. Ginger.
**Finish:** Medium. Quickly fading. A bit thin. Smoked hazelnuts. Becoming astringent.

**8¼ Dave: You could sit and suck on a bottle of this all day long. Worryingly drinkable.**
**Nose:** Clean and light. Gentle grated nutmeg, cumin, vellum, roasting coffee bean then into honeycomb. Rose petal.
**Palate:** A clean very honeyed palate with a crisp spice from the oak which then softens into melted chocolate.
**Finish:** A zippy lift which freshens everything. Sandalwood.

### W.L. WELLER 19 YEARS OLD 45%
Bourbon - Kentucky

**8 Michael: A bourbon of some presence and elegance. With dessert, or after dinner?**
**Nose:** Fruity and toffeeish. Polished oak.
**Palate:** Lighter-bodied than the full colour might suggest, but firm and textured.
**Finish:** Hint of char. Firm and clinging.

**8 Jim: A busy, beautifully constituted bourbon that gracefully defies the years.**
**Nose:** Toast and marmalade with coffee.
**Palate:** Dry and spicy start. The oak is pierced by a decent corn richness that hangs on the oily middle.
**Finish:** Remains vanilla-rich and oaky.

### W.L. WELLER 19 YEARS OLD 45%
Bourbon - Kentucky

**7¼ Michael: If this had been bottled for six or seven years ago, I would probably have loved its big flavours. I like oak, but this is too much, and too old, for me. If you are an oak extremist, rush out and buy this one.**
**Nose:** Nutty, wheaty. Cinnamon. Earthy, oaky.
**Palate:** Smooth. Some winery notes. More oak.
**Finish:** Dried fruits. Black chocolate. Cedary.

**9¼ Dave: The wood is perfect balance. Complex and very sophisticated.**
**Nose:** Rich and elegant with gunky, fugal notes mixed with soft honeysuckle, gingerbread, banoffee pie/pecan pie, chocolate covered cherries.
**Palate:** Mellow, funky and perfumes with layers of complex dark fruit: blackberry, prune, clove-spiced honey, cooked apple, raisin/sultana, spice, old leather, earth, soot, orange butter icing.
**Finish:** Gentle and soft.

### WILD TURKEY 10 YEARS OLD, RUSSELL'S RESERVE 50.5%
Bourbon - Kentucky

WHISKY Magazine Recommended

**8¼ Michael: Slightly austere and cerebral. One to sip while watching a video of an art-house movie.**
**Nose:** Slightly smoky. Char. Oak. Leather. Tightly combined aromas and flavours.
**Palate:** Dry maltiness. Raisins. Fruitiness. Fudge. A hint of dusty chocolate.
**Finish:** Fruity, sappy.

**Dave: A complex, serious, sipping bourbon.**
**Nose:** Spicier than 101 but with weight and fragrance. As it opens (and it needs time) out come classic WT notes: ripe fruits, rich dark honey, with added cigar box, leather, peach, honeysuckle.
**Palate:** A little more wood than 101 but balanced. Chewy weight with an extra layer of dried spice: garam masala.
**Finish:** Long and rich.

## WILD TURKEY 17 YEARS OLD 50.5%
Bourbon - Kentucky

**Michael: I like this very much, for its complexity and originality. As a bourbon?** The useful phrase 'something else' comes to mind.
**Nose:** Red summer fruits. Cherry pits. Almonds.
**Palate:** Big, firm, smooth. Much drier than a typical Turkey, or any other bourbon. Flowery. Lavender.
**Finish:** An explosion of dry, cedary flavours.

**Dave: All the power you expect from this distillery. Late at night.**
**Nose:** Heavy and powerful. Rum-like: black fruits, molasses sugar. Caramelised orange, leather and dark chocolate (mint?). Black honey. Woody notes.
**Palate:** Massively powerful, sits on the tongue like a grizzly bear. Chestnut honey but with a teasing savoury edge and a lift from the rye.
**Finish:** A little woody, then sweet spices.

## WILD TURKEY 8 YEARS OLD, 101 40%
Bourbon - Kentucky

**Michael: Yes it is big and wild, but far more sophisticated than the name suggests.**
**Nose:** Dry. Molasses. Vanilla.
**Palate:** More malty flavours than might be expected in a Bourbon. Suggestions of Assam tea. The char flavours are not tea but wood.
**Finish:** Oaky, winey, raisiny. Very long.

**Jim: A drier version of the old No. 8 101 brand, with the honey trademark keeping a low profile. Not quite so** complex but a sturdy bourbon for all that.
**Nose:** Heavy oak and vanilla, sweet and quite fat.
**Palate:** Rich and mouth-coating from the start, with a surprising burst of oaky spice at the centre. The honey sweetness lurks in the background.
**Finish:** Rye depth and fruitiness but unusually dry and oak-heavy.

## WILD TURKEY 8 YEARS OLD, 101 50.5%
Bourbon - Kentucky

**Michael: A huge whiskey. Put together with style and sophistication, but still with** all the robustness of a true bourbon. A classic, of course. A Clint Eastwood of whiskeys.
**Nose:** Robust. Leather saddlery. Molasses.
**Palate:** Firm. Deep. Very malty-tasting, yet assertively a bourbon. Malt-loaf. Cookies. Raisiny.
**Finish:** Rummy. Powerful. Soothing.

**Dave: This is what great bourbon is all about. Languorous, rich, elegant and powerful.**
**Nose:** Big, fruity and complex. Ripe dark fruits: blackberry, prune, wild honey, caramelised fruit, leather, chocolate. Luscious and beautifully balanced.
**Palate:** Big, no, make that huge. Ripe, treacle, chocolate mousse, with a ripe rose petal/violet high. Thick layers of honey and nut and balanced spicy oak.
**Finish:** Long and complex.

## WILD TURKEY 80 40%
Bourbon - Kentucky

**Michael: No fancy tricks here but a big, complex, regular bourbon.**
**Nose:** Aromatic. Polished leather.
**Palate:** Big. Smooth. Almost slippery at first, then developing an interesting interplay of sweetness and dryness. Cereal grains. Pecan nuts. Tobacco-like.
**Finish:** Spicy. Toothsome.

**Dave: Firm and dry, but has none of Wild Turkey's signature depth and sweet power.**
**Nose:** Dry and spicy with treacle, cigar smoke/ash. Pretty dry.
**Palate:** As the nose suggests, dry and tight with a little honeyed lushness mid-palate.
**Finish:** Long and sweet.

## WILD TURKEY KENTUCKY SPIRIT 50.5%
Bourbon - Kentucky

**Michael: Wild Turkey in a coat and tie.**
**Nose:** Soft, deep. Mint cream chocolates.
**Palate:** Smooth and sweet at first. Then developing bigger flavours. Lots of oaky woody extract.
**Finish:** Very lively and and appetising. Root ginger and bitter chocolate.

**Jim: Deceptively delicious: threatens to erupt but ends up relatively meek and well behaved.**
**Nose:** Loads of fruit, rye and malt. Big and bristling.
**Palate:** Rich chocolatey orange with toffee fudge but then lightens to allow the corn through.
**Finish:** More corn and dries as oak arrives.

## WILD TURKEY KENTUCKY SPIRIT 50.5%
Bourbon - Kentucky

**Michael: My descriptors make it sound like a dessert whisky, but it is also very appetising. Just a tad too** sophisticated for me.
**Nose:** Soft and luscious. Fruity, orangey. Chocolate. Mint.
**Palate:** Big, lively, flavours with ginger and more chocolate.
**Finish:** Especially gingery. Root ginger? More chocolate.

**Dave: As sexy as Isaac Hayes' Hot Buttered Soul. One to savour all night.**
**Nose:** The most herbal and spicy of the WT range: wild thyme, sage, fennel, coriander, nutmeg, cumin. Also smokier than the rest with notes of molasses, chestnut honey, crème brûlée.
**Palate:** Complex and very soft. Raisin bread, butter, tupelo honey/maple.
**Finish:** Huge and everlasting. Highly complex.

## WILD TURKEY RARE BREED 54.2%
Bourbon - Kentucky

**Michael: This is more like a supercharged Wild One. Defiantly robust, but with** Devilish charm. I love it.
**Nose:** Soft, oaky, fresh earth. Peaches.
**Palate:** Toffeeish. Fruity. Raisins. Remarkably smooth, but packed with energy and power.
**Finish:** Creamy, aromatic.

**Jim: A big bourbon with the proportions being generous and almost perfectly proportioned.**
**Nose:** Gorgeous honey, diced dates, old leather and rye with a teasing sprinkling of spice. Magnificent.
**Palate:** Massively intense launch, waxy honeycomb with fabulously controlled Demerara sweetness and an edge of rye.
**Finish:** Long lightly liquoriced with the honey hanging on, as does the rye and a soft build up of cocoa.

## WILD TURKEY RYE 50.5%
Rye - Kentucky

**Michael: The wildness of 101, tempered with the extra rye, makes for a very distinctive whiskey.**
**Nose:** Molasses. Hickory. Briar. Herbal, tea-like, rye notes.
**Palate:** A powerful whiskey. Spicy rye against a big corn background. Some malt, too.
**Finish:** Vanilla. Spiced rum. Charred oak.

**Dave: A classic big-boned style that gets maximum extraction of flavours.**
**Nose:** Big and perfumed: dried lavender, honey, cake mix, black cherry and rye pepperiness.
**Palate:** Huge, heavy and oily, then the acidic rye blasts its way in like Jesse James and takes control souring things up and giving a powerful mouthful that balances sweet and savoury beautifully.
**Finish:** Long with wonderful balance.

# American Wild - Woodford

## WILD TURKEY SHERRY SIGNATURE 43%
Bourbon - Kentucky

**7½ Michael: Bourbon and sherry? Is this allowed? I'm not sure it should be. I didn't order this, I ordered 101.**
**Nose:** Cherries. Almonds. Bakewell tart fresh out of the oven.
**Palate:** Creamy. Cedary. Smoky.
**Finish:** Drying.

**7½ Dave: Seems to come in two distinct parts. Of interest, but by no means the best Turkey.**
**Nose:** Rich and concentrated. Raisin, walnut, sour cherry syrup, clove and cocoa. Oak with sherry.
**Palate:** Rounded and rich. Chocolate and vanilla, nutmeg and red/black fruits. Then comes sherry; raisined fruits and lightly grippy oak.
**Finish:** Thick and sweet. Liquorice. Tannin.

## WILD TURKEY SINGLE BARREL 101 PROOF 50.5%
Bourbon - Kentucky

**7½ Arthur: Good dram, lacked the greatness you'd hope for with such age.**
**Nose:** Hazelnuts, dark chocolate, tropical fruit. With water up came some aloe vera with peaches.
**Palate:** Peaches and sweet mint and lots of American oak.
**Finish:** Like sucking an apricot stone: fruity, woody and bitter.

**8 Dave: A well-balanced slightly lighter style of Turkey, but another finer addition to the range.**
**Nose:** Intense. Amaretto, cherry stone, pine, light rye dustiness, bitter chocolate, spiced buns. Wood oil, into varnish, citrus zest and firmness.
**Palate:** Clean and precise with good grip. The chocolate reappears alongside some tobacco, then masses of spice, maraschino, caraway, rye.
**Finish:** Tinned cling peaches, oak.

## WOODFORD RESERVE KENTUCKY STRAIGHT BOURBON WHISKEY 45.2%
Bourbon - Kentucky

**8½ Michael: Seductive. I found myself using such post-prandial language. Will she respect me in the morning?**
**Nose:** Minty. Oily. Parma violets.
**Palate:** Hard bitter chocolate. A praline filled with almond cream. Faintly smoky, suggesting coffee being roasted for espresso.
**Finish:** Rich black coffee, a quick splash of rum and crisp, stem-ginger, petit-fours.

**8½ Dave: Sophisticated stuff with a subtle southern charm. Classic Manhattan material.**
**Nose:** Hauntingly perfumed. Complex, honeyed and soft: orange blossom, tangerine peel, poached peach, mint, smoky oak.
**Palate:** Ripe and soft, like orange honey dribbled on top of Greek yoghurt. Caramelised fruits, it gets creamier as it opens.
**Finish:** Dry and elegant with a little grippy wood.

## WOODFORD RESERVE KENTUCKY STRAIGHT BOURBON WHISKEY 45.2%
Bourbon - Kentucky

**8½ Michael: Encouraged by the dark-orange colour, descriptors sound sweet. Overall effect is one of pithy dryness, with great finesse.**
**Nose:** Cigar-boxes. Hint of charcoal.
**Palate:** Very firm. Full of flavours, tightly combined. Whole almonds, marzipan.
**Finish:** Very long. Flowery. Violets.

**8½ Jim: More oak and age than normal. Being small batch, it does vary but is always delicious.**
**Nose:** Pronounced oak softened by fruity rye and gentle vanilla. A little toffee and honey.
**Palate:** Big, big lift off with a powering oaky-rye surge and an immediate arrival of spice. Toasty towards the middle with the corn arriving late on.
**Finish:** Long, cocoa and oak finale; burnt toast with a spread of honey.

## WOODFORD RESERVE SONOMA-CUTRER FINISH 43.2%
Bourbon - Kentucky

**5¾ Dave: Very poor. Still, after this and the Buffalo Trace experiments we can say that bourbon and Chardonnay don't mix. So, let's move on.**
**Nose:** Odd. Bread and butter pudding, soft fudge. Behind a dry grassiness teetering into off notes. Becomes cloying with water. Cold caramel pudding.
**Palate:** Oxidised wine, blackberry and in time a buttermilk sourness. Clumsy.
**Finish:** Claggy.

**5¾ Dominic: An oddball. Like an over-thin model: neither very attractive and not much in the way of body.**
**Nose:** Lightweight, grassy, over-ripe fluffy apple.
**Palate:** Winey, young fruit, more wet grass than bluegrass.
**Finish:** Over-polite for a bourbon.

Heaven Hill's warehouses are an imposing sight in the Kentucky dusk

**Clockwise from top:** The opening of Washington's Distillery at Mount Vernon; Race horses feature prominently at Woodford Reserve; The Maker's Mark spirit safe; Mash fermenting at Barton Distillery; The Beam flag flying proudly over its warehouses and land; Barrels resting in George Dickel's warehouses

# Canada

We should not forget that once Canada was one of the biggest whisky producing nations. Large distilleries across the country pumped out millions of gallons of spirit. By the mid-20th century companies like Seagram's and Hiram Walker & Son built huge kingdoms surrounding their whiskies, with Seagram even building Allt a' Bhainne and Braeval back in Scotland.

Now this time has passed and once where hundreds of distilleries created an empire just a dozen follow in the footsteps of this illustrious history, still producing a significant amount of whisky each year. In fact it still ranks as one of the biggest producing countries in volume terms.

With massive growing capacity in the prairie lands, the most important grain here is rye, and the production of rye-based spirits is central to distillers.

The classic method in Canada for making whisky has taken the traditional Scottish blending example and added a Canadian twist on it.

In general most distillers blend rye, perhaps with other whiskies made in the style of malts and bourbon. Rye adds the pep and spice to the flavour and aroma.

These rye-centred blends create a clean, gentle whisky, which is different to the ryes of America. A fine example comes from the Alberta Distillery in the shape of Alberta Premium 25 Years Old rye.

© WILLIAM M DOWD / DOWD ON DRINKS

**This page top and bottom:** John Hall at Kittling Ridge; The Hiram Walker building, part of the Canadian Club legacy
**Opposite:** A collection of Canadian whiskies

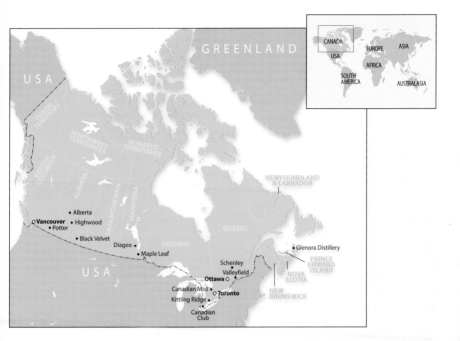

That is the traditional approach. Some smaller distillers such as John Hall, the owner of Kittling Ridge distillery, have set about making whisky that takes the tradition in a new direction.

John makes his own rye, malt whisky and bourbon and blends all three to create some fine whiskies.

Looking over the tastings from the past years, perhaps it is time that the world started to listen to some of the Canadian distillers once more.

**DID YOU KNOW...**
- The two potstills at Glenora Distillery in Cape Breton were sourced from Scotland
- The super premium brand Crown Royal was created to honour King George VI and Queen Elizabeth's visit to Canada in 1939
- The first distillery was opened by Hiram Walker in Windsor, Ontario in 1858, with Canadian Club launched in 1884

## CADENHEAD'S CANADIAN INDIAN CORN 15 YEARS OLD 54.9%
Single Grain

**7¼ Martine:** Quite young and green, with a nice fresh tang, especially when diluted. But this cardboardy flavour hangs on.
**Nose:** Spirity, slightly cardboardy at first then fruity notes. With water, a wet earthy note.
**Palate:** Silky with sweet notes (red fruit in yoghurt). Funny enough, the cardboardy flavour comes after. Distant mint.
**Finish:** Dry, slightly burning, spicy.

**7¾ Dave:** A total change from the first quartet with good drive and energy which sets it apart.
**Nose:** Higher alcohol and a crisper attack. Scented, fruit sirop. Flowers. Perfumed. Lime. Attractive. Obviously sweet.
**Palate:** Direct and tight mid-palate with slight acidity giving interest. A charred note with water then floral lift. Better grip.
**Finish:** Spicy yet sweet.

## CANADIAN CLUB 100 PROOF 50%
Blended

**8¼ Michael:** About as robust a whisky as I have tasted from the established Canadian distillers.
**Nose:** Freshly chopped almonds. Then toasted almonds.
**Palate:** Oily. Lots of flavour development. Figs, peaches, prunes.
**Finish:** Soft, syrupy, anis, sweet.

**6 Dave:** Poor. Unbalanced. In your face. Terrance and Phillip.
**Nose:** Light, numb, hard and a little dumb.
**Palate:** Hard and powerful. The alcohol dominates.
**Finish:** Hard and slightly metallic.

## CANADIAN CLUB 6 YEARS OLD 40%
Blended

**6¼ Martine:** Hard to believe this is a whisky. Closer to a rum.
**Nose:** Sweet and sugary. Cane syrup with a hint of liquorice and barley sugar. The sweetness reminds more of a liqueur than a whisky.
**Palate:** Sweet with a strong Demerara flavour. A rum in disguise? More burning than spicy.
**Finish:** Bittersweet, not holding long but leaves an astringent aftertaste.

**7 Dave:** Nothing to write home about.
**Nose:** Medium intensity, slightly leafy with a hint of caraway. In time a youthful edgy note is added. Green with water, quite hard. Green garden twine. Plant like.
**Palate:** Soft start only getting some grip in the centre and then builds in intensity to the finish. Better neat than diluted. A bit rigid and slightly.
**Finish:** Metallic on the finish.

## CANADIAN CLUB 8 YEARS OLD, SHERRY CASK 41.3%
Blended

**7¾ Michael:** Does Canadian work with sherry? I think bourbon wood has more to offer, but this is a nice try.
**Nose:** Maple syrup.
**Palate:** Smooth, nutty, rich.
**Finish:** Some rye coming through.

**7¼ Dave:** Whisky-flavoured sherry. Bit too sickly sweet for me. Celine Dion.
**Nose:** Amber/copper. Slick, slippery nose: caramel, Gonzalez-Byass Alfonso sherry, wholemeal bread, fruit cake.
**Palate:** Ultra-soft like buttered walnut bread and a dry, nutty, mid-palate.
**Finish:** Drying but soft.

## CANADIAN CLUB CLASSIC 12 YEARS OLD 40%
Blended

**7¾ Michael:** That medicinal touch gives this whisky an appetising edge.
**Nose:** Drier, pruney, slightly medicinal.
**Palate:** Rounded. Tightly interlocked flavours.
**Finish:** Milk chocolate. Sweet. By far the biggest finish in this group of Canadian Clubs.

**7¾ Dave:** Rye bite with butter and vanilla coating. Cowboy Junkies.
**Nose:** Understated and buttery. There's vanilla slice/custard, soft silky fruits, some nuttiness.
**Palate:** That buttery quality continues: mellow and honeyed, like soft toffee cream, then crisps up towards the finish.
**Finish:** Spice and harder than you'd initially expect.

## CANADIAN CLUB CLASSIC 12 YEARS OLD 40%
Blended

**6½ Martine:** Again, this rum taste, in a sharper and richer version than the first one.
**Nose:** Sweet with a floral note and a touch of beeswax. A distant echo of toffee trying to cover up the spirity olfactory frame.
**Palate:** Extremely sweet at first, on the Demerara side like the first one, then getting really bitter. A touch of ginger.
**Finish:** Drier, bitter, rather short.

**7½ Dave:** Well-balanced and pleasing.
**Nose:** Dry crackers, but underlying sweetness. Kumquat and pomegranate. Shows a decent layering effect. Sweet/sour with balanced caramelised oak tones. Soft with water, if a little one-dimensional.
**Palate:** Very sweet. Vanilla ice cream and coffee. A little mango. Tongue clinging, but with an early, zesty bite.
**Finish:** Flattens a little. Soft.

## CANADIAN CLUB RESERVE 10 YEARS OLD 40%
Blended

**7½ Michael:** Straight-ahead Canadian whisky, as I remember it from my early days as an eclectic drinker.
**Nose:** Fruity. Rye. Smoky.
**Palate:** Bigger, rounder, spicier.
**Finish:** Spicier, drier.

**7¾ Dave:** Easy going, middle of the road. Needs another layer of complexity to lift it into greatness. Bryan Adams.
**Nose:** Mellow toffee sweetness with cooked fruits, honey/syrup, apple and a whiff of camphor.
**Palate:** Soft, round and silky with lifted orange/tangerine notes.
**Finish:** Tingling. The toffee comes back.

## CANADIAN CLUB RESERVE 10 YEARS OLD 40%
Blended

**7¼ Martine:** The sweet Demerara taste is still there but "enriched" with a spicy note.
**Nose:** Spirity at first then sweetness wraps up the nostrils with chocolate syrup and a touch of vanilla. A citrussy breath comes in behind. Hint of varnish.
**Palate:** Quite balanced. Velvety texture. The sweetness is not overpowering. Spices open up. Ginger and white pepper.
**Finish:** Medium, dry, with a bitter edge.

**7¼ Dave:** It's sweet...and then sweeter.
**Nose:** Fat and corn-sweet. Popcorn and meal. Melted milk chocolate, mango, banana milk shake. Very light spice.
**Palate:** Just a hint of dried fruit on the start then dried pineapple and papaya. Quite simple and slightly one-dimensional.
**Finish:** Only starts to firm here.

## CANADIAN CLUB SHERRY CASK 40%
Blended

**7½ Martine:** A fruity/spicy profile. Rye whisky shines through. Refreshing on a hot summer day.
**Nose:** Shy, fruity sweetness. Apple blossom and apple jelly with a creamy toffee touch.
**Palate:** Sweet and fruity. Quite refreshing. Apple juice. Candied ginger. Water brings out citrussy aromas and a touch of sawdust.
**Finish:** Dry and spicy with an oaky grip.

**7 Dave:** Everything turned up to 11, but that can't hide its clumsy character. More bolted together than blended.
**Nose:** Stewed plums, grape must with some butteriness behind.
**Palate:** Very scented. Rosewater then the classic Canadian flow of sweet cream and a little nuttiness. Dried fruits dominate. Collapses with water.
**Finish:** Splits into spirit and dried fruit.

## CANADIAN CLUB SHERRY CASK 41.3%
Blended

**7½ Martine:** More smooth than the previous ones. But I still can't find if it's whisky there.
**Nose:** Oaky. Quite dark too. Sherry influence. Prune juice. Strong coffee. Less spirity than the younger ones. But the rum influence is still there.
**Palate:** Sweet, smooth. Sugar prevails. Coffee liquor. Crushed walnuts. Demerara again.

**Finish:** Short and quickly vanishing. A trace of oak.

**5½ Dave: This is confected rubbish.**
**Nose:** Soft and sweet. Gives the illusion of age, but is simply sweeter and over extracted. Figgy, stewed tea, pomegranate syrup, some rye/chicory notes.
**Palate:** Not as grippy as nose suggests. Camp coffee (undiluted), toffee, prune juice, molasses. Thick.
**Finish:** Bitter. Liquorice, claggy.

## CANADIAN MIST 40%
Blended

**7¾ Martine: Probably rich in rye. Quite a nice sweet and sour profile. With a good oaky frame. An unusual taste which reminds French gin spirit.**
**Nose:** Fruity. A touch of rose scent. Sweet vanilla rises up with a hint of marzipan. Apple skin.
**Palate:** Sweet but crisp. Peach cooked in vanilla. Dusty spices.
**Finish:** Dry, spicy, quite lingering.

**7 Dave: Trying to please too many people therefore has no individuality, other than aggression.**
**Nose:** Red grape, fruit kernel, quite lean. Citrus zest, touch of lavender and a little metallic. Water makes it akin to cold stewed tea. Firm. Green.
**Palate:** You almost don't notice it in the mouth to begin with. Dumbed down with water. Bland.
**Finish:** Firm and a touch edgy.

## CANADIAN MIST ORIGINAL 40%
Blended

**7½ Martine: The nose is more elegant than the palate. Water washes that whisky out.**
**Nose:** Fragrant. Light flowery bouquet. Carnation. Gorse. Watermelon. A touch of coconut. Fudge. With water, lots of white fruit (conference pear).
**Palate:** Demerara sweetness at start then oak tends to grip. Sour apple compote.
**Finish:** Quickly fading. Spicy. A bitter touch.

**7¼ Dave: Comes in two distinct and unlinked parts which would knit if longer in cask.**
**Nose:** A blurred quality as if aromas are being obscured. Tinned pineapple, orange pulp/jelly. Aggressive oak. More perfumed with some strawberry when water is added.
**Palate:** Fruit syrup, mashed banana and oak. Under the wood the spirit is tight and slightly thin.
**Finish:** Short.

## CENTENNIAL PREMIUM RYE 10 YEARS OLD 40%
Rye

**7 Martine: The nose makes you expect a more original profile. Lack of balance. Too much of that "rummy" sweetness.**
**Nose:** Rather bland at start. Cheers up on a fruity note. Apples in caramel. Touch of freshly cut grass.
**Palate:** Sweet, too sweet. Again, a demerara rum flavour hides the cereal notes. Drying on hot spices.
**Finish:** Slightly bitter, grippy.

**7½ Dave: Decent structure saves it.**
**Nose:** Iced gem biscuits. Slightly hard. Lemon and linoleum. Cereal notes and a touch of the farmyard. Overall it's lean.
**Palate:** Seems to split in the mouth. Hard on the start, then clamps onto the palate before light chocolate. Becomes fruitier towards the finish.
**Finish:** Berry fruits.

## CENTURY RESERVE 15 YEARS OLD 40%
Blended

**7½ Michael: Very light-tasting. Some delicacy.**
**Nose:** Very faint liquorice.
**Palate:** Light-bodied. Satiny. Gently fruity. Dry.
**Finish:** Hint of sweetness.

**7½ Dave: A little short but more to it than meets the eye. Alanis Morissette.**
**Nose:** Fragrant, high-toned and estery. Lemon, anise/fennel seed, plum brandy, oily.
**Palate:** Light and perfumed that attacks the mouth well then softens into a sugar-sweet centre.
**Finish:** Soft clean and spicy.

## CENTURY RESERVE 15 YEARS OLD 40%
Blended

**7¾ Martine: A very pale whisky, tastes young but has got a fresh citrussy elegance which would make it a nice dram to be enjoyed on a summer evening. Why not on the rocks?**
**Nose:** Light and mild. A delicate citrussy note. Touch of lemon posset.
**Palate:** Fruity like a bowl of mixed sweets. Hint of liquorice. Nice lingering spiciness.
**Finish:** Dry, spicy, nutty.

**7 Dave: A wraith of a whisky. The spirit is OK, the cask has let it down.**
**Nose:** Very light nose with a hint of lemon and some rye flour but fairly insubstantial. Fragrant with water. Oak is firm and dry. Immature.
**Palate:** Limeade, quite grippy and tight and quickly runs out of steam. Strangely like a young Jamaican rum, all perfume and attack.
**Finish:** Slightly metallic again.

## CENTURY RESERVE 21 YEARS OLD 40%
Blended

**7¾ Michael: Substantially more character than the 15 Years Old.**
**Nose:** Honey. Honeydew melons.
**Palate:** Smooth. Honeyish. Developing appetisingly rounded rye flavours.
**Finish:** Crisp.

**8 Dave: Seems light and approachable but carries a switchblade in its pocket. Robbie Robertson.**
**Nose:** Floral and estery with biscuity wood, rye spice, yellow plums. Seems filled with pent-up energy.
**Palate:** Spicy yet slow-moving good mix of oily rye and fine weight. Smooth and mouthcoating, yet grippy.
**Finish:** Oak tones.

## CROWN ROYAL 40%
Blended

**7½ Michael: Like Seagram's VO Gold, a delicate but wonderfully dextrous blend.**
**Nose:** Soft, sweet toffeeish. Rounded.
**Palate:** Oily. Drier. Fudge-like.
**Finish:** Slight rye dryness, rounded out with a touch of bourbon.

**8½ Dave: Mellow elegance. Joni Mitchell.**
**Nose:** Complex yet restrained with depth and a subtle charm. Poached pear, peach, creamy toffee/sweet vanilla and hint of light rye notes, lemon nut and hickory.
**Palate:** Sits on the tongue nicely with an almost dense chewiness. Starts softly then a gentle, subtle lift of lemon icing, sultana cake, rye and soft sweet honey.
**Finish:** Soft and long.

## CROWN ROYAL 40%
Blended

**8¼ Martine: A characterful and clean whisky, with a rich proportion of rye in the mashbill. Oak is well integrated. Would be pleasant with a pecan pie.**
**Nose:** A good rye sour fruitiness. Blackcurrant, red apple. Then comes a touch of roasted coffee beans and a distant grassy note.
**Palate:** Sweet, with that tangy edge you get from rye. Damson plums, hint of prune. Milk chocolate.
**Finish:** Medium, spicy, nicely clings to the palate.

**7½ Dave: Better balance between this sweet, easy-going Canadian character and some grip.**
**Nose:** Melting ice cream on warm leatherette. Clean rye notes, lightly oily. Water brings oak and a light toasty quality. Red fruits, honey and hazelnut.
**Palate:** Drier than the nose suggests. Runny toffee with a firmness underneath. Almost Cognac like grip. Dried apricots. Well balanced.
**Finish:** Slightly tight and fading quickly.

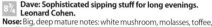

## CROWN ROYAL SPECIAL RESERVE 40%
Blended

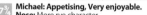

**7¾ Michael: Much more character.**
**Nose:** Minty rye notes.
**Palate:** Firm but smooth. Milk chocolate.
**Finish:** More complex and lively than its younger brothers.

**8¾ Dave: Sophisticated sipping stuff for long evenings. Leonard Cohen.**
**Nose:** Big, deep mature notes: white mushroom, molasses, toffee, vanilla/butterscotch, black fruits with teasing spiciness. Leathery and oaky, but balanced with smooth coffee and cream.
**Palate:** Smooth and elegant, sweet deep and slow: cigar smoke, raspberry, soft centred yet spicy.
**Finish:** Big and long.

## CROWN ROYAL SR SPECIAL RESERVE 40%
Blended

**7½ Martine: A mild character, soft and pleasant but lacking nerve. Fine for a sweet tooth.**
**Nose:** Perfumy. Floral. Carnation. Dry cider. Crushed fresh hazelnuts. Quite a rich aromatic profile.
**Palate:** Sweet, with a good fruity profile. Wine gums. Nice creaminess.
**Finish:** Medium, pleasant sweetness.

**8¼ Dave: This has better balance than most of the rest on show. Dares to show individuality.**
**Nose:** Allspice, light cooked fruit, green plum, sour cherry, pomegranate, apple skin, a little hint of musk. Ripe tropical fruits. Rich and layered.
**Palate:** As sweet as the nose suggests, but this has an extra grip and acidic kick to add interest and structure. Better without water, but well balanced.
**Finish:** Firm mix of fruit and oak.

## CROWN ROYAL XR EXTRA RARE 40%
Blended

**7¼ Martine: Maple syrup taste works more like an additive than natural aroma gained through maturation.**
**Nose:** Bland at first then getting rather expressive. Releases a lot of sweet notes. Maple syrup, toasted pecan nuts. A touch of cider apple.
**Palate:** Sweet with a distinctive apple and maple syrup flavour. Oak is overwhelming in a grippy bite.
**Finish:** Dry, oaky, slightly bitter.

**7¾ Dave: Bolder and beefier than the standard.**
**Nose:** Ripe with lots of American oak, sweet cooked fruits, apple, oak lactone, butterscotch. Water broadens it even further.
**Palate:** Plump, round and full. Sinks on to the tongue but lacks a little definition. Water crisps things up, but only a little. Seems slightly off balance. Has length and depth but almost too fat.
**Finish:** Candy floss sweetness. Long.

## FORTY CREEK BARREL RESERVE 40%
Blended

**8 Martine: A gentle dram. Soft and rich. Soothes your worries away.**
**Nose:** Floral, aromatic. Lilac, narcissus. Becomes creamier in time. Vanilla custard, dried apricot. Quite tantalizing.
**Palate:** Velvety texture. Lot of smoothness. Flows gently on the tongue. Fruity and creamy with a pleasant tickling spiciness.
**Finish:** Medium, warm but not burning.

**7½ Dave: Well put together.**
**Nose:** Very creamy. In fact, it's cream buns with strawberry jam along with overripe banana and with water Caramac bars. In time, cigar box.
**Palate:** Tastes strangely dilute. Fresh fruit juices overlaid with cherry. Slightly tannic. Water brings out cocoa and cappuccino and then a nuttiness. Good depth.
**Finish:** Bourbon-like with a bit of a kick.

## FORTY CREEK BARREL SELECT 40%
Blended

**8½ Michael: The richest-tasting Canadian whisky I have tasted. Wins points for luxury.**
**Nose:** Soft, nutty (walnuts). Rich, spicy.
**Palate:** Smooth, cream, rounded. Bittersweet chocolate.
**Finish:** Black chocolate. Long.

**8 Dave: Good balance with lots of extractive flavours. Oscar Peterson.**
**Nose:** A sweetly perfumed nose: all coffee bean, chocolate and coconut: like Bounty bar and Milky Way smooshed together along with honey/vanilla, smoky wood and winey notes: dried apricot, soaked raisins.
**Palate:** Silky texture which grips nicely mid-palate. Flavours of honey, violet, spices, soft black fruits.
**Finish:** Spicy with little oak.

## FORTY CREEK JOHN K HALL SMALL BATCH RESERVE 40%
Blended

**7½ Martine: Interesting nose but the palate does not quite fulfil the expectations. Oak speaks too loud at times.**
**Nose:** Balsamic. Eucalyptus. Cigar box. Oak is present.
**Palate:** Dry and crisp. Burnt apple wood. Chestnut cake. Oak is prevailing but in a pleasant way.
**Finish:** Dry, quite short.

**7½ Dave: The oak is a little heavy-handed and though it has character, there's a lack of balance.**
**Nose:** Ripe with lots of new wood and with that a light charred/hickory note. Some hickory. Semisweet and bourbon, but has a certain complexity.
**Palate:** Briar, polished wood. Dry and slightly tannic. Very firm meaning that the sweetness is obscured by the oak. There's nutmeg, allspice and some black fruit.
**Finish:** Long slightly tannic.

## FORTY CREEK THREE GRAIN 40%
Blended

**8¼ Michael: In palate, the closer of the two to the Canadian tradition. Wins points for that attribute. I could drink quite a few of these.**
**Nose:** Nutty (almonds), cookie-gingery, sweet.
**Palate:** Orange blossom. Creamed corn. Toffee.
**Finish:** Light, crisp, toasty. Spicy. Rye.

**7¼ Dave: Young and not quite fully mature but worth watching. Nelly Furtado.**
**Nose:** Young, with spicy oak, orange peel, a hint of lemon and a whiff of tobacco.
**Palate:** Soft, chewy butterscotch with a positive spicy kick from the rye on the back palate.
**Finish:** Orange.

## GIBSON'S FINEST 12 YEARS OLD 40%
Blended

**7½ Michael: Pleasant and well-balanced, with a freshness and confidence.**
**Nose:** Spicy. Herbal.
**Palate:** Smooth, rounded, malty.
**Finish:** Long, flavoursome. Rye. Oak.

**8¼ Dave: Attractive, lifted, spicy yet soft. K. d. lang.**
**Nose:** Discreet and slightly shy. Oak tones with creamy weight behind: milk chocolate, butter toffee, vanilla, sultana and rye oil.
**Palate:** Understated. Good feel balancing a chewy orange butter/ Butterkist popcorn mid-palate with feisty zip.
**Finish:** Just a little short.

## GIBSON'S FINEST 18 YEARS OLD 40%
Blended

**7¾ Michael: Appetising, Very enjoyable.**
**Nose:** More rye character.
**Palate:** Bigger, drier, spicier. Still very well rounded.
**Finish:** Nutty dryness. Warming. Long.

**8¾ Dave: Gentle but big and feisty. Neil Young.**
**Nose:** Aromatic, assertive and spicy, it smacks you in the nose with its mix of Christmas spice (ginger, cinnamon, allspice, nutmeg), bitter orange, but behind is mellow chewy toffee. Delicious!
**Palate:** A big mouthful. Gentle and chewy, mixing vanilla, chocolate pepper and spice. Great exchange between spice and mellowness.
**Finish:** Chocolate then dry and tingling.

## GIBSON'S FINEST STIRLING 40%
Blended

**7¾ Michael: Is there enough of a bridge between the youngest and oldest whiskies?**
**Nose:** Drier.
**Palate:** Buttery. Then drier. Vegetal. Slightly sour.
**Finish:** Peppery.

**7¾ Dave: It's almost as if the energy has gone. Steven Stills.**
**Nose:** Wood. Soft and creamy caramel-toffee, but with a slightly hard centre – particularly when you add water.
**Palate:** Soft yet strangely bland.
**Finish:** Short, slightly hard.

## LOT 40 POT STILL SINGLE CANADIAN 43%
Rye

**7¾ Michael: Rich, sweet, liqueur-like. I would like to get to know this one better.**
**Nose:** Flowery. Slightly herbal.
**Palate:** Smooth, sweetish, fruity. Orange liqueur.
**Finish:** Vanilla, toffee. Gently warming.

**7¾ Dave: A mellow Canadian take on things with enough peppery bite to keep rye fans happy.**
**Nose:** Light but exotic with some marzipan, varnish, Turkish delight, apricot (orange muscat) orange pith and milky coffee.
**Palate:** Light with sweet spices and a light bite. All on the sweeter more fragrant side of the spectrum.
**Finish:** Clean with light peppery rye tingle. Still that sweetness.

## SEAGRAM'S VO 40%
Blended

**8 Martine: A well put together dram with a solid oak frame.**
**Nose:** Sweet. Crème caramel, hint of brown sugar. Raisins in a vanilla syrup. A touch of raspberry juice. Touch of resin.
**Palate:** Crisp and dry, bursting into a gingery spiciness.
**Finish:** Spicy and dry, oaky, quite lingering.

**7 Dave: Clean and light and sweet, but it's merely another...and lesser...variation on the clean light and sweet theme.**
**Nose:** Light and understated. In fact, so understated it's barely there. Oh no! there's some orange.
**Palate:** Slightly more substantial than the nose, with a touch of cocoa, but all very young and dilute.
**Finish:** Dies quickly.

## SEAGRAM'S VO GOLD 40%
Blended

**7¾ Martine: Rye is well brought in without oak over-whelming. Water brings in a nice minty freshness.**
**Nose:** Not very intense but with a distinctive rye presence. Ripe apricot, cider apple.
**Palate:** Smooth, fruity, opening on an elegant rye spiciness.
**Finish:** Warm and lingering.

**7¼ Dave: Perfectly nice, but nice isn't enough! There's such a bland similarity between most of these you wonder if it's whisky-making by committee.**
**Nose:** Corny, grainy. Seems young, or at least aggressive. Light though there's also a touch of cardboard and, weirdly, ricotta cheesecake.
**Palate:** Plain start then developing some marmalade, some thick Greek yoghurt and honey.
**Finish:** Sweet and clean. Little caramel.

## SEAGRAM'S VO GOLD 8 YEARS OLD 40%
Blended

**7½ Michael: Light and delicate, but beautifully composed.**
**Nose:** Creamy oak.
**Palate:** Creamy, oily, delicate.
**Finish:** Lightly spicy, but long.

**8½ Dave: Creamy and lovely. A great introduction to the Canadian style. Buffalo Springfield.**
**Nose:** Big fat, muscular, creamy nose, all apple pie and custard, toffee brittle and ginger snaps.
**Palate:** A rich soft vein of melted milky toffee peppered with spice. Rounded and well covered. Chewy mocha.
**Finish:** Soft and sweet with teasing spiciness.

## WINDSOR CANADIAN 40%
Blended

**6¾ Martine: Another example of a "worked upon" whisky. Rather dismantled in its sweetness.**
**Nose:** Sweet and sugary. Candylike. A floral note. Syrup with a drop of orange blossom.
**Palate:** Sweet and oaky. Velvety texture; reminds of a VSOP cognac. Watery in the middle. As if syrup had been added to the spirit.
**Finish:** Tangy, bitter, abrupt.

**6 Dave: An explosion at a beauticians. Nail varnish raining down while the bored Saturday assistant chews bub-blegum amidst the chaos.**
**Nose:** This is different, though not in a good way. Solvent, bubblegum and acetone.
**Palate:** Better than the nose. Perfumed with a firm structure. A little jangly on the finish. Seems young, green and slightly sappy. In time the solvent reappears.
**Finish:** Somewhat abrasive.

## WISER'S DELUXE 40%
Blended

**6¾ Martine: Does not reflect a quality spirit. Looks as if it had been sweetened.**
**Nose:** Fruity. Cider apple. Crème brûlée. A wave of vanilla slowly emerges. Candied chestnut. Slightly grainy.
**Palate:** Sweet and smooth. The grainy character lingers. Not integrated caramel syrup? Weak at mid palate.
**Finish:** Sweet, bland.

**8 Dave: Spicy rather than blandly sweet.**
**Nose:** Perfumed and grassy, cumin and cinnamon, fresh fir, curry leaf/methi. Exotic and some complexity.
**Palate:** A floral start: freesia. The Turkish yoghurt (it's different to Greek) and apricot giving a thick feel before yielding to spiciness. Good length.
**Finish:** Guava.

## WISER'S RESERVE 43%
Blended

**6¾ Martine: All that caramel dress up seems to hide an immature spirit. Has it been aged in decent wood? One can wonder.**
**Nose:** Sweet, lots of caramel that obliterates all other aromas. Just a hint of mint coming through.
**Palate:** Sweet at first then shifts on to the oaky side. A hint of liquorice and a bitter astringency.
**Finish:** Short, bitter.

**8¼ Dave: It's almost like a pudding whisky, but has balance.**
**Nose:** Planed oak fir, pine but this also has apple, barley-sugar. Honeycomb on toast.
**Palate:** Sweet, but also nutty. Marzipan, an estery lift alongside that distinctly Canadian silky feel. Good length.
**Finish:** Long mingling sweet and spicy.

## WISER'S VERY OLD 18 YEARS OLD 40%
Blended

**8 Martine: A well integrated combination of fruit and oak. A dram for uplifting hikers back from a wet walk.**
**Nose:** Earthy with a distant mushroom aroma. Wild mint. A very autumnal aromatic profile. Gets more dessert-like in time.
**Palate:** Crisp, medium bodied. Clings on the palate. Nice spicy display. Rye shows up. Apple skin, fresh ginger.
**Finish:** Dry, spicy. With a nice warm kick.

**8½ Dave: This has structure and character, one of the few to show some personality. Pleasant to start with but ultimately you're driven mad by the saccharine niceness of it.**
**Nose:** Rich and powerful. Banana, raspberry, clotted cream cut with orange and lime zest. Generous and succulent.
**Palate:** Good balance. Has extra weight and depth and manages to play dry and sweet off each other.
**Finish:** Long, rich silky.

# Ireland

One of the fun things about compiling such a tasting guide is looking back over the history and events that have shaped the industry, and so it is with Ireland. Once a power-house of whiskey distilling, the Irish distillers refusal to assist American bootleggers during the prohibition period became a contributing factor to the industry's decline.

For a period of time, 1966 to 1988, there was just the behemoth of Irish Distillers Limited (IDL) which had a strangle-hold on all Irish whiskey, until recently.

The rise of Cooley can be charted through the tastings. Founder John Teeling bought the distillery off the Irish Government in 1987 with the idea of selling it later as a going concern replete with whiskey filled warehouses. Yet in a climate of belt tightening by the industry, Teeling eventually had to mothball the distillery. However after an offer by Pernod Ricard was blocked by Ireland's Competition Authority, Teeling managed to convince his backers and in 1995 he fired up the stills again. His approach to the category has led to some fascinating whiskies being made, including Greenore, Locke's and Tyrconnell and a phenomenal growth in interest in Irish whiskey across the globe.

Bushmills was originally family owned until 1964 when it was sold to an English brewing company who then sold it to Seagram's (later to be part of IDG) and has finally rested in the hands of drinks giant Diageo, which is now investing in the production. Bushmills is again on the prowl through the bars and imagination of drinkers across the world.

Apart from the Connemara brand, you do not find peat in Irish whiskey. This is due to the fact that distilling became big business in Ireland early on, long before peat cutting was mechanised, so coal and wood was used to meet the demand. Also the powerhouse distillers were urban and had access to coal. It is interesting to note that Bushmills was peated until the 1960s.

Let's not forget as well that Ireland gave us one of the significant developments in distilling – the column still.

This was perfected by Aeneas Coffey in the early 1800s, patented in 1831, and has changed the face of distilling completely,

allowing producers to make whiskey cheaply and quickly without sacrificing any quality.

The connoisseur will often head for the pure pot still whiskey style of brands such as Redbreast and Green Spot. Pot still whiskey is defined as spirits distilled from malted and unmalted barley. The resulting liquid has a viscosity to it.

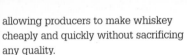

**Clockwise from top:** The imposing chimney at Locke's Distillery; Old Bushmills; A column still; Pot stills at Cooley

## DID YOU KNOW...

- The still at Midleton, near Cork, is the biggest in the world. Built in 1825, and now retired from service, this wash still could accommodate 152,966 litres
- Cooley distillers began distilling again at Locke's Distillery in 2007 after it fell silent in 1953
- Dublin was once home to great whisky names such as Powers and Jameson, now the city has no distilleries as production has moved to Midleton
- Bushmills is the only distillery based in Northern Ireland and before branching out into malts concentrated on two blends, Black Bush and Bushmills, giving it great market visibility

## ADELPHI SUIR PEATED MALT 40%
Single Malt

**7¾ Michael: Lacks the rich smokiness of Connemara.**
**Nose:** Lightly grassy dryness. Burnt grass.
**Palate:** Light but textured. Grassy. Burnt grass. Fruity.
**Finish:** Lively, spicy, dry. Bitter.

**8 Doug: Intriguing combination of flavours. Sweet meets peat.**
**Nose:** Sultry, sultanas, smoke and brine. Some Cognac characters and even a whiff of tandoori food.
**Palate:** Smoky, viscous sweet pears, salty and peppery with a malty body.
**Finish:** Sherry shadowing the salty and peaty, warming aftermath.

## BLACK BUSH 43%
Blended

**9 Michael: Long one of my great favourites. In composition, it is the simplest of** blends, yet it demonstrates how malt can someimes be enhanced by a leavening of grain.
**Nose:** Fresh oak, softened with sherry.
**Palate:** Full of flavours, and such a beautifully balanced, rounded whiskey: oaky, fudgy, buttery, with that Bushmills rosewater character.
**Finish:** A grainy, but more-ish, dryness.

*WHISKY Magazine Recommended*

**8½ Jim: One of the world's finer blends, though again showing more sherry character than before. Obviously** some extremely fine quality sherry casks have been introduced for this vatting.
**Nose:** Multi-layered and seductive. The sherry is clean, medium sweet and a good foil for the malt and grain.
**Palate:** Amazingly soft. The grain ensures clarity and lightness, highlighted by peppery spice.
**Finish:** Long, spicy and grapefruity with some toasty, oaky notes.

## BUSHMILLS 10 YEARS OLD
Single Malt

**7½ Dave: Lovely nose (once again). . Lacks a bit of depth (once again).**
**Nose:** Light, youthful and floral. A mix of cut grass, clover, tinned fruit salad and lots of cream. Loses impact with water.
**Palate:** Gentle sweetness. Sponge cake, sweet orange peel. The grass becomes drier, adding a firm edge.
**Finish:** Gentle. Soft.

**7¾ Gavin: Pleasant enough, but straightforward!**
**Nose:** Initially very delicate, with developing floral and plum notes.
**Palate:** Straightforward, with eating apples, cream, and a hint of honey.
**Finish:** The cream from the palate persists as acceptable oakiness develops.

## BUSHMILLS 10 YEARS OLD 40%
Single Malt

**6 Michael: All the woods are influential, especially the port in the finish. A very dexterous balancing act, but is the** house character eventually overwhelmed?
**Nose:** Distinctly almondy. Some soft, perfumy, winey spiciness.
**Palate:** Toasted almonds, raisins, slightly burnt toffee.
**Finish:** Delicate, elusive, flavours. Long, soft, soothing.

**7½ Jim: A bigger whisky than of a year or two back with the sherry making a much bigger impression. Quite fruity** and full where once it was slightly powdery and over-dependent on the malt character alone.
**Nose:** Intense malt with a unmistakable sherry richness. Quite firm, fruity and clean.
**Palate:** Sweet, quite lush start: malt, sherry and soft spice.
**Finish:** Lashings of toffee with bigger sherry than of old. Dark fudge sweetness gives way to much drier cocoa notes.

## BUSHMILLS 10 YEARS OLD 40%
Single Malt

**8 Peter: After years of being overshadowed by its older wood finished cousins, this 10 Years Old is finally coming** into its own.
**Nose:** Very lightly scented with nutty ice cream and sherry.
**Palate:** Rich dried fruit and chewy toffee, quite a mouth filling shock after the very delicate nose.
**Finish:** Fudgy.

**7½ Dave: Light and clean, delivers well on the palate.**
**Nose:** Malty, toasted meal. Hint of cream, slight grassy/vegetal edge, cocoa powder, light citrus. Floral.
**Palate:** Clean, light and spicy. Apricot to start, then toast, cereal. Some chalky notes, nutty oak.
**Finish:** A burst of soft fruit, flowers.

## BUSHMILLS 12 YEARS OLD DISTILLERY RESERVE 40%
Single Malt

**7¾ Michael: Despite being a malt, it still, somehow has an Irish accent. Slightly more personality than the Bushmills** malt at 16 Years Old. Drinkable and sociable.
**Nose:** Warm. Suede. Leather. Linseed.
**Palate:** Toasted almonds. Pistachios. Fudge. Fruity. Flowering currant. Good flavour development.
**Finish:** A hint of sherry. Apricot-like, oily sweetness.

**7¾ Jim: Cleaner than of old but no less characterful. Quite a cerebral whisky.**
**Nose:** The sherry is light and clean and gives way to a lovely hint of orange and spice. Impressively stylish and assured.
**Palate:** A highly developed and confusingly complex middle tends to nudge back towards sherry dominance.
**Finish:** Dries as the richer sherry notes fade and the oak takes hold.

## BUSHMILLS 12 YEARS OLD 'DISTILLERY RESERVE' 40%
Single Malt

**8¾ Dave: A leap in quality above the rest on show here. Worth a trip to the still just to buy one.**
**Nose:** Toasty and sweet, ripe and juicy. Bread pudding, light treacle, dried fruit but there's still a grassy freshness along with oolong-like perfume.
**Palate:** Soft, generous and with a slow, unfolding quality. Ripe fruits. Rich and mouthfilling with light grip. Big and chewy, but balanced.
**Finish:** Gentle. Passion fruit juice.

*WHISKY Magazine Editor's choice*

**8 Gavin: Moreish!**
**Nose:** Malt, honey and citrus notes, freshly squeezed oranges and barley sugar.
**Palate:** Oily, mouth-coating, dry and attractively winey.
**Finish:** Long and drying, with liquorice and treacle.

## BUSHMILLS 16 YEARS OLD 40%
Single Malt

**8½ Michael: All the woods are influential, especially the port in the finish. A dextrous balancing act.**
**Nose:** Distinctly nutty, but also with those linseedy Irish flavours. some soft, perfumy, spiciness.
**Palate:** Toasted almonds, raisin, slightly burnt toffee.
**Finish:** Delicate, elusive, flavours. Long, soft, soothing.

*WHISKY Magazine Recommended*

**8¾ Doug: Absolutely charming Bushmills. Expertly composed.**
**Nose:** Beautifully scented with honey, sweet apples, pears, bananas and sherry.
**Palate:** Delicious, malt roundedness, rich fruit and nuttiness peep through the sherry and port structure.
**Finish:** Lingering sweet fruit salad character and the lightest trace of peat.

## BUSHMILLS 16 YEARS OLD 40%
Single Malt

**7½ Peter: Triple distilled whiskey drawn from bourbon, sherry and port wood...what a balancing act. It usually** works a treat, but this time the elements are strangely out of kilter.
**Nose:** A delicate waft of mashed banana and spice jars.
**Palate:** Soft gentle nuttiness, echoes of fortified wine.
**Finish:** Spirity.

**8 Dave: Plenty of oak but the spirit holds its own. An extra dimension to the 10.**
**Nose:** Big, fat and sweet. Butter and raisins. Forms slowly with pineapple, stewed fruits, malted milk, coconut, cereal, cocoa, orange. Big (but balanced) oak.
**Palate:** Round and rich. Sweet dried fruits, brazil nut, coffee, soft malt, popcorn. Good grip. Oak in balance.
**Finish:** Long. Hazelnut.

## BUSHMILLS 16 YEARS OLD 40%
Single Malt

**7½ Dave: A touch slick and a little one-dimensional.**
**Nose:** Big, fat and wine like. Sweet and jammy with hot raspberry jelly alongside dry roast peanut, (over) cooked apple and cinnamon.
**Palate:** Sweet red fruits. Hint of sloe-scented sweetness. Fresh, but as fat as you like in the middle, then comes the cereal.
**Finish:** Falls away on the back palate.

**8 Gavin: Attractive and eminently quaffable.**
**Nose:** Wine gums and wet garden undergrowth.
**Palate:** Bright and fruity, a fresh, lively mouthfeel.
**Finish:** Drying steadily with vanilla and rye.

## BUSHMILLS 16 YEARS OLD 40%
Single Malt

**8½ Michael: Is the house character overwhelmed by the three woods (bourbon, sherry and port)? I'll give it the benefit of the doubt.**
**Nose:** Fruity and flowery. Roses. Fragrant. Hint of smoke.
**Palate:** Mouth-filling, tongue coating, soothing, soft. Marshmallow. Slightly burnt toffee.
**Finish:** Fruity again. Raspberries, prunes, raisins? Winey. Some balancing dryness.

**8 Jim: This whiskey benefits from warming in the hands. Opens like a flower as the temperature rises into something very beautiful, indeed.**
**Nose:** A basket of fruits with apples and grape prominent here. Even some curious smokiness...
**Palate:** Seismic waves of spicy fruit with an earlier than usual surge of cocoa.
**Finish:** A slightly thinner, harder finale than the norm.

## BUSHMILLS 1608 RESERVE 40%
Blended

**8¼ Michael: Very rich and sweet, but still a Bushmills.**
**Nose:** Distinct rose-like aroma of Bushmills. Sandalwood.
**Palate:** Syrupy, sherryish. Nutty. Almondy.
**Finish:** Hard liquorice. Late rootiness.

**8¾ Dave: A less exuberant Black Bush: richer and more brooding.**
**Nose:** Rich, soft and deep with sherry well in evidence. Turned earth, charred wood, raspberry, currant, hedgerow fruits. Almost jammy with a crisp cereal centre and some vanilla.
**Palate:** Big, soft and very smooth. A silky mouthful.
**Finish:** Starts juicily, then becomes dry and malty.

## BUSHMILLS 1982 BOURBON CASK 57.8%
Single Malt

**7¾ Michael: An unusually dry expression of Bushmills. Complex. Austere. Bushmills needs a touch of sherry sweetness.**
**Nose:** Warm. Nutty. Marzipan. Pistachios. Appetising.
**Palate:** Leafy. Spicy. Rosewater. Garden mint.
**Finish:** Dry. Drying on the tongue. Coriander. Slightly bitter. Slightly sharp.

**8¾ Dave: Who said this was an insubstantial malt?**
**Nose:** Big and sweet with layers of fruit: butterscotch, cinnamon, citrus peels. With water, more spice, ripe oranges and a clover-like grassy/malty note.
**Palate:** Medium-bodied. Spices burst in the mouth. Masses of US oak, balanced with gentle, soft maltiness. Explosive, sweet, delicious.
**Finish:** Malty.

## BUSHMILLS 21 YEARS OLD 40%
Single Malt

**7 Michael: A delicious whisky. The sweetness and nuttiness of Bushmills whiskey and of Madeira are an enjoyable double-act. The whiskey has to work hard to avoid being upstaged.**
**Nose:** Pronounced Madeira ' toffee' character.
**Palate:** Smooth, sweet, succulent. Marzipan. Glazed almonds.
**Finish:** Dusting of ginger.

**8½ Dave: Lovely balance. A whisky for those who like things on the fruity side.**
**Nose:** A lifted, perfumed fruit-filled nose, soft and pulpy, apricot yoghurt and crannachan (raspberry oats sugar and cream).
**Palate:** Starts sweet, soft and juicy starting with apricot ending up with redcurrant and cherry.
**Finish:** A very light smokiness.

## BUSHMILLS 21 YEARS OLD 40%
Single Malt

**8½ Peter: This whiskey has changed quite a bit in the last few years. It's now less subtle, more forthright, but no less delicious.**
**Nose:** A stunning assault of Demerera sugar, roasted nuts and fruity yoghurt.
**Palate:** Very sweet and juicy, then dried apricots before moving on to rich fruitcake.
**Finish:** A tart, dark marmalade tingle.

**7¾ Dave: It's balanced but it lacks the vibrancy of the 16 Years Old.**
**Nose:** Full, rich and woody. Light spiciness, varnish, toffee, orange peel. Good mature notes: overripe fruit, spruce, spent firework. Old...too old
**Palate:** Wood has strong influence. Some sweet dried fruits, amontillado-like, roasted almond. A touch winey, then the wood firms a little.
**Finish:** Biscuity, dusty, splintery.

## BUSHMILLS 21 YEARS OLD MADEIRA FINISH 40%
Single Malt

*WHISKY Editor's choice*

**8¼ Dave: Good flow, balance and grip. A powerhouse.**
**Nose:** Big and generous. Shifting into coffee cake with butter icing. Water makes it reminiscent of a bodega then comes mint, citrus zest and in time tanned leather. Grist-like sweetness.
**Palate:** Better grip, some substance and a dried fruit edge along with red liquorice.
**Finish:** Firm, nutty and clean.

**8¼ Gavin: A whiskey with complexity, character and some age to it.**
**Nose:** Initially rather reticent, with acetone and developing grain giving way to a treacly, slightly smoky nose.
**Palate:** Medium-bodied, with a hint of honey, then darker treacle and stewed fruits dominate.
**Finish:** Liquorice and oak – quite lengthy.

## BUSHMILLS BLACK BUSH 40%
Blended

*WHISKY Recommended*

**8 Dave: Beautifully balanced.**
**Nose:** Rich and ripe, with some dark (cooked) black fruit. Raisin, cocoa, praline, coconut. Substantial smooth succulence.
**Palate:** Sweet start then it firms up in the centre where the nuts return melting into the chocolate and raisin. Chewy and tongue coating. Showing some complexity.
**Finish:** Long, sweet.

**8¼ Gavin: A confident whiskey that feels as though it has some age to it.**
**Nose:** Baked apples and spicy malt. A pleasingly mature character to it.
**Palate:** Big bodied, slightly oily, with nutmeg and red wine. Sophisticated and assured.
**Finish:** Notably long, drying with dark syrup and liquorice notes.

## BUSHMILLS MILLENNIUM 40%
Single Malt

*WHISKY Recommended*

**8½ Michael: Tightly combined flavours. Delicate. Elegant.**
**Nose:** That leathery, saddlery, Irish note. Linseedy, nutty, grassy. Soft but wonderfully scenty.
**Palate:** Fresh. Lightly creamy. Develops nuts and marzipan.
**Finish:** Faintly spicy. Orange zest. Dessert apple.

**9 Jim: This is Bushmills at its peak.**
**Nose:** Understatedly rich, with a glorious yet subtle honey sweetness which is in total harmony with the banana custard background. Fabulous.
**Palate:** Brilliant intermingling of malt and honey which makes way for a deftly oaked middle. The tantalising spicy buzzes complement the complexity.
**Finish:** Medium long with the remnants of a honey-comb sweetness jousts with the soft spice.

# Irish Bushmills - Connemara

## BUSHMILLS ORIGINAL 40%
Single Malt

**7¼ Dave: Its youth just gives it a hard quality.**
**Nose:** Young. That grassy edge once again this time reminiscent of wet raffia. A nutty, floury note. Firm with a very slight metallic edge.
**Palate:** Light and sweet but a youthful cereal, slightly hard core before a tantalising burst of peachy fruit at the back of the palate.
**Finish:** Becomes dry. Quite short.

**7¼ Gavin: Gives the impression of needing time to grow into itself.**
**Nose:** Green grain, fresh fruit and acetone.
**Palate:** Clean, slightly spirity, simplistic.
**Finish:** Short and spicy, with a fresh oak feel.

## CLONMEL PEATED 8 YEARS OLD, CELTIQUE CONNEXION 40%
Single Malt

**8 Michael: Another smoky whiskey is always welcome, but I think I may have tasted this under another name.**
**Nose:** Peaty and smoky, but with a burnt and cooked character.
**Palate:** Very dry and quite intensely phenolic. Grassy. Then some sweeter flavours. Baked plantains?
**Finish:** Warming. Soothing.

**7¾ Dave: Well made, clean and balanced. Worth a punt.**
**Nose:** Oily. Fried mackerel, soot, seems young. Singed rope, lino. Attractive.
**Palate:** Opal fruits, hazelnut and a smokiness which picks up towards the finish.
**Finish:** Medium length. Lightly smoky.

## COLERAINE 40%
Blended

**7 Michael: A pleasant whiskey for everyday drinking.**
**Nose:** Fresh leather. Oil.
**Palate:** Fruity. Honeydew melon. Honey.
**Finish:** Grainy. Sunflower seeds.

**5 Jim: Not to be confused with great malt by the same name. Pretty poor stuff.**
**Nose:** Lots of caramel and soft grains. Flat, one dimensional and uninspiring.
**Palate:** Caramel-sweet and very soft at first; then hard, bitter grains and vanilla.
**Finish:** Dry with an almost apologetic spiciness.

## CONNEMARA 12 YEARS OLD 40%
Single Malt

**8¾ Peter: This is a bottling of 28 casks of the 1991 vintage, so it is particularly rare and therefore collectible. When it's gone. It's gone.**
**Nose:** Roses, heavy musk, damp conifers and bog.
**Palate:** Very soft, round and complex. The flavours are hard to unpick, but there's warm honey, buttered crumpet and a hint of sweet pipe smoke.
**Finish:** Long and chewy.

**7¾ Dave: Good balance. Doesn't like water. Start here.**
**Nose:** Pungent, intense, marine-like, a sweet minty note backed with a touch of lanolin. Good balance, with some creamy popcorn notes.
**Palate:** Fragrant but almost friable character: cashew, brittle toffee. Peat smoke, light nuttiness.
**Finish:** Honey, then ash.

## CONNEMARA 12 YEARS OLD 40%
Single Malt

**7¼ Martine: That lactic note overwhelms nose and palate. Not sure that a dairy whiskey is something to look forward to! Surprisingly, a dash of water makes more palatable.**
**Nose:** Lactic, sour milk and buttermilk. Then a grassy note (camomile and lemon grass).
**Palate:** Sweet but with a sour note. Buttery. Creamy cheese. Quite watery at midpalate. Gets fruity with water.
**Finish:** Soothing, nutty with a hint of spice.

**8 Dave: Proof if it were needed that Cooley is now really up and running. Atypical for an Irish whiskey insofar as it is peated (as Bushmills was 'til the 70s).**

**Nose:** Intensely scented. Cut grass, green leaves, dried apple and a touch of peat. Young and oaky.
**Palate:** Lychee and soft fruits. Light almond note and fennel seed then nutmeg and oak. Mashed banana and light smoke. Balanced.
**Finish:** Gentle and smoked.

## CONNEMARA CASK STRENGTH 59.6%
Single Malt

**8½ Michael: The paler colour suggests less interesting casks. The higher the alcohol adds to the pepperiness. The end result is drier, more cutting, but less rounded than the 40%.**
**Nose:** Slightly sooty.
**Palate:** Sweeter than the 40%.
**Finish:** Spicy, grassy, smoky, slightly hot. Peppery.

**7½ Jim: Hmmm. Not quite the babe I was expecting. Due to the rarity of this malt vattings do tend to travel the quality spectrums.**
**Nose:** Less intense peat than the standard version. It is the dollop of marmalade that stars.
**Palate:** The peat forms a sweet and silky layer. Oak tends to be lumpy.
**Finish:** A toasty, dry finale. Maybe a little off key.

## CONNEMARA CASK STRENGTH 60%
Single Malt

**9¼ Peter: I just love this un-chill filtered version; it's fat, it's loud and it's fun. In this price bracket, there are very few Scottish single malts that can match it.**
**Nose:** Liniment and farmyard.
**Palate:** Honey on hot porridge, before a mushroom cloud of peat blows your head off.
**Finish:** A rollercoaster ride of pepper, huge amounts of billowing smoke, then vanilla, mint and choc fudge.

**7¾ Dave: Not surprisingly the punchiest – and the peatiest of these two.**
**Nose:** Muted nose before vanilla, nuts, violet and a mix of estery notes and perfumed peat smoke. Kippers.
**Palate:** A very sweet start, lemon barley water, then the smoke builds in intensity, perfumed, touch of sheepskin. Good intensity.
**Finish:** Long, smoky. Slightly hot.

## CONNEMARA PEATED SINGLE MALT 40%
Single Malt

**7¾ Dave: There's real substance here. Well-integrated.**
**Nose:** Sweetly peaty: smouldering bonfire, violet, hazelnut/pecan pie. Gutsy.
**Palate:** Lots of orange peel, dried fruits giving another layer of interest to the slow-burning fire which starts from the middle of the tongue.
**Finish:** Little green, suggesting it could improve still further.

**8 Gavin: A very drinkable and comparatively complex dram.**
**Nose:** Floral, with a background note of silage.
**Palate:** Nicely balanced, with sweet, warm leather, fruit notes, and a hint of fresh peat.
**Finish:** Lengthy, quite sophisticated, slowly drying.

## CONNEMARA PEATED SINGLE MALT 40%
Single Malt

**8¾ Michael: Lots happening. Chimney pots of smoke. I love this whiskey.**
**Nose:** Pronounced smoke, rather than peat, though both are evident.
**Palate:** Syrupy. Sweet grass. Smoky, some drier hints of phenol. A suggestion of juicy wood extracts, or sherry, rounding out the flavours.
**Finish:** Smoky and emphatically grassy. Sweet grass but also spicy dryness.

**8¾ Jim: Not as complex on the palate as before. This is a truly great whiskey developing in the mould of a youngish Port Ellen.**
**Nose:** An elegant floral style of peat, iodine laced with heather offering a deliciously sweet maltiness. Excellent.
**Palate:** Intensely malty at first. Immaculately clean and juicy, almost.
**Finish:** Medium, melt-in-the-mouth and luscious.

## CONNEMARA PEATED SINGLE MALT IRISH WHISKEY 40%
Single Malt

**7½ Martine: Characterful, vivid but not complex. "Tastes" stronger than 40%. A body warmer for cool evenings.**
**Nose:** Intense, waxy and malty. Lemon granité. A medicinal touch. Herbal. Opens on toasted hazelnuts and green tomatoes.
**Palate:** Smooth, thick, rich and coating. Creamy at first (toffee) then getting very peppery.
**Finish:** Very hot with a touch of green oak and almond milk.

**7½ Dave: Just lacks the energy and extra dimension of the 12 Years Old.**
**Nose:** Coconut again, but this time shell. Beeswax. Lightly grassy. Light smoke.
**Palate:** Light fruit. Nutty and polished. Smoke is there but not as well knitted as the 12 Years Old.
**Finish:** Short. Smoked.

## CONNEMARA SINGLE MALT IRISH WHISKEY 40%
Single Malt

**WHISKY** Recommended

**8½ Michael: The revival of rustic peatiness adds a whole new element to today's palette of Irish whiskey flavours.**
**Nose:** Wonderfully peaty and smoky.
**Palate:** Smooth, oily. Sweet, perfumy, smoke.
**Finish:** Smoky. Sweet grass.

**9 Jim: This single malt had suffered from an identity crisis over the last year or so. Some vattings had become slightly off-key, dirty even, and the malt had lost direction. This bottling, however, is back to its brilliant best.**
**Nose:** Sweet, clean peat, vanilla and-floral notes. One of the most profound and complex of Irish noses.
**Palate:** Again very sweet, peaty. Softly honeyed and oily Mild molasses, fabulously smoky.
**Finish:** Becomes drier as some oak bites, but the peat just keeps on rumbling along.

## COOLEY, WORLD WHISKIES 12 YEARS OLD, CADEN-HEAD'S 60%
Single Malt

**9¼ Peter: This is some bottling; great distillate matured to perfection in excellent casks. One for the Islay bore in your life.**
**Nose:** A stonker of a nose: damp cellars, waxed canvas, peat smoke and brine.
**Palate:** Barry White smooth. This is good; fresh soda bread, marshmallows toasting on open peat fire. Vanilla ice cream and now wood smoke.
**Finish:** Long and unctuous. Chilli chocolate.

**7¼ Dave: Has impact and aggression, but a bit one dimensional.**
**Nose:** Peaty, slightly greasy/lanolin/wet sheep. A little numb (high alcohol) then plenty of sooty smoke. Wet army blankets. Seems young.
**Palate:** Explosion of oily notes, oats. Has balance, but the spirit seems gawky. A pure sweet centre. Smoke is like hot tar on a road.
**Finish:** Slightly musty.

## CRAOI NA MONA 40%
Single Malt

**6 Dave: Ominously pale and initial suspicions were proved correct. This has been bottled way too young.**
**Nose:** Phenolic, with turfy smoke. Seems very young, with a sulphury edge. A greasy and slightly feinty note.
**Palate:** Sweeter than the nose suggests. The peat is better behaved than you expect. Slightly medicinal and slightly better with water.
**Finish:** Charred sticks.

**6¾ Gavin: Is this old enough to be out by itself?**
**Nose:** The yeasty, fresh nose of new make, plus a whiff of peat.
**Palate:** Again, the dominant impression is of youth. Yeast and vibrant spices.
**Finish:** Short and spicy.

## CRESTED TEN IRISH WHISKEY, 10 YEARS OLD 40%
Blended

**7 Michael: This is a highly respected 'sophisticated' whiskey, but it has never done anything for me. Good sherry character, but the whiskey itself is just too thin in the middle. I find it unbalanced.**
**Nose:** Light, dry. Slight nutty sherry. Melon skins.
**Palate:** Smooth, honeyish. Toffee wafers. Lean, clean.
**Finish:** That sherry again. Nutty, but a bit dry and papery.

**8½ Jim: A shade more sherry-intense than it used to be, so some of the finer notes have been swamped. If anything the sherry is of too fine a character. Even so, tremendous.**
**Nose:** Enormous pot still presence softened by a hint of sherry and a sprinkling of ginger.
**Palate:** Perfect balance of sherry, malt and oak with a pot still backbone. Warming spiciness.
**Finish:** Hints of cocoa, lingering spice.

## GREENORE 8 YEARS OLD 40%
Single Grain

**7¼ Michael: Bourbon Lite might taste like this.**
**Nose:** Sweetly appetising. Toasty, lemony.
**Palate:** Clean, sweet. Vanilla. Some resiny, lemon peel notes. Honey.
**Finish:** Firm, dryish.

**6 Dave: Water kills this stone dead.**
**Nose:** Light. Seems young. Quite grassy (grass box clippings) with light, sappy, oak.
**Palate:** Soft and nutty with a sweet centre. Pleasant and light.
**Finish:** Short.

## GREENORE 8 YEARS OLD 1996, SINGLE GRAIN IRISH WHISKEY 40%
Single Grain

**7½ Dave: The best Greenore yet. Worth a look.**
**Nose:** A wildly spiced nose: caraway, turmeric, dried mint (freshly made mint sauce), banana chips, plain wood. Cereal. Bourbon like.
**Palate:** Light. The mintiness carries through. Some hard youth battling against sweetness from the oak. Cinnamon balls.
**Finish:** Short.

**7¾ Arthur: A simple but satisfying whiskey that almost tricked me into thinking it was a bourbon at times. Good stuff for its age too.**
**Nose:** Crab apple and redcurrant jelly. A bourbony, grain-like character is more evident. A little cloying after a time, like the sweetness of jam cooking.
**Palate:** Lots of vanilla, filled with new sawn oak.
**Finish:** That vanilla oozes back like a half-sucked caramel chew.

## HEWITTS IRISH WHISKEY 43%
Blended

**7 Michael: Soothing. A touch of more-ish dryness.**
**Nose:** Polished oak.
**Palate:** Very lively. Sweet maltiness. Touch of vanilla, developing to a perfumy spiciness.
**Finish:** Falls away somewhat. Grainy.

**8 Jim: A favourite. The sherry also has a kind of port-wood fruitiness to it, but it is the malt that is so memorable.**
**Nose:** A big, intense heavy malt-rich nose with the cleanest of sherry backgrounds. Dark cherries and ripe plums.
**Palate:** Intriguingly deep; packed with grapey fruitiness. The malt clings to the mouth; the body is oily and full. A much lighter grain note thins it slightly.
**Finish:** Custard-cream sweetness gives way to drier grains plus some juniper on the very end.

## INISHOWEN BLENDED WHISKEY 40%
Blended

**7½ Michael:** More complex, and fuller in flavour, than many Irish blends. Very well balanced. Just a hint of a Scottish accent.
**Nose:** Perfumy, linseedy, cereal-grain.
**Palate:** Firm, smooth, sweetish. Touch of peaty rootiness.
**Finish:** Faint balance of orange-peel dryness.

**8 Jim:** A superb blend that is more complex than it used to be.
**Nose:** That rarest of beasts: a peaty aroma on a blended Irish. Softer than it used to be, but with trademark apples and grapes; fine balance.
**Palate:** Full, fat and much richer than of old. The sweetness holds longer and the smokiness has to battle through the intense malt. The grain adds a refined dryness.
**Finish:** Dry, spicy, and hauntingly smoky. Some deep vanilla and sweeter malt.

## THE IRISHMAN 70 SUPERIOR 40%
Blended

**6¼ Dave:** A promising nose, but doesn't deliver on the palate.
**Nose:** Lightly floral, with apple skin, lemon peel but with a dry, biscuity undertow. Good with water.
**Palate:** Cracked wheat, very light and is destroyed by water which splits it into its constituent parts.
**Finish:** Insubstantial and quite hard.

**7¼ Gavin:** Again, an attractive nose is confounded by a lacklustre experience in the mouth.
**Nose:** High, sweet, with a pleasing note of peaches.
**Palate:** Nutty and oaky.
**Finish:** Medium, oaky, drying to something quite astringent.

## THE IRISHMAN AGED SINGLE MALT 40%
Single Malt

**7 Dave:** Once again the nose offers up hope only for it to be dashed on the palate. It's not so much these are light, it is that they lack substance.
**Nose:** Plump and fleshy with apricot/pear and light liquorice. Coconut cream and some muscle.
**Palate:** Peachy once more, but thins quickly. Very light in the mouth with a nutty/vanilla mid-palate.
**Finish:** Biscuity. Light.

**7¾ Gavin:** Lively spices dominate this expression, but perhaps slightly on the youthful side?
**Nose:** Delicate, with pleasing aromas of pears and spring flowers.
**Palate:** Malt and ginger, slightly assertive.
**Finish:** Attractive ginger/spice notes, but not much length to it.

## JAMESON 12 YEARS OLD 40%
Blended

**9 Peter:** For the money, this is the best damn blend you will ever, ever taste.
**Nose:** Leather handbags, new car smell. Seville oranges and dusk in Valencia.
**Palate:** I have died and gone to heaven. Warm oily spice, cardamom, cinnamon and some damn fine sherry notes.
**Finish:** Rumbles on for ages. Tickling pepper and milk chocolate.

**8¼ Dave:** Much more like it. Has the rich, velvety, juicy, fruitiness of good Irish.
**Nose:** Lush and rich. Some oily pot still notes. Ripe fruit, melon, spices, oak notes, charcoal, some raisin/sultana. With water: cocoa butter, tea cake.
**Palate:** Clean and slightly malty start. Stretches across the palate. Semi-dried peach softness, crisp cereal/oak. Balanced, honeyed and soft.
**Finish:** Herbal.

## JAMESON 12 YEARS OLD 43%
Blended

**8 Michael:** The aroma that I associate with a traditional Irish. A superb example for everyday drinking.
**Nose:** Leather-like. Saddlery. Orange skins.
**Palate:** Fruits, nuts, sugared almonds. Silky-smooth. Well-rounded.
**Finish:** Juicy. Lively. Late touch of peppery earthiness.

*WHISKY Magazine Recommended*

**9 Jim:** Never lets you down and offers the most old-fashioned and complex of Irish blended character. No nonsense but stunningly beautiful.
**Nose:** This offers the lot: sherry, fine pot still, lighter grains, a dash (but no more) of oak.
**Palate:** Firm, oily and spicy at first, then wonderful interlocked spice and sherry. A bittersweet heart.
**Finish:** Long, pretty lush, drying towards cocoa, vanilla and toast.

## JAMESON 12 YEARS OLD, OLD DISTILLERY RESERVE 40%
Blended

**7½ Michael:** I find the aroma quite sexy. The palate is big, but the finish leaves me wondering about the casks.
**Nose:** Creamy. Cedary. Fresh sweat. Aromatic.
**Palate:** Firm. Full flavours. Nutty. Very toffeeish. Apricot-like.
**Finish:** Spicy. Slight sulphur.

**9 Jim:** This is a great Irish whiskey where the faultless sherry is played and controlled to near perfection.
**Nose:** Sherry so thick you can cut through it.
**Palate:** Gloriously fat and rich; delicious barley, intermingling with juicy plums. Big and sturdy throughout.
**Finish:** A peppery spice begins to formulate, as does the drier oak. But it is the softness of the grain which impresses most.

## JAMESON 15 YEARS OLD LIMITED EDITION 40%
Pot Still

**8¾ Michael:** Those oily aromatics are quite a shock at first. Shows just how different a true 'Irish' character was 15 years ago, or does Jameson benefit greatly from age?
**Nose:** Fresh sweat. A shower with Badedas. Arousingly aromatic. Perfume. Rose water.
**Palate:** Creamy. Turkish delight.
**Finish:** Very emphatic tea character.

**8¾ Jim:** Sensational stuff of a style universally unique to Irish whiskey, the Midleton distillery in particular. A classic.
**Nose:** The raisiny, deftly honeyed brittle pot still eventually dominates the spice. Brooding stuff.
**Palate:** Shafts of honey pierce the oaky, barley-rich intensity. Excellent bittersweet balance, but tending on the sweetish side.
**Finish:** Docked marks for a slight briefness of finish. Hints of cocoa towards the end.

## JAMESON 18 YEARS OLD 40%
Blended

**8¾ Peter:** Even after 18 years, the pot still refuses to be mastered by the wood. Very drinkable.
**Nose:** A gentle caress of apricots and carbolic soap.
**Palate:** That firm, linseed crackle of pot still whiskey, the edges rounded by sultanas.
**Finish:** Mince pies then a farewell buzz from the unmalted barley.

**8½ Dave:** Seems drier than I remember but still well balanced.
**Nose:** Rich fruit and nut. Good weight with positive (resinous) oak notes. Linseed oil, black butter, moss, dried apricot and honey, toffee apple. Mature.
**Palate:** Rolls around the mouth, becoming intensely exotic. Dried peels, peach, honey, Turkish Delight. Nutty grip, fruit cake, bitter chocolate and cream.
**Finish:** Firm, oak.

## JAMESON 18 YEARS OLD MASTER SELECTION 40%
Blended

*WHISKY Magazine Editor's choice*

**9 Michael:** Robustly sexy. I always enjoy Jameson, but I really relished coming to grips with this one.
**Nose:** Fresh, clean linen. Alder. Bath oil.
**Palate:** Oiled wood. Out of the sauna to a cup of tea. Quite strong flavours. Aromatic and refreshing.
**Finish:** Gunpowder tea. A minor explosion.

**9 Dave:** I could drink this all day. A classic Irish whiskey.
**Nose:** Soft, rich, juicy: apricot, dried fruits, orange, butterscotch, hazelnut butter. Water brings out sherry, becoming chocolate and bourbon biscuit.
**Palate:** A luscious, oily sweetness with a crisp solidity on the palate, then a burst of dried fruits, spices and citrus fruits.
**Finish:** Rich, soft honeyed.

## JAMESON GOLD 40%
Blended

**7¾** **Michael:** There is some virgin oak in this one, along with bourbon casks. Bonus points for trying something new, but would have expected more interesting results. I find it a bit light tasting. Try it with fresh brown bread and Dublin Bay prawns.
**Nose:** Light. Fresh wood. Vanilla. Distinctly buttery.
**Palate:** Creamy. Vanilla. Fresh apple. Honey.
**Finish:** Lightly toasty. Fresh-cut cedar.

**9½** **Jim:** No two vattings are ever the same. However this is, astonishingly high quality every time. The most complex Irish of them all; a blender triumph.
**Nose:** Layered elements of soft honey and subtle oak criss-crossing the crisp port-still.
**Palate:** Truly magnificent honey-barley notes.
**Finish:** Silky and subtle, an essay in bittersweet balance with the final, drier, bitter notes reminding you of some decent age.

## JAMESON IRISH WHISKEY 40%
Blended

**8** **Michael:** A superb Irish for everyday drinking. I love this, though not quite as much as the 1780.
**Nose:** Very aromatic. Waxy orange skins. Linseed oil. Leather.
**Palate:** Big, oily, creamy, sociable.
**Finish:** Delicate. Peppery. More-ish.

**8** **Jim:** Five or six years back I panned this whiskey: it was lacking in pot still character. Not any more. Now genuinely impressive, charming and characterful.
**Nose:** A meeting of Oloroso and crisp pot still character. Malty, too. Lovely fruitcake richness, though not as sweet as in recent years.
**Palate:** Very firm, oily, intense and mouthfilling.
**Finish:** A hint of spice counters an increasing oaky bitterness though the barley and sherry lasts to the very end.

## JAMESON LIMITED EDITION, 15 YEARS OLD 40%
Blended

**8½** **Michael:** Distinctive. A very full pot-still Irish.
**Nose:** Superbly aromatic. Cedary.
**Palate:** Dried apricots. Marshmallow. Syrup-soaked seed cake.
**Finish:** Wafers. Peppery dryness.

**8¾** **Jim:** A really clean, compact whiskey which expands in a controlled but mouthwatering manner.
**Nose:** Spicy start is a detour to the sweet unmalted barley.
**Palate:** Mouth-watering start with enormous pot still arrival. But the impact is cushioned slightly by a silky sweetness.
**Finish:** Hardness remains but is softened by a cocoa/caramel thread.

## JAMESON ORIGINAL 40%
Blended

**7¼** **Peter:** Not as interesting as it used to be, this brand is teetering on the brink of bland.
**Nose:** Musky vanilla and mashed linseeds.
**Palate:** Firm citrus fruitiness, viscous and mouth coating.
**Finish:** Tonic water dryness, light sherry.

**6¾** **Dave:** Distinctly average. Very disappointing.
**Nose:** Soft and creamy (coconut), acetone, then a hard metallic note reminiscent of aluminium cigar tubes. Peanut brittle. Has some sweetness with water, but there's some young stuff in there.
**Palate:** Light, soft, grassy. Vanilla, cane juice, apricot jam. With water a nagging harshness.
**Finish:** Dry raffia, wet reeds.

## KILBEGGAN 15 YEARS OLD 40%
Blended

**7¾** **Dave:** Proof (if it were needed) that Cooley is a serious player.
**Nose:** Full and thick with decent intensity. American oak: hot sawdust, cherry, spices. Sugared almond.
**Palate:** Sweet with banana and coconut to the fore. Ripe with just sufficient grip. A drop of water brings out the grass, giving it a fragrant edge.
**Finish:** Medium.

**7¼** **Gavin:** The luxurious nose raises expectations that the palate can't quite match.

**Nose:** Quite bourbon-like. Vanilla, maple syrup, and even a suggestion of menthol. Ice cream and fudge sauce.
**Palate:** Initially, drier and more oaky than the nose promises, but with developing stewed fruits.
**Finish:** Short and slightly bitter. Disappointing.

## KILBEGGAN BLENDED IRISH WHISKEY 40%
Blended

**7** **Michael:** Light but firm and satisfying. A welcome newcomer for everyday drinking.
**Nose:** Lemongrass. Lime.
**Palate:** Medium. Smooth. Sweetish, very toasty, malt character. Well-balanced.
**Finish:** Nice balancing dryness. Leafy.

**7** **Jim:** A satisfying, finely balanced dram which again shows Cooley's decent grain to good effect.
**Nose:** No shyness to the firm, extra-clean grain, but the malt does balance things out beautifully. The fruit has receded in recent years but there are still hints of apple and grape.
**Palate:** Fabulously lush, honeyed and delicately malted. The grain adds complexity.
**Finish:** Still lush, moderately sweet, slightly grapey. The early spices vanish and leave some oak and a grainy firmness.

## KILBEGGAN FINEST 40%
Blended

**7¼** **Dave:** An attractive sipper, but only in decent mouthfuls. A good session whiskey...if one is allowed to say that in these moderate times.
**Nose:** Warm straw, honey and lemon. Water makes it drier and brings out wet green ferns.
**Palate:** Clean light and crisp with a soft, vanilla led, mid-palate. Tropical fruit and a slightly chalky quality.
**Finish:** Clean and lightly nutty.

**7½** **Gavin:** A pleasant enough dram, but lacking real personality.
**Nose:** Hand-rolling tobacco, a hint of ginger. More floral and fragrant notes emerge in time, and finally vanilla.
**Palate:** Oily mouthfeel, quite dry, with fudge and emerging spices.
**Finish:** Starting out spicy and drying.

## KNAPPOGUE CASTLE 1993 40%
Single Malt

**7** **Michael:** The vinho verde colour suggests a very light whiskey, and this certainly is, in both body and flavour. Seems markedly thinner than the last vintage I tasted.
**Nose:** Gently fruity, perfumy, smoky.
**Palate:** Light on the tongue. Flowery. Oat-like flavours. Some maltiness. Vanilla sweetness.
**Finish:** Light. A touch of spiciness.

**8** **Dave:** Hugely drinkable. Young but sweetly vibrant.
**Nose:** Attractive, obviously young but not immature. Grassy with a touch of muesli, sweet almonds and juicy malt. Sauvignon Blanc/green rhubarb ferment notes.
**Palate:** Sweet and fresh all the way through: peaches, blossom and clover. Light nutty malt mid-palate with that winery/grapey note at the back.
**Finish:** Peaches in syrup (en regalia?) then dry cereal.

## LOCKE'S 8 YEARS OLD 40%
Single Malt

**8** **Peter:** A very enjoyable, no nonsense malt.
**Nose:** Camphor, hints of peat and loads of vanilla.
**Palate:** A full on tongue riot as melons and custard creams go at it big time.
**Finish:** The lurking peat finally makes itself felt.

**7½** **Dave:** In a Speyside mould. Well made and a good drink.
**Nose:** Estery. Hint of putty, cake mix, macadamia, lawnmower box. Then dry oak, pencil shavings, nectarine and light (dried) floral notes.
**Palate:** Starts all delicate and perfumed then firms up. Lean and balanced with a zesty citric lift and touches of nougat, clean oak and vanilla.
**Finish:** Peppery and spicy, then shaved oak.

## LOCKE'S BLENDED IRISH WHISKEY 40%
Blended

**7** **Michael: Very appetising.**
**Nose:** Grassy. Lemongrass. Lemons.
**Palate:** Spearmint, oily, smooth. Becoming sweet. Mint-toffee. Nicely rounded
**Finish:** Minty, fruity.

**8** **Jim: Perhaps the most improved blend in the Cooley range. A massive assertiveness throughout.**
**Nose:** Massive fruit onslaught: apples and oranges and well structured sweetness. The grain lightens the proceedings.
**Palate:** Big and boisterous and enormously sweet from the start. Rich maltiness, a slight smokiness and an almost metallic honey sheen.
**Finish:** Drier with some cocoa. Quite gristy.

## LOCKE'S SINGLE MALT 40%
Single Malt

**8** **Michael: Beautifully balanced with toasted dryness.**
**Nose:** Fragrant, with just the tiniest hint of peat. Grassy. Lemon grass.
**Palate:** Honeydew melons.
**Finish:** Full. Firm. Juicy. Peachy maltiness.

**7½** **Jim: Hmmm...Not quite up to what it was, but still a pretty interesting and enjoyable dram.**
**Nose:** Slightly musty, coal-gassy, but with a sultana-currant bun, spotted dick suet doughiness.
**Palate:** Archetypal Cooley malt intensity which clings to the mouth with a firm, fruity oiliness. One dimensional but rather tasty.
**Finish:** Some oakiness begins to dry out the proceedings, leaving a vanilla-banana residue. Some caramel and demerara sugar adds a lingering sweetness.

## MAGILLIGAN 1991 LIMITED EDITION, SHERRY WOOD FINISH 46%
Single Malt

**7¼** **Peter: Finishing Cooley's peated malt in a sherry wood for a year works a lot better than I imagined, and makes me wonder what an unpeated malt would taste like after a year in Jerez.**
**Nose:** Tobacco tins and lemon grass.
**Palate:** A huge sherry embrace, which gives way to mince pies and very juicy peat.
**Finish:** Tickly spicy marmalade.

**7½** **Dave: The wood becomes a little obvious.**
**Nose:** Light fruits: citrus pith, grapefruit, tinned peach, marzipan. Light smoke, tea caddy. Sweet and lightly juicy with crispness. In time, menthol whittled sticks and apricot stone.
**Palate:** Sweetness and juicy oiliness. Hazelnut, bitter orange, orange peel.
**Finish:** Nutty.

## MAGILLIGAN 1991 SHERRY WOOD FINISH 46%
Single Malt

**7¾** **Michael: I liked the lively 8 Years Old version. Would I be tempted away by something smoother, more mature? I would think about it...maybe.**
**Nose:** Oily. Lemon grass. Sweet lemons.
**Palate:** Fruity. Lemon curd. Marshmallows. Pastry. Icing sugar.
**Finish:** Spiciness and biscuity maltiness provide a balance.

**7½** **Dave: A boisterous, roistering, very quaffable malt.**
**Nose:** Quite rich and sherried. Cake mix, dried fruits, tobacco, date and syrup you get in tins of fruit. Light milky note.
**Palate:** Big and robust with good malty attack. Fine, sweet mid-palate, but a little bitter on the sides.
**Finish:** Burnt orange, bitter.

## MAGILLIGAN 8 YEARS OLD, IRISH PEATED MALT 43%
Single Malt

**7¾** **Michael: A lovely, clean, malty, easily drinkable, whisky. The label promises peat, but that is hard to find.**
**Nose:** Sweet and syrupy without being cloying. Fruity. Sweet lime juice. Very faint grassy peatiness.
**Palate:** Soft, fresh, pillowy. Very clean, marshmallow.
**Finish:** Light, sweet. Biscuity. Hint of toasty dryness.

**8** **Dave: Well balanced and juicy.**
**Nose:** Initially a farmyard aroma, then lots of smoke, turned earth, grass, cereal and some soft ripe fruits.

**Palate:** Very smoky but with a soft juicy texture. Well balanced.
**Finish:** Long, becoming sweet.

## MAGILLIGAN PURE POT STILL 43%
Single Malt

**7** **Peter: Although it says 'pure pot still' on the label, this is a single malt, there's no unmalted barley here. At 5 or so years old this malt is still a bit green.**
**Nose:** Malt and grain, boiled sweets. A less aromatic and interesting bouquet than Cooley's Tyrconnell.
**Palate:** Lime and biscuits washed down with cream soda.
**Finish:** Spicy and strangely dry.

**7½** **Dave: Developing some weight. An older example will be interesting.**
**Nose:** Light, nutty edge, moving into dried peach, mixed herbs, turf and wood shavings. Seems young with an aroma akin to wet pavements after the rain.
**Palate:** Buttery and tongue-coating. Sweet: a juicy centre then a crisp maltiness. Like eating Smarties.
**Finish:** Peppery and spicy.

## MICHAEL COLLINS BLEND 40%
Blended

**9¼** **Michael: Visually, a very attractive whisky – rich amber and gloriously viscous. If my suspicions are correct, an earlier expression of this whisky reminded me of a Peshwari Nan. Must be shared and discussed with friends.**
**Nose:** Delicate, sweet short crust pastry. Marzipan and raspberry jam. Raisins.
**Palate:** Oily, vaguely fruity, honeyed. Faintly herbal.
**Finish:** More like a dessert wine than a whisky. Rich, creamy and filling.

**7½** **Arthur: Pleasing, bright, and easy-going. A good gift whiskey, but not one for the new breed of crusading Whiskey Adventurer.**
**Nose:** Honey porridge, coconut and a savoury, clove-like spice. Fresh orange: zest and pithy.
**Palate:** Raisiny, slightly spicy with lots of vanilla.
**Finish:** Citric and lightly bitter.

## MICHAEL COLLINS SINGLE MALT 40%
Single Malt

**7½** **Dave: A little lacking in impact after such a big nose. Worth a look though.**
**Nose:** Lightly oily with some plasticene/pear drop/green plums. This then shifts into drumskin, oiled leather and candlewax. Some soft stone fruit notes in time.
**Palate:** Sneaks into the mouth and seeps across the tongue. Mango. Broadens and sweetens in the mid-palate but then starts to fade rapidly.
**Finish:** Thin and short.

**7½** **Arthur: A session malt, pure and simple.**
**Nose:** Fruit salad chews, strawberries and lemon balm. A bit of fermenting grass and some background sourness to balance out the cuteness.
**Palate:** Soft, sweet and malty, with more strawberries.
**Finish:** Short, with a gentle oakiness and maybe a little smoke.

## MIDLETON VERY RARE 40%
Blended

**8¾** **Peter: Don't know how Barry Walsh keeps this standard up year on year, the most robust MVR in ages. Bravo!**
**Nose:** Furniture polish and mixed spice.
**Palate:** The familiar vinatge DNA of cream soda, melting into vanilla toffee.
**Finish:** An unusual vigorous climax to a stunning offering.

**8¾** **Dave: Leave a glass of this to breathe for 24 hours and you're blown away by its complexity.**
**Nose:** Subtle and complex. Very spicy with sandalwood, discreet oakiness, cereal and peach. In time even more spice and a lovely juiciness.
**Palate:** Long and very perfumed with layers of flavour: lilac, oak, toffee. Finer than the others.
**Finish:** Long, spices, oak.

## MIDLETON VERY RARE 40%
Blended

**8¾ Michael: In general, Midleton is a bit too elegant for me, but this is a lovely vintage. The Yquem of whiskies?**
**Nose:** Clean, fresh, dessert apple skin. Honeycomb toffee
**Palate:** Soft, smooth, caressing. Very lightly fruity. Zabaglione. White peaches. Amaretto macaroons.
**Finish:** Toasty. Winey. Malaga?

*WHISKY Magazine Recommended*

**8¾ Dave: Not one, but two world-class whiskeys. All hail the two Barrys!**
**Nose:** Quite lean, aromatic and complex: sandalwood, polished furniture, nutmeg and spice. Oak tones alongside crème caramel, oil, tobacco.
**Palate:** Rounded with treacle toffee and a mix of dried spice, oak and a rich, oily texture with a crunchy centre.
**Finish:** Long.

## MILLARS SPECIAL RESERVE 40%
Blended

**6½ Michael: Perfectly pleasant but very light in flavours.**
**Nose:** Flowery, herbal.
**Palate:** Very light. Fresh.
**Finish:** Hint of liquorice-like sherry.

**7½ Jim: Wonderfully balanced and quite chewy. Has shifted its shape a little: the spice now starts earlier and fizzles out before the finish.**
**Nose:** Unusually sherried for a Cooley blend; sweet blackcurrant jelly fruit. Pretty decent malt involvement, grapey and firm grain. Impressive.
**Palate:** Immensely rich, fruity and chewy by Cooley standards. Fine malt sweetness balances oaky dryness.
**Finish:** An oaky buzz sits well with the sweeter remnants of the fruit and malt. Slightly roasted.

## MURPHY'S BLENDED IRISH WHISKEY 40%
Blended

**6 Michael: Pleasant but a little one-dimensional.**
**Nose:** Lightly malty. Fudgy.
**Palate:** Light butter and toffee.
**Finish:** Crisp. Peanut brittle.

**7 Jim: Lacks depth: a simple but pleasant blend.**
**Nose:** Delicate and immediately malty. A sound, slightly toffee grain presence. Not as smoky as a few years back, but salty for an Irish.
**Palate:** A complex maltiness – both grassy and intensely barley-rich – dominates. The oak is quite drying, though a hint of wild fruit offers some extra compexity.
**Finish:** Lightly spiced, malty with some vanilla from the grain.

## OLD MIDLETON 1967, 35 YEARS OLD, THE WHISKY EXCHANGE 41.1%
Blended

**8½ Michael: Post prandial. After the aloo.**
**Nose:** Fresh bread. Fruit. Nuts. Peshwari nan.
**Palate:** Big and creamy. Walnut bread. Walnut oil. Peach kernel. Fresh white peaches.
**Finish:** Toasty, biscuity, cookie-like dryness.

**7¾ Dave: A smooth tongued charmer.**
**Nose:** Fresh, silky and gentle with good weight. Malt, butter, lemon, milk chocolate and the smell of spring meadows.
**Palate:** Sweet, malty and attractively oaky. It starts all very charming with lemon cake and cream then there's a hard, crunchy, nutty centre.
**Finish:** Dried mint. Slightly sour.

## PADDY OLD IRISH WHISKEY 40%
Blended

**7½ Michael: A classic Irish, though less full in flavour than Jameson.**
**Nose:** Very linseedy, flowery and appetising.
**Palate:** Smooth, perfumy.
**Finish:** Mustard.

**5 Jim: An unwieldy blend which disappoints thanks to its refusal to offer anything but a grainy, almost metallic hardness against an uncomplex softness.**
**Nose:** Grainy from the off, but just a little more pot still sturdiness than of yore. A touch fruity but overall quite uninspiring.

**Palate:** Much more toffee-vanilla than in recent years; enormously soft and completely lacking richness.
**Finish:** Dries as the oak takes over; becomes even bitter.

## REDBREAST 12 YEARS OLD 40%
Blended

**9 Peter: This is what real pure pot still whiskey is all about, a glorious contradiction of soft fruit and firm grain, oily seeds and sweet wood. World beating stuff.**
**Nose:** The very Irish nose tweak of resin, sherry and linseed.
**Palate:** Fat and oily. Layers of satin ginger, silk honey and hints of spicy liquorice.
**Finish:** Vanilla pods and marsala.

*WHISKY Magazine Editor's choice*

**9 Dave: Whiskey covering the entire spectrum of aroma, taste, feel, flavour. World class.**
**Nose:** Intense and full blooded. Pot still richness: citrus oils, hot sealing wax, leather, tobacco, tea, maraschino, overripe fruits, marzipan. Exemplary.
**Palate:** Ridiculously big. Oozes into the mouth and erupts. Spices galore to the finish. Oily and unctuous.
**Finish:** Long, rich, oily.

## REDBREAST 12 YEARS OLD 40%
Blended

**8¾ Michael: Those oily, cakey aromas still have me hankering for a weekend in Dublin. Tea and cakes at the Shelbourne, then off to the Horseshoe Bar for the first whiskey of the evening.**
**Nose:** Nutty oiliness. Nuts and sultanas in a fruitcake.
**Palate:** Tangerines. Brazil nuts. Toasted almonds. Sherry. Lots of flavour development. Complex, but slightly less rich than I remember.
**Finish:** Vanilla. Spicily warming. Long.

**9 Jim: Remains an all-Ireland great and one of the few true pure pot still whiskies around. A treat for even the most experienced connoisseur.**
**Nose:** An unhurried display of ripe fruits. The sharpness of the pot-still always reminds me of a firm pure rye, only this is spicier.
**Palate:** More spice, though not before the early shock-waves of complex, mouth-watering barley notes.
**Finish:** Lingering sherry-toffee.

## SHANNON GRAIN 1991, 9 YEARS OLD, CASK 10839, ADELPHI 67.3%
Single Grain

**7 Michael: For a grain whiskey, it has plenty of flavours, but they do not hang together very well.**
**Nose:** Lemon grass. Garden mint. Ground almonds.
**Palate:** Firm. Starts dry but some peppery sweetness develops. Fuller flavour than its sister, Greenore.
**Finish:** Slightly sticky. Fruity. Hot.

**6¼ Dave: Easy going.**
**Nose:** Damp grass and wood. Nutty with a slight musty edge.
**Palate:** Sweet and thick to start, seems a little unbalanced.
**Finish:** Short.

## SHANNON GRAIN SINGLE MALT IRISH WHISKEY, ADELPHI 67.3%
Single Grain

**7 Michael: Flavoursome for a grain, but neither especially clean nor well rounded.**
**Nose:** Lemon grass. Lemon rind.
**Palate:** Very light, but firm and dry. Sherbety. Lemony. Peppery. Some pepperminty sweetness.
**Finish:** Papery. Sticky. Fruity. Hot.

**6½ Doug: Charming but unemphatic. The nose promises more than delivers.**
**Nose:** Gentle oaky herby floral traits, hints of caramel, raisins and reminiscent of plastic paddling pools.
**Palate:** Delicate, sweet to dry peppery swing. Sweet and sour grain.
**Finish:** Dryish, the grain teases against some salty extremes.

## SLANEY SINGLE MALT IRISH WHISKEY, ADELPHI
Single Malt

**7¾ Michael: Pleasant, soothing, sociable.**
**Nose:** Light cereal grain and fruit.
**Palate:** Lightly oily. Creamy, nutty. Hazelnut. Fruity. Candied angelica.
**Finish:** Dry. Hint of charcoal.

**7 Doug: Showing some nice complexities. Drier than younger offerings.**
**Nose:** Dry overall, despite some butterscotch, pear drops and a hint of chocolate orange.
**Palate:** Aniseed, a wave of brine then more chocolatey and citrus notes.
**Finish:** Dry, spicy and chocolatey.

## TULLAMORE DEW 40%
Blended

**6 Dave: This metallic edge suggests the use of young grain that hasn't matured out fully.**
**Nose:** Edgy and slightly metallic. Seems young; green walnut, unripe fruits. Slightly sweeter with water, but still hard overall.
**Palate:** Some daffodil-like floral aromas. Light pear, but very thin with water.
**Finish:** Sudden. Dry and hollow.

**7½ Gavin: A curious beast, indeed.**
**Nose:** A most unusual, high, furniture polish and spirity nose. Acetone and meths, yet not unattractive.
**Palate:** Oily, with dark berries and malt.
**Finish:** Quite short and nutty. Lingering vanilla behind oak.

## TULLAMORE DEW 12 YEARS OLD 40%
Blended

**8 Peter: This is a super little whiskey; a premium Jameson clone. And a good one too.**
**Nose:** Fruit scones with burnt raisins.
**Palate:** That crackling pot still and sherry wood combination is knockout here, beautifully balanced with toasted vanilla notes and sunflower seeds.
**Finish:** Slightly bitter. Burnt hops, toffee on the stove. Very long.

**7½ Dave: Well made and quite delicate. Decent balance.**
**Nose:** Firm with some unmalted barley notes. Rich tea biscuit, slightly grassy and oily. Wild herbs (tarragon) and a hard note right in the centre.
**Palate:** Light bodied. Chewier than the nose suggests with nutmeg and a mouth filling character.
**Finish:** Nutty, good, spicy.

## TULLAMORE DEW 12 YEARS OLD 40%
Blended

**7¾ Michael: Sophisticated and seductive, but I always find it a little lacking in substance.**
**Nose:** Perfumy, grassy. Sesame seeds. Data-like sweetness.
**Palate:** Light, elegant, sweetish, and raisiny, with some sherry.
**Finish:** Lightly spicy, gingery.

**8½ Jim: The injection of rich, exotic fruit along with the bigger pot still feel improves it almost beyond measure. The finish is still weak, though.**
**Nose:** A rigid backbone of pot still is softened by massive and quite startling fruit arrival.
**Palate:** Remains grain orientated, though quite mouth watering.
**Finish:** Pretty dry and thin, but just enough sweet oil to keep the oak in check.

## TULLAMORE DEW HERITAGE 40%
Blended

**8 Michael: Deserves points for daring to be so sweet.**
**Nose:** Soft, very grassy and linseedy.
**Palate:** Remarkably syrupy. Very sweet and spicy. Lemon grass.
**Finish:** Lemon sherbet fizzing on the tongue.

**7¾ Dave: Have with Guinness to soften the slightly hard edges.**
**Nose:** Intense, lightly fragrant nose: some grassiness and juicy fruits but this is a prickly character that's more austere than it initially seems.
**Palate:** Gutsy and zesty with an oily crunch mid-palate. Light and straight down the middle of the palate.
**Finish:** Zesty, peppery. Little short.

## TULLAMORE DEW HERITAGE 40%
Blended

**8 Peter: A very decent and reserved blend that is simply overshadowed and outclassed by the 12 Years Old.**
**Nose:** Pot still and candied peel.
**Palate:** An almost too subtle combination of dry biscuits and lush sherry. The pot still is a bit too well behaved for my liking.
**Finish:** Malted milk drink for adults.

**8 Dave: Big-boned, but the most restrained of the big boys.**
**Nose:** Has complexity and maturity. Full pot still weight, lush and oily with rye, stewed apple, malt loaf, burnt raisin, cooked pear, vanilla pod, dubbin, cocoa.
**Palate:** Slides into the mouth. A good firm structure with light wood then semi-dried fruits and peels.
**Finish:** Refreshingly crisp. Big and fruity.

## TYRCONNELL 40%
Single Malt

**7½ Michael: A pleasant, light-tasting malt.**
**Nose:** Very scented, appleskin dryness. Oily, cereal-grain.
**Palate:** Light, oily, grassy. Lightly malty and cookie-like. Some vanilla sweetness.
**Finish:** Crisp, clean. Hint of charcoal.

**6 Jim: Perhaps the most inconsistent brand from Cooley. Not the finest expression of its normally impressive single malt; usually there is greater clarity and depth.**
**Nose:** Fresh, malty, and amazingly fruity. Loads of citrus and traces of apple. There is just a very faint touch of ammonia to this vatting, which is not normally the case.
**Palate:** Intense malt with a distinctive, coppery richness. Spicy, with a fine sweet/dry balance. But the oak does start making a point.
**Finish:** Dry and lacking true depth.

## TYRCONNELL 40%
Single Malt

**7½ Peter: This malt used to be a tad young, the current bottling is older and certainly works better.**
**Nose:** An intense assault of pear drops, lime peel and Haribo jelly sweets. Incredibly fruity.
**Palate:** Very creamy but not as sweet as the nose would lead you to believe. Loads of grassy spice with honeyed oak after a moment.
**Finish:** Quinine dry.

**6¾ Dave: Young, hard to back.**
**Nose:** Oaky. Balsa wood, young spirit. Malt husks and a green, grappa-like note.
**Palate:** Thin and dilute. Soft fruits in centre, but overpowered by tightly gripping oak and lemony spirit.
**Finish:** Dry, short.

## TYRCONNELL 40%
Single Malt

**7½ Michael: Pleasant, light. For sociable drinking.**
**Nose:** Grassy, leafy. Herbal. Hint of charcoal. Dry.
**Palate:** Firm, silky, oily. Some vanilla-pod. Cereal-grain flavours.
**Finish:** Garden mint. Very late sweetness.

**7¾ Jim: By no means complex but not a single wayward note, either. Perhaps too one dimensional for some, this expression proves what excellent malt Cooley produces.**
**Nose:** Very sweet and clean aged malt.
**Palate:** Light but intensely malty with a gathering of oaky spice. Excellent sweetness.
**Finish:** Lingering oak helps the malt keep an impressive shape on the palate.

## TYRCONNELL 14 YEARS OLD 46%
Single Malt

**7½ Dave: A decent drink, but the port finish is the winner out of the trio.**
**Nose:** Hunter Valley Semillon. Green, grassy slightly stony. Then there's pineapple, tinned pear and becomes increasingly sweet.
**Palate:** The pears are to the fore for me. Marzipan/amaretto.
**Finish:** Very gentle.

**7¾ Arthur: Balanced and pleasant.**
**Nose:** Malty.

**Palate:** Basically sweet with acacia honey, custard crèmes and a little candied nuts. Syrupy exotic fruit and caramel too, like fairground toffee apples. A macaroon biscuit.
**Finish:** Caramel.

### TYRCONNELL MADEIRA FINISH 10 YEARS OLD 46%
Single Malt

**8** **Dave: Well put together, the finish not too obtrusive.**
**Nose:** Firm and malty yet with a scented exotic fragrance: orchid/ flight frangipan. Wood.
**Palate:** Soft and seemingly simple start then things pick up. A juicy mouthwatering quality reminiscent of mango. Balanced. Some chocolate.
**Finish:** Fruit juice.

**8¼** **Arthur: I've nothing against finishes, especially when they work as well as this one!**
**Nose:** A vibrant initial nose with forest fruits, strawberries and orange frozen yoghurt. Vanilla and nuts, like nut sprinkles on ice cream.

**Palate:** Rich and creamy with caramel sweetness on the tongue with lots of dried fruit (papaya, raisins, apricots, pineapple). Strawberry jam.
**Finish:** More jammy sweetness.

### TYRCONNELL PORT FINISH 46%
Single Malt

**7¾** **Dave: This just balances the whiskey and the finish.**
**Nose:** Looks like a rose wine, smells like a rose wine. Straw and strawberry. Sweet shop/dolly mixtures. Herbaceous.
**Palate:** Seems slightly confected but this is knocked aside as malt comes through. Soft fruits. Has balance.
**Finish:** Jammy.

**8** **Arthur: Another success. It walked that fine line between jammy and cloying, just about staying on the right side.**
**Nose:** Strawberry jam, pineapple and apples. Forest floor (earthy and leafy).
**Palate:** Victoria sponge. Very sweet and confected, but not in a nauseating way and underpinned with a little malty, cereal character.
**Finish:** More sweetness.

Kilbeggan Distillery, home of Locke's Irish whiskey, basks in the glory of an Irish summer's day

Yoichi •

HOKKAIDO

• Noheji

HONSHU

Sendai •

• Shirakawa

JAPAN

Karuizawa •
Hakushu •          • Hanyu
Mars Shinshu •         ○ **Tokyo**
Yamazaki •          Gotemba •

SHIKOKU

KYUSHU

# Japan

Despite the fact that some of *Whisky Magazine*'s tasters, Dave Broom and Michael Jackson foremost, have been plugging away that Japanese whisky is something very special and has a lot to offer the whisky lover, it probably took the 2003 film *Lost in Translation* to put the idea of whisky from the East in the minds of most drinkers.

The Japanese whisky-making tradition is based on a love story that spans the globe, from the now defunct Hazelburn distillery in Campbeltown to the stills of Yamazaki. The man regarded as one of the two fathers of Japanese whisky, Masataka Taketsuru, learnt his passion for the water of life during a series of distillery apprenticeships in Speyside and Campbeltown.

While working he met his future bride, Rita Cowan, and so when he returned to start distilling in Japan in about 1923, Rita travelled with him. Thus Japanese whisky was born out of the tale of two lovers. Taketsuru, while being the first master distiller at Suntory where he was hired to create whisky, also founded the other Japanese distiller Nikka.

Both companies are now among some of the most influential distillers in the world and also own some Scottish distillery companies; Suntory owns Morrison Bowmore and Nikka has Ben Nevis.

One slight quirk is that the two companies do not trade barrels like their Scottish counterparts, so the distilling teams need to produce a wide selection of different whiskies, everything from grain to unpeated and heavily peated whiskies. This gives the blending teams all styles under the sun to work with. Suntory deals with this by having an impressive mix of stills, whereas Nikka uses different strains of yeast and varies its fermentation times to create different flavours.

In recent years we have also seen a small revival in the use of Japanese oak for maturing which gives the whisky a distinctive incense-like aroma.

In the tasting notes you will find the one exception to the rule in Japan. Ichiro Akuto, who is currently rebuilding the Hanyu distillery, decided to blend together whiskies from the main Japanese distilleries to create Gingko. This is a great starting point for those wanting to embark on a voyage of what the East has to offer.

**Clockwise from top left:** Yoichi Distillery in the snow; The entrance to Yamazaki Distillery; The stillroom at Yamazaki; The iconic Mount Fuji

## DID YOU KNOW...

- The pagodas of the Japanese Buddhist temples are said to have inspired the vents on Scottish maltings designed by Charles Doig in the 1890s
- Yoichi is a coastal distillery on the northern island of Hokkaido. The rest of Japan's distilleries are on the main island of Honshu. Sendai, Karuizawa, Hakushu and Gotemba are near Tokyo, while Yamazaki sits a Bullet train ride away to the south nearer Kyoto
- Hakushu is one of the world's biggest malt distilleries at full capacity and sits higher than any in Scotland at 700m above sealevel. (Dalwhinnie is Scotland's highest distillery at 350m)
- Nikka's distilleries at Yoichi and Miyagikyo (Sendai) are both coal fired, with the coal imported from Eastern Europe. While some stills at Yamazaki use direct gas firing and some have internal steam coils

### EVERMORE 2004 BLEND, 21 YEARS OLD 40%
Blended

8½ **Martine: Perfect blend of aromas and textures. Really appealing. Makes you feel romantic.**
**Nose:** Complex, rich. Intriguing combination of earth and sea aromas. Wet leaves. Sea spray on warm bitumen. Touch of fried bacon. Vanilla waffle.
**Palate:** Attractive sweetness. Layers of fruit. Dark cherries. Marmalade, dates, raisins, roasted nuts.
**Finish:** Subtle but lingering. Hint of phenols. Liquorice.

7¼ **Dave: An old whisky and of interest, but beginning to fade.**
**Nose:** Brandy and sweet. Touches of rose petal perfume/orange muscat and sweet pine. Slightly dusty with water but has breadth.
**Palate:** Nut oil, chocolate, pecan. Still sweet. Becomes sappy to finish. Orange.
**Finish:** Dry, slightly dusty.

### FUJI SANROKU 18 YEARS OLD 43%
Single Malt

7¾ **Martine: The complexity of the nose is not reflected on the palate. But the clean dryness makes it refreshing and enjoyable.**
**Nose:** Estery and buttery with a slight butyric note. A phenolic hint tangled up with a fresh liquorice fragrance. Opens up on a smooth grassy note. Quite a complex interlaced aromatic profile.
**Palate:** Dry and fruity, giving way to bitter notes.
**Finish:** Rather short, clean and dry.

7½ **Dave: Very clean and precise. Charming.**
**Nose:** High toned and estery. Quite restrained. Polished wood, peach stone, violet. With water there's white flowers, grapefruit.
**Palate:** Sweet, fragrant and honeyed. Very light grip with a little lemon and hot sawdust.
**Finish:** Gentle. Lychee.

### FUJIGOTENBA 15 YEARS OLD, SINGLE GRAIN 43%
Single Malt

7¾ **Martine: Characterful but I would have easily mistaken it for Cognac.**
**Nose:** Assertive. Apples in caramel. Damp earth. Musty. Cider cellar.
**Palate:** Round. Fruity. A good deal of vanilla.
**Finish:** Spicy, warm and fruity. With a dry oakiness.

7¾ **Dave: A delicious whisky.**
**Nose:** Very sweet, liqueur like. Honey, light oil, sesame, orange pulp, coconut. Gentle and approachable.
**Palate:** Very soft. Good oak extract balancing the buttery quality. Juicy and soft.
**Finish:** Sweet. Marshmallow. Polished oak.

### FUJIGOTENBA 18 YEARS OLD, SINGLE MALT 43%
Single Malt

8 **Martine: I like its balance and elegance. Again in a cognac style like a mature X. O. from 'fins bois terroir'.**
**Nose:** Mellow. A lovely nuttiness. Candied chestnut. Fruity. Cider apple cooked in vanilla syrup.
**Palate:** Smooth. Velvety. Elegant balance between sweet and sour. Toasted cereal.
**Finish:** Whispering, soothing, nutty. Liquorice. Some dry oak on the sides.

7¼ **Dave: All oak. Good oak, but oak nonetheless.**
**Nose:** Quite light, moving into crumbling biscuit. Then leather, deck oil, hot fences in the summer sun. Touch of pear. Mature. Higher alcohol.
**Palate:** Very dry and quite tannic. Some sweet digestive biscuit. Hint of tobacco and dry nuts.
**Finish:** Tight, oaky, bitter almond.

### GOLDEN HORSE CHICHIBU 10 YEARS OLD 43%
Single Malt

7½ **Michael: Fresh, lively, flirtatious but slightly tart and astringent.**
**Nose:** Herbal. Fruity. Lemony. Ground coriander seeds.
**Palate:** Vegetal. Thick green grass. Burnt grass. Peaty bitterness.
**Finish:** Quite oaky for a 10 Years Old.

7¼ **Dave: Well-made, clean, light and drinkable.**
**Nose:** Cereal, sugar puffs, hazelnut. There's cream amongst the wood shavings.
**Palate:** Soft and rounded with creamy toffee, green plum and nut. Good weight, attractive.
**Finish:** Smoke. A little dry/planed wood.

### GOLDEN HORSE CHICHIBU 12 YEARS OLD 50%
Single Malt

7¾ **Michael: Bittersweet, sophisticated.**
**Nose:** Fruitier. Orange. Clotted cream. Vanilla. Sponge.
**Palate:** Candied citrus peels. Zest of orange and lemon.
**Finish:** Marmalade-like bitterness. Orange bitters.

6 **Dave: A quick-maturing spirit that needs to be watched like a hawk.**
**Nose:** A bit dull to start. Faded maltiness. Wood.
**Palate:** The wood is now beginning to dominate what seems to be essentially a light spirit.
**Finish:** Very woody. Tannic.

### GOLDEN HORSE CHICHIBU 8 YEARS OLD 43%
Single Malt

7½ **Michael: Well-balanced. Elegant.**
**Nose:** Sweet. Slightly vegetal. Lavender.
**Palate:** Straight ahead. Silky, scenty. Pistachio ice cream.
**Finish:** Dry. Slightly smoky.

6¾ **Dave: A fight between a sweet, light, attractive young spirit and firm wood.**
**Nose:** Bran flakes, nutty, sour cream. Slightly green and young.
**Palate:** Light. Clean and crisp start, then it starts to grip and close.
**Finish:** Immature.

### HAKUSHU 12 YEARS OLD 43%
Single Malt

8 **Martine: A perfectly balanced dram. Fruit and spices mingle gently.**
**Nose:** Fruity and sweet. Ripe cherry plums, almond milk, acacia honey.
**Palate:** Smooth and velvety. A caressing feel, quite thick. Good balance. As fruity as on the nose. Plums with a hint of prunes.
**Finish:** Medium, with a pleasant dry spiciness. Soothes down on an almondy note.

7½ **Dave: Delicacy to the fore. A breakfast dram if there were ever one.**
**Nose:** Light and grassy and slightly stony to start. In time there's sweet persimmon and nut.
**Palate:** Pure and very clean. Sweet lime, green fruits then a hint of smoke and a buttery meadow sweet/chamomile note. Light to the point of fragility.
**Finish:** Honey, lemon and a little ginger.

### HAKUSHU 12 YEARS OLD PURE MALT 43%
Single Malt

WHISKY Magazine Recommended

8½ **Michael: A beautifully structured, appetising, whisky. Captivating.**
**Nose:** Honey, Heather, camomile. Vanilla.
**Palate:** Firm. Honeyish. Heathery. touch of peat.
**Finish:** Long, warming. Marshmallow. Sweet grass.

8½ **Jim: A first rate malt.**
**Nose:** Fruity: stewed gooseberries, raspberry juice and intensely sharp malt
**Palate:** Fat, leaving a coating of gently peated malt all round the palate
**Finish:** Long with a mixture of cocoa and peat notes

### HAKUSHU 18 YEARS OLD 43%
Single Malt

8¼ **Martine: A colourful character, lively and dancing on nose and palate.**
**Nose:** Intense. Sunny country fragrances. Dry hay, wild flowers. Sunflower honey. Then apple blossom and ripe apples. A touch of new leather.
**Palate:** Oak grip. Silky texture. Fruit is released at midpalate with a burst of spice. A mix of pears, peach, ginger cooked in a vanilla syrup.
**Finish:** Sherbety, dry and lingering. Slightly dusty.

7½ **Dave: Another lighter one which only gets going in the middle of the mouth.**

**Nose:** Splintery attack. Fresh wood, a walk in a warm summer forest. Marzipan, wet raffia, green grass/blackcurrant leaf.
**Palate:** Off-dry and perfumed with good length. Melon balls and gentle soft fruit. Then the grassiness returns.
**Finish:** Dry.

## HAKUSHU 1981, 21 YEARS OLD, 120.1, SCOTCH MALT WHISKY SOCIETY 60.7%
Single Malt

**8¼ Michael: A very enigmatic malt. Lighter in body but drier and more assertive in flavour than Yamazaki. A digestif.**
**Nose:** Very dry, leafy and earthy.
**Palate:** Light but firm and smooth. Dry. Like leaves of cilantro or garden mint on a crème brûlée. Some vanilla, some oakiness.
**Finish:** Spicy but soothing.

**7¾ Dave: A lot of oak on the nose, but has good balance.**
**Nose:** Toasty, oaky, extractive: spices, hot sawdust, nutmeg, apple skin butterscotch, pine.
**Palate:** The weight of the spirit manages to cope with the lashings of oak. Good weight and power. Red fruits, cherry, leafy.
**Finish:** Oaky.

## HAKUSHU 1982 SHERRY CASK 61%
Single Malt

**8¼ Michael: I would love this whisky if it had a little less wood. I want to love it, but in the end the wood defeats me.**
**Nose:** Smoky. Treacle toffee.
**Palate:** Chewy. Fruity. Cherries. Chocolatey.
**Finish:** Bitter chocolate. Concentrated. Intense.

**7½ Dave: A fine example of European oak in action.**
**Nose:** Powerful intense and resinous: treacle, raspberry, coffee. Light smoke giving a burnt note. Gutsy European oak in spades.
**Palate:** Rich and mouthfilling, reminiscent of Brandy de Jerez: stewed plum, leather, PX, burnt raisins. Dry and densely wooded.
**Finish:** Fruit cake.

## HAKUSHU 1984 WHITE OAK CASK 61%
Single Malt

**8½ Michael: Its edgy assertiveness might bother aesthetes but I warm to a whisky that knows its own mind.**
**Nose:** Very aromatic. Fresh cedar. Coconut.
**Palate:** Intense. Tar-like. Rooty. Sappy. Earthy. Piney.
**Finish:** Liquorice. Spicy. Peppery.

**7½ Dave: Packs a real impact.**
**Nose:** Very intense and hot without water, quite oaky. Sharpened pencils and orchard fruits. Water brings a sauna-like piney oiliness. Clean, citric.
**Palate:** Softer and more zesty than you'd expect, though it carries the heat of high alcohol all the way. A fiery beast.
**Finish:** Becomes perfumed in the drying glass.

## HAKUSHU 1988 BOURBON CASK 61%
Single Malt

**8¼ Michael: Lean, limber and characteristically smoky. A clear sense of Hakushu malt without heavy wood influence.**
**Nose:** Clean. Dry. Perfumy. Apple skins.
**Palate:** Vanilla. Freshly cut oak. Forest floor. Pine. Resin. Menthol.
**Finish:** Smoky. Char.

**8 Dave: More gentle than the rest of the range.**
**Nose:** Peaty, heading to the medicinal side of the spectrum. Some sweet fruit and a light menthol note, applewood fires.
**Palate:** Dry. The smoke hits at the deepest point of the palate but a real sweet fruity/lemony note softens things nicely. Fairly firm but has a good range of flavours.
**Finish:** Peppery.

## HAKUSHU 30TH ANNIVERSARY BOTTLING 43%
Single Malt

**8¾ Michael: A beautifully composed whisky. No aggression, but a great sense of authority.**
**Nose:** Toffeeish. Fruity.
**Palate:** Roses. Fruits. A suggestion of milk chocolate.
**Finish:** Firm balancing oaky dryness.

**7¾ Dave: A dry whisky that wakes the palate up.**
**Nose:** Fairly rich: dried fig, hard toffee, chocolate, light smoke. Rich and fruity with drier notes of sacking, redwood, walnut.

**Palate:** Firm with positive grip. Dried fruits/coffee grounds sit in the centre surrounded by oak. Tea-like tannins, dry spices.
**Finish:** Dusty.

## HIBIKI 17 YEARS OLD 43%
Blended

**8¼ Martine: An elegant and satisfying dram. Well educated, in good quality casks.**
*WHISKY Magazine Editor's choice*
**Nose:** Beeswax, polished floor, church bench, candle wax. A tar hint in the back. When aerated, opens up on citrussy notes and barley sugar before a wave of vanilla brings in a sweet brine.
**Palate:** Smooth, mellow. Velvety. Oak and citrus fruit are intertwined in an elegant two step dance.
**Finish:** Medium, smooth, hardening up on a more assertive oaky note. Touch of bitter chocolate.

**8½ Dave: Relaxed and laid back. This is excellent blending.**
**Nose:** Ripe soft and pillow like with hints of smoke and toasty wood. Citrus leaf, cocoa, cooked apricot, ripe banana, hazelnut giving a crunch.
**Palate:** Toffee sweetness stretches along the palate. Very clean and clear. Sweet with sultana and cherry.
**Finish:** Long and silky.

## HIBIKI 21 YEARS OLD 43%
Blended

**7¾ Michael: Leaner, drier, less estery and more oaky than the version that has no age statement. I like each equally, in its own right.**
**Nose:** Chocolates in a cedar box.
**Palate:** Firm. Tightly combined flavours. Chocolate. Faint hint of ginger.
**Finish:** Gentle, long, warming. More obvious ginger.

**8¾ Jim: A classic whisky in any language or any culture.**
**Nose:** Notes of cherry and sherry with malt, peat smoke and oak combining for maximum complexity.
**Palate:** Fat and oily; like the nose hinting slightly at bourbon.
**Finish:** Long and intense with more smoke and a build up of drier, spicier oak.

## HIBIKI 21 YEARS OLD 43%
Blended

**8¼ Martine: Its wide aromatic palette is well displayed. Nothing is missing except a longer finish maybe. A second sip keeps the pleasure on.**
**Nose:** Malty. Cereal bowl with fresh hazelnuts. Creamy and fruity notes like pears in a Greek yoghurt. Cider apple. Hint of peat.
**Palate:** Minty, very refreshing. Sour apple. Excellent balance between sweet and sour.
**Finish:** Elegant, clean and delicately spicy. A touch of peat.

**7½ Dave: Just a little too fat for me.**
**Nose:** Herbal with a dry, twiggy, nuttiness though there's some sweetness behind which emerges in time. Sensual and weighty with stewed fruit, black butter and a touch of sandalwood.
**Palate:** Quite fat and maybe just lacking in grip. Dried flower, violet. Rich dried fruits.
**Finish:** Ripe and rich. Balanced.

## HIBIKI 505 17 YEARS OLD, NON CHILL FILTERED 50.5%
Blended

**8¾ Martine: Virile. Rich display of flavours. If I was to climb up the Fujiyama, I'd take a flask with me.**
*WHISKY Magazine Editor's choice*
**Nose:** Rich, creamy. Milk chocolate. Hay, meadow flowers. Cappuccino. Dried banana. Pepper.
**Palate:** Full-bodied. Waves of flavours. Stewed peaches, coffee, walnuts. Aniseed. With water, toffee and more cream.
**Finish:** Quite dry, thinner than palate. Nutty. Spicy.

**8½ Dave: Sweet and soft but with some creamy oak notes. Syrup/honey. Dried orange peel. Light cocoa butter. Violet. Has elegance.**
**Palate:** Mouthfilling and sweet to start. Red fruits, stone fruits, caramel toffee. A procession of flavours. Balanced dry oak. Good weight.
**Finish:** Good length. Brazil nut. Dry grass. Residual sweetness.

## HIBIKI SUNTORY 43%
Blended

**7¾ Michael: Very easily drinkable. Well matured, as the label suggests. Enjoyable. Appetising. Slightly drier with a splash of water, but not too much. Too good for a mizuwari.**
**Nose:** Soft, rounded. Polished walnut.
**Palate:** Smooth, malty, honeyish, slightly syrupy.
**Finish:** Honeyish. A touch of orange.

**7¾ Jim: Enjoyable if simplistic, the grain holds power here. An attractive session whisky.**
**Nose:** Light for all its colour-attractive green fresh grain with some caramel.
**Palate:** Lively. A deep grain middle on which the most delicate of malt notes hang. Firm, but deliciously sweet.
**Finish:** Chewy with a strong build up of oak, suggesting decent age.

## HOKUTO 12 YEARS OLD 40%
Single Malt

**7¾ Martine: A pleasant summery dram. Keeps fruity all the way.**
**Nose:** A bit restrained. Fruit and oak are well integrated. Watermelon. White peach. A touch of rose syrup. Opens on sweet syrupy notes. Tangerine juice. Polished floor.
**Palate:** Light and silky. Fruit basket. Malty sweetness at midpalate then drying out on an oaky touch.
**Finish:** Dry and nutty.

**7¼ Dave: All front loaded, but doesn't deliver all the way through.**
**Nose:** Crisp and floral with cedar and wood ash/dead BBQ. Once again an almost wheat-like dusty sweetness. Slightly unripe (green banana, floral) and immature.
**Palate:** A very bright start, crisp, clean and gingery/japaleno. Then becomes a little too sweet: flat Irn-Bru and bubblegum.
**Finish:** Rather short. Dilute.

## ICHIRO'S MALT 1985 ACE OF SPADES 55%
Single Malt

**8 Martine: When oak is elegantly mastered, no problem. Same with the alcohol. A beautiful example of controlled maturation.**
**Nose:** Distinguished, aristocratic. Rich but without ostentation. Old leather. Antique shop. Cloved orange. Candied orange and hazelnuts cake.
**Palate:** A good mix of sweet and sour flavours with oak in the first place, firmly dominating but not in an aggressive way. Candied citrus fruit.
**Finish:** Beautifully lingering. Liquorice.

**7¾ Dave: If you like your whisky in yer face then this is for you.**
**Nose:** Rich and quite fat. Chocolate-covered raisin with a hint of creosote and treacle. Yet still very pure with some complexity. Shows maturity.
**Palate:** Thick and very chewy, like melting toffee in the mouth balanced by an intense, savoury edge which then shifts into prunes macerated in brandy. Huge impact.
**Finish:** Dusty and lightly tannic.

## iCHIRO'S MALT 1988 KING OF DIAMONDS 56%
Single Malt

**7¾ Martine: Water undoubtedly tames the alcohol but alters the freshness and enticing natural sharpness of that bold whisky.**
WHISKY *Editor's choice*
**Nose:** Tangy (alcohol tickles nostrils). Lots of cereal notes. Cooked grains. Oatcakes. Cowshed. Creosote with fresh mint aromas. Lemon juice.
**Palate:** A very short sweet start, bursting out into a spicy circus of aromas. Quite sharp but challenging. Less creosote on the palate.
**Finish:** Concentrated, citrussy, minty and spicy.

**9 Dave: This has classic Japanese finesse (and excellent viscimetry). Great whisky is about balance and this has it...in diamonds, not spades.**
**Nose:** Immediate complexity. Cheddar cheese, cream, but also a firm nutty quality. A touch of burlap, smoke and then with water it shifts into sandalwood, citrus, pineapple, pine.
**Palate:** Dances in the mouth, moving from spice into flowers then to smoke, which builds subtly.
**Finish:** Long, mixing spice and sweetness.

## ICHIRO'S MALT 1988 SINGLE MALT VINTAGE 56%
Single Malt

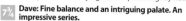

**7¾ Martine: A pungent character. Warm phenolic and uncompromising but hiding a pleasant cereal sweetness. The alcoholic strength is somewhat burning though.**
WHISKY *Recommended*
**Nose:** Marine and phenolic. Seawashed pebbles. Creosote whiff. Sweet cereals. Crème caramel.
**Palate:** Definitely a mariner. Smoked fish and some oiliness. Tangy spicy feel. Black pepper.
**Finish:** Dry, smoky. Slightly sooty. Hint of tar.

**8½ Dave: Another which typifies the Japanese style of light pure whiskies with amazing precision.**
**Nose:** Packed full of intense, bright aromas: vanilla pod, lemon zest, white chocolate. There's a strange exoticism like Tibetan salt chocolate and a whiff of black olive tapenade. The light smoke adds another touch to the pattern of aromas.
**Palate:** Good breadth of character and intensity with a light smokiness. Water needs to be added.
**Finish:** Tarry rope. Great length.

## ICHIRO'S MALT 1990 QUEEN OF HEARTS 54%
Single Malt

**7¾ Martine: A well balanced and refreshing dram. Try it with raw fish and ginger in vinegar.**
**Nose:** Fresh and assertive. Aniseed. Digestive biscuits. Lime juice. White chocolate. Rhubarb crumble. Opening up on spices.
**Palate:** Luscious silky feel. Sweet and spicy. Cooked bananas. Lime syllabub. Complex spicy display. Oak underlines the flavours.
**Finish:** Crisp and clean. Drying out on spices. Slightly nutty.

**7¾ Dave: Fine balance and an intriguing palate. An impressive series.**
**Nose:** Round, tangy and slightly fat. Plaster, raspberry, tablet and vanilla. A touch of smoke mingling with estery perfume.
**Palate:** Lighter than the nose suggests and slightly drier. An interesting battle between deep sweetness in the mid-palate and fizzing spiciness. Good balance.
**Finish:** Zesty soft fruits. Pecan.

## ICHIRO'S MALT 20 YEARS OLD 46%
Single Malt

**7¾ Martine: The nose is more enticing than the palate. Water reduces the gap, bringing in a velvety texture.**
**Nose:** Clean, rich, buttery, sweet. Butter and ground almond cakes. Hazelnut milk chocolate. Oak elegantly intertwines with rich date aromas.
**Palate:** Sweet and spicy. Oak speaks up, covering fruit with spices. Nutmeg, ginger.
**Finish:** Dry, assertive. Dark chocolate. Bitter root. Toasted nuts.

**7½ Dave: Well made, but lacks the complexity and range of the best.**
**Nose:** Full and fudge-like cut with green orange peel, herbs and marzipan. Well-balanced.
**Palate:** A fresh clean nutty start with notes of patisserie, powdered almond before a hint of incense/Turkish delight. Concentrated.
**Finish:** Spicy and dry.

## ICHIRO'S MALT ACE OF HEARTS, 22 YEARS OLD 56%
Single Malt

**7¾ Martine: Water cuts the edges a little but does not mellow the sourness.**
WHISKY *Recommended*
**Nose:** Tangy, malty and fruity. Raw bread dough with a hint of yeast. Sour apples. Cider cellar. A dash of water releases earthy notes.
**Palate:** Oak speaks up. A bitter/sour note of fermenting apple with a touch of must.
**Finish:** Oaky and spicy (white pepper).

**8¾ Dave: Fascinating. Hanyu does it again!**
**Nose:** Full, sweet and concentrated. Semi-dried summer fruits, banana, dried coconut, sandalwood. Exotic and complex.
**Palate:** Smoky and rich yet still lifted. Imagine barbecueing fresh pineapple. Good grip and some acidity. Wet chamois leather clinging to the tongue, while above is almond and unripe melon.
**Finish:** Long and elegant.

## ICHIRO'S MALT KING OF SPADES, 21 YEARS OLD 57%
Single Malt

**8¾ Martine: A liquid dessert. Reminds me of a rich Balvenie. Superb dram.**
WHISKY *Editor's choice*

**Nose:** Sweet and enticing. Crème caramel, orange cake, short-bread. Barley sugar. Touch of water chestnut.
**Palate:** Rich, sweet and mellow. Mouth coating. Alcohol is perfectly tamed. Very satisfying. Cooked fruit with soft spices.
**Finish:** Intense, warm and lingering.

**8 Dave: Best neat. Has that classic 'open' character that typifies Japanese whiskies.**
**Nose:** Gentle. Bread pudding, stewed apple, toasted rice. Slightly oily with some dried fenugreek, mace, apple skin. Has finesse.
**Palate:** Delicate smoky start. Cognac like: dried fruit, grilled nut alongside a haunting dried rose petal perfume.
**Finish:** Ripe, sesame, waxy.

### ICHIRO'S MALT THREE OF DIAMONDS 56%
Single Malt

**7½ Martine: Lacks balance. Alcohol is quite fierce. Water tames it down but needs to be strictly dosed as it enhances bitterness. Some character but quite sharp.**
**Nose:** Citrussy and buttery. Orange curd. Earthy and musty. Moss, fern. Hint of rose.
**Palate:** Sweet at first, then gets close to medlars. Spices wipe out this unpleasant note.
**Finish:** Dry and spicy. Rather tangy.

**8¼ Dave: Perfume and smoke? It's a Japanese Ardmore.**
**Nose:** High-toned and estery but with a deep caramel toffee from the oak. Super-ripe fruits and a smoky edge.
**Palate:** Praline, runny toffee, sultana. Somewhat rum like: allspice, ginger, brazil nut, cool mint, rice crackers. Smoke hangs above like a veil.
**Finish:** Clean and gentle. Medium.

### ICHIRO'S MALT TWO OF CLUBS 57%
Single Malt

**7½ Martine: The nose is more appealing than the palate. Water tames it.**
**Nose:** Estery. Exotic. Ripe bananas, coconut milk. Another raw bread dough profile with a strong yeasty note.
**Palate:** Quite assertive. The alcohol bite gives a fizzy feel on the tongue. Some fruit then a cardboardy note. A phenolic hint in the back.
**Finish:** Dry, tangy with a nutty aftertaste.

**8½ Dave: An amazing array of flavours and aromas from one so young.**
**Nose:** Succulent and vibrant. Mint sauce, camphor, dessicated coconut and cocoa powder. In time, quince. Powerful.
**Palate:** Pure, sweet and tongue coating. Sour cherry, liquorice and candlewax. The note is a little like incense cut with aged tea.
**Finish:** Ash and then ginger.

### KARUIZAWA 12 YEARS OLD 40%
Single Malt

**7¾ Michael: I found myself writing some of the same descriptors as I did 15 or 20 years ago. That says something for the consistency of this product.**
**Nose:** Sherry. Peaches. Raisins. Lemon skins. Lemon pith.
**Palate:** Firm. Emphatic malty sweetness, then leafy dryness. Earthy. A hint of peat. Also some oak.
**Finish:** Crisp to the point of being sudden.

**6 Dave: Disappointing. Seems to have the elements of a good whisky but nothing has knitted.**
**Nose:** Malty, leathery with some soft fruit and a slightly feinty note. Water brings out smoky notes oak, vanilla.
**Palate:** Some smokiness here as well though a fairly dry mid-palate. Water thins it very disappointingly.
**Finish:** A little feinty.

### KARUIZAWA 12 YEARS OLD 40%
Single Malt

**8 Martine: Reveals more balance on the palate than expected. Certainly on the wood side but in a rich and complex way.**
**Nose:** Woody. Rich oak. Burnt wood. But also a touch of wet damp cellar with some notes on the walls.
**Palate:** Thick, syrupy. Smooth and sweet. Chestnut purée. Wood is more integrated than expected. Coffee toffee.
**Finish:** Long, peppery.

**7 Dave: Can't quite get over that odd nose.**
**Nose:** Very odd: turnip skin, bread crust, burning wood. With water, Indian spices and blonde tobacco notes.

**Palate:** Liquorous. Marsala-like burnt edge. A little tannic and tight in the mouth. Water loosens things up bringing out orange and chocolate.
**Finish:** Short, slightly bitter.

### KARUIZAWA 15 YEARS OLD 40%
Single Malt

**7¼ Martine: I would have enjoyed the whisky more if I had stuck to nosing.**
**Nose:** Grassy and fruity. Butterscotch. Shortbread. Beeswax. Water chestnut. Quire rich. Sour apple.
**Palate:** Sweet and syrupy but slightly prickly. As if spirit and sugar were dislocated.
**Finish:** Quire short and evolving on bitter notes. As if you were chewing some grass stalk.

**8 Dave: Has maturity and masses of charm.**
**Nose:** Firm but light. Crisp, dry grass, overripe pear, baked peach, honey, cereal.
**Palate:** That grassiness again, chewy soft fruits. Good presence. Balanced oak. Milky coffee. Hint of smoke/bung cloth. Soft feel then dry oak.
**Finish:** Strawberry.

### KARUIZAWA 17 YEARS OLD 40%
Single Malt

**7¾ Michael: Pleasant as a 'dessert whisky', but lacks complexity.**
**Nose:** Earthy. Riesling. Linseed oil.
**Palate:** Sweetish. Chocolatey. Sliced toasted almonds.
**Finish:** Warming. Soothing.

**8 Dave: Well-made and best neat, when that rich spirit comes through.**
**Nose:** Weighty with almost carbonised notes (roasted nut/burnt almond), cooking chocolate, leather, fruit cake, spice and some smoke (turf/moss).
**Palate:** Soft, ripe and fruity with that burnt edge. Malaga. Soft, rounded and slightly dry. Good balance.
**Finish:** Dry with a nodule of sweetness. Good length and power.

### KARUIZAWA 17 YEARS OLD 40%
Single Malt

**7¼ Martine: A marine character but more whispering than speaking up.**
**Nose:** Discrete. Rather bland. A medicinal touch (tar cream). Wood varnish.
**Palate:** Sweet. Peaty, medicinal. Hint of seaweed and iodine. But not as pungent as an Islay malt. A cardboardy note.
**Finish:** Dry; slightly hot. Spicy.

**6½ Dave: Just plain odd.**
**Nose:** The first whisky I've ever come across which smells like hickory-smoked dry roast peanuts. Pimenton. Dense and oily, but that hickory note is all pervading.
**Palate:** And it's there on the palate as well alongside a slightly artificial rose note. Splits on the palate, between the slick and the dry.
**Finish:** The slick wins on the finish.

### KARUIZAWA 1974 65%
Single Malt

**6¾ Martine: Can't see the point in offering such an unbalanced oaky profile. It is whisky we want to enjoy, not a wood infusion.**
**Nose:** Spirity. Waves of liquorice. Freshly squeezed oak juice? Hint of candied chestnut purée.
**Palate:** Bittersweet. Very oaky. Spicy. A touch of coffee toffee. But alcohol harshness makes the tastebuds uncomfortable. And water releases more bitterness.
**Finish:** Dry, bitter, oaky.

**7 Dave: Just old and by now lacking balance.**
**Nose:** Very savoury with high intensity thanks to the alcohol. Old chocolate, tomato ketchup, wood varnish, raisin and prune, roast chestnut.
**Palate:** Decent mid-palate sweetness. Liquorice water, dandelion and burdock, pot pourri.
**Finish:** Fades quickly.

*WHISKY Magazine Recommended*

### KARUIZAWA 1988 59.3%
Single Malt

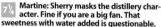

7¼ **Martine: Sherry masks the distillery character. Fine if you are a big fan. That sweetness with water added is questionable.**
**Nose:** Spirity at first then vanilla smooths the rough edges. Sherry shows up. Plum jam, fig molasses. Oak makes its way assertively.
**Palate:** Definitely sherried. Chocolate, dried fruit. Develops on dry bitterness. Water takes astringence away, then too much sugar.
**Finish:** Dry, oaky, astringent.

8¾ **Dave: Excellent backbone and manages to integrate fully the bitter edge that creeps into many of these.**
**Nose:** Exotic: flat cola, wet bamboo, hedgerow, sour black cherry mixed with coconut, chocolate and green fig. With water, eucalyptus.
**Palate:** Shows real maturity, complexity and balance. Tongue-coating with layers of flavour and good weight. The oiliest so far.
**Finish:** Long, with a refreshing tart grip.

### KARUIZAWA 1988 CASK 3397 59.8%
Single Malt

7¾ **Martine: The nose does not say it all. The old man is still sprightly.**
**Nose:** Rich, complex oaky notes which slowly unwind to release stewed fruit. Cooked apricots. Apple compote. Wood is well integrated. When aerated, some luscious coffee notes.
**Palate:** Frisky, a bit sharp. Gets sherbety. Then a malty sweetness tries to calm the game but spices block the way.
**Finish:** Dry, biting, spicy.

7¾ **Dave: Does that paradoxical, very Japanese thing, of having real lift while going deep at the same time.**
**Nose:** Deep and mature yet with sufficient freshness to give it lift. Humus and fresh fennel. Quite restrained yet funky.
**Palate:** Good feel. Creamy, sweet and quite hot with a deep, solid centre. Light tannins. Powerful with real depth. Blossoms on the back palate.
**Finish:** Rich and fruity.

### KARUIZAWA 1992 CASK 5978 62.8%
Single Malt

7½ **Martine: A sharp character which needs a good dash of water. Quite refreshing.**
**Nose:** Tangy, a little spirity. Floral. Geranium. Quite perfumy. In the back, a note of wet leaves and moss.
**Palate:** Sweet at start, with a cotton wool feel. Then the alcohol makes a hefty come back but in a pleasant way. Lots of oak.
**Finish:** Warm, spicy, oaky. A grassy aftertaste.

6¾ **Dave: One dimensional and rather simple.**
**Nose:** Plain and slightly harsh. Linoleum with a vegetal note. Cinnamon and mashed banana.
**Palate:** Better on the palate. Smooth yet tingling attack and a Madeira-like nuttiness. Very direct.
**Finish:** Dry. Slightly aggressive.

### KARUIZAWA 1993 60.1%
Single Malt

7½ **Martine: A herbal tea for those who like it hot and pungent. Lovely nose. Good balance. Definitely needs water to tame the strength.**
**Nose:** Grassy, herbal. Dry hay, angelica, lemon grass. Fresh lemon. Very zesty. Young and vibrant.
**Palate:** Unexpected sweetness at start. A zesty tanginess with a pleasant cereal note. Alcohol strength is not easy to cope with.
**Finish:** Long, warm, slightly burning. Oaty dryness.

7 **Dave: Has that slightly edgy quality of a spirit that hasn't quite resolved itself with the oak.**
**Nose:** Light and quite high-toned, even slightly yeasty with a hint of grass, melon. Fairly plain. Stewed fruit, quince jam, rhum vieux.
**Palate:** Dusty. Powdered lime, yeast and decent intensity. Fresh and fruity and young with good mid-palate sweetness.
**Finish:** Slightly sour and not wholly balanced.

### KARUIZAWA MASTER'S BLEND, 10 YEARS OLD 40%
Blended

7¾ **Martine: For once, a whisky that delivers more on the palate than the nose. Could make a pleasant summer dram.**
**Nose:** Very caramelly. Quite bland. Slightly grainy. Rather shy.
**Palate:** Sweet, smooth. Quite refreshing. Pleasant mintiness. Citrus fruit.
**Finish:** Keeps up with fresh minty and citrus notes.

7½ **Dave: A great session whisky.**
**Nose:** Clean and soft. Pear, tinned peach (syrup) glace/crystallised fruits. In time, sugared almond, damp raffia, bran, oak. Attractive and sweet.
**Palate:** Soft and gentle with summer fruit, vanilla. Light charred oak frame. Broadens to finish.
**Finish:** Strawberry.

### KIRIN 18 YEARS OLD 43%
Single Malt

7½ **Arthur: Pretty, light in body, with the smoky/savoury element providing interest.**
**Nose:** Peaches and cherries, scented candlewax. Dusty and floral too, like dried roses.
**Palate:** Apricots, then burnt wood and a savoury character.
**Finish:** Dried mushrooms.

8¼ **Owen: Japanese whisky is frequently surprising and rarely disappointing. This whacky, outside the box, example is no exception.**
**Nose:** Strangely flat and waxy on top; yet underneath, some sharp orange-citrus notes. After time, some biscuit notes with chocolate.
**Palate:** Sweet and waxy. Orange squash. Ginger ale. Sweetshop flavours.
**Finish:** Some cedary cigar box notes. Ginger and cinnamon. Very late citrus character emerges.

### KIRIN 18 YEARS OLD, FUJI-SANROKU 43%
Single Malt

7¾ **Martine: For those who like cider rather sour than sweet! interesting combination for a whisky cooler. A refreshing aperitif.**
**Nose:** Intense. Sweet and sour. Fruity. Apple and pear cider. Vanilla toffee gradually emerging. Touch of chicken broth.
**Palate:** Sweet start then oak comes in the front, in an elegant manner though. Good sweet and sour balance. Keeps the fruit up. A distant peaty echo.
**Finish:** Well balanced, rather short but clean.

8¼ **Dave: Once again here's a great example of that Japanese lightness of character.**
**Nose:** Lightly oiled soft leather, old peach, pine sap/yew tree. With water an incredible citrus oil lift: pine, elderflower, honeycomb, lime blossom. Estery and perfumed.
**Palate:** This floats across the palate having both delicacy and complexity. Honeycomb (sweetness and waxiness). Good feel.
**Finish:** Clean medium length good sweetness.

### MERCIAN 1987 SINGLE CASK 58.7%
Single Malt

7¾ **Michael: More complex than the younger vintage.**
**Nose:** Cedary. Faint hint of peat.
**Palate:** Orange essence, then anise.
**Finish:** Toasted oak. Slightly sappy. Warming. Rather astringent.

7¼ **Dave: Good weight, wood is beginning to show.**
**Nose:** Mossy and nutty (pecan) with soft fruits and some smoke. Slightly hard with water: tea leaves, wholemeal toast, a spicy tobacco note. A clean, quite light spirit.
**Palate:** Spicy and sweetly concentrated: pecan pie, ripe fruits.
**Finish:** Hint of smoke.

### MERCIAN SHIP 40%
Blended

7 **Martine: A promising nose but a somewhat worn out palate.**
**Nose:** Resiny. Freshly cut oak. A forestry bouquet reluctantly leading way to fruit. Stewed plums. Vanilla and caramel shines through. Grilled sausage.
**Palate:** Very sweet if not too soft. Watery in the middle. Sugary and not much else.
**Finish:** Short, vanishing, colourless.

7¼ **Dave: Is this whisky? Part 2. Seems to be flavoured. Good for cocktails, but this is weird.**
**Nose:** Sugar icing. Starts with sweet biscuits, orange then it's all strawberry jam.
**Palate:** Light to medium-bodied. Intensely jammy, almost like strawberry/raspberry essence.
**Finish:** Sweet, quite long.

## MERCIAN SINGLE CASK , 1991 62.8%
Single Malt

**7½ Michael: Pleasant. Could be slightly rounder.**
**Nose:** Aromatic. Honeyish. Flowery, with a slightly sharp, herbal, dryness.
**Palate:** Orangey. Developing suggestions of toasted coconut and cedary notes.
**Finish:** Oily dryness. Warming.

**6¾ Dave: Concentrated and tense, a little immature.**
**Nose:** Slightly raw note: crisp and sappily green, lead pencils. There's also a tarry note that reminds me of Pontefract cakes.
**Palate:** Sweet and malty with raspberry, but overall pretty hard and young. The spirit seems concentrated, still sleeping.
**Finish:** Sweet.

## MIYAGIKYO 10 YEARS OLD 45%
Single Malt

**7¼ Martine: Nose is more attractive than the palate. Lacks elegance and cohesion.**
**Nose:** Floral. Peppery. Prickly. Cider apple. Becomes buttery with toffee notes. Distant echo of creosote.
**Palate:** Sweet and sour. Pear-drop, pineapple. Varnish. Tangy in the middle.
**Finish:** Dry and assertive. Concentrates on spices and oak.

**8½ Dave: Just beginning to pick up complexity. Try this distillery at 12 or 15! World class.**
**Nose:** Pure and light. Lifted, lightly floral. Lily, broom, fennel, fruit. Hint of nut (hazel/brazil). Pine. Sweetly refined with an extra level of complexity.
**Palate:** Medium-bodied and lively. Silky, soft fruits. Graceful and smooth with balanced oak.
**Finish:** Broad. Cedar. Winey.

## MIYAGIKYOU 1987, CASK NO. 60236 61%
Single Malt

**6½ Martine: How can whisky leave its signature behind that thick oak panelling? No chance.**
**Nose:** Flat and bland at start then oak leads the show. Liquorice, chocolate and walnuts.
**Palate:** Sweet and sugary. Oak infusion conducting bitter tanginess. Touch of black pepper.
**Finish:** Oaky, dry.

**7¾ Dave: The oak is slightly too dominant to elevate it into the next category.**
**Nose:** Mature. Cedar, tobacco, and light charred note (burning embers), turned earth then a herbal lift of fresh bay, dried sage and beeswax.
**Palate:** A palate spreader. Liquorous and rich with real intensity and a slightly acidic quality which is just balanced by that honeyed sweetness. Oak is quite firm and grippy.
**Finish:** Tight, slightly lean.

## MIYAGIKYOU 1987, CASK NO. 89714 61%
Single Malt

**7½ Martine: Another example of sherry domination. Where's the balance?**
**Nose:** Sherry, ground coffee. Morello cherries. Grapefruit juice. A distinctive sourness combined with dry oaky notes. Liquorice. Opening on sweet creamy custard. Hint of damp wall.
**Palate:** Sweet but oaky. Sherry is in control. Burnt caramel. Bitter tang.
**Finish:** Dry, oaky, dark chocolate, liquorice.

**7¾ Dave: Good, but again not quite the extra dimension that's needed.**
**Nose:** Ripe and sweet with dried fruits, nuts and candied peel shifting into marmalade, persimmon. Shows good balance with a sweet blackberry note cut with saddle soap.
**Palate:** Once again, really piercing concentration which goes into a mix of dry, crisp oak this time with cigar leaf, oak and sandalwood.
**Finish:** Red grape skin, redcurrant tartness.

## MIYAGIKYOU 1991, CASK NO. 117705 61%
Single Malt

**7½ Martine: Quite a nice refreshing dram when generously diluted.**
**Nose:** Grainy. Linseed oil. Pumpkin seeds. Peanut butter. Fresh garden mint. Almonds. With water, pear drops.

**Palate:** Sweet for the strength. The alcohol tickles tastebuds though. Nice syrupy feel with water. Releases floral and estery notes; banana, pear.
**Finish:** Oily, with a spicy fringe.

**7½ Dave: There's often a battle between sweet and savoury in Japanese whisky...this time the balance hasn't been achieved.**
**Nose:** Ash-like, though strangely sappy as well with a wheat-chaff like simplicity. There's a light perfume like linden blossom and with water a nectarine note and some After Eight mint.
**Palate:** Sweet and sour again. Highly fragrant almost confected and slightly unbalanced.
**Finish:** Tart, long, quite hot.

## MIYAGIKYOU SINGLE CASK SENDAI, 1990 60.6%
Single Malt

**7¾ Michael: The orangey colour suggests some sherry. Nikka's Sendai distillery has in this instance produced a nuttier, maltier style of whisky than Yoichi.**
**Nose:** Appetising citrus (tangerine?).
**Palate:** Malty, textured. Crunchie bars. Cinder toffee. Softening to marshmallow. Cream. Strawberries.
**Finish:** A sprinkling of lemon juice.

**7¾ Dave: An intriguing mix of sweet wood, crisp malt and toasted nuttiness.**
**Nose:** Intense, aromatic, rich yet dry: resin, oil, dried fruit, plum pudding, coffee. In time, mushroom, damp earth.
**Palate:** Sherried/walnut flavours, resinous. Chocolate. The wood hits half way through but there's just enough sweet weight to carry.
**Finish:** Rich.

## NIKKA 34 YEARS OLD 43%
Blended

**8 Michael: Big and complex. Slightly drying but avoids excessive woodiness.**
**Nose:** Rich. Powerful, Freshly cut oak.
**Palate:** Oaky. Sherryish (notice the full, reddish amber colour) Cakey. Marzipan.
**Finish:** Long. Rooty. Slightly peaty.

**8½ Jim: A whisky of antiquity that has survived many years. Quite excellent.**
**Nose:** Bourbony and rich; over-ripe cherries and wet tobacco.
**Palate:** Big and fruity and then a surge of oak.
**Finish:** Wonderfully spicy and mouth filling.

## NIKKA ALL MALT 1989 43%
Blended

**7½ Michael: An interesting idea, and it produces for Nikka a much sweeter style of whisky.**
**Nose:** Soft. Malty. Buttery. Hint of cedar
**Palate:** Sweet. Very creamy and toffeeish, but light on the tongue. Very clean.
**Finish:** Light. Cedary.

**8 Jim: The best example of an almost unique style of blended whisky.**
**Nose:** Delicate yet intensely malty.
**Palate:** Fresh and then sharply intense.
**Finish:** Late arrival of drier vanilla, oaky tones and Java coffee.

## NIKKA BLACK 8 YEARS OLD 40%
Single Malt

**8 Martine: Easy-going, well-balanced. To be enjoyed as a refreshment with water and ice.**
**Nose:** Fresh pear, then richer notes quickly develop. Custard, apricot, touch of hazelnut. Hint of pine. Delicate smokiness in the back. Caramel with water.
**Palate:** Sweet and flowing. Well balanced. Nutty. Drying on light oak.
**Finish:** Medium, firm but retains sweetness. Ginger.

**7½ Dave: A well balanced session drink.**
**Nose:** Clean and soft. Green grass, light vanilla, soft grain. With water, some red fruit. Fresh.
**Palate:** Barley sugar. Lightly chewy and soft with some toffee and caramel notes. Good structure.
**Finish:** Dry, quite short. Refreshing.

# Japanese Nikka - Yamazaki

## NIKKA SINGLE MALT YOICHI NON AGED 43%
Single Malt

**7½ Dave: Not Yoichi at its most full-blooded and a little gawky but worth a look.**
**Nose:** Smoky and quite dry with a hint of rubber suggesting youth. Underneath this is a subtle perfume: moist banana, cumin powder.
**Palate:** Oak and smoke but there's dried peel, crème brûlée, orange peel and tropical fruit in the centre. Youth showing still.
**Finish:** Light smoke.

**8¾ Martine: A superb combination of fruit and oak, so well integrated.**
**Nose:** Intense. Intricate bouquet of wood notes. Sandalwood, floor polish. Antique shop. Elegantly combined with floral aromas (rosehip, freesia). Sweeter notes break through. Toffee. Liquorice.
**Palate:** Smooth, round and delicate. Perfect balance between wood, fruit and spices.
**Finish:** Soothing on dried fruit and nuts.

## NIKKA SUPER 43%
Blended

**7½ Michael: Easily drinkable. Very pleasant. Refreshing. Not especially complex.**
**Nose:** Clean, dry, lemony. Firm.
**Palate:** Very clean. Fresh, Lemony. Quite sweet.
**Finish:** Dry, crisp.

**8½ Jim: A very, very fine blend that which makes no apology for the peaty complexity of Yoichi malt. Classy stuff.**
**Nose:** Excellent firm, grassy malt base. A hint of peat.
**Palate:** A starburst of rich, mouth watering and malt.
**Finish:** Soft, fabulously intrinsic peaty notes from the Yoichi school give brilliant length and depth.

## NIKKA TSURU 43%
Single Malt

**7¾ Michael:** Clean. Light. Fresh. Polished oak.
**Palate:** So smooth that it is almost slippery. Syrupy sweet. Tangerines. Perfume.
**Finish:** Creamy, oily, then firm. Long, warming.

**8½ Jim: Gentle and beautifully structured.**
**Nose:** Apples, cedar, crushed pine nuts.
**Palate:** As clean and fresh as the nose.
**Finish:** A continuation of soft malts and oak.

## NIKKA TSURU, 17 YEARS OLD 43%
Single Malt

**7¾ Dave: The finish pulls it down. Other than that, very approachable and highly drinkable.**
**Nose:** This is filled with the aromas of ripe apple, nutmeg, oak lactone and a soft sweet chocolate fragrance that brings to mind crème eggs.
**Palate:** A well integrated mix. Stewed rhubarb, apple and that creamy oak note. Water brings out a slightly bitter note on the finish.
**Finish:** Just a little too hard.

**8¼ Martine: A complex lad. Needs time to smooth and release its sweetness. But worth giving it attention.**
**Nose:** Fruity, juicy. Sour fruit. Fresh paint. Quite sharp but very pleasant. Vivid. Develops on deep oak and orange custard. Faint smoke.
**Palate:** Velvety. Oily. Mouth coating. Multilayered. Spicy. Ginger and white pepper.
**Finish:** Long, loads of liquorice. Nutty aftertaste.

## SENDAI 12 YEARS OLD 45%
Single Malt

**8 Michael: A totally different style from Yoichi malts. A very enjoyable, sweet, pick me up. After a round of golf?**
**Nose:** Faint tobacco. Autumn leaves. Hint of pine.
**Palate:** Sweet. Cereal grains.
**Finish:** Very sweet. Cookie-like.

**8¾ Jim: A greatly improved malt.**
**Nose:** Thin, austere and mildly feinty.
**Palate:** Vanilla is the main theme and there is a fresh, fruity, mouth-watering quality.
**Finish:** Surprisingly long and increasingly oily. A hint of smoke adds to the complexity.

## TAKETSURU 17 YEARS OLD 43%
Single Malt

**7¾ Martine: The creamy notes on the nose suggest more sweetness on the palate. Oak speaks up.**
**Nose:** Oaky. Beeswax. Cooked apples. Crème brûlée. Raw bread dough. Peat in the back.
**Palate:** Sweet at start but spices put taste buds on fire. Passion fruit. Oak gradually takes over.
**Finish:** Dry, dusty, spicy, slightly astringent.

**8¼ Dave: Images of a weatherbeaten oak. Mature, but sweet-hearted.**
**Nose:** Clean, with layered tropical fruit. Eucalyptus, red fruit, vanilla. Oak. Good weight and breadth.
**Palate:** Oily, fruity and juicy. Almost Irish. Firm with obvious oaken structure but sufficient sweetness (cocoa, liquorice, vanilla) to carry.
**Finish:** Lightly gripping.

## YAMAZAKI 10 YEARS OLD 40%
Single Malt

**8¼ Martine: A charming summery dram. The perfect "herbal tea" to savour while gazing at the moonlit sky.**
**Nose:** Summery, light and fragrant. Grassy. Freshly cut lawn, green oak. Lemon grass. Herbal tea. Lemon sherbet. Reminds me of a chartreuse.
**Palate:** Unctuous, sweet. A slight watery gap at midpalate. The palate is true to the nose. The same herbal notes are delivered. Wild chervil, dill.
**Finish:** Sweet, minty with a spicy dryness.

**7 Dave: More about potential. For me this is too young and needs time to come together.**
**Nose:** Edgy and young. Minty (toothpaste) flaming orange oils. A little stony.
**Palate:** Clean and floral with a soft apricot like richness in the centre. Good length. More to it than the nose suggests.
**Finish:** Quick, biscuity oak.

## YAMAZAKI 12 YEARS OLD 43%
Single Malt

**8 Michael: A pioneering malt in Japan, for which Suntory deserve great credit. In its early days, it was rounded and delicate, as though wary of offending anyone. Now it is more intense, confident and elegant.**
**Nose:** Flowery. Fresh herbs. Biscuity.
**Palate:** Lightly clean and sweet. Honeyed. Intense.
**Finish:** Burst of concentrated perfumy sweetness, balanced by cereal-grain notes and Japanese oak.

**7½ Dave: Well made. An honest citizen.**
**Nose:** Clean and crisp: dried herb, oak, nuts and slightly dusty malt.
**Palate:** A sweet start, some light smoky notes. Well-rounded with a dense, fruity mid-palate, though a little firm on the sides of the mouth.
**Finish:** Rich Tea biscuits, dried fruit and nut.

## YAMAZAKI 12 YEARS OLD 43%
Single Malt

**7¾ Michael: This was a pioneering malt in Japan, for which Suntory deserve great credit.**
**Nose:** Sweet, malty, flowery.
**Palate:** Crisp. Grassy. Almost herbal.
**Finish:** Long, perfumy. Parma violet sweets? Becoming drier. Slightly biscuity.

**7½ Jim: Impressive nose and excellent body is undone slightly by the untidy finish.**
**Nose:** Finely balanced; with assorted citrus notes.
**Palate:** Warming to the point of spicy. Lots of custardy vanilla and butterscotch.
**Finish:** Thinly textured. Disappointing.

## YAMAZAKI 12 YEARS OLD 43%
Single Malt

**7¼ Martine: The palate does not keep what the nose promises. Disappointing. Sweetness does not make up for flavour.**
**Nose:** Prickly at first but soon softening on fruity notes. Apples and pineapple in caramel. Creamy. Rhubarb flan. Blancmange.
**Palate:** Very sweet. A bit too soft. Then oak has its grip. But the appetising fruity basket of the nose is hidden in the oak cupboard!

**Finish:** Sweet with a bitter grip spicy aftertaste.

**7¼ Dave:** Yamazaki needs time and 12 years ain't enough.
**Nose:** Broad and quite sweet, reminiscent of roasting sweetcorn. Vanilla, spice, dried citrus peels, tomato leaf. On top, there's light freesia blossom. Cigar box.
**Palate:** Quite long and deepens in the middle into peach and a little sultana.
**Finish:** Ginger biscuits.

## YAMAZAKI 18 YEARS OLD 43%
Single Malt

**8 Michael:** Well-balanced. Full of flavour.
**Nose:** Cream. Toffee.
**Palate:** Spicy. Complex. Maple syrup. Fruity, cinnamon. Brown sugar, baclava pastry.
**Finish:** Balancing dryness. Very slight woodiness. Firm, gripping.

**8 Dave:** Strikes an excellent balance between those spicy high tones and a sweet but nutty palate. A little slick.
**Nose:** Slick and fruity (toffee apple), becoming buttery with water. Malt, nuts, sesame oil and some sherried notes. Plenty going on.
**Palate:** Rounded and soft with a burst of spiciness mid-palate. There's some smoke as well. Complex and soft with excellent balance.
**Finish:** Dry, a little short?

## YAMAZAKI 18 YEARS OLD 43%
Single Malt

**8 Michael:** Big flavours, and a lot happening, but could be rounder.
**Nose:** Quite assertive. Sherry, oily, nutty.
**Palate:** Nutty, sweet, chewy. Cinnamon. Toast.
**Finish:** Oily, perfumy. Cypress? Sweet leaves. A hint of peat. A touch of oak.

**7 Jim:** The nose is outstanding, but not a patch on Hibiki 21.
**Nose:** Sweet with a beeswaxy texture.
**Palate:** A slightly battered array of oaky notes limps alongside the strained malt.
**Finish:** Superficial smoky malt notes but out of sorts.

## YAMAZAKI 18 YEARS OLD 43%
Single Malt

**8 Martine:** Surprisingly, water tones the oaky flavours down, bringing out more malty sweetness. Quite a self-indulgent dram.
**Nose:** Malty with a floral note (meadow flowers). Toasted oatmeal. A touch of salty butter. On time displays richer aromas. Toffee, liquorice. Apple flan.
**Palate:** Sweet and smooth. Pear poached in syrup. Estery. Oak envelops fruit in a firm, dry and grippy veil, releasing spices.
**Finish:** Long, dry and spicy.

**8¼ Dave:** This is a real jump in quality and shows great finesse.
**Nose:** Rich and slightly sweet though with a balanced oakiness. Walk in the woods: apple and violet, an old log cabin in the summer heat.
**Palate:** Though lighter than the nose suggests this has class. Leafy, almost mossy. Pine woods, violet again and a dusty rooty quality but sufficient sweetness to add depth and complexity.
**Finish:** Good length. Pomegranate.

## YAMAZAKI 1979, JAPANESE OAK CASK, 119.2, SCOTCH MALT WHISKY SOCIETY 57.4%
Single Malt

**8¾ Michael:** A breakfast malt? Splendidly complex, with Japanese oak adding that extra touch of distinctiveness.
**Nose:** Incense, beeswax, cedar, roasted coffee, ripe fruits (kumquats cherries, plums).
**Palate:** Dense. Slippery. Toasty malt. Coffee, with figs and chicory.
**Finish:** Black treacle toffee. Perhaps even maple syrup.

**8¾ Michael:** A tremendous malt. World class.
**Nose:** Complex, head-filling aromas. Perfumed, intense. Walking in a damp pine forest (needles, sap, spruce) pear, spice, malt, toasted nuts, light oak, crystallised ginger, sandalwood, deck varnish.
**Palate:** Crisp, clean and malty. Mature with balanced oak. Some light smoke in the background. All the flavours on the nose.
**Finish:** Long and complex.

## YAMAZAKI 1980 JAPANESE WHITE OAK CASK 58%
Single Malt

**8 Michael:** The most herbal and spicy of these three bottlings, and the most distinctive.
**Nose:** Very aromatic. Floral, but flowers with a heavy scent, like a geranium. Or perhaps a tropical flower. Leafy. Herbal. Minty. Oily.
**Palate:** Fragrant, with lots of flavour development. Cedary notes, orange and maple syrup.
**Finish:** Sweet but also peppery.

**7½ Dave:** Aged in a Japanese-made, second-fill, US white oak cask, so no bourbon ageing involved. A worthwhile experiment typical of this enterprising distillery.
**Nose:** Medium-weight, quite oaky sawmills, cedar logs, varnish. A sweetness akin to maple syrup or candy floss and an orangey note.
**Palate:** Soft. Clean, fresh maltiness. Grips from mid-palate, building up charred notes. Clean, spicy.
**Finish:** Clean. Soft.

## YAMAZAKI 1980 VINTAGE MALT 56%
Single Malt

**8½ Dave:** Big but balanced. Shows complexity.
**Nose:** Sweet slightly peppery oak, rock candy, cocoa. Has age. Lightly oily with scented wood and plenty of sweet-hearted spirit to balance. Tickle of smoke.
**Palate:** Meaty, charred wood. Musky and intriguing. Deep sweet black fruits with a touch of liquorice bed it down in the middle of the tongue. Good length.
**Finish:** Mixing fragrance, light smoke and deep oak.

**8½ Martine:** A warm expression of sherry. Quite sensuous if not fiery. Rich and deep.
**Nose:** Warm, rich, deep. Prickly. Damson jam. Blackcurrant. Orange caramel. Freshly brewed coffee. Needs time to release all its richness.
**Palate:** Velvety, almost syrupy, smooth at start then a spicy burst (fresh grated ginger) which dries up the mouth.
**Finish:** Dry, spicy, oaky. A sweet malty touch in the back.

## YAMAZAKI 1980, WHITE OAK CASK, 119.1, SCOTCH MALT WHISKY SOCIETY 50.9%
Single Malt

**8½ Michael:** Elegant, and more flavoursome than Suntory bottlings I think.
**Nose:** Lightly malty. Creamy. Vanilla. Ripe bananas.
**Palate:** Light to medium. Very smooth. Creamy. Cinnamon. Brown sugar. Anis.
**Finish:** Some tart apple tannins, and a surge of gingery spiciness.

**7¾ Dave:** A little bigger, but slightly duller than 119. 2.
**Nose:** Medium to full-bodied. Perfumed. Floral, rose-like, mint, toffee apple, polished oak, walnut, raffia, nutty malt.
**Palate:** Ripe sweet and chewy. Toffee, cream with light touches of leather. Dried fruits. Has maturity.
**Finish:** Tingling oak.

## YAMAZAKI 1991 BOURBON CASK 60%
Single Malt

**7½ Michael:** An interesting interplay of flavours. Comes to rather an abrupt halt.
**Nose:** Perfumy. Hint of burnt orange.
**Palate:** Surprisingly rich, vanilla toffee flavours, drying to flowery, herbal (camomile?) notes.
**Finish:** Slightly short, drying. New wood.

**8¼ Dave:** Great balance between sweet fruit, nutty flavours and oak. Very good.
**Nose:** Initially not much, then sweet, perfumed, floral, malt; lemon, sesame oil. Water brings out vanillins, sweet oak, tobacco. Complex yet discreet.
**Palate:** Long, ripe with sweet fruitiness. Flows beautifully, mouth-coating nut oil, a hint of resinous oak, honey, nuts, spice. Charming and mouth-filling.
**Finish:** Dry but not woody.

### YAMAZAKI 1991 SHERRY CASK 61%
Single Malt

7¾ **Michael: Can the elegant Yamazaki whisky stand up to heavy sherry? Yes. A dexterously balanced malt.**
**Nose:** Very fruity, and nutty. Dark fruits, like figs.
**Palate:** Walnuts. Brandy butter. Big, sweet, malty background.
**Finish:** Cigar tobacco. Lingering warmth.

8 **Dave: An elegant, beautifully balanced whisky.**
**Nose:** Overt 'sherry' notes: dried fruit, nuts etc. Similar to a palo cortado. A lovely red fruit quality alongside butter, raisin and, in time, toffee apple/baked apple and a hint of smoke.
**Palate:** Good rich weight and a soft feel. Chewy. Great balance.
**Finish:** Rounded.

### YAMAZAKI 1991, 11 YEARS OLD, 119.5, SCOTCH MALT WHISKY SOCIETY 62.2%
Single Malt

8 **Michael: Saves all the action for the finish. Very appetising.**
**Nose:** More aromatic. Very fresh, delicate, fragrant, floweriness.
**Palate:** Lightly syrupy. Perfumy. Very delicate. Creamy honey.
**Finish:** Very big. Spicy and long.

8¼ **Dave: Has some elegance.**
**Nose:** Good structure. Dried flowers, dilute orange squash, violet, oak, hint of rubber.
**Palate:** Sweet and rich. Cooked fruits, marzipan/almond and sweet malt. Oak in balance.
**Finish:** Nutty and long.

### YAMAZAKI 1993 BOURBON CASK 58%
Single Malt

7½ **Michael: The Yamazaki I know well; but with a more obvious and robust hint of bourbon character.**
**Nose:** Vanilla. Fresh oak. Earthy. Pine cones on the forest floor. Ferny.
**Palate:** Toast. Bean curd. Walnut. Dry. Drying. Strong flavours.
**Finish:** Lean but limber. A muscular punch. Bourbon-like.

7½ **Dave: A good addition to the range, maybe just a little young.**
**Nose:** Peaty (sooty) yet fragrant, solid but pretty (it's young). As it opens there's vanilla, syrup/barley sugar and in the background some orange and a wood fire, the memory of bubbling sap.
**Palate:** A dry start, then opal fruit sweetness, then smoke and that attractive sappy quality.
**Finish:** Slightly hot. The youth shows.

### YAMAZAKI 25 YEARS OLD 43%
Single Malt

7 **Martine: A PX sherry first fill? Fine if you like oak infusion. Clings on your palate for ages. Too oaky to be OK.**
**Nose:** Assertive sherry. Rich chocolate. Walnut peel. Dates. Raisins. Prunes. Overcooked plum jam. Burnt applewood. Bittersweet apples.
**Palate:** Sweet at start then astringent wood raids tastebuds, sweeping out the dried fruit sweetness.
**Finish:** Dry, grippy, bitter. A touch of sweetness coming back.

6½ **Dave: Old and over the hill.**
**Nose:** Very deep in colour and aroma. Big, resinous and perfumed: fig jam, autumn bonfire, late-blooming roses, PX, musky. Leather.
**Palate:** Dull and over-wooded. High tannins and over-stewed tea. A tale of two halves. Inhale only.
**Finish:** Bitter bitter bitter. Mouth drying.

### YAMAZAKI 80TH ANNIVERSARY BOTTLING 43%
Single Malt

8¼ **Michael: A lovely, elegant, delicately malty Yamazaki.**
**Nose:** Like walking into an expensive sweet shop. The sweets are all in boxes, perhaps even gift-wrapped, but the aromas of fudge, chocolate, mint and Parma violets linger in the air.
**Palate:** Honeyed. Cinder toffee. Shortbread.
**Finish:** Balancing flowery dryness.

8¼ **Dave: Excellent balance and intriguing complexity.**
**Nose:** Round and creamy with underlying sweetness. Apricot, mango, cooked apple; runny honey, malt and a forested note: moss, sandalwood.
**Palate:** Gentle and lightly chewy: yellow wine gums, vanilla sugar. Balanced between dry oak and sweet spirit. Gets spicier towards the finish.
**Finish:** Nutty.

### YAMAZAKI BOURBON CASK, 1993 59%
Single Malt

7¾ **Michael: Lots happening, lively, enjoyable.**
**Nose:** Dryish, fresh oak. Ferns, forest flowers.
**Palate:** Firm, toffee, coconut.
**Finish:** Dry, spicy. Vanilla pod. Hint of char.

8 **Dave: A fascinating package with unlikely flavour combinations. Barmen will love this.**
**Nose:** Peaty (smoked fish) but with some perfume (lemon, pot pourri, dried heather) and softness (nut oil).
**Palate:** Rounded and sweet. Very sweet in fact: like cinnamon toast with demerara sugar, but there's smoke as well, and it's in balance.
**Finish:** Medicinal. Smoked fish again.

### YAMAZAKI OAK CASK , 1979 58%
Single Malt

8¼ **Michael: Scores points for its robust distinctiveness.**
**Nose:** Very aromatic. Cypress. Beeswax.
**Palate:** Leafy, bittersweet, kumquats. Very distinctive.
**Finish:** Fruity, zesty.

7¼ **Dave: The wood is a bit too much, but good base spirit.**
**Nose:** Resinous, bay leaf, perfumed and slightly nutty.
**Palate:** Clean and quite sweet mixing a good, fairly weighty spirit with a mixed bag of nuts and spices. All pretty dry.
**Finish:** Quite lifted.

### YAMAZAKI SHERRY CASK, 1984 63%
Single Malt

7¾ **Michael: A huge whisky but overwhelmingly fruity and alcoholic.**
**Nose:** Sandalwood. Cedar. Oak tannins. Some phenols. Cough sweets. Morello cherries. Passion fruit.
**Palate:** Sour cherry pie. Blackcurrants. Coconut.
**Finish:** Huge. Peppery.

7 **Dave: Way too much sherry for me. It's too strong without water but splits when you add some.**
**Nose:** Dense, almost burnt. Rum truffle, chocolate, prune.
**Palate:** Thick. Robust, smoky, black treacle toffee. The wood and the sherry dominating.
**Finish:** Bitter chocolate.

### YAMAZAKI SHERRY WOOD, 1982 45%
Single Malt

8 **Michael: Any whisky-lover would be glad of the chance to taste this, even if it is on the woody side.**
**Nose:** Oak, cedar, spearmint.
**Palate:** Cypress. Sweet leaves. Fruity, winey, oaky.
**Finish:** Hint of peat. Powerful. Slightly woody.

7½ **Dave: Well made, but there's just too much sherry character which diminishes any complexity. A shame for the spirit which seems very good.**
**Nose:** Fat and very sherried: walnut, treacle toffee, sticky toffee pudding, raisin and a strangely vegetal note.
**Palate:** Full-on sherry. The wood seems to have taken charge, giving it a slight astringency.
**Finish:** Long. Walnut bread. Dry.

### YAMAZAKI, 10 YEARS OLD, 119.3, SCOTCH MALT WHISKY SOCIETY 56.2%
Single Malt

8¼ **Michael: A surprising amount of peat in this usually very delicate malt.**
**Nose:** Soft. Very flowery. Nasturtiums? Garden bonfires.
**Palate:** Light to medium. Smooth. Flowery but substantial. Orange blossom honey.
**Finish:** Spicy, long, dry peaty.

9 **Dave: If you're not a member, sign up now!**
**Nose:** Fragrant, smoke: smoked meats, medicinal, but also flowers and citrus. Great complexity.
**Palate:** Layers of complex, balanced, flavours. Wonderful weight: thrift, flowers, smoked meat, spice. Precise and balanced.
**Finish:** Long and slightly dry from the smoke but complex.

### YOICHI 10 YEARS OLD 43%
Single Malt

9 **Michael: This is a wonderful whisky at 10 Years Old. I love the almost shocking hit of heavy peating.**
**Nose:** Pronounced, astonishingly fresh, dry, peat.
**Palate:** Mint creams, then orangey.
**Finish:** After the creaminess, the peat surges back. Clean, sweetish, soft smokiness.

8¼ **Jim: In my books, whisky from one of the worlds top half dozen distilleries. One of my day-to-day drams.**
**Nose:** Soft, sensuous, peaty tones.
**Palate:** Immediately sweet and oily, with a chewiness.
**Finish:** Bittersweet balance borders on perfection!

### YOICHI 10 YEARS OLD, SINGLE CASK 59.9%
Single Malt

8¾ **Michael: A terrific whisky, beautifully rounded, with lots of everything.**
**Nose:** Smoky, phenolic, but restrained.
**Palate:** Oily, creamy, juicy, sherryish, raisiny, nutty, almondy, spicy.
**Finish:** Big. Sappy, oaky.

9¼ **Jim: Huge and uncompromising, this is true classic among the world's single malts.**
**Nose:** Well restrained despite enormity.
**Palate:** Massive peat surge countered by an oaky dryness. But soon the peat returns.
**Finish:** Remains oily to the death.

### YOICHI 12 YEARS OLD, PEATY AND SALTY 55%
Single Malt

8 **Martine: An interesting combination of fruit and peat. They don't mingle, they keep playing hide and seek. More complexity than it appears. Water makes it caressing.**
**Nose:** Phenolic and fruity. Demerara sugar, hint of molasses. Kippers on toasted bread. Ozonic. Malty sweetness.
**Palate:** Thick, syrupy, sweet and oily. Tar sweets, liquorice. Opening up on spices. Malty crunchiness.
**Finish:** Dry, fruity, spicy.

8¼ **Dave: While the oak has grip the whole package has great balance. Excellent.**
**Nose:** Initially sweet with plenty of American oak (vanilla, cream) then comes tinned apricot, something akin to a buttered scone.
**Palate:** Very smoky, much more than the nose suggests. An explosive peaty attack which is overlaid with intriguing floral notes: tar and blossom. Oily, yet sweet, rich but fragrant.
**Finish:** Iodine. Black grapes.

### YOICHI 12 YEARS OLD, WOODY AND VANILLIC 55%
Single Malt

7¼ **Martine: Soft and smooth whisky which seems tired. Not particularly exciting.**
**Nose:** Restrained. Fruity. Apple and pear pie. Cider cellar. Vanilla slowly emerges, bringing out sweeter notes. Touch of floor polish.
**Palate:** Sweet and surprisingly watery at midpalate. Oak and fruit are well integrated though. Summer fruit. Vanilla biscuits. Dusty.
**Finish:** Dry, spicy, dusty.

9 **Dave: Flawless, sweet, dry, deep, light, smoke, flowers, cream, toasty oak. Elegant.**
**Nose:** Smoke again, this time with briny notes and plain oak (almond, pine). There is also real weight behind this. Subtly perfumed mixing heavy flowers with soft/semi dried fruits and hints of cocoa.
**Palate:** An excellent spread of flavours: cooked apple, fresh apricot, toasted nuts, madeleines, tickle of smoke and a waxy depth.
**Finish:** Smoked vanilla pod.

### YOICHI 15 YEARS OLD 45%
Single Malt

8½ **Michael: Creamier than the 10 Years Old, but that softens the peatiness. Between these two, I preferred the peatier ten.**
**Nose:** Polished oak, then smoky.
**Palate:** Lots of malt. Chewy, creamy, oily.
**Finish:** More crisply peaty.

9¼ **Jim: Sheer brilliance. An absolute must for anyone who regards himself a whisky connoisseur.**
**Nose:** Lychees and sweet white grape.
**Palate:** Immediately sweet with a slow implosion of peat that seems to arise from nowhere.
**Finish:** Long, lingering, massive malt frame.

### YOICHI 1985, CASK NO. 250216 58%
Single Malt

7¾ **Martine: A sharp character, full of life. Needs water to tame the alcohol. For an outdoor invigorating crisp morning walk.**
**Nose:** Sweet maltiness tangled up in oak. Cedary, creamy. Almond toffee, touch of sour apple. A distant smoky hint. With water, more fruitiness.
**Palate:** Vibrant prickling, with a big burst of smoke and spices. Apricot and almond flan. Hot paprika.
**Finish:** Warm, dry and spicy. Oak shows up.

7¾ **Dave: Slightly diminished by quality of its colleagues.**
**Nose:** Reed bed/wicker chair. Dry and crisp, slightly nutty with plenty of toasty pine-like oakiness. Water brings out smoke and some fragrance.
**Palate:** A momentary pause and then a huge blast of smoke, this time bonfire-like; drying crab shell, lightly perfumed. Another which starts hard (think of Port Ellen). Intense and quite dry.
**Finish:** Sweet. Medium length.

### YOICHI 1991, CASK NO 129504 64%
Single Malt

8¼ **Martine: Another outdoor drink combining estery elegancy and phenolic pungency. High strength must be monitored with water.**
**Nose:** Floral. Estery. Exotic fruit. Mango, pineapple. Echo of vetiver. Enticing bouquet.
**Palate:** Appetising, with a light sweetness which brings out briny phenolic puffs and delicate fruit. Quite a good control of alcohol given the strength. Spicy bite. Touch of cinnamon and ginger.
**Finish:** Long spicy feel. Smoky aftertaste.

8½ **Dave: A real head opener which is slightly of the wall, but wonderfully likeable.**
**Nose:** That exotic caraway, vetiver and eucalypt aroma with a touch of incense and a little acetone. There's also autumn fruits and a light meatiness.
**Palate:** Highly fragrant and intense. Sandalwood, citrus oils, preserved lemon, fragrant herbs, light smoke. Powerfully aromatic, balanced and with real class.
**Finish:** Maraschino, herbs and smoke.

### YOICHI SINGLE CASK, 1986 61.3%
Single Malt

7¾ **Michael: The typical fruitiness of the Yoichi whiskies, but less peat than I remember.**
**Nose:** Lemony. Fragrant.
**Palate:** Tongue-coating. Spicy. Intense. Victoria sponge. Marmalade. Oranges and lemons.
**Finish:** Big, zesty. Long.

7¾ **Dave: The driest and leanest of this flight, but has some complexity.**
**Nose:** Dry. Turf/turned earth, smoke, green sticks. With water, apple becomes the dominant aroma, with lemon, crisp (nutty) malt, tea and oak.
**Palate:** Quite intense to start, but opens well. Apple and nut, dried fruit, spice, ginger biscuits, pepper and dry wood. Light and dry.
**Finish:** Good length but maybe a little woody.

### YOICHI SINGLE CASK, 1989 60.8%
Single Malt

7½ **Michael: Again, very fruity, but lacking in other flavours.**
**Nose:** Very aromatic. Spicy. Vanilla-like.
**Palate:** Cookie-like. Dusty. Sherbety. Orange oil. Very lively indeed.
**Finish:** Woody, drying.

7½ **Dave: Well-made and gentle, but straight down the middle rather than mouth-filling.**
**Nose:** Peaty: smoked meat, a just-dead bonfire, dry leaf with light oil/resin. Fragrant. With water a hint of sulphur, bay, and a nutty maltiness.
**Palate:** Bone dry, smoky: burning timbers. Light butteriness/sweet macadamia nuttiness.
**Finish:** Bone dry, smoky.

# Japanese Yoichi

## YOICHI SINGLE CASK, 1990 61.5%
Single Malt

**8** **Michael: A big whisky, with some of the smokiness I remember.**
**Nose:** Treacly. Icing sugar. American cream soda.
**Palate:** Good malt background. Vanilla. Liquorice. Slight coal/tar smokiness.
**Finish:** Soothing rather than aggressive.

**7½** **Dave: It just might benefit from a little more time in the cask.**
**Nose:** Rich, malty, sweet: nutty toffee, caramelised apple, vanilla, butterscotch. With water, light spice and smoke, balsa wood and a sappy youthfulness.
**Palate:** A sweet, nutty start, then dries. Good weight with slightly hard spirit. Decent balance.
**Finish:** Dry, fresh.

## YOICHI, 116.1, SCOTCH MALT WHISKY SOCIETY 56.6%
Single Malt

**8½** **Michael: A whole sequence of flavours emerges in this vintage. These are flavours** I have found before in Nikka whiskies, but they have not been especially evident elsewhere in this flight.
**Nose:** Smoky. Peaty. Leafy. Minty. Menthol.
**Palate:** Good malt background. Piney. Intense. Complex.
**Finish:** Dry, resiny.

**7¾** **Dave: A sweet cask and a firm spirit more or less in harmony.**
**Nose:** Good rich, toffeed maltiness. Water brings out American oak and lemon, mink oil/dubbin, dry grass and cold tea. Becomes crisp and nutty.
**Palate:** Rounded, medium-sweet start. Crisper and nuttier later with smoke and light toasted oakiness on the back palate. Nice weight.
**Finish:** Dries suddenly leaving a little bitterness.

## YOICHI, 116.4, SCOTCH MALT WHISKY SOCIETY 64.9%
Single Malt

**8¼** **Michael: Lots happening. Nice interplay of elements.**
**Nose:** Hints of bitter chocolate.
**Palate:** Clean, syrupy. Brown sugar. Butter. Dark chocolate. Mint. Kendal mint cake.
**Finish:** Late hint of peat.

**8** **Dave: A lot to it. Everything has knitted together well.**
**Nose:** Rich and rounded: toffee (Werthers Original) orange, light spice/leaf. Pretty rich, good balance.
**Palate:** Thick in the mouth. A chewy weight, any woodiness is balanced by buttered nuts, citrus and a slightly earthy smokiness. A lush package.
**Finish:** Dry and nutty with good balance.

**Above:** The magnificent stillroom at Yamazaki
**Main:** The picturesque Yoichi distillery with a covering of snow

# Rest of World

There is plenty of whisky on offer from the rest of the world, and looking at our tasters' reactions some pretty fine stuff too. The innovative newcomers from Finland to Australia are really making waves in the whisky world.

Making the most of a rising tide of drinkers searching for something different is the Swedish company Mackmyra. Bottles of Preludium have known to sell out in a matter of hours when they arrive on the shelves.

Across the rest of Europe micro-distillers are showing too that they can make some very pleasing whiskies.

In France, particularly in Brittany, small-scale distillers have been up and running for a while. Amorik, from the Warenghem distillery is probably the best-known, together with Eddu from La Distillerie des Menhirs, which is produced using buckwheat giving a distinct flavour, nose and aroma.

Various distilleries have sprung up round Germany, Austria, Switzerland, Turkey, Czech Republic, Spain, Pakistan, Taiwan and Russia all taking their cues from different inspirations.

The New World is also reaching out to the Old World with its whiskies. Pioneering the rise of Australian whisky was Lark's distillery in Tasmania, which has a cool climate closer to Scotland, and produces a complex and slightly smoky spirit.

Now Sullivan's Cove, Tasmania, and Bakery Hill, Melbourne, are also enjoying success following Lark's.

India may be one of the key markets most whisky companies are looking to crack, but in terms of a domestic distilling industry using only cereal crops only a few producers have emerged. One of the better known outside of India is Amrut.

Although Scotland is famed for its whisky making the English and Welsh are fast catching on.

Penderyn in Wales is the most established and is already producing some great whisky using wash from a local beer brewer. The company also matures its spirit in predominately bourbon casks, before finishing the whisky off in Maderia wood.

Circles show country location, not distillery

**Opposite:** Bottles running off the Penderyn lines
**This page top to bottom:** The stills at Mackmyra; Barrels of Penderyn maturing

In England, the St George's Distillery has been up and running since 2006. It has been laying down spirit since 2007. Although it is too early to tell how it will turn out, the new make is certainly impressive.

All in all the rest of the world is waking up to whisky making, and although some of the enterprises are still in the fledgling stages, the future looks bright for these emerging whisky nations.

**DID YOU KNOW...**

- Germany's distilling culture blossomed after the Second World War with more whisky becoming available
- The first German whisky made to Scottish production methods appeared in 1984
- The Guillon distillery in the Champagne region of France uses smoke from beech and oak leaves to dry the barley
- The Lark Distillery received the first distiller's licence to be issued in Tasmania since the 1830s
- Mackmyra distillery has been experimenting with Swedish oak and juniper wood to give their whiskies a distinctive Nordic twist

## AMRUT 40%
Single Malt - India

**7** **Martine: Quite an appetising nose but mid palate is faint and watery. Too quick a dilution?**
**Nose:** Fragrant, fruity and floral. Medlar, raisins, stewed rhubarb. A hint of rose syrup. Opens up on bakery notes (ginger biscuits, apple and vanilla flan) and lingers on heady vanilla notes.
**Palate:** Smooth and soft. But mid palate is flat and watery. Then a pleasant spicy fit of energy.
**Finish:** Sweet, with a nutty tang. Touch of mint.

**7¾** **Dave: Well made. A good session drink. Have it with ice.**
**Nose:** Lightly oily: nut oil, mutton fat, vanilla. Ripe and soft, lightly spiced, coconut, peach and malt. Medium-bodied.
**Palate:** Decent balance. Juicy soft fruits, toasty oak, malt flour. The palate has a kick to it adding interest. Good.
**Finish:** Dry, short, refreshing.

## ARMORIK 40%
Single Malt - France

**7** **Michael: An enjoyable after dinner malt, though not especially complex.**
**Nose:** Woody. Logs in a wood yard.
**Palate:** Silky. Black chocolate. Brazil nuts. Hard toffee. Some orangey notes. Orange creams.
**Finish:** Spicy. Gingery.

**8** **Dave: An extremely well-made, if young, spirit. One to watch.**
**Nose:** Rounded and fruity to start: baked apple, honey, peach stone. Water brings out a damp straw/hay note and more 'foresty' aromas of nut, moss, fern and leaf.
**Palate:** The baked apple note is there along with a youthful spiciness. A sweet mid-palate and good balance.
**Finish:** A little short.

## BAKERY HILL CLASSIC 60%
Single Malt - Australia

**7¼** **Martine: Unusual. Very tickly but water tames it and brings a fresh fruity flavours out.**
**Nose:** Spirity. Jumps right up your nostrils. After a while, develops sweeter notes. Lemon drops, barley sugar, vanilla syrup.
**Palate:** Tangy, fizzy in a refreshing way. Yeasty. Tastes like a dry pear cider. Tickles the tongue.
**Finish:** Dry, slightly burning. Touch of ginger. Bitter apple skin.

**6¾** **Dave: This needs more time in cask. Well distilled though.**
**Nose:** Light and fragrant, daffodil, slightly sappy, perfumed lemon (slightly artificial). Water exposes a hard edge, grappa-like.
**Palate:** Very sweet and sugary to start. High alcohol. Floral notes. Apple purée. Spices.
**Finish:** Barley sugar.

## BAKERY HILL PEATED 61%
Single Malt - Australia

**6** **Martine: It seems to have retained all the back side of an animal farm. An attempt to replicate some long ago illicit still stuff?**
**Nose:** Sour. Butyric, slightly rancid. Wet decaying straw. Tangy.
**Palate:** Sweet but tangy. The same unclean cereal notes from the nose linger on the palate.
**Finish:** Dry, a bit heavy. Fresh oak.

**7¾** **Dave: Again, well distilled but still young.**
**Nose:** Clean and fresh. Smoked cheese, apple wood. Water shows it to be slightly gawky but the smoke gives it another dimension.
**Palate:** Clean and quite light. Citric and intense. Has a charred quality and a certain swagger. Nutmeg.
**Finish:** Toasty, smoked.

## CRADLE MOUNTAIN DOUBLE MALT 46%
Single Malt - Australia

**8** **Michael: Plenty of flavours, but they need to be better combined and rounded.**
**Nose:** Slightly dry. Faint suggestion of peat. Perhaps it's just a grassy note.
**Palate:** Concentrated sweetness. Fruity. Lemony.
**Finish:** Spicy. Warming.

**8¾** **Dave: Of the two Cradle Mountains I have tasted, this is the better.**
**Nose:** Sweet with a dry undertow and some depth. Fruity, with orange concentrate, lemon icing/cupcakes and some dry maltiness. In time, a real creaminess.
**Palate:** Good weight, though slightly slick on the palate. Plenty of fruit balanced by a crisp nuttiness and a strange roasted quality: highly roasted coffee bean/bourbon biscuit.
**Finish:** Soft and long.

## HARRIER WHISKY 43%
Blended - South Africa

**7¾** **Martine: A good development, even if astringence shows up at times.**
**Nose:** Sylvestry. Wet leaves, humus. Cooked mushrooms. Chicken broth. With aeration, carries on creamier notes. Vanilla custard.
**Palate:** Round, almost syrupy. Then orange marmalade. Stem ginger.
**Finish:** Warm. Oaky, bitter orange.

**7** **Dave: A theme seems to be emerging. Light spirit, plenty of oak, not long enough in cask to mellow.**
**Nose:** Singed grass moving into sulphur (boiled cabbage). Earthy with some estery notes, black peppercorn, nuts.
**Palate:** Clean and rounded and vanilla soft from the oak with pumpkin seed crispness coming from the cereal.
**Finish:** Finishes half way up the palate.

## KNIGHTS 43%
Blended - South Africa

**8** **Martine: A fruity character. Well-balanced.**
**Nose:** Intensively fruity. Notes of ripe banana. Lemony. Scent of a garden after a summer rainfall. Lemony.
**Palate:** Sweet and smooth. Good fruity sensation. Melon. Pears poached in a spicy syrup. Almond cake.
**Finish:** Medium, spicy.

**7** **Dave: Lacks any real individual character – or middle palate.**
**Nose:** Clean and sweet. Baked banana, vanilla sugar, mango, just mown grass drying in the sun. New oak. Destroyed by water.
**Palate:** Quite light and slightly hollow. Lacks a mid-palate and becomes coarse to the finish.
**Finish:** Hard.

## LAMMERLAW 10 YEARS OLD, CADENHEAD'S 49.1%
Single Malt - New Zealand

**7½** **Michael: This bottling is much more aggressive, and drying, than I remember. What happened to the soft maltiness and apricot fruitiness?**
**Nose:** Oily. Sun-dried grass.
**Palate:** Sweet for a moment, then intensely peppery.
**Finish:** Lingering. Dry. Ground white pepper. Peat.

**8½** **Dave: Well-balanced and characterful. Worth seeking out.**
**Nose:** A lot going on here: lifted notes of lemon balm/menthol, tangerine peel over a nutty/toasty background and, as it opens in the glass, vanilla and butter.
**Palate:** Silky and well-rounded. All the aromas come through making it creamy, fruity and spicy at the same time. Lovely balance and some complexity.
**Finish:** Well-rounded, mealy.

## LAMMERLAW 12 YEARS OLD, PEATED MALT FINISHING 40%
Single Malt - New Zealand

**7¼** **Michael: The peat is so light that it is barely perceptible in the nose and palate, but it's dryness creates a contrast that lifts the sweeter notes.**
**Nose:** Light smoke, as though from a nearby lone chimney. Just a hint on the breeze.
**Palate:** Creamy. Custard. Marshmallow. Toasted coconut.
**Finish:** Toasty.

**6¾** **Dave: More weight is needed in the spirit.**
**Nose:** Light and quite attractive, with a touch of smoke. Toasty (wholemeal bread) caramel, barley sugar, American cream soda.
**Palate:** A strange smoky perfume like burning orange tea. Light and gentle, but thin.
**Finish:** Sweet.

## LAMMERLAW 12 YEARS OLD, SPECIAL FINISHING 40%
Single Malt - New Zealand

**Michael: I thought the earlier, younger bottling had more vigour.**
**Nose:** A field of straw stubble drying in the sun.
**Palate:** Silky. Grassy. Nutty. Bean-sprouts.
**Finish:** Ground white pepper. Long. Lingering.

**Dave: Well enough made, just insubstantial.**
**Nose:** Young slightly immature. Barley sugar/boiled sweets, slightly artificial. Water removes the harshness, leaving some peach, though the confected Irn-Bru type note remains.
**Palate:** Light and a little thin. There's some orange and marzipan in the middle, but its hard round the edges.
**Finish:** Short and a little sour.

## THE MACKENZIE 40%
Blended - New Zealand

**Martine: A very strange aromatic profile. Nose is not very pleasant at start then it delivers more.**
**Nose:** Slightly butyric. Wet floor in a dairy. Touch of pinewood. Fungus. Barleysugar. Touch of apple juice. Elderberry wine.
**Palate:** Sweet at first sip then very spicy with an unusual taste. Physalis, poppy drop, elderberry. Going definitely on the hot side. Tabasco.
**Finish:** Dry, burning.

**Dave: Bonkers stuff.**
**Nose:** Rooty, then peach, fruit salad. Hot rocks. With water becomes hugely perfumed, lavender, then camomile blossom. Bizarre.
**Palate:** Immediate hit of marzipan, then angelica. Almost off-puttingly confected. A scented boudoir.
**Finish:** Camomile tea with a touch of echinacea.

## MACKMYRA PRELUDIUM 01 55.6%
Single Malt - Sweden

**Arthur: Lowland-like, extremely pretty and characterful. Good by any standard, excellent given its youth. Welcome to the gang Mackmyra!**
**Nose:** Apples, lemon, and a light yeastiness. Newly sawn wood. Meadow flowers and garden mint.
**Palate:** Fresh and young, with a baked apple flavour.
**Finish:** Floral, citric and a touch of toffee.

**Owen: As a cask sample of a maturing whisky, I'd say it had definite potential, but otherwise, it's jailbait.**
**Nose:** Traces of vanilla and fudge, but largely dominated by the acetic dryness of new spirit. Menthol or Eucalyptus.
**Palate:** Flat, dusty, chalky. Big alcohol burn, even with water. Big, but unsophisticated, vanilla notes.
**Finish:** Definite peppermint/menthol character. With water, more toffee develops.

## MACKMYRA PRELUDIUM 02 54.2%
Single Malt - Sweden

**Dave: Another nipper. That tropical fruit will develop over time as everything settles down. Like Ballechin, this is one to watch.**
**Nose:** Very fresh and grassy, with some fresh fruit salad and then Crunchie bars. Water brings out graphite and freshly mown grass. Still a little stony.
**Palate:** Fairly rigid light powdered ginger. Seems a little unformed, as if the constituent parts are still pulling together. Water helps.
**Finish:** Short, little hard. Young.

**Arthur: Very unusual and now knowing what it is, this one was hard to assess blind, as it feels very different to Scotch malt, just as it should do.**
**Nose:** Gala melon, juniper and Ouzo. A clay-like mineral quality. Linseed oil, with an intensely floral nose too. Some sherry-like toffee notes.
**Palate:** Unusual and difficult to place. Something herbal, possibly burnt sage or even more of that juniper. Some vanilla and fruit toffee.
**Finish:** Oily, like a cooking oil.

## MACKMYRA PRELUDIUM 03 52.2%
Single Malt - Sweden

**Dave: A theme emerges...**
**Nose:** Fresh and clean to start with an almond note. Once again though the development is poor with chemical notes emerging, this time Brasso. Dry cereal/straw behind.

**Palate:** Light and, once again, aggressive. Some nuttiness as well.
**Finish:** Chemical notes to finish. Brutally young?

**Ian: Not very inspiring.**
**Nose:** Very little on nose. Straw?
**Palate:** Raw, sharp, spirity. Unduly assertive.
**Finish:** Harsh and spirity, blessedly short.

## MACKMYRA PRELUDIUM 04 53.3%
Single Malt - Sweden

**Dave: If you want to build a new distillery you have to be willing to take the financial hit of waiting until the whisky is ready.**
**Nose:** Light to the point of neutrality. A whiff of cut grass, a hint of lemon juice, but little else.
**Palate:** Light, hot. Bypasses the taste buds and goes for sensation rather than flavour.
**Finish:** Hot.

**Ian: Not unpleasant.**
**Nose:** Grassy, fruity, citrus notes and some smelly socks.
**Palate:** Quite assertive.
**Finish:** Short finish with little development and complexity.

## MACKMYRA PRELUDIUM 05 48.4%
Single Malt - Sweden

**Dave: We're moving in the right direction here.**
**Nose:** Once again alcohol is the main characteristic. High-toned and slightly soapy. Light mint, fir trees. Plastic here as well.
**Palate:** Quite sweet and rigidly structured. Not bad with water. A clean sweet centre suggesting a spirit which is beginning to come together, but is far from complete.
**Finish:** Some length and residual sweetness.

**Ian: May develop with time.**
**Nose:** Spirity, anaesthetic, faded vanilla extract.
**Palate:** Flavour notes seem under-developed and overwhelmed by the spirit.
**Finish:** Spirit dominates.

## MACKMYRA RESERVE SWEDISH OAK FINISH 58.5%
Single Malt - Sweden

**Dave: Another let-down. Lacking in coherence.**
**Nose:** Flat and soft. Acetone once again, biscuit, hot crumpet, oily and slightly smoky with water.
**Palate:** A somewhat unhappy amalgam of the oak and a young spirit. The former is beginning to soften and bring out some sweetness but is also quite grippy. All rather uneasy.
**Finish:** Hard.

**Ian: Probably the best of the bunch.**
**Nose:** Biscuits. Wood smoke. Complex.
**Palate:** Smooth and rounded.
**Finish:** Long and consistent.

## MACKMYRA SINGLE CASK SWEDISH OAK FINISH 56.5%
Single Malt - Sweden

**Dave: It's not hard, it's not chemically, it doesn't have a bitter edge, or taste of glue, it is actually good!**
**Nose:** Fragranced. Wild and herbal: coumarin, bergamot, wild thyme. With water some smoke, shoe polish and an oiliness.
**Palate:** This is roundness with an interesting fragrance and lightly smoky. The oil gives a fatness, texture and middle.
**Finish:** Not to mention an aromatic finish.

**Ian: More than just acceptable.**
**Nose:** Thin – peat smoke.
**Palate:** Peat smoke very forward and consistent.
**Finish:** Consistent, develops some complexity.

## MCDOWELL'S SINGLE MALT 42.8%
Single Malt - India

**Michael: Somewhat one-dimensional.**
**Nose:** Oily. Cereal grain. Malty.
**Palate:** Malty dryness. Vegetal.
**Finish:** Slightly medicinal, very warming.

**Dave: Well-made, light and clean. Good distilling.**
**Nose:** Light, attractive, gentle. There's some barley sugar, soft fruits, banana. With water there's milk chocolate/vanilla and a spicy, biscuity, woody note.
**Palate:** Soft, juicy style with a rounded, peachy, fruity mid-palate.
**Finish:** Sweet, syrupy.

## MILFORD 10 YEARS OLD 43%
Single Malt - New Zealand

**6½ Michael: Good flavour development.**
**Nose:** Dry. Lightly fragrant.
**Palate:** Cream flavours. Maltiness. A short burst of extreme sweetness. Then peppery.
**Finish:** Hot. Warming.

**7½ Dave: Well-made, light and clean. Good balance.**
**Nose:** Dry and malty/oaty (accentuated with water). Light vanilla, crème caramel, some dried apricot.
**Palate:** Herbal tea with some citrus notes and nutmeg. A little too light with water.
**Finish:** Dry, slight wood.

## MILFORD 10 YEARS OLD 43%
Single Malt - New Zealand

**8½ Martine: A good combination of fruit and oak. Wood is well integrated. Quite a moreish dram.**
**Nose:** Aromatic. Fresh aniseed aromas. Marzipan. Apple blossom. Juicy peaches. A touch of new leather
**Palate:** Rich, mellow, fruity. The same herbal freshness. Lemon balm, star anise. A delicate oak touch.
**Finish:** Dry, fresh oak. Walnut peel. Sweet liquorice.

**7¼ Dave: Technically excellent...but an extra dimension is needed. None of these are complex.**
**Nose:** Oily almost greasy. Wood preserver, slightly flabby. Moss and grass, green fern, hot bracken. With water, some camphor.
**Palate:** Light malt, dry oak, clean and citric.
**Finish:** Apple and nutmeg.

## MILFORD 15 YEARS OLD 43%
Single Malt - New Zealand

**8¼ Martine: Like a sweet chariot. Puddings on display...-Keeps fresh and lively.**
**Nose:** Creamy. Cereals bowl. Custardy. Syllabub. Tangerine. Lemon and meringue pie.
**Palate:** Smooth, silky. Rewarding and refreshing. Pear drop. Touch of gingerbread. Warms up on allspice and long peppercorns. Hint of liquorice.
**Finish:** Warm, sherbety. Tickly. Toasted hazelnuts.

**7½ Dave: At least this has some depth.**
**Nose:** Dumb. Putty/plasticene, green fruits, unripe pear. Once again sweetness and some pear juice as well. Sweet and pleasant.
**Palate:** Nothing to start, then a light juicy fruit spreads across the middle of the palate. Has some weight, but shatters with water.
**Finish:** Oat. Dry.

## PENDERYN GRAND SLAM 46%
Single Malt - Wales

**8½ Martine: A well structured whisky. Oak frames the aromatic palette without overpowering. Quite a complex dram.**
**Nose:** Fruity. Cider apples. A bit sharp at start but quickly turns biscuity. Sweet vanilla notes. As it opens, the appley character breaks through to lead way to fudgier aromas.
**Palate:** Thick, oily. Creamy fudge, raisins and milk chocolate. A sensuous spicy wave.
**Finish:** Lingering, peppery. A bitter oaky edge.

**8 Dave: Another great session drink, this has the sweeter edge. Good distilling. Stylish.**
**Nose:** Rounded. The first with any extra complexity to it. Plenty of vanilla, butter and a hint of pine. Light spices and sweet citric notes, apricot and banana. Orange peel and zest.
**Palate:** Very pure flavours. Clean with a mix of nuts and spice from the oak and a sweet spirit. Vanilla cinnamon, pepper spiced apple.
**Finish:** Vanilla. Very smooth. Medium length. Spicy.

## PENDERYN PEATED LIMITED EDITION 50%
Single Malt - Wales

**7¾ Martine: A thin but palatable smoky whisky. Tells more on the palate than on the nose. For a rainy afternoon with blue cheese and toasted bread.**
**Nose:** A smoky whiff. Creosote. Aerial peatiness. Reminds me of a faint Caol Ila. Strawberry yoghurt.
**Palate:** Sweet and light. Smoky. Green fruit. Kiwi. Very pleasant flowing feel.
**Finish:** Short, quickly fading. Gentle spicyness. Nutty touch.

**6¾ Dave: In bottle too quickly.**
**Nose:** Very pale. Light and malty with a hint of smoke. Clean, but seems very young. Little substance.
**Palate:** A mix of sweet and dry sensations but there is little real flavour. Dry, green, light smoke.
**Finish:** Short.

## PENDERYN WELSH WHISKY 46%
Single Malt - Wales

**7¾ Gavin: The process is unusual, and so are the resultant flavours, but this is a very drinkable whisky in its own right. I was a sceptic, but no longer.**
**Nose:** Sweet. Herbal, vegetal, notes, but also meaty yeastiness. Some madeira wineyness.
**Palate:** Dense body. Rye-like mintiness. Sweet and vegetal again. Flavours reminiscent of snow peas.
**Finish:** Spicy. Hint of ginger. Warming, soothing.

**7 Dave: Dangos cyntaf eithriadol o dda gan y chwisgi (ifanc iawn) yma. Un i'w wylio, yn sicr. As they say in Wales.**
**Nose:** Young. Lightly nutty with hints of cream, pear/cooking apple. Sherberty with some pine needle. With water a burnt note. Raisin bread.
**Palate:** Smooth and fairly sweet. Vanilla, lemon and currant. Clean and gentle.
**Finish:** Young, green. Pencil shavings.

## PENDERYN WRU 125TH ANNIVERSARY LIMITED 50%
Single Malt - Wales

**8½ Martine: The oaky start leads way to a cheerful fruity and floral profile. Marked by the sherry but not on the dark (woody) side. Avoid water.**
**Nose:** Oaky. Antique shop, cigar box. A meaty note, dark chocolate. A hint of geranium. Getting more floral and sweeter on time. Cloved orange.
**Palate:** Sweet at start then drying out on a very spicy kick. Bitter orange marmalade. Ginger. Oak is well integrated.
**Finish:** Dry, spicy and fruity. Cider apple.

**6 Dave: I was expecting the atypicality to be the world's first Malibu finish, but no...maybe it is just atypical for Welsh whisky.**
**Nose:** A lurid colour reminiscent of Lucozade. Masses of coconut: cream; dessicated; flesh; oil; bounty bars. Hot gorse. Underneath there's lime, banana split and chocolate.
**Palate:** Slick and sweet. Seems as if this thick veneer of sweet oak is smothering the spirit.
**Finish:** Guess? Yup. Coconut.

## SULLIVANS COVE BOURBON MATURATION 60%
Single Malt - Australia

**6¾ Dave: The overriding impression is of young whiskies released too soon.**
**Nose:** Hot with alcohol, with a sweet lemon drop nose. Quite acidic as well. As it opens notes of hot rabbit hutches. Has decent concentration.
**Palate:** Penetrating and alcoholic. Mix of dusty cereal (malt bins) and some fruit pastille, then like England's midfield it collapses in the centre. Lacks harmony.
**Finish:** Short.

**6½ Ian: Showing some promise. Might develop with age.**
**Nose:** Sweets, gum, ripe fruits.
**Palate:** Assertive but not actively unpleasant.
**Finish:** Chewy.

## SULLIVANS COVE FRENCH OAK CASK 60%
Single Malt - Australia

**6¾ Dave: Here's oak being used as a Romulan cloaking device to hide young(?) spirit. I can see what they're trying to do, but this needs tweaking.**
**Nose:** A somewhat alarming Lucozade-like colour. Vegetal, with notes of hamster cage, sunflower seed, then masses of oak.
**Palate:** HUGE, sweet oak extract. Leather laid over charred wood and a machine-oil note that brings to mind a cooperage workbench.
**Finish:** A bit grubby.

**5½ Arthur: A dirty, grizzly thing which dolls out some rough, tough flavours. Be (slightly) delighted and (mostly) disgusted all at the same time. Never ever boring, but very far from perfect.**

**Nose:** Grapes, rye bread, bruised cooking apples. With water up comes some chemical stinkiness, like boat diesel. Gooseberries and marzipan.
**Palate:** Rye, earthiness and rubber tyres. Intense.
**Finish:** Lots of European oak rubberiness, like gnawing on a Wellington boot.

## SULLIVANS COVE PORT MATURATION 60%
Single Malt - Australia

**6½ Dave: It sticks to the tongue and you can't get rid of it.**
**Nose:** Boiled and oxidised. Grape must. Perfumed.
**Palate:** Greasy and thick of the tongue. It's like drinking varnish. Some bitterness and burning plastic.
**Finish:** Cloying.

**6¾ Ian: I have hopes for this.**
**Nose:** Rich wine, smooth, comparatively subtle vanilla.
**Palate:** Develops complexity in the mouth.
**Finish:** Holds together comparatively well.

## THREE SHIPS 10 YEARS OLD 43%
Single Malt - South Africa

**7¾ Michael: Some odd esters on the nose, but a nicely festive whisky.**
**Nose:** Powerful. Ground almonds. Rum. Coconut. Lemons. Pear-drops.
**Palate:** Creamy. Rum butter on Christmas pudding. Steamed pudding.
**Finish:** Lightly soothing. Balancing root-ginger dryness.

**7 Dave: Well made spirit that would probably benefit from slightly less aggressive oak.**
**Nose:** Very fruity start, moist cake, light honey, orange. Lots of vanilla and toffee apple. Becomes bourbon-like.
**Palate:** Light and clean with a slightly oily texture. Lots of new oak putting a fairly firm grip on things.
**Finish:** Oak.

## THREE SHIPS 5 YEARS OLD 43%
Single Malt - South Africa

**7½ Martine: A decent dram, a little heavy on the palate though. You need to like oaky aftertaste to fully appreciate it.**
**Nose:** Buttery but with a butyric edge. Herbal, aniseed. Shortbread. Dry hay.
**Palate:** Fresh, clean, sweet. Malty and minty.
**Finish:** Medium, some spices (paprika, ginger). A bit grippy. An earthy touch.

**7¾ Dave: Has some varied character. Good.**
**Nose:** Light smoke? Salami, pulpy fruits, crisp oak, gentle malt, some resin, toasted.
**Palate:** Oxidised and fruity. Old pears, slightly chewy. Wood smoke from the middle. Slightly green, seems young.
**Finish:** Fruity then spiced.

## WALDVIERTLER FEINSTER ROGGENWHISKY 42%
Single Malt - Austria

**6¾ Michael: A winter whisky. Points for assertiveness.**
**Nose:** Slightly spicy and medicinal.
**Palate:** Light. Slightly soapy. Scenty. Very spicy. More rye character.
**Finish:** Sharp. Astringent.

**6½ Dave: Well-made, just lacks some complexity.**
**Nose:** Gentle yet crisp. Some leather, marzipan and rounded fruits: apple/apple wood, banana. Water makes it slightly harder and woodier.
**Palate:** Crisp, clean and slightly grassy. A bit immature.
**Finish:** Good length with some spiciness.

## WALDVIERTLER ROGGEN-MALZWHISKY 42%
Single Malt - Austria

**6½ Michael: One to put in the hip-flask for a walk in the forest.**
**Nose:** Fruitier and more resiny.
**Palate:** Creamier. Suggestions of clove. Menthol. Woody.
**Finish:** Green. Like biting on young twigs.

**7½ Dave: Good balance, with zesty rye touches.**
**Nose:** Clean, fragrant and attractive. Marzipan and light rye notes: sourdough, fennel seed. With water the bready notes dominate. Floury (and flowery).
**Palate:** Slightly muted to start then lovely spicy attack. The rye flour re-emerges. Light but well balanced.
**Finish:** Clean with a hint of sweetness.

## WHISKY BRETON SINGLE MALT WHISKY 40%
Single Malt - France

**6¾ Michael: Pleasant enough, but a Breton whisky should surely offer some kind of regional difference?**
**Nose:** Dryish. Vanilla-pods. Fragrant.
**Palate:** Lightly malty character. Some caramel-like flavours.
**Finish:** Faint suggestion of peat (or char?).

**7½ Dave: Approachable. I like it.**
**Nose:** Light fruits and floral notes. An intriguing mix of citric and savoury: orange bitters and boot polish. Water gives it a lovely spring-like lift: leafy, damp and a light buttery edge.
**Palate:** Sweet and medium-bodied, the flavours all concentrated on the middle of the tongue. Dries quite quickly with a hint of charcoal. Strangely attractive.
**Finish:** Smooth.

**Above:** The picturesque setting of Mackmyra Distillery

# Scotland

For those wanting to venture into the big world of whiskies, Scotland offers a huge range of tastes and styles, from graceful and floral to hard hitting and medicinal, with all the taste ranges in between.

Looking back through the tastings you can see how some distilleries have shaken off their mothballs and started to produce again. In fact, the rise of some distilleries to prominence in the market can be traced through the tasters' comments.

Scotland is divided into six main areas of production, Highland, Islands, Lowlands, Islay, Campbeltown and Speyside.

Single malts have strong links to the areas they are produced in.

As a very rough guide, Islay whiskies are phenolic and medicinal with plenty of peat; Islands have hints of smoke and salt; Highland malts are big and malty; Speysiders are sweet and fruity; Lowlanders are more floral and delicate and Campbeltown whiskies are complex with brine, peat and fruit.

As with all rules there are many exceptions. All this adds to the complex tastes of single malts.

Distillers in Scotland have changed the way they approach whisky in the time *Whisky Magazine* has been bringing readers all the best bottlings from the industry.

In recent years we have seen the rise of 'wood finished' whiskies. These are whiskies that have been left to mature for a final period in different casks, usually former wine casks.

Another innovation that has taken off is bottling non chill-filtered whiskies, often weighing in at the 60% ABV mark.

Essentially chill-filtration removes certain compounds from the liquid by lowering its temperature and pushing it through a card filter. This means when you add water the whisky stays clear.

Some connoisseurs prefer to have the compounds left in, which results in a haze when water is added.

Scottish blends have also played a very important role in the rise of their single malt siblings.

Blends also make the lion's share of world Scotch sales, accounting for 93 per cent of global sales.

Drinkers often start their journey with blends and then want to explore further, leading them down the path of single malts.

The master blenders of Scotland pioneered the marriage of different whiskies with a grain backbone, and indeed blended single malts to produce vatted or blended malts.

The idea was simple; to produce a drink that was lighter and that had a certain mass-market appeal.

Most whisky lovers liken these blends to a symphony of tastes, and some say that they offer more complexity than single malts.

# Scotch

## DID YOU KNOW...

- Speyside has the greatest concentration of malt whisky distilleries in Scotland and the world
- Dalwhinnie Distillery is situated at the confluence of old drovers' trails and is the highest and coldest distillery in Scotland
- Highland Park on Orkney is the most northerly distillery with Pulteney in Wick taking the title of most northern mainland distillery
- Glasgow once had about 20 malt distilleries surrounding it, now only Auchentoshan survives, with Glengoyne not too far away. Port Dundas and Strathclyde in Glasgow are both still producing grain whisky
- Campbeltown suffered the same fate, but is now experiencing a mini revival with the latest distillery Glengyle coming of age

NORTH ATLANTIC OCEAN
SCOTLAND
Edinburgh
NORTH SEA
IRELAND
ENGLAND

Scapa • Highland Park
Pulteney
Clynelish
Balblair • Glenmorangie
Teaninich
Dalmore
Glen Ord
Glenugie
Speyside region
Talisker
HIGHLANDS
GRAMPIAN
Speyside • Royal Lochnagar
Glenury Royal
Dalwhinnie Fettercairn
Ben Nevis Blair Athol • Edradour Glencadam
Aberfeldy
Tobermory TAYSIDE
Glenturret • Tullibardine
Oban Deanston • Cameronbridge
FIFE
Glentauchers
Loch Lomond Glengoyne
Inverleven St. Magdalene Edinburgh
Bunnahabhain Auchentoshan Rosebank Glenkinchie
Jura Dumbarton North British
Bruichladdich Caol Ila Port Dundas
Kilchoman Bowmore Strathclyde
Port Ellen Ardbeg Arran STRATHCLYDE BORDERS
Lagavulin
Laphroaig SCOTLAND
Glen Scotia DUMFRIES & GALLOWAY
Springbank • Glengyle
Ladyburn
Bladnoch ENGLAND

Speyside region

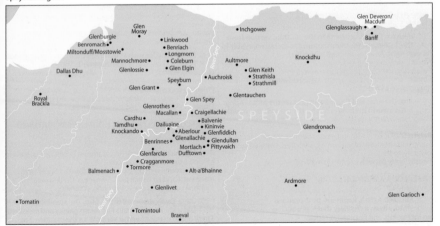

Glen Deveron/ Macduff
Glen Moray Inchgower Glenglassaugh
Glenburgie Banff
Benromach Linkwood
Miltonduff/Mosstowie Benriach Knockdhu
Mannochmore Longmorn
Glenlossie Coleburn
Dallas Dhu Glen Elgin Aultmore
Speyburn Glen Keith
Glen Grant Auchroisk Strathisla
Strathmill
Royal Brackla Glen Spey
Glentauchers
Glenrothes
Macallan Craigellachie
Cardhu Balvenie Glendronach
Tamdhu Dailuaine Kininvie
Knockando Aberlour Glenfiddich
Benrinnes Glenallachie Glendullan
Mortlach Pittyvaich
Glenfarclas Dufftown
Cragganmore
Balmenach Tormore Alt-a'Bhainne
Ardmore
Glenlivet Glen Garioch
Tomatin
Tomintoul
Braeval

## ABERFELDY 12 YEARS OLD 40%
Single Malt - Highland

**7½ Michael: Refreshing and light-hearted. Almost too playful to take seriously.**
**Nose:** Fragrant. Orange-zest. Light smokiness. Incense. Touch of sherry.
**Palate:** Light on the tongue. Oily. Emphatically clean fruitiness. Tangerines. Very lively, fresh, flavours.
**Finish:** Like biting into a kumquat. Then a long, fruity glow.

**8½ Jim: Really outstanding example of massively complex, classy but undiscovered malt.**
**Nose:** Beautifully intense malt with a cidery-apple fruitiness. Gentle oak and honey round off superbly.
**Palate:** Fresh, almost crisp mouthfeel with outstanding sweet maltiness and an almost Irish pot-still firm fruitiness. Mouthwatering.
**Finish:** Softly spiced with a long, rich malt follow-through.

## ABERFELDY 1974, COOPER'S CHOICE 46%
Single Malt - Highland

**8 Michael: All the classic flavour elements. With its character "freshness", Aberfeldy often shines at younger ages. Here it excels in middle age.**
**Nose:** Warm, sweet, nutty, appetising.
**Palate:** Very full flavours, beautifully rounded. Rich maltiness; orange fruit; slight smokiness; but no astringency; perfectly balanced.
**Finish:** Fresh, sweetish, spiciness and smoky dryness. Both restrained. Perfect balance.

**8¼ Dave: A gentle dram from a strangely forgotten distillery. More like this please.**
**Nose:** Rich and soft with an oily feel. Raisin, dried fruits, turf, oak, malt, heavily perfumed roses, orange peel. Good balance.
**Palate:** Gentle, oily and soft. Macadamia nut, toffee.
**Finish:** Dies a little. Dried fruits.

## ABERFELDY 1978, GORDON & MACPHAIL 40%
Single Malt - Highland

**7¾ Michael: Delicate but not bland. Real subtlety. Very mature, but not a Highlander. A Highlander, but blindfold I would have placed it as a Speysider.**
**Nose:** Still very fresh, but drier, with a touch more smokiness, and no obvious sherry.
**Palate:** Oilier. Very tangerine-like. Sweeter. Scenty. More complex.
**Finish:** Attractively appetising late echo of peat smoke.

**8½ Jim: Held its age well and another gem for the sweet-toothed. Excellent.**
**Nose:** Stupendous aroma: a posy of lilacs and blue bells which is heady and rich.
**Palate:** Drier than the nose suggests with an early arrival of firm oak. Sweetens as the malt arrives.
**Finish:** Decent bitter-sweet balance which perhaps levels out on the former but always with a barley-sugar undercurrent.

## ABERFELDY 1978, SIGNATORY 43%
Single Malt - Highland

**7½ Michael: Less structure than the youthful version from the distillery or the more mature choice, but enjoyable in its own right. As a dessert malt with trifle?**
**Nose:** Lightly dry. Incense. Flowery.
**Palate:** Oily, orangey, but more creamy in style.
**Finish:** Seems very sweet indeed, then suddenly the peat-smoke emerges. Very long.

**7½ Jim: The nose and finish do little to set the pulse racing. But it's worth the boring bits for the magnificent middle.**
**Nose:** Heady stuff with the oak. Good sweet/dry balance, nonetheless.
**Palate:** Begins lazily with some non-specific oakiness offering a bland start, then takes off with a malty sweetness tweaked by some peppery notes.
**Finish:** Pretty flat with a soothing malt-oak finishing.

## ABERLOUR A'BUNADH 59.6%
Single Malt - Speyside

**8½ Michael: A dark, luxurious, post-prandial whisky from a distillery that is producing an increasing, and impressive range.**
WHISKY Recommended
**Nose:** Sherry, mint, pralines. Luxurious.

**Palate:** Very rich and creamy, with just a hint of mint and cherries behind.
**Finish:** Nougat, cherry brandy, ginger, faint smoke. Definitely an afterdinner whisky.

**8½ Jim: Surprising complexity; very, very good.**
**Nose:** Incredibly aromatic, thanks partly to a subtle peatiness. The sherry notes are concentrated and there is massive fruit ranging from mango to apples. Enormous.
**Palate:** The sherry tries to dominate but fails. Peppery spices, lightly smoked malt, clean sherry mingling with paw-paw and a vague nuttiness.
**Finish:** Long, clean sherry, hints of citrus fruit and cocoa. The peppers linger.

## ABERLOUR A'BUNADH, LIMITED EDITION 59.6%
Single Malt - Speyside

**8¾ Michael: Darker, drier and more spicily assertive than the earlier version, despite only a slight difference in ages.**
WHISKY Recommended
**Nose:** Sherry, mint, pralines. Oakier (and smokier?) than the earlier version of a'bunadh.
**Palate:** Very rich, and creamy. Cherries. Ginger.
**Finish:** Nougat, cherry-brandy, ginger, fragrant smoke.

**9 Jim: Wow!! Who would have thought a mere Speysider could offer such personality and depth?**
**Nose:** Heavier and oakier than the age suggests but with a big, waxy, sherry note offering a cleaner, richer dimension.
**Palate:** Quite massive with a big sherry surge that breaks against a big malt middle and delicious spices.
**Finish:** Long, magnificently oaky and proud. Some cocoa and sherry fight for the finish but intertwine.

## ABERLOUR 10 YEARS OLD 40%
Single Malt - Speyside

**8¼ Michael: Sophisticated but very approachable.**
**Nose:** Very distinctively nutty, with a touch of sherry.
**Palate:** Nutty maltiness. Unusually textured. Nougat-like. A hint of cherries. Beautifully balanced.
**Finish:** Long. Gentle but firm. Subtle spiciness. Nutmeg? Cinnamon?

**6¾ Dave: Lacks integration with the wood. Like some middle-weight malts, it needs time to reach full maturity.**
**Nose:** Quite light, slightly immature nose. There's (green) melon balls, ginger, a hint of cream, sultana and sherry.
**Palate:** The fruit cake/sherry begins to emerge but it's a bit thin and simple.
**Finish:** Slightly bitter.

## ABERLOUR 12 YEARS OLD, SHERRY CASK MATURED 40%
Single Malt - Speyside

**8¼ Michael: Well-rounded, but the balancing dryness can be slightly bitter.**
**Nose:** Sweet. Marzipan. Notably nutty. Very heavy sherry (slightly tar-like, iron-ish). First-fill dry Oloroso? It tastes more like Pedro Ximenez.
**Palate:** Soft, smooth, juicy. Malty nuttiness. Liquorice.
**Finish:** A firm, assertive, hug. Enwrapping.

**8 Dave: Good for such a young Aberlour. Sherry in balance.**
**Nose:** Mellow, sherry-dominant nose. Tobacco leaf, orange pekoe tea, walnut, caramelised fruit. Mint, leather, toffee and butter. In time it gets even sweeter.
**Palate:** Sweet and silky with well integrated sherry wood overlaying the creamy/minty character. Ripe and soft.
**Finish:** Light chocolate and some dried fruit.

## ABERLOUR 15 YEARS OLD, DOUBLE CASK MATURED 40%
Single Malt - Speyside

**8½ Michael: Drily flowery-herbal aromas. Roses. Vanilla. Moving to a suggestion of tobacco.**
**Palate:** Smooth, with tightly-combined flavours. Some buttery maltiness. Candied lemon peel. Cinnamon. Garden mint.
**Finish:** A surge of spiciness. Very long. Warming.

**7¾ Dave: Easily drowned with water. The standard 15 Years Old is stunning, but this just seems gawky and awkward. There are so many Aberlour variants on the market – I'm getting mightily confused.**

**Nose:** Initially quite crisp with a fairly hot nose burn and citric. Seems strangely immature with very faint sherried notes.
**Palate:** A creamy centre, but everything is muted.
**Finish:** A little short with minty tones.

## ABERLOUR 15 YEARS OLD, OLD DOUBLE CASK 40%
Single Malt - Speyside

**7½ Martine: A well balanced dram. Would have got more nerve with a bit of extra strength.**
**Nose:** Fragrant, intense. Fruity. Greengage. Vanilla biscuits. Gets creamier in time. Almond and pear tart. A refreshing touch of fresh oak. Aromas are pleasantly intertwined.
**Palate:** Smooth, oak is well integrated. Custard and apricots. A light spicy fringe. Lacks a little muscle though.
**Finish:** Drying, green oak shows up.

**7¼ Dave: Decent, but you get the feeling it needs more time to soften down.**
**Nose:** Malty and a little oily: mash tun, bran, bracken and moor. Though there's some soft characters (toasted pineapple, whole nut chocolate, tangerine marmalade) it has a hard edge. Rather blunt.
**Palate:** Less dry. Sweet, creamy, toffee start, then freshly oiled oak, shoe polish and a sudden drying.
**Finish:** Toasted cereal.

## ABERLOUR 15 YEARS OLD, SHERRY WOOD 40%
Single Malt - Speyside

**WHISKY** ⒸRecommended

**8½ Michael: Complex and sophisticated.**
**Nose:** Roses, candyfloss, slightly buttery.
**Palate:** Perfect balance of sherry and the malty, spicy, house character. The two elements are tightly combined, with the spicy flavours emerging slowly: nutmeg, aniseed and emphatic orange-flower.
**Finish:** Liquorice toffee. Mint.

**9 Doug: A biggish-bodied Aberlour which helps to lengthen the complex effects of the double maturation.**
**Nose:** Beautifully mellow, sherryish, grassy with a little marzipan and mint toffee.
**Palate:** Enveloping, creamy and nutty with a teasing sherry and gentle peaty twist. Peppermint prickle.
**Finish:** Long, soothing, with a minty and spicy end.

## ABERLOUR 1976 43%
Single Malt - Speyside

**8 Michael: Had I not known that it was matured in first-fill bourbon barrels I would have guessed that there was some sherry.**
**Nose:** The faintest hint of peat, quickly developing to big heather-honey, then lots of berry-fruit and raisins.
**Palate:** Toffeeish. Apricots. That typical Aberlour nutmeg. Crème brûlée. Anise.
**Finish:** Spicy, with a hint of lemon. Vanilla. Oak.

**8½ Jim: A pleasant and well-measured oldie without blemish but perhaps lacking complexity before the excellent finale.**
**Nose:** Suet and sultanas liberally sprinkled with vanilla.
**Palate:** Dry and spicy start with wave upon wave of encroaching oak.
**Finish:** More vanilla but some pleasant malty tones stretch out the length to a surprising degree.

## ABERLOUR 1988, DISTILLER'S SELECTION 40%
Single Malt - Speyside

**8½ Michael: An astonishingly malty whisky. For someone who wants to taste the eponymous ingredient, this shows it at its best.**
**Nose:** Oaky, nutty, fudgey.
**Palate:** Good depth of deliciously fresh, layered, malty, butterscotch flavours, developing to liquorice-toffee and anise.
**Finish:** Crystalised ginger. Warming.

**7 Jim: To taste, this is a lively malt of pleasing depth. Only the nose somewhat spoils the show.**
**Nose:** Light, malty and vaguely citric, the weight is supplied by some soft sherry tones spoiled slightly by a tad too much sulphur.
**Palate:** Immediate flavour explosion of quite fabulous sweet, buttery malt and richer sherry tones. Just a hint of smoke fills out the middle.
**Finish:** Caramel, sherry and liquorice make for a rich finish. The drier vanillins come in at the death.

## ABERLOUR 1990 40%
Single Malt - Speyside

**8¾ Michael: On this occasion the vintage bottling had the most typical Aberlour character, especially in its spiciness. I also enjoyed its liveliness and complexity.**
**Nose:** Fresh. Momentarily sweet, then cedary and grassy, with a gentle suggestion of peat.
**Palate:** Light to medium. Firm. Smooth. Malty. Lots of flavour development. Nutmeg is very evident.
**Finish:** More spices. Peppery. Some sweetness.

**7½ Dave: Young and light but a bit flat with a wet newspaper note that could be light corkiness.**
**Nose:** Initially quite light and lean. Water is needed to bring out a hot bracken, toffee note with US wood: light hickory, honey and spice. Flat.
**Palate:** A burst of soft toffee, loads of honey and a dry cereal, peanut brittle edginess. A little musty.
**Finish:** Chewy, medium length, a little minty.

## ABERLOUR 1994, BERRY'S OWN SELECTION 46%
Single Malt - Speyside

**8½ Martine: Kicking up your heels as well as soothing. To be sipped far from the city buzz.**
**Nose:** Perfumy. Light and delicate. Floral. Sweet peas, wild rose. Opens on slightly sour fruit. The sour edge is swept out by vanilla and custard.
**Palate:** Drier than expected. Very lively and refreshing. Cooked apples and pears. Almond and apricot pudding. Quite fizzy. Water soothes the feel down.
**Finish:** Steady, dry, quite lingering.

**7½ Dave: A lovely very summery aperitif.**
**Nose:** Light, slightly volatile estery and youthful. Dilute lemon and ginger cordial. With water there's dried banana chips and some fragrant floral aromas.
**Palate:** Clean lifted and perfumed. Elderflower. Quite lacy and fragile.
**Finish:** Vanilla and then the ginger returns.

## ABERLOUR 21 YEARS OLD 43%
Single Malt - Speyside

**8 Michael: Great to see this once-reticent distillery releasing some really expressive bottlings.**
**Nose:** Sherry, oak, polished leather.
**Palate:** Firm, smooth, lightly creamy. Packed with lively flavours: malt, cookies, fruit, mint.
**Finish:** Spicy, rooty, dry, very long.

**7 Jim: 11 years ago I tasted some 10 Years Old Aberlour and wasn't too impressed. It has matured well but not all the kinks have been ironed out, especially towards the finish.**
**Nose:** A first class aroma of honey and sliced almonds. Very sweet for the age with the oak being surprisingly subdued, perhaps by the delicate sherry/apricot fruitiness.
**Palate:** Much drier from the start with the oak steaming in. Fills out in mouth well, with an almost metallic hardness to the malt-honey sweetness, softened only by an oily tang.
**Finish:** Very hard and quite grainy with the malt lengthening out. Perhaps just slightly off key.

## ABERLOUR 30 YEARS OLD 43%
Single Malt - Speyside

**WHISKY** ⒸEditor's choice

**8½ Michael: More sophisticated, especially in the finish. Better balanced, but less voluptuous maltiness.**
**Nose:** Polished leather. Mature, finessed.
**Palate:** Firmly malty. Hint of smoky peat, plus rooty liquorice and anise. Tightly combined flavours.
**Finish:** Surprisingly fresh oak. Sappiness and log fires; warming.

**9 Jim: A really excellent and classy Aberlour showing amazing complexity for its age.**
**Nose:** A faultlessly clean and deep sherry aroma with a mint residue and beautiful lemon notes. Compelling.
**Palate:** Deep, moderately dry throughout with a slow build up of peppery spices and smoke. Malty, grapey succulence with some cocoa bitterness giving extra complexity.
**Finish:** Amazingly long and brilliantly weighted, the fruitiness sweetens the malt gracefully.

## ABERLOUR WAREHOUSE NO.1 59.1%
Single Malt - Speyside

**7¾ Martine: Quite simple and light. But pleasantly refreshing. For a summer evening aperitif.**
**Nose:** Close to a pear eau-de-vie. So fruity. William pears soaked in a vanilla syrup. Alcohol tickles. Some grassy notes. Freshly cut lawn. Garden mint.
**Palate:** Fresh and clean. Keeps a pear eau-devie profile.
**Finish:** Dry. Quickly vanishing.

**7½ Dave: Decent.**
**Nose:** Straw/lawnmower box. Sappy and sugary and slightly metallic note.
**Palate:** Water improves things making it soft and sweet. Very direct.
**Finish:** Clean short, lightly citric.

## ALLT-A-BHAINNE 1992, 9 YEARS OLD, CADENHEAD'S 59.4%
Single Malt - Speyside

**7½ Michael: A rare opportunity to serve this summery whisky.**
**Nose:** Heathery. Ferny. Forest floor after rain. Sweet wild flowers.
**Palate:** Fiddlehead ferns with butter.
**Finish:** Green peppercorns. Quite assertive.

**7 Dave: A well-made light and clean dram. Will Pernod get rid of this distillery as well?**
**Nose:** Clean, fresh and lively. Pretty estery: flowers, pears, dolly mixture. All high-toned with some dried grass. Malty note with water.
**Palate:** Soft, quite sweet (sugared almond), light and fairly creamy spirit.
**Finish:** Short. Immature.

## ALLT-A-BHAINNE 1995 10 YEARS OLD, JAMES MACARTHUR 58.9%
Single Malt - Speyside

**7 Martine: Quite harsh and burning. Alcohol is not tamed at all.**
**Nose:** Floral and citrussy. Rose syrup, lime. Quite prickly. Green oak. Seems young. A soapy note.
**Palate:** Sweet. Grassy then getting dry and spicy. Zesty. Alcohol is quite aggressive. Peppermint.
**Finish:** Dry and grassy. Fresh chewed stem.

**6 Michael: An aggressive young punk of a dram: Sid McVicious? It might have a gastronomic application as a marinade for oily fish or perhaps in a dressing.**
**Nose:** Acetic acid with some butteriness (should be a Hollandaise, but it's not). Underlying menthol and acetone.
**Palate:** Crude. Alcoholic. Intensely acetic. Tropical fruit.
**Finish:** Reluctant to swallow: Sweet and bitter.

## AN CNOC 13 YEARS OLD, LIMITED EDITION HIGHLAND SELECTION 46%
Single Malt - Highland

**7¾ Michael: A pale, shimmery gold dram with flavours one expects from a bigger, darker, whisky. Slightly odd, but enjoyable. Could be a flavoured spirit from a little-known, newly independent republic in Central Asia.**
**Nose:** Light, dry. Slight burnt grass. Then lemongrass and mint.
**Palate:** Lightly syrupy. Herbal, minty, rummy.
**Finish:** Hint of cloves. Warming. Soothing. Very long.

**8 Dave: Lifted and aromatic. Who said malt whisky had to be all about smoke and bluster?**
**Nose:** Fragrant and soft with lemon sherbet, crisp apple/apple blossom. Long and soft.
**Palate:** Soft with creamy notes. The fragrant spirit and the (apple) wood in superb balance. Attractive and delightful.
**Finish:** Dry then syrup sponge pudding.

## ANTIQUARY 12 YEARS OLD 40%
Blended - Scotland

**7¾ Michael: Feminine. Elegant. Having talked myself into an oriental mind-set, I begin to wonder whether this whisky would accompany some Asian dishes.**
**Nose:** Faintly peaty, herbal. Chinese tea. Jasmine.
**Palate:** Smooth, dry maltiness. Perhaps that tea was Lapsang Souchong. Then sweeter flavours develop. Darjeeling? Eventually, a honeyish sweetness.
**Finish:** Flowery. Crisp, clean.

**8 Dave: On the lighter side but attractive.**
**Nose:** Clean and initally dry nose which sweetens up in time: vanilla/butter, light spice and cereal.
**Palate:** Fairly dry start: spicy and nutty with lemon-accented fruit then a creamy soft centre. A lovely medium-rich rich nuttiness. Evolves well.
**Finish:** Soft with a spicy tingle.

## ANTIQUARY 21 YEARS OLD 43%
Blended - Scotland

**8 Michael: Robust, hearty, embracing. Not much subtlety, but it knows its own mind. Very enjoyable. I imagine this with a decadent meal in Tangier.**
**Nose:** Sweet. Lemongrass. Honeydew melon. Sweet lime.
**Palate:** Big body. Hard toffee. Liquorice. Juicy, with a suggestion of anise. Lots of late flavour development.
**Finish:** Floral (jasmine?) but firm and gripping.

**8½ Dave: Complex and ever-changing.**
**Nose:** Elegant and complex. There's an instant turfy/peaty lift mixed with moist fruit cake, nuts, cooked fruits, dark honey and burnt sugar.
**Palate:** Sweet toffee/treacle start. Juicy malt and soft grains with puffs of smoke give it an extra layer of complexity.
**Finish:** Long, quite nutty and lightly smoky.

## ARDBEG 10 YEARS OLD 46%
Single Malt - Islay

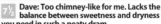

**8½ Michael: Not from a particularly peaty period, but packed with Ardbeg's other flavours. Wonderfully distinctive.**
**Nose:** Tar-covered rope.
**Palate:** Tar-like. Medicinal. Seaweedy. Salty. Behind all of those dry flavours, a background of light, clean, fresh, maltiness and lemon skin fruitiness.
**Finish:** Sandy, peppery.

**9 Dave: A punch in the chops from a stroppy Islay middleweight. Flavour-packed yet delicate.**
**Nose:** Astoundingly smoky, yet delicate with subtle tarry notes behind. With water the smoke dies a little and raisin and caramelised apple notes emerge.
**Palate:** An immediate waft of peat smoke. Full, robustly flavoured with turf and lapsang souchong tea.
**Finish:** Salty, long and filled with fragrant peat reek.

## ARDBEG 10 YEARS OLD 46%
Single Malt - Islay

**4½ Martine: The same phenolic profile as in very young but more disciplined and rounder.**
**Nose:** Phenolic. Burning tyre. Soon covered by more marine scents. Something mineral, brown seaweeds, a light note of fragrant sea air. The distillery character shining.
**Palate:** Sweet and velvety. The peat comes through smoke and a dry sooty feel. A touch of smoked haddock.
**Finish:** Dry, sooty, fresh.

**4 Dave: The feeling is of better integration and balance.**
**Nose:** Overtly peaty, sweeter than the Young One, lime marmalade, oak, floral, peat fire smouldering on the beach. With water, light soot and a balancing creaminess.
**Palate:** Sweet start. Phenols come in middle and towards the back, adding weight to the middle palate. Smoke moving into medicinal flavours.
**Finish:** Oatcake, smoke, lingering.

*Peat rating out of 5*

## ARDBEG 15 YEARS OLD, OLD MALT CASK 50%
Single Malt - Islay

**7½ Dave: Too chimney-like for me. Lacks the balance between sweetness and dryness you need in such a peaty dram.**
**Nose:** Charred embers/charcoal/coal dust shifting into juniper and pine. Lightly smoked fish.
**Palate:** A dry and smoky start. Foggy smoke that knocks back the sweetness which is there: sultanas packed inside a baked apple.
**Finish:** Dry and smoky again.

**8½ Arthur: Took a while to show its true colours as an Ardbeg, but developed into a good example.**
**Nose:** Dried fruit, rum butter and mixed peel. An occasional waft of struck flint, morphs into a clearer smokiness. Mint toffee, lint bandages and citrus.

**Palate:** Sultanas, wood smoke, apple, ship rope and Christmas pudding spice.
**Finish:** Smokiness and dry rope.

## ARDBEG 17 YEARS OLD 40%
Single Malt - Islay

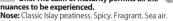

**8½ Michael: Not the most muscular Ardbeg, but still robust.**
**Nose:** Assertive, briny, seaweedy, tar-like. Hint of sulphur.
**Palate:** Sweetish. Cereal grains, oil, gorse. Tightly combined flavours.
**Finish:** Oily. Lemon skins. Freshly-ground white pepper. Very appetising.

**9 Jim: I admit to being a little biased here as I did have a hand in putting this whisky together. But I must say I adore it for its wonderful balance.**
**Nose:** A gentle, seductive sweet peat leads the way to a complex arrival of malt and vanilla.
**Palate:** Soft and languid at first, brilliant chewy malt and cocoa adds the depth and balance.
**Finish:** There is a delightful level of residual peat which ensures a long finish.

## ARDBEG 1974, CONNOISSEUR'S CHOICE 43%
Single Malt - Islay

**9 Michael: Less boisterous than The Young One. The calm of maturity permits all the nuances to be experienced.**
**Nose:** Classic Islay peatiness. Spicy. Fragrant. Sea air.
**Palate:** Dusty. Earthy. Iron-ish. The flavours of a dunnage warehouse.
**Finish:** Sea spray. Wet earth. Seaweed.

**8½ Dave: A classic Ardbeg.**
**Nose:** Fragrant and smoked. Coal bunkers and rose bushes. Perfumed wood, apple loft, peat smoke in background, antiseptic, coal tar.
**Palate:** Dry, firm. Sweet oak and a burst of smoke. Timbers on a beach. Marine notes. Seashells. Great flowing feel.
**Finish:** Mixing sweet and dry.

## ARDBEG 1975 58.1%
Single Malt - Islay

**9 Michael: Ardbeg is one of my great favourites, and this is one of the best versions I have tasted recently.**
**Nose:** The complexity starts here. Heathery, rooty, burned notes. Fruity (applewood barbecue, grilled tomatoes, roasted peppers?) Hint of the typical Ardbeg 'leafy bonfire' character. Tar. Rope. Seaweed.
**Palate:** Sappy, earthy, peppery.
**Finish:** Salt. Lemon skins. Barbecue smokiness. Very long indeed.

## ARDBEG 1976, DISTILLERY MANAGER'S CHOICE 56%
Single Malt - Islay

**9 Michael: Real Ardbeg peatiness and smokiness.**
**Nose:** Driftwood bonfires on the beach, then home to a hot, steamy bath in coal-tar soap.
**Palate:** Syrupy, sensuous, tar-like.
**Finish:** Charcoal. Perfumy. Fresh. Therapeutic.

**9½ Jim: The nose may be a little disappointing, but in all a glorious experience not to be missed.**
**Nose:** Heavily oaked and richly sherried, salty heavy weight aromas. Prickly spice adds to the aroma.
**Palate:** Absolutely mind-blowing. The sweet peat is dense and chewy but also offers lighter smoky tones, too and eventually oak and iodine.
**Finish:** Sweet and toasty, some hickory and highly roasted coffee blends well with the massive peat.

## ARDBEG 1976, SINGLE CASK COMMITTEE BOTTLING 51%
Single Malt - Islay

**8¾ Gavin: A 'no bones about it' Islay whisky, and a fine example of Ardbeg.**
**Nose:** Assertive, with soot, dry sherry, raisins and claret.
**Palate:** Dry, lots of smoke-both wood and peat, aniseed and fishermen's ropes.
**Finish:** Long and loud.

**8½ Dave: Not exactly discreet...but it's Ardbeg!**
**Nose:** Mature, liquorous and sweet. There's prunes, coffee grounds, cream sherry and dried mushroom; funkier notes of moss, creosote, bung cloth, resin and chimney smoke. A big bugger.
**Palate:** Immediate, all-enveloping smoke. Rich, mature with good grip: dried fig, turf, nuts. Mellow.
**Finish:** Big, intense, smoky. Touch of rubber.

## ARDBEG 1977 46%
Single Malt - Islay

**9 Michael: Cleaner, more lemony and oily, and less assertive, than the 24 Years Old duty free edition.**
**Nose:** As it warms, bonfires on the beach. Boats caulked with pitch. The tar-like Ardbeg trademark
**Palate:** Light-bodied but oily. Clings to the tongue. Lemony sweetness. Barbecue wood.
**Finish:** Clean coal-tar. Warming. Lingering.

**9¼ Dave: A stunner.**
**Nose:** Complex and strangely delicate. Seashore aromas but also fruit. Tangerine, marmalade, cream.
**Palate:** Complex and mouth filling. A lovely soft start with that elegant fruit. The smoke builds in power as it moves through the mouth, drying as it goes.
**Finish:** Immense. Incredibly long. You'll taste it the next day.

## ARDBEG 1980 KILDALTON 57.6%
Single Malt - Islay

**7¼ Michael: Where's the peat-smoke? Not very Islay.**
**Nose:** Nutty. Marzipan.
**Palate:** Very sweet. Develops some dried fruit. Nutty maltiness. A hint of lemon peel. Saffron.
**Finish:** Quick. Hot.

**8¼ Dave: A substantial drink with an all-enveloping charm.**
**Nose:** Hefty with toasty oak, sweet mandarin, orange blossom, oat, then piney notes. A substantial elegant nose.
**Palate:** Smooth and silky. The orange reappears with honey and cooked fruits. Concentrated and rich.
**Finish:** Long, silky.

## ARDBEG 1990, CONNOISSEUR'S CHOICE 40%
Single Malt - Islay

**8½ Michael: The palate seemed almost disappointingly cosy, but the wildness of Islay was recalled in the finish.**
**Nose:** Expressive. Fresh smoke and, again, the aromas of the seashore. Tar, caulked ropes, weatherbeaten wooden boats on a pebbled beach.
**Palate:** Oily, smooth, creamy. Clean, fresh, maltiness. Rounded with a touch of sherry?
**Finish:** Light leafy spiciness. Long and warming.

**7¾ Dave: All of Ardbeg and some more. Uncompromising.**
**Nose:** Intense and smoky: tar, bitumen, beach bonfires, drying seaweed. Mouth watering. A lean and dry young pup.
**Palate:** Bone-dry to start, the smoke parches the throat, saved by a light tickle of fruit.
**Finish:** Tarry and intense with glimmer of seaweed.

## ARDBEG 1992 12 YEARS OLD, RUM FINISH, PARK AVENUE LIQUORS, DOUGLAS LAING 50%
Single Malt - Islay

**8½ Michael: With smoked salmon and a squeeze of lemon.**
**Nose:** Fragrant. Saffron.
**Palate:** Delicate. Slips down like a freshly shucked oyster. Sweet, then smoky, then toasty.
**Finish:** Sharply appetising acidity.

**8¼ Dave: Good balance between heavy phenols and sweet creamy oak. Along, generous, palate filler.**
**Nose:** Cooked fruit, light medicinal notes, fish oil, black olives in brine, dried seaweed. Vanilla.
**Palate:** Layered flavours. Starts sweet (banana) then Savlon, seaweed, tar-covered pebbles, with perfumed smoke on top. Balanced.
**Finish:** Tarry. Peat.

## ARDBEG 24 YEARS OLD, OLD MALT CASK 50%
Single Malt - Islay

**9** **Michael: Full of flavour and complexity, but less challenging than some Ardbegs. More peaty than the bottling reviewed among new releases. Some woodiness.**
**Nose:** Seaweed. Tar. Peat.
**Palate:** Starts assertively dry, but quickly reveals a soft centre. Tar-like. Sweetish. Oily. Lemon.
**Finish:** Dry, Drying, Sandy, Warming, Long. Notably big finish.

**8¾** **Dave: Slightly sweeter than the 1977 but equally good. The sulphury note lets it down.**
**Nose:** Soft. Light sherry. It's like a box of spent matches next to a slumbering peat fire.
**Palate:** Sweet, almost oily, start then comes a lovely interplay between pulpy fruit and dry sooty smoke.
**Finish:** Very long. Smoky chimney.

## ARDBEG 28 YEARS OLD, THE ARDBEGGEDDON 1972, SHERRY CASK, OLD MALT CASK 48.4%
Single Malt - Islay

**9¼** **Michael: One of the best Ardbegs I have ever tasted. Full range of the distillery's typical flavours, lyrically combined.**
**Nose:** Rich, soft, oily, smokiness. Very appetising.
**Palate:** A dexterous interplay of grassy peatiness; oiliness; just lurking suggestions of lemony fruitiness, sherry and oak.
**Finish:** Lively, evocative, maritime flavours. A long walk on a sandy beach, with a vigorous, salty spray.

**7¾** **Dave: For true believers only. The most intense, full-on Ardbeg I've ever come across.**
**Nose:** Dry, amazingly intense. Incredibly concentrated aromas: tarry rope, peat oil, lanolin, red herrings dangling from hooks in the smokehouse. Huge.
**Palate:** Sweet, concentrated, pent-up start. Then lime, lanolin, coal tar soap and all those weird aromas.
**Finish:** Bone dry.

## ARDBEG 6 YEARS OLD, COMMITTEE BOTTLING 58.9%
Single Malt - Islay

**8** **Michael: I like young Islays, but this hyperactive whisky is just too frisky. The flavours need time to meld. Even with those shortcomings, it is an Ardbeg …**
**Nose:** Deceptively restrained.
**Palate:** Spicy. Saffron. Garden mint. Lemon juice. Tea.
**Finish:** Smoky.

**8½** **Dave: A swaggering young dude.**
**Nose:** Intense and vibrant. Lime zest, green grass, smoked fish and peat fires. Quite dry.
**Palate:** Initially seems like an explosion in the peat shed, but has great balance: sweet centred, malt, citrus. Fresh and exciting.
**Finish:** Oatcakes and smoke. Long.

## ARDBEG AIRIGH NAM BEIST 1990 16 YEARS OLD 46%
Single Malt - Islay

**8** **Dave: A welcome addition to the range.**
**Nose:** Weighty, phenolic. Foggy coal smoke, then more lifted and complex. Arbroath smokie, tar.
**Palate:** A lick of cream brings to mind an alcoholic Cullen skink. Shows maturity along with toasted almond, biscuity cereal. Not overly heavy, a good tongue-coating texture with persistent smoke.
**Finish:** Caramelised, smooth, then smoke returns.

**9** **Arthur: For all its chest-beating, smoking-gun aroma, the palate is softer and more approachable. Compelling.**
**Nose:** Ashy, smoky and lemony. Seaweed, apple, mint and tea tree oil. Intense, snarling and complex.
**Palate:** Not quite the assault I'd expected but delicious all the same. Lots of sweetness, tea tree, ash and a vegetal/autumn leaf flavour.
**Finish:** Smoked meats and a persistent seaweed.

## ARDBEG ALMOST THERE 54%
Single Malt - Islay

**8** **Dave: This is seamless stuff and despite the smokiness is unshowy. Only 9 Years Old? Great things are on their way.**
**Nose:** Smoky with seaweed and burned wood. Slightly vegetal/ eucalypt with a hint of firelighter.

**Palate:** Immediate hit of smoke, cubeb berries but then a silky sweet mid-palate with touches of citrus. Then the smoke returns.
**Finish:** Salty and a little tann.

**9** **Arthur: A breathless, smoky charge with great clarity of flavour.**
**Nose:** Woodsmoke, raisiny fudge and burning field stubble. Smoked almonds.
**Palate:** A real witches' cauldron. The smokiness is very dense. With time green apple, lime and Werther's Original caramels come through.
**Finish:** Fading smoke and some pepper, but not as intense and lasting as I'd expected.

## ARDBEG LORD OF THE ISLES 46%
Single Malt - Islay

**3½** **Martine: The less phenolic of all the Ardbeg tasted in this session. Merging with oak, phenols have developed an enticing and original bouquet.**
**Nose:** Very nutty. Almond. Resiny. Oak is not assertive but, combined with peat phenols, brings out balsamic aromas. Eucalyptus. Very fragrant. Tarred timber.
**Palate:** Sweet, unctuous. Barley sugar. Toasted oatmeal. Tar losanges. Peat merges in the back.
**Finish:** Dry, spicy, smoked salty almonds.

**3½** **Dave: Peat is a supporting element. A reflective dram, looking back at its gallus youth.**
**Nose:** Mature, complex with balsamic notes. Rosemary thrown on a barbecue, marmalade, dried leather, apple skin. A hint of smoke given by moor burn, moss-covered wall. Finesse.
**Palate:** Layered smoke with complex mix of dried fruits and peels. Sweet, dry with a peatiness most expressive on the finish.
**Finish:** Perfumed. Kipper? Fading.

*Peat rating out of 5*

## ARDBEG LORD OF THE ISLES, 25 YEARS OLD 46%
Single Malt - Islay

**9** **Michael: Lots of flavour development, complexity and refinement. Very elegant, but where is the clamour of battle?**
**Nose:** Sea air and smokiness – evocative sootiness.
**Palate:** Silky. The touch of fruitiness, usually reminiscent of lemons, is sweeter, with a momentary suggestion of cherries. The flavours become almondy and walnut-like, then rooty and peppery.
**Finish:** Long, haughty.

**8¼** **Dave: Mellower than you'd expect but beautifully balanced.**
**Nose:** Gentle and complex: orange/marmalade, sponge cake with pink icing, calfskin leather, angelica and smoke.
**Palate:** Soft and fragrant, light leathery notes then a smoky bonfire.
**Finish:** Light medicinal (Savlon/Germolene) then smoke.

## ARDBEG LORD OF THE ISLES, 25 YEARS OLD 46%
Single Malt - Islay

**8½** **Michael: Becomes more complex with age. I admire its style, but hanker for the bravado of the younger Ardbegs.**
**Nose:** Fragrant. Sea air. Distant smoke.
**Palate:** More fruitiness than any other Ardbeg. Candied orange peel and cherries. Walnuts, almonds. Marzipan. Bittersweet. Spicy. The roundness of flavours masks the peat.
**Finish:** Long, haughty. Steely.

**8½** **Dave: All of Ardbeg's uncompromising directness with extra complexity.**
**Nose:** Phenolic: sooty smoke, beach bonfire, creosote, ozone, brine but with some sweet, biscuity malt. Complex.
**Palate:** Quite dry, but enough oiliness and sweet fruit to balance the sootiness. Good balance.
**Finish:** Long, firm.

## ARDBEG OLOROSO FINISH, CASK 4704 47.2%
Single Malt - Islay

**8¼** **Michael: Nothing too elaborate here. Good honest Islay whisky. Have this with breakfast and you will live forever, or feel that way.**
**Nose:** Fresh sea air. Soft smoke. Both restrained.
**Palate:** Tongue-coating. Honeyed. Sweetcure smoked bacon. Slight laver-bread or spinach.
**Finish:** Spicy. HP Sauce, gingery.

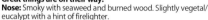

**8¼ Dave: Not for the fainthearted. A hairy beast.**
Nose: Dull greenish amber hue. Rich, mellow and well peated. Kippers, wet coal, pipe smoke, walnut. Slightly medicinal. It's standing beside the Port Ellen maltings going at full blast while drinking a glass of dry Oloroso. Development moves into balsamic notes, furniture polish, violet. Complex.
Palate: Robust and smoky from the start. Ash like, suggesting maturity. Still sweet in centre.
Finish: Treacle and some tar.

### ARDBEG PROVENANCE, 1974, BOTTLED 1998, 24 YEARS OLD 55.6%
Single Malt - Islay

WHISKY *Editor's choice*

**9 Michael: Rich and creamy, with huge flavour development.**
Nose: Sea air. Seaweed. Oak, rope, leather.
Palate: Malty, toffeeish, sweet, fruity. Barbecue wood. Mustard. Salt.
Finish: Distinctly sappy, smoky and very warming.

**9¾ Jim: This is the finest whisky I have ever tasted. As close to perfection as makes no difference.**
Nose: The peat courses through the aroma, in perfect balance and harmony with the oily malt.
Palate: The malt is soft at first but then, the peatiness gathers pace and intensity until it positively glows.
Finish: The oak Bourbon-malt-peat-cocoa characters all ebb and flow but is joined by a late fruity ripeness and a sprinkling of peppers.

### ARDBEG UIGEADAIL 54.2%
Single Malt - Islay

WHISKY *Editor's choice*

**9¼ Michael: The elemental opposite of the sophisticated Lord of the Isles.**
Nose: Intensely smoky. Dry, clean, tangy smoke. Like standing downwind of the barbecue while steaks are char-grilled on the beach.
Palate: Firm, very smooth, then explodes on the tongue.
Finish: Hot. Alcoholic. A shock to the system.

**8½ Dave: Some dram!**
Nose: Sweet yet pungently smoky: lime marmalade and peat fires on the beach, malt, cocoa powder, salted herring.
Palate: Rich, concentrated and powerful. Sooty with light tarry/liquorice touches. The lime returns. Great presence but subtle in its own way.
Finish: Long. Biscuity malt.

### ARDBEG VERY YOUNG 58.3%
Single Malt - Islay

**4½ Martine: great interplay of sweet and dry flavours. More phenolic at start, smoke is more integrated than in Bowmore or Caol Ila.**
Nose: Spirity, prickly. A definite phenolic expression. Boat tar, coal dust, kippers. With lighter grassy and herbal aromas. Smoke from the kiln with a pungent peat scent.
Palate: Same sweet maltiness. Then a huge smoky taste, a salty feel on the tongue.
Finish: Dry, spicy, with a light smoky "leftover".

**4½ Dave: Not yet opened up. Dry smoke, malt and some sweetness still sizing each other up.**
Nose: Intense and pungent with dry smoke and a cereal edge. Dried seaweed, into soot and light creosote, slightly Arbroath smokie. Under this is a sweet zesty lime note, Oddfellows.
Palate: Intensely phenolic. A fug of dry smoke hits dominating a mix of salt and sweet. Soot, lanolin and white pepper. Gallus as we say in Glasgow.
Finish: Hot, smoky, lingering. Dry.

*Peat rating out of 5*

### ARDMORE 1977 30 YEARS OLD, OLD MALT CASK 50%
Single Malt - Speyside

**7¾ Dave: Has maturity and presence. Ardmore: a complete package.**
Nose: Warm. Cow's breath and sweet hay with a hint of scented smoke, lemon. Mature. Becomes fresher and greener in time, hedge clippings.
Palate: Clean, leafy with an acidic energy. Good orchard fruits in, then hazelnut and light smoke. Good balance.
Finish: Tight and slightly smoked.

**7½ Martine: Oak is prevailing, especially on the palate. Lacks balance and charm.**
Nose: An unwelcome note of damp wood at start which gives way to wet straw then citrus fruit (orange pulp). Takes time to open up. Grated coconut.
Palate: Smooth at start then getting drier and slightly sour. Grippy oak, Touch of leather.
Finish: Dry, spicy (paprika).

### ARDMORE 1985, GORDON & MACPHAIL 40%
Single Malt - Speyside

**7½ Michael: I have always thought of Ardmore as having a rather bluff character, but on this occasion I found it both welcoming and comforting.**
Nose: Carbolic soap. Smoke, beeswax, church-like.
Palate: Flavours tightly bound together, and reluctant to unfurl. At first, a retrained, malty sweetness, then suddenly a surge of incense-like smokiness, this happens more easily after a dash of water.
Finish: Cereal-grain oiliness. Fairly dry, but soothing.

**7½ Doug: Big and old fashioned feel.**
Nose: Heady, fruity and faintly medicinal.
Palate: Big, malty, sherryish with background sooty smoke.
Finish: Spicy, smoky and dry.

### ARDMORE 1987, GORDON & MACPHAIL 40%
Single Malt - Speyside

**8¼ Martine: Very elegant and fragrant. As an apéritif with melon, basil and Parma ham.**
Nose: Soft, sweet and tender. Lots of fruit (orange, grapefruit, almond). Hint of hawthorn blossom.
Palate: Smart combination of fruit and oak, uncovering peat on the move. Mouthfilling and appetite-arousing.
Finish: Clean, dry, crisp and gently smoky.

**7¼ Dave: All the qualities of this distillery: fragrance, good feel, little smoke but not one of the best.**
Nose: Freshly-turned earth, apple blossom, a little smoke. Fragrant, medium-bodied. Water brings out apple wood, cream and a citric lift. Smoke remains.
Palate: Light start, good mid-palate weight but not very broad or overly complex. Smoke and soft attractive fruits.
Finish: Short.

### ARDMORE 1990 CASK STRENGTH, GORDON & MACPHAIL 55.8%
Single Malt - Speyside

**7½ Michael: Starts slowly, and seems uncertain as to where it is going.**
Nose: Slight peat. Burnt wood. Faintly astringent.
Palate: On the light side for this whisky. The big, creamy maltiness that I expect in Ardmore seems to have attenuated instead to a papery, metallic, thinness.
Finish: Quick. Astringent.

**8 Dave: A good example from an underrated distillery. Now all we need is an Allied bottling.**
Nose: Light. Sweet eating apples (Cox), crusty bread, banana, sage. It's a bloody picnic! Perfumed with light smoke and a vegetal note. Hint of linoleum.
Palate: Soft. Medium bodied. Cooked apple, lemon and lime zest and sweet spices. Understated.
Finish: A wisp of peat smoke.

## ARDMORE 1990, CASK STRENGTH, GORDON & MACPHAIL 55.8%
Single Malt - Speyside

**8** **Martine: A hidden complexity on the palate. A malt to give you a tender kick on "one of those days, you know …"**
**Nose:** Floral, tangy. Honeysuckle. Green oak. Lemon balm. A briny hint. Develops into creamier aromas. Vanilla waffles.
**Palate:** Unexpectedly smooth and sweet. Grassy, malty with a touch of bitter almond. Pear drops. Dries out on a dusty hint.
**Finish:** Sweet, long, almondy. Touch of mint.

**7¾** **Dave: Jim Beam, will you PLEASE do what Allied failed to and release Ardmore as a single malt? It's criminal this distillery isn't better known.**
**Nose:** An oily peatiness then comes mustard powder and freshly bleached lino floor and a hint of rubber (not necessarily a bad thing).
**Palate:** Initially more on the lifted, lemony, estery side undercut with smoke. Very sweet with good balance. With water the smoke returns.
**Finish:** Oily, phenolic.

## ARDMORE 1990, GORDON & MACPHAIL 43%
Single Malt - Speyside

**7½** **Martine: A pleasant dram, especially with a splash of water but lacks nerve and buoyancy.**
**Nose:** Perfumy. Delicate. Garden mint and honeycomb. A touch of smoke. Apple juice and dry hay when diluted.
**Palate:** Smooth at start but a bit too soft. The delicacy of the nose is not there. Malty with a toffeish mintiness. A cardboard touch underneath. Appley with water.
**Finish:** Not very exciting. Clean though.

**7¾** **Dave: The smoke is a surprise, but well put together.**
**Nose:** Light with distinct smoke. Behind there are fragrant white fruits, crab apple, crystallised fruits. In time, a light nuttiness.
**Palate:** Soft sweet start the peat held in check by balancing acidity. Fresh, lightly smoky and clean.
**Finish:** Sweet, with smoke drifting by.

## ARDMORE 1990, SIGNATORY 46%
Single Malt - Speyside

**7¾** **Michael: Robust as ever, but much more peatiness than I associate with this distillery. Oaky, too, for a relatively young whisky.**
**Nose:** Fresh, fragrant, peat-smoke.
**Palate:** Peaty, tar-like, against an oily, cereal-grain sweetness.
**Finish:** Rooty, liquorice. Medicinal. Soothing. Extraordinarily long.

**8¾** **Dave: What will happen now that Allied has ruined the new make by ripping out the coal fires?**
**Nose:** Light but complex: an apple orchard after rain with pear, baked apple, cream and raisin and a balancing smoky sootiness.
**Palate:** There's lots going on: butter, cream, apple, fruit blossom, white pepper. Great balance and youthful vigour.
**Finish:** Long sooty, kiln.

## ARDMORE 1994 11 YEARS OLD, SINGLE MALTS OF SCOTLAND 60.8%
Single Malt - Speyside

**7¾** **Arthur: Speyside you say, eh? A real region buster, and I loved that sootiness.**
**Nose:** Seaweed, creosote, and fish. Potent, sweet and sour. With water there are jelly sweets and silage, horse dung and fag ash.
**Palate:** Sweet, peaty, and a little coal tar soap.
**Finish:** Dry and ashy.

**7¾** **Dave: Thanks for bottling this Sukhinder, now, Jim Beam...follow that!!**
**Nose:** Light and perfumed top notes (green apple, lemon zest, lily) with some sweet hay, then comes a smokiness like burning stubble. Black pepper.
**Palate:** Sweet floral start, an rounded centre mixing grass (silage), smoke and a dusty note like angelica. Some coconut.
**Finish:** Smoked chilli.

## ARDMORE, SCOTT'S SELECTION 58.1%
Single Malt - Speyside

**7½** **Martine: Not a model of subtlety but a well-knitted character, in the light heavyweight category.**
**Nose:** Assertive. Aniseed. Artichoke. Acacia flowers. Green fruit. Vetyver. Lingering peat in the back. Straw. Alcohol tingles.

**Palate:** Sweeter than expected. Oily. Thick. Very refreshing. Grated lemon. Liquorice mingled with toffee.
**Finish:** Peppery. Dry. Bitter chocolate.

**7** **Dave: Can't get hugely excited.**
**Nose:** Fennel seed and lemon. A twiggy, slightly grubby note.
**Palate:** Very sweet in the centre with some demerara sugar, slivered almond.
**Finish:** Earthy.

## THE ARRAN MALT COGNAC FINISH 58.6%
Single Malt - Island (non Islay)

**7½** **Michael: I have observed few happy marriages between whisky and Cognac. Perhaps the rivalry is just too obvious.**
**Nose:** Toffee and chocolate.
**Palate:** Lightly creamy. Becoming abrasive and hot.
**Finish:** Snappy. Somewhat aggressive.

**7** **Dave: French oak can be pretty aggressive. Here it's got a vice-like grip on what is a gentle fragrant spirit.**
**Nose:** Fragrant, exotic, nose. Dried apple. Incense and grass. Dusty with water.
**Palate:** Fairly strong oakiness. One-dimensional and slightly tannic.
**Finish:** Cooked apple. Nutty.

## THE ARRAN MALT, GORDON'S DRAM 46%
Single Malt - Island (non Islay)

**7½** **Dave: A gentle and sweet farewell to one of the gentlest and sweetest men in the industry. Farewell Gordon, we'll miss you.**
**Nose:** Sweet and slightly malty. Wheat chaff, green oak, banana skin, boiled sweets. Good nutty concentration and a hint of dried grass.
**Palate:** Light honey and macadamia nut and a hint of barley sugar. The middle is little lacking in power.
**Finish:** Light malt.

**9** **Martine: Takes you on a wonderful sensory journey. Like walking on an orange orchard.**
**Nose:** Perfumy. Citrussy. Lime and citron (cédrat). Touch of orange blossom. Delicate and intriguing. Opens up on sweet orange marmalade.
**Palate:** Rich, deep. Coating. Releases a full basket of fruit: the citrus fruit captured on the nose and also exotic fruit wrapped in a fresh minty mist.
**Finish:** Everlasting. Sensuous. Delicately spicy.

## AUCHENTOSHAN 10 YEARS OLD 40%
Single Malt - Lowland

**WHISKY MAGAZINE Recommended**

**8½** **Michael: Very expressive when young – as might be expected from a classic Lowlander.**
**Nose:** Perfumes of lemongrass, linseed oil and vanilla.
**Palate:** Zest of lemon, marshmallow. Sweet but not cloying.
**Finish:** Vanilla, perfumy. Good balance, nicely rounded. Soothing. Long.

**8½** **Jim: A highly sophisticated dram. Intensely malty. Has improved enormously over the last few years.**
**Nose:** Lively and enticing: soft peppers, citrus and oak. Superb.
**Palate:** Surprisingly oily for a triple-distilled malt. Mouthwatering fresh barley and a superb crisp, slightly sweet malt-chocolate interplay – like a Malteser candy.
**Finish:** A sweet malt glow.

## AUCHENTOSHAN 10 YEARS OLD 40%
Single Malt - Lowland

**8½** **Michael: At 10 years, Auchentoshan makes an expressive, eloquent claim to being the classic Lowlander.**
**Nose:** Scenty. Definite linseed. Lemon grass. Vanilla.
**Palate:** Light, soft, oily, mashmallow-like. Good flavour development. From lemony to cedary.
**Finish:** Rounded. Soothing, long.

**6¾** **Dave: Undemanding but pleasant.**
**Nose:** Loght, crunchy and very malty: wholemeal bread, bran flakes, then an intense orange zestiness.
**Palate:** Clean, pretty and citric, with a sudden drying sensation from halfway.
**Finish:** Crisp and clean.

## AUCHENTOSHAN 10 YEARS OLD 40%
Single Malt - Lowland

**7** **Arthur: Lots of American Oak, and a super clean character. Nowt wrong, but not quite enough right.**
**Nose:** Marzipan, quince, apples, peach slices and the top of a crème brûlée.
**Palate:** Vanilla, apples, and chewy toasted oak.
**Finish:** A tinny bloodiness.

**7½** **Dave: A malty nose but balanced and quite sweet on the palate. A drinkable session dram.**
**Nose:** Light. Wholemeal bread/dry grass/bran/Ryvita, with some fresh soft fruits behind (raspberry). Brown boot polish, freshly baked bread.
**Palate:** Light still, but with more fruit. Vanilla and caramelised fruits. Good silky, rounded, feel.
**Finish:** Smooth, liquorous.

## AUCHENTOSHAN 10 YEARS OLD, JAMES MACARTHUR 64.2%
Single Malt - Lowland

**8¼** **Michael: I have not previously encountered such a full expression of Auchentoshan, but the style suits the whisky.**
**Nose:** Perfumery. Light vanilla. A suggestion of tangerines. A hint of very dark chocolate.
**Palate:** Rich. Cream-filled pralines. Hazelnuts.
**Finish:** Gingery. Spicy.

**7** **Dave: Sweet and simple.**
**Nose:** Very citric: tangerine, lemon, almost orange muscat, with light malt. Sadly, water drives the top notes away leaving mealy malt.
**Palate:** Sweet. Orange jelly. The sweetness stays alongside the malt. There's also a slight metallic edge.
**Finish:** Crisp.

## AUCHENTOSHAN 15 YEARS OLD, DEWAR RATTRAY 59%
Single Malt - Lowland

**8** **Martine: A well-balanced dram, as malty as fruity with a luscious toffee tempting character.**
**Nose:** Biscuity. Shortbreads. Oak comes through. Tangerine, orange icecream. Rum toffee.
**Palate:** Delicate sweet maltiness at start. Orange blossom. Wood is well integrated. Vanilla mascarpone mousse.
**Finish:** Long, lingering, with a citrus touch and ginger in the back.

**7** **Dave: A bit flabby and dry.**
**Nose:** Bread mix/malted grain still steaming from the oven. Rich with peach stone. With water a bung cloth note, eccles cake, stewed milky tea.
**Palate:** Flowers, privet then bread flour. Moves increasingly towards this dusty dry malty note.
**Finish:** Raisin.

## AUCHENTOSHAN 17 YEARS OLD, BORDEAUX WINE 51%
Single Malt - Lowland

**8½** **Martine: The wine finish brings in sweetness and fruitiness but without masking the delicate grassiness and lightness of the Lowland style. A real cracker, perfect for a wake up call.**
**Nose:** Grassy and floral. Meadow flowers. Bursting with spices. Gently toasted hazelnuts. Greengage jam. Opening up custardy notes.
**Palate:** Sweet and elegant. Rich creamy scrumptious flavours. Like a liquid bakewell tart.
**Finish:** Lingering, nutty and fruity. So satisfying.

**7½** **Ian: A dram that combines disciplined flavours with delightful variations on a theme.**
**Nose:** Elegantly poised, dried truffle reclining on a bed of caramel sauce and butterscotch, with roasted almonds and spiciness midway.
**Palate:** Smooth, velvety texture with an integrated package of crème brûlée and chocolate sweetness, fruit trifle, hints of espresso, nutmeg and butterscotch.
**Finish:** Fruity chocolate with dry spicy oak.

## AUCHENTOSHAN 18 YEARS OLD, OLOROSO 55.8%
Single Malt - Lowland

**7¾** **Dave: An underrated malt. Check it out.**
**Nose:** Slightly dusty, like an old attic, but shows good maturity. Pine, cake mix, Weetabix, allspice, clove. A polished oak quality. This improves in the glass.
**Palate:** Sweet to start moving immediately into red fruit, blueberry juice then the malty nuttiness takes over. Good depth and and well balanced.
**Finish:** Bran muffin.

**7** **Arthur: I was surprised to discover that this is sold as a sherry-matured bottling...where is that sherry cask character?**
**Nose:** Icing sugar, fruit and breakfast cereal. Orange bitters, Demerara and banana. With water it becomes doughier, like banana bread. Almonds.
**Palate:** Silken, sweet then drying and dusty. Difficult to pick out distinct flavours.
**Finish:** A buttery, corn-like graininess.

## AUCHENTOSHAN 1966, 31 YEARS OLD 45.8%
Single Malt - Lowland

**8½** **Michael: A fine whisky, but does something as fresh and soft benefit from quite so much ageing?**
**Nose:** Lemon, oil, cedar. Spicy.
**Palate:** Oil, lemon, orange. Fruity (apricot?), nutty, toffee. Cookie-like maltiness. Falls away somewhat in middle.
**Finish:** Soothing. Very long. Cedary dryness and grassy hints of peat in a very slightly woody finish.

*WHISKY Magazine Editor's choice*

**9** **Jim: A rare treat for a Lowlander and the most complex on the market by a mile.**
**Nose:** Half bourbon, half malt. A quite brilliant honey-rich oakiness in perfect harmony with kumquats, a sprig of mint and a touch of menthol. Stunning.
**Palate:** Enormous start with the oak taking command immediately. The very sturdy malt fights through to ensure a fabulous sweetness that counters the toasty dryness and biting spice.
**Finish:** Long; reverts to oaky vanilla when toffee dies. Unbelievably complex.

## AUCHENTOSHAN 1973, 29 YEARS OLD 55.8%
Single Malt - Lowland

**7¾** **Michael: The chestnut colour betrays the time this whisky has spent in oak. I have tasted much woodier whiskies - but not oakier Auchentoshans.**
**Nose:** Varnish. Shellac. Linseed oil. A French polisher's shop.
**Palate:** Thinnish. Drying. Wood shavings. Resin. Liquorice root. Opens with water. Soft liquorice.
**Finish:** Woody. Drying.

**8¼** **Dave: Has held its own very well for such an allegedly light spirit. Mature and substantial.**
**Nose:** Rich, resinous: coffee grounds, treacle toffee, Dundee cake, walnut, molasses, floral top notes.
**Palate:** Powerful. Oak, that treacle toffee again, spices, tobacco, Tunnock's caramel wafers, coffee cake. Good balance and feel.
**Finish:** Fairly dry.

## AUCHENTOSHAN 1976 30 YEARS OLD 41.8%
Single Malt - Lowland

**7½** **Dave: Better on palate than the nose, but so fragile it shatters easily.**
**Nose:** Distant. Dry grass, wood shavings/green oak with a mashtun like aroma to the back. Florist shop buckets. With water, cereal and moss.
**Palate:** Very light. Light grip (rice crispies) becomes softer to the back palate. A splash of water smoothes it showing soft fruit, a floral touch. Juicy cereal.
**Finish:** Short, clean, nutty.

**7¼** **Martine: Did that whisky stay too long in cask? It certainly is not at its best.**
**Nose:** Nutty, with a beautiful display of elegant fruity notes. Multi layered. Pears cooked in a vanilla syrup, cider apples, flaked almond pie.
**Palate:** Mellow but does not infuse the palate. Flavours are vague, like lost in a mist. A watery touch. The nose promised more aromatic delivery.
**Finish:** Gentle but fading quickly.

# Scotch Auchentoshan

## AUCHENTOSHAN 1976 40 YEARS OLD 41.6%
Single Malt - Lowland

**7½ Dave:** Old but still fresh. All very discreet. At its best neat.
**Nose:** Similar to the 30 Years Old, this time with extra coconut and fragrance (green fig, lemon, marshmallow) then there's cooked pear. Becomes waxy with some pollen.
**Palate:** An ash-like quality then a subtle, fragrant, palate. Aromatic woods, pot pourri. Light and creamy with a lovely texture that lifts into. After Eight mint.
**Finish:** Dries to cereal again.

**8 Martine:** An appetising dram, more complex than it seems. Still alert though quite matured (quite a comforting thought !)
**Nose:** Floral, perfumy. Cedary with a pleasant earthy note (pine needles). The floral note is swept by fruit (apple juice).
**Palate:** Smooth and velvety. Very fresh and inviting. Liquorice losanges. Hint of toffee.
**Finish:** Biscuity, lingers on liquorice, with a hint of oak.

## AUCHENTOSHAN 1978, 18 YEARS OLD 58.8%
Single Malt - Lowland

**8¾ Michael:** This seems to me the definitive light tasting (triple-distilled) Lowlander. In theory, such whiskies mature young, but this has aged beautifully.
**Nose:** Dubbin. Linseed. Flowery
**Palate:** Pastry. Malty. Sweet. Butterscotch. Spicy. Straight-ahead. Uncomplicated.
**Finish:** Very clean and crisp.

**8¾ Jim:** A must for those in search of the best a distillery can offer. Distilled when the stills performed in perfect harmony.
**Nose:** Gooseberries with delightfully fresh barley, a sprinkling of unrefined sugar and gentle oak.
**Palate:** A busy malt boasting an extraordinary degree of complexity for a lowlander.
**Finish:** Light and elegant with the fabulous malt lingering to the death.

## AUCHENTOSHAN 1978, OLD MALT CASK 50%
Single Malt - Lowland

**7 Martine:** Promising nose. Palate hard to tame, disappointing.
**Nose:** Floral, estery. Lavender. Lemon sherbet. Melon balls. Liquorice. Chocomint. Quite complex. Creamy porridge. Slightly fiery.
**Palate:** Tangy mouthfeel. Fiery. Reserved maltiness. Water dampens the fire down but disperses the magical fragrances.
**Finish:** High on the fire scale. Slowly calms down with sweet almondy notes.

**7¾ Dave:** Lovely.
**Nose:** Clean, dry, slightly perfumed malt: toast, wholemeal flour, oolong tea, lemon and a light touch of chocolate.
**Palate:** Attractive, dry and spicy plus a creamy light toffee note.
**Finish:** Dry liquorice.

## AUCHENTOSHAN 1983, BERRY'S OWN SELECTION 46%
Single Malt - Lowland

**7¾ Michael:** Subtle aromas and flavours, but beautifully composed.
**Nose:** Toasted sesame seeds.
**Palate:** Dry, nutty, with a suggestion of lemongrass in the background.
**Finish:** Soothing.

**7¾ Dave:** One of those 'light' drams which sneaks up and beguiles you.
**Nose:** Creamy and sweet. Loads of vanilla. Some flowers, dandelion and burdock, tinned apricot, baked apple, toasted nut. Delightful.
**Palate:** Sweet with tinned fruit syrup. Tongue coating. Whipped cream with chocolate sprinkles. Ripe and sweet offset by crisp oak.
**Finish:** Very flowery.

## AUCHENTOSHAN 1990 16 YEARS OLD BOURBON MATURED 53.7%
Single Malt - Lowland

**7¾ Dave:** Draff mixed with whipped cream? It's a Glaswegian cranachan.
**Nose:** Immediate oak lactone (coconut) over praline and a hint of chocolate. As it opens there's redfruit and madeleine. A little fusty with water, the sweetness of draff and vanilla.
**Palate:** Hint of orange peel, then chocolate shifting to tinned peach and malt. Good feel. Water brings out the cereal note; wholemeal bread and creamy butter.
**Finish:** Dusty malt. Fades a little quickly.

**7¾ Martine:** A well educated dram, pleasant, balanced. Maybe just lacking the sparkle which would make it gain a better score.
**Nose:** Intense, fruity, with a luscious cakey fragrance in the back. Greengage flan, shortbread, honey syrup. Oak is well integrated...
**Palate:** Crisp and firm but releasing a well controlled sweet maltiness. Well balanced, with a tangy feel which dries the flavours. Oak is more perceptible at midpalate.
**Finish:** Dry with a slight bitterness and a leafy note.

## AUCHENTOSHAN 1990, 13 YEARS OLD, DEWAR RATTRAY 60%
Single Malt - Lowland

**7¾ Michael:** I would never have identified this as an Auchentoshan. Proves 'the Glasgow malt' has plenty of character, but this expression lacks subtlety.
**Nose:** Chocolate mints. Dark chocolate. Wax paper. Straw.
**Palate:** Chocolatey. Crunchy. Root ginger. White pepper.
**Finish:** Hot. Alcoholic. Aggressive.

**7¼ Dave:** Decent but lacking true balance.
**Nose:** A strange nose: farmyards and mash gas to start, then malt extract, damp raffia and then a dominant raisin-like Marsala-type note.
**Palate:** Sweet and slightly burnt treacle toffee. Slightly unbalanced.
**Finish:** Dry and crisp. Char.

## AUCHENTOSHAN 21 YEARS OLD 43%
Single Malt - Lowland

**8¼ Michael:** Gently restorative. Subtleties gradually become apparent. Not quite as complex as I remember it.
**Nose:** Soft. Warm grass on a summer's day. Pastry. Custard tarts. Vanilla.
**Palate:** Sesame. Nutty. Oily.
**Finish:** Candied citrus peel. Orange zest. Cedar. Oak.

**7 Dave:** Pleasant, undemanding.
**Nose:** A mealy, floury nose with light citric notes. It's all very up.
**Palate:** Clean. That mealy crispness comes through. Dry and slightly wooded. Attractive and balanced, quite nutty and feisty.
**Finish:** Fresh and clean.

## AUCHENTOSHAN 21 YEARS OLD 43%
Single Malt - Lowland

**8 Arthur:** A fruity rumble in the hay. Oo arr missus.
**Nose:** Lime marmalade on malt loaf. Opal fruits. Bales of damp hay.
**Palate:** Appetising apricot jam in the middle of the palate, followed by some oaky maturity.
**Finish:** Drying, brown toastiness.

**8 Dave:** More weight and interest than the 12 Years Old.
**Nose:** Fruity (quince, bletted fruits, plum, orange spangles) sweet and concentrated with hints of honey and flowers. Some dry oak and a hint of bran-like maltiness.
**Palate:** Zesty with dried peels and berry fruits. Rounded.
**Finish:** Medium dry. Jammy fruit.

## AUCHENTOSHAN THREE WOOD 43%
Single Malt - Lowland

**8¼ Michael:** Matching Auchentoshan with Pedro Ximenez is like putting Benny Lynch in the ring with Marciano. What do you get? It's unimaginable, but in whisky it works.
**Nose:** Fruity. Raisins, especially dates, orange peel.
**Palate:** Beautiful balance of dark, syrupy, fruity, maturation flavours and cedary, oily, marshmallow, characteristics from the spirit itself.
**Finish:** Gentle, long, warming, lemon grass, spice.

**7 Dave:** A lot of wood-derived flavours and aromas here. Has a certain swaggering style.
**Nose:** Malt along with dried fruit and nut, then burnt toffee, red fruits and real sherried quality. Water shows cake mix and prune.

**Palate:** Very sherried with a certain soft, sweet fruitiness in the centre and dry maltiness underneath.
**Finish:** Dry, burnt fruit.

### AUCHENTOSHAN THREE WOOD 43%
Single Malt - Lowland

WHISKY Magazine Recommended

8¼ **Arthur: Lowlands just as aperitifs? Pah! A well constructed malt with varied wood flavour, although the prevalence of sherry flavours makes it atypical of the region.**
**Nose:** Armagnac and cognac, prunes, and treacle cake.
**Palate:** Complex and long-lasting, with raisins, cherries and chocolate. European oak to the fore.
**Finish:** A sophisticated complex of flavour, with maple syrup, dark fruits and apples.

8 **Dave: As warm and welcoming as a real Glasgow kiss.**
**Nose:** Deep and rich. Stewed fruit, raisins, molasses, roasted red pepper, violet. In time, there's resinous notes, tamarind concentrate, walnuts then cocoa. Malt way underneath.
**Palate:** Sweet and sour. Pomegranate/grenadine, dried orange peel thick berry juice. Lightly tannic, treacle, black fruits. Splits with water (don't dilute).
**Finish:** Tingling and thick.

### AUCHROISK MEDOC, CHIEFTAIN'S CHOICE 43%
Single Malt - Speyside

7 **Martine: A port finish? Rather brutal and overwhelming. Was the distillery character so bland?**
**Nose:** Heavy with wood influence. Wet cellar, damp wood. Earthy notes. Distant floral touch. Fading rose.
**Palate:** Wood speaks up on the palate as well. Dark chocolate, raisins, burst of spices. One by one, unmelted. Pretty harsh.
**Finish:** Dry, bitter. Woody.

7¾ **Ian: Evolves with poise and self assurance, retaining controlled sweetness.**
**Nose:** Rich dried fruit, with underlying toffee, butterscotch and digestive biscuits, chocolate, then apricot jam appears.
**Palate:** Creamy créme caramel and butterscotch lead to orange marmalade, apricot jam, then a serving of chocolate mousse with subtle, dry oak.
**Finish:** Dried fruit, shortbread and spicy oak.

### AUCHROISK 10 YEARS OLD 43%
Single Malt - Speyside

8 **Michael: This version is not obviously sherryish, but still manages very big flavours indeed. I'm very impressed.**
**Nose:** Hugely aromatic. Lemony, estery. Hint of smokiness. Malty.
**Palate:** Quite big. Firm. Appetising and full of flavours. Sweetish. Distinct anis. Liqueur-ish.
**Finish:** Cookie-like dryness.

7¼ **Dave: Very soft, direct. Good blending material, but as a single?**
**Nose:** Light soft and creamy. American cream soda, custard and cooked apple/bread and butter pudding with nutty malt underneath.
**Palate:** Very soft and sweet. Straight down the middle.
**Finish:** Soft.

### AUCHROISK 11 YEARS OLD, CHIEFTAIN'S CHOICE 43%
Single Malt - Speyside

8 **Michael: The port threatens to dominate the malt. I can't recall tasting such a powerful wood finish. Could seduce people who believe they don't like whisky. For that purpose, I would use this rather than a lighter, blander, malt.**
**Nose:** Slightly smoky fruitiness (cherries?).
**Palate:** Lightly syrupy. Very fruity and winey. A firm embrace of big flavours. Quite sweet.
**Finish:** Fruity, perfumy, almost jammy. Lingering.

7½ **Dave: Has retained the distillery character but given it a sweeter lift.**
**Nose:** Nutty malt with a red jelly centre. Cakey and mellow.
**Palate:** Very sweet and rounded. Redcurrants and peaches with nuts sprinkled on top.
**Finish:** Malty. Soft.

### AUCHROISK 28 YEARS OLD, RARE MALTS 56.8%
Single Malt - Speyside

8¼ **Michael: Carries its age effortlessly. Approachable, clean, sweet-tempered. Unlike The Singleton version, no obvious sherry.**
**Nose:** Faint hint of peat. Cinnamon. Dusty liquorice.
**Palate:** Full flavours. Spicy. Liquorice root. Anis.
**Finish:** Cough sweets. Smokiness (again, just a hint).

7½ **Dave: Delightful nose, palate pretty firm.**
**Nose:** Gentle, spicy and attractive. Cereal/bran, nutmeg, allspice, dried lavender, vanilla. Malty.
**Palate:** Clean and sweet with water. Still some floral notes (dried). Apple, dry grass. Has a slightly hard, woody, edge towards the finish.
**Finish:** Nutty. Long.

### AULD REEKIE 12 YEARS OLD 46%
Single Malt - Islay

8¼ **Gavin: A drinkable, if relatively undemanding whisky. Perhaps a good introduction to Islay.**
**Nose:** Old-fashioned sticking plasters, herrings in a barrel.
**Palate:** Lively, brine and limes, backed by delicate peat-reek.
**Finish:** Lengthy and increasingly salty, with cereal 'new make' notes lingering.

7¾ **Dave: Reekie certainly, but auld? Good fun.**
**Nose:** Hugely smoky. Jalapeno peppers, kippers, soot. Becomes fragrant and increasingly medicinal.
**Palate:** Balancing biscuity/salted crackers crispness. Burning dry leaves, smoked fish. Ointment (Savlon) in taste and texture.
**Finish:** Quite perfumed, fragrant smoke. Scallop.

### AULTMORE 16 YEARS OLD, DEWAR RATTRAY 57.9%
Single Malt - Speyside

8½ **Dave: It's not my preferred style of whisky, but this has real class and excellent balance.**
**Nose:** Very rich and heavily sherried. Fig rolls, fruit cake, bitter orange and a light almost tarry note. becomes ever sweeter with luscious coffee notes and a subtle fragrance on top.
**Palate:** Ripe with tomato leaf, black cherry and walnut and a hint of smoke. Good grip balancing a very silky feel.
**Finish:** Long and generous.

7¾ **Martine: An old fellow on the oak side but with elegancy.**
**Nose:** Unmistakably sherried. Wood gives the pitch. Damp warehouse walls, wet pine needles, humus, earthy roots. It's like walking in a thick sun deprived forest.
**Palate:** Sweet at start. Velvety. Then begins the tastebud dance. Spicy and tickly, with a bitter edge toward the finish. But deep and rich.
**Finish:** Long, spicy, slightly bitter.

### AULTMORE 1989, 16 YEARS OLD, OLD MALT CASK 50%
Single Malt - Speyside

7¼ **Dave: Don't get me wrong, there's nothing bad with this it's just amazingly bland.**
**Nose:** Singed, like a burning carpet, or burning hair (maybe a flaming toupee?) Malty, with cocoa nibs and an earthy weight.
**Palate:** A similarly charred start. Clean enough, with a burnt almond edge. Grippy but it is killed with the addition of water.
**Finish:** Firm and nutty.

7 **Arthur: OK, fine, solid. Whisky should be more though, right?**
**Nose:** Metallic and meat: like the roasting tin as you pull out the joint of pork. Grassy, citric and a bit earthy.
**Palate:** Baked ham, toffee and some tinned peaches.
**Finish:** Spices, perhaps morrocan.

## AULTMORE VINTAGE CASK, SQUARE BARREL 49%
Single Malt - Speyside

**7¾ Dave: Hardly the most subtle whisky you'll ever meet, but if you love em big and bouncy, this is for you.**
**Nose:** Heavy. Floor polish, then barley straw and some burnt orange. Sweetens into banana split, white chocolate, raspberry. Almost OTT.
**Palate:** Very thick, almost cloying, but the oak is grippy enough to give it structure. Hugely sweet.
**Finish:** Super-ripe fruits. Long.

**7½ Arthur: Cask driven and enjoyable without being particularly exciting.**
**Nose:** Treacle, mixed with orange liqueur and herbaceous grassiness.
**Palate:** Sweet, with treacle toffee, ginger and some European oak tannins.
**Finish:** Molasses.

## BAILLIE NICOL JARVIE 40%
Blended - Scotland

**8½ Michael: Demanding and stern. Take some time to understand it. A complex whisky as it reveals its secrets.**
**Nose:** Sweet limes. Leafy. Cypress or sandalwood.
**Palate:** Marshmallow maltiness, rose-water, then cedary, briar-like dryness. A remarkable integration of sensuousness and severity.
**Finish:** Joss-stick smokiness.

**9 Dave: A superbly balanced blend. You can't fail to love it.**
**Nose:** Charming mellow, but slightly exotic nose; fenugreek, coconut/gorse with vanilla, orange, pears and apple blossom.
**Palate:** Very soft and clean with a zesty tangerine/orange peel touch and a delicious hazelnut/almond crunch in the centre.
**Finish:** Soft and juicy.

## BAILLIE NICOL JARVIE 8 YEARS OLD 40%
Blended - Scotland

**7¼ Martine: A pleasant drink with an interesting freshness. Leaves a burning sensation with a spirity feel back in the throat though. No reason to get excited.**
**Nose:** Shy at the beginning. Then opening on sweet notes: vanilla fudge. An insistent oaky note. Slightly grainy.
**Palate:** Smooth, hesitating between cereal and fruit. Pear. A citrus touch. Porridge.
**Finish:** Fades quickly. Lack of firmness. Dry oak.

**8 Dave: Another which shows that delicacy is as much of an asset as weight and power.**
**Nose:** Fresh and floral. Green fruits: peach, greengage, grass. Lifted and buttery. Pear and spring flowers. Malted milk. More oak with water.
**Palate:** Sweet, clean and fragile floral notes with balanced nutty structure. White chocolate, spice.
**Finish:** Hazelnut. Smooth.

## BALBLAIR 10 YEARS OLD 40%
Single Malt - Highland

**7¾ Michael: Approachable and well structured, with delicious flavours.**
**Nose:** Fresh. Salty. Vanilla. A hint of chocolate.
**Palate:** Light on the tongue. Malty dryness. Shortbread sprinkled with sugar. Custard. Summer pudding.
**Finish:** Concentrated fruity dryness. Summer pudding. Comforting.

**7¼ Dave: Charming and highly drinkable.**
**Nose:** Malty-all bran/shredded wheat, then a toffee-apple sweetness. With water there's dry oak and a light (attractive) earthiness.
**Palate:** Medium-weight and quite sweet, it sits on the tounge nicely with light oakiness on the sides. Toffee-soft and easy with touches of buttered fruit loaf.
**Finish:** Lightly dry.

## BALBLAIR 16 YEARS OLD 40%
Single Malt - Highland

**7¾ Michael: Much more life and structure.**
**Nose:** Clean, soft, peatiness. Fresh spiciness. Apricots.
**Palate:** Cream-toffee. Hints of chocolate, cinnamon, oranges and lemon grass.
**Finish:** Lightly peaty. Cedary.

**9 Jim: This is startlingly wonderful. Only for those who prefer a malt that talks. Brilliant.**
**Nose:** Quite lush and fruity. Medium sweet, softly malted but lashings of vanilla.
**Palate:** Confident and assertive-then the taste buds are treated to an outrageous outbreak of spicy, multi-layered oaky complexity. Earthy stuff.
**Finish:** Dark chocolate and raisins. Very, very long.

## BALBLAIR 16 YEARS OLD 40%
Single Malt - Highland

**7¾ Martine: An attractive character. Too much sweetness on the palate though.**
**Nose:** Light sea-breeze. Touch of wet cardboard. Pine needle. Milk chocolate. Honey. Apricot jam. Cider apples. Develops on soft creamy aromas.
**Palate:** Very sweet and smooth. Pears poached in spices. Marzipan. Caramelised apples.
**Finish:** Spicy, weakening steadily. Toasted almonds. Nutty.

**8 Dave: Just a tiny splash of water is needed. A lovely drink.**
**Nose:** Gentle and rounded. New pigskin leather, dried flower. Moves into passion fruit, creamy toffee, ginger, ripe stone fruits and some light oak.
**Palate:** Good concentration: crisp cereal then runny chocolate and hazelnut, spices yet sweet and very soft.
**Finish:** Quite short, clean, spicy.

## BALBLAIR 1966, GORDON & MACPHAIL 40%
Single Malt - Highland

**8 Martine: The nose is rich and harmonious. The palate not so lavish, somewhat dulled by wood dominating. It would have shown better at a higher strength.**
**Nose:** Intensely fragrant. Fruity and buttery. Stewed plums, custard, white pepper. Vanilla fudge. Mint chocolate. Very dessert-like.
**Palate:** Mellow, elegant. Fruit and oak interlaced.
**Finish:** Unexpected dryness with a bitter note.

**7½ Dave: Another which picks up well on the palate.**
**Nose:** Rounded. Dried grasses, coconut, honeydew melon. Tree blossom (lime tree/linden). Slightly lean.
**Palate:** Touch of smoke, firm structure then a liquorous syrupy quality. Coconut again.
**Finish:** Sweet then dries into nut.

## BALBLAIR 1969 VINTAGE 45%
Single Malt - Highland

**8 Michael: For a whisky that is very light when young, this matures surprisingly well and for long periods**
**Nose:** Very aromatic and appetising. Hints of the sea. Some earthiness. Surprisingly peaty.
**Palate:** Seed cake. Textured, sweet. Some creaminess. Vanilla.
**Finish:** Lemony. Slightly sharp. A touch of salt.

**9 Jim: Unquestionably one of the finest Balblairs released.**
**Nose:** Butterscotch, kumquats and almonds combine to offer a most tantalising and complex nose.
**Palate:** Shuddering arrival of firm oak. Softened by a voluptuous sweet malt concentrate.
**Finish:** Finely balanced with some smoke and chocolate drifting serenely over the sweet malt and oak.

## BALBLAIR 1973, PRIVATE COLLECTION 45%
Single Malt - Highland

**9¼ Michael: Elegant and uncomplicated. Refreshing and appetising.**
**Nose:** Youthfully acetic with a whiff of spirit above gentle smoke (bbq?) and a cereal base. Some caramel. Honey?
**Palate:** Quite light and dry at first; then surprisingly rich and gingery. Gingerbread.
**Finish:** Mild. Lovely late smoke development.

**8 Arthur: A sherry beast with rubbery horns. A drink to be chewed rather than sipped. It caught me in the right mood and I liked it.**
**Nose:** Lots of sherry, wood polish, tiramisu, tobacco and cinnamon toast.
**Palate:** Coffee drunk through a snorkel mask.
**Finish:** Bitter chocolate.

## BALBLAIR 1979 VINTAGE 43%
Single Malt - Highland

**8¾ Dave: Needs time to grow in the glass. A dream.**
**Nose:** Aromatic with good American oak notes. Hot gorse, drying lilac, scented grasses and frangipan. Mango, pineapple. Complex, elegant.
**Palate:** Supple and silky. Mouthfilling. Peaches and yoghurt, orange blossom, light acacia honey mixed with nutmeg.
**Finish:** Chocolate. Sensual. Amazing length.

**8¾ Arthur: A vibrant and enticing nose. Really good stuff though.**
**Nose:** A sensuous dessert-like experience. Amaretto biscuits and apricot jam. Trifle with good custard and raspberry soaked sponge. High bourbon impact. Orange flavoured Turkish Delight.
**Palate:** The fruitiness doesn't follow to the palate, but an attractive dram with orange and grippy oak.
**Finish:** Dry leafiness.

## BALBLAIR 1989 VINTAGE 43%
Single Malt - Highland

**7½ Dave: Seems young, but very attractive.**
**Nose:** Clean and dry to start (muesli) then becomes increasingly fragrant (pear drops and pineapple, passion fruit, orchid, apricot skin). Touch of wax. Quite discreet.
**Palate:** Soft and slightly fuller than on the nose. Sweet and peachy in the middle good with a zingy lemon/lime character.
**Finish:** Soft, gentle.

**7¾ Arthur: Very American oak, and a pretty young thing. A summer sipper.**
**Nose:** Pear drops and a light freshness which at times was almost metallic. Damp leaves, chocolate milk and a bit of foamy banana.
**Palate:** Sweet, syrupy and chocolatey, with some pepper. Dried papaya.
**Finish:** Vanilla sweetness cut with tingly pepper.

## BALBLAIR 1990 15 YEARS OLD, DEWAR RATTRAY 62.9%
Single Malt - Highland

**7¼ Martine: The nose is more attractive than the palate, rather restrained.**
**Nose:** Grassy and malty. Barley sugar, Weetabix. Cowshed. Corn syrup. Opens up on fruity notes. Summer fruit. Cherry jam.
**Palate:** Incredibly sweet for the strength. Flowing, custardy, then breaks into a spicy burst.
**Finish:** Dry and short. Slightly astringent.

**7¼ Dave: Once again not sufficient complexity or balance to elevate it to greatness.**
**Nose:** Clean and leafy (green leaves), light nutty/hay-like maltiness, pie crust, macaroon and a hint of phenols. Water reveals a note like firelighters/leaking primus stove.
**Palate:** Incredibly hot when taken neat. Water calms it and initially shows hazelnut and attractive sweetness. Then it collapses.
**Finish:** Light smoke.

## BALBLAIR 1990, DEWAR RATTRAY 62.9%
Single Malt - Highland

**7¼ Martine: The strength is a bit aggressive. And oak is not well-integrated. Tastes like a too young fellow.**
**Nose:** Tangy. Slightly butyric. Boiled vegetables. Dry hay. White chocolate.
**Palate:** A bit harsh. Astringent. Cereal bowl. Honey comb. Pear compote.
**Finish:** Lingering but astringent. Drying on toasted nuts.

**7½ Dave: Not quite enough interaction between wood and spirit.**
**Nose:** Orange Smarties! Very candied then comes balsa wood, dust and very high alcohol burn. Despite that, it's a little dull. Water makes it slightly musty with a note reminiscent of woollen jumpers.
**Palate:** Much, much better than the nose. Quite high-toned: powdered almond, chalk, grass; then the sweetness unfolds into gentle, pure apricot fruit.
**Finish:** Jalapeno peppers. Slightly grubby.

## BALBLAIR 1997 VINTAGE 43%
Single Malt - Highland

**9 Dave: A stunner.**
**Nose:** Substantial with good maturity. Orange peel and ginger, drying grass, barley sugar, passion fruit, banana skin and a wholemeal maltiness.
**Palate:** Very silky with marzipan, sweet nut and dried tropical fruits, peach. Honeycomb, chocolate and mint. Multi-layered and surprisingly deep.
**Finish:** Immensely long. Trickles down the back of the throat.

**8½ Arthur: Again, pleasant very pretty. A really good example of American oak maturation.**
**Nose:** Baked bananas, green apples and pear drops. An attractive and subtle meadow note. Custard. A little pencil shavings woodiness.
**Palate:** Sweet banana custard, toffee apple followed by drying spice.
**Finish:** Cinnamon.

## BALBLAIR 33 YEARS OLD 54.4%
Single Malt - Highland

**8 Michael: A whisky that starts life with some restraint has certainly developed over the years.**
**Nose:** Peaty, earthy, almost pungent.
**Palate:** Oily. Seed cake. Banana cake. Spicy.
**Finish:** Big. Spicy. Lemon grass. Fragrant peat. Long.

**8¾ Jim: Few malts reach this age intact. This has - and with some considerable panache.**
**Nose:** Pipe smoke, citrus and waxy leather: beautifully sweet despite the big oak. Overall, somewhat bourbony.
**Palate:** Intense toasted malt-oak intensity before it drifts back off into bourbon-land.
**Finish:** Slightly bitter honeycomb and waxy-though the demerara sweetness continues.

## BALBLAIR 38 YEARS OLD 44%
Single Malt - Highland

**9 Martine: An enticing expression of old age. Forever young! With elegance and style.**
**Nose:** Rich, oaky. Resiny. Cedar. Honey. Antique shop. Cappuccino, tiramisu. Toasted hazelnuts in caramel.
**Palate:** Silky, very smooth. A refined creamy delicacy. Develops on drier oaky notes but keeps it round.
**Finish:** Long, reluctantly fading away on toffee and nutty notes.

**9 Dave: Subtle and mature. This is one of those drams you need to take hours over.**
**Nose:** Mature, complex and powerful. Cold tea, leather, overripe apple, fruit sugars. A lovely, mature mix of brioche, orange, dried peach, black banana, tea leaves, chocolate, almost rum and raisin.
**Palate:** Old but has sufficient spicy energy. Good depth of fruit, custard-like vanilla. Balanced oak.
**Finish:** Long sweet.

## BALBLAIR 40 YEARS OLD, SINGLE MALTS OF SCOTLAND 42.8%
Single Malt - Highland

**8½ Martine: Old and complex but keeping fit. A rich character, to be enjoyed right now.**
**Nose:** Musty. Apples and pears drying on racks. A hint of crystallised violet. Then a more earthy profile. Wet pine needles. Dead leaves.
**Palate:** Fresh but mellow. Lots of honey. Roasted almonds. Currants and dried apricots. Candied pineapple. Spices take over fruit.
**Finish:** Long, lingering, warm. Star anise, drying out on an oaky edge.

**8 Dave: Highly perfumed. This needs time to open. Worth a look. Good price!**
**Nose:** Everything here is pastel-shaded: flowers, Edinburgh rock, apple cake, grass, ginger. Well balanced. Highly oily, suggesting good age almost into varnish, old book shop, dried fruit, beeswax.
**Palate:** A little disappointing after such an excellent nose. Like many old whiskies it has a fragility to it. Tannins a little high. The fungal depth of old Cognac.
**Finish:** Long, tannic then fades quickly.

### BALBLAIR 40 YEARS OLD, THE WHISKY EXCHANGE 47.2%
Single Malt - Highland

8¾ **Dave: Yet another superb Balblair which chimes perfectly with the official bottlings.**
**Nose:** Mature and deep with a superb layering effect: ripe fleshy autumn fruits. Then fudge, citrus and a leather/bung cloth note.
**Palate:** Deep with good grip. Real power and a figgy depth, but then it lifts once more into cherry stone/maraschino. One to sip slowly.
**Finish:** Long, silky.

8¼ **Martine: Quite a warming fellow. A real character. For winter … or a rotten summer!**
**Nose:** Nutty, oaky. Malt and oak are well integrated. Sherry in the back. Strong coffee.
**Palate:** Rich with lots of caraway and curry (not revealed by the nose!). Warm feel.
**Finish:** Dry oaky and spicy.

### BALBLAIR ELEMENTS 40%
Single Malt - Highland

7½ **Michael: Gentle, but complex as the flavours open.**
**Nose:** Lightly salty and peaty. Black chocolate.
**Palate:** Light shortbread. Creamy. Hint of raspberries. Spiciness emerging. Very slightly peppery.
**Finish:** Gentle fruity dryness.

7½ **Jim: Takes time to get going, but worth the wait.**
**Nose:** A lively aroma bristling with heather and a hint of honey and prickly malt notes.
**Palate:** Firm and dry mouthfeel suggests a busy malt: after a short lull much fruitier, fleshy notes appear.
**Finish:** This is where it comes good: massive complexity sparked off by a touch of smoke and more heather. Fabulous and faultless bittersweet balance.

### BALLANTINE'S 12 YEARS OLD, PURE MALT 40%
Blended Malt - Scotland

8 **Martine: Elegantly restrained. An excellent pure malt for socialising.**
**Nose:** Buttered toast, peaches poached in syrup, touch of heather root.
**Palate:** Fade-in-fade-out of malty and fruity flavours. Biscuity. Orange zest and nougatine.
**Finish:** Reasonably long, echoing maltiness and almond milk.

7¾ **Dave: Mellow and soft. It doesn't quite deliver the promise of the nose but a fine example.**
**Nose:** An attractive and approachable, malty nose with coconut, vanilla (melting vanilla ice cream) and citric top notes. Water brings out nutty nougat and some good peachy/banana softness.
**Palate:** Mixes sweet fruits and slightly bitter nuttiness well along with a gentle smoky thread. Well balanced.
**Finish:** Nutty again with a hint of smoke.

### BALLANTINE'S 17 YEARS OLD 43%
Blended - Scotland

8½ **Michael: The blending skills at Ballantine have long been renowned. The 17 has always seemed to me the most eloquent demonstration of that. Beautifully composed and mature.**
**Nose:** I could be in a leather armchair before a peat fire in the Highlands. Tinge of soot-very evocative.
**Palate:** An astonishing freshness. Some cereal-grain sweetness. Grassy. Burnt grass. Peat.
**Finish:** Dry. Elegant.

8 **Dave: I was surprised when the bottle was revealed. This has been a favourite for a while, but not on this occasion.**
**Nose:** This needs water to reveal smoke, cooked vegetable, cocoa, walnut, wet leather and coffee.
**Palate:** A soft and quite creamy start then a burst of coal-like smoke halfway through. Hint of vanilla, orange juice, cream and biscuity crunchiness.
**Finish:** Medium length and very juicy.

### BALLANTINE'S 17 YEARS OLD 43%
Blended - Scotland

7½ **Martine: Quite a rustic profile, warmed up when aerated. Seems to have retained the waterfalls from all Scotland!**
**Nose:** Musty. Earthy peat notes. Mushrooms, wet leaves. Oozing dampness. Then rich biscuity notes. Lemon cake. Touch of beeswax.
**Palate:** Enticing sweetness. Silky feel. Salty sensation. Peaty, rooty. Teasingly tingling. Spicier with water.
**Finish:** Dry, sherbety. Nutty. Dry walnuts.

8¼ **Dave: An example of superb blending skills. If this tasting is about balance then this is a perfect example, every element pulls together in harmony.**
**Nose:** Gentle and soft: green banana, coconut milk, hot gorse, honey, whipped cream. With water, there's subtle smoke and summer fruits.
**Palate:** Very smooth start, then lifts into dry smoke and spicy oak which balance the citric juiciness, gooseberry jam, vanilla and general fruitiness.
**Finish:** Light sherried notes and smoke. Gentle.

### BALLANTINE'S 21 YEARS OLD 43%
Blended - Scotland

8¼ **Michael: My personal taste is more robust, but I am in awe of the precision and refinement of the older Ballantine's.**
**Nose:** Very delicate. Fleeting fragrance of peat smoke. Hints of sweet orange, apricot, toasted nuts.
**Palate:** Light, but with a good malt background. Developing creamy butterscotch flavours, a hint of vanilla. Moderating the sweetness, a little lemon zest.
**Finish:** Interplay of fruitiness and older oak.

8¼ **Dave: This has great balance and the light smoke gives it extra interest.**
**Nose:** Clean, medium-bodied and quite citric. Water brings out orange and a lovely smoky note which builds as the whisky develops but never overpowers.
**Palate:** Very sweet. A soft gentle grain with pops of spice, honey, nougat and smoke weaving in and out.
**Finish:** Rich and soft.

### BALLANTINE'S FINEST 40%
Blended - Scotland

8½ **Michael: Very gentle, but a precise clarity of flavours. Drink while listening to Vivaldi.**
**Nose:** Perfumy. Very fragrant smokiness.
**Palate:** Soft and light. Silky, oily peaty. A therapeutically medicinal relaxant.
**Finish:** Lemon-honey. Some late sweeetness. Late surge of gentle warmth.

6½ **Paul: For those imbibers who relish a honeyed/caramel core to their whisky. If you prefer the more sinewy, definitive elements of oak or smoke, stay clear.**
**Nose:** Sweet and grainy, like cereal with honey. No discernible hints of wood, smoke or peat. A no-frills aroma, solid, likeable, undemanding.
**Palate:** Unabashedly sweet and near syrupy from palate entry through mid-palate. The sweetness is grainy, not fruity or flowery. Light-to-medium bodied.
**Finish:** Notes of caramel and nougat are featured in the ultra-sweet aftertaste.

### BALLANTINE'S GOLD SEAL, 12 YEARS OLD 43%
Blended - Scotland

7¾ **Michael: Gold seal is a particularly rich version of Ballantine, but this bottling seems even sweeter and less peaty than I remember. For me, the syrupiness swamps the house character.**
**Nose:** Honey. Tropical fruits. Burnt currants.
**Palate:** Buttercream. Chocolate. Coffee.
**Finish:** Rummy for a moment, then lightly soothing.

7 **Dave: Balances all its elements very well. One to work on.**
**Nose:** A sulphur/rubber note, mixed with light smokiness unreduced. With water comes a decidedly jaunty, maritime air with lovely soft grain behind.
**Palate:** Soft and clean building into a vinous, Fino sherry quality. Soft, juicy grain appears mid-palate while smoke wreathes itself about. Good feel.
**Finish:** Smoke. Little short.

### BALLANTINE'S LIMITED 43%
Blended - Scotland

8¾ **Michael: Much more sherryish than the colour suggests. Sweet. Sponge fingers. I wouldn't have recognised it as a Ballantine's.**

**Nose:** Clean. Melba toast.
**Palate:** Silky. Very sherryish, juicy.
**Finish:** Sherry trifle, with chocolate. Some balancing dryness.

**8¼ Dave: Subtle and complex. A very gentle giant**
**Nose:** Gentle with a hint of light coal smoke/tar, balanced with soft rich fruit (apple/plum/cherry), sultana cake, cream toffee, citrus peel, heather, spice.
**Palate:** Soft with lovely feel which moves nicely in the mouth. Soft fruit/butter tablet mixed with citrus freshness and smoke drifting in and out.
**Finish:** Medium. Fruity.

## BALMENACH 1972, 30 YEARS OLD PORT WOOD, HART BROTHERS 50.1%
Single Malt - Speyside

**7¾ Michael: Very distinctive. Bring on the chicken mole.**
**Nose:** Honey with a suggestion of chocolate, but also herbal notes.
**Palate:** Peppery and dry, but also creamy.
**Finish:** Orangey, zesty. Appetisingly spice. Cilantro?

**7 Dave: A shame as you don't find many wholly port pipe matured whiskies, but this has lain in the cask too long.**
**Nose:** Rich, wooded. Like a dunnage warehouse. Molasses, Christmas cake. European oak.
**Palate:** Charred timbers. The spirit has a fruity weight but the wood is in charge. Too dry and tannic.
**Finish:** Dry.

## BALMENACH 1990, 11 YEARS OLD, CASK 507, ADELPHI 59.7%
Single Malt - Speyside

**7¾ Michael: Can whiskies be handsome and romantic? This is a seductive bottling.**
**Nose:** Linen. Hessian. Pot pourri.
**Palate:** Big, soft, pillowy. Heather. Honey. Sweet. Sugared almonds.
**Finish:** Balancing peaty dryness. Warming as an open fire.

**8¼ Dave: This can cope with plenty of water.**
**Nose:** Good legs. A succulent yet floral nose: apples with custard, spice, sugared almond, marshmallow.
**Palate:** Medium-bodied but juicy and elegant. The first hit is a spicy one, then a fragrant, floral yet chewy, mid-palate.
**Finish:** Sweet then nutty.

## THE BALVENIE 10 YEARS OLD, FOUNDER'S RESERVE 43%
Single Malt - Speyside

**8½ Michael: The most honeyish of Speyside malts?**
**Nose:** Orange-honey perfume. Musky, faint hint of peat.
**Palate:** Honeyed sweetness drying to lightly spicy notes. Very lively. Just a hint of sherry.
**Finish:** A tingly, almost aggressive, surge of flavours, with lingering, syrupy honey.

**9 Jim: Balvenie has long been a favourite, and this expression is sublime. A riposte to any who claim that all Speysiders are much of a muchness.**
**Nose:** Dazzling complexity; light yet softly smoked, with both youthful grassy notes and heavier, richer ones. A treat.
**Palate:** Rich, faintly honeyed malt tones, underpinned by smokiness. The fruitiness is faint but essential to the complexity.
**Finish:** Dry malt and gentle peat take equal and alternate stage. Some lovely cocoa notes on the finish.

## THE BALVENIE 12 YEARS OLD, DOUBLE WOOD 43%
Single Malt - Speyside

**9 Michael: Yet richer, and fruitier.**
**Nose:** Sherry and orange skins.
**Palate:** Beautifully combined mellow flavours: nutty, sweet, sherry, very orangy fruitiness, heather, cinnamon spiciness.
**Finish:** Long, tingling. Very warming.

**9 Jim: A more intense malt than the Founder's Reserve. Despite its finesse, it is just shaded in regard to all-round complexity. Still nothing short of glorious.**
**Nose:** A close relation to the Founder's Reserve, with extra vanilla and honey plus the subtlest of Oloroso influences. Delicate for its age.

**Palate:** Sweet and honeyed with intense malt meeting the soft peat and controlled sherry fruitiness.
**Finish:** Smoky and a little spicy with a bigger vanilla tang.

## THE BALVENIE 12 YEARS OLD, DOUBLE WOOD 43%
Single Malt - Speyside

WHISKY
Recommended

**8¾ Michael: Delicious.**
**Nose:** The skins of Seville oranges. The apricot note of Oloroso sherry.
**Palate:** Beautifully combined mellow flavours: nutty, sweet, juicy sherry, very orangey fruitiness, heather, cinnamon. Very spicy.
**Finish:** Long, tingling. Very warming.

**8½ Doug: Some of the 10 years brandyish elements subdued to give a rounded gentle being.**
**Nose:** Entrancing, lightly honeyed, sweet and gentle.
**Palate:** Full, succulent and buttery, whafts of sherry, nuttiness and wavering spice.
**Finish:** Long and warming, cinnamon prickles through the lingering sweet sherry.

## THE BALVENIE 15 YEARS OLD 50.4%
Single Malt - Speyside

**8¼ Michael: A very interesting whisky, but the distillery character is better served with a dash of sherry.**
**Nose:** Cedary. Vanilla. Custard. Honey.
**Palate:** Toffee. Sweetish. Cedary. Scenty. Talc-like.
**Finish:** Coconut. Indian spices. Very long indeed.

**8 Dave: A subtle expression of The Balvenie.**
**Nose:** A malty, intense and slightly hard nose. Water tones it down showing sweet fruit, malt and bracken.
**Palate:** Totally different to the nose. Luscious and mellow with honey, chestnut, honeysuckle and cream. Builds beautifully still, with firm wood.
**Finish:** Sugared almond.

## THE BALVENIE 15 YEARS OLD SINGLE BARREL 50.4%
Single Malt - Speyside

**8 Michael: Certainly robust. Perhaps a little harsh?**
**Nose:** Assertive. Dry, fresh oak. Heather. Rooty. Coconut. Lemon pith.
**Palate:** Lively. Cedar. Orange skins, fruity, pineapple-like sweetness and acidity.
**Finish:** Very dry. Peppery alcohol.

**9½ Jim: Arguably the ultimate Speyside dram, though the Glenfiddich Solera gives it a close run. A kaleidoscope of flavours.**
**Nose:** Again, closely related to the Founder's Reserve. More vanilla, with the honey a degree lighter than some previous bottlings. Even so, this is just wonderful.
**Palate:** An explosion of bittersweet flavours. Incredible depth and complexity with the trademark Balvenie maltiness. Lots of spicy peat notes.
**Finish:** Amazingly long with some chewy smoke, even a hint of liquorice. Some chocolate for good measure.

## THE BALVENIE 17 YEARS OLD SHERRY OAK 43%
Single Malt - Speyside

**8 Dave: Good but the oak has leaned a little too heavily on the expressiveness of the whisky.**
**Nose:** Chocolate covered raisins, dried fruit. Heavily sherried. Varnish, black banana and toffee apple. Shows some power. Freshly polished oak. In time (and with water) the nose firms up. Furniture polish and antique shops. Hint of sulphur.
**Palate:** Sweet start, melting dark chocolate. Firm enough grip which slightly mutes the mid palate and hides the sweetness behind.
**Finish:** Long mixing light spice, dried fruit, drying tannin and a nutty honeyed note. Ultimately dry.

**7½ Martine: The sherry influence conveys a certain dourness to the malt. Not fully convinced by this finish.**
**Nose:** Sherried. Toffee, marrons glacés. Rich chocolate. A hint of rubber. Wet ground coffee. Maraschino. Walnut.
**Palate:** Smooth start with lots of chocolate fudge, then oak has its word, tightening up taste buds.
**Finish:** Woody and spicy.

### THE BALVENIE 17 YEARS OLD, NEW WOOD 40%
Single Malt - Speyside

**7¼ Michael: Attractive in the glass, with a pleasant nose, rich in dessert notes, but is let down by a slight astringency in the palate.**
**Nose:** Rich. Warming. Malty and sweet. Malt and creamy vanilla high notes.
**Palate:** Fairly dense, yet initially dry. A hint of chocolate cookies, with a cherry-like sharpness.
**Finish:** A little more oily and slightly burnt. Hints at cough mixture. Tarry?

**7 Arthur: Dramatic, like a kiddie's sweetshop in a sawmill. One to try for interests sake, but I suspect that many hard-men malt fans will be put off by the perfumed character.**
**Nose:** An explosion of fruits: peach, bruised apples, black cherry, strawberry milkshake. In the background there is a sappy, hay-like quality.
**Palate:** Milk chocolate, spice and toasted oak.
**Finish:** More toasted oak and dry spice.

### THE BALVENIE 1968 50.8%
Single Malt - Speyside

**9 Michael: Tasting from the cask resulted in slightly different descriptors whereas these notes were based on a sample sent to Whisky Magazine.**
**Nose:** Clear liquid honey. Orangey with water.
**Palate:** Fudge. Almonds. Honey. Orange. Minty.
**Finish:** Lemony. Dry. Warming. Very long.

**8¼ Jim: A rather unusual Balvenie but delicious nonetheless!**
**Nose:** Deep oak with hint of berry fruits and buttered crumpets. Very firm.
**Palate:** Clean surge of unspecified fruitness.
**Finish:** Hardens into a very brittle maltiness and oak.

### THE BALVENIE 1970 VINTAGE CASK 44.6%
Single Malt - Speyside

**9¼ Michael: Extraordinarily distinctive. All the characteristics I expect in Balvenie, but I have never experienced them in such a concentrated intensity.**
**Nose:** Fudge. Honey. A hint of heather. Very soft.
**Palate:** Intensely sweet and Sauternes-like. Or perhaps orange muscat? With water, yet sweeter and fruitier.
**Finish:** Becoming more like dark, clear, liquid, honey.

**9 Dave: Complex, luscious, gorgeous.**
**Nose:** An elegant, soft, luscious, nose that reminds you of pancakes dripping with butter and honey.
**Palate:** Soft and mouthfilling with little spikes of wood notes and citrus. Dries as it develops.
**Finish:** Ripe soft and long, drying into wood then burnt orange.

### THE BALVENIE 1972 VINTAGE CASK 49.4%
Single Malt - Speyside

**9¼ Michael: The ultimate dessert dram. Beautifully composed.**
**Nose:** Buttery richness. Butterscotch pudding. Bread and butter pudding. Honey.
**Palate:** Astonishingly syrupy smooth. Still evoking thoughts of the sweet trolley, but farther south; the honeyed pastries of the Balkans. Then a suggestion of chocolate powder hints at tiramisu.
**Finish:** Bitter chocolate. Terry's chocolate oranges.

**9 Dave: Proof, if it were needed, that this is a first-growth distillery.**
**Nose:** Hugely complex: perfumed with dried apricot, pear, orange and cinnamon. There's honey, hazelnut, orange blossom water, spices and light smoke.
**Palate:** Intensely concentrated mid-palate with a mass of honeyed red and black fruits, spice, apple. Superb balance and harmony between all the elements.
**Finish:** Sweet toffee. Smoke.

### THE BALVENIE 21 YEARS OLD PORTWOOD 40%
Single Malt - Speyside

**9 Michael: The full, honeyed, richness of the malt combines beautifully with what seems to be a generous kiss of port.**
**Nose:** Perfumey. Passion fruit. Nutty. Marzipan.
**Palate:** Rich. Complex. Honeyed, creamy, winey, aniseed, almonds.
**Finish:** Long, cedary, dryish. A wonderful digestif.

**9 Doug: An extremely graceful and charmingly feminine dram.**
**Nose:** Intensely perfumed, ladies powder pack, passion fruit and toffee banana, and walnuts.
**Palate:** Creamy, soothing, nutty, with a warm augmenting portwine influence.
**Finish:** Smooth, cedary with a warming spice.

### THE BALVENIE 25 YEARS OLD 46.9%
Single Malt - Speyside

**8½ Michael: A very sophisticated malt. Beautifully combined flavours.**
**Nose:** Honey, the dark, liquid kind. Flowery. Acacia-like.
**Palate:** The honey is there in the first taste, then it lingers behind the other flavours. Lightly syrupy. Mirabelle plums. Oranges. Lively, lemony flavours, especially when water is added. A hint of clove. More peat than I remember.
**Finish:** Firm, tingly.

**8¼ Jim: A rare treat. A malt that, despite an obvious over oakiness, retains a truly impressive complexity and charm.**
**Nose:** Mouth-watering malt surrounded by an almost minty freshness. Some tired oak but beautifully couched.
**Palate:** Every bit as lively as the nose suggests; waves of intense malt but of varying sharpness.
**Finish:** Some oiliness appears, generating length to that fabulous malt and bitter chocolate.

### THE BALVENIE 25 YEARS OLD, SINGLE BARREL 46.9%
Single Malt - Speyside

**8½ Michael: Seemed a little lighter all round than I remember.**
**Nose:** Orange flower water. Soft. Honey-sweet.
**Palate:** Marshmallow-like. Cereal grain. Cream. Orange peels.
**Finish:** Faintly smoky dryness.

**7¾ Dave: Understated, just a bit shy.**
**Nose:** Gentle, discreet even. Raisin bread/pannetone, apple, light honey, peach. Toasty, lively.
**Palate:** Delicate with soft layers of flavour. Wood gives a good frame for the light gentle honeyed fruit. Very light.
**Finish:** Long, slowly fading fruits.

### THE BALVENIE 30 YEARS OLD 47.3%
Single Malt - Speyside

**8 Gavin: This expression wears its years well.**
**Nose:** Initially curiously unyielding, slight perfume, even-tually warm horse (in a good way) and cloves.
**Palate:** Confident. Golden syrup, slight oiliness balancing dry sherry notes, moving into soft peat and a little smoke.
**Finish:** Long lasting, more delicate, fragrant notes appear as it fades. Slightly smoky.

**8¾ Dave: Fantastic length. A truly three-dimensional malt.**
**Nose:** Dry and ash-like: cedar, cigar ash, charred. Softens, showing honeycomb, candied peel, acacia, honey, kumquat, orange pekoe tea, powdered ginger.
**Palate:** Soft, unctuous feel. Cream, orange peel, that cigar box note again, hint of nut. Fine grained tannin. Great balance with depth and texture.
**Finish:** Soft and gentle, fades discreetly.

### THE BALVENIE ISLAY CASK, 17 YEARS OLD 43%
Single Malt - Speyside

**9 Michael: Reminiscent of the days when Speysiders were peatier.**
**Nose:** Garden bonfires, or perhaps steam trains. A picnic in the park? After a number of nosings, there's seaweed and salt. Make that a picnic on the cliffs.
**Palate:** Honey. Sugar glazing and caramelising slightly. Nuts. A touch of candied orange peel. Lemon.
**Finish:** Fresh. Fragrantly smoky.

**7¾ Dave: Cheaper than buying a distillery on Islay but what's next? Speyside finished Caol Ila or a cask aged in every region?**
**Nose:** Well rounded. Honey and cream with some sultana and light phenolic notes.
**Palate:** An immediate sootiness. Soft, dessert like with a dry smouldering border. Lovely, if a bit schizoid.
**Finish:** Gentle with teasing smokiness.

## THE BALVENIE PORTWOOD 1989 40%
Single Malt - Speyside

**7¾ Martine:** Not the depth of the PortWood 21 Years Old, but thoroughly enjoyable.
**Nose:** Shy initially, then blossoms. Wood and fruit gracefully interlace. Muscat grape. Dates. Vanilla rice pudding. Carnations.
**Palate:** More wood than on the nose. Creamy. Sweet stewed plums. Oaky.
**Finish:** Quickly fades with sweet fruity notes.

**7¾ Dave:** Well-mannered and well-balanced.
**Nose:** Sweet, quite winey, reminiscent of old Tavel rose. There's some honey, spices, charred fruits and red fruits. Subtle.
**Palate:** Soft and honeyed with a sweet redcurrant jelly flavour. Good weight and balance. A sweet gentle malt.
**Finish:** Soft.

## THE BALVENIE PORTWOOD 21 YEARS OLD 40%
Single Malt - Speyside

**9 Michael:** Bring on the petits-fours.
**Nose:** Perfumy, fruity. Passion fruit. Raisiny. Nutty dryness, marzipan.
**Palate:** Very complex. Toffee, creamy, winey, aniseed.
**Finish:** Long, cedary, dry.

**8 Jim:** The port wood has altered the shape of the whisky. The malt plays a less significant part, which means limited complexity.
**Nose:** Fruity and ripe; lovely and grapey yet smoky, too. Finely tuned.
**Palate:** Silkier than the other Balvenies, and with greater fruit and spice. Yet some how lacks their complexity.
**Finish:** Enormous. Wave upon wave of deep smoky/oaky notes. A slight hint of sap towards the finish, though, as the whisky heads in a bourbony direction.

## THE BALVENIE PORTWOOD 21 YEARS OLD 40%
Single Malt - Speyside

**8¾ Michael:** This expression beautifully highlights the qualities of The Balvenie as a whisky that is full of rich flavours yet gentler and less robust than, for example, Glenfarclas or The Macallan.
**Nose:** Rich, creamy, malty.
**Palate:** The maltiness becomes creamy, then honeyed, then develops raisiny notes (Scottish black bun) and nutty dryness. An inviting, seductive dryness.
**Finish:** Bitter black chocolate.

**8¾ Dave:** Finishing is all about striking a balance. Here, the port just nudges the spirit into a new space but never dominates. Classy.
**Nose:** Elegance personified. Rich and soft with peach, fudge, red fruits (cherry especially) and a tiny cough of smoke. Sexy stuff.
**Palate:** Very soft and quite sweet: acacia honey, red fruit and a gorgeous silky feel.
**Finish:** Orange peel.

## THE BALVENIE ROASTED MALT AGED 14 YEARS 47.1%
Single Malt - Speyside

**7¾ Dave:** Give this time and you'll find a delicious dram.
**Nose:** Fleshy, sugared almond. Needs time to open when you can find clover honey, violet. Quite syrupy and sweet. Water gives it a lift.
**Palate:** Light touch of pear drop. Immediate sweetness with a crunchy middle. Cheesecake base.
**Finish:** Long, sweet.

**8¼ Arthur:** There's something breakfasty about this, like a good bowl of honeyed and well-fruited porridge.
**Nose:** Pale sultanas, exotic fruit, kiwi and a pencillike woodiness. Cocoa.
**Palate:** Honeycomb sweetness, kiwi, oats, some floral notes and lemon Turkish delight. Well balanced, fruity goodness.
**Finish:** Dusty cocoa and a shake of spice.

## THE BALVENIE RUM WOOD 47.1%
Single Malt - Speyside

**7¼ Dave:** A disappointment after the class of the 1972.
**Nose:** Quite plain and oaky: cigar box, pine flooring, dry bracken, sweetening into sponge cake, date. With water a lightly doughy note and a hint of cold green tea.

**Palate:** Sweet...then dry...then sweet. Spreads well initially but becomes rather dull and flat.
**Finish:** Custard and then spice. Woodsmoke.

**7½ Arthur:** The overall experience was harmed by the bitterness.
**Nose:** Orange liqueur sweetness and a sweet chlorine. Orange peel and banana. With water a little more sherbety, then grassiness, vanilla and blossom. More baked banana.
**Palate:** Lots of bourbon cask character, with toasted oak and vanilla.
**Finish:** More US oak and a burnt twig bitterness.

## THE BALVENIE RUMWOOD 14 YEARS OLD 47.1%
Single Malt - Speyside

**8¼ Martine:** A rich whisky which has taken some exotic and sensuous notes from the rum. Stiffens up on the finish.
**Nose:** Fruity and creamy. Luscious caramel aromas. Candied orange. A touch of praline.
**Palate:** Velvety, coating. Orange custard. Gets very spicy, cinnamon and ginger. Exotic citrus, vetiver. A distant note of coconut.
**Finish:** Spicy, dry. Dark chocolate bitter bite.

**8¼ Dave:** A classy package with the rum adding its character to an already well-matured spirit. This is what finishing is about.
**Nose:** Oak driven. Crushed toasted hazelnuts on top of a banana and chocolate dessert. Needs time to open and show its full rich sweet depth.
**Palate:** Gentle and well layered. Cigar, caramelised peach. Deep and balanced.
**Finish:** A rich concentrated fruitiness that then gives way to a crisp oak.

## THE BALVENIE VINTAGE CASK 1967 40%
Single Malt - Speyside

**9 Michael:** A beautifully balanced classic Speyside whisky.
**Nose:** Very aromatic. Butterscotch, honey. Acacia. Faint peat.
**Palate:** Buttery maltiness. Honey. Orange. Linctus-like. Hint of vanilla. Juicy oak.
**Finish:** Orange skins. Lemongrass. Lightly peaty balancing dryness.

**9 Jim:** An astounding whisky for its age; head and shoulders above its Glenfiddich stablemate.
**Nose:** Beautifully delicate and floral with a layer of peat. Bourbon-style vanilla adds age, approaching perfection in Balvenie terms.
**Palate:** Oily rush of malt. Vanilla and bourbon kick and then infusion of spices and bitter chocolate.
**Finish:** Dries out and becomes vanilla rich. Remains cocoa dominant.

## THE BALVENIE VINTAGE CASK 1972 47.3%
Single Malt - Speyside

**8¾ Dave:** This oozes class and, for me, is streets ahead of everything else in this group.
**Nose:** Shows real maturity, but with a lifted, elegant rather than woody nose: light dried fruit, resin, sandalwood, hint of varnish and slightly rum-like notes moving into malted milk.
**Palate:** Silky palate mixing honey scented with rosemary, and layered fruits. Very well balanced.
**Finish:** Long, smooth.

**8 Arthur:** The nose is greeted by a massive estery whoosh! Banana, very ripe pineapple and rum butter. Yum. Cocoa. Mango. More yum. Bounty bars. With time it moves towards a floral style.
**Palate:** Orangey, but not as much fruit as the nose, but lots of smoky-oaky cocoa character. Perfumed.
**Finish:** Mixed spice in sugar. Overall: good, and nearly great.

## BANFF 1966, 31 YEARS OLD, OLD MALT CASK 50%
Single Malt - Speyside

**6½ Michael:** Banff was never a classic, but it is an evocatively old-fashioned Highland malt, and it has stood up reasonably well to great age.
**Nose:** Faint, fragrant, burnt grass.
**Palate:** Clean, distinctly sweet, peachy, malty. Rather neutral in the middle. Becoming smoky and peaty.
**Finish:** Sweetness and dryness, becoming astringently peaty. Long, warming.

**9 Jim:** A fabulous whisky for its age.
**Nose:** Big age oakiness with hints of lavender and a pleasing saltiness. Still malty, very lightly smoked, but a little sappy, too.
**Palate:** Sweet and bourbony early on with lashings of honeyed finesse. Very intense and pleasantly oily; slightly plummy.
**Finish:** Medium to long with some impressive vanilla. Remains thick on the palate for a long time with the toastiness at last drying things a little.

## BANFF 1978, SHERRY WOOD, CHIEFTAIN'S CHOICE 46%
Single Malt - Speyside

**6¾ Michael:** Too burnt and dry. Not for everyone. Reminds me of a particular espresso and grappa, standing outside the Arsenale, on a winter's morning.
**Nose:** Reticent. After some coaxing, dried fruits – apricots, figs. Oily, monster nuts – Brazils?
**Palate:** Dark, burnt cake (Dundee cake perhaps?). Liquorice. More oiliness, treacle toffee, bitumen.
**Finish:** Burnt. Bitter notes. Drying but warming.

**8¼ Dave:** This has complexity, though does lose some intensity and mouth feel with water.
**Nose:** Big and mature with a hint of smoke. Quite resinous: liquorice and leather, wood oil, sultana fruit cake, clinker. In time there's a note of wrinkled apple, baked fruits.
**Palate:** Very soft and rounded and less dry than the nose suggests. Honeyed with a layered feel: marzipan, turmeric/curry leaf even some peach.
**Finish:** Very spicy.

## BANFF 1979, AGED 23 YEARS, CHIEFTAIN'S CHOICE 46%
Single Malt - Speyside

**6¾ Michael:** I thought this whisky had died in the bottle, but water brought it back to life.
**Nose:** Slightly smoky.
**Palate:** Sweet, then woodily dry. With water, creamy and much improved.
**Finish:** Lemon tarts.

**7¾ Dave:** Delicious and very drinkable.
**Nose:** Attractive and malty with dry grass, cooked fruit, apple pie (and pie crust) and orange. Mature, but crisp and toasty.
**Palate:** Sweet as a nut with Highland toffee, a hint of peat and crisp malt.
**Finish:** Sweet.

## BANFF 24 YEARS OLD, CADENHEAD'S 58.3%
Single Malt - Speyside

**7 Michael:** The best Banff I have tasted. Shows its age but the finish reveals real depth and staying power.
**Nose:** Clean, dry, peat-smoke fragrance. A hint of the sea?
**Palate:** Vanilla. Syrupy-sweet flavours. Grassy. Sundried grass.
**Finish:** Lemon grass. Complex spiciness. Gingery, dry. Very long.

**6¼ Jim:** This was probably a half decent dram 12 years ago.
**Nose:** Over ripe banana and papaya star in this fruity production. Otherwise hot and slightly over oaked.
**Palate:** For all the alcoholic oomph, it's rather thin taste-wise, except for an exceptionally sweet maltiness which grows rather charmingly and is the high point.
**Finish:** Thinner still, despite a hint of cocoa. Still hot and off-balanced by the bullying oak.

## BANFF 34 YEARS OLD, SIGNATORY SILENT STILLS 50.1%
Single Malt - Speyside

**6½ Michael:** Just too woody for me.
**Nose:** Very woody. Discourages further exploration.
**Palate:** Surprisingly fresh and fruity. What happened to the woodiness? Suddenly, it smacked me in the mouth.
**Finish:** Some fruity, mint-toffee flavours struggle through.

**8½ Dave:** Old, mature, showing its age a bit, but still a remarkable dram.
**Nose:** Big and perfumed, with notes of coffee cake, chestnut, treacle, burnt orange, mulled wine spice.
**Palate:** A little woody and firm, but has just sufficient sweet spirit to carry. Oak, spiced orange, dried fruit, nutmeg. Spicy and quite full with a light touch of burnt sugar. Cognac-like.
**Finish:** Fresh ginger. Oak.

## BELL'S EXTRA SPECIAL AGED 8 YEARS 40%
Blended - Scotland

**8½ Michael:** Assertive but rounded. A wonderfully satisfying whisky. Enormously improved since its (and my) younger days.
**Nose:** Briney. Fresh earth. Arousing.
**Palate:** Grassy, juicy. Malty, firm, chewy. Shortbread. Cookies. Lemon marmalade. A lot happening.
**Finish:** Distinctly oily aromatics coming through. Long, peppery, dry.

**8 Paul:** I favourably responded to the oily texture and laser beam graininess of both the flavour and finish phases. Approaches genuine complexity. Bravo.
**Nose:** Softly grainy, with nuances of heather and moss. Dry.
**Palate:** Starts moderately sweet at entry, then turns more hard candylike and caramelly at mid-palate, with not-so-subtle notes of stone dry resiny oak. Oily texture and medium bodied.
**Finish:** Medium long and mildly floral/ripe/sweet in the throat.

## BEN NEVIS 10 YEARS OLD 46%
Single Malt - Highland

**7¾ Michael:** The sweetness could be excessive, but it is saved by the stogie.
**Nose:** Perfumy. Waxed fruits. Hard black chocolate. Cedar.
**Palate:** Oily, syrupy, sweetish. Belgian toffee wafers. Orange-cream pralines.
**Finish:** Stewed apricots. Crème Anglaise. A late whiff of cigar smoke.

**9 Jim:** This is a solid, gutsy whisky with wave-upon-wave of rich flavours and textures. A truly great malt. Older in style than the label suggests.
**Nose:** Much weightier and characterful than most 10 Years Olds. Toffee and fresh figs. Enticing.
**Palate:** Glorious mouth feel: chewy and lush with cream toffee giving way to a sprinkling of demerara.
**Finish:** Brilliant! Just a hint of fettered spice, and then waves of oak and malt with vanilla.

## BEN NEVIS 12 YEARS OLD, GLENKEIR TREASURES 40%
Single Malt - Highland

**7½ Dave:** A slightly uneasy balance between cereal, fruit and oak. Do not water.
**Nose:** Has depth and presence: liquorice, fruits de bois. Slightly oily almost like mutton fat with a touch of buttermilk underneath. Water makes it drier: nut shell, cereal, spice.
**Palate:** Covers the tongue, but the oak is quite grippy. Decent spread of flavours.
**Finish:** Long, mixing toasted cereal and dried fruit.

**8¼ Arthur:** Tasty stuff.
**Nose:** Sultanas and butter. A little sweet mint and some chestnuts. Candied peel and ginger, with a little citrus.
**Palate:** Very sweet, velvety and viscous. Sexy texture with satisfying balance of orangey fruitiness, flowers and malt.
**Finish:** Gingerbead.

## BEN NEVIS 1984 RAW CASK, BLACKADDER 61.2%
Single Malt - Highland

**8 Michael:** Extraordinarily red colour. The sweetness is almost overwhelming. The ultimate dessert whisky.
**Nose:** Raspberry vinegar. Winey. A fruity, French Syrah, perhaps?
**Palate:** Firm, sweetly fruity. Extraordinarily so. Kumquats. Brown sugar. Crêpes Suzette.
**Finish:** Crème Anglaise. Vanilla. Oak.

**7¼ Dave:** Rich and heavy. Plenty of nutty sherry-derived notes. It's good but just lacks complexity.
**Nose:** Dry, savoury/wooded notes though there's some butter that softens things a little. A mix of walnut, cherryade and clootie dumpling.
**Palate:** Powerful, intense and full-bodied with a leathery tone. Sweet. Solid ripe and rich.
**Finish:** Almost tarry. Marmite.

## BEN NEVIS 1986, 16 YEARS OLD, CADENHEAD'S 61.9%
Single Malt - Highland

**7¼ Martine: Hard to guess at the high alcohol strength from the nose. Not the usual big, oily Ben Nevis character. A pleasant fruitiness keeps the sweet notes dominant.**
**Nose:** Lots of fruit. Pear drops. Summer fruit pudding. Apples cooked in the oven.
**Palate:** Quite smooth. Light-bodied. Lots of fruit again. Blackcurrant.
**Finish:** Crisp and dry. Warm all the way through.

**7¼ Dave: Builds from a slightly disappointing nose to a solid sweet palate.**
**Nose:** Slightly indistinct but in time a rich sweetness.
**Palate:** Incredibly sweet: demerara sugar and malt. Has good weight, vanilla, almond. Well-rounded and silky.
**Finish:** Nutty and long.

## BEN NEVIS 1992 14 YEARS OLD, DEWAR RATTRAY 57.2%
Single Malt - Highland

**7 Dave: I find it a little grubby.**
**Nose:** Damp hay and coal dust with some farmyard notes. Cheese rind and penetrating alcohol. Sulphurous.
**Palate:** Biscuity, then liquorice soon overtaken by a dank note like a wet cellar. Lacks mid-palate oomph.
**Finish:** Suddenly appears to improve, but then the sulphur returns.

**7½ Arthur: Put off slightly by that combination of sharpness and sweet egg, but pleasant enough.**
**Nose:** Butter, kiwi, apples and peardrops. Spritzy with grapefruit and lime, but a little sharp and bordering on metallic. An ovaltiney background and a sweet egginess, like custard tarts.
**Palate:** A robust cereal character, plums, vanilla and some nutmeg.
**Finish:** Milk chocolate.

## BEN NEVIS DEW OF THE BEN 21 YEARS OLD 43%
Blended - Scotland

**7¾ Michael: Somewhat lacking in complexity. For the drinker who wants an easily drinkable whisky with some maturity.**
**Nose:** Beeswax. Tropical fruits. Raisins. Sweet, sugary.
**Palate:** Creamy but light. Fruity, refreshing. Orangey.
**Finish:** Lightly smoky. Slightly bitter. Appetising.

**8 Dave: Fine, pretty classy stuff.**
**Nose:** Round and soft and very creamy. Tangerine, chocolate, toffee, some oak.
**Palate:** Rounded. A real wave of chocolate flavours hits you, along with nut, a hint of oak and an earthy powerful undertow. Solid stuff.
**Finish:** Might just be a tad short.

## BEN NEVIS, OLD & RARE PLATINUM 45%
Single Malt - Highland

**7½ Gavin: Just about holds its own against the effects of excessive age. On the cusp!**
**Nose:** Very fragrant, violets and honey. A great nose.
**Palate:** Not surprisingly, some flat, oaky notes, but the honey, robust maltiness, and a tinge of smoke hold together to make this work rather well.
**Finish:** Drying sherry and oak, ultimately quite bitter and tannic.

**7½ Dave: Strange nose but good flavours.**
**Nose:** Plenty of wood. Plasticene, emulsion paint and amyl nitrate. Water reveals toasted oak, rich dried fruits, cumin/coriander powder.
**Palate:** Soft demerara sweetness. Toasted almond, grilled nut. Acquires some elegance, almost Cognac like. A floral, pot pourri note. Grippy oak.
**Finish:** Marzipan. Almond slices.

## BENNACHIE 10 YEARS OLD 40%
Blended Malt - Scotland

**7 Michael: Light but pleasant.**
**Nose:** Heathery. Honeyish. Peaty. Slightly burnt.
**Palate:** Light. Grassy. Lemongrass. Falls away somewhat.
**Finish:** Late surge of spiciness.

**6½ Dave: Decent but unexciting.**
**Nose:** Light gold. Straw, light wood. Aromatic with hints of heather, apple, bran flakes and faint sulphur.
**Palate:** A sweet start reminiscent of Juicy Fruit chewing gum. Crisp and nutty mid-palate.
**Finish:** Medium length with dried fruits, heather honey and a drift of smoke.

## BENNACHIE 17 YEARS OLD 40%
Blended Malt - Scotland

**7½ Michael: Light but pleasant, with some delicacy and complexity.**
**Nose:** Lemony, flowery, honeyed, grassy, peaty.
**Palate:** Soft, smooth, malty. Lightly creamy. Some good Speyside fruity-flowery flavours.
**Finish:** Flowery dry.

**6 Dave: No great distinguishing features.**
**Nose:** Light gold. Unreduced it shows fruit cake, heather and apricot. With water a strange fizzy quality appears. Sherbet dab, heather-honey and light smoke.
**Palate:** The fizziness continues on the palate. There are some sherry notes, but oak dominates.
**Finish:** Oaky and dry.

## BENNACHIE 21 YEARS OLD 40%
Blended Malt - Scotland

**7 Michael: It would take a particularly good parcel of this malt to mature for 21 years.**
**Nose:** Sweet. Oak. Hint of sulphur.
**Palate:** Sweetish. Vanilla. Lemony. Some maltiness. Somewhat woody.
**Finish:** Slightly sappy. Smoke. Bergamot. Hint of spice.

**7 Dave: A slightly bizarre malt.**
**Nose:** Light gold. An amazing nose, like walking into a branch of Body Shop – all passion fruit, overripe mango, ripe banana, cocoa butter and vanilla.
**Palate:** As you'd expect, the ripe fruity theme continues in the mouth with a glint of sweet sherry-accented fruit mid-palate.
**Finish:** Dry to start then softens leaving traces of raisin and soft tropical fruit.

## BENRIACH 15 YEARS OLD, CASK COLLECTION, DEWAR RATTRAY 59.9%
Single Malt - Speyside

**7¼ Martine: Quite an energetic guy which needs water to be tamed. A classic light Speysider, lacking elegance though.**
**Nose:** Light, tangy. Mustardy. Spirity. Dry hay, mint. A touch of tangerine. Water enhances a butyric note.
**Palate:** Sweet at start then developing on mustard and spices. Biting. Fresh oak. A musty note.
**Finish:** Lingering and spicy. A bitter edge with water.

**7½ Dave: Call me a wimp if you want, but the high alcohol has just blurred everything here.**
**Nose:** High nose-burn without water. Very buttery with lots of top-notes: freesia, citrus peels, jasmine, lilac, estery, green pear, dolly mixtures.
**Palate:** Very sweet and hot without water but jammed full of fruit. Slight pooling of fruits in centre.
**Finish:** Citric and punchy. Short.

## BENRIACH 1981, CONNOISSEUR'S CHOICE 43%
Single Malt - Speyside

**7½ Martine: The bourbon cask influence is obvious. A refreshing dram but simplistic. Water ruins it.**
**Nose:** Buttery. Nutty. Pine nuts. Vanilla. Aniseed. Hint of coconut milk.
**Palate:** Smooth. Grassy. Green apples. Kiwi. Star anise. A certain weakness at mid-palate. Fresh feel all the way through.
**Finish:** Grassy, slightly astringent.

**8¼ Dave: Seems delicate but has real presence.**
**Nose:** Light and fragrant. Perfume-like. Hyacinth. American cream soda, apple pie. Balanced, vanilla, oakiness. Some weight and complexity.
**Palate:** Sweet and direct with an unctuous feel. Apples, raspberry shifting into papaya and, with water, peanut oil. Blossom-like.
**Finish:** Fresh, clean and zesty.

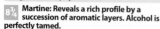

## BENRIACH 21 YEARS OLD 56.7%
Single Malt - Speyside

**8¾ Martine: Reveals a rich profile by a succession of aromatic layers. Alcohol is perfectly tamed.**
**Nose:** Silvestry. Damp earth, pine needles. Chestnut purée. Vanilla merges through the wood. Peppermint tea. A smoky medicinal whiff coming through with a creosote note.
**Palate:** Velvety, smooth. The creosote is coming through grassy flavours. Fresh cider. Lemon pie.
**Finish:** Slightly fizzy then fruit (lemon drops).

**9 Dave: Atypical for a Speysider for sure but what a phenomenal dram this is.**
**Nose:** Elegant and refined with peat smoke to the fore. Raisin, heather and dried fruits. Has real maturity. Light spice and coal dust.
**Palate:** Rich ripe and long with great layers of dried fruit and subtle scented ash like woodsmoke. Some sweet spice. Multifaceted.
**Finish:** Spicy. Ashes yet a real life.

## BENRIACH 21 YEARS OLD, THE WHISKY EXCHANGE 56.7%
Single Malt - Speyside

**8¾ Dave: Complex with excellent balance. Atypical for a Speyside, but it's one hell of a dram!**
**Nose:** Initially, stewed fruit/marmalade and roasted nuts, then the smoke begins to build. This melange of fruit, nut and peat fires makes it multi-faceted.
**Palate:** Immediate overwhelming smokiness which hangs there as the spirit slowly unfolds. Pecan, hazelnut. Sweet spices. Great length.
**Finish:** Ash and pepper. Tingling.

**9¼ Arthur: Complex and balanced. Excellent.**
**Nose:** Very estery, pear drops and pineapple cubes. With water some complex and subtle phenols, as it settles autumn woodsmoke and dry ash. With plenty of time to settle in the glass a subtle tone of roasted peanuts or peanut butter.
**Palate:** Woodsmoke, and parma ham, with a vanilla sweetness. Some salty nuts too.
**Finish:** Pink dettol, estery.

## BENRIACH 25 YEARS OLD 50%
Single Malt - Speyside

**8¾ Dave: Another killer from Mr Walker's warehouse. Distillery of the year for me.**
**Nose:** Shows maturity, with a lifted estery quality. More perfumed and floral with water. Digestive biscuits and nutmeggy spiciness then clove.
**Palate:** Seamless and highly energetic. Layered fruits, dark chocolate and a dazzling array of spices that fly over the tongue.
**Finish:** Sparkling. Complex.

**8½ Arthur: Proudly and confidently mature.**
**Nose:** Honeysuckle, gala melon and some sweet, oily terpentine notes. Vanilla-infused rice pudding, baked sweet gammon and powdered almonds.
**Palate:** Peaches in sweet syrup, orange, grass. Marzipan and sultana cookies, made with nutmeg.
**Finish:** Drying tannins that balance the earlier sweetness.

## BENRIACH 30 YEARS OLD 50%
Single Malt - Speyside

**9 Dave: Soft, subtle and not overwooded. Just shades it over the 25yo this time.**
**Nose:** Good oak extract and layering effect: vanilla, hard barley sugar, pecan nut, coconut, dried apricot. Lightly oily, cooked custard.
**Palate:** Sweet start. Nuts and honey. Spreads well across the palate. White chocolate, shortbread, nutmeg, Turkish delight/rose. Excellent length.
**Finish:** Cereal then raisin and toffee.

**9 Arthur: Some older whiskies smell great but are world-weary on the palate. This is vibrant with a palate that matches or even exceeds its nose.**
**Nose:** Fruit and nut toffee, refresher sweets and a lemony sourness. Ginger and spices.
**Palate:** A burst of complex Oloroso wood and smoky notes, with ginger cake iced with lemon.

**Finish:** That fizzing rich woodiness lasts long after the maltiness passes.

## BENRIACH AUTHENTICUS PEATED SINGLE MALT 21 YEARS OLD 46%
Single Malt - Speyside

**8½ Arthur: Another region-buster and a good one too.**
**Nose:** Pink Germolene, sultana and nutmeg cookies, burning wet wood, orange juice.
**Palate:** A thick and juicy texture, sweet and spicy with plenty of peat in between.
**Finish:** Tea tree and sweet woodsmoke.

**8 Owen: Utterly confused here, I thought I was on Speyside.**
**Nose:** Sugary and unmistakably phenolic. School woodwork room aromas of pine resin and glue.
**Palate:** Sawdust. Charcoal. Smoky wood fires. Sweet and then bitter. A sneeze inducing pepperiness. Pleasant smoke, liquorice. Clean.
**Finish:** Oily, and less phenolic than the nose would suggest. Appetising smoke.

## BENRIACH BOTTLED FOR CRAIGELLACHIE HOTEL 1976 57.6%
Single Malt - Speyside

**8½ Arthur: Very enjoyable and marked up for balance and poised integration.**
**Nose:** Peach and strawberry yoghurts, Refresher sweets, carrots and pears. With time and water a slightly silagey element appears, but recovers to show admirable balance of fruit, earth and wood.
**Palate:** Buttery, fruity and a slurpy suck of toffee.
**Finish:** A light burnt-woodiness indicating some age and a slight minerally, coal-tar edge.

**7¾ Owen: Rich and viscous and packed with flavour. Develops some elegance with water.**
**Nose:** Light and sweet. Coconut ice. Some marshmallow and vanilla. Creamy.
**Palate:** Oily, fiery, sugary. Some vegetal bitterness. Creamier and more rounded with water.
**Finish:** Warming. Late, sweet and bitter, liquorice notes. Remember "Imps"?

## BENRIACH CURIOSITAS PEATED MALT, 10 YEARS OLD 40%
Single Malt - Speyside

**7¾ Martine: A Speyside? The most Islayish of all the Speysides I have ever tasted. Interesting as a freak even if wood toughens the whole profile a little.**
**Nose:** Incredibly phenolic. Creosote. Meaty. Bacon. A slight butyric note in the back. Ash. Smoky when diluted.
**Palate:** Smooth and sweet then an explosion of pepper and ginger, fading on dry nuttiness.
**Finish:** Lingering. Liquoriced, with a dry woody bitterness.

**8 Dave: A shock to find something this phenolic in this part of the world – but a great dram.**
**Nose:** Peat. Smoky and turfy moving into coal tar/bitumen with real baked fruit sweetness behind. Opens up into dried heather and turf.
**Palate:** Immense smoke, then sweet rich mouthfeel with nuttiness and a slight medicinal edge.
**Finish:** Cereal and smoke. Long. Bitumen. Embers.

## BENRIACH CURIOSITAS PEATED MALT, 10 YEARS OLD 46%
Single Malt - Speyside

**7¾ Martine: Quite a nice dram but a bit edgy.**
**Nose:** Intense. Old parmigiano. Medlars. Then becoming creamier, molasses toffee with a hint of burnt coffee. A touch of sultanas.
**Palate:** Sweet, velvety. Sticky toffee pudding. Smoky (burnt wood and dry ashes). Getting quite peppery.
**Finish:** Warm, dry, rather long. Tabasco. A minty touch.

**7½ Dave: Well balanced. Though peaty it doesn't have the marine phenolics usually encountered on the coast.**
**Nose:** Raffia/weetabix to start then dry wood smoke/charred sticks. With water a cooked vegetable note and old trainers.
**Palate:** Sweet oak when neat. Lightly nutty with a hint of smoke. Water maintains the balance.
**Finish:** Long and lightly smoky.

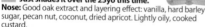

## BENRIACH DARK RUM FINISH 46%
Single Malt - Speyside

**8** **Martine: A cheery dram, opening up on the sunny side with definite rum colours on the nose. A dash of water sweetens the palate.**
**Nose:** Sweet and intense with a fruity twinkle. Porridge, fresh hazelnuts. Marshmallow. Rum influence peeps through the creamy fruitiness.
**Palate:** Quite crisp though with a syrupy texture. Less mellow than expected. A spicy explosion at mid palate with a slight bitter edge.
**Finish:** Spicy, slightly dusty. Nutty aftertaste.

**7¾** **Dave: Works pretty well. Rum in a supporting role, putting a different spin on the whisky.**
**Nose:** Sweet. Banana jam, guava juice, floral with a light cereal maltiness. Plenty of vanilla.
**Palate:** Smooth with bags of vanilla soft fruits and a lightly floral touch. Lots of character and good balance between the two elements.
**Finish:** Medium length. Touch of deeper rum notes.

## BENRIACH MADEIRA WOOD FINISH 46%
Single Malt - Speyside

*WHISKY Magazine Recommended*

**7¾** **Dave: Balanced and with good weight. A good addition to the range.**
**Nose:** Lightly malty with plenty of sweet spices. Water brings a fluffy citrus quality and butteriness.
**Palate:** Acetone and menthol. Deepens in the middle where it becomes quiet chewy. Better with water, those dusty spices adding interest.
**Finish:** Nutty and clean, with decent length, some concentrated fruit.

**8¼** **Arthur: Yummy. Luxurious texture and sweetness.**
**Nose:** Bananas, green apples and lots of dry woody spices. Mango lassi.
**Palate:** A big broad texture on the tongue with sweet pale sultanas, caramel and a sweet breadiness.
**Finish:** A little drying spice.

## BENRIACH OVER 12 YEARS OLD 43%
Single Malt - Speyside

**7** **Martine: Herbal in the dry way. Leaves a bitter grassy note in the finish. I'd rather have a cup of tea.**
**Nose:** Sappy. Grassy. Coriander. Forestry touch (mushrooms, wet leaves). Water releases caramel sweetness. Waffles.
**Palate:** Sweet and smooth. Herbal. Rosemary.
**Finish:** Short and dry. Touch of dusty finger.

**7¾** **Dave: Good balance. A great aperitif.**
**Nose:** Very delicate, floral/estery, pear drop, peppermint. Stewed apple, oak, lemon. Bubblegum. Seems young. Wood shavings.
**Palate:** Sweet and softly creamy, then fresh limey acids. Floral peachy notes in mid-palate. Has a piercing quality and real charm.
**Finish:** Chewy, into oak.

## BENRIACH OVER 20 YEARS OLD 43%
Single Malt - Speyside

**7½** **Martine: Muscular. Welcome in a blizzard but don't expect Mozart when you are likely to get Wagner.**
**Nose:** Rich antique bouquet. Exotic wood. Polished floor. Galanga. Creamy. Vanilla toffee. Orange and chocolate biscuit.
**Palate:** Smooth, syrupy. Raisins. Marmalade. Chocolate mousse. Wood never gives away.
**Finish:** Dries off on wood notes. Spicier as time goes.

**8¼** **Dave: Long, elegant and soft.**
**Nose:** Mature. Dry oak, wood oil, cedar, eucalypt, tobacco, chocolate, vanilla. Has weight behind: big, lush fruitiness, apricot, marzipan.
**Palate:** Soft fruits crisped up by oak. Well integrated flavours. Smooth and not as oaky as nose. Lightly honeyed, coconut.
**Finish:** Dry, bracken like, then toffee.

## BENRINNES 10 YEARS OLD, CHIEFTAIN'S CHOICE 43%
Single Malt - Speyside

**7** **Dave: For me this has been bottled too early and before the sulphuriness of youth has been fully matured out.**
**Nose:** Rubbery, firm with a strange mealy dustiness. Sulphur obscuring other character.

**Palate:** Light smoke with a deep and heavy midpalate. A powerful flavour though with water that youthful sulphury note comes back.
**Finish:** Earthy and deep.

**7** **Arthur: Relatively uneventful.**
**Nose:** Green plums, roasted cheese, a slightly prickly, chemically note. With water there is a doughy note, with a bit of bran husk like a bran scone. Plum or cherry sauce.
**Palate:** Quite broad on the palate, a youthful maltiness and some apple.
**Finish:** Light, sweet breadiness.

## BENRINNES 13 YEARS OLD, CASK 7014, HARRIS WHISKY 55.9%
Single Malt - Speyside

**7¾** **Michael: This youngster has some hidden depths. Promising.**
**Nose:** Gooseberry. Youthful, fresh, tart, green fruits. Some menthol. Forest odours. More citrussy with water.
**Palate:** Instantly drying. Caramel. Cereals. Oat cakes?
**Finish:** Warming. Biscuity with a hint of cocoa. Cleansing. With water, chocolate chip cookies.

**7½** **Arthur: Some attractive elements but a little clumsy and adolescent.**
**Nose:** An effervescent nose: lime chews and lemongrass. Lemon flavoured vitamin C tablets. Hay. With water some more youthful bran/brown bread cereal notes appear, but ultimately it remains a bright and fruity, but slightly sharp spirit.
**Palate:** Bready maltiness and peaches.
**Finish:** Drying, with slightly earthy bitterness.

## BENRINNES 14 YEARS OLD, DEWAR RATTRAY 59.3%
Single Malt - Speyside

**7¼** **Martine: Nose and palate are a bit agressive with a lingering sourness which is disturbing. A prickly character. Water smooths the flavours over but this is not enough.**
**Nose:** Tangy, somewhat spirity. Cider cellar. Wet leaves. Touch of earthy mushrooms. Pear drop. Becomes cheesy.
**Palate:** Biting. Sour apple, pear drop. The cheesy notes show up.
**Finish:** Fizzy, spicy and nutty. Turning bitter.

**7¾** **Dave: This is still improving. A couple more years in cask would have improved it further.**
**Nose:** Smooth and soft to begin, then some light smoke, bourbon biscuit, roast beef gravy, mint all balanced by gentle vanilla ice cream.
**Palate:** Praline, butter/cream. Meaty and rich in the centre with gentle oak. Substantial with richness.
**Finish:** Sweet then smoky/burnt.

## BENRINNES 1989, BERRY'S OWN SELECTION 46%
Single Malt - Speyside

**7¼** **Dave: Bizarrely, the nose reminded me of an Argentinian Torrontes. Where's the famed Benrinnes meatiness?**
**Nose:** Light and discreet with some grass, limeade and a macadamia nuttiness. In time there's lemon and a wine-like perfume.
**Palate:** Very sweet with lifted aromatics. Delicate but with a subtly rich middle palate. Soft fruits.
**Finish:** Sweet grassy.

**7¼** **Arthur: Pleasant enough.**
**Nose:** Lots of cereal character: Shredded Wheat, hay, wet earth, and some sweet biscuits. Some fruit syrup and lemon peel.
**Palate:** Light and sweet, with no off-notes. Vanilla cream, peach and some cereal.
**Finish:** Hay.

## BENRINNES 1990 14 YEARS OLD, SINGLE CASK SHERRY FINISH, DOUGLAS LAING 50%
Single Malt - Speyside

8¼ **Michael: Beautifully full flavoured whisky. Manages to be both elegant and robustly expressive. Very appetising.**
**Nose:** Floral. Camomile. Honey. Herbal tea.
**Palate:** Fruity, morello cherries. Fresh, woody, rooty, liquorice?
**Finish:** Spicy dryness.

7 **Dave: Needs a bit more in the middle.**
**Nose:** A light, malty spirit. Almost frothy with some vanilla, Ovaltine and US oak. Hot without water.
**Palate:** Sweet and gentle, but you need water to reduce the edge, then lose character.
**Finish:** A bit flat.

## BENRINNES 21 YEARS OLD, RARE MALTS 60.4%
Single Malt - Speyside

8 **Michael: One of Speyside's secret delights. But a hard whisky to know. Big flavours, but tightly combined and unyielding.**
**Nose:** 'Green' aromas. The forest floor.
**Palate:** Oily. Nutty. Creamy flavours. Sweet.
**Finish:** Firm. Robustly spicy. Long.

7¾ **Dave: Soft yet savoury. Mortlach's little brother and a forgotten classic.**
**Nose:** Rich, oily with a meaty edge. Dubbin. Smoke, fruit and nut and surprisingly fragrant top notes.
**Palate:** Oily rather than silky texture: then a nutty smoky bite and citrus. A full-blooded, mouth-coating experience, and for all its robust, meaty nature, quite gentle.
**Finish:** Long. Meaty.

## BENROMACH 18 YEARS OLD, GORDON & MACPHAIL 40%
Single Malt - Speyside

8 **Michael: The best Benromach I have tasted. I wonder what she should expect in a few years from the new stillhouse.**
**Nose:** Perfumy. New leather upholstery in a luxury car. Mint imperials for the road.
**Palate:** Butterscotch sauce. Peaches and cream. Sherry trifle.
**Finish:** Deliciously rounded. Some garden mint. A hint of peat. Balancing dryness. Gently warming.

8¼ **Martine: A vibrant, characterful malt, drier on the palate and finish than expected from the nose.**
**Nose:** Intense and colourful. A basket of ripe summer fruit (apricot, peach) with a fresh lemony character. Becomes biscuity (short-bread) with water. Pleasant dry oakiness in the back.
**Palate:** Smooth and velvety. Oak and spices tend to prevail over the fruit.
**Finish:** Dry, spicy and slightly astringent.

## BENROMACH 1969 40%
Single Malt - Speyside

8 **Michael: An old-fashioned whisky for an old-fashioned winter's evening. Wins points for being cuddly rather than complex.**
**Nose:** Cough sweets. Mint boiled sweets.
**Palate:** Syrupy without being cloying. Fisherman's Friend. Delicious.
**Finish:** Gently warming. Soothing.

7 **Marcin: As a fan of Benromach, I was surprised at how little character came through and felt that the whisky had been overpowered.**
**Nose:** Not too much going on – dumb nose flattens out further when reduced.
**Palate:** Lots of wood influence dominating the whisky. Dried out and lacking passion.
**Finish:** Medium and warming.

## BENROMACH 1973, GORDON & MACPHAIL 40%
Single Malt - Speyside

7¾ **Michael: After a weekend walk in the country? Mid to late afternoon. Who needs tea? Just a slice of fruit pie and a generous dram of Benromach.**
**Nose:** Flowery, Lime tea, lemongrass, light peat.
**Palate:** Key lime pie. Lemon meringue. Marshmallow. Candied angelica. Shortbread.
**Finish:** Icing sugar. Dusty dryness.

7¾ **Dave: Good. Well-balanced. An attractive anytime malt.**
**Nose:** Fresh and attractive. Green walnut, oats and then lily/freesia. Cut grass.
**Palate:** Light smoke but all ripe, soft and chewy. It's light but has a good sweet mid-palate with touches of fig and nut. Don't add water though.
**Finish:** Dry with some smoke.

## BENROMACH 1974, GORDON & MACPHAIL 40%
Single Malt - Speyside

8 **Michael: I have always found Benromach assertively flowery, herbal, almost cedary. Will this highly distinctive character prevail in the new, smaller, stills introduced since the change of ownership? Tastings on a recent visit suggest that it might.**
**Nose:** Garden mint. Marijuana. Incense. Joss sticks.
**Palate:** Creamy and oily. Peppermint.
**Finish:** Tobacco. Faint peat smoke.

8 **Jim: Something of a delicate flower, lacks a certain 'oomph' to rant it amongst the greats.**
**Nose:** At once flowery and fruity. Marmalade and very sweet vanilla.
**Palate:** Excellent bittersweet kick-off, complex and tangled but settling for a medium sweet wine gum fruitiness.
**Finish:** Lots of vanilla intermingling with gentlest arrival of smoke. Rather thin at the death, though.

## BENROMACH 1976, 27 YEARS OLD AUTHENTIC COLLECTION, CADENHEAD'S 57.1%
Single Malt - Speyside

7½ **Martine: The nose promised more smoothness. Quite an austere character on the palate but with a lot of class.**
**Nose:** Resiny. Intense. An elegant oaky profile with a concentrated fruity richness. Apricot and marzipan pie. Toasted raisin buns. Beautiful creaminess.
**Palate:** Dry at the start then opening up on creamy toffee flavours. Oak is never far away though.
**Finish:** Dry, slightly bitter. Liquorice, chocolate, coffee.

8½ **Dave: Layered, multifaceted, excellent.**
**Nose:** Rich and mature. Syrupy notes, ginger preserve, fudge, steamed spice pudding, marmalade, honey, hard toffee. Layered, nutty.
**Palate:** Ripe. Very full bodied. Explosive spiciness: nutmeg, clove, cinnamon, but all bedded down in sweet ripe fruits. Even some passion fruit. Complex.
**Finish:** Spicy, tingling.

## BENROMACH 1980, GORDON & MACPHAIL 58.6%
Single Malt - Speyside

8 **Martine: A wake up dram. Not a great deal of complexity but an enjoyable fruitiness to make you think of springtime.**
**Nose:** Fruity. Zesty. Vanilla rises up in sweet waves. Orchard fruits. Fresh and lively. Needs time to open.
**Palate:** Surprisingly sweet in spite of the high strength. Coating. Ripe apricots, peaches.
**Finish:** Lingering, slightly heavy but satisfying. Candied ginger. Almondy.

7½ **Dave: Another vibrant springtime aperitif.**
**Nose:** Lively and young. Green oak, balsa wood, lemon. With water, green fig, marshmallow, summer fruits and aromatic top notes.
**Palate:** Alcohol obscures the sweet centre. Water opens up grassiness, pear, baked apple. Concentrated.
**Finish:** Clean and short.

## BENROMACH 21 YEARS OLD, OLD TOKAJI FINISH 45%
Single Malt - Speyside

7¼ **Martine: Rather unbalanced. The nose is far more promising than the palate. What's the point of the finish?**
**Nose:** Floral (Ivy flowers) at first then heading to heavier scents. Caramelised walnuts, cloved orange. Toffee.
**Palate:** Sweet and sour, then bitter. Bitter orange juice, unsweetened coffee. Close to astringent.
**Finish:** Dry with an oaky grip. Quite sweetly lingering but the wood bite does not give up.

7¾ **Ian: Inhaling provides 'aroma-therapy', while the palate shows that mixing the grape and the grain can be thoroughly rewarding and risk-free.**

**Nose:** Rich gingerbread, chocolate, honey, then poached fruit with a hint of Christmas pudding.
**Palate:** Velvety, luscious thick honey with hints of fruity mulled wine, apricots, sloes, then butterscotch and dark chocolate.
**Finish:** Créme brûlée, fruit with spicy oak garnish.

## BENROMACH 22 YEARS OLD, PORT WOOD FINISH, GORDON & MACPHAIL 45%
Single Malt - Speyside

**7¼ Michael:** Should the pink tangerine blush of this whisky hint at Bacchus? He may have glanced at the cask, but I can't find him in the glass.
**Nose:** Digestive biscuits (shortbread?) in the foreground, give way to distant background of ripe tropical fruits. Banana? Vanilla, too.
**Palate:** Viscous. Well done toast, unsalted butter and maybe home-made lemon curd.
**Finish:** Fruity? Faintly citric with traces of cocoa.

**8 Dave:** A generous distillate given a little nudge by the finish. Very well balanced.
**Nose:** Distinctly pinky with a sweet, slightly jammy nose: rosehip jelly, rasps, stewed fruit tea, sweet apple and a hint of smoke.
**Palate:** Sweet start, a (balanced) grippy mid-palate then a slow, sweet wine gum like centre. Bittersweet wild fruits (rowan) balanced by oak.
**Finish:** Long and sweet.

## BENROMACH ORGANIC 43%
Single Malt - Speyside

**6¾ Dave:** This suggests a young spirit and lots of oak. Not balanced.
**Nose:** Oak driven. Edgy and plain with hard malt and freshly planed wood.
**Palate:** As the nose suggests. A picture of oak shavings piled on top of a fruit salad. Hollow midpalate. There's two elements to this and they ain't talking to each other.
**Finish:** Hard and lean.

**8¼ Arthur:** The 'organic' bit feels like first-ism to me, and not as important as the 'virgin oak' part. The first new oak malt that has worked for me.
**Nose:** Spicy, sappy oak. Pine, cloves and fudge. Some apple and lemon peel. Danish pastry overspiced with nutmeg. Pencil shavings.
**Palate:** Toffeeish and spicy
**Finish:** Great texture and body of youth, cut through by bold oak.

## BENROMACH PEAT SMOKE, GORDON & MACPHAIL 46%
Single Malt - Speyside

**7½ Dave:** Once the middle fills out will be a lovely addition to the range.
**Nose:** Ultra-fresh fish, rainwashed pebbles, light smoke which develops as it opens. Clean and quite sweet behind.
**Palate:** Light clean with a delicate oiliness. Mixing fragrance delicate fruit and smoke well but needs a little more weight.
**Finish:** Light smoke.

**7½ Martine:** Fresh and frisky. A welcome body warmer.
**Nose:** Light, fresh, lemony (unripe lemon). Earthy and rooty. Distant smoke.
**Palate:** Sweet, keeps that refreshing character. Peaty, even sooty. Woodsmoked ham. Minty.
**Finish:** Dry, dusty. Spices keep the palate warm.

## BENROMACH SASSICAIA WOOD FINISH, GORDON & MACPHAIL 45%
Single Malt - Speyside

**8 Dave:** A success.
**Nose:** Strawberry and rosehip once more but this has some greater substance and depth. Some smoke in there as well. Slight touch of youth.
**Palate:** Sweet quite concentrated fruits. Again hinting at depth. Lightly phenolic.
**Finish:** Good length mixing woodsmoke and hedgerow fruits.

**WHISKY** *Magazine* *Recommended*

**8 Arthur:** Another successful finish where the cask input seemed to work with the spirit.
**Nose:** Some sherry-like dried fruit notes, with some berries and spice too. There's smoke too with a little oaty cereal character.
**Palate:** Very sweet initially, with vanilla and treacle toffee, with cinnamon spice and dryness coming through later. Some berry fruit is in the delivery too.
**Finish:** A thread of smoke.

## BENROMACH TRADITIONAL, GORDON & MACPHAIL 40%
Single Malt - Speyside

**8¼ Michael:** This one really does have subtlety. A lovely, delicate aperitif.
**Nose:** Vanilla. Sweet gale. A hint of sea air.
**Palate:** Perfumey. Floral. Heather. Juniper.
**Finish:** Sweet lemons. A light dusting of ginger.

**WHISKY** *Magazine* *Recommended*

**8½ Dave:** Young, but what a well poised session dram this is.
**Nose:** Floral to start (freesia, stock) with light vanilla notes and a hint of pine. In time a drift of peat smoke, cashew, gingerbread and clover honey.
**Palate:** Soft to start then butterscotch, spices. Excellent breadth. Oak in balance.
**Finish:** Light oak, orange peel.

## BERRY'S BEST LOWLAND 12 YEARS OLD 43%
Single Malt - Lowland

**7¼ Arthur:** A fine dram to start off a tasting, but not enough interest to engage you the whole night long.
**Nose:** Lemony, doughy and floral. Orange blossom and warm bread.
**Palate:** A rounded maltiness and a little ripe fruitiness.
**Finish:** Drying, earthy and slightly bitter. Not its strong point.

**7 Dave:** Just needs a middle palate lift…and a bit more mature stock vatted in?
**Nose:** Light, floral and a little dumb. Butter (unsalted!), scone mix, a hint of jasmine, broom flower (pea pod) slightly immature. In time, damp washing, putty, earth (a little grubby).
**Palate:** Light, muscat like, delicate. A hint of sweetness in the centre but pretty ethereal stuff. You feel it could blow away like a dandelion fluff.
**Finish:** Slightly green. Sugary.

## BERRY'S BEST ORKNEY, 14 YEARS OLD 43%
Single Malt - Island (non Islay)

**8¼ Michael:** Intense salt. Very slight iodine.
**Nose:** Pale greeny gold.
**Palate:** Very restrained. Soft. Sea air.
**Finish:** Very fresh. Malty nuttiness. Becoming gritty and sandy.

**WHISKY** *Magazine* *Recommended*

**7¾ Dave:** A delicious session dram but could do with more oomph.
**Nose:** Light juicy fruits (apricot jam, lemon barley water, orange pith, mango). Like a Trinidadian rum. Light tropical fruit and coconut. Attractive and subtle.
**Palate:** Very light with this juiciness slowly seeping out. Oak grips very lightly . Lightly oily in texture.
**Finish:** Fruity with some white pepper.

## BLACK BARREL 40%
Blended - Scotland

**7½ Michael:** The name does not imply a dark whisky – the colour is a good full gold – but the barrel may have been well-charred. There is plenty of juicy wood-extract there.
**Nose:** Faintly smoky. Sweetish. Lemon zest. Pancakes.
**Palate:** Assertively sweet. Slightly syrupy.
**Finish:** Spicy (cinnamon?) dryness.

**7½ Dave:** A lovely easy going, approachable dram.
**Nose:** Soft and gentle with a light, crisp, cereal note. Water brings out milk chocolate, fruit and sultanas.
**Palate:** Very soft, gentle and sweet. A ripe whisky with chewy toffee.
**Finish:** Citrus sweetness.

## BLACK BOTTLE 10 YEARS OLD 40%
Blended - Scotland

**9 Michael: A delicious, appetising, new expression of Black Bottle. As a blend, it is a star.**
**Nose:** Very fragrant. Slight sherry, lots of seaweed, hint of salt and soda-bread.
**Palate:** Malty. Soft, syrupy. Marzipan. Almonds. Grassy.
**Finish:** Peat comes surging through.

**9 Jim: Simmering, full-blooded blend that celebrates its 100% Islay malt roots by taking no prisoners whatsoever. Brilliant.**
**Nose:** Grassy grain thins out the deep peat. Saltiness adds depth and compliments peppery notes.
**Palate:** Chewy and smoky. Flavours intensify as the rich, clean and oily peat really kick in. Malty too.
**Finish:** Sensational. Waves of peat give way to cocoa/coffee effect. Unbelievably long for a blend.

## BLACK BOTTLE 10 YEARS OLD 40%
Blended - Scotland

**8 Martine: An uncompromising Islay blend. Washes along sea fragrances. But reveals a sweet nature on the palate. Grain and malt are well married. A good cure for Islay-sickness.**
**Nose:** Tangy. A definite marine breath. Creosote. Drying sea-weeds. Coconut. Bogmyrtle. A hint of tar. Sour apple. Vanilla breaks through after a while.
**Palate:** Smoky. Sweet fruit notes. Malt extract.
**Finish:** Warm. Hint of soot. Light oak.

**8½ Dave: Holding all those expressive peaty malts in check is a difficult task. This does so with poise.**
**Nose:** Phenolic: tarry rope, seashell, salami. With herbs, seaweed, cereal notes. Coal scuttle.
**Palate:** Explosive smokiness balanced by a silky soft mid-palate. Seashore aromas, fish oil, light ginger, lavender. Sooty. Great balance.
**Finish:** Smoke and ginger.

## BLACK CUILLIN 8 YEARS OLD, COOPER'S CHOICE 40%
Single Malt - Island (non Islay)

**7¾ Michael: A substitute for the much-missed Talisker eight year-old? Perhaps, but neither as complex nor as robust.**
**Nose:** Smoky. Lightly peaty. Dry.
**Palate:** Oily at first, becoming lightly smoky, then a gritty minerally character.
**Finish:** Earthy, smoky dryness and a lingering suggestion of iron.

**7 Dave: A straightforward young dram.**
**Nose:** Malty and crisp. It seems pretty young with hard, lean immature notes of crab apple, unripe pear and light smoke.
**Palate:** Softer and sweeter than the nose suggests.
**Finish:** A little hard.

## BLADNOCH 10 YEARS OLD 43%
Single Malt - Lowland

**7½ Michael: Lots of aromas and flavours, but lacks structure. Curiously flat.**
**Nose:** Candyfloss (cotton candy). Some oxidation.
**Palate:** Sweet. Spicy. Muscovado sugar. Digestive biscuits.
**Finish:** Cedary dryness.

**6½ Dave: A very peculiar beast.**
**Nose:** Robust. Is that a hint of Irn Bru? There's oranges stewing in a pan and an aroma reminiscent of badly maderized wine (not Madeira) slightly off-putting.
**Palate:** Dominated by wood, then maderized character reappears.
**Finish:** Flat.

## BLADNOCH 12 YEARS OLD, JAMES MACARTHUR 43%
Single Malt - Lowland

**7¼ Michael: Gentle to the point of reticence. Aperitif. Or try it with Morrocan food.**
**Nose:** Sage. Chestnuts. Marron glacé.
**Palate:** Sweet. Very restrained. Almonds. Fresh, pronounced, garden mint. Aniseed.
**Finish:** Spicy. Soothing.

**7¾ Dave: I'm not fat, I'm just big boned.**
**Nose:** Lean yet gentle. Some cereal, flour, then comes polished oak. Water moves it towards orange and grapefruit zest.
**Palate:** Good flow with some spiciness, floral notes and a tingle of red peppercorn deepening into runny toffee and vanilla pod. Soft and substantial with creamy weight.
**Finish:** Gentle, if short.

## BLADNOCH 15 YEARS OLD, DOUGLAS LAING 50%
Single Malt - Lowland

**7 Martine: Not a very exciting whisky. Too edgy. Not delivering much on the palate. And lacking finesse. A bland cask?**
**Nose:** Heavy, buttery. Melting cheese. Quite unidimensional and restrained. Dry cider.
**Palate:** Sweet with a velvety feel. Oily. Malt teasers. Cereal bowl. Nescafé.
**Finish:** Tangy, chewed stalk.

**7 Dave: A whisky on the verge of a nervous breakdown.**
**Nose:** Plain, as if little has passed by way of conversation between cask and spirit. Lime, chalk dust. Little grubby with water.
**Palate:** Very light even fragile running scared down the middle of the tongue.
**Finish:** Simply disappears.

## BLADNOCH 15 YEARS OLD, JOHN MCDOUGALL'S 55.8%
Single Malt - Lowland

**8¼ Arthur: Distinctive and fascinating sourness: a complex, tangy old tart.**
**Nose:** Melted butter, apples and lemon rind (the preparatory stage of a crumble). Wet paint and plasticene. With water lots of sourness: gooseberries, soor plooms and grapefruit.
**Palate:** Mouthfilling and challenging with lime marmalade on brown bread and a dry finish.
**Finish:** A little sourness and perhaps some soap.

**7¼ Dave: It's a decent dram, but the soapiness just knocks it back a few points.**
**Nose:** Spicy! Curry leaf/fenugreek. Lightly floral, cooked pear, melted butter, linden blossom, light grass and a charred smokiness. Has character and quality.
**Palate:** Round and balancing between the tart and the sweet. Sadly there's also a slightly soapy quality.
**Finish:** Unripe fruit.

## BLADNOCH 17 YEARS OLD, DUN BHEAGAN 43%
Single Malt - Lowland

**7¾ Michael: Drier and thinner than Bladnoch at it's best.**
**Nose:** A suggestion of dried banana. Lightly vegetal. Grassy. Earthy.
**Palate:** Thin, dry. Herbal. A hint of garden mint. Dried citrus peels.
**Finish:** Orange pith.

**7¾ Dave: The nose is a distillation of a summer's day. The palate suggests there's a few clouds blocking out the sun.**
**Nose:** Fragrant and sweet: freesia, white fruits, puréed apple, green grapes, light malt. Delicate yet complex.
**Palate:** Light, sweet and charming, but not quite the delivery you expect after such a gorgeous nose.
**Finish:** Dries nicely. Honey.

## BLADNOCH 18 YEARS OLD SHERRY WOOD, CHIEFTAIN'S CHOICE 46%
Single Malt - Lowland

**7¾ Martine: A distinguished expression of sweet Oloroso, even if it seems a bit ostentatious on the palate. For afterdinner enjoyment.**
**Nose:** Nutty and spicy. Dominated but not drowned in sherry. Cherries in chocolate. Dried fruit. Kumquat.
**Palate:** Sherry leads the way. Candied chestnut. Fudge. Leather.
**Finish:** Robust. Warm. Spicy.

**8 Dave: A cracking Bladnoch. Let's have more like this.**
**Nose:** Sweet with toasted nuts, dried fruits and spices. Some light oaky tones and bracken. Water makes it slightly more fragrant: sweet hay, flowers, more spice.
**Palate:** A sweet yet savoury start. Caramelised fruit and nut. A good, quite chewy mid-palate but all very nicely underplayed.
**Finish:** Soft, hay-like.

## BLADNOCH 1974, SIGNATORY 50.6%
Single Malt - Lowland

**8** **Michael:** A whole range of aromas and flavours that are hard to pin down. Sent me into a reverie: a long weekend in a big house, kippers for breakfast, toasted brown bread and good marmalade. The house also smells of furniture polish.
**Nose:** Appetisingly piney.
**Palate:** Slippery smooth. Oily. Fragrant. Sappy.
**Finish:** Powdery. Spicy.

**7¼** **Dave:** Lovely, but the oak is just maybe a little too firm.
**Nose:** Fragrant, blossom-like and lifted, with some grass and oaky notes reminiscent of hot sawdust. After a while there's macaroon bars, lots of vanilla and blossom-like grassiness.
**Palate:** Oaky to start. A pretty firm structure, but attractive quite delicate spirit.
**Finish:** Dry.

## BLADNOCH 1977, 23 YEARS OLD, RARE MALTS 53.6%
Single Malt - Lowland

**7¾** **Michael:** Rather aggressive for a malt that is usually delicate and sweet, but still very distinctive. Will stand softening with a good splash of water.
**Nose:** Straw, grass, lemongrass.
**Palate:** Light, oily. Dry. Bamboo-like woodiness. Some vanilla smoothness after a few minutes in the glass. Aromatic. Exotic.
**Finish:** Grassy again. Hot. Chillies.

**8½** **Dave:** Delicate yet complex.
**Nose:** Delicate and summery but with guts. Aromatic nose: lemon, icing sugar, almond slice, vanilla, red fruit and with water basil leaf/anise.
**Palate:** Light to medium bodied. Floral with a sweetly attractive start but good texture mid-palate.
**Finish:** Strawberries then dry and malty.

## BLADNOCH 1980, 17 YEARS OLD, CADENHEAD'S
Single Malt - Lowland

**8** **Michael:** Slightly lean. Where is the fruity softness of Bladnoch?
**Nose:** Grassy, dry.
**Palate:** Dry, grassy, leafy.
**Finish:** Dry, herbal (bay leaves?)

**6½** **Jim:** An uncomplicated but less exhausted, more even Bladnoch than Adelphi's, offering pleasing balance. Past its best, though.
**Nose:** Subtle, silky and sweet; the maltiness is all-embracing and clean. Soft vanilla and coriander add depth.
**Palate:** Early dry oak suggests decay but powering, intense, if unsophisticated malt gives balance.
**Finish:** Vanilla, toffee and cocoa.

## BLADNOCH 1986, GORDON & MACPHAIL, CONNOISSEUR'S CHOICE 40%
Single Malt - Lowland

**8½** **Michael:** The light touch of sherry helps bring out the soft, fruity, flavours.
**Nose:** Slight nutty sherry. Dried citrus skins. Sweet grass.
**Palate:** Orange zest, lemons, faint syrup. Cream. Honey.
**Finish:** Orange zest. Gently gingery balancing dryness.

**6** **Jim:** Starts brightly enough but the caramel character prevents the whisky taking off.
**Nose:** Sharp lemon drops are blunted by caramel but the fruity, lime-zest freshness is appealing and intense.
**Palate:** Immediate fruitiness; very chewy malty middle with some bitter oak. The caramel slowly dulls everything.
**Finish:** Again, the caramel dominates. Flat, uninteresting, lacks length and depth.

## BLADNOCH 1989, 12 YEARS OLD, CADENHEAD'S 56.3%
Single Malt - Lowland

**7¾** **Martine:** A neat, summery comforter. Perfect dram for hillwalkers.
**Nose:** Flowery. Carnation. Pear-drop. Reminiscent of a grappa. Touch of hazelnut and date.
**Palate:** Very sweet. Cereals sweeping up fruit. Grassy. Wholegrain bread. Cooling mintiness.
**Finish:** Hot, intense, slightly fiery.

**8** **Dave:** Delicate but intense with great energy and zesty drive.

**Nose:** Light, crisp and intense with dry malty notes alongside lemon zest/leaf, flowers, almond and a crisp hay/grassiness.
**Palate:** Sweet, fragrant start, a flowery mid-palate with white currants, violet grass. Concentrated.
**Finish:** Light and quite dry.

## BLADNOCH 1989, 13 YEARS OLD, CADENHEAD'S 54.9%
Single Malt - Lowland

**7¾** **Michael:** Tired and irritable when first poured, but gradually opens up, more so when water was added.
**Nose:** Light, dry, lime peels?
**Palate:** Light, dry. Petal-like. Green. Chlorophyll. Some late vanilla. Herbal.
**Finish:** Dried out. Drying.

**7¾** **Dave:** A good example from a shamefully overlooked distillery.
**Nose:** Very pretty, lightly floral. Cut grass, lemon peel, Edinburgh rock, sweets, coconut cream. With water, spikier and a hint of immaturity.
**Palate:** Clean and crispier than the nose suggests. Fresh flowers, light summer fruits. Floats over the palate. Fragrant and attractive.
**Finish:** Soft.

## BLADNOCH 1991, GORDON & MACPHAIL 54.8%
Single Malt - Lowland

**7¼** **Martine:** The nose is unusual, closer to a sour Chinese broth than a whisky! But the palate restores an expected floral Lowland freshness.
**Nose:** Tangy. Mustard poultice, shallot dressing.
**Palate:** Sweeter than expected. Floral. Orange blossom. With water, honeyed cereal bowl.
**Finish:** Warms up on a gingery and peppery tanginess. A pleasant toasted hazelnut come back.

**8** **Dave:** Proof that a whisky can be delicate yet complex.
**Nose:** Mouthwatering. Florist shop: lily, freesia, then comes apple: blossom/sweet eating apple. Fragrant with a light malty note.
**Palate:** Delicate but vibrant with good feel and a fresh natural ripeness. Orchard fruit, boiled sweets, gentle oak. Good balance.
**Finish:** Lightly dry.

## BLADNOCH 1992 12 YEARS OLD, OLD MASTERS 56.1%
Single Malt - Lowland

**7¾** **Michael:** Quite assertive for Bladnoch. Not keen on the papery character. Quality of wood?
**Nose:** Lemon grass. Dry grass. Reedy. Cereal grain. Papery. Newsprint.
**Palate:** Starts with a dry maltiness. Lively development. Fruit pies: lemon meringue; gooseberry; pumpkin, the latter dusted with cinnamon and ginger.
**Finish:** Spicy, hot.

**8** **Marcin:** Unusual but a bit of a crowd pleaser.
**Nose:** High alcohol and quite medicinal. Butterscotch hiding in background. Lightly vegetal when reduced.
**Palate:** Great presence. Forceful masculine and relatively unsophisticated. Banana and toffee.
**Finish:** Freshly cooked and buttered, al dente green beans. Gutsy but not long.

## BLADNOCH 1992 13 YEARS OLD, OLD MASTERS 56.9%
Single Malt - Lowland

**6¾** **Arthur:** I know, I know – it's a Lowland! Still, I want a little more from a whisky. Full stop.
**Nose:** Cress, Jif lemon, pizza dough, bran and wet grass. Lemon pith.
**Palate:** Spirity, sweet and a little bland. A faint woodiness at the end.
**Finish:** Largely absent, but a soggy biscuit character.

**7** **Dave:** Not much interaction between spirit and wood immature. Light and clean but lacking in oomph.
**Nose:** A quite distant, slightly lean, unformed nose. Sugared almond, fondant icing, pear drop, muddy field, peanut skin.
**Palate:** Fine-boned and intense. Good quite vibrant, youthful feel. Alcohol.
**Finish:** Very short.

## BLADNOCH 1992, BERRY'S OWN SELECTION 46%
Single Malt - Lowland

**7½** **Arthur: So subtle it's barely there, but an intriguing mystery.**
**Nose:** Lime cordial, blackcurrant Chewitts and warm plasticene. All in wispy, etheral levels.
**Palate:** Sweet, then grassy then dry.
**Finish:** A ghost of dry maltiness and hot hay.

**8¼** **Dave: Gentle with excellent balance. Ridiculously lovely, like an Edwardian beauty.**
**Nose:** Pretty. Cereal, macadamia nut, meadow flowers, white fruit, light apple, herbal, medlar jelly. With water there's increased perfume reminiscent of an old-fashioned talcum powder flowers and some lime zest.
**Palate:** Sweet and light with a soft elegant mid-palate. Hints of vanilla, coconut and flowers.
**Finish:** Sweet then lightly drying.

## BLADNOCH 1992, OLD MASTERS 58.5%
Single Malt - Lowland

**7¼** **Martine: A two-sided malt, with two different expressions on the nose and on the palate. The alcohol needs to be tamed with water.**
**Nose:** Floral. Grassy. Gillyflower. Freshly mown lawns. Honeycomb. Barley sugar. A touch of linseed.
**Palate:** Oily and fat. Very fruity and sherbety. A big mouthful of William's pear.
**Finish:** Slightly biting. Warm and lingering.

**7¾** **Dave: Great delivery, all coming together on the finish.**
**Nose:** Intense, attractive quite 'green' nose. Water reveals a lovely fragrance: a posy of wild flowers but also some rooty notes and a hint of malt bins.
**Palate:** Great explosion of flavour unreduced. Dried flowers, crisp malt. Water calms it down making it creamy, soft and gentle. Lovely.
**Finish:** Floral, spicy, complex.

## BLADNOCH 22 YEARS OLD, DOUGLAS LAING 50%
Single Malt - Lowland

**8** **Michael: Good balance of the fruity acidity and sweeter juicy notes.**
**Nose:** Soft. Green. Lightly spicy.
**Palate:** Fruity and spicy. Juicy. Sweet lime cordial. Then fresh lime juice. Becoming syrupy. Then peppery.
**Finish:** Lively. Spicy.

**8** **Dave: It's held up superbly well and has good weight for such an apparently gentle spirit.**
**Nose:** Floral, the barley sugar, stewed apple, dry grass, toasted marshmallows, butter, light spices and balanced oak.
**Palate:** Sweet and light, but with a full, soft centre, the floral notes balanced by the oak.
**Finish:** Clean and dry.

## BLADNOCH 22 YEARS OLD, SINGLE CASK, ADELPHI 46%
Single Malt - Lowland

**8** **Michael: On the dry side for this whisky.**
**Nose:** Grassy, earthy, allspice.
**Palate:** Grassy, herbal, dry.
**Finish:** Herbal, dry. Late rooty bitterness.

**6** **Jim: Struggles to find a rhythm. Lowlanders weren't built to last to this age. Nevertheless, it has its delightful moments. Best at full strength and at about 46%.**
**Nose:** Over-aged, sappy and astringent oak redeemed by bourbony sweetness and by an undertone of amazingly fresh barley.
**Palate:** Excellent, oily maltiness at first. The middle is an oaky mess.
**Finish:** Dries too harshly. Long, tapering finish saved by late and enjoyable complexity.

## BLAIR ATHOL 12 YEARS OLD 43%
Single Malt - Highland

**7¾** **Michael: The obvious sherry ageing really suits Blair Athol. It is a malt that matures quickly, and this is very sophisticated for its age. A lovely whisky.**
**Nose:** Creamy, nutty, lightly peaty.
**Palate:** Full-bodied. Decidedly silky-smooth. Spiced cake. Candied lemon peels. Lots of flavour development.
**Finish:** Smoky, rooty, treacly. Impeccable balance between sweetness and dryness.

**7¼** **Jim: About as uncomplicated as it gets. Has improved on recent years, though.**
**Nose:** A clean, uncomplicated and rather sweet sherry aroma partially smothers a slightly off-key sub strata.
**Palate:** Again more massive sweet sherry and surprisingly smoky amid the malt.
**Finish:** A bitter, rather sharp finale which becomes increasingly dry.

## BLAIR ATHOL 1973, SIGNATORY 55%
Single Malt - Highland

**8** **Michael: Has matured superbly. I love the interplay of sweet and fruity, hot and dry. The orange colour distinguishes this from Signatory's earlier bottling.**
**Nose:** Rummy cake. Hints of banana. Restrained sherry.
**Palate:** Sweeter, spicier cake (more gingery). Very rich and long. Good balance of dry smokiness.
**Finish:** Very distinct black treacle. Toasted nuts. Burnt crust on a cake.

**8¾** **Jim: It has been 20 years since I came across a BA this fine. There is an after life...**
**Nose:** Ripe, rich and clean, honey and kumquats take a delicious centre stage.
**Palate:** Immensely intense, the honey malt has first say before oak crushes all in its path. Miraculously, the malt re-emerges rich, biscuity and better than ever before.
**Finish:** Rumbling oak after-shocks do little to hamper the honeyed barley. Stunning.

## BLAIR ATHOL 27 YEARS OLD, RARE MALTS 54.7%
Single Malt - Highland

**7¾** **Michael: The flavours seem to be held back, then suddenly released. This whisky might have been less inhibited at a younger age.**
**Nose:** Lemon peel on a cake.
**Palate:** Dry, drying. Darjeeling tea. Ginger cake. Restrained. A little lacking in complexity.
**Finish:** Big, long, lively, gingery, spicy.

**7¼** **Dave: Attractive but slightly flabby.**
**Nose:** Medium rich. Polished oak, chestnut purée, butter, cake, chocolate chip cookie.
**Palate:** Very nutty. Hazelnut spread, chestnut. Soft and sweet with dundee cake sweetness towards the back.
**Finish:** Orange peel. Chocolate.

## BLAIRFINDY 1980 RAW CASK, BLACKADDER 57.6%
Single Malt - Speyside

**7** **Michael: Those flavours in mid-palate afford a glimpse of a delicious malt but the wood is very dominating.**
**Nose:** Very woody. Leathery.
**Palate:** Slight toffee. Malty. Oily. Touches of mint, spiciness and hay. Quickly moving to woodiness.
**Finish:** Earthy, peaty, woody, drying.

**8½** **Dave: Huge! A machiatto to the Glen Grant espresso.**
**Nose:** Dried fruit, earth, smoke. Water brings out rubber and pipe tobacco (a rough shag this one).
**Palate:** Sweet and savoury at the same time with real charred tones all the way through.
**Finish:** Starts crisp, then comes dried fruit, then those charred/singed fruits and finally earth and smoke.

## BLUE HANGER 25 YEARS OLD, SECOND RELEASE 45.6%
Blended - Scotland

WHISKY Recommended

**7¾** **Michael: The nose suggests a winter warmer, but the palate performs as a summer refresher.**
**Nose:** Very expressive. Classic whisky aromas. A greenwood bonfire. Yorkshire parkin. Ginger biscuits.
**Palate:** Rounded, tangerines.
**Finish:** Lemon juice.

**8¼** **Dave: A rich, ripe and well-balanced dram.**
**Nose:** Concentrated and mature. Oak, bounty bar, grilled nut, treacle. Very spicy and complex. Some tablet sweetness and touch of Jaffa Cakes. Smoke.
**Palate:** Softer than the nose. Silky and slightly waxy feel with cooked plummy fruit/plum skin. Light oaky grip. Well balanced.
**Finish:** Spicy, nutmeg.

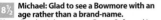

## BOWMORE 12 YEARS OLD 40%
Single Malt - Islay

**8½ Michael:** Glad to see a Bowmore with an age rather than a brand-name.
**Nose:** Emphatic burnt grass. Peaty. Soft smokiness.
**Palate:** Fragrant smokiness seems to waft against an oily, earthy, background. Some seaweed. Some sherry.
**Finish:** Not only is the smokiness sustained all the way through, it surges in the finish. Lots of salt, too.

**8½ Dave:** Great balance between dry smoke and soft fruits.
**Nose:** Attractive, perfumed fairly intense maritime nose: dark chocolate, orange peel, quite buttery with dry lavender-tinged smoke.
**Palate:** Rounded, and soft, then it dries half-way as the peaty notes (hessian, smoke) take over, then comes flowers, parma violet, rose and always those soft fruits.
**Finish:** Nut and fragrant smoke. Light touch of buttered kippers (a breakfast dram?)

## BOWMORE 12 YEARS OLD 40%
Single Malt - Islay

**2½ Martine:** Peat is integrated in oak though wood is not overwhelming. Water changes the rules, bringing peat and smoke forward.
**Nose:** Floral and peaty. Wet earth. Cold fireplace. Opening on briny notes, fishing net. Smoke is rather distant.
**Palate:** Smooth, sweet. Peat is not discernable at first. Then a light smoky flavour.
**Finish:** Medium, drying on lime peel. A hint of dry ashes.

**2½ Dave:** The smoke and oak now working together, everything shaken loose of the oaky cereal shell.
**Nose:** Plenty of American oak showing lots of vanilla, quite toasty. Smoke a subtle presence, fresh seashells, woodsmoke, seashores. Light cigar smoke/cedar wood, malty. Clean.
**Palate:** Rounded feel with a light maltiness, smoke to the back palate, seaweed, turfy.
**Finish:** Fragrant peat.

*Peat rating out of 5*

## BOWMORE 14 YEARS OLD, DEWAR RATTRAY 57.8%
Single Malt - Islay

**8½ Martine:** A beautiful Islay malt in a sherry refill dressing. Rich aromatic development, great combination of strength and sweetness.
**Nose:** Pungent, definitely coastal. Creosote. Touch of TCP. Tarry rope. Kippers. Hint of broom.
**Palate:** Silky and soft. A well integrated sherry influence. Floral. Candied grapefruit. Plum jam.
**Finish:** Long, lazily fading out on fruity and liquoriced notes. With light smoke floating around.

**8¾ Dave:** A fantastic dram and proof that Bowmore is back.
**Nose:** A creamy start then creosote on hot wood, dried fruits and a sooty thread of smoke. Behind is a melon-like softness. Even better with water. Burnt toast, sultana, fruit cake. Complex.
**Palate:** A touch of smouldering wood, Arbroath smokie, soft fruits and then bitumen and soot.
**Finish:** Black olives in brine.

## BOWMORE 15 YEARS OLD, DEWAR RATTRAY 52.9%
Single Malt - Islay

**7½ Michael:** Some of the classic Islay elements are there, but discordant. Not well rounded.
**Nose:** Sooty. Treacle toffee.
**Palate:** Peaty, earthy, cedary. Charcoal.
**Finish:** Robust. Sharp. Hot.

**7¼ Dave:** A good spirit dented by that essential oil quality.
**Nose:** Sweet, poached pear with a nutty malt at back. Coconut and vanilla. In time sage perfume which with water becomes more oily and lavender like.
**Palate:** Very perfumed. Has become essence like. The overt lavender is calmed with water, making it sweet and lightly smoky once more.
**Finish:** Smoke.

## BOWMORE 16 YEARS OLD 53.8%
Single Malt - Islay

**7¾ Dave:** The nose is fantastic, like the fug in an old Scottish pub: coal fires, cigarette smoke, damp clothes. The perfume pulls the score down.
**Nose:** Big smoke. Quite fragrant with cigar smoke, heather, chocolate covered raisin, liquorice, walnut and sweet mash underneath.
**Palate:** Robust, dry and slightly perfumed a hint of lavender (though this is reduced with water). Smouldering peat, hard toffee.
**Finish:** Little perfumed.

**7¾ Arthur:** The keynotes are the intense floral and a meaty sherriness, which aren't my favourite flavours in a whisky, but I can see this being popular with many.
**Nose:** Raisins, then peat ash and swimming pools and Love Heart sweeties. A fruitcake character wafts in and out of focus.
**Palate:** Intensely floral: lavender, parma violet and dried roses.
**Finish:** A meaty, burnt character.

## BOWMORE 17 YEARS OLD 43%
Single Malt - Islay

**8½ Michael:** A touch of astringency that seems to be more than Islay iodine.
**Nose:** Smoothly aromatic. Nutty malt. Smoky. Very good, appetising medicinal Islay character.
**Palate:** Rounded, firm, malty, dry creaminess. Tightly combined flavours.
**Finish:** Leafy, ferny, malty, sandy, smoky.

**8 Jim:** A quite delicious version but not anything like the heavier, more complex 17 Years Old of old.
**Nose:** Understated peat offers no more than a smoky sprinkling on the juicy apple and vanilla.
**Palate:** Much fuller and fatter in the mouth with an immediate outbreak of spices. Impressively delicate.
**Finish:** Medium length and perhaps just a little thin. The coffee feature of old is less intense. Holds its age impressively.

## BOWMORE 17 YEARS OLD 43%
Single Malt - Islay

**3 Martine:** More integration but a real earthy presence. Water does not make a drastic change.
**Nose:** Flowery, peaty. Mix of turf, dried herb and heather, lightly smoked. Briny notes emerge. A delicate intricacy of aromas.
**Palate:** Very smooth and velvety. Malty with an assertive smoky tone soothed by liquorice and coconut. Wood keeps control of peat and smoke. A salty feel.
**Finish:** Dry, liquoriced, with an oaky edge.

**3 Dave:** The peat is fully integrated, beginning to play a supporting role to the oak.
**Nose:** Richer with scented peat hanging above it all: heather, hint of lavender essential oil, then into cod liver oil, shoreline. Less overtly briny. Well balanced notes of brazil nut, moist tobacco, resin, liqueur chocolate, walnut, dried fruit, Jaffa cake.
**Palate:** Chewy and soft. Peat has a bigger say in centre, chocolate, mint. A slightly soapy note.
**Finish:** Perfumed, slightly cloying.

*Peat rating out of 5*

## BOWMORE 17 YEARS OLD, DEWAR RATTRAY 49.6%
Single Malt - Islay

**7½ Martine:** The nose is more interesting than the palate. A full bodied character which has flirted a bit too long with wood. Might suit cigar palates.
**Nose:** Enticing. Cloved orange. Moth balls. A touch of old leather armchair. Shoe polish. Smoky. Cold ashtray. A marine hint.
**Palate:** Sherry. A bit cardboardy. Distant coaltar. Date chutney. Getting bitter. Oak speaks out.
**Finish:** Dry, bitter.

**7 Dave:** This is where Bowmore was stuck for too long.
**Nose:** Dullish green rim. Dried sage and lavender/parma violet, seashore. Water increases the perfume lavender eau de toilette.
**Palate:** Soapy and sweet though with plenty of smoke trying to cover it up. A peat fire in a lady's bathroom?
**Finish:** Nutty yet tacky.

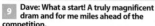

### BOWMORE 1968 43.4%
Single Malt - Islay

**9 Dave: What a start! A truly magnificent dram and for me miles ahead of the competition.**
**Nose:** Scented, spicy with some Seville orange, cedar then sweetness into poached tropical fruit, and mint. A complex aroma with hints of rancio.
**Palate:** Oak lends a firm edge, balancing concentrated raspberry fruit initially fragrant before deepening into dark vegetal areas.
**Finish:** Long, fruity, silky.

**9½ Arthur: Head and shoulders above the others in this batch.**
**Nose:** Fermenting gala melons, overripe kiwis, creamy strawberry sweets, and banana milkshake. A light chemical note: like petrol or a black truffle without the mushroominess.
**Palate:** Fruit salad, Carnation cream, aniseed and crème de menthe.
**Finish:** Zesty sourness, with a musty woodiness.

### BOWMORE 1968, CELTIC HEARTLANDS 40.6%
Single Malt - Islay

**8½ Michael: Fresh, very drinkable. Doesn't remotely taste it's age.**
**Nose:** Very aromatic. Fruity. Smoky. Ortega grape.
**Palate:** Light to medium. Firm. Slippery smooth. Ripe banana. Pineapple. Grape.
**Finish:** Fragrant smoky dryness. Ferny. Just a hint of the sea.

**8¼ Dave: Bowmore? Where's the smoke? Who cares, this is a beautiful whisky.**
**Nose:** Incredibly fruity: melon, lychee, peach, kiwi. Gentle and soft; very light oak, a hint of smoke.
**Palate:** Good grip balanced by that fruit salad that runs from start to finish. Soft and plump with enough zestiness to stop it being flabby.
**Finish:** Long, drying.

### BOWMORE 1968, SIGNATORY 46%
Single Malt - Islay

**7¾ Michael: At first tasting, I was hard-pressed to find any Islay character at all. On a second tasting, the next morning, I began to find some smokiness. Even then, it seemed to emerge on the tongue for two or three minutes.**
**Nose:** Salty. Parsley. Vegetal. Rooty. Possibly iris root and even a hint of gin?
**Palate:** Light, firm, smooth, ferny. Some lavender.
**Finish:** Herbal. Very restrained peat-smoke.

**8¾ Jim: One of the lightest, least peaty Bowmores I've tasted. Really delightful.**
**Nose:** Sweet (ish) with a peculiarly limp peatiness that has to be searched for. Very odd!
**Palate:** Light and exceptionally malt-rich at first, salivatingly so. The smoke is no more than a wisp, followed by an absorbing mix of bittersweet spices.
**Finish:** Soft peppers, chocolate, vanilla and an almost apologetic, yet delicious, hint of peat.

### BOWMORE 1975 CASK STRENGTH, SIGNATORY 51.8%
Single Malt - Islay

**8 Michael: Has mellowed with age. I missed the more assertively maritime characteristics in some younger Bowmores.**
**Nose:** Reedy, leafy. Dry, smoky. Burnt grass. Sun-dried grass. Hay.
**Palate:** Cereal grain. Nutty. Malty dryness, and some oaky sweetness.
**Finish:** Very dry maltiness. Vegetal. Lavender. Parsley. Sea air.

**8½ Dave: A big, elegant, powerful dram that's beautifully balanced.**
**Nose:** Rich and powerful with a slight biscuity edge. Leather, smoke, burnt orange peel, sultana, Dundee cake. Lovely elegance, mixed nuts, heather, seaweed.
**Palate:** Really sweet start, walnut cake, peach, treacle, then the peat surges through along with chocolate powder, wood.
**Finish:** Fruit cake, peach dry and smoky.

### BOWMORE 1989, BLACKADDER 63.3%
Single Malt - Islay

**8¼ Michael: All the elements of Bowmore, and plenty of alcohol, but extra dimension.**
**Nose:** Straight-ahead fragrant peat smoke.
**Palate:** Oily. Good Bowmore character: reedy, smoky, sandy, salty.
**Finish:** Appetising. Long, late, peppery dryness.

**7½ Dave: A solid Bowmore that's lighter than the distillery bottlings.**
**Nose:** Slightly lean with touches of vanilla, shaved wood, butter and green plum.
**Palate:** Clean and sprightly, sugary: orange marmalade with smoke from about half way in. Round and gentle.
**Finish:** Light smoke.

### BOWMORE 1989, LOMBARD 50%
Single Malt - Islay

**7¾ Michael: For a relatively young Bowmore, this seems somewhat tired.**
**Nose:** Reedy, leafy. Smokiness disappointingly light. Hay.
**Palate:** Oily, very vegetal, distinctly mustardy. Sweet-and-sour. Parsley.
**Finish:** Quick, gritty, sandy.

**5 Dave: This is a whisky from a 'neutral' cask where there has been no interchange between wood and spirit, giving a neutral end result. A distillery owner would be able to blend this away.**
**Nose:** Dull and flat. Damp wood and some smoke.
**Palate:** Some light smoke.
**Finish:** Smoke.

### BOWMORE 1990, 15 YEARS OLD, DEWAR RATTRAY 55.7%
Single Malt - Islay

**8 Martine: Straightforward and uncompromising. Very good balance. The classic Islay outdoor dram for simple enjoyment.**
**Nose:** Phenolic. Creosote. Sweet malty notes. Briny. Young leather. Lemon peel. Tangerine juice. Morning dew on moss. A touch of smoked mackerel.
**Palate:** Sweet and smoky. Oily. Refreshing. Smoke lingers all the way to the finish.
**Finish:** Slightly sooty, tangy, dry. White pepper.

**8¼ Dave: A cracking whisky from a distillery that's right back on form.**
**Nose:** Intense. A fluxing mix of barbecue sauce, seaweed, wet sand, hot shells, chocolate, jalapeno, ripe pear/melon, smoked fish. Great balance between the maritime and the fruits.
**Palate:** Light to medium bodied. Once again great impact: lanolin, cordite, peat smoke, creels, seaweed, seashore. A weird elegance.
**Finish:** Long, smoked with a sweet finish.

### BOWMORE 1990, 16 YEARS OLD 58.5%
Single Malt - Islay

**7¾ Dave: Water smooths it down, but the rugged edge is what makes this a winner.**
**Nose:** Fish market, light smoke and flowers. Weetabix and bourbon biscuits. Very intriguing.
**Palate:** The chocolate hit is immediate. Explosive smoke ignites in the middle. Deep and quite rugged. Well put together.
**Finish:** Long, gently smoky.

**6¾ Arthur: Some off-notes which I really didn't like, although the smokescreen saved it.**
**Nose:** Grubby and leathery initially, with a mushy old orange and a bit of woodsmoke. With water a bit of soapiness came up.
**Palate:** Woodsmoke to the fore, with some baked apple.
**Finish:** A little burnt plastic.

### BOWMORE 1990, 16 YEARS OLD, DEWAR RATTRAY 54%
Single Malt - Islay

**8 Dave: Has richness and some finesse.**
**Nose:** Mature. Light leather and maltiness. In time, violet then a shift to vanilla, brazil nut, polished oak. Light smoke.
**Palate:** Oily start, creosote with a balancing crisp nuttiness. Slow, peaty fog then tobacco and the cinders of a woodland bonfire. Water brings out damp mash, lanolin, heather and a briny note.
**Finish:** Long, perfumed, salty.

**8¼ Arthur: A good complex mix of floral flavours, fruit and smoke.**
**Nose:** A handful of lightly peated barley, tea tree and a musky, perfumed element. Band Aids. A creaminess, like a creamy coffee. Crème de dulce.

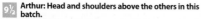

**Palate:** Forest fruits and charcoal, with bonfire smoke.
**Finish:** A little more smoke fading to burnt sage.

## BOWMORE 1991, 12 YEARS OLD, OLD MALT CASK 50%
Single Malt - Islay

**7½ Gavin: Lightweight, but very drinkable.**
**Nose:** Sweet, breakfast muesli with fresh fruit and milk. The smoke is so reticent you could miss it.
**Palate:** The 'breakfast' nose comes through, with a little more banana, and the same shy smoke.
**Finish:** Elegantly fruity, with a little more smoke at the last.

**7½ Dave: A good aperitif. Strangely like a Rockley Still rum.**
**Nose:** Sweet. Cereal, Sugar Puffs, banana, nuts, violet, sesame. Gentle smoke. Delicate and pretty.
**Palate:** Gentle, light and smooth. Kiln-like with notes of bran along with lychee and apricot. A smoky centre. Precise.
**Finish:** Nutty. Light smoke.

## BOWMORE 1991, 14 YEARS OLD, DEWAR RATTRAY 59.6%
Single Malt - Islay

**8¼ Dave: Old Bowmore is fascinating: it either becomes light and tropical with no smoke or reduces into this anchovy like concentration.**
**Nose:** Immediate smoke and light sootiness. Mint chocolate mixed with Soreen malt loaf.
**Palate:** Fishy.
**Finish:** The slight mustiness of age mingled with rose petal, then smoke descends like a fog. When it lifts there's a flavour akin to old kipper boxes.

**7 Arthur: A little mucky on the nose when diluted.**
**Nose:** Floral phenols and pencil shavings. Smoker's toothpaste and floral air freshener. Damp autumn leaves and river mud.
**Palate:** Treacle, burnt sugar and cinnamon sticks.
**Finish:** Coffee-like bitterness.

## BOWMORE 1995, BERRY'S OWN SELECTION 56.2%
Single Malt - Islay

**7½ Martine: A sunny malt. Quite sharp and spirity but a pleasant aromatic freshness. Could be a thirst quenching for some. Water does not cut all edges.**
**Nose:** Grassy. Freshly cut grass including a bunch of garden mint. Turf. Malt flour. Alcohol tickles. A hint of smoke.
**Palate:** Sweet maltiness. Hay loft. Wild chervil. A spicy burst at mid-palate.
**Finish:** Dry, very spicy. Chilli.

**7¾ Dave: Drink over ice.**
**Nose:** Neat there's apple skin, some earthy smokiness and a slightly musty wood. Hay. Water brings out peat which grows in intensity. Pretty tense.
**Palate:** Highly aromatic and zesty with apple blossom then the smoke begins to drift through. Shows very good balance when water is added. Cayenne. Appetising. Just entering maturity.
**Finish:** Lightly nutty.

## BOWMORE 1995, RARE CASK, QUEEN OF THE MOOR-LANDS 57.2%
Single Malt - Islay

**7 Dave: Nothing wrong, just bottled too early.**
**Nose:** Fruit juice, melon, banana milkshake and a tight grassiness coupled with whittled sticks, woodsmoke. Water makes it more plain with a light marine touch. Seems young.
**Palate:** Very hard and quite firm with a sweet centre lurking. Water doesn't loosen it. Immature with a slight chemical flavour.
**Finish:** Flinty, hard then starts to loosen.

**8¼ Arthur: Fairly typical of the distillery, and a solid, tasty example.**
**Nose:** Lots of vanilla sweetness, pears, smoked almonds, and wood smoke. A minerally character with creosote and ash. With time and water, more floral, pot pourri elements appear. Parma violets.
**Palate:** Again, minerally with that floral element lying above the earth and smoke.
**Finish:** Ash and parma violets.

## BOWMORE 20 YEARS OLD, DOUGLAS LAING 50%
Single Malt - Islay

**8¾ Michael: Bowmore is a great malt. Let's see more of it in straightforward ages.**

**Nose:** Very aromatic. Distinctive. Fresh. Lavender. Ferny. Peat smoke.
**Palate:** Soft but insistent smokiness over a clean, sweetly malty background.
**Finish:** Creamy, with a savoury note reminiscent of seaweedy pretzels.

**7½ Marcin: Confusing. Lightness of nose is contradicted by strident palate. It promises a lot but doesn't deliver.**
**Nose:** Complex and fresh scented. Lightly maritime. Concentrated light honey flavours and maple syrup when reduced.
**Palate:** Maritime. Pretty friable; the addition of water doesn't help.
**Finish:** Very short and drying.

## BOWMORE 2000 (CASK SAMPLE FROM BOURBON CASK)
Single Malt - Islay

**3 Martine: Peat plays the major part in the aromatic display, with an assertive sea influence.**
**Nose:** Tickling. Fresh. Straightforward. First, wet seaweeds and herbs steaming on a bonfire, then a touch of smoked meat and back to burning grass. Followed by lingering creosote.
**Palate:** Sweet maltiness at first, then a fizzy feel and a huge invasion of smoke and seaweeds. Drying off on a more "tactile" smoke.
**Finish:** Dry, grassy, sooty.

**2½ Dave: This is young and everything seems locked in.**
**Nose:** Young and vibrant. Sweet. Wood sugars. Light bran, hint of heathery smoke, marine/beach like. Very pure with a touch of dried herbs, soft fruit, burning turf.
**Palate:** Clean, if slightly aggressive. Malt, oak and peat. Dolly mixtures. Smoke builds near the finish.
**Finish:** The peat is here, damp seaweed, heather.

*Peat rating out of 5*

## BOWMORE 22 YEARS OLD, DUNCAN TAYLOR 62.5%
Single Malt - Islay

**1 Martine: An almost unpeated version of Bowmore? A (too) perfect integration of peat in wood? Unusual.**
**Nose:** Spirity. Alcohol tickles nostrils, a creamy custardy sweetness in the back with a fruity sourness. Peat is hardly discernable.
**Palate:** Sweet and sour. Smooth too. Peat and smoke have been melted into a fruit basket. An earthy touch.
**Finish:** Dry, peppery. Not smoked nor peated.

**1½ Dave: An old lady, but a feisty old lady. The smoke is a memory.**
**Nose:** Salty and vibrant with a spicy nature. Hint of salted anchovy, creamy malt, mint chocolate, orange Club biscuits. What smoke there is suggests bitumen and dried lavender.
**Palate:** Orange crates, sweet yet tart. A wisp of subtle smoke hits mid-palate. Still a marine freshness into salt offsetting the sweetness.
**Finish:** Dry, oak.

*Peat rating out of 5*

## BOWMORE 25 YEARS OLD, GORDON & MACPHAIL 43%
Single Malt - Islay

**1 Martine: Old age has completely integrated peat and smoke. Oak overpowers the marine character. A splash of water does not help.**
**Nose:** Oak has the word with a sherry accent. Damp cellar, earth floor, dark chocolate. Hard to find a peat note.
**Palate:** Sweet and bitter. Oak dominating. Oxtail broth. Can't find the peat.
**Finish:** Bittersweet. Lingering. Drying off on spices.

**2 Dave: The peat drifts in and out like cigar smoke on your skin the morning after.**
**Nose:** Concentrated. Dry amontillado sherry, toasted almond. Fungal, rancio notes: cheese rind, porcini water. Phenolics have also reduced to their essence: lobster creels, brine. Spent fire.
**Palate:** Nutty oak with some tinned fruit salad coming through. A slight resinous quality alongside ashes.
**Finish:** Lightly spiced, slightly bitter.

*Peat rating out of 5*

# Scotch Bowmore

## BOWMORE CASK STRENGTH ISLAY SINGLE MALT 56%
Single Malt - Islay

**7½ Gavin: Doesn't leap out of the glass at you, but well balanced and unthreatening.**
**Nose:** Fragrant, oak and malt, very delicate wood smoke.
**Palate:** Some oiliness, orange juice, again delicate smoke, suggestion of peat.
**Finish:** Dry, slightly acrid, smoke from cheroots.

**7¾ Dave: A good introductory malt.**
**Nose:** Initially malty, becoming rounded and buttery with water. There's olde English marmalade, delicate woodsmoke wood shavings, log, cigar ash.
**Palate:** Lightly perfumed and quite sweet. Orange peel, stewed apricot, tinned prune and aromatic smoke. Long and smooth.
**Finish:** Dry, ash-like.

## BOWMORE CLARET
Single Malt - Islay

**9 Michael: The fighter beat the boxer, but it was a wonderfully enjoyable contest.**
**Nose:** Very aromatic. A robust struggle between the claret's fruit-and-cedar notes and a confident Bowmore smokiness.
**Palate:** Bowmore beats Bordeaux.
**Finish:** Toffeeish (more port-like) fruit fights back convincingly. Oak keeps the contestants apart. Finally a salty battle is won by the distillery character.

**6½ Jim: Worth trying for novelty value alone. Too much rough to go with the smooth.**
**Nose:** Truly bizarre: the peat seems to have vanished and in its place is a distinctly winey spiciness.
**Palate:** A biting, puckering zingy, hot spicy attack that in some ways is not too far off a very young Talisker.
**Finish:** Rich, fruity, almost blackcurrant, then drier cocoa-coffee notes.

## BOWMORE CLARET
Single Malt - Islay

**9 Michael: The fighter beat the boxer, but it was a wonderfully enjoyable contest.**  WHISKY Recommended
**Nose:** Very big in both departments. Lots of recognisably claret-like fruit-and-cedar notes-and a powerful response from Bowmore smokiness.
**Palate:** Bowmore beats Bordeaux.
**Finish:** Toffeeish (more port-like) fruit fights back convincingly. Oak keeps the contestants apart. Finally a salty battle is won by the distillery character.

**9 Doug: An elaborate malt which enhances Bowmore's association with perfume. Good enough to wear!**
**Nose:** Intensely perfumed, ripe summer fruits, bubble gum and honey melon? Evolving to show base notes of peat and more concentrated fruits.
**Palate:** Delicate to medium bodied. A gentle oiliness carries initial bursts of fruit to drier complexities.
**Finish:** Teasing, lingering, quite feminine until that Islay smoke kicks in.

## BOWMORE DARKEST 43%
Single Malt - Islay

**9 Michael: Not that dark – just tawny. Whisky in its mid teens, I would say, but from superb sherry casks.** WHISKY Recommended
**Nose:** Fragrantly smoky. Perfumy, very floral. Hessian. Sea air. Astonishingly fresh, delicious, appetising, complex.
**Palate:** Perfumy start. Hint of flowering currant. Nutty. Layers of dry, black treacle, maltiness.
**Finish:** Smooth. Polished stone. Hard, salty, liquorice.

**8½ Jim: Really delightful whisky which suggests youth but offers a faultless peat/sherry combination.**
**Nose:** Fresh, wonderfully clean Oloroso clings to the oak and peat to form a wonderful trio.
**Palate:** Big and chewy with the sherry and the peat in perfect harmony. Perhaps uncomplex and lacking sophistication, but the balance is quite stunning.
**Finish:** Long with a hint of molasses/liquorice adding to the toasty malt and rumbling smoke.

## BOWMORE DARKEST 43%
Single Malt - Islay

**9 Michael: Let the flavours unfold. Enjoy the complexity.**
**Nose:** Hessian. Sea air. Smoke. Complex, distinctive and appetising.
**Palate:** Perfumey. Satiny. Mint humbugs. The smokiness of burning grass. Hint of flowering currant.
**Finish:** Hard, salty, liquorice.

**8½ Doug: Forget expresso and cappuccino, try this for breakfast with a fat Havana. Hedonistic!**
**Nose:** Heady, toffeeish and promising with a lurking smoky backdrop.
**Palate:** A magic carpet of sherry, dark toffee, coffee and smoke hover above Bowmore's more delicate structure.
**Finish:** Cocoa and roaster coffee abound until all the peaty and perfumy liquorice notes emerge.

## BOWMORE DAWN 51.5%
Single Malt - Islay

**8¼ Michael: Wood finishes are still fun and may recruit new enthusiasts for malt. Dawn, Dusk, Voyager...this is becoming confusing. Of those three (Port, Bordeaux and Port again), Dawn seems the lightest all-round.**
**Nose:** Soft, gentle, sooty smokiness.
**Palate:** Textured, lightly toffeeish. Fruity. Interplay of brown-sugar sweetness and tar-like dryness.
**Finish:** Peaty, leafy, reedy. A certain sandy grittiness.

**8¼ Dave: Like sucking a wine gum in a kiln. A little too winey for me.**
**Nose:** Perfumed and winey: lavender, peat smoke, red fruits, strawberry jam, rhubarb and custard sweeties. Water intensifies the perfume: sage, peat smoke, orange, drying seaweed, heather.
**Palate:** Mulled wine beside a peat fire. Hessian, clove, sour cherry.
**Finish:** A little hot. Sweet. Smoky.

## BOWMORE DAWN ISLAY SINGLE MALT 56%
Single Malt - Islay

**8 Gavin: Complex and curious!**
**Nose:** Quite heavy sweet notes – dates and figs – initially, before malt and faint smoke is detected.
**Palate:** Thick mouthfeel, red grapes, more complex soft fruits and smoke develop with water.
**Finish:** Gentle, some peat, balanced by sweeter malt notes, but plums linger too insistently.

**7 Dave: Just plain weird. Don't know whether to dab it behind my ears or drink it.**
**Nose:** Firm, concentrated start. Floor wax, cigar smoke. Then a strange artificial perfume: attar of roses, orange blossom water, lavender.
**Palate:** The essency, gin like, notes continue. Then smoke and a nice hit of red fruits.
**Finish:** Soft, light smoke.

## BOWMORE DUSK 50%
Single Malt - Islay

**8¾ Michael: After that smoky start, becomes much more toffeeish than most Bowmores. But is this a good thing?** WHISKY Recommended
**Nose:** Seems fractionally smokier than the earlier version labelled Bowmore Claret. Peaty. Grassy. Linseed. Leather armchairs. Deliciously evocative.
**Palate:** Rich, fruity, smoky. Lots of flavour development: perfumy fruit, nuts (almonds?), vanilla.
**Finish:** Toffeeish, cedary, oaky, smoky. Long.

**8¼ Jim: Brilliantly balanced and a fabulous addition to the rich tapestry of Islay malts.**
**Nose:** A dextrous aroma, beautifully sculpted. The peat is even and forms merely a backdrop; in the foreground are rose petals, apple and grape.
**Palate:** A soft, controlled explosion of peat that reaches all parts of the palate.
**Finish:** Only now some age and oak appear, drying out the easy sweetness of the peat malt and grape.

## BOWMORE LEGEND 40%
Single Malt - Islay

**8 Michael: A light, young version, at a competitive price:**
**Nose:** Peaty, smoky, very appetising.

**Palate:** Light but textured. Flavours very singular, and not yet melded. A fresh, young whisky, but no obvious spiritiness.
**Finish:** Sweet, then salty.

**7 Jim: An almost teasing Islay, with peat but never really taking off. Never more than pleasant.**
**Nose:** Young, sweet, slightly under-ripe and malty. The peat is surprisingly subdued.
**Palate:** Enormously sweet to begin, with an almost gristy, mealy presence. Dries out towards the middle but the peat appears light and clean.
**Finish:** Surprisingly long with the peat at last gathering forces. Very little complexity or direction.

## BOWMORE SURF, 25 YEARS OLD 43%
Single Malt - Islay

**7¾ Michael: A light, smooth, Bowmore that might attract younger drinkers.**
**Nose:** Fresh peat smoke.
**Palate:** Seems very tame at first, with a cookie-like maltiness, but the characteristic ferny lavender, fragrant smoke and sea air gradually emerge.
**Finish:** Sweet smokiness. With water, late saltiness. honey-roast peanuts.

**8 Dave: A fine introduction to peated Islays and a good session malt.**
**Nose:** Fragrant with clean cereal notes. Heather, peat smoke and lanolin (woolly jumpers). Dried thyme. Young.
**Palate:** Mid-weight with tangerine and incense in the mid-palate mixed with fragrant smoke which builds towards the back of the mouth.
**Finish:** Good length, quite juicy.

## BOWMORE VOYAGE 56%
Single Malt - Islay

**8½ Michael: Port often leaves a toffeeish note, but not in this case. Perhaps needs a bit more maturity.** *WHISKY Editor's choice*
**Nose:** Less obviously smoky than the Bordeaux finish. More perfumy. Drier. Dried fruit?
**Palate:** Smooth, light on the tongue. Develops some fruitiness.
**Finish:** Spicier. Very lively. Seems crisp at first, but lingers very warmly, with late brown sugar and salt.

**8¾ Jim: Really impressive balance and complexity. Very laid-back and understated. Great stuff.**
**Nose:** Light and juicy, the peat is little more than a distant echo. Sweet malt adds weight, but not much.
**Palate:** Much more peat on the early arrival, several layers of oak and then a brilliant rush of fruit and then more clean peat and a wave of spice.
**Finish:** Medium length but remains clean, crisp and softly peated.

## ROYAL MILE WHISKIES BOWMORE 1999, YOUNG PEATY ISLAY 61.5%
Single Malt - Islay

**8½ Michael: Bring on the kippers.** *WHISKY Editor's choice*
**Nose:** Big, soft, smokiness.
**Palate:** Assertive. Attention-grabbing. Lively acidity. The faintest dash of malt vinegar. Malty. Bittersweet.
**Finish:** Long, warming.

**8½ Ian: Sweet-dry-savoury-fruit balance, intense but elegant. A dram with drama.**
**Nose:** Gentle waft of creosote and embers, above which a jasmine flower blossoms, accompanied by pear drops, linseed notes and a hint of vanilla.
**Palate:** Luscious sweetness with creamy crème caramel, background waft of sweet, earthy peat and chargrilled notes, before jasmine tea.
**Finish:** Creamy crème caramel and digestive biscuit sweetness with a waft of dry peatiness.

## BRAES OF GLENLIVET 1985, CELTIQUE CONNEXION 50%
Single Malt - Speyside

**7¼ Michael: The cask character somewhat dominates this zesty but delicate whisky.**
**Nose:** A Christmas stocking that contains toffees, chocolates, perfume and soap.
**Palate:** Very lightly syrupy. Chocolate. Soft caramel. Suggestions of Mars Bars or Rolo chocolates.
**Finish:** Fruity, with a touch of winey acidity.

**7¾ Martine: The Sauternes finish mellows the oak; but unsatisfying, except for fans of wood.**
**Nose:** Woody, resiny. Oak with cedar. Good variety of spices (cloves, cardamom). Fruit aromas hardly emerge, just an orangey hint.
**Palate:** Robust without being agressive. Sweet malty and honeyed flavours, then liquorice.
**Finish:** Warm and lasting. Liquorice and spices.

## BRECHIN 28 YEARS OLD 53.3%
Single Malt - Highland

**8 Martine: A warm character, just a little too assertive when it comes to oak but so uplifting.**
**Nose:** Nutty, fresh and lively. A delicate touch of wild rose pops up before being submerged by liquorice and vanilla toffee. Quite tickling. Water releases more sweet toffee notes.
**Palate:** Smoother than expected at first then bursting out. Tangy mouthfeel. Not unpleasant though. Barley sugar. Gripping oak in the end.
**Finish:** Dry, oaky. Liquorice and nuts.

**7½ Michael: Curious balance of firm earthiness and acidity.**
**Nose:** Soft and warming. Ripe apples. Some pear notes. Hints at brownies with mango tartness balancing.
**Palate:** Sharp with slightly earthy background. Late solid cereals.
**Finish:** Firm, becomes creamy, with some hints of acetone and phenol(?).

## BRORA 18 YEARS OLD, OLD MALT CASK 50%
Single Malt - Highland

**8 Michael: More Islay-like than its Clynelish brothers. Was this some of the last made with highly peated malt?** *WHISKY Editor's choice*
**Nose:** Earthy, salty, iodine.
**Palate:** Very drying, falls away in the middle.
**Finish:** Stinging. Fresh limes (or does the green-tinged colour suggest that?). Very long saltiness.

**9¼ Jim: This Brora is close to perfection. To ignore would be your eternal loss.**
**Nose:** A curiously sweet/dry peatiness. Almost chewy oak/malt resonance that forms an ever greater backbone than the soft but significant smoke.
**Palate:** Wave upon wave of gentle, slightly crusted peat couched in a sweet bedrock of malt.
**Finish:** Slightly peppery with drier oaky tones. Almost too beautifully balanced to be true.

## BRORA 1977 24 YEARS OLD, RARE MALTS 56.1%
Single Malt - Highland

**8½ Michael: Lively, fruity, refreshing. Distinctive. Does the 19th hole at Brora serve sushi?**
**Nose:** Very flowery. Camomile. Suggestion of sweet lime.
**Palate:** Lightly oily. Gorse or whin; that coconut flavour. Then fresh lime, then peppery seaweed.
**Finish:** Sandy, grainy, mustardy. Wasabi?

**8½ Dave: Discreet on the nose but rages in like a north-eastern storm on the tastebuds.**
**Nose:** Clean, dry, coastal aromas. Slightly muted with hints of smoke, oil and brine.
**Palate:** Big, robust and quite oily with rounded waxed leather flavours. Sea breezes lash your tastebuds.
**Finish:** Lightly smoky with a salty tingle.

## BRORA 1977, 21 YEARS OLD, RARE MALTS 56.9%
Single Malt - Highland

**8½ Michael:** A lovely coastal malt. It's a shame that its surviving brother Clynelish is more muted.

**Nose:** Very appetising. Fresh sea air. Salty. Seaweed on the rocks. Fragrant, smoky.
**Palate:** Oily, tarry, chewy. Very spicy indeed. Stinging flavours. Lots of flavour development. Grassiness. Gorse. Flowering currant. Sweet mustard.
**Finish:** Pepper. Hot mustard. Grainy. Cumin.

**9 Jim:** What a fabulous whisky of extraordinary complexity and wonderful balance. Masterful.

**Nose:** Bracing and intense. Sea-spray and sawdust and the lightest of smoke. Marvellously evocative and appealing.
**Palate:** Fat, massively bodied with powerful peat that was missing on the nose. The saltiness seeps through and the malts remains clean and chewy.
**Finish:** Intense vanilla and then drier oaky tones battle against the lingering sweet peat.

## BRORA 1981 25 YEARS OLD 56.5%
Single Malt - Highland

**7½ Dave:** Lacks balance.
**Nose:** Very hot nose. Hints at peatiness. Wood ash mixed with freshly sawn timber: it's the shop floor of a cooperage.
**Palate:** Smoky and quite dry. The wood is a little exposed and the spirit is struggling to make itself heard above the cooper's hammers. All that comes out is a sweet spiciness...
**Finish:** ...which continues on the finish.

**7½ Martine:** The nose is enticing but the palate rather restrained.
**Nose:** Biting. Alcohol teases the nostrils. Nature after a summer rain. Wet straw. Hint of squeezed orange. A slight cardboardy touch.
**Palate:** Sweeter than expected. The cardboard is more distinctive. Almond custard.
**Finish:** Dry, almost dour.

## BRORA 1981 UNCHILLFILTERED, SIGNATORY 46%
Single Malt - Highland

**8¼ Michael:** What a distinctive malt Brora was, and there are some excellent bottlings available.
**Nose:** A walk across the grassy dunes to a clean beach in a light, fresh breeze.
**Palate:** Teasing balance of sweet, creamy maltiness and salty, savoury, vegetal flavours. After the walk, warming soup.
**Finish:** Peppery dry. Bring on the cullen skink.

**6½ Dave:** Not sufficient drive being given by the cask.
**Nose:** Light and slightly numb. Wet stones, thrift flowers, herbs, smoke.
**Palate:** Dry and unyielding. Those herbs again, some almond and a light maritime character.
**Finish:** Short.

## BRORA 1981, 23 YEARS OLD, SHERRY FINISH, CHIEFTAIN'S CHOICE 46%
Single Malt - Highland

**8 Michael:** Rich flavours. A chestnut-coloured whisky for people who like very grown-up sweetmeats: Marron glacé, for example. Unlikely to be enjoyed by anyone younger than the whisky.
**Nose:** Mint toffee.
**Palate:** Treacle toffee. Bittersweet chocolate.
**Finish:** Oily. Praline with angelica filling. Slightly resiny.

**7 Dave:** This is decent, just slightly dull.
**Nose:** Dusty, leafy, dry with a hint of sweetness, all the signs of ex-sherry butts. Walking into a warehouse: all fungal, earth and clinker. Shifts into leather and dark chocolate. A little distant.
**Palate:** Mix of savoury and sweet. Bruised fruits, walnut, treacle, Sumatra coffee, tobacco (shop/moist pouch). Firm grip. Splits with water.
**Finish:** Grippy.

## BRORA 1982, 19 YEARS OLD, SHERRY BUTT, CHIEFTAIN'S CHOICE 46%
Single Malt - Highland

**8¾ Martine:** Pure mastered (and mastering) Oloroso style. But where is the spirit contribution?

**Nose:** Sherry, tobacco leaf. Huge notes of sweet Oloroso. Shoe polish. Cloved orange, smoky wood.
**Palate:** Smoothness meeting sweetness. Christmas cake flavours, dark chocolate.
**Finish:** Sensuously lingering, laced with spices. Smoky aftertaste.

**7 Dave:** Good, but it could be any heavily sherried malt. Lacks an individual personality.
**Nose:** Lots of Oloroso notes: rubber, walnut, dried fruits.
**Palate:** Good weight, nutty, soft, silky and fruity with some turfy smoke.
**Finish:** Sweet and sherried.

## BRORA 1982, 20 YEARS OLD, RARE MALTS 58.1%
Single Malt - Highland

**8½ Michael:** Refreshing start; soothing finish. Quite a trick.
**Nose:** Perfumy. Very floral. Rose petals.
**Palate:** Light, cleansing. Long, spicy, flavour development. Very fresh ginger character. Cumin?
**Finish:** Liquorice. Gin-like. Gin-and-tonic.

**9 Dave:** A complex, subtle malt.
**Nose:** Creamy. Complex. Candle wax, lilac, bitumen, lemons a-plenty, pear, honey, light marine notes, dry seaweed, smoke.
**Palate:** Oily and smooth with a light waxiness. Eases onto the palate. A concentrated bundle with hints of lemon myrtle. Great balance.
**Finish:** Smoke leaks out. Dry.

## BRORA 1982, LOMBARD 50%
Single Malt - Highland

**8¾ Michael:** Every time I pick up the glass, I find new flavours. A Scottish aquavit to send the Danes packing.
**Nose:** Grassy dunes, the seashore, seaweed on a gusty day.
**Palate:** Powerful. Pronounced peatiness. Vegetal, but pleasantly so (salsify?). Peppery. Mustardy.
**Finish:** Iodine. Medicinal.

**7¾ Dave:** A big package, yet quite restrained.
**Nose:** Dry meadow grasses, heathery smoke from a distant peat fire. Fruit. With water, bosky: privet blossom/box hedge/yew. Lean.
**Palate:** Medium-bodied with better weight than expected. A teasing mix of dry sides, oily middle and smoky finish, all beautifully integrated. Smoke rounds it out rather than dries it up.
**Finish:** Smoky and slightly oily.

## BRORA 21 YEARS OLD, RARE MALTS 56.9%
Single Malt - Highland

**8½ Michael:** A good example of Brora as a distinctive maritime malt. Very appetising indeed, but quite different from Talisker, for example.
**Nose:** Dry, vegetal. Seaweed. Sea air.
**Palate:** Firm, malty background. Becoming grainy, earthy, tar-like and chewy. Then dry, smoky and sandy.
**Finish:** Salty. Peppery. Mustardy too. A long, powerful assault from the spice-rack.

**9 Dave:** A richly-flavoured malt with a punchy delivery. Another silent still. Bloody typical!
**Nose:** Pungent, rich, oily. Peaty but also a lifted, almost floral top note. BIG. Chocolate and cream. Robustly elegant and increasingly complex as it warms.
**Palate:** A lovely mix of sweet and dry flavours. Very rich and mouth-coating. Almost briny: nuts, lemon, oil and gentle smoke underneath. Has weight and power.
**Finish:** Slight peppery kick.

## BRORA 24 YEARS OLD, CHIEFTAIN'S CHOICE 46%
Single Malt - Highland

**8 Dave:** Elegant and highly individual. Takes no prisoners.
**Nose:** Big and oily but with a wild fruit character: rowanberry jelly, tomato purée, Madeira cake.
**Palate:** Drier than expected with a peppery kick. The waxiness is immediately there, clinging to the tongue while the smoke emerges half-way along. Great length and best with a drop of water.
**Finish:** Rich, clinging lightly smoked.

**8¾ Arthur:** A big spirit tempered by a characterful cask. Very enjoyable.

**Nose:** Christmas cake mix. All spice. There is also evidence of phenols, though not peat or smoke, more like oil paints or floor polish.
**Palate:** Some burnt buns, a rich underlying raisin toffee sweetness and a grassy peat.
**Finish:** Light rubberiness and some more of that peat, although in subtle quantities.

## BRORA 30 YEARS OLD 52.4%
Single Malt - Highland

WHISKY
*Editor's choice*

**8¾ Michael: Those startling, appetising aromas and flavours had me cooking in a new kitchen. I must have let the Sabatier slip. Why else the TCP?**
**Nose:** Hugely aromatic. Very distinctive. Resiny. Balsamic vinegar.
**Palate:** Spiced olive oil. A sweet mustard, then a hot one. White pepper. Cumin. Stinging, lively, with lots of flavour development.
**Finish:** Salty. Medicinal. Sudden TCP/Listerine.

**9 Dave: Complex. A remarkable malt that thrills but saddens. Here's another light that's gone out.**
**Nose:** Hugely complex. Big, powerful, rich. Heathery smoke, lanolin. Sweet notes from oak, soft caramelised fruits. Also liquorice, light roasted coffee, serrano ham, candle wax and spent wick.
**Palate:** Fantastically complex, the notes on the nose plus a mouthfilling mix of sweet, smoky and dry.
**Finish:** Very long, spices, oil, fragrant smoke.

## BRORA 30 YEARS OLD 55.7%
Single Malt - Highland

WHISKY
*Recommended*

**7 Dave: A big beast, but the butiric knocks its score down.**
**Nose:** Foursquare and solid. Musk. Lanolin and a butiric note. Smoke, cigar leaf, wet leather.
**Palate:** Immediate robust smokiness. Coal scuttle. Slightly biscuity. In time wood and a coriander seed spiciness. Slightly salty. The butiric note is just apparent. Rich and powerful.
**Finish:** Oily and long. Robust.

**9¼ Arthur: A real bruiser, that comes out with fists flying.**
**Nose:** Intense, with a sweet burning rubber, scorched treacle toffee, peat. An essential oil character too, somewhere between rosemary and tea tree. Some coal tar soap and ghee.
**Palate:** Sweet, peaty: kappow! The peatiness and the spices remind me of Moroccan food.
**Finish:** Harissa paste.

## BRORA 30 YEARS OLD 56.3%
Single Malt - Highland

**8 Martine: Dour at first then opening up in a delightful way. Take your time to get acquainted with this fellow and you'll like it.**
**Nose:** Slightly butyric at start. Wet straw. Cowshed with a whiff of creosote. Dry seashells, tar rope. Vanilla rising up with caramel notes.
**Palate:** Very sweet then drying out on smoke and soot. Definitely phenolic. Earthy roots.
**Finish:** Dry, sooty, vanishing quite quickly then sweet maltiness coming back.

**7½ Michael: Reticent at first, shows itself to be a well structured whisky delivering mature flavours.**
**Nose:** Slow to develop. Delicate. Pine resin, wood glue, shavings. Toffee base notes.
**Palate:** Drying, then malty. Nice cereal development. Fresh egg pasta? Fruity (muesli?) character with water.
**Finish:** Smooth, confident. Sherry and bitter cacao in the tail.

## BRORA 30 YEARS OLD, LIMITED EDITION 55.7%
Single Malt - Highland

WHISKY
*Editor's choice*

**8¾ Michael: Exuberant interplay of sweet and dry flavours, pivoted on a firm malt background.**
**Nose:** Fresh limes. Vegetal. Sea air.
**Palate:** Medium. Firm. Sweet start. Truffle oil. Whole-grain mustard. Salt.
**Finish:** Stingingly appetising. Long.

**9 Dave: OK, so who is going to stump up the cash to get Brora up and running again?**
**Nose:** Complex. Vanilla, poached pear, wax, peat, seaweed, Danish oil and a whiff of the cowshed.

**Palate:** Rich and complex, this unfolds slowly and has richness, balance, texture, sweet waxy fruits and a lift of smoke. Some package.
**Finish:** Cigar ash.

## BRORA 30 YEARS OLD, THE WHISKY SHOP 47.4%
Single Malt - Highland

**7¼ Michael: For the collector.**
**Nose:** Extreme resin. Pitch pine. Railway sleepers.
**Palate:** The chestnut colour is a warning. Although the spirit is very lively, and toffeeish fruitiness and spiciness manage to put in an appearance, none of these flavours can fully express themselves under the burden of such sherry and wood.
**Finish:** Woody, astringent.

**7½ Dave: More Motorhead than Mozart.**
**Nose:** Rich, thick and concentrated. Like stumbling into a warm fuggy pub after a long walk over the hills: tobacco, lanolin, Madeira, smoke.
**Palate:** Big fruit, smoke and firm wood makes for a serious impact. Robust and rugged but with a sweet centre. For those who like 'em BIG, smoky and sherried.
**Finish:** Long, drying, slightly tannic.

## BRUICHLADDICH 10 YEARS OLD 46%
Single Malt - Islay

**8¼ Michael: Not only the liveliness of youth but also the least wood influence. The use of second-fill casks leaves the fruity flavours of Bruichladdich to express themselves more freely.**
**Nose:** Fresh, clean, flowery. Primroses.
**Palate:** Lightly creamy. Peaches. Summer fruits. Passion fruit. Zesty, almost effervescent.
**Finish:** The flavours meld, with a touch of sharpness.

**7¾ Dave: Best as a wake-up call at 10 a.m.**
**Nose:** Very light and fresh. Floral, with crunchy green apple, verjus, lemon, fresh malt.
**Palate:** Clean, zesty and direct. Apples, lanolin, cream. A perky little number. A port finish version would be pinky and perky.
**Finish:** Feisty and breezy.

## BRUICHLADDICH 10 YEARS OLD 46%
Single Malt - Islay

**7½ Michael: Very slightly spirity, but appetising.**
**Nose:** Very flowery, heathery, light seaweedy, emphatically salty.
**Palate:** Firm and dry at first, with a touch of iron. Slight oiliness, and a suggestion of peat. Becoming maltier and sweeter, with touches of heather.
**Finish:** Long, with a range of subtle flavours.

**7 Jim: This dram has changed in recent years; less silky and more malt sharp but very easy going.**
**Nose:** The lightest, creamiest of all Islay's noses, but contains a surprising richness. There is also a fruit salad sweetness with diced apples.
**Palate:** Fresh, intense malt which clings to the roof of the mouth alongside some slightly bitter oaky notes.
**Finish:** Pleasant, medium length but rather one dimensional. A chalky, vanilla finale.

## BRUICHLADDICH 13 YEARS OLD, ADELPHI 40%
Single Malt - Islay

**7 Michael: Interesting, but not typical.**
**Nose:** Heather. Flowery. Mint. Menthol. Faintly medicinal. Salt.
**Palate:** Very light but oily. Passion fruit. Grassy.
**Finish:** Minty. Peppermint. Drying.

**8½ Jim: Better than either standard bottling and true to the style which has made this Islay's most popular dram.**
**Nose:** Classically malty and fat on the nose but with an exceptional fresh fruit richness. Quite lovely.
**Palate:** Gloriously oily and malty. Fabulously clean malt interspersed with gentle spice and vanilla.
**Finish:** Long and simple. Little complexity but an attractive malt glow lingers, helped by the rich oils.

## BRUICHLADDICH 15 YEARS OLD 46%
Single Malt - Islay

**8** **Michael: More rounded and restrained than I remember, but lots of flavour development in that long middle. Bring on the Islay oysters.**
**Nose:** Fresh, clean. Distinctly flowery. Slightly oily.
**Palate:** Starts with a light, clean, taste of barley-malt. Then grassy sweetness. Becomes peppery in a series of small eruptions. Very lively. Very long.
**Finish:** Characteristic salt and iron emerging.

**8¾** **Dave: This has an extra maritime edge and is disgracefully (dangerously) drinkable.**
**Nose:** Fresh. Ozone and oak. Lifted aromas: sea thrift, lemon, malt/tablet, cinnamon bun, peaches in cream. A lovely nutty seaside (beech nuts?) air: brine, hot shells.
**Palate:** Fresh and bracing with mellow fruit (mango/orange) in yoghurt, lemon, almond and then the sea.
**Finish:** Long, warm, soft.

## BRUICHLADDICH 15 YEARS OLD LIMITED EDITION 54%
Single Malt - Islay

**7** **Martine: The nose puts you off, the palate tries to make it up but the result is not exciting.**
**Nose:** A sour scent of dry cider. Tangy, not pleasant. Unripe orange. A yeasty and sulphury note in the back.
**Palate:** Sweeter than the nose but still the citrussy sourness of unripe fruit. Touch of beeswax. Getting spicy.
**Finish:** Smoother than at start, biting in the back.

**8¼** **Dave: To me it is a classic balanced fresh sweet Laddie.**
**Nose:** Slightly edgy. Dry and slightly malty, a hint of dunnage warehouse then comes banana, crisp green eating apple.
**Palate:** Very lifted and effervescent. Light estery fruits to the fore. Lemon, lime and then Turkish yoghurt and honey cut with almond. Fragrant.
**Finish:** Spicy.

## BRUICHLADDICH 15 YEARS OLD, (JBB BOTTLING) 46%
Single Malt - Islay

**8** **Michael: An easily drinkable yet satisfying malt. Has definitely benefited from the extra five years.**
**Nose:** Intense. Drier, flowery, seaweedy, salty.
**Palate:** Flowery, seaweedy, salty. Flavours very well-combined and rounded. An easily drinkable yet satisfying malt. Has definitely benefited from the extra five years.
**Finish:** Long, warming, salty.

**7½** **Jim: Wondrously peat-free for an Islay but lacking in depth. Even so, this is rather lovely stuff.**
**Nose:** Peat-free (contrary to label) and clean – even cleaner than 10 Years Old. The malt is sweeter, too, with more vanilla, and a hint of butterscotch.
**Palate:** More discreet malt this time, with a pleasing built up of spices and oak.
**Finish:** Dry and extremely malty. The oak adds a bitter chocolate finale.

## BRUICHLADDICH 1969, 33 YEARS OLD, DUNCAN TAYLOR 48.7%
Single Malt - Islay

**8½** **Gavin: Good balance – has stood up to its cask well, retaining a zest not overwhelmed by age.**
**Nose:** Initially zesty, perfumed, with developing vanilla and leather. Finally, as it dries out, lemons.
**Palate:** Assertive oak, becoming into sherry and toffee.
**Finish:** More delicate oak, with attractive caramel notes cutting in later.

**9** **Dave: Fantastic for its age. Has retained the signature freshness.**
**Nose:** Toasty. Plenty of oak, pine sap, sawn wood, floor polish, then Lockets, mint nutmeg, praline.
**Palate:** A mix of soft and dry. Creamy texture balanced by sweet grippy oak. Guava, ripe orange, deck oil, biscuit, butterscotch toffee.
**Finish:** Light oak, coconut, toffee.

## BRUICHLADDICH 1969, OLD MALT CASK 53.5%
Single Malt - Islay

**8** **Michael: Shows that this whisky can handle some age and sherry.**

**Nose:** Salty. Seaweedy. Oily. Passion fruit. Spicy. Mace?
**Palate:** Light touch of sherry and toasty malt. Spicy. Pepper.
**Finish:** Firm, dry, appetising.

**8¾** **Jim: Why don't Gordon & MacPhail bottle at cask strength more often? This is fabulous.**
**Nose:** Some rich, softly honied, gently waxed, leathery Bourbony notes; a good age and a light malt.
**Palate:** Truly stunning balance achieved by the massive sweet malt and the old oak. Deep Bourbon-style notes offering a coffee fudge depth.
**Finish:** Some demerara sweetness but is over whelmed by the mounting sweet oak. Never dries.

## BRUICHLADDICH 1970 44.2%
Single Malt - Islay

**8** **Michael: Lively, expressive, enjoyable.**
**Nose:** Heavy, blossomy aroma. Fruit trees. Fresh limes.
**Palate:** Gentle, slow start. Leafy, malty. Brooding.
**Finish:** Surge of spicy, sandy flavours.

**8¾** **Dave: A whisky which needs time, thank god we're seeing some great old examples.**
**Nose:** A barrel in a dunnage warehouse. Green oak with a fresh floral note playing against earthy notes. Layers of fruit, vanilla, chocolate, sugared almonds.
**Palate:** Spicy, elegant, wood in perfect balance. Apricot, dried apple, spice. Orange, cakey, sweetness.
**Finish:** Fresh, then soft, sweet fruit.

## BRUICHLADDICH 1984 VINTAGE 46%
Single Malt - Islay

**7¾** **Michael: A more familiar Islay style, with plenty of pep.**
**Nose:** Very restrained. Flowery, leafy. Dry earth, sand. Sea air.
**Palate:** Lightly creamy. Drying. Salt and pepper.
**Finish:** Sandy. Cayenne pepper. Passion fruit.

**7½** **Dave: A good addition to an impressive range.**
**Nose:** Fresh and lively with light toffee, nutmeg, vanilla ice cream and then melted milk chocolate. With water there's malt and toasted wood.
**Palate:** A sweet start with light oak tones and a freshness which clears the head. Chocolate with vanilla. Good balance.
**Finish:** Vanilla.

## BRUICHLADDICH 1991 12 YEARS OLD, OLD MASTERS 58.7%
Single Malt - Islay

**7¾** **Michael: The Laddie in austere mood. Best before dinner.**
**Nose:** Dry. Herbal. Wild garlic. Appetising.
**Palate:** Bison leaf. Cut grass. Vanilla. A brief crunch of hard, nutty maltiness.
**Finish:** Peppery. Warming. Entrapping.

**7¾** **Dave: Well balanced, delicate and attractive.**
**Nose:** Perfumed and floral: iced gems, icing sugar, vanilla pod, crème anglaise. Sweet, light and appetising. In time, lino and plain oak.
**Palate:** Very sweet and fragrant. Alpine blossoms. Delicate and delicious.
**Finish:** Light oak.

## BRUICHLADDICH 1991, 12 YEARS OLD, DEWAR RATTRAY 60%
Single Malt - Islay

**9¼** **Michael: Savoury. Summery. A picnic malt. Or eating freshly shucked oysters with Jim McEwan.**
**Nose:** Fresh, fragrant. Light peatiness. Late hint of sweet seaweediness.
**Palate:** Complex. Lots of flavour development. Light oily hint of seaweed, passion fruit. Lively interplay of sweetness and saltiness
**Finish:** Sweet mustard.

**7¾** **Dave: A very pretty whisky.**
**Nose:** Almost rum-like: light spirit allied with tropical fruit/melon/zesty notes. Opal fruits and lilac. In time a hint of crystallised ginger. Fades relatively quickly.
**Palate:** Plenty of (balanced) oaky notes. Quite a thick feel with fresh fruit all the way.
**Finish:** Just a touch metallic.

## BRUICHLADDICH 1991, 12 YEARS OLD, PORTWOOD, COOPER'S CHOICE 46%
Single Malt - Islay

**8¼ Michael: Very appetising. Long, lingering.**
**Nose:** Warm nuttiness. At length, sea air.
**Palate:** Surprisingly big body. Emphatic. Marshmallow maltiness. Lots of flavour. Toffeeish Port notes add a whole new dimension to the estery, fruity subtleties of Bruichladdich.
**Finish:** Gentle blend of fruits and spices. Pepper comes into play.

**6½ Dave: The Port has the upper hand here. Unbalanced.**
**Nose:** Sweet. Wine gums, cranberry, raspberry ripple and light oak.
**Palate:** Again, a sweet, winey, start with some mushed up strawberries/raspberry sauce. The malt fights back mid-palate...
**Finish:** ...but back comes the port.

## BRUICHLADDICH 1992 SPIRIT SAFE & CASK SELECTION, CELTIQUE CONNEXION 43%
Single Malt - Islay

**8 Michael: It took me a while to get past the very pale colour (white wine) and the distinctive aroma but, in the end, I liked this manifestation of The Laddie.**
**Nose:** Fresh brie cheese.
**Palate:** Lightly creamy. Cereal grain. Digestive biscuits.
**Finish:** Quince jelly. Pepper.

**7½ Dave: As good as the OB 10 year-old.**
**Nose:** Young, vibrant and zingy. Lemon and lime, cut flowers. Thins a little as it develops.
**Palate:** Sugared almond. Clean and very fresh with a tingle in the centre. Holds its sweet fresh character well.
**Finish:** Short, fresh.

## BRUICHLADDICH 1993 12 YEARS OLD, DEWAR RATTRAY 55.1%
Single Malt - Islay

**7½ Arthur: Complex, subtle and interesting, but not a dram to stay at home for. Go out, have fun!**
**Nose:** Poached pears, autumn leaves and rockpools. With water there is wet clay, lemon balm, warm brown bread and damp woodland.
**Palate:** Lemony, malty and dry to finish.
**Finish:** Digestive biscuits.

**7¾ Owen: Youthful, and slightly understated, but heading in the right direction.**
**Nose:** Restrained at first, but developing coastal aromas: salt, iodine, drying seaweed.
**Palate:** Salty. Drying. Some lime and lemon notes (Margarita with a salted rim)? Cereal. Flavours become more precise with water.
**Finish:** Clean, crisp, and phenolic. Some late oily, caramel notes.

## BRUICHLADDICH 20 YEARS OLD 46%
Single Malt - Islay

**8½ Michael: Rounded, balanced and complex. Too expensive to pour on my porridge** before an early morning walk on the Big Strand? I'll economise. I'll skip the porridge.
**Nose:** The fresh flowers by the shore are now being blown by sea air gusting off Loch Indaal.
**Palate:** More cereal grain oiliness. More fruit. More salt. More of everything.
**Finish:** Again, salt and iron. Warming and appetising.

*WHISKY Editor's choice*

**9 Dave: Elegant. You'd never guess it's 20 Years Old. Great balance between salt and soft fruit.**
**Nose:** Charming, juicy, gentle and ripe. Succulent fruit (cooked apple, poached pear) balanced oak (vanilla). Water brings out dry bracken, thrift and sea spray.
**Palate:** Very soft malt. A sweet, succulent, subtly balanced malt that rolls around the mouth.
**Finish:** Hint of salt, butter and light smoke drifting by.

## BRUICHLADDICH 30 YEARS OLD, ADELPHI 49.4%
Single Malt - Islay

**8 Michael: It is more substantial than people think, as this bottling shows.**
**Nose:** Almonds, passion fruit.
**Palate:** Quite full in body and palate. Firm, dry, malt background. Toasty. Very spicy.
**Finish:** Long. A very late crescendo. Warming.

**7¾ Jim: Don't look for a big array of flavours: just variations on a theme, and most of them quite lovely.**
**Nose:** A little strained, honey-suckle sweetness.
**Palate:** Immediate bittersweet complexity.
**Finish:** Getting seriously old, but the oak remains the right side of delicious.

## BRUICHLADDICH CELTIC NATIONS 46%
Blended Malt - Scotland

*WHISKY Recommended*

**8½ Martine: Seems to have stored all the ingredients for a healthy breakfast. A** morning dram? Quite inviting.
**Nose:** Malty. Fruit and fibre cereals. A touch of burnt applewood. Strawberry yoghurt. An intriguing floral note (wild rose?).
**Palate:** Sweet with a sour touch. Smooth, refreshing. With a wave of liquorice dying out on a spicy fringe. A hint of yeasty wash behind.
**Finish:** Medium, tangy, dusty. A nutty aftertaste.

**8 Dave: As a blend of Scottish and Irish whiskies this is certainly atypical, but it works well.**
**Nose:** Very sweet, almost liqueur like with a green fruit note underneath: unripe plum mixed with kumquat and a sweet syrup note. Very creamy.
**Palate:** Big impact. Tingling alcohol. Some herbal notes. Gentle and clean with a hint of smoke.
**Finish:** Long, full and clean.

## BRUICHLADDICH INFINITY SECOND EDITION 52.5%
Single Malt - Islay

*WHISKY Recommended*

**8 Martine: Alcohol is perfectly tamed. No burn or tang. A cheery dram for a sunny** afternoon.
**Nose:** Fruity and malty. Lemon syllabub. Fresh leather. Demerara sugar. Apple pie. A touch of tangerine. Breath of grass.
**Palate:** Crisp, firm. But a sweet luscious start. Quite thick on the tongue. Mouthcoating. Pear poached in a vanilla syrup.
**Finish:** Long, nutty spicy.

**9 Dave: A blend of lightly peated older laddie and some new heavily peated Port Charlotte it is typical for Islay, but atypical for Bruichladdich.**
**Nose:** Sweet. Reminiscent of throat sweets, then nettle cordial and macaroons before the smoke begins to drift out. Light seashore aromas.
**Palate:** Burst of phenols to start, then parma violet. Concentrated and lightly perfumed. Hint of lavender. Silky and smooth with excellent length.
**Finish:** Ever lasting mixing smoke and vanilla.

## BRUICHLADDICH 'ISLANDS' THIRD EDITION, 20 YEARS OLD 46%
Single Malt - Islay

**7¾ Arthur: Surely a finish, but I couldn't quite place the influence, despite it having the malt in a half-nelson.** Curious, but I liked it.
**Nose:** Swimming pools, grass, mint toffees, sulphur (French bangers), mud and wax.
**Palate:** Woody with complex underlying sweetness and nut character. A touch sour and burnt (roasted pork), but with syrup to balance.
**Finish:** European tannins and lots of nuttiness.

**8 Dave: Old and gentle with a broad smile.**
**Nose:** Rounded, rich and elegant with a lightly charred nose. Burnt raisin, light prune, fruit cake with a hint of clove, walnut. Good concentration.
**Palate:** Well-rounded. A sweet, mellow quality with an intriguing burnt edge. Beech nut. Very soft and subtle with gentle, deep plummy fruits. Starts slightly muted, then the flavours are slowly revealed and keep building. Subtle and elegant.
**Finish:** It is, isn't it? Treacle toffee and cold tea.

## BRUICHLADDICH LEGACY 1966 VINTAGE 40.6%
Single Malt - Islay

**8¼ Michael: An especially characterful 'laddie from its sunny hue and lean, firm body to its touch of tartness.**
**Nose:** Estery. Apple crumble.
**Palate:** Estery. Calvados. Cider. Some fruity acidity.
**Finish:** Passion fruit. Iron. Salt. Blood and sand.

**8 Dave: A cracker.**
**Nose:** Sultry: heather, pot pourri, oak, orange, dark chocolate. Rich, mature and elegant.
**Palate:** Luscious. There's a crisp quality given by the oak, but some dried flower/heather and almond paste. Great balance.
**Finish:** Long, soft.

## BRUICHLADDICH LEGACY SERIES II 1965 41.8%
Single Malt - Islay

**8 Michael: Does Starbucks know about this?**
**Nose:** Choux pastry fresh out of the oven. Pain au chocolat.
**Palate:** Lean and chewy, like the inside of a croissant. Passion fruit. Sweet red peppers.
**Finish:** Ground black pepper.

**8½ Dave: Lighter and more lean than the '73.**
**Nose:** Fresh, vibrant and clean. Pine/forest floor, tangerine zest. Becomes sweeter and more chocolatey in time.
**Palate:** Light and fresh with a tingle akin to hot sand. A bleached maritime feel to start though it sweetens as it opens.
**Finish:** Dry, tingling.

## BRUICHLADDICH REDDER STILL 50.4%
Single Malt - Islay

**7½ Dave: A plump fruity number.**
**Nose:** Big and sweet with lots of childhood aromas: rosehip syrup, travel sweets, stewed rhubarb, ginger snaps filled with cream and strawberry jam. High tea in a glass.
**Palate:** Very thick and mouthfilling, mixing oak, red fruit coulis. Juicy and fat. Best neat, though water brings out a light leafy quality.
**Finish:** Sweet chestnut.

**7½ Martine: Quite a punchy lad. Water calms it but that colourful fruit basket loses its brightness.**
**Nose:** Tangy, slightly spirity. Very fruity. Tangerine juice, grapefruit (the pulp not the peel), plum jam. Gives a fresh feel. A touch of nougat. Opens on cappuccino. Touch of leather.
**Palate:** Smooth and sweet at first then abruptly shifts to hot spices (tabasco). A touch of cocoa bean.
**Finish:** Dry and warm.

## BRUICHLADDICH SECOND EDITION 15 YEARS OLD 46%
Single Malt - Islay

**7¾ Michael: I seem to have fallen into a breakfast reverie. This would be best with a Japanese breakfast.** WHISKY Recommended
**Nose:** Seaside bouquet, but delicate rather than intense.
**Palate:** Dusty. Peppery. Seaweedy, but not overtly medicinal.
**Finish:** Appetising sourness.

**8¼ Ian: Elegant and seductive, while also offering depth and range.**
**Nose:** Toffee, butterscotch overture, followed by vanilla, citrus and apricots, with a final touch of malt, and underlying toastiness throughout.
**Palate:** Ultra-delicate, creamy, apricots, hint of orange marmalade lusciousness, spicy fruityness.
**Finish:** Rich dried fruit with butterscotch, chocolate sweetness and growing toastiness.

## BRUICHLADDICH VINTAGE 1973 40.2%
Single Malt - Islay

**8½ Michael: The whisky for a Baltimore crab feast. Why not a Bruichladdich crab feast, come to that?**
**Nose:** Very aromatic. Quite heavy. Unusually peaty. A touch of sulphur.
**Palate:** Creamy. Passion fruit. Iron. Then sandy and salty.
**Finish:** Crescendo of spicy flavours, especially cayenne pepper.

**9 Dave: Superb balance and complexity. A belter.**
**Nose:** Elegant, complex and layered: pot pourri, dried peel, cashew, lightly caramelised fruits, praline, pistachio, vanilla, clootie dumpling.

**Palate:** Builds very very slowly in the mouth. Fresh, and though seems delicate has a mellow weight. Complex.
**Finish:** Long, softens.

## BRUICHLADDICH XVII, 17 YEARS OLD 46%
Single Malt - Islay

**8½ Michael: I shall try this in a Caipirinha, with a CD of Annie Ross at her peak.** WHISKY Recommended
**Nose:** A rock pool by the shore.
**Palate:** Soft, clean, sweet, becoming sandy, salty and spicy. Huge flavour development. Beautifully structured.
**Finish:** Lemon zest. Fresh limes. Lively. Irrepressible.

**8¾ Dave: What is it about Islay whiskies in their mid-teens? A masterclass in subtlety.**
**Nose:** Gentle and soft. Sweet oak, flowers, vanilla, nutmeg, dried apple, apricot. Water brings out more toasty notes, hazelnut and milk chocolate.
**Palate:** Rounded and creamy, with a subtle interplay between vanilla-like oak, macaroon bars, nut and fruit.
**Finish:** Fresh and crisp.

## BUNNAHABHAIN 12 YEARS OLD 40%
Single Malt - Islay

**7½ Michael: Appetising and remarkably refreshing.**
**Nose:** Remarkably fresh, sweet, sea-air and perfume.
**Palate:** Gentle, clean, nutty-malty sweetness.
**Finish:** Herbal. Sage?

**7½ Jim: This malt is on its way back. This is a big, big improvement – which will continue if sherry content is reduced.**
**Nose:** A slight sulphury note spoils the party. Underneath lovely soft sherry and crisp briny, malty notes.
**Palate:** Delightful with an astonishing arrival of malty-sherry notes. Low-key saltiness reveals extra depth.
**Finish:** Strange, sulphur-sherry style returns and not for the better. Remains salty with bitter-chocolate.

## BUNNAHABHAIN 14 YEARS OLD PORT FINISH 53%
Single Malt - Islay

**6¾ Dave: Front-loaded, clumsy and forced. Bunna's good enough on its own.**
**Nose:** Distinctly odd. A child's coat pocket; strawberry chewits and melted toffee. Hugely sweet, butterscotch.
**Palate:** A tight start, but a flabby centre. Stewed red fruit and caramel. Strangely dilute.
**Finish:** Disappears in a haze of saccharine sweetness.

**7¾ Arthur: Rather subdued on the nose, but a lovely, texture malt to drink.**
**Nose:** Fudgy, raisiny sweetness, green apples and fresh cut parsnips. An antiseptic, floor polish.
**Palate:** A good, oily and unchillfiltered texture, with jam, fruit and nut toffee, a little creosote and some orange.
**Finish:** Some sweet medical character, like Savlon.

## BUNNAHABHAIN 18 YEARS OLD 43%
Single Malt - Islay

**7 Arthur: I couldn't get past that taste of overfried bacon. This is a great malt distillery, and one of my favourites, so I am a little disappointed.**
**Nose:** Savlon, pizza dough and red apples. Spray-can paint.
**Palate:** Astringent, then dry. Burnt pork.
**Finish:** That lingering burnt meat and a balsa woodiness.

**7½ Owen: A very rich nose is slightly let down in the palate. On the whole, it's respectable enough.**
**Nose:** Some tart red fruits hover above a buttery, chocolate croissant base. Pleasant malt notes.
**Palate:** Sweet (green apples?) and fiery at first. Some buttery notes. Warm fruit scones?
**Finish:** On the short side, with a memory of well done toast.

## BUNNAHABHAIN 1963 42.9%
Single Malt - Islay

**8¼ Michael: The Islay origins become more obvious the more mature Bunnahabhain is. This one would be comfortable in distant Cathay or in Tokyo or even 42nd Street.**
**Nose:** Cashew nuts.
**Palate:** Gunpowder tea. Ginseng.
**Finish:** Just enough bitterness to be appetising. Salty.

**8 Dave: Another cracker from the vaults. Burn Stewart must be rubbing their hands with glee.**
**Nose:** Colour suggests real age, as does the initially muted nose but in time there's crystallised ginger, raisin, mushroom, peach, fondant icing and hint of peat.
**Palate:** Very gentle but still sweetly fruity and spicy and a crackle of energy in the middle.
**Finish:** Light peat. Fades away gently.

## BUNNAHABHAIN 1966 46.1%
Single Malt - Islay

**8 Michael: The blood-orange hue suggests that this Bunnahabhain will in all senses be more colourful than the gentle 12 Years Old we normally encounter. Sun-dried whisky?**
**Nose:** Smoke melding with fresh sea breezes. Could that be the puffer leaving for Glasgow?
**Palate:** Rich, creamy body. Fresh flavours. Unusually estery. Ginger toffee. Becoming nutty.
**Finish:** Dusty. Spice-shop. Long and warming.

**7½ Dave: It's more Jerez than Islay. I can't help feeling this would have been a cracker a few years ago.**
**Nose:** Heavy wood influence hits immediately. Leather, pipe smoke, Armagnac like (prune nut and earth).
**Palate:** A sweet start, the (tannic) wood puts a grip on things pretty quickly but there's still some attractive sweet honey notes/apple sponge in centre.
**Finish:** Ginger then roses and spice.

## BUNNAHABHAIN 1968 AULD AQUAINTANCE, HOG-MANAY EDITION 43.8%
Single Malt - Islay

**8½ Michael: A brilliantly sunny winter's day; a walk by the sea in late afternoon; a dram at dusk. Still Bunnahabhain, but so different.**
**Nose:** A rich, moist Dundee cake. Toasted nuts. Salty. Sea breezes.
**Palate:** Malted milk. Chocolate. Nonetheless avoids being cloying. Deftly balanced.
**Finish:** Dark cocoa powder.

**8½ Martine: A truly distinguished acquaintance.**
**Nose:** Rich, delicate. Bouquet of granny's wardrobe. Gingerbread, orange peel. Dried roses. Prunes. exotic wood. Old furniture.
**Palate:** Creamy, sweet. Wood apparent with liquorice and eucalyptus notes. Hint of resin.
**Finish:** Nice orangey aftertaste. Slight bitterness in final notes. Shorter than the nose suggests.

## BUNNAHABHAIN 1968, THE FAMILY SILVER VINTAGE RESERVE 40%
Single Malt - Islay

**8 Michael: Because it is less aggressive than some of its neighbours, Bunnahabhain is often regarded as not being a proper Islay malt. This proves it can be.**
**Nose:** Fragrant. Sea air. Very lightly briney.
**Palate:** Firm. Hint of iron. Oaky. Oily. Developing almondy, nutty maltiness. Deft balance of flavours.
**Finish:** Edible seaweed. More salt.

**8¼ Jim: Another example of an aged malt that, for all its obvious charm and class, has been just a tad too much oak. A delicious experience, nonetheless.**
**Nose:** Subtle sherry aroma balanced by a fresh salty breeze. Mildly bourboned.
**Palate:** Marginally fatter than the average Bunna, a quick rush of oak countered by malt and sherry.
**Finish:** Remains oaky and oily with some cocoa notes popping through.

## BUNNAHABHAIN 1969, 36 YEARS OLD, DUNCAN TAYLOR 40.7%
Single Malt - Islay

**7¼ Gavin: Hasn't held up for its age anything like as well as the previous thirty-something Bruichladdich. The cask has won this battle.**
**Nose:** Leather, saddle soap, 'fousty'.
**Palate:** Quite thick mouthfeel, dominant dry oak.
**Finish:** Mixed spices and raisins behind the oak, but struggling.

**7 Dave: Gone, just spent too long in the cask.**
**Nose:** Old, mature. Bung cloth, raisin, cereal, boot polish, lardy cake. Like an old warehouse. Becomes mustier with time. Damp wood.
**Palate:** Mixed dried fruits, dry clootie dumping mix. Old and fading fast.
**Finish:** Light tingle of ginger.

## BUNNAHABHAIN 1979 BOURBON BARREL, MURRAY MCDAVID 43%
Single Malt - Islay

**8 Michael: Surprising peatiness, but without smokiness.**
**Nose:** Salt. Fresh limes. Citrus peel.
**Palate:** Lightly nutty. Creamy, oily. Clean, grassy, peat.
**Finish:** Fragrant.

**5½ Jim: One to forget.**
**Nose:** A disappointingly dirty, off aroma more akin to a curry than a single malt.
**Palate:** Much better than the nose suggests but beyond a sweet maltiness it doesn't travel far before something thin and not quite right makes an entry.
**Finish:** Malty with vanilla but very little depth.

## BUNNAHABHAIN 1979 SHERRY CASK, MURRAY MCDAVID 43%
Single Malt - Islay

**7 Michael: For an allegedly light malt, the flavours sing through but, as the dark colour suggests, there really is too much wood.**
**Nose:** Salt and oak.
**Palate:** Vanilla, toffee, oil, salt.
**Finish:** Dry, gingery, spicy, woody.

**8 Jim: An immensely drinkable malt that is the alter ego to its sibling cask.**
**Nose:** The Hyde to the Bourbon barrel's Jekyll. The cleanest, deepest sherry aroma you could ever pray for offering subtle spices and delicate malt. To die for.
**Palate:** Massively chewy with sherry making all the play. The malty background is off-key by comparison but the nutty, plummy fruit-cake tones win through.
**Finish:** Medium length and massively fruity.

## BUNNAHABHAIN 1989, GORDON & MACPHAIL 40%
Single Malt - Islay

**8 Michael: A breakfast whisky for the truly decadent.**
**Nose:** Lots of sherry. Ginger marmalade and toast.
**Palate:** More of the same, but the grassy, briny, distillery character emerges later.
**Finish:** Salty and appetising.

**7½ Jim: One of the most enjoyable Bunnas I've tasted though missing that breathtaking freshness.**
**Nose:** An attractive mix of fresh cherries, sweet, over-ripe grapes and much earthier, drier malt.
**Palate:** Clean, intense malty start which continues. Fruitiness arrives towards the middle with toasty oak.
**Finish:** A dry finish with that massive malt still pursuing its relentless course.

## BUNNAHABHAIN 25 YEARS OLD 43%
Single Malt - Islay

**8 Arthur: A bold spirit, tempered by well-timed matura-tion. A little flat to be truly great.**
**Nose:** Vanilla ice cream, milk bottle chews, sultana bran, dried coconut. With time grassiness, and a farmyard whiff.
**Palate:** Mouth filling and malty, with a shake of spice.
**Finish:** Woody, drying and with complex bitterness of quality dark chocolate.

**7½ Owen: Not a big whisky, but comforting.**
**Nose:** Traces of caramel and fudge at first, with developing oily (metal polish?) notes.
**Palate:** Lightly oily. Digestive biscuits. Toffees and toffee apples. Mint.
**Finish:** A warming, and curiously more-ish finish.

WHISKY
Editor's choice

### BUNNAHABHAIN 27 YEARS OLD, DEWAR RATTRAY 49.9%
Single Malt - Islay

8 **Michael: Not as elegant and complex as some in this flight, but the breakfast it evoked was hearty and delicious.**
**Nose:** Toast with raspberry jam, for breakfast by the sea.
**Palate:** Almond croissants. Darjeeling tea.
**Finish:** A bit sandy. It's a windy day.

8¼ **Ian: Softly spoken but plenty to say, being elegantly delicate but delivering real range.**
**Nose:** Rich dried fruit wafts above underlying toastiness, brioche with fruit sauce, then vanilla, créme brûlée and apple skins emerge mid-way.
**Palate:** Rich gingerbread, brioche, baked apples with vanilla sauce and cloves, while underlying toastiness continues with digestive biscuits.
**Finish:** Fruity, malty combination, toastiness lingers.

### BUNNAHABHAIN 27 YEARS OLD, THE WHISKY EXCHANGE 46%
Single Malt - Islay

7½ **Dave: A welcome addition.**
**Nose:** Slightly plain, yet fragrant with wet green grass, anise, marzipan. Lightly dusty. Sweeter with water.
**Palate:** Very sweet again. The anise note returns along with meadow sweet. Firm but charming.
**Finish:** Clean and soft.

7¾ **Martine: A summer dram. Quite thirst quenching with its bitter profile.**
**Nose:** Fragrant. Lemon juice and pulp. Gooseberry. A hint of verbena herbal tea.
**Palate:** Sweet at first then getting bitter. Strange hoppy taste, like a beer. Peppermint.
**Finish:** Dry, spicy, sherbety.

### BUNNAHABHAIN 35 YEARS OLD LIMITED EDITION 44.9%
Single Malt - Islay

8¼ **Dave: You'd never guess this was 35. Great life, balance and bags of character. A beauty.**
**Nose:** Mature notes cut with celery salt, sweet oak. Dried peach, musk, and coconut. Complex.
**Palate:** Good flow of flavours: Bounty bars, light cinnamon, then ginger, stewed rhubarb, clove and ripe fruits. There's a strawberry lift and some marzipan as well. Medium weight.
**Finish:** Long and elegant.

8¼ **Arthur: No water required, as this brought out a soapiness for me. A very satisfying old malt.**
**Nose:** Raisins, Madeira cake and ginger thins. Underneath this is a melange of fruits: baked apples, pineapple and strawberry. Perhaps a light, sweet soapiness.
**Palate:** A silky almost soapy texture, with blueberry muffin, and strawberry-flavoured toffee.
**Finish:** Burnt wood and more strawberry.

### BUNNAHABHAIN, 10.56, SCOTCH MALT WHISKY SOCIETY 59.4%
Single Malt - Islay

7½ **Michael: I admired its feistiness, but I might be more comfortable with a greater degree of maturity.**
**Nose:** Aromatic. Somewhere in the distance, they are burning heather.
**Palate:** Malty dryness. Straight-ahead attack. Powerful. Grips the taste sensors and won't let go.
**Finish:** Sweet but peppery.

8½ **Dave: A big soft beast of a dram. More please!**
**Nose:** Rich and soft. Ridiculously creamy: blackberry cheesecake, semi-dried fruits, roasted nuts. Voluptuous.
**Palate:** Spicy and dark with ginger notes. Fruit cake, smoked paprika, butter, dried fruit.
**Finish:** Palo Cortado, nutty, marzipan.

### CADENHEAD'S CLASSIC RANGE, CAMPBELTOWN 50%
Blended Malt - Scotland

8 **Michael: Seems simple at first, but gradually reveals subtleties. Stylish, teasing.**
**Nose:** Crème caramel. Rosewater.
**Palate:** Am I being suggestible? That famous Campbeltown coconut character seems almost tangible. Dry and straw-like at first, then a surge of grassy sweetness. Dusting of powdered sugar. Garnish candied angelica.
**Finish:** Cookie-like dryness.

7½ **Ian: An animated and flirtatious nature, with engaging gestures and a lovely smile.**
**Nose:** Apricots, baked apples, mellow spice and underlying oak, brioche and gingerbread.
**Palate:** Elegant though with a certain richness, balancing cooked fruit and apricots with subtle spices, créme brûlée sweetness balanced by oak.
**Finish:** The same flavours but the volume rises, and lasts.

### CADENHEAD'S CLASSIC RANGE, HIGHLAND 50%
Blended Malt - Scotland

7¾ **Michael: How nice this would be with one of those tasteful desserts that involves a 'sugar nest' and some fresh fruit.**
**Nose:** Spicy, lemony freshness (ginger?), becomes sweeter with ripe raspberries, a dusting of icing sugar and a garnish of fresh garden mint.
**Palate:** Firm yet light. Sweet, then burnt sugar. Brandy snap and zabaglione.
**Finish:** Caramel. Buttered toast. Lingering.

7¾ **Dave: A very decent dram with good balance and structure.**
**Nose:** Very sweet with vanilla, barley sugar, candied fruits, linden, fried banana and citrus. With water, more oak.
**Palate:** The oak is quite firm but acts as a frame for some sweet fruit. Gentle and tongue-coating. Some bubblegum sweetness...
**Finish:** ...then a bitter catch like rue.

### CADENHEAD'S CLASSIC RANGE, ISLAY 50%
Blended Malt - Scotland

8¼ **Arthur: You can see why the Germans get so obsessed with this stuff. A peaty happy-slap.**
**Nose:** Burnt sticks, lemon flavoured toilet cleaner (in a good way), and tarry rope.
**Palate:** A big, sweet, citric peat-boff, followed by a whiplash of dry, moreish ropiness.
**Finish:** Storm-lashed rope.

7½ **Dave: A slap in the face with a wet haddock.**
**Nose:** Slightly stony, with smoked meat, juniper, aniseed, rock pools, wet face cloth and paint thinner (??!). Clean, assertive with a little immaturity.
**Palate:** Very dusty start. Coal shovel, damp nutty slack, zesty, wet rope. Bigger than you'd expect, but a little one-dimensional.
**Finish:** Crisp, phenolic.

### CADENHEAD'S CONVALMORE-GLENLIVET 26 YEARS OLD 61.4%
Single Malt - Speyside

7 **Michael: A welcome opportunity to taste a rare whisky, though it was never a classic, and in this instance is over the hill (or the Conval Hills?).**
**Nose:** Cidery. Oily. Earthy.
**Palate:** Cooked apples. Over-ripe bananas.
**Finish:** Cloves. Medicinal. Tight on the tongue.

7¼ **Dave: Just lacks some depth. All a bit nervy, but worth seeking out.**
**Nose:** Incredibly sweet and estery. Lemon, candy floss, Sugar Puffs, honey, mint, touch of smoke and cocoa. The oak emerges with water but ends up slightly flat with time.
**Palate:** Lemon-fresh and sugary sweet all the way. Cinnamon. Just a dab of water is needed here.
**Finish:** Light but intense.

### CALEDONIAN 1976, 23 YEARS OLD, SIGNATORY 58.5%
Single Grain - Scotland

6¾ **Michael: Despite their lightness, some grains can stand up to long periods in wood.**
**Nose:** Old books. Vegetal. Cedary.
**Palate:** Dryish. Grassy. Then some pleasant sweetness.
**Finish:** The hit of alcohol and some oaky vanilla help round out the woodiness.

8 **Dave: Great contrast; a pretty dry nose, a lush soft palate and that complex finish where it all comes together. Seamless.**

**Nose:** Very clean and medium-bodied with a good spiky lift. Dry to start, but in time it gets creamier with hints of light toffee.
**Palate:** Much softer than the nose suggests. Ripe and chewy with lovely flavours of fresh melon juice, with nutmeg spiciness.
**Finish:** Bursts into life with gorgeous soft apricot.

## CAMBUS 1964, 31 YEARS OLD, SIGNATORY 43.8%
Single Grain - Scotland

**7** Michael: A good example of a single grain as a pleasant dram. If someone gave me this whisky in a bar, I would enjoy it, but I have yet to find a single grain that has the complexity of a great malt.
**Nose:** Sweet, clean, almost malty.
**Palate:** Sweet syrupy, perfumy.
**Finish:** Cedary, dryish. Appetising.

**8¾** Dave: Can a whisky be mellifluous? If so, this is it. Needless to say the distillery has been bulldozed. Ironic, huh?
**Nose:** Very gentle and soft with sweet spice notes. Vanilla, toffee, lemon/orange and cigar smoke.
**Palate:** As the nose suggests with an extra (Greek yoghurt?) creaminess. Soft, sweet and gentle though the spiciness stops it becoming too soft. Great texture.
**Finish:** Long and soft. As on the palate it's the feel which seduces you as much as the flavour.

## CAMERON BRIG 40%
Single Malt - Scotland

**7¾** Michael: I have long enjoyed this whisky. It's own subtle character shines through, despite the influence of the wood being so obvious.
**Nose:** Honeyish and spicy.
**Palate:** Smooth. Nutty. Firm.
**Finish:** Faintly coffeeish. Smoky. With a slight, appetising, bitterness.

**7** Dave: Attractive, quite light.
**Nose:** Rich with some vanilla, soft fruits, dry grass and a slight dry/metallic note.
**Palate:** Crisp in the mouth to start, with an attractively soft mid-palate. Slightly hard on the sides of the tongue but softens in time.
**Finish:** Tingling and a little short.

## CAMPBELTOWN 1970, THE ALMOND TREE 46%
Single Malt - Campbeltown

**8** Dave: Great balance. Worth a look.
**Nose:** Odd winey notes, slightly sour. Green plum and pear drops, then a note like warm Fino sherry. Touch of saltiness and a little smoke. In time oilskins. Water adds complexity. Seems old but very fresh.
**Palate:** Rounded and sweet. Deep palate where the vanilla/coconut notes mix with nutmeg and that briny quality. Olive. Succulent and long.
**Finish:** Coal dust.

**8½** Martine: A superb dram combining fruit and spice in the most elegant way.
**Nose:** Enticing, sweet and fresh. A full basket of juicy fruit. Ripe pears, quince, white peaches. With luscious creamy notes topping the fruit. Hint of grapefruit and tangerine.
**Palate:** Just as enticing. What you nose is what you get. Clean and crisp with a good depth.
**Finish:** Drier with a pleasant display of soft spices.

## CAMPBELTOWN LOCH 21 YEARS OLD 40%
Blended - Scotland

**8** Michael: A good, solid blend. Serve chilled, neat, with Loch Fyne oysters, pickled herrings and scallops.
**Nose:** Leather luggage.
**Palate:** Oily. Full cereal-grain maltiness. Quite steely. Restrained fruity esters. Passion fruit.
**Finish:** Coconut sweetness. Peppery dryness. A pinch of salt.

**8¼** Dave: Firmer than the legendary 25 year-old, but a fine replacement.
**Nose:** Rounded and peachy. Oak, vanilla, marshmallow, sultana, toffee. Has complexity.
**Palate:** Starts spicy (cinnamon/allspice) and lightly, then a soft fruity (dried tropical) mid-palate before a lightly smoky oaky lift.
**Finish:** Crisp, oak.

## CAMPBELTOWN LOCH 25 YEARS OLD 40%
Blended - Scotland

**8** Michael: Easily drinkable but with a distinct regional character and plenty of flavour. This could become one of my favourite blends.
**Nose:** Grass verges overgrown with whin, leaving its curiously fruity, banana and almond aromas.
**Palate:** Lightly syrupy. Clean. Teasing, gentle, dexterous interplay of sweetness and smokiness.
**Finish:** Flowery, dryish, restrained.

**7½** Dave: A pretty phenolic example.
**Nose:** Dry, lean and woody. Fairly phenolic. Water shows the wood, but also sugared almond, cigar smoke/cedar.
**Palate:** Has honeyed sweetness and good weight. The smoke dominates the back palate. Perfumed but dry.
**Finish:** Smoky.

## CAOL ILA 10 YEARS OLD, RARE CASK, QUEEN OF THE MOORLANDS 46%
Single Malt - Islay

WHISKY
Recommended

**8** Arthur: Very good, but better without water. Is Caol Ila the most consistent distillery ever? So many indies, so few duff drams.
**Nose:** Lime, vanilla ice cream flecked with peat. Cold salty butter. With water there is stable hay, peat-flavoured Shredded Wheat.
**Palate:** Pleasant buttery texture and a good balance between sweet and savoury barbecue character.
**Finish:** Coal tar.

**8½** Owen: Nice interplay of youthful flavours. Puts me in mind of a popular late 1980s aftershave. (Good pairing for a Cohiba Robusto).
**Nose:** Clean. Fresh. Pine resin notes complement a drying, adolescent, acetic background. Icing sugar.
**Palate:** Woody. Faintly astringent. Fresh. New sawdust. Citrus and pine resin.
**Finish:** Medium. Again, piney, but with a faint trace of peppermint.

## CAOL ILA 11 YEARS OLD, ADELPHI 40%
Single Malt - Islay

**6** Michael: A curiously insipid bottling.
**Nose:** Very light for this distillery. Sweetness and pepper. Seaweed.
**Palate:** Oily, lightly malty, sweetish.
**Finish:** Light pepper.

**7½** Jim: About as subtle as a Peckinpah film and about as violent on the palate, too. Monster stuff.
**Nose:** Slightly astringent and lower peated than one might expect. Remains fresh, but a little green and a tad feinty.
**Palate:** Big and cumbersome on the palate with most extra-ordinary malty, gristy sweetness. Quite brawny.
**Finish:** Long and oily with some drier, almost bitter almond notes.

## CAOL ILA 12 YEARS OLD 43%
Single Malt - Islay

WHISKY
Editor's choice

**8** Michael: All the classic Caol Ila aromas and flavours are there, with no sharp edges. Vatted for drinkability?
**Nose:** Juniper. Garden mint. Burnt grass, but soft.
**Palate:** Lightly oily. Soothing at first. Lots of flavour development.
**Finish:** Spicy (nutmeg, pepper). Warming. Very long.

**8½** Dave: Great balance.
**Nose:** Oily yet fruity. Linseed oil, green olive, smoked fish. Lightly medicinal, wet grass, linseed oil, smoky wood (balsa wood?). With water good biscuity malt and smoky bacon notes.
**Palate:** Rounded, mid-weight. Good smoky intensity mid-palate. Clean juicy fruits, oil and dry smoke.
**Finish:** Long smoky, fishy.

## CAOL ILA 12 YEARS OLD 43%
Single Malt - Islay

**3** **Martine: A balanced expression of peat in this version. A lot of intricate aromas in this dram.**
**Nose:** Lively. Marine. Morning sea-breeze. Wet rocks. Phenolic. Warm tar. Cough medicine. Burning seaweed.
**Palate:** Round, mellow. A full bite of sea-shore. Hint of scallop. Smoked mackerel. Salty. Smokiness comes in the back.
**Finish:** Spicy, lingering, dry on cold ashes. Smoked oysters.

**3½** **Dave: Better balance than the cask strength. The peat is at same level, but a greater range of aromatics has been brought out. Complexity emerges.**
**Nose:** Crisp. Hot-smoked salmon, wet seaweed, smoked paprika. New aromas of parma violet, liquorice, wet canvas shoes.
**Palate:** Soft and clean. The smoke teases you at the front, then erupts in middle and back. What is most noticeable is how the middle has fleshed out.
**Finish:** Blackberry leaf. Beach bonfire. Smoky.

*Peat rating out of 5*

## CAOL ILA 12 YEARS OLD, THE WEE DRAM 40%
Single Malt - Islay

**8¾** **Michael: I like this young man: he's showered and shaved, suited and booted, and off for a night on the town.** *WHISKY Magazine Editor's choice*
**Nose:** Elegant smoke masks a youthful, cleansing acidity, and belies a fresh sweetness.
**Palate:** Light and crisp. Above a cereal base, lemony smoke cleans without compromise.
**Finish:** Simple and refreshing – yet nothing is missing. Confident.

**8** **Dave: More expressive than the other peated one. Very good.**
**Nose:** Smoky and intense. Good delivery of sweet peat smoke. Balanced, subtle and rounded. A fleshy smoked fish, olive oil, vegetal. Good breadth of flavour. Intriguing. Hint of coconut.
**Palate:** Very smoky start, then medicinal notes, then macaroon with a floral sweetness underpinning it. Lightly oily texture.
**Finish:** Long, smoky, peppered mackerel.

## CAOL ILA 13 YEARS OLD, BOTTLE FOR THE WHISKY FAIR 54.2%
Single Malt - Islay

**8¾** **Michael: Beautifully complex.** *WHISKY Magazine Editor's choice*
**Nose:** Vanilla. Perfumy. Dry grass. Then late smokiness. Grilled sardines.
**Palate:** Slides off the tongue. Oily. A creamy risotto, with spinach, lemon and saffron.
**Finish:** Smoky again.

**8¼** **Dave: The key, as ever is balance offsetting dry smoke with a sweet spot in the centre. Good.**
**Nose:** Highly smoked: smoked ham, fat, the tar on the wooden walls of a smokehouse, but then the door is opened to let in a grassy fragrance. Goes very cloudy with water, then some coal tar.
**Palate:** Fragrant and floral (violet) then a blast of tarry rope. Good balance.
**Finish:** Lingering smoke.

## CAOL ILA 13 YEARS OLD, CHIEFTAIN'S CHOICE 46%
Single Malt - Islay

**8½** **Dave: Here we go again...Caol Ila hits the nail on the head yet again.** *WHISKY Magazine Recommended*
**Nose:** Fragrant smoke, light tar, wet grass, burning fish boxes. In time there's Old English marmalade and fish oils and a hint of seaweed.
**Palate:** Immediate thrust of smoke with lots of oil, leather, plum and a vanilla smoothness. Long layered and balanced.
**Finish:** Superb length.

**8¼** **Arthur: Bristling with all those flavour spikes that make the Peat Freaks grin. Like a mint choc chip and peat ice cream.**
**Nose:** Youthful and intense with plenty of peat, wet grass and fish oil.
**Palate:** Dark chocolate and sweet vanilla. Earthy and grassy, with silky, creamy mint. Like peat-flavoured bubblegum.
**Finish:** Earthy.

## CAOL ILA 15 YEARS OLD 43%
Single Malt - Islay

**8** **Michael: A wonderful aperitif. Smoked fish to follow?**
**Nose:** Aromatic, complex. Peaty, seaweedy, fruity.
**Palate:** Peaty, spicy, olive-like. Flavours beautifully rounded.
**Finish:** Oily, peppery.

**8½** **Jim: Complex with the oak making an ultra impressive foil to the peat. Excellent.**
**Nose:** Charming sea spray dilutes the soft, deep peat. Shades of vanilla and iodine.
**Palate:** Brilliantly oily, offering a magnificently lingering peaty sheen. Lovely maltiness giving way to some rich dark chocolate.
**Finish:** The oaky dark cocoa fuses effortlessly with the pulsing peat.

## CAOL ILA 15 YEARS OLD, DEWAR RATTRAY 56%
Single Malt - Islay

**8½** **Martine: An enticing young beauty. Matches subtlety with character.** *WHISKY Magazine Recommended*
**Nose:** Delicate, fruity and creamy. Peaches in syrup. Rhubarb marmalade. Burnt twigs. Pine cone. Hint of mushroom broth. Wet sand. Touch of bog myrtle and pepper. Develops on buttery notes. Shortbread. Quite complex for a teenager.
**Palate:** Sweet and sour. Lemon meringue pie. Soot and smoke. Candied rhubarb. Luscious.
**Finish:** Gingery and dry.

**8½** **Dave: Faultless balance. Has an extra dimension which just edges it past the Bowmore.**
**Nose:** Moderate intensity showing beautifully integrated phenols: lightly perfumed (herbs), farmland, then sea spray, bitumen and finally smoked ham, kippers. Vibrant and complex.
**Palate:** Great mix of sweetness and phenolic depth: rosemary oil, bayleaf. An oily quality which allows the flavours to extend across the palate.
**Finish:** Cooked meats, sweet smoke.

## CAOL ILA 16 YEARS OLD, THE WHISKY EXCHANGE 57.9%
Single Malt - Islay

**8½** **Dave: Just one of a great clutch of smoky drams this time around.** *WHISKY Magazine Recommended*
**Nose:** Once the alcohol flashes off the smoke rushes out along with citrus, freshly cut green grass, oyster shells and a youthful bleachy note.
**Palate:** Good mix of intense leafy smoke and an oily succulent feel. Melon. Fresh fish. Generous and silky.
**Finish:** Smoky. Lobster creels.

**8½** **Arthur: Lively, lip-smacking Islay. More good stuff from Sukhinder and his Whisky Exchange gang.**
**Nose:** White/lemon pepper, some cereally sweet oat notes of youth.
**Palate:** Lemon puff biscuits, vanilla and a leafiness. A chalky smokiness, and maybe like barbecued fish at times.
**Finish:** A lingering, tingling pepperiness.

## CAOL ILA 18 YEARS OLD 43%
Single Malt - Islay

**8½** **Michael: The most vegetal and assertive of the three expressions. Lots of contribution from the wood.**
**Nose:** Fragrant. Menthol. Markedly vegetal. Vanilla pod. Creamy.
**Palate:** Firmer. Much bigger. Much more expressive. Sweeter. Leafy sweetness. Spring greens. Crushed almonds. Rooty, cedary.
**Finish:** Some peaty bitterness. Big. Long, warming.

**7¼** **Dave: Dry, crisp and mature with more of a contribution from the cask (not OTT though).**
**Nose:** Darker in colour, some vanilla and a heavy floral note (bluebell). Light oaky notes, orange/lemon and some smoke.
**Palate:** Rounded and quite sweet to start then begins to dry in the centre. Good weight. Some oak.
**Finish:** Lightly smoky and herbal (dried thyme).

## CAOL ILA 18 YEARS OLD 43%
Single Malt - Islay

**2½** **Martine: Oak seems to have "digested" peat. The smokiness is restrained on nose as well on palate but surprisingly comes back on the finish.**
**Nose:** Grassy and herbal. A faint smoke scent from a distant dying bonfire. Oak covers the peat character and releases sweet herbal notes.

**Palate:** A smooth, mellow, sweet, malty. Herbal character as announced on the nose.
**Finish:** Lingering, with a swift smoky come back. And a phenolic touch. Ends on dry ashes.

**3** **Dave: The peatiness is less 'peaty' and is more in the area of light phenols. It's there though.**
**Nose:** Intense with an oyster like freshness, fish in early stages of being smoked, slightly medicinal. In time a note reminiscent of a muggy day in Islay.
**Palate:** The smoke travels low and fast across the top of the tongue, then the rich, textural oiliness calms it down and mixes it with light fruit.
**Finish:** Still a mix of oils and dry smoke, then a hint of tinned fruit.

*Peat rating out of 5*

### CAOL ILA 1969, GORDON & MACPHAIL 45%
Single Malt - Islay

**4** **Martine: Surprisingly, the distillery character resists in this oldie. And peat "revisits" the aromatic palette. Integration again but no fusion.**
**Nose:** Lively oak with a sherry character. Toned down creosote. Moss and mushrooms. Smoked chestnuts. Lapsang souchong tea. Then sweet notes come up. Vanilla, toffee, butter scotch.
**Palate:** Sweet and bitter. Sherried. Smoke hangs above wood.
**Finish:** Dry, oaky, sooty with a hint of tarred timber.

**3½** **Everything has deepened and become richer but those oils have been retained and the smoke has controlled everything.**
**Nose:** High concentration with an immediate wisp of perfumed smoke. Peat retained. An elegant mix of phenols, honeyed sweetness, toffee, and even some pineapple. Robust yet complex.
**Palate:** Peat from the start. Slightly dry tannins and dry smoke. Singed grass. Hessian.
**Finish:** Dark chocolate, undergrowth, ashes.

*Peat rating out of 5*

### CAOL ILA 1969, PRIVATE COLLECTION 45%
Single Malt - Islay

**7¾** **Michael: After a few of these, the rebel leader (played by Anthony Quinn) toasts freedom, and we start firing our carbines in the air.**
**Nose:** Honey. Syrup. Figs. Dry spiciness. Slightly medicinal.
**Palate:** Astonishingly fig-like. Earthy. Dusty.
**Finish:** Tastes stronger than the claimed 45%. Restorative.

**8¾** **Dave: Do NOT add water. Remarkable for its age.**
**Nose:** Obviously old: concentrated rancio/balsamic notes, wild mushroom liquor. Fragrant smoke, coffee grounds, arbroath smoke, amontillado.
**Palate:** An intriguing and complex mix of dried fruits, oak, wet coal, fish oils.
**Finish:** Long oaky, rancio.

### CAOL ILA 1977, 20 YEARS OLD, RARE MALTS 61.3%
Single Malt - Islay

**9** **Michael: A wonderful aperitif. Who would have thought of a Scotch to precede Greek food?**
**Nose:** Powerfully aromatic. Roasted peppers. Olives. Salt.
**Palate:** Oily, soothing. Roasted peppers, olives, lemon juice.
**Finish:** Dry, junipery, vine-leaves, stemmy. Intense, expressive.

**7½** **Jim: A big malt, but carrying little of the magic that sets Port Ellen apart in this group. A stark reminder of what Islay has lost.**
**Nose:** Fat, oily and lazilly smoky. Slightly kippery with salt and vanilla.
**Palate:** Sweet at first then a massive oaky intervention which dries the malt. Peat and dark chocolate.
**Finish:** Dark chocolate digestive biscuits with a peaty, toasty edge. Some saltiness comes through on the clinging, oily finish. Slightly tired oak spoils the balance.

### CAOL ILA 1979 25 YEARS OLD, DOUGLAS LAING 50%
Single Malt - Islay

**8¼** **Martine: An attractive character. Phenolic but with much more.**
**Nose:** Phenols. Creosote. Briny. Burning dried seaweeds. Lemon essence. Restrained smoke. Like the vapour rising from hot bitumen after a storm.
**Palate:** Sweet and malty. Very oily. Crystallized violets. Liquorice losenges. Refreshing. Kippers.

**Finish:** Dry. Vanilla breaks through. The smoke disappears gradually.

**7¾** **Dave: Austere but with a restrained power.**
**Nose:** Firm. Sun-baked bare rock, acetone, then medicinal. Water releases peat smoke, juniper and marine character.
**Palate:** Beach bbq, creosote. Becomes very medicinal. Clean with some softening vanilla creaminess in the centre of the palate.
**Finish:** Explosive. The phenolics appear. Fish oil.

### CAOL ILA 1979 26 YEARS OLD, THE WHISKY FAIR, DOUGLAS LAING 57.2%
Single Malt - Islay

**7¾** **Arthur: Should have been taken out of the cask a few years back. Easy to say now of course.**
**Nose:** Tropical fruit flavoured Germolene. Artificial strawberry flavour. Yacht varnish. A sweet floral note too. With water, cigarette ash and horses. Lemon and mothballs.
**Palate:** Antiseptic, ropey, then leathery. Some fruitiness tucked in somewhere.
**Finish:** Salted cashews rolled in cigarette ash.

**8¼** **Owen: Smoked malt aromas and flavours remind me of early morning mashing at a Bavarian smoked beer brewery. Stunningly balanced.**
**Nose:** Delicate, but undeniable phenols waft above a cream soda/candy floss base. Pear drops, too.
**Palate:** Sweet 'n' salt. Beautiful biscuity fresh flavours of toasting malt.
**Finish:** Sweet, smoky and medicinal.

### CAOL ILA 1981 CASK STRENGTH, SIGNATORY 62.5%
Single Malt - Islay

**7¾** **Martine: Quite sharp at the beginning then gradually softening. Fruitier than previous Signatory bottlings. Very sensitive to dilution.**
**Nose:** A bit spirity. Sea-washed dune grass. Hint of camphor. Phenolic whisper.
**Palate:** Burning, stout. Slowly releases fruity sweetness. Melon, strawberry, vanilla ice cream.
**Finish:** Dry again with an afterglow of kiln embers.

**7¾** **Dave: Another Caol Ila? I like the softer, more succulent expression.**
**Nose:** Good mix of fragrant orange/tangerine notes, malt and smoky bacon along with real end-of-the-pier stuff. A lightly medicinal note but plenty of soft fruit and a floral lift (parma violet?).
**Palate:** Scented smoke, heather blossom, soft pulpy fruits in the middle.
**Finish:** Sweet smoky malt, then dries.

### CAOL ILA 1981, GORDON & MACPHAIL 62.7%
Single Malt - Islay

**8** **Michael: A beautifully balanced, rounded, example of this distinctive malt.**
**Nose:** Juniper, seaweed, tobacco.
**Palate:** Hint of nutty sherry. Leafy, junipery, tobacco-like, long.
**Finish:** Teasing, appetising, interplay of distillery flavours and sherry.

**7** **Jim: Can't put my finger on it: it's okay, but a bit boring and passionless for a Caol Ila.**
**Nose:** A measured, almost sulking peatiness breaks through some flat and uninspiring fruity, oaky tones.
**Palate:** Surging peat and sweet malt are given their usual oily treatment with some extra peppery spices making a change. But the middle seems a little jaded.
**Finish:** Some flat peatiness flies alongside the oak, too lazy to battle for supremacy.

## CAOL ILA 1982 25 YEARS OLD 62.5%
Single Malt - Islay

**8½ Dave:** Perfect balance. An extremely good Caol Ila. Recommended.
**Nose:** Big. Early morning fishing trip: bait box (dried fish scales and lugworm extract), alongside a bacon sandwich (white bread/butter/smoked bacon). In time, smoky fish stock. Sea breezes. Real freshness.
**Palate:** Smoke at the front of the mouth. Tongue coating. Smoked fish cooked in hay. Great feel and delivery.
**Finish:** Angelica. Oyster with a drop of tabasco.

**7¼ Martine:** Like an unripe fruit. Too biting, too thin flavourwise. Possibly a tired cask.
**Nose:** Pungent if not spirit. Spirity. Smells young. Iodinic. Medicinal. With water, barley sugar.
**Palate:** Deceptive sweetness at first, quickly wiped out by an aggressive bite. Tar, once diluted, gets malty with a citrussy touch.
**Finish:** Short with a sooty hint.

## CAOL ILA 1982, CELTIQUE CONNEXION 43%
Single Malt - Islay

**7¼ Michael:** A confusion of flavours that don't seem to have rounded in the cask
**Nose:** Dry. Slightly vegetal. A hint of lime peel.
**Palate:** Oily. Cinnamon. Dusty.
**Finish:** Spicy. Aromatic. Slightly medicinal. Menthol.

**9¼ Martine:** Sauternes adds fruity mellowness without obstructing the splendid sea influence. A real beauty.
**Nose:** Fruit by the sea … A distinct veil of smokiness subtly hovering over a full basket of fruit (melon, grapefruit, apricot) and toasted almonds.
**Palate:** Oily and silky. Sweet, mellow, candied quinces and orange. Dried seaweed. Drying, smoky notes.
**Finish:** Warm, spicy with a touch of hot pepper and curry. Caramelised almonds.

## CAOL ILA 1984, SIGNATORY 40%
Single Malt - Islay

**8¼ Michael:** An excellent example of Caol Illa, a highly distinctive malt that is gaining in recognition.
**Nose:** Fragrant. Tobacco. Floral. Juniper. Some seaweed.
**Palate:** Sweet, seaweed, juniper, Guinea pepper. Drying.
**Finish:** Stalky. Late surge of flowery, peppery, dryness. Very Long.

**9 Jim:** This is a very high quality, complex version of an underestimated malt at an optimum age. Fabulous!
**Nose:** Pulsating peat, hint of lavender and mint. Some vanilla sweetens it with the malt.
**Palate:** Rich, oily, fat, chewy and then peaty malt that is almost perfectly sweet and clean.
**Finish:** Multi-layered with the peat forming the mighty base and then some supremely toasty malt notes arrive.

## CAOL ILA 1988 COGNAC FINISH, PRIVATE COLLECTION 40%
Single Malt - Islay

**WHISKY** Magazine *Recommended*

**8½ Michael:** All the action is in that finish. A clear points victory for the whisky, with brandy going the distance.
**Nose:** Junipery, but less robustly peaty.
**Palate:** Much sweeter. Creamy. Oily.
**Finish:** Juniper and sea-salt in a savoury struggle against gingerbread and quince.

**8½ Jim:** A much truer translation of Caol Ila.
**Nose:** Bolder peat. Sweet enticing.
**Palate:** Sweet and chewy malt and then an eruption of peat and spice.
**Finish:** Long and lingering, a simplistic, entirely uncluttered infusion of malt and peat.

## CAOL ILA 1988 SHERRY WOOD FINISH, PRIVATE COLLECTION 40%
Single Malt - Islay

**8 Michael:** Less complex, with the distillery character coming through much more strongly.
**Nose:** Sweet. Hard toffee.
**Palate:** Silky. Starts dry, then nutty and luscious.
**Finish:** Lingering brown sugar-and-spice finish, with a balancing savoury touch from the salty Sound of Islay.

**7¼ Dave:** The sherry gives roundness but doesn't dominate Caol Ila's characteristic energy.
**Nose:** High sherry notes: almond, nut bowl, spice. A clootie dumpling thrown athwart a peat fire.
**Palate:** Well covered and rich but with great smoky/kippery depth.
**Finish:** Long nutty/fruity then suddenly dies and a medicinal note comes out.

## CAOL ILA 1988, CONNOISSEUR'S CHOICE 40%
Single Malt - Islay

**8 Michael:** Caol Ila can be a little gin-like. This bottling could be served like a Pimms. Mind you, no gin has such a long finish.
**Nose:** Dry. Junipery.
**Palate:** Flowery, creamy. Berry fruits. In the background, a cucumber-like vegetal character.
**Finish:** Very mild, but some leafy, herbal, dryness and late salt. Very long.

**7¼ Dave:** A good attractive introduction.
**Nose:** Fragrant peat with a kumquat lift and a slightly bitter edge. Medicinal with a touch of beach bonfire, fishing nets. Light and straightforward.
**Palate:** Bone-dry it starts with crisp malt, then dry smoke. A slightly perfumed quality. Gentle.
**Finish:** Smouldering and dry.

## CAOL ILA 1989, CASK 3322, MACKILLOP'S CHOICE 57.7%
Single Malt - Islay

**7¾ Michael:** If Caol Ila can evoke the aroma and flavour of junipers, perhaps it can also suggest olive oil, vine leaves, couscous, baked aubergines. I have had great martinis in Tangier. Next time, a Caol Ila Sour?
**Nose:** Lightly dry. Vegetal. Slight sulphur.
**Palate:** Lightly oily. Cereal grain. Leafy. Then late, very distinctive, fruitiness.
**Finish:** Big and peppery.

**Dave:** The smokiest of the bunch. A big boy.
**Nose:** Vanilla and soft fruit, then charred notes: smoky wood, singed heather, and a sulphury/burnt match heads note.
**Palate:** Powerful, medicinal and very smoky. It fills the mouth well, the light creaminess just about binding the prickly heathery/seaweedy smoke together.
**Finish:** Big and long.

## CAOL ILA 1989, CASK STRENGTH, SIGNATORY 58.3%
Single Malt - Islay

**8 Michael:** The more typical of the two 1989 versions. For me, classic Caol Ila, with a touch of peat, noses ahead of the fruitier, more sensuous, expression.
**Nose:** Smoky, with hints of oak and sherry.
**Palate:** Syrupy, surprisingly sweet and nutty, with very late development of appetisingly grassy, peaty, smokiness, slight seaweed and saltiness.
**Finish:** Long and warming.

**8½ Dave:** The biggest and the most complex.
**Nose:** Elegant, powerful and muscular. Stewed pear, cream and dried peel/orange marmalade. Great energy. All the phenolics come from the end of the pier.
**Palate:** Big and chewy, the smoke acting as a counterpoint to maritime/medicinal notes. Heather perfumed smoke and rich fruit in perfect balance.
**Finish:** Long and smoky, a touch of Germolene, then almond/cream.

## CAOL ILA 1989, MURRAY MCDAVID 62.7%
Single Malt - Islay

**7½ Michael:** On the light side, but with some delicacy and complexity.
**Nose:** Light peat and iodine.
**Palate:** Junipery. Interplay of stemmy dryness and sweetness.
**Finish:** Tobacco-like.

**8½ Jim:** Caol Ila is not renowned for its complexity but this is as good as it gets at what its best at: offering big peat in a sweet, oily manner. Excellent.
**Nose:** Classic and quite unmistakable Caol Ila with its ultra-clean, delightfully oily gristy peatiness.
**Palate:** Malt-sweet at first and them an intense build-up of clean, uncomplex peat. Chewy and fat.

Finish: Long, sweet and gristy with just a gentle oak follow through.

## CAOL ILA 1989, SIGNATORY 46%
Single Malt - Islay

**8 1/4** **Michael: A fine example of Caol Ila – in one of its peatier moods.**
Nose: Briny sea air. Juniper skins.
Palate: Olivey. Oily. Light. Junipery. Aromatic. Medicinal. Spicy, peppery.
Finish: Clean, dry. Tree-bark. Complex. Long.

**8 1/2** **Dave: A beauty from Islay's forgotten giant. UDV are you listening?**
Nose: Dry smoky perfumed medicinal (Savlon) aromas. Herring nets drying on the beach with someone caulking a boat in the distance. Appetising.
Palate: Smoke wreathing around a soft centre. Dry and savoury smokehouse flavours with some dried lavender.
Finish: Dry, yet malty. Banana.

## CAOL ILA 1990 DEMERARA RUM FINISH, PRIVATE COLLECTION 45%
Single Malt - Islay

**7 3/4** **Martine: A bit puzzling at start. Seems somewhat austere and restrained. Then releases sweet notes. Is it an effect of the rum finish?**
Nose: Créosote, straw in a cowshed. Moss, damp fence. Opens up on sweeter notes. Hint of demerara sugar.
Palate: Flowing nicely on the tongue. Fresh, appetising. A good mix of sweet maltiness and smoky dryness. Touch of ginger.
Finish: Dry. Lingering smoke. Liquorice.

**7 3/4** **Dave: Islay moved to the tropics.**
Nose: Smoky and very fruity. Welly boots and mango. Lanolin and banana split. Water tames the ripe fruits and brings out a briny manzanilla like character. Green olive.
Palate: Rooty smoke tongue coating. Water helps this smoothing all the elements out. Fruit salad on an Islay beach.
Finish: Has that mellow slightly decayed vegetation note of a good Guyanese rum.

## CAOL ILA 1990 PORT WOOD FINISH, PRIVATE COLLECTION 40%
Single Malt - Islay

**8 1/2** **Michael: No contest, the Inner Hebrides quickly overwhelms the Duoro.**
Nose: Dry, fruity, salty.
Palate: Instant salt and pepper, against firm, hard toffee, malt background.
Finish: The Port arrives late. Fruity and winey. It struggles with the junipery, orris-like, characteristics of Caol Ila.

*WHISKY Magazine Editor's choice*

**8 1/4** **Dave: This works. The Port gives a new spin to the distillery character without swamping it.**
Nose: Charred, smoky notes: smoked meat, hot dry bracken, redcurrant and haddock. Sweet lift.
Palate: Good attack. The sweet fruit sits on the tongue, the smoke hanging above. A hint of berry fruits before the smoky bacon returns.
Finish: Long. Smokehouse. Subtle sweetness.

## CAOL ILA 1990 VINTAGE RUM FINISH, PRIVATE COLLECTION 45%
Single Malt - Islay

**7** **Martine: Hang on! Is that a single malt with a rum finish or a good rum matured in a bourbon cask? An exemplary phagocytosis or a magical trick. But we wanted whisky!**
Nose: Immediate rum aromas. The ones of a "grand arôme" rum. Slightly medicinal, hint of camphor. Lot of cloves. Touch of mango.
Palate: Sweet at start then very spicy. Cane syrup infused with spices. Touch of eucalyptus.
Finish: Rummy, rummy, rummy.

**7 1/4** **Dave: This is a great drink but seems more like a whisky finished rum than the other way around, so have marked it accordingly.**
Nose: Very plain and very rum-like. Good pungent Jamaican high ester lift, wet cane, pineapple. Lightly oily phenols. Lots of acetone.
Palate: This is all rum and a pretty decent rum at that. Water shows light smoke but it is all to do with wet cane, molasses and punchiness.
Finish: Finally some smoke. Slightly medicinal.

## CAOL ILA 1990, 14 YEARS OLD, COOPER'S CHOICE 46%
Single Malt - Islay

**7 3/4** **Michael: A middleweight Islay malt.**
Nose: Gently sooty.
Palate: Lightly syrupy. Long development: smoky sappiness, briar-like woodiness, passionfruit, wild garlic, medicinal.
Finish: Long. Slowly stoking up the warmth.

**8** **Dave: A lively smoky little number. One for a walk.**
Nose: Rock pools, wet stone. Quite tight and young with a struck match note. Clean phenolics with good intensity. Sooty with some sweetness behind.
Palate: Medium-bodied. Very pure and fresh. Light oak. Interesting mix of sweetness with spiky peppermint, then smoke. Good balance.
Finish: Fresh.

## CAOL ILA 1990, BLACKADDER 58.5%
Single Malt - Islay

**8 1/4** **Michael: Light in the middle, and delicate throughout, but lovely Islay flavours.**
Nose: Aromatic. Dry. Medicinal. Juniper.
Palate: Interplay of creamy sweetness, graininess and saltiness. Reminiscent of Japanese seaweed crackers.
Finish: Sea flavours building up for a storm in the sound.

**8** **Martine: Young, easygoing, vibrant. Absolutely unfiltered judging by charcoal particles in the sample.**
Nose: Light, cheerful. Vanilla pod. Fresh garden herbs. Hint of butterscotch, orange blossom. Smoke.
Palate: Palatable sweetness. Barley juice. Appetising cereal notes tinged with mint. Water releases exotic fruity notes (juicy pineapple) and peat reek.
Finish: Short but pleasant.

## CAOL ILA 1990, CHIEFTAIN'S CHOICE 43%
Single Malt - Islay

**8 1/4** **Michael: The more Caol Ila makes itself available the more I seem to enjoy it.**
Nose: Junipery, medicinal.
Palate: Lightly creamy. Sudden rush of peat. Freshly burnt grass. Big, fresh flavours.
Finish: Oily, salty, peppery.

**7 3/4** **Dave: A very good, well-balanced Caol Ila, but not enough happening to make it complex. Ideal for beginners.**
Nose: Canvas, wood smoke. Like being on Scout camp. Wet grass, smoky bacon. Water softens it.
Palate: Intense dry smoke hits immediately, then the smoked meat and singed heather.
Finish: Dry and long.

## CAOL ILA 1990, GORDON & MACPHAIL 58.2%
Single Malt - Islay

**8** **Gavin: Very decent example of Caol Ila, nothing jars here.**
Nose: Acetone, oak leaves, wood adhesive.
Palate: Fresh oak, classic Caol Ila 'TCP', delicate peat smoke.
Finish: Smoky and dry, herrings, crumbly peat.

**8** **Dave: A very good introduction to Caol Ila.**
Nose: Creamy oak. Hint of sulphur alongside bonfire smoke, fish smokehouse and fishing nets.
Palate: Clean and balanced. Tinned fruits and hot-smoked salmon. Quite oily in feel.
Finish: Dry. Driftwood. Smoke.

## CAOL ILA 1991, 12 YEARS OLD, OLD MALT CASK 50%
Single Malt - Islay

**8** **Gavin: Conclusion: Another perfectly fine Coal Ila, but nothing to blow the mind.**
**Nose:** Wood smoke, pears, mild antiseptic, old-fashioned wound-dressings.
**Palate:** Rich leather and vanilla, dry oak and bonfire smoke.
**Finish:** Lingers well, increasingly dry. Touch of Germolene?

**8¾** **Dave: An extra dimension over the OB.**
**Nose:** Complex and rich: burnt stick, wood ash, smoked ham and haddock, roasted pepper, chamois, Savlon, toasted oats. Creaminess.
**Palate:** Smoky and powerful with a dry start. Big and broad with layers of flavour: smoke, fish, coconut, wet grass, harbour fronts. Great balance.
**Finish:** Lightly medicinal.

## CAOL ILA 1991, 15 YEARS OLD, COOPER'S CHOICE 46%
Single Malt - Islay

**7¾** **Dave: A perfectly decent dram, but just lacks the required interaction between wood and spirit.**
**Nose:** Clean and limey, scallop shells, brine, fresh salted fish. Slightly plain: hot pebbles on a beach.
**Palate:** Smoky with light juniper and thyme notes. Sufficient sweetness to offset the sooty smoke.
**Finish:** Becomes citric, this time lemon, and slightly floral.

**7½** **Arthur: Fell apart with water, but fun to tussle with neat.**
**Nose:** Tea tree, a handful of peated malted barley. Apple skins and compost. Damp woodland floor and burning wet leaves. Cigarette ash. Turned a bit grubby with water.
**Palate:** Sweet, then composty, almost like silage.
**Finish:** Wet ashtrays.

## CAOL ILA 1991, 15 YEARS OLD, DEWAR RATTRAY 56.7%
Single Malt - Islay

**8½** **Dave: Fishy yet sweet. Kipper crumble in a hospital anyone?**
WHISKY Magazine Recommended
**Nose:** Intense. An immediate hit of Dettol and hospital corridors then a switch to oyster shell freshness. The smoke drifts away in time revealing a complex fruity centre.
**Palate:** Still medicinal and briny seashore aromas above an oily softness. Great impact.
**Finish:** Phenolic, coal tar lozenge. Fantastic length.

**8¼** **Arthur: Another good example from Mr Consistency, Caol Ila.**
**Nose:** The memory of grazed knees (pink dettol), pickled ginger and rescue remedy. Creosoted fenceposts and a little chlorine whiff. Some earthiness and lavender, and becoming floral.
**Palate:** Creosote, coal tar and aniseed. Smoked hickory.
**Finish:** Burnt twigs after a marshmallow toasting.

## CAOL ILA 1991, GORDON & MACPHAIL 57.4%
Single Malt - Islay

**9** **Martine: What you nose is what you get. A beautiful uncompromising version of Caol Ila. More enjoyable when neat.**
WHISKY Magazine Recommended
**Nose:** Genuine Caol Ila. Creosote, lobster pot, wet sand. Big thick smoke. White pepper. With water, lime and smoked meat.
**Palate:** Sweet, despite strength. Lovely malty feel.
**Finish:** Long, warm, lingering, with lots of liquorice coming through.

**8** **Dave: A good example of how peaty drams need a balance of sweetness. Another Caol Ila cracker.**
**Nose:** Smoked ham/salami, then perfumed peat, coal bunker. Like the burnt grass at the edge of a campfire with slightly damp socks drying beside it.
**Palate:** Dry and sooty offset by a slightly oily texture and sweet soft fruits. Has complexity.
**Finish:** Short, crisp, smoky. Smoked fish.

## CAOL ILA 1991, PORT WOOD, SIGNATORY 46%
Single Malt - Islay

**8** **Michael: I would like to try this with lamb.**
**Nose:** Soft fruit. Brambles. Juniper, sea air.
**Palate:** At first the port seems to have sweetened the spirit, and accentuated its estery fruitiness. Then Caol Ila comes through: sandy, dry, junipery.
**Finish:** A nice, lively touch of appetising bitterness.

**8** **Dave: It's a weird one but everything is in balance. Worth a shot.**
**Nose:** Pale onion skin colour. Clean smooth peatiness. If you could smoke strawberries they'd smell like this.
**Palate:** An interesting mix of pastille-like red fruits/cherry with subtle smoke. A sweet centre with the peat wrapped around.
**Finish:** Sweet, winey, then dry smoke.

## CAOL ILA 1992, 13 YEARS OLD, COOPER'S CHOICE 46%
Single Malt - Islay

**8¾** **Michael: Incredibly appetising. Perhaps a touch more acidity somewhere would balance the sweetness.**
WHISKY Magazine Recommended
**Nose:** Glorious clear crisp woodsmoke, followed by the slow steady thump of the phenols – some tar, some burnt wood. Salty, savoury undertones.
**Palate:** Sweet smoke. Wood (not peat) fires. Embers. Ash. Honey. Salty.
**Finish:** The smoke cuts through any residual cloying honey. Medicinal.

**7½** **Dave: This is good, but seems to still be building in complexity. If there's any of this batch left...keep 'em in cask for a few more years.**
**Nose:** Light, but immediately peaty. Seashore aromas, quite salty, dried seaweed, smoked haddock. With water more like a dentist's surgery.
**Palate:** Light, but sooty. Have to fight to get past the smuts to discover cooked fish. Water calms it down and brings out lychee, then smoke.
**Finish:** Dry, kipper-like (a pick-up of intensity).

## CAOL ILA 1996, BERRY'S OWN SELECTION 57%
Single Malt - Islay

**7¾** **Dave: Intense and in character. A fairly simple Caol Ila but a goody.**
**Nose:** Aromatic and fresh with, initially, a touch of the dentist's surgery, then linden tree blossom. In time it conjures up an image of chewing a grass stalk next to a dying bonfire as someone passes you an oatcake with smoked mackerel paté on it.
**Palate:** Well balanced. The peat slides through the Germoline. Sweet mid-palate with light grassiness.
**Finish:** A little short.

**7¾** **Arthur: Distinctive, and not the usual Caol Ila, and Talisker fans should find this one fun.**
**Nose:** Grape juice carbolic, vanilla pannacotta and chocolate limes. With more time an intense earthiness comes through, with moss and seaweed thrown in.
**Palate:** Earth, spice and vanilla. Smoked fish rolled in ash. A little simple, and too dominated by that earthy, sphagnum character.
**Finish:** Peppercorn spice.

## CAOL ILA 1998 CALVADOS, PRIVATE COLLECTION 40%
Single Malt - Islay

**8¼** **Michael: The Calvados character is almost overwhelming but Caol Ila comes surging through in the finish.**
**Nose:** Apples? Apple skins perhaps.
**Palate:** Tannin. Apple. Toffee. Vanilla. Sulphur.
**Finish:** Whisky wins convincingly against the Calvados, but it's still a very interesting struggle.

**7½** **Jim: A highly unusual Caol Ila mysteriously lacking in complexity.**
**Nose:** Sharp burst of flighty peat, etheric apple based fruitness.
**Palate:** Lively and fresh.
**Finish:** Thin despite a hint of spice and surprisingly short for a Caol Ila.

## CAOL ILA 1998 CLARET FINISH, PRIVATE COLLECTION 40%
Single Malt - Islay

**8** **Michael: The least characterful of the three Caol Ila wood finishes.**
**Nose:** Peat. Juniper. Fruit skin, or am I being suggestible?
**Palate:** Very peaty. Some creamy, sweeter, nutty fruitiness coming along behind. Iron.
**Finish:** Saltiness reasserts the coastal identity.

**7** **Jim: There are times when whiskies can be just a little too gentle....and this is one.**
**Nose:** Ripe fruit covers the peat but leaves the vanilla unscathed.
**Palate:** Unbelievably soft, with a hint of cherry.
**Finish:** No more than an echo of smoke and spice.

## CAOL ILA 21 YEARS OLD, RARE MALTS 61.3%
Single Malt - Islay

**8¼ Michael: Confident. Austere.**
**Nose:** Fresh. Dry. Oaky. Steely. Tannic apples. Juniper. Peppery (especially with water added).
**Palate:** Creamy. Oily. Briar-like dryness. Peppery. Salty.
**Finish:** Very dry. Intense. Long. Very warming.

**8¼ Dave: Complex, great balance. Hidden malt? Not any more.**
**Nose:** A smoky delivery. Wet grass, cod liver oil, tar, heather root, slightly medicinal. A very clean peatiness in which everything seems well-defined and which builds to a smoky bacon note.
**Palate:** Powerful smokiness balanced by an oily centre. Smoky, but with a fragrant nature and sweet, juicy centre. Rich.
**Finish:** Dry. Smoked fish. Hessian.

## CAOL ILA 23 YEARS OLD 60%
Single Malt - Islay

**7¾ Michael: All the oily, waxy, junipery, bush-like flavours of Caol Ila, but the whiff of the sea comes late.**
**Nose:** Light. Juniper. Blackcurrant.
**Palate:** Smoky. Sweet. Malty. Peppery.
**Finish:** Light, leafy, sweet, refreshing, therapeutic. Sea air. With water, a touch of salt.

**9 Jim: Top drawer stuff that balances out beautifully, retaining a stupendous freshness for its age.**
**Nose:** A lazy, sweet peatiness contains some resounding oaky elements. Finely tuned.
**Palate:** A massive blast of seaweedy iodine leaves no doubt to its origins and the follow through of delightfully sweet malt and brine is awesome.
**Finish:** Long, lingering peat lives contentedly with the drying oak.

## CAOL ILA 23 YEARS OLD, HART BROTHERS 43%
Single Malt - Islay

**7 Michael: For its age, not at all woody, but lacking in roundness. The flavours seem to be coming apart.**
**Nose:** Intensely junipery.
**Palate:** Sweet, junipery, salty. Stony. Ironstone.
**Finish:** Juniper. Mint.

**7½ Jim: A noble, attractive if rather tired version of one of the first ever makes of the new-style Caol Ila after it's rebuilding in 1974.**
**Nose:** The peat plays a surprisingly minor role with the acacia-honey and malt starring. Oak wins.
**Palate:** Some deep oak sweetens out to welcome the malt and when peat arrives it takes a firm hold.
**Finish:** Medium length with lots of chocolate among the peat. Quite bitter on the finish.

## CAOL ILA 25 YEARS OLD, SPECIAL RELEASE 58.4%
Single Malt - Islay

**8 Dave: Not instantly welcoming, this takes time to get to know...but it is worth the effort. Subtle complexities at work.**

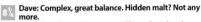

**Nose:** Light and grassy, then some Arbroath smokie. Lightly perfumed (sage, juniper?) with a vanilla lift, hot sand, ash-like smoke. Good balance and intensity. Needs water.
**Palate:** The sweetness continues. Light fruits, some creaminess. Quite firm without water.
**Finish:** Dry, long, lightly grassy. Ash.

**7¼ Arthur: Old, phenolic but just not pleasant enough for me. I think I just prefer Caol Ila young.**
**Nose:** Lemon, tiger balm, eucalyptus, lime, citrus flavoured bathroom cleaner.
**Palate:** Some buttery character, but fairly woody and with a dirty smoke.
**Finish:** Ash.

## CAOL ILA 28 YEARS OLD 1979, OLD & RARE 54.6%
Single Malt - Islay

**7¼ Dave: Good but pretty tired.**
**Nose:** Light as rainwater. Needs time for a lint-like aroma to emerge followed by melon, oyster liquor, wet bracken and light smoke. Hint of phenols, though it's more ozone than fire. Swimming pool.
**Palate:** Good feel. Much sweeter than the nose and the smoke also comes through, adding another dimension, but it falls apart easily and quickly.

**Finish:** Bandages.

**7½ Martine: A kick you up dram. Becomes more interesting with a dash of water. To keep for a wintery miserable day.**
**Nose:** Grassy. Lemon balm. Touch of aniseed. Quite prickly but clean. Opens up on fruit notes (cider, lemon zest).
**Palate:** Sweet but assertive. Flowing nicely on the tongue. Pineapple drop. Faint smoke in the back.
**Finish:** Dry, grassy.

## CAOL ILA 7 YEARS OLD, 53.50, SCOTCH MALT WHISKY SOCIETY 62.1%
Single Malt - Islay

**8¼ Michael: Young and hot. If that sounds flirtatiously sexy, you have the right idea.**
**Nose:** Vegetal. Green. Or is that suggested by the Chartreuse colour? Or the shade of undiluted real absinthe. A very pretty whisky.
**Palate:** Light but oily. Fragrant. Junipery, fruity. Peppery. Phenolic.
**Finish:** Very dry. Reminds me of alder smoke.

**7¾ Dave: You can see why blenders adore this. For those who like their Islay malts aggressive, zesty and smoky.**
**Nose:** Juicy, smoky with iodine notes. There's sooty chimneys, rock pools, seaweed, crepe bandages and burnt sticks on the beach.
**Palate:** Slightly bitter with some citric notes which are then given a blanket of peat smoke and iodine.
**Finish:** Long. Smoky. Medicinal.

## CAOL ILA 8 YEARS OLD UNPEATED 59.8%
Single Malt - Islay

**7¾ Martine: A straightforward example of a bourbon cask maturation. A bit burning on the tongue for me but some like hot, don't they?**
**Nose:** Tingly, a bit spirity. Vanilla toffee, a touch of blancmange. White currant, lemon pulp. Quite fresh and perky. In the back, dry hay and a touch of honeyed white flowers (acacia).
**Palate:** Sweet, malty. Oily. Tangerine and lemon fruit salad. Garden mint. White chocolate.
**Finish:** Fizzy, spicy, lingering. A slight bitter edge.

**8 Dave: Not what you expect from Caol Ila though this unpeated style has been made for blending for 20 years or more.**
**Nose:** Very clean fresh and slightly sweet with touches of raspberry leaf, melon balls/rind, green banana. Fruity and gentle but seems young.
**Palate:** Light and lively. Juicy mid palate with that melon character coming to the fore. Delightful.
**Finish:** Fresh, slightly green grassy.

## CAOL ILA 9 YEARS OLD, CADENHEAD'S 43%
Single Malt - Islay

**7½ Michael: Youthfully powerful. Almost raw flavours, without being in any way spirity. Many Islay-lovers enjoy their whiskies young. This is a robust example.**
**Nose:** Powerful seashore aromas.
**Palate:** Firm, dry, salty. Olivey bitterness. Black olives.
**Finish:** Intensely pepper, salty. Slight iodine.

**8 Jim: Peatiness is unyielding and unsubtle but enormously enjoyable.**
**Nose:** Fresh and slightly green, subtle and very sweet pea. Quite oily and gristy.
**Palate:** Immediately sweet with a consuming and fabulously oily peatiness. Little complexity beyond peppery smoke and the youth of the malt.
**Finish:** Remains young and wonderfully intense with the peat clinging on as some drier oaky tones emerge.

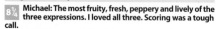

## CAOL ILA CASK STRENGTH 55%
Single Malt - Islay

**8¼ Michael: The most fruity, fresh, peppery and lively of the three expressions. I loved all three. Scoring was a tough call.**
**Nose:** Intensely aromatic. Very light, sweetish, smokiness. Coconut. Grapefruit.
**Palate:** A lively interplay of flavours, with both malty sweetness and dryness and peppery dryness. Perfumy, with suggestions of thyme.
**Finish:** The flavours come together in a rousing finale, with the alcohol providing a back-beat.

**7¾ Dave: A young, in-your-face style that still has some complexity. Really delivers on the palate.**
**Nose:** Perfumed and marine: hot seashells, medicinal, pancetta. Water (and it can take a fair bit) brings out smoke, fennel seed/anise, nut, wet grass, pepper.
**Palate:** Sweet with gingery spices. The smoke builds and builds on top of the oily texture.
**Finish:** Long, smouldering.

## CAOL ILA CASK STRENGTH 55%
Single Malt - Islay

**8¾ Gavin: Bold, well-balanced example, most drinkable.**
**Nose:** Fresh and nutty, raw green vegetables and phenols.
**Palate:** Toffee, cooking oil and insistent smoke.
**Finish:** Almost herbal, with increasing peat reek.

*WHISKY Magazine Recommended*

**8½ Dave: A young cracker. Don't pass this up.**
**Nose:** Direct and phenolic. Frying bacon fat, cabbage, silage, fish boxes, damp coal bunker. Some lifted citric notes, camomile. Smoke.
**Palate:** Young with real power and attack. The smoke appears from half way but is balanced by a sweet centre. Oily, rich, even salty (oops!).
**Finish:** Smoky bacon, camomile, clove.

## CAOL ILA CASK STRENGTH 55%
Single Malt - Islay

**3½ Martine: Wood shows up more. Smoke is heavier and less sea-sprayed than the Bowmore.**
**Nose:** A mix of damp wood and peat. An earthy scent. Thick smoke, hoovering low. Fainter aromas shine through BBQ flavoured crisps, a big floral note, nutty hints. Opens on creosote.
**Palate:** Sweet, malty, smoky. Soot quickly stick to the tastebuds. The sweetness tames down the high strength. A burst of spices.
**Finish:** Drier but smooth. Spicy and slightly sooty.

**3½ Dave: Peat has the upper hand, oilier than these other youngsters.**
**Nose:** Crisp and punchy. Sweet grass, dry smoke. Lit kindling, peppered smoked mackerel. Behind is a perfumed juniper note. Light oily/fatty notes.
**Palate:** Quite light, sweet to begin, then a peppery note. Smoke starts to ramp up, dominating the back palate. Marine character, bacon fat, given a lift by light grassiness.
**Finish:** Cereal and smoke. Rooty.

*Peat rating out of 5*

## CAOL ILA VINTAGE 1981, SIGNATORY 59%
Single Malt - Islay

**7½ Gavin: Significantly drier than the other Caol Ilas sampled.**
**Nose:** Delicate, slightly scented. Hazelnuts.
**Palate:** Fresh peat, peppery, sharp oak, increasingly dry.
**Finish:** Slightly woody and overly dry.

**7¾ Dave: The driest of the bunch.**
**Nose:** Oily. Wood-burning stove. Sweet fruits and dried grasses, nutty oak, chamois leather, macadamia. Quite edgy.
**Palate:** Sweet to start but dries. Grippy oak, pear, dry grass. Hot tarmac, peat smoke in the distance.
**Finish:** Long, quite hot. Peat.

## CAPERDONICH 16 YEARS OLD, CASK STRENGTH EDITION, CHIVAS BROTHERS 55.8%
Single Malt - Speyside

**7¾ Michael: Promises more than it delivers. Try it with sweet Turkish coffee or espresso.**
**Nose:** Figs.

**Palate:** Like eating a fresh fig. Seedy. Sweet. Crystalised fruits, sprayed with sugar. Fig Newtons. Biscuity. Floury. Dusty. Falls away.
**Finish:** Stingingly warming.

**8 Dave: Fragrant and fine. A Caperdonich? I'm amazed.**
**Nose:** Fragrant. Icing sugar, freesia, lemon, wood shavings (becoming like balsa wood), light vanilla. Hint of plasticene behind. Becomes drier, but still with cut flower stems, jasmine.
**Palate:** Very sweet. Gooseberry, green apple, just ripe melon. An interesting mix of fragrant flowers, light spice and firm oakiness. Holds well in glass.
**Finish:** Slightly grippy.

## CAPERDONICH 1968, LOMBARD 46%
Single Malt - Speyside

**7½ Michael: Less fruity than I remember. An unusual afterdinner malt.**
**Nose:** Cereal grain. Stoney. Metallic.
**Palate:** Much more yielding. Lightly oily. Vanilla. Grassy. Coconut. Cherry syrup. Juicy.
**Finish:** Subtle. Soothing. Warming.

**5 Dave: Like an old dusty house that's being cleaned up for the new owners.**
**Nose:** Lightly citric, then old apples (wrinkled Cox) straw, dry wood. Becomes quite sharp in time, then dusty, with notes of floor polish and yellow dusters.
**Palate:** Carbolic soap. A greasy feel.
**Finish:** Blessedly short.

## CAPERDONICH 1968, MURRAY MCDAVID MISSION II 46%
Single Malt - Speyside

**7¼ Michael: Good structure, but spoiled by bitterness and woodiness.**
**Nose:** Aromatic. Restrained peat smoke.
**Palate:** Peaty, grassy, potpourri. Bath Olivers.
**Finish:** Dry, intense. Slightly bitter. Woody.

**7¾ Dave: A charming dram from a still which usually is pretty bland.**
**Nose:** Blossom (cherry/apple). Lightly spicy and young. Pine. With water Roquefort cheese (!) and nut oil.
**Palate:** Sweet and sugared light and lemony. The cheese is still there.
**Finish:** Clean fresh and short.

## CAPERDONICH 1969 34 YEARS OLD, DUNCAN TAYLOR 41%
Single Malt - Speyside

**7¼ Michael: Quite engaging, but just past its best.**
**Nose:** Fruits, whole and unpeeled. The aromas of a greengrocer's shop. Grapes.
**Palate:** Soft but rounded. Sliced cooking apple. Hazelnuts.
**Finish:** Becoming hotter, sharper. Some tannin. A touch of woody dryness.

**8 Dave: A little simple, but again a perfectly pleasant whisky.**
**Nose:** Starts with linseed oil/play-doh, then becomes buttery with light marzipan, dried orange peel and some apricot jam. Wood oils, peanut and a tickle of smoke. Pretty.
**Palate:** Clean and light. Parma violet. Sweet centre with dry oak and a concentrated mid-palate.
**Finish:** Fades a little quickly.

## CAPERDONICH 1977, 24 YEARS OLD, CADENHEAD'S 46%
Single Malt - Speyside

**7¾ Martine: Heavily sherried. Rich and full-bodied but the distillery character is hidden by the wood. For the sherry fanatic.**
**Nose:** Undoubtedly sherry first-fill. Intense, perfumy. Musty. Mushroom. Buttered fruit cake. Vanilla fudge. Roasted coffee beans. Smoke.
**Palate:** Elegant oaky notes. Dark chocolate. Bread and butter pudding. Mixed spice. Cloves.
**Finish:** Lingering, sweet and so sherried.

**7¼ Dave: Clean, dry. Perfectly drinkable.**
**Nose:** Richly coloured. Sweet, golden syrup, toffee, wood. Nutty with some fig, dried apricot, orange. Autumnal.

**Palate:** Cake spices. Attractive, light-to medium-weight. Seems to stop halfway through. Wood apparent all the way.
**Finish:** A little short and dry.

## CAPERDONICH 1980 25 YEARS OLD, DEWAR RATTRAY 53.1%
Single Malt - Speyside

**7¼ Dave: A shy little furry woodland creature peeking out, then hiding again.**
**Nose:** High nose burn and another which is a bit reluctant to open. Musky, wet leaves. Seems mature but also quite piercing.
**Palate:** Another which disappoints on the palate. A slight clinging quality with some sweet citrus notes, but overall it is light and short.
**Finish:** Little soapy.

**6¾ Arthur: A bit dull, and there's no excuse for dull whisky.**
**Nose:** Pears, lemon pith, soap suds and Swizzler lollies. With water more floral with a fragrant apple note like a Pink Lady. Almonds, Battenburg and a fading bouquet of lilies. A bit flat.
**Palate:** Sweet, with floral, some nectarine and a dried hay flavour. Thin.
**Finish:** Drying, with grassiness and oat biscuits.

## CAPERDONICH 33 YEARS OLD, DUNCAN TAYLOR 41.9%
Single Malt - Speyside

**7½ Martine: A well knitted dram. On the fruit side. More complex than it appears. Oak is well integrated. A pity such a treasure is lost!**
**Nose:** Sweet and sour. Gooseberry. Cranberry. Blancmange. A juicy fruit smoothie. Gets creamy in time. Apple toffee.
**Palate:** Smooth. An appetising sweetness releasing fruity flavours. Touch of blackcurrant.
**Finish:** Pleasantly drier. Fresh liquorice.

**7¾ Michael: Has some strange (and compelling) woody flavours. Not entirely unpleasant. If you can, try before you buy.**
**Nose:** Salicylic top notes. Celery? Furniture polish.
**Palate:** Chalky and thin. Chipboard. Dusty.
**Finish:** Not unpleasant. Wine like. Grape seeds?

## CAPERDONICH RUM FINISH, 33 YEARS OLD 49.2%
Single Malt - Speyside

**7 Dave: They've done their best to improve a poor cask, but it's one note all the way.**
**Nose:** Take some butter. Add more butter. Then some sugar. Mix them together. Smell.
**Palate:** The butter now deepens into cream with some vanilla sugar or maybe even white chocolate Light grip. Touch of tangerine peel. Thins with water.
**Finish:** Short and drying.

**8½ Arthur: First taste was amazing, second a little bit flat.**
**Nose:** Lots of zest citrus character, especially grapefruit. Lemon fudge.
**Palate:** An old and complex malt with great progression in the mouth. More of that citrus, backed with sweet caramel.
**Finish:** Dry woodiness.

## CARDHU 1973 27 YEARS OLD, RARE MALTS 60%
Single Malt - Speyside

**7¾ Michael: They made bigger, peatier whiskies in those days.**
**Nose:** Sweet. Hint of hessian. Very peaty for a Cardhu.
**Palate:** Sweet. Malty. Toasted marshmallows. Quite mouth-filling.
**Finish:** Liquorice. Tangerines. Crystallised lemons. Syrup. Late surge of sherbety spiciness.

**6¾ Jim: I think I remember a 25 year-old Cardhu of far better charm and balance.**
**Nose:** Tangy oranges where grass once grew.
**Palate:** A surge of spicy oak yields little to the malt.
**Finish:** Over roasted, almost bitter coffee but then softens for the highlight of the experience as the oak and mild liquorice offers a long, lingering and, at last, balanced, finale.

## CARDHU 1973, 25 YEARS OLD, RARE MALTS 60.5%
Single Malt - Speyside

**7½ Michael: For teatime – more fun than Darjeeling.**
**Nose:** Faint peat-smoke fragrance. Flowery. Greengage fruitiness. Custard.
**Palate:** Lively, very sweet, fresh marshmallow, crystallised fruit.
**Finish:** Light, dryish, tangerine-like, refreshing.

**7½ Jim: A very pleasant dram which shows Cardhu in its usual ultra-genteel light. Hardly complex, but a delightful dram from first to last.**
**Nose:** Trademark malty, grassy simplicity, with an extra dollop of vanilla oakiness for depth.
**Palate:** Sweet and spicy with a biscuity, doughy firmness.
**Finish:** Sweet finale, lacking complexity. Demerara sweetness wins through.

## CARDHU SPECIAL CASK RESERVE 40%
Single Malt - Speyside

**7¾ Dave: Well balanced and worth seeking out.**
**Nose:** Fragrant and quite grassy (hay). Light wood oil notes, almost varnish like with peach, strawberry stewed apple and green plum. With water there's a toasty note, cigar box light caramel and a little mint. Interesting.
**Palate:** Good feel medium bodied mixing a dominant crisp dried grassy note with orange peel, chocolate and a creamy mid palate.
**Finish:** Spicy with chocolate but dries fairly quickly.

**7½ Martine: The first nose is not promising then the sweet maltiness wraps it in a more pleasant dress. You've got to have a taste for sweet drinks.**
**Nose:** Slightly butyric. Touch of rancid butter. Malty, wet draff. Peaches in a honeyed syrup. The buttery aroma comes out more pleasantly.
**Palate:** Mouth coating, nearly syrupy. Very sweet. Malteasers, liquorice toffee.
**Finish:** Medium length. Sweet to the end. With a taste of stewed grass. Dry dust feel.

## CARME 43%
Blended Malt - Scotland

**7¾ Arthur: Put off slightly by a fatty edge, but otherwise a balanced and satisfying malt.**
**Nose:** Sherry, pineappple, lemon peel and spice.
**Palate:** Sherry sweetness, cooked pineapple and an all-spice character. A good chunky texture.
**Finish:** Lightly spicy, with a fatty edge.

**7 Dave: The elements are fighting against each other rather than pulling together. Needs something to bind them in...or time to marry?**
**Nose:** Hazy (even without water). Peeled turnip, herbal. Smoke, sulphur/struck match and in ime some inner tube. Estery.
**Palate:** Off-dry. Seems to have distinct zones: a sweet bit, a coal-like smoky bit and a dry, structured bit. Spicy, better than the nose. Plump.
**Finish:** Sweet and long.

## CELTIQUE CONNEXION 1993 MONBAZILLAC WOOD FINISH 43%
Single Malt - Speyside

WHISKY
*Recommended*

**7¾ Martine: Quite a strong character. Uncompromising warmth. Good balanced. You need to like it hot to enjoy the dram.**
**Nose:** Rich, intense. Fruity. Fig molasses. Overcooked plum jam. Prunes. Tamarin juice. Maple syrup. What an aromatic concentration!
**Palate:** Smooth at first then developing into a dry spiciness. Ginger, tabasco. Dried apricot. A smoky hint.
**Finish:** Dry, warm and lasting.

**8¼ Ian: Composed of two distinct parts that add up to an impressive and balanced total.**
**Nose:** Crème brûlée, chocolate, sticky toffee pudding with dried fruit emerging mid-way, accented by citrus freshness.
**Palate:** Creamy, silky, beguiling, with crème brûlée, fruit trifle, chocolate cake, then luscious fruitiness, orange marmalade, apricots and citrus.
**Finish:** Subtle, dry oak balances creamy, fruity, citrus and chocolate notes.

## CELTIQUE CONNEXION CADILLAC WOOD FINISH 1990 43%
Single Malt - Speyside

**8½ Martine: A whispering dram. Nothing wrong with that. You've just got to tune in** to its delicacy. The character is full and complex. Dangerously enticing especially with a dash of water.
**Nose:** Delicate, lacey. Sweet pastry notes. Shortbread, syllabub. Blancmange, lemon curd. Lemon balm. Tangerine.
**Palate:** Sensually smooth. Coating, then covering the mouth with spicy flavours. Ginger, star anis.
**Finish:** Spicy, nutty, gently dry. Touch of liquorice.

**7¾ Ian: A comprehensive digestif, combining the benefits of an afterdinner chocolate, a coffee and a whisky.**
**Nose:** Gingerbread with vanilla custard, baked apples with raisins, and a hint of spicy honey.
**Palate:** Velvety with creamy vanilla sweetness, underlying spicy oak dryness, continues with butterscotch, chocolate and cappuccino notes.
**Finish:** Chocolate, cappuccino with a subtle fruit, oaky garnish.

## CELTIQUE CONNEXION SPEYSIDE 1989, ARMAGNAC WOOD FINISH 43%
Single Malt - Speyside

**8 Michael: Still sweet, but much more rounded. Real depth of flavour, tastes more like Armagnac than whisky. I** would like to try it with pecan pie.
**Nose:** Fruity, sweet, sticky. Prunes in a pie?
**Palate:** Hard sponge cake, soaked in syrup. Reminded me of the Turkish cake called Kateife.
**Finish:** Nutty. Walnuts, mint toffee.

**8 Dave: The best balanced of the three.**
**Nose:** Ripe and perfumed: black fruit, wild flowers, apple, candle wax, cereal/hay loft, dry oak. Sweetens with water.
**Palate:** Sweet with a silky feel. Black fruit in centre alongside crisp malt. Decent grip.
**Finish:** Sweet fruits then dry oak.

## CELTIQUE CONNEXION SPEYSIDE 1989, SAUTERNES WOOD FINISH 43%
Single Malt - Speyside

**7¾ Michael: Which Sauternes? The flavours of childhood, rather than sophistication.**
**Nose:** Coconut ice.
**Palate:** Sherbet. Lemonade. Becoming. Honeyish.
**Finish:** Rose's lime marmalade, on well-done buttered toast.

**7½ Dave: The wood has a fair say in things, the Sauternes playing a subtle role in it all.**
**Nose:** Sweet and malty: hay, fruit salad, ripe pear, pineapple, quince, lemon, barley sugar, candy floss. Gets drier, and woodier, with time.
**Palate:** Silky and soft with fair balance. The sweetness goes quickly, leaving crisp malt and light spices.
**Finish:** Bitter orange nut.

## CELTIQUE CONNEXION SPEYSIDE 1990, VIN DE PAILLE DU JURA WOOD FINISH 43%
Single Malt - Speyside

**8¼ Michael: I am totally seduced by its eccentricity and intensity. Where's the whisky? who cares? Pour me** another. Bring on the chicken mole.....
**Nose:** Musty. Sweet-and-dry.
**Palate:** Chocolatey. Coco beans. "Cream sherry". Also meaty yeast notes. Reminiscent of barley wine or Lambic beer.
**Finish:** Very vinous. Again, the wine dominates.

**7¾ Dave: A new flavour and a valid one. Well handled. Just a little grippy for me.**
**Nose:** Exotic. Damp straw, nut, malt, acacia. In time there's caramel, tarte tatin, dried pear, nuts.
**Palate:** Sweet, but with a dry, grippy, undertow. Good concentration: nuts, toffee. Firms towards the finish.
**Finish:** Where it happens: hazelnut, pears, dried fruits and nut bowl.

## CELTIQUE CONNEXION VIN DE PAILLE DU JURA WOOD FINISH 1994 43%
Single Malt - Speyside

**8¾ Martine: A rich and comforting character. Complex but not complicated. To warm** you up on a dull evening. Play Beethoven Symphony N7 (second movement) and you'll be in heaven.
**Nose:** Rich, bold. Beeswax, antique shop. Old leather. Chestnut purée.
**Palate:** Round, sweet, velvety. A beautiful development on fruit and wood. So well integrated. All spice, cinnamon, candied ginger. Dried raisins.
**Finish:** Dry, warm, spicy.

**8 Ian: Like a platter of various desserts, why choose one when you can have them all.**
**Nose:** Mellow, rich dried fruit, spicy oak with a burst of fresh citrus zest mid-way, and opening up further with apricot jam, cocoa powder and vanilla.
**Palate:** Creamy vanilla, chocolate, fruit trifle sweetness, with more fruit opening up: orange marmalade, apricot jam then some chocolate, nutmeg and cappuccino notes.
**Finish:** Citrus, vanilla, butterscotch, dry spicy oak.

## THE CENTURY OF MALTS BLENDED SCOTCH WHISKY 40%
Blended - Scotland

**9 Michael: Gentle, smooth and delicately balanced, but with some underlying muscle. Complex and sophisticated. More of a James Bond than a Braveheart.**
**Nose:** Very big. Cream, toffee, hazelnuts, potpourri notes. With water, faint peat.
**Palate:** Fudgy, creamy, nutty. Rosewater, potpourri, developing peaty dryness.
**Finish:** Firmly enwrapping, soothing. Long, developing a hint of aniseed. Dryish.

## CHIEFTAIN'S CHOICE IMPERIAL SPEYSIDE 24 YEARS OLD 46%
Single Malt - Speyside

**7½ Dave: One for the palate and not the nose.**
**Nose:** Acetone and burning plastic. Light and rumlike fragrance. Citrus oils.
**Palate:** A positive change from that slightly odd nose. Scented grass, apple blossom. A lacy feel to it. A drift of smoke just discernible.
**Finish:** Gentle and sweet. Orchard fruit.

**8 Arthur: Good sipping malt with pleasing sweetness and satisfying texture.**
**Nose:** A perfumed fruitiness, like a very ripe and fragrant pear. Lemon fudge.
**Palate:** A viscous, oily texture, and more of that lovely pear and some apple crumble.
**Finish:** Sponge cake.

## CHIVAS BROTHERS 100 PIPERS, 8 YEARS OLD 40%
Blended - Scotland

**7¾ Martine: A very gentle and fruity whisky. Would have benefited from a balancing dryness.**
**Nose:** Biscuity, buttery. Apple jelly. Like walking in an orchard in September and stamping on fruit fallen from the tree, dried leaves and wet grass.
**Palate:** Oily, thick, very sweet. Autumn fruit syrup. Apples, a touch of quince. Wood well integrated.
**Finish:** Sweet, with a slight dry spiciness. Some nuttiness maybe.

**7½ Dave: Starts out as a great big floppy labrador of a whisky, then there's an abrupt change in gear towards the finish.**
**Nose:** Broad. Dried mango, light cereal, furniture polish. Very soft and fruity. Slightly dulled by water.
**Palate:** Macadamia nut and cooked apple, toasted almond and then into black fruit.
**Finish:** Dries suddenly.

## CHIVAS REGAL 12 YEARS OLD 40%
Blended - Scotland

**7½ Michael: The flavours tail off, as though the whisky is going to sleep. Smooth and easy, but lacks liveliness.** Springtime never quite blossoms into summer.
**Nose:** Distinct marshmallow. Peach blossom. Faint cocoa.

**Palate:** Light. Hazelnuts. Cream. Buttercups. Violets. Lavender. Herbal.
**Finish:** A little snappy and aggressive.

**9 Paul: The blend for grown-ups, for people who have made their rites of passage and are ready to enjoy their success. Sweet, but not cloying. Buxom, but not overblown. Balanced.**
**Nose:** Absolutely beguiling perfumed bouquet that features multi-layered and mature scents of apricot, pear, sweet cereal, and honey. Enchanting.
**Palate:** The palate entry speaks of Strathisla smoke. The mid-palate offers complex tastes of oaky vanilla, cocoa and butterscotch. Medium to full-bodied.
**Finish:** It glides down the throat in embers-warm, silky and mildly peaty tastes.

## CHIVAS REGAL 12 YEARS OLD 40%
Blended - Scotland

**7¾ Michael: Delicately balanced. Clean. Drinkable. There is an element of luxury, but never quite the frisson of luxury that the marketing implies.**
**Nose:** Peach or orange blossom. Lemon. Hazelnuts.
**Palate:** Pancakes with cream. Orangey. Buttercups. Herbal.
**Finish:** Tingly dryness.

**7½ Dave: A good mouthful. OK, its not hugely demanding but a great introduction.**
**Nose:** A little soapy without water, but with attractive perfumed floral notes and a hint of tangerine. Water pulls out some butter toffee, cream and orange/mint.
**Palate:** A lovely soft, grassy start which then opens into a lovely interplay between the soft toffee centre and the high citric notes. Good weight.
**Finish:** Pretty short which lets it down a little.

## CHIVAS REGAL 18 YEARS OLD 40%
Blended - Scotland

**8½ Michael: A bit overbalanced by sherry, but nicely rounded by the smoky finish.**
**Nose:** Creamy. Mint humbugs. Mint toffee.
**Palate:** Sherryish. Nutty. raisins. Vanilla. A suggestion of trifle.
**Finish:** Quite big. Soothing. Slightly smoky.

*WHISKY Magazine Recommended*

**9 Dave: Like a gentleman's club: all leather chairs, cigar smoke and murmured conversations.**
**Nose:** A little closed without water; hints of grass, crystallised fruits and butter toffee. Water brings a note of dry cracker which mellows into juicier aromas.
**Palate:** Solid rich stuff that stays in the mouth, all polished wood, soft leather, chocolate, black fruits, pipe smoke and balancing crunchiness.
**Finish:** Lush and fruity slowly crisping up.

## CHIVAS REGAL 18 YEARS OLD 40%
Blended - Scotland

**9 Martine: This jewel is bursting with life and joie de vivre, like a bright aromatic rainbow. Want a wee refill?**
**Nose:** Nutty and cakey. Walnut oil. Fresh orange peel.
**Palate:** Oily, nearly viscous. Dried apricot. Roasted pinenuts. Candied chestnut. Toffee, mocha ice cream.
**Finish:** Warm, sensuous, so elegantly satisfying. Liquorice and chestnut again.

*WHISKY Magazine Editor's choice*

**9 Dave: More lifted than others of this age. Just has the edge in terms of complexity and balance.**
**Nose:** Lifted and elegant. Spicy. Citric. Malty notes along with toffee. Grows in the glass. Complex.
**Palate:** Gentle yet broad and mouth-filling with orange peel, balanced oak. A clever, subtle package with a surge of flavour on the finish.
**Finish:** Long, oaky, fantastically complex.

## CLAN CAMPBELL 8 YEARS OLD 40%
Blended Malt - Scotland

**7¼ Martine: To stimulate a sweet tooth when served with a fruit cake.**
**Nose:** Fairly intense. Citrus fruit. Cumin and orange blossom.
**Palate:** Spiciness dominates throughout. Ginger shortbread, butterscotch.
**Finish:** Firm, a bit insistent, dries out on oaky notes.

**6½ Dave: Lacks direction and energy. A simple starter for a malt novice but I'd rather have a good blend.**
**Nose:** Big and malty, with caramel toffee, honey, cream and toasted nuts. With water some citrus notes, stewed fruits and dried herbs. It has impact but no great complexity.
**Palate:** The toffee dominates but it fades a bit too quickly and fails to fill the mouth or excite the taste buds.
**Finish:** Nutty. Short and dry.

## CLAN CAMPBELL HIGHLANDER 12 YEARS OLD 40%
Blended - Scotland

**7¾ Michael: Rounded. On the sweet side.**
**Nose:** Fragrant, with that hint of nutmeg, but subtle and complex spiciness.
**Palate:** Rich, with cream and honey flavours. Reminded me of Atholl Brose.
**Finish:** Firm spicy.

**7 Dave: The oak is a little heavy.**
**Nose:** Slightly turfy nose with orange peel, saddles and dried heather but also a touch of solvent. Water makes it a little more scented-geraniums, wood polish. Pretty rich but also dry.
**Palate:** The oak is well-polished and maybe a little too upfront but there's a good mix of ripe, dark fruit and walnut behind.
**Finish:** Fruit, then dries.

## CLAN CAMPBELL LEGENDARY, 18 YEARS OLD 40%
Blended - Scotland

**8 Michael: With a light, fragrant cigar?**
**Nose:** Some oaky, cedary, leathery notes.
**Palate:** Rich and very creamy indeed. Still nutty. Some cereal-grain notes. Hazelnuts. Grassy peatiness.
**Finish:** Long, soothing, warming. Becoming drier.

**8 Dave: A big whisky which needs time in the glass to open.**
**Nose:** Nose shows stewed prunes, coal sack, walnut, honey, mint toffee, vanilla and reminiscent of an old bureau: polished wood, dust and leather.
**Palate:** Thick and oaky with deep, rich, silky black fruit flavours. Leather, coffee grounds and a little smoke.
**Finish:** Dry and slightly woody with a puff of fragrant, heathery smoke.

## CLAN DENNY LOCHSIDE 1963, GREAT SINGLE GRAIN 50.2%
Single Malt - Highland

**8¾ Martine: A liquid pudding! Rich and old.**
**Nose:** A full bodied of sweet aromas. Crème brûlée, toffee, vanilla. Chestnut purée, dry raisins. Rich, enticing dessert-like notes.
**Palate:** Sweet and oaky. Opens up on spicy notes. In the back, a sherry influence. Touch of sulphur (not detected on the nose). Plum jam. Dried dates.
**Finish:** Long, lingering. Oak, milk chocolate with nuts and raisins.

*WHISKY Magazine Recommended*

**8 Michael: Did I tell you how cool, creamy and minty it was?**
**Nose:** Cautious at first. Tropical fruits (ripe bananas, flambéed). Faintly minty.
**Palate:** Cool and creamy. Oily. Minty. A mint Kulfi (Rye-like notes).
**Finish:** More of the same.

## CLASSIC CASK SCOTCH WHISKY, 35 YEARS OLD 40%
Blended - Scotland

**7½ Michael: Slightly woody in aroma, but develops nicely.**
**Nose:** Rhododendrons. Cereal-grain nuttiness but also sherry. Linseed oil on a cricket bat.
**Palate:** Fruit, raisins, fudge, cream.
**Finish:** Well balanced with a light oak dryness.

**8 Jim: An enormous whisky which hangs together impressively for its great age.**
**Nose:** Massively bourbony; a roasty, slightly nutty-sweet, cocoa-dry aroma. Fascinating sub-strata of bamboo shoots and malt. Big and complex.
**Palate:** Aged from the off: very dry oaky tones and roast malt. Very chewy.
**Finish:** Sweetens drastically with toffee-vanilla and some fading coffee on the long, tapering finish.

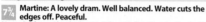

## CLYNELISH 43%
Single Malt - Highland

**7¾ Martine: A lovely dram. Well balanced. Water cuts the edges off. Peaceful.**
**Nose:** Perfumy. Floral. Lilac. Malt flour. Toffee. Touch of resin. Wet paint. Lime juice.
**Palate:** Smooth. Mouthfilling. Charming interplay between malty and fruity flavours. Pistachio. Nougat.
**Finish:** Spicy and dry. Gingery.

**8 Dave: A textural whisky.**
**Nose:** Rounded with a hint of sweet spice. Sultana, marshmallow, apricot (jam), honey. Beeswax. Big, soft and pillowy.
**Palate:** Herbs and peach, then orange blossom honey, cherry, apple wood and a smooth waxy texture (candlewax).
**Finish:** Long, soft, succulent.

## CLYNELISH 10 YEARS OLD 59.8%
Single Malt - Highland

**8½ Michael: The true maritime taste of Clynelish.**
**Nose:** Hint of the sea.
**Palate:** Textured, sweet, mustardy, iron iodine salty. Very lively. Lots of flavour development. Light but warm smokiness.
**Finish:** Salty. Long. Stinging. Very appetising indeed.

WHISKY *Magazine* Recommended

**8½ Jim: A full-blooded Highlander. Another gem from a usually first-class bottler.**
**Nose:** Wow! Sumptuous barley, healthy smokiness.
**Palate:** Fat and fantastic! Lovely honey sweetness.
**Finish:** Long and continually malty with some soft smokiness lingering.

## CLYNELISH 11 YEARS OLD, ADELPHI 59.8%
Single Malt - Highland

**7¾ Michael: I normally rate Clynelish very highly, but this bottling leaves its fireworks until the last minute, and with more heat than light.**
**Nose:** Unusually buttery for this malt. Some herbal, spicy notes.
**Palate:** Malty. Syrupy. Black treacle. Woody.
**Finish:** Peaty, salty, peppery, mustardy, hot.

**8 Dave: In the classic distillery style, but a pretty feisty young punk for all that.**
**Nose:** Light straw. Waxed jackets/beeswax/oily with some bracing saltiness.
**Palate:** A sweet oily start, then it rolls around the palate nicely. Rich, waxy with a hint of sea spray livening things up.
**Finish:** A vibrant mix of oily fruit and sour/salty notes.

## CLYNELISH 12 YEARS OLD, CASK 3280, ADELPHI 57.2%
Single Malt - Highland

**7¼ Martine: Pungent and vibrant but lacks the beautiful Clynelish style.**
**Nose:** Shellfish, caramelised pecan, overripe medlar. Chocolate fudge. Spirity, biting. A breath of smoke.
**Palate:** Harsh at the start, calming down when tamed with a good dash of water, but still on the fiery side.
**Finish:** Hot, spicy and sappy.

**7¾ Dave: All the classic Clynelish characteristics with added youthful intensity. Already complex.**
**Nose:** Intense with lovely waxy weight. Honey and sea breezes with lightly phenolic notes behind.
**Palate:** Luscious, silky fruits: honey/beeswax, coconut. Well-balanced with the high alcohol giving it a good bite.
**Finish:** Fresh.

## CLYNELISH 13 YEARS OLD, CHIEFTAIN'S CHOICE 46%
Single Malt - Highland

**7¾ Martine: The perfect whisky with farm cheeses.**
**Nose:** Cheerful. Lots of butterscotch. A sweet grassy profile. Dry hay. Toasted buns.
**Palate:** Rich and sweet with a fresh lemony touch. Malt sugar. Honeyed cornflakes.
**Finish:** Long and warm. Crushed almonds. Green cardamom.

**8 Dave: Very good with a slight maritime edge.**
**Nose:** Rich, fat, oily/waxy. Ripe, soft fruits, fruit jelly, pork fat, and also honey on buttered white loaf. Big, oily (waxed jackets/wet kelp), toasty. Gutsy.

**Palate:** Great texture with a slight (balanced) toastiness. Soft orangey fruit. The oily/waxy feel smooths it all together. Rich and mouthfilling.
**Finish:** Long and lush.

## CLYNELISH 14 YEARS OLD 43%
Single Malt - Highland

**8¼ Michael: The fuller gold colour suggests more contribution from the wood.**
**Nose:** Sweet grass. Lightly peppery/mustardy.
**Palate:** Creamy maltiness. Big flavours. Peaty. Seaweedy-fruity.
**Finish:** A fresh, mustardy attack. Some salt, too.

**8½ Jim: A disarming malt that exudes sheer class.**
**Nose:** Excellent complexity with diced carrots adding to the earthy, salady aroma. Some sweetness but drier than usual.
**Palate:** Fruity, grapey and beautifully mouthwatering: quite different from the nose. Brilliant sub-strata of peat runs throughout and adds a luscious sweetness to compliment the sultanas and spice.
**Finish:** Smoky and dries rapidly to allow in a cocoa effect.

## CLYNELISH 14 YEARS OLD 46%
Single Malt - Highland

**8 Michael: Full of flavour. Full of interest. A good, complex bottling.**
**Nose:** Good firm aromatics. Fennel. Liquorice.
**Palate:** Malty. Sweetish, especially with water. Seville orange peels.
**Finish:** Fruity-spicy. Chilli-like. Explosion of spicy flavours. Hot peppermints. Pepper.

**8¾ Dave: Wonderfully textural, sexy, dangerous. Unconventional beauty.**
**Nose:** Oily/beeswax, dried tropical/citric fruits, honey. Water brings out waxy oiliness, the (nice) smell of new welly boot. Exotic, individual.
**Palate:** Drier and crisper than expected, the oak merged well with light smoke and oiliness. Great balance. Really delivers. Succulent but dry.
**Finish:** Dry, light pepper, becomes gentle.

## CLYNELISH 14 YEARS OLD, CADENHEAD'S 57.6%
Single Malt - Highland

**8¼ Michael: Firm, dry, confident. Not quite as expressive as the best bottlings.**
**Nose:** Warm. Gently smoky and peaty.
**Palate:** Big, syrupy-smooth. Dry maltiness. Again, gentle smokiness. Touch of the vegetal character typical in Clynelish.
**Finish:** Dry. Slightly bitter. Leafy. Appetising.

**7½ Dave: I love Clynelish to bits but this was almost too much even for me.**
**Nose:** A contrary nose: clotted cream, honeycomb, green mango/peach stone, orange honey and welly boots. Water brings out burnt grass and wax.
**Palate:** Rounded, sweet and rich: peach juice with a soft, waxy texture. Candle wax and overripe fruit.
**Finish:** Dry and firm.

## CLYNELISH 16 YEARS OLD, ADELPHI 54%
Single Malt - Highland

**8¼ Michael: The most oily of the three, and very assertive in the finish.**
**Nose:** Peatier.
**Palate:** Firmer. Green, oily, becoming dry and leafy.
**Finish:** More assertive pepper and mustard.

**8½ Jim: Impressive, smokeless and delicate for its age. A finely tuned malt.**
**Nose:** Wonderfully fresh and clean but not without character: grassy malt and crushed pine nuts. Mouth-wateringly beautiful.
**Palate:** Drier on the palate, the vanilla bites early but is still unable to dampen that succulent grassiness.
**Finish:** Finely balanced but frying with oaky-cocoa notes. Very long finale.

## CLYNELISH 16 YEARS OLD, COOPER'S CHOICE 43%
Single Malt - Highland

**8 Michael: The most gritty and seaweedy.**
**Nose:** Very fresh. The most aromatic of the three. Pears. Cress. Pepper.
**Palate:** Light olive oil. Falls away in the middle. Then develops sweet mustardy notes.

**Finish:** Grassy, sandy, peppery.

7¾ **Jim: A simple amazingly clean dram that belies its years.**
**Nose:** Amazingly green and young. Grassy and slightly tart. The oak is sweet and relaxed.
**Palate:** As mouth-watering as it gets: outwardly young at first, sweet and then the spiced oak intensifies.
**Finish:** Medium length, vanilla rich with an oaky fuzziness at the finale. Also a late barely audible echo of smoke.

## CLYNELISH 19 YEARS OLD, DUN BHEAGAN 57.5%
Single Malt - Highland

8 **Michael: A surprisingly sweet expression of Clynelish. Lots of flavour and plenty of charm.**
**Nose:** Sweetish seaweed.
**Palate:** Lightly creamy. Viscous. Creamed spinach with toasted almonds.
**Finish:** Sweet lemons. Sea salt.

8¾ **Dave: A top example from one of the greats.**
**Nose:** Oily/waxy with dried apricot, vanilla, heather, wild herbs and mink oil. A touch of light peatiness. With water it louches like absinthe. Beautiful, but slightly alarming.
**Palate:** Medium-bodied, but a real mouthfiller which coats and clings to the palate. There's smoke, that lovely oiliness and a fruity sweetness. Ripe, rich.
**Finish:** Dry, peppery and long.

## CLYNELISH 1969, PRIVATE COLLECTION 45%
Single Malt - Highland

8¼ **Michael: A hint of sulphur in the nose had me dismissing this whisky. It seemed young, immature, callow – but we finishing up flirting.**
**Nose:** Party balloons. Lemon jelly and custard.
**Palate:** Dolly mixtures. Children's party, but now the adults have arrived. The sweetness now is brown sugar, in Earl Grey tea.
**Finish:** Port. Thinly sliced Stilton. Saltines.

8¼ **Dave: Complex. This has a layered effect which elevates it above most of the rest.**
**Nose:** Mature and sweet with a little touch of oak. Coconut, beeswax, honey, apple skin.
**Palate:** Slow moving and expansive. Mature notes again, powdered nut, custard cream. Becomes more oaky, but balanced by silky fruits. and a growing flavour of almond. In time a hint of heathery smoke.
**Finish:** Long. Hardens slightly.

## CLYNELISH 1971, 30 YEARS OLD, OLD MALT CASK 50%
Single Malt - Highland

8¼ **Martine: There's more in the nose than in the finish. A really characterful malt. Interesting. This is one of the more medicinal expressions of Clynelish I have come across.**
**Nose:** Medicinal, peaty. Camphor. Seaweed drying in the sun. Absolutely marine. Exotic touch of pineapple.
**Palate:** Oily. Sweet. Well-balanced. Sea salt. Barley.
**Finish:** Neither pronounced nor lingering.

7¼ **Dave: It's just too old and struggles to fight its way out of the wood.**
**Nose:** Some fragrance with melon/orange. With water it smells like a lumber yard.
**Palate:** Thick and sweet with good concentration, a little smoke, waxiness. The wood starts to tighten becoming increasingly aggressive and tannic.
**Finish:** Very long and perfumed as if the whisky has finally escaped the oaky grip.

## CLYNELISH 1972, CASK 15619, SINGLE MALTS OF SCOTLAND 49.9%
Single Malt - Highland

8¼ **Arthur: Good, mature but still lively.**
**Nose:** Posh, scented candlewax (like the type one might buy in Jenners, doncha know). Warm baking and a slight phenol character, like floor polish or swimming pools. Honey.
**Palate:** Lots of maltiness, more wax and an astringent citrus.
**Finish:** Grassy and slightly peaty.

6¾ **Owen: Simple blocks of flavour and aroma come together to form a whisky that might have benefited from a few more years maturation.**
**Nose:** Light and clean but spirity. Faint tangy orange with a biscuity base note.
**Palate:** Sugary and citrussy. Marmalade notes. Silver Shred? Somewhat reminiscent of old fashioned Lucozade.
**Finish:** Sweet and warming. Late dusty cocoa dryness.

## CLYNELISH 1972, MURRAY MCDAVID MISSION 46%
Single Malt - Highland

8½ **Michael: Spectacular aperitif. I wanted to eat a whole salmon.**
**Nose:** Hugely aromatic. Spicy. Mustardy.
**Palate:** Oily. Very lively. Extraordinarily spicy. Mustard, cumin seeds, coriander seed, Chinese parsley (cilantro).
**Finish:** Slightly sour, acid tang.

7¾ **Dave: Typical Clynelish in its texture but a smokier than usual example.**
**Nose:** Light smoke with gentle soft fruits and hints of orange leaf, hot bracken, privet blossom and a maritime edge. Quite sexy.
**Palate:** Oily jumpers and a silky texture. Well balanced with smoke kicking in. Light.
**Finish:** Soft.

## CLYNELISH 1989 SOUTH AFRICAN SHERRY BUTT, SIGNATORY 58.7%
Single Malt - Highland

7¾ **Michael: A very unusual expression of Clynelish.**
**Nose:** Buttery sweetness. Rum. Bananas. Is this the 'sherry' of South Africa or the whin of the Highlands? I am not sure.
**Palate:** Banana liqueur. Then smoky, like a pancake that has burned slightly.
**Finish:** Soothing, caramel-ish, with some leafy spiciness.

7¼ **Dave: At the risk of being pedantic are you allowed to call it South African sherry?**
**Nose:** Smoky. Some waxiness and a grapey note as well. Madeira cask like in its charred dry notes.
**Palate:** Better than the nose, sweet and rich and coats the mouth. Another which is all feel. The singed note comes back towards the finish.
**Finish:** A little dirty?

## CLYNELISH 1989, 13 YEARS OLD, ADELPHI 56.7%
Single Malt - Highland

8¼ **Michael: Not the most peaty Clynelish I have tasted, but a lovely, distinctive whisky.**
**Nose:** Aromatic, fruity, flowery, vegetal (dock leaves?), appetising.
**Palate:** Biscuity, cracker-like. Edible seaweed. Interplay of sweetness, spicy mustard and vegetal dryness.
**Finish:** Peppery. Very salty.

8¼ **Martine: A light-bodied lovely outdoor dram, to serve with barbecued fish. Fresh like a sea-breeze.**
**Nose:** Vivid, nutty. Custard, lemon curd, aniseed. A smoky hint like a distant bonfire. Toffee notes.
**Palate:** Sweet, quite smoky (cold ashes). Curd-like texture. Apricot jam. Very refreshing, delicate spiciness. With water, a spice explosion.
**Finish:** Slightly dry. Lovely citrus and walnut notes.

## CLYNELISH 1989, OLD MASTERS 59.1%
Single Malt - Highland

8 **Michael: Very much in line with recent bottlings. Not especially peaty, but crisp, clean and decisive in it's flavours.**
**Nose:** Very fresh. Fresh apple.
**Palate:** Oily but also grainy. Sweet start, becoming grassy and mustardy.
**Finish:** Firm, long, appetising.

7¼ **Dave: A good one, though spoiled by that slightly grubby character.**
**Nose:** Waxy. Dried and overripe fruit. Becomes creamier with water. The waxiness is always there, but there's a slightly dirty note.
**Palate:** Honey, some sweetness. Engine oil.
**Finish:** Soft.

## CLYNELISH 1990, 12 YEARS OLD, PORT FINISH, COOPER'S CHOICE 46%
Single Malt - Highland

**8 Michael:** Not one of the peaty vintages, and would have benefited from some other element to lift the creaminess.
**Nose:** Fresh sea smells. A walk in the dunes.
**Palate:** Fresh, creamy. Reminded me of a mustardy hollandaise sauce (perhaps served with samphire).
**Finish:** Fruity, mustardy, dry.

**7¾ Dave:** Gentle and well-balanced.
**Nose:** A very fruity nose: tangerine peel, marmalade, tinned peaches, slightly waxy.
**Palate:** Best drunk neat. A gentle, quite sweet palate. There's a little woodiness, but the main effect is of ripe sweet fruit.
**Finish:** A hint of smoke.

## CLYNELISH 1990, AMONTILLADO SHERRY CASK, KINGSBURY
Single Malt - Highland

**8¼ Michael:** That distinctive pine-nut character perhaps derives from the Amontillado sherry, but its influence is otherwise restrained.
**Nose:** Very oily. Orange zest. Citrus peels. Lemon.
**Palate:** Oily. Lemon. Mustard. Pine nuts. Cream.
**Finish:** Late cress. Bitter salad leaves. Powerfully dry.

**8½ Jim:** This is sophisticated stuff and complex.
**Nose:** Amazingly dry for this distillery, showing a touch of heather and the faintest hint of something citrus.
**Palate:** Explosive start by contrast to the nose, quite peppery throughout but allowing grapey, oak depth.
**Finish:** The oak continues to fill out with vanilla.

## CLYNELISH 1991, CONNOISSEUR'S CHOICE 43%
Single Malt - Highland

**8 Gavin:** Well-balanced and complex as a Clynelish should be. A good, solid afterdinner dram.
**Nose:** Ozone, brine, peardrops, with malt emerging in time.
**Palate:** Dry, spices, some peat notes, robust malt, French mustard. Silky mouth-feel.
**Finish:** Long and spicy.

**7¼ Dave:** That peachiness made me think of a Clynelish Bellini.
**Nose:** Soft. Baked white peach, hint of candlewax. Juicy Fruit chewing gum, thick fruit syrup. With water becomes more oily (dubbin). Some soft pear. Overall quite light.
**Palate:** Silky texture with a bouncy rubbery feel. Oak in balance. A little flat.
**Finish:** Tightens slightly to oakiness.

## CLYNELISH 1992, BERRY'S OWN SELECTION 46%
Single Malt - Highland

**7 Dave:** Tight and hard to love.
**Nose:** Seems young. Slightly stony, shifting to nuttiness and a touch of kiln-like smoke. Plain and pretty hard.
**Palate:** As the nose suggests, penetrating alcohol and a lean flinty quality. Water is needed to bring out balancing sweetness. Direct and ultimately pretty hard.
**Finish:** Fades quickly.

**8 Arthur:** A bright, sparkling nose and slightly less exciting on the palate but still good.
**Nose:** Chopped, mixed nuts and a buttery pastry. Amaretto biscuits, honeydew melon and Granny Smith apples. Lemon meringue pie.
**Palate:** A sweet syrupy texture with vanilla, melons and lemon rind. Victoria Sponge.
**Finish:** Minerally and lightly earthy.

## CLYNELISH 1995, CASK 12783, ADELPHI 59.3%
Single Malt - Highland

**8½ Martine:** Quite a character. Water mellows the spicy burn. Would match well with a chicken "à la crème".
**Nose:** Musty. A walk in a pinetree forest on a rainy day. Damp walls. Develops into creamy aromas. Vanilla toffee. Hint of polished floor.
**Palate:** Lusciously sweet with a tender bitter sour bit (sloe). Syrupy. Butterscotch. Turns tickling. Sherbety. Nutmeg and ginger.
**Finish:** Creamy, spicy, everlasting.

**7½ Dave:** This delivers on palate rather than nose. Oak is just a little hard though.
**Nose:** Fresh and clean with a sweet hay note. There's also oak, light peach and coconut. In time a smokiness emerges. Citric and zesty with water.
**Palate:** Good intensity with fine grip showing good balance between the char and a mouthcoating, sweet, sensual mid-palate of nougat, cream, tinned fruit and orange blossom honey.
**Finish:** Light smoke. The sweet citrus notes return.

## CLYNELISH 23 YEARS OLD, OLD MALT CASK 50%
Single Malt - Highland

**8 Dave:** All comes together at the end.
**Nose:** Tobacco pouch and crisp wood with some signs of maturity. Black banana and a herbal note. Oak driven.
**Palate:** Sweet start banana and raspberry sweets. The oak is quite grippy but not unpleasantly so. Oranges and a silky texture. Long and juicy.
**Finish:** Soft and then drying and then returns to an apricot note and some cocoa.

**8¾ Arthur:** Good complexity and typical of this hearty distillery.
**Nose:** Light fruity notes such as honeydew melon, pineapple and lychee are underpinned by a wax jacket/candlewax element. White chocolate and some drying spice. The chlorine whiff of a swimming pool possibly there too.
**Palate:** Pineapple and nutmeg spice.
**Finish:** Chocolate.

## CLYNELISH 27 YEARS OLD, CASK 2568, ADELPHI 56.3%
Single Malt - Highland

**8½ Michael:** A robust, straight-ahead Clynelish, which is a great thing.
**Nose:** Wet grass, fresh earth, peat.
**Palate:** Deliciously smooth. Syrupy without being cloying. Malty. Then developing peaty flavours. Grassy dunes on a rainy day.
**Finish:** Cress. Warming mustard.

**8¼ Dave:** The 12 Years Old is good but this has another layer of complexity.
**Nose:** Another big one, this time with lots of pipe smoke, apricot, wax, pine needles. Elegant with light smoke in the background.
**Palate:** Big silky/waxy texture, peaches and beeswax with a peaty lift. A beauty.
**Finish:** Long and complex.

## WHISKY FAIR CLYNELISH 32 YEARS OLD 58.6%
Single Malt - Highland

**7¾ Martine:** A muscular yet elegant old malt. Brisk and complex. Alcohol is somewhat insistent.
**Nose:** Old oak floor. Antique shop. Varnish and a hint of burnt plastic. Touch of linseed. Nutmeg. Cooked plums. Orange marmalade. Complex.
**Palate:** Assertive bit with a good integration of oak. Layers of liquorice, fruit and toffee lusciously intertwining.
**Finish:** Oaky, bold. Walnut come back.

**8¼ Dave:** This shows the delicate savoury spiciness of age. Good.
**Nose:** Very precise and biscuity, coal dust, light dried mint then thyme.
**Palate:** A soft smooth flow showing good maturity and complexity. Fine spread of flavours. Caramelised apple.
**Finish:** Long, teasing.

## COCK O' THE NORTH LIQUEUR SINGLE MALT WHISKY LIQUEUR 35%
Whisky Liqueur - Scotland

**7 Michael:** The less obviously whiskyish of these two liqueurs.
**Nose:** Honey, butter, fruit-cake.
**Palate:** Condensed milk, moving to ginger biscuits.
**Finish:** Warming-hot, even.

## COLEBURN 1979, RARE MALTS 59.4%
Single Malt - Speyside

**7¼ Michael:** The best Coleburn I have tasted.
**Nose:** Flowery, dry. Zest of lemon. Resiny. Leafy. Hint of peat.
**Palate:** Creamy mint toffee. Sweet, smooth, start, falling away somewhat.
**Finish:** Ginger. Spicy, medicinal. Warming. Soothing.

**7** Jim: Despite the low mark, pretty good by Coleburn standards. The nose and finale are impressive.
**Nose:** A floral perfume of bluebells and damp moss.
**Palate:** An early sprinkling of clean malt quickly disintegrates into something too oaky, hot and rugged for it's own good.
**Finish:** Tired, one-dimensional malt and offers a degree of sweetness against the drying and bitter oak.

### COLEBURN 1991, SIGNATORY 46%
Single Malt - Speyside

**6¾** Michael: I'm glad still to be able to taste a whisky from this long-gone distillery, but it's really one for the collectors.
**Nose:** Resiny. Lemon skins. Leafy. Boiled potatoes. Earthy.
**Palate:** Creamy. Vegetal. Sweet. Parsnips?
**Finish:** Slightly sour. Grassy. With water, a late, sudden, hint of peat.

**7¾** Dave: Good everyday kind of dram.
**Nose:** Chewy, soft and cuddly. Ovaltine, hot cross bun, coconut, green fruit/olive oil, light smoke, sulphur.
**Palate:** Fairly dry but attractive mix of chewy malt, nut and light oiliness. Good texture with some white fruit, dry edges and a wisp of smoke running through the centre.
**Finish:** Sweet.

### COMPASS BOX ASYLA 40%
Blended Malt - Scotland

**7¾** Martine: A refreshing dram. Straightforward, clean. No complexity but it does not boast sophistication. Simplicity and natural are also great qualities.
**Nose:** Fresh and lively. Green fruit. Kiwi. Honeysuckle. Pear drop. Muesli. Dried apple skin. Lemon.
**Palate:** Round, sweet, fruity. Citussy. A little grainy.
**Finish:** Fades away quickly but leaves a pleasant feel. Almond. A touch of chives.

**8¼** Dave: Holds its own beautifully against some heavyweight competition. Subtle.
**Nose:** Fragrant and gentle. Coconut, tangerine, white fruits, elderflower, peach blossom, apple skin, freesia. Sweetly pure.
**Palate:** Perfumed, delicate and silky. Balsa wood, cream, coconut, citrus peels, light oak, candle wax.
**Finish:** Spicy, floral and lightly drying.

### COMPASS BOX ASYLA 43%
Blended Malt - Scotland

**7¾** Michael: Plenty of attack, but straightforward rather than complex. Suggested as a base for cocktails. I'll work on that...
**Nose:** Vanilla. Green herbs. Aromatic. Dry.
**Palate:** Sweet limes. Leaf mint. Woodruff. Resiny. Oily.
**Finish:** Dry. Soothing. Long. Gently warming.

**7** Dave: The nose is a little unrewarding but the palate has a delicate refreshing quality that lingers nicely.
**Nose:** A light, fresh nose with touches of cereal, lemon, apple and a sandalwood-like spiciness.
**Palate:** White chocolate and almond, banana, lemon. Decent mouthfeel with soft grain and balanced wood.
**Finish:** Spicy/ginger nut, biscuity.

### COMPASS BOX ELEUTHERA 46%
Blended Malt - Scotland

**8½** Martine: Hold your glass to your ear and listen to water lapping against the tarred boat hull.
**Nose:** A hearty whiff of marine air with phenolic notes in the background. White currant and lemon zest. Tender vanilla echoes.
**Palate:** Silky. Coating. Oily mouthfeel. Sea lettuce.
**Finish:** Big, warm, exploding waves of spices. Water disciplines the outburst.

**8¼** Dave: Superb balance. Shows how classy and complex a vatted malt can be.
**Nose:** Oily/waxy with peach, honey and some subtle smoky bacon/pancetta notes that grow in time.
**Palate:** Sweet start. As luscious as the nose suggests. Great texture, with the peppery smoke weaving seamlessly around the soft fruits and gingery spices.
**Finish:** Full. Rounded.

### COMPASS BOX FLAMING HEART 48.9%
Blended Malt - Scotland

WHISKY *Magazine* Recommended

**7¾** Dave: Worth a try but not the most subtle or refined of the range.
**Nose:** Impressive, manages to be light, creamy, oily and smoky at the same time. Ice cream on a seaweed strewn beach, macadamia nut.
**Palate:** Smoke to start, then immediately sweetens into fat ripe fruits. A peppery attack then smooths and softens.
**Finish:** A bit cloying which disturbs the balance.

**8¾** Arthur: Delicious combination of intense sweetness with moreish smoke.
**Nose:** Jelly babies, ripe banana and pineapple and a persistent and brooding woodsmoke. Strawberry jam, sweet mint and creamy vanilla.
**Palate:** Creamy and viscous with a lovely meld of sweet and smoky flavours. Smoked almonds and woodsmoke, more of those jelly babies.
**Finish:** Jam and smoke. Relatively short.

### COMPASS BOX HEDONISM 43%
Blended Grain - Scotland

**8** Michael: Someone knows what they are doing. Who would have thought grain whisky could taste so good?
**Nose:** Fresh, lightly fruity (roasted peppers?). A hint of charcoal.
**Palate:** Creamy. Polenta-like. Sweet, appetising.
**Finish:** A hint of lemon.

**8½** Dave: THIS is innovation at work in whisky.
**Nose:** Soft and creamy but with good intensity. Ripe, elegant and lush with wild strawberry, Milky Bar (white chocolate) and Butterkist popcorn. Sexy.
**Palate:** Soft, silky and chewy, with a spicy lift and touch of ripe cherry.
**Finish:** Fragrant. The chocolate comes back with some mint and cream.

### COMPASS BOX HEDONISM 43%
Blended Grain - Scotland

**7½** Michael: Compass Box knows how to stay on course. Its whiskies are well-judged and consistent.
**Nose:** Perfumy. Vanilla pod. Sweetly appetising.
**Palate:** Soft. Oaty. A bit empty in the middle.
**Finish:** A hint of lemon. Cedary, bittersweet, balancing dryness.

**8½** Dave: Subtle and soft are the key words here. Like the best of these whiskies, this might not be as challenging as a peated Islay or sherried Speyside but it is bloody drinkable!
**Nose:** Gentle and creamy. Chocolate, vanilla and some red fruitiness (raspberry yoghurt?).
**Palate:** Very soft with great silky texture and a good cinnamon spiciness giving the mid palate a lift.
**Finish:** Rounded, fruity and soft.

### COMPASS BOX HEDONISM 43%
Blended Grain - Scotland

**7¾** Michael: Remarkably flavoursome and enjoyable for a blend of grain whiskies.
**Nose:** Earthy. Surprising suggestions of smokiness.
**Palate:** Very firm. Steely. Hints of charcoal in the flavour. Roasted peppers. Chilli.
**Finish:** Very Warming.

**8¼** Jim: Quashes the theory that grain whisky cannot be taken seriously. Marvelously complex, surely containing the fabulous Cambus. The first classic of its genre.
**Nose:** A classic amalgamation of prime and old grain. Very sexy, indeed.
**Palate:** A crisp, clean mouth arrival.
**Finish:** Oaky tones fill the spectrum from cocoa to vanilla.

## COMPASS BOX OAK CROSS 43%
Blended Malt - Scotland

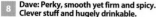

**8** **Dave: Perky, smooth yet firm and spicy. Clever stuff and hugely drinkable.**
**Nose:** Light, grassy and floral with subtle perfumed mixed spice. In time there's vanilla sugar, tangerine, lemon, a whiff of dry stuff, some old apple and with water an exotic note like hoisin sauce.
**Palate:** A direct, sweet start smooth middle then a gear shift, spices come through with sweet citrus.
**Finish:** Sweetness and spice. Tingling, then dry.

**8¾** **Arthur: Structured and classy, an anytime drinking. Inclusive and populist without being dull.**
**Nose:** Warm and enticing, honey and Kalhua. Sweet, toasted oats and golden syrup. Mint chocolate, some orange and peach. Some ginger and cloves too.
**Palate:** Soft and honeyed. Sweet maltiness and brown toast, a little grass and fruit.
**Finish:** A little toasty oak.

## COMPASS BOX ORANGERIE 40%
Whisky Liqueur - Scotland

**8** **Michael: It is not a whisky, so it cannot be scored as one. In character, I would regard it as an aperitif liqueur, rather than an-after dinner drink. In a category of its own, it secures a high score.**
**Nose:** Orange zest. Very restrained.
**Palate:** Light. Silky. Scenty. Delicate. Orange junket or blanc-mange.
**Finish:** A hint of bitterness to provide a balancing dryness.

**7** **Marcin: Very pretty. An unusual and interesting post-prandial option.**
**Nose:** Chocolate covered orange peel.
**Palate:** Luscious. Orange and cinnamon. Good weight of alcohol; strength disguised by attractive mouthfeel.
**Finish:** Luxuriant.

## COMPASS BOX THE PEAT MONSTER 46%
Blended Malt - Scotland

**8¼** **Michael: A monster? As compared to earlier creations from the same house, but don't expect mass hysteria on Park Avenue.**
**Nose:** Vegetal peatiness, but hardly a monstrous note.
**Palate:** Crisp, clean, peaty dryness. Develops some medicinal notes.
**Finish:** Bittersweet.

**8¼** **Marcin: More dour than I was expecting but this whisky will have many devoted adherents. Another winner from Compass Box.**
**Nose:** Vanilla, cream, smoke. Very intriguing. Draws you in.
**Palate:** Peat, smoke. Burning peat fires.
**Finish:** Long but relatively austere.

## COMPASS BOX THE PEAT MONSTER 46%
Blended Malt - Scotland

**8¾** **Martine: A warm, clean and charming whisky. The Islay influence is there but gently flirting with a mainland fellow. An accomplished character.**
**Nose:** Enticing, lively and aerial. Light smoke mingled with summer flowers fragrances.
**Palate:** Velvety, gently spreading on the tongue. Creamy light toffee teased by a hint of smoke. A mouth-watering texture.
**Finish:** Balanced, smoke over dry grassiness.

**8** **Dave: As much about texture and balance as it is about smoke. Not as monstrous as I recall, but very good.**
**Nose:** Smoky, bacon fat mingling with peach, cocoa powder. Aromatic and almost floral.
**Palate:** Very focused in the front of the mouth giving a really sweet start. Fragrant vetiver grassiness, then butterscotch. Good length. Oily.
**Finish:** Long, creamy.

## CONVALMORE 1960, RARE OLD 40%
Single Malt - Speyside

**7** **Michael: Try it with a book at bedtime.**
**Nose:** Aromatic, oily, with very clean smoke.
**Palate:** Begins with a good malt background. Distinctly oily. Again, lightly smoky.

**Finish:** Light malt and a hint of honey and yet more oiliness. Hint of sulphur and clean peatiness, warming and long.

**7** **Jim: Not the greatest malt when reasonably youthful. As a near 40 Years Old it has gained some tasty character, though most of it is of the bourbon variety.**
**Nose:** Shades of violets and cloves with a lightly honeyed maltiness. The oak is commendably restrained for its age, though a little bourbony.
**Palate:** Big malt and honeycomb, lots of oak. That bourbon feel powers through with a toffee-treacle sweetness.
**Finish:** Long and oily. The oak gives a deep, drying vanilla intensity and some liquorice and chicory.

## CONVALMORE 1975 28 YEARS OLD, DUN BHEAGAN 46%
Single Malt - Speyside

**8** **Michael: Ascetic. Complex. Cosmopolitan.**
**Nose:** A basket of breakfast breads, but in what country? Evokes memories of soda bread in Ireland, cherry muffins in Washington state, buttery croissants in Paris.
**Palate:** Warmed brioches. Chewy. Sweet without being cloying. Becoming drier. Slightly herbal. Focaccia with rosemary. Sophisticated.
**Finish:** Extraordinarily long. Teasing.

**7¾** **Dave: Better on nose than palate where it's just tipping over into the woody stage. Good though.**
**Nose:** Elegant and mature with a spicy attack, some coconut. With water, there's milk chocolate, charred smokiness over apricot juiciness.
**Palate:** More wood smoke and ashes, kumquat, red apple, mixed nuts. Water makes it more tannic.
**Finish:** Tight.

## CONVALMORE 1977, 21 YEARS OLD, CADENHEAD'S 64.4%
Single Malt - Speyside

**7½** **Michael: The best Convalmore I have tasted, with the typically big, fruity syrupiness. After dinner.**
**Nose:** Oily. Passion fruit. Iron-ish. But sweet.
**Palate:** Drying on the tongue. Clinging syrupiness. Gritty. Dry. Sherbety. Peppery.
**Finish:** Big, long, rummy, warming.

**7½** **Martine: Straightforward. Needs a splash of water, but much smoother than expected.**
**Nose:** Not very intense to start with. Light, grassy, ethereal. Fresh oak, sawdust. Touch of leather.
**Palate:** Rather sweet. Well-balanced. In tune with the nose. Oak mingles with spices (peppermint, candied ginger).
**Finish:** Dry, nutty and spicy.

## CONVALMORE 24 YEARS OLD, RARE MALTS 54.9%
Single Malt - Speyside

**8** **Michael: The second good Convalmore I have tasted. It was not highly rated in its lifetime, but could win friends now.**
**Nose:** Gently sweet. Oily cereal character. A fresh day on Speyside, with a little smoke wafting past.
**Palate:** Chocolate cream in a cookie sandwich. Becoming less chocolatey, more biscuity and drier.
**Finish:** Fruity. Lemon pith. Slightly woody. Alcoholic. Warming. Long. Powerful.

**8½** **Dave: Holds itself back a little, but delicious.**
**Nose:** Gentle and perfumed with good complexity. Raffia, planed wood, florist shop, fennel. Merest touch of smoke.
**Palate:** Spring-like freshness. Floral with good balance. Light vanilla notes, peaches. Elegant.
**Finish:** Becomes firm and oaky.

## CONVALMORE 28 YEARS OLD 57.9%
Single Malt - Speyside

**7½** **Martine: Interesting, not very well balanced but enjoyable on a cold frosty morning (or after having vacuum cleaned !).**
**Nose:** Clean and crisp. Nougat, white chocolate. Dusty smell (the inside of a vacuum cleaner). Lemon chewing-gum.
**Palate:** Velvety, mouthcoating. Quite herbal. Distant peat. A bit harsh.
**Finish:** Dry, spicy. Hot chilli.

**8¼** **Michael: A lot going on in this whisky; can't help thinking about a Mint Julep, though.**
**Nose:** Cream soda sweetness punctuated by gluey hints.
**Palate:** Smooth, slightly drying. Hot and a little salty. Pastis. Mint.
**Finish:** Silky, warming and curiously reminiscent of mint imperials. (Drier with water).

## CONVALMORE 30 YEARS OLD 1976, OLD MALT CASK 50%
Single Malt - Speyside

**7½** **Dave: Shows maturity but very front loaded.**
**Nose:** Cream and tangerine peel with some ras el hanout, dried thyme, coal smoke. With water there's toasted oak then coconut wax. Lightly earthy. Coal smoke.
**Palate:** As expected, a big creamy hit with a silky feel to start; the dry but fragrant spices hitting on the back, though the oak creaks through to dominate slightly. Not a lot in the middle.
**Finish:** Dry, slightly smoky.

**7½** **Martine: An unusually fragrant dram. Palate does not totally follow though.**
**Nose:** Perfumy. Freshly cut wood. But an unusual wood aroma. Then opens up on fruit. Reminds of the spicy candies that are served in Indian restaurants after the meal.
**Palate:** Sweeter than expected. Wood is well integrated but perceptible. Beeswax. Spicy. Cinnamon.
**Finish:** Medium length. Nutty. Ends on a bitter note (walnut peel).

## COOPER'S CHOICE GLENLIVET 1991 43%
Single Malt - Speyside

**8¼** **Michael: A delicious afterdinner malt.**
**Nose:** Fresh, ripe, sweet, apples (a burnished gold, like the whisky). Mouthwateringly appetising.
**Palate:** Perfumy. Expressive. Rounded. Greets with a firm kiss. Intense. Pastis. Crèpes. Tarte tatin. Clovey.
**Finish:** Spicy but very gentle. Caressing, soothing.

**7¾** **Dave: Well balanced if just a little oaky.**
**Nose:** Light, creamy and sweet. Toast, vanilla ice cream, basil/anise, butter and sugar folded together. In time a note of pewter and bracken.
**Palate:** Gentle and light, though leaner than the nose. Tight grippy oak, glimpses of peach between the slats. Fine grip. Cashew nut with water. Butter.
**Finish:** Softens slightly, custard.

## COOPER'S CHOICE MORTLACH 1990, SHERRY CASK 46%
Single Malt - Speyside

**8** **Michael: Delicious, especially if you have a sweet tooth.**
**Nose:** Butter. Shortbread.
**Palate:** Lots of flavour development. Slowly revealing layers of spiciness. Lemon zest. All spice. Ginger. Expressive, diverting.
**Finish:** Teasing waft of smokiness on the tongue.

**8½** **Dave: The wood is ever present but it is working in harmony with the spirit – which has the depth of character to cope. At its peak.**
**Nose:** Autumnal. Old leather, gun oil, dried flowers with a lift of raspberry. Rich, burnt/roasted meaty notes with treacle and light smoke.
**Palate:** Seems old. Truffles, smoke, Seville orange peel, antique shops, leather and a Sunday roast on the table.
**Finish:** Long and balanced.

## CRAGGANMORE 12 YEARS OLD 40%
Single Malt - Speyside

**8¾** **Michael: Very accessible, and not given to grandiosity, but it's one of the Speyside greats. Good with some desserts. Try it with cassata.**
**Nose:** Honeyed. Floral. Herbal. Full of subtleties.
**Palate:** Lightly syrupy. Sweet. Delivers what the bouquet promised.
**Finish:** Starts gently dry, but quickly soars to spicy heights.

**8¾** **Dave: Balances richness and fragrance superbly.**
**Nose:** Complex, rich mix of flowers, fruit (dried and caramelised), plum, baked apple, currant, honey, roast chestnut, meat and toffee. Phew.
**Palate:** A soft start, then dark fruits mixed with light honey and cooked peach. A rich, elegant, silky texture that fills the mouth. Highly complex.
**Finish:** Soft with a gentle hint of smoke.

## CRAGGANMORE 12 YEARS OLD 40%
Single Malt - Speyside

**9** **Michael: It's worth taking the trouble.**
**Nose:** Very expressive. Notably herbal. Grassy.
**Palate:** Having flirted, plays hard-to-get. Interplay of teasing sweetness and stony dryness. Promises of orange blossom. Honey. Anise.
**Finish:** Slow seduction in the flower beds.

**8¾** **Dave: The most complex of the flight by some margin.**
**Nose:** Silky, elegant and rich: currant bushes, sweet fruits, honey, cream, leather, rich malt, chestnut. Water makes it smokier. Fruity with a savoury edge.
**Palate:** Lovely weight: honey, blackberry, cooked fruits, walnut, dried apricot. A mid-to back-palate whisky which is robust, yet silky; meaty but elegant. The word is complex.
**Finish:** Tingle of heathery smoke binding it together.

## CRAGGANMORE 17 YEARS OLD 55.5%
Single Malt - Speyside

**9** **Dave: Give this lots of time. Do so and you will be richly rewarded.**
**Nose:** Touch of smoke, dried grass, moss. Then apple, nut oils, toasted coconut, vanilla pod. Finally out come sweet spices and calf leather, toffee. Complex and sophisticated.
**Palate:** Intense and highly spiced. Honeyed with a sweet/savoury/spiced combination.
**Finish:** Very long and silky. Smoke gives another dimension.

**8½** **Arthur: Elegant, complex and still forceful. It took water and developed well, holding its structure and continuing to interest.**
**Nose:** Sweet sponge cake, marzipan, iced gems and a little chalkiness. With a little time and water pale sultanas, root ginger and floral notes appear among a strong lemon character.
**Palate:** Sweet, lots of vanilla, but with ginger powder spice too.
**Finish:** Candied fruits and a touch of smoke.

## CRAGGANMORE 1984 DISTILLERS EDITION, RUBY PORT FINISH, 12 YEARS OLD 40%
Single Malt - Speyside

**9** **Michael: Connoisseurs might miss the austerity of the original – or enjoy the added layer of fruity, winey, sweetness.**
**Nose:** Scented. Beeswax.
**Palate:** Delicate orange-blossom. restrained fruitiness: sweet oranges, cherries, port.
**Finish:** Flowery balancing dryness. Warming. Soothing.

**8** **Doug: For coffee, cigar and chocolate lovers.**
**Nose:** Promising, delicate orangey spiciness, fruity, toffeeish backdrop with subtle hints of madeira wine.
**Palate:** Full caramel and coffee textures emerge from initial floral and spicy, prickling characters. Lingering until the gentle sweetness yields to reveal more coffee, crème brûlée and soft peat.
**Finish:** Smooth, smoky and chocolatey. Very dry at the death.

## CRAGGANMORE 1989, SIGNATORY 55.7%
Single Malt - Speyside

**8½** **Michael: Not very old, but was the cask a little tired?**
**Nose:** Creamy, herbal, flowery.
**Palate:** Complex, with very tightly combined flavours, gradually revealing cut grass and thyme, but somewhat dried out.
**Finish:** Austere even by Cragganmore standards.

**6¾** **Dave: Lacks the complexity you expect from Cragganmore.**
**Nose:** Obvious alcohol when neat. Slightly hard and austere: graphite, oak, some heather, grass and very light touches of vanilla and fruit.
**Palate:** Sweet and gentle. Very light.
**Finish:** Lightly fruity.

## CRAGGANMORE 29 YEARS OLD 52.5%
Single Malt - Speyside

**9¼ Michael: At this age, more complex and elegant than ever. No obvious sherry.**
**Nose:** Fragrant. Herbal.
**Palate:** Silky. Soft and embraceable but reluctant to yield its secrets. Orange blossom. Absinthe.
**Finish:** Dryness and sweetness tightly combined. Thyme. Still teasing. Long.

**8 Dave: Complex, intriguing.**
**Nose:** Orange peel, smoke, light leather, burnt toast, plum. Has depth and at the same time is very precise.
**Palate:** Medium-bodied. Smoky, cashew, floor polish, savoury notes underneath. Some deep, carbonised notes. Oaky.
**Finish:** Runny honey, acacia.

## CRAIGELLACHIE 15 YEARS OLD, DEWAR RATTRAY 54.9%
Single Malt - Speyside

**8¾ Martine: A model of balance and elegance. A first class Speysider.**
**Nose:** Pure, clean and fresh. Malty and minty. Green apple. Freshly squeezed tangerine. Hint of resin. Tantalizing. Honeycomb.
**Palate:** Deceptively sweet. Spices burst in a beautiful circus of warm flavours. Drier than expected from the nose but still so satisfying.
**Finish:** Dry, spicy. Toasted almond with an oaky grip.

**7½ Dave: Seems young.**
**Nose:** Creamy and quite simple. Lightly floral, green apple, nut, sap. Water brings out copper coins.
**Palate:** Lifted, slightly smoky (burnt grass). Firm, toasty oak, heather. Peppery from mid-palate on.
**Finish:** Hot and peppery. Nettle.

## CRAIGELLACHIE 15 YEARS OLD, DEWAR RATTRAY 59.9%
Single Malt - Speyside

**6½ Martine: On top of a maturation in poor wood, seems to have undergone problems at distillation. Disappointing.**
**Nose:** Unusual. Boiled Jerusalem artichoke. Hint of petrol. Linseed oil.
**Palate:** Harsh and pungent. A burnt taste. Quite unpleasant. Cardboard.
**Finish:** Dry, bitter.

**7½ Dave: Though it feels good just lacking in weight. Maybe it would have improved with another five years in cask.**
**Nose:** Earthy with dry, dusty smokiness. Garden bonfire (dead), then crème brûlée/marshmallows; reminiscent of clay soil. Water calms it, brings out a hidden silkiness. That said, it lacks substance.
**Palate:** Immediate smoke. Best with a little water which allows banana creaminess to develop.
**Finish:** The smoke returns.

## CRAIGELLACHIE 15 YEARS OLD, THE WEE DRAM 43%
Single Malt - Speyside

**6½ Michael: Metallic flavour seems dominant, and the rest doesn't hold together.**
**Nose:** French polish.
**Palate:** Metallic. Or is it metal polish? I want to dismiss that idea, but can't get it out of my head. The palate picks up toward the finish, with some passion fruit and honeyed, cedary notes.
**Finish:** Quick alcohol warmth.

**7½ Ian: Individual flavours open up and then group themselves into a neat package, before whispering good-bye.**
**Nose:** Toffee apples, sticky toffee pudding with caramel sauce, coconut, macaroons, maltiness.
**Palate:** Crème caramel sweetness and toffee lead, before the light spiciness of gingerbread, rich dried fruit and a hint of cloves.
**Finish:** Light and compressed with a subtle sweet-dry balance.

## CRAIGELLACHIE 1989 16 YEARS OLD, DEWAR RATTRAY 54.7%
Single Malt - Speyside

**7½ Dave: The different elements haven't been pulled together. A better cask would have given some order and control.**

## CRAIGANMORE 29 YEARS OLD continued
**Nose:** Mature, cooked apple, quite chewy. Attics. Spent candles. Reminiscent of a chocolate chip cookie after being dunked. Becomes very sooty.
**Palate:** More like chimneys than attics. The chocolate is still there as are the aromatics. Hot!
**Finish:** Still soot.

**7¾ Arthur: An elegant oaky whisky, but the dried fish element was only apparent after half an hour in glass; most people will have glugged this by then.**
**Nose:** Gooseberries, rhubarb and watermelon flavoured Jolly Ranchers. Hay and wet varnish.
**Palate:** Vibrant fruitiness and textured sweetness. More watermelon sweets and Turkish Delight. With time a dried fish or prawny element appeared.
**Finish:** Green, sappy oakiness, some smoked fish.

## CRAIGELLACHIE GLENLIVET 12 YEARS OLD, WILLIAM CADENHEAD 58.3%
Single Malt - Speyside

**7½ Dave: Saved by the water and though too insubtantial to get a high mark would make a good aperitif.**
**Nose:** Sweet and malty. Green melon, frying turmeric powder and little lime zest and a floral touch. Delicate and slightly chalky.
**Palate:** This needs water which has a softening effect, bringing out lemon, banana milk shake and hazelnut. Very light and delicate.
**Finish:** White pepper.

**7½ Martine: A very refreshing dram, most enjoyable for a summer evening (one can dream!). The alcohol is more aggressive on the palate.**
**Nose:** Citrussy. Lemon posset. The alcohol bite is quite prickly but in a nice way. Herbal tea (lemon balm). In time, sweet notes softens the spirit tang. Guava jelly. Mandarine.
**Palate:** Silky. More orangey than lemony. Water brings out a touch of cardboard. Spicy tang.
**Finish:** Dry, spicy, gingery. Almond milk.

## CRAIGELLACHIE HOTEL CRAIGELLACHIE 1982, 2003 SINGLE CASK BOTTLING, 21 YEARS OLD 57.7%
Single Malt - Speyside

**7¾ Michael: I hope we will be seeing a little more of Craigellachie.**
**Nose:** Warm. Fresh earthiness. The forest floor. Wild mushrooms. Chanterelle vol-au-vents.
**Palate:** Creamy. Slight accent toward maltiness, but very well balanced. Starts sweet, but develops some fruity acidity. Apricots. Apple. Fruit pie and custard.
**Finish:** Soothing warmth.

**7¾ Dave: Decent balance, but very nervy.**
**Nose:** Straw/nut, slightly earthy, wet grass. Hint of tangerine. Slightly fuzzy with alcohol.
**Palate:** Pretty firm and malty. Glucose, lemon, sweet fruits in centre, dry malt on the sides. A little acidic.
**Finish:** Light oak.

## CUTTY SARK 12 YEARS OLD 40%
Blended - Scotland

**7¾ Michael: Clean, fresh and refreshing. A whisky for the beach?**
**Nose:** Edible seaweed. Estery. Fruity. Children's sweets. Jelly beans.
**Palate:** Lightly syrupy. Rose-water, sweet lemons, coconut.
**Finish:** Late saltiness. Cedary balancing dryness.

**7¾ Dave: Has more substance than the nose suggests. Subtle.**
**Nose:** Soft and mealy with aromas on the orange/lemon side. There's some chocolate, cereal, dry grass and a sulphury note.
**Palate:** Light and soft with sweet vanilla mid-palate. Iced Gems and cake.
**Finish:** Gentle.

## CUTTY SARK 25 YEARS OLD 45.7%
Blended - Scotland

**8¾ Michael: The extra years serve Cutty well. It is confident, expressive, expansive.**
**Nose:** Mint, liquorice, anise, raisins.
**Palate:** The same components in the flavour. Against a rich, velvety, malt background. Nutty malt flavours, too.
**Finish:** Faint balancing peat and smoke. Quite long.

**9** **Dave: Cutty with rippling well-oiled muscles. Well done!**
**Nose:** Rich, muscular, sherried nose: liquorice, tar, runny treacle, incense. Water brings a light mintiness with a drift of perfumed smoke.
**Palate:** Big soft and sweet. Treacle again, this time with cold tea, chocolate orange and beautiful balance between grain and malt.
**Finish:** Long and soft.

## CUTTY SARK IMPERIAL KINGDOM 40%
Blended - Scotland

**8** **Martine: A smooth and caressing blend. Full of charm.**
**The balance is superb. Gives a sense of comfort and relief.**
**Nose:** Fragrant. Floral. Carnation. Dry meadow flowers. Apple blossom. Cider apple. Touch of leather. Toasted almonds.
**Palate:** Silky. Mellow. Fruity. Stewed apple. Madeira cake.
**Finish:** Soft, elegantly spicy. Nutmeg. Pepper.

**8¾** **Dave: A big, sweet-hearted giant.**
**Nose:** Mature with good power. varnish, golden syrup, oak. Cognac like: spices (allspice/clove), semi-dried/caramelised fruit, grilled nut. Resinous, walnut, stewed tea, baked banana, leather.
**Palate:** Soft with a clear progression of flavour. Flows like syrup. Lockets (honey and spices).
**Finish:** Raisined and rich.

## CUTTY SARK ORIGINAL SCOTS 40%
Blended - Scotland

**8** **Michael: The flavours are tightly combined. I imagine**
**exploring them late at night in a vaguely disreputable bar in the tropics. Perhaps it's the name.**
**Nose:** Very faint seaweed. Estery. Fruity.
**Palate:** Very light-bodied, but with interesting flavours. Coconut. Pistachio nuts. Rosewater.
**Finish:** Hessian, cedar and oak. Salt, very definitely. Seems to lift in the finish.

**5** **Paul: I find it too manipulated and, as a result, painfully**
**bland. A cardboard cut-out.**
**Nose:** Intensely grainy and cereal sweet, with background touches of toasted almond and nougat. The aroma is vivacious at first, then it fades to obscurity with frightening velocity.
**Palate:** Ethereal to light-bodied. Pleasant, if one-dimensional on the tongue, showing mild, grain mash, manufactured, sweet flavour notes of light toffee and cane sugar.
**Finish:** Thin. Highland Spring mineral water shows more depth of character.

## DAILUAINE 16 YEARS OLD 43%
Single Malt - Speyside

**7¾** **Michael: Almost too perfect. Beautifully put together, but**
**not quite memorable.**
**Nose:** Clean. Sweetish. Pronounced barley sugar. Some sherry.
**Palate:** Medium-bodied. Very smooth indeed. Clean, malty, nutty.
**Finish:** Nice balance of fragrant smoky dryness.

**7¼** **Dave: Substantial. One for a cigar.**
**Nose:** Spicy oak tones along with fig rolls, soft baked fruit, Dundee cake and roasted walnut. Hint of rubber.
**Palate:** Soft, but the weighty spirit holds its own pretty well against the pretty assertive wood. A big fruity boy.
**Finish:** Tight and a little tannic.

## DAILUAINE 1975, CONNOISSEUR'S CHOICE 40%
Single Malt - Speyside

**7¾** **Michael: Characterful. Individualistic.**
**Nose:** Quite heavily aromatic. Tropical flowers. Smoky. Lemony.
**Palate:** Lemon zest. Oily. Good malt background. Morrocan pastilla.
**Finish:** Perfumy. Falls away somewhat.

**7¾** **Dave: A rich beast of a dram from another often**
**overlooked still.**
**Nose:** Deep, almost earthy with soft power. Chocolate, dark fruits. Hint of smoke.
**Palate:** Very chocolatey, soft and rounded. Some meaty depth.
**Finish:** Lightly peaty.

## DAILUAINE 1985, BERRY'S OWN SELECTION 46%
Single Malt - Speyside

**7½** **Dave: A good example of a little seen**
**distillery.**

*WHISKY Magazine Recommended*

---

**Nose:** Quite deep and hairy with a slightly charred, meaty edge. Into the earth again, this time with a sulphur edge. Medlar-like fruit with water.
**Palate:** Big, robust and mouthfilling. Long and quite deep with rooty, almost smoky notes.
**Finish:** Meaty again.

**8½** **Martine: An excellent whisky which has reached its peak.**
**More time in oak and it would lose its charm.**
**Nose:** Grassy. Cereal. Muesli. Dry hay. A slight sour note in the back. Fermenting pears.
**Palate:** Round, mouthcoating. Delightful feel. Rich fruity and oaky combination. Sweet. Plum and date chutney. Spicy (ginger).
**Finish:** Lingering, sweet and elegant.

## DAILUAINE 21 YEARS OLD, CASK 4150, ADELPHI 56.1%
Single Malt - Speyside

**7¾** **Michael: The confident virtues of a good**
**Speyside whisky: malt, heather and peat.**
**Well-combined but without either refinements or flourishes.**
**Nose:** Soft. Fresh. Heather. Grass. Sweet. Vanilla. Oak.
**Palate:** Very malty. Cookie-like. Pale toast. Very dry. Some bitter-orange marmalade.
**Finish:** Cereal grain. Some peat. Earthy.

*WHISKY Magazine Recommended*

**9** **Dave: A gorgeous, refreshing summery glass.**
**Nose:** Assertive maltiness with cooked apple, sweet hay and an intense fragrant/perfumed lift. Delicate but seductive.
**Palate:** A sweet, perfumed start then that dry malt/nut cuts through to balance well. Some smoke.
**Finish:** Dry, hay like. Crisp malt.

## DALLAS DHU 1970, 32 YEARS OLD, COOPER'S CHOICE 46%
Single Malt - Speyside

**8** **Michael: Delicious Dallas Dhu does it**
**again. How long can this go on?**
**Nose:** Warm. Malty. Buttery. Cinnamon.
**Palate:** Textured. Crunchy, chewy and creamy. Like eating cannoli while drinking grappa. (Less Dallas than South Philly).
**Finish:** Powerful. Fruity. Warming.

*WHISKY Magazine Recommended*

**9** **Dave: How old? Would never have guessed it. Complex,**
**balanced and elegant.**
**Nose:** Lovely, mature (but not wood). Honey, clover, dried fruit. Sweet and rich with toffee, apple, caramelised fruits. Elegant is the word.
**Palate:** Fruit cake: cherry, sultana. Lovely feel with a soft, gentle spiciness, caramel, dried fruits.
**Finish:** Spicy, long and tingling.

## DALLAS DHU 1978, SIGNATORY 59.7%
Single Malt - Speyside

**7¾** **Michael: More woody and astringent than earlier**
**bottlings at similar ages.**
**Nose:** Quick hit of intense syrupy fruit.
**Palate:** Very pleasant grassy and smoky aspects. Creamy in the middle. Suggestion of white chocolate.
**Finish:** Quite hot. Ginger cookies.

**7** **Jim: A big malt, but there are some flaws suggesting this**
**has passed its best.**
**Nose:** A curious balance of cream, fruits and smoke.
**Palate:** Quite fat with a sweet stratum of malt hemmed in by some full on oak.
**Finish:** Chocolate but definite signs of over-ageing.

## DALLAS DHU 1979, MURRAY MCDAVID MISSION 46%
Single Malt - Speyside

**8¼** **Michael: The most elegant bottling of the three from**
**Dallas Dhu in this tasting. Soft, soothing.**
**Nose:** Lightly fragrant. A hint of orange blossom honey.
**Palate:** Crème caramel, dusted with cinnamon.
**Finish:** Fruity tartness. Raspberries? Lemons.

**7½** **Dave: This take a LONG time to open, but is worth it when**
**it does.**
**Nose:** A bit unyielding on the nose but there's some apple, baked banana and chocolate milk.
**Palate:** Medium bodied with gentle soft chewy feel. Sinks into the middle of the palate well. Rolos and then spices.
**Finish:** Clean with some fruits.

# Scotch Dallas - Dalmore

### DALLAS DHU 23 YEARS OLD, CADENHEAD'S 60.8%
Single Malt - Speyside

**WHISKY** Magazine Editor's choice

**8** **Michael: I think I have discovered a breakfast whisky. They can call it Dallas Dhu. I'll dub it "Death in the Morning."**
**Nose:** Expressive, distinctive, appetising. Orange, apricot, anis.
**Palate:** Apricot jam on buttered toast.
**Finish:** Orange juice with a shot of Pernod.

**8½** **Dave: An elegant, sophisticated malt. On this evidence, a real loss to the industry.**
**Nose:** Big, creamy and sweet. Plenty of fruit, cocoa, butterscotch, honey and oak. Complex.
**Palate:** Medium weight but mouthfilling with a punchy, rich middle palate. Sweet, ripe toffee fruits: sultana cake, cinnamon, apple, butterscotch, spicy. Real drive.
**Finish:** Long, complex, sweet.

### DALLAS DHU 24 YEARS OLD, DOUGLAS LAING 50%
Single Malt - Speyside

**7¾** **Michael: Much more herbal than other bottlings of Dallas Dhu.**
**Nose:** Warm, oaty, cookie-like, grassy.
**Palate:** Creamy and minty, with a suggestion of anis.
**Finish:** Fennel. Flowery.

**8** **Dave: Not so much who shot JR, but who killed Dallas Dhu?**
**Nose:** Nutty, sweet and rich. Cereal notes, toasted almond, dried apple. More complex with water: sweet spices, Toffee Crisp, cedar.
**Palate:** Medium weight with good texture and sweetness. Hay, nutmeg, sultana. Good presence.
**Finish:** Spicy.

### DALLAS DHU 26 YEARS OLD RUM FINISH, CHIEFTAIN'S CHOICE 48.5%
Single Malt - Speyside

**7½** **Martine: I wonder what type of rum casks were used. I couldn't find any hint to a finish here. Don't look for delicacy but fine if you look for a wake up call.**
**Nose:** Grassy with a smoky echo. Very fruity. Poached pears. A sweaty touch.
**Palate:** Sweet but crisp sensation. Tinned peaches. Savoury taste with a tangy bite. Wasabi. Dry spiciness which tickles the tongue.
**Finish:** Dry with a slight bitterness in the back.

**7¼** **Dave: The rum acting as a cover for what you suspect is a whisky which suffered from being in a tired cask.**
**Nose:** Slightly abrasive. Some high estery/glue like notes. Immature. Water shows a smoky edge. Damp grass.
**Palate:** Better than the nose with a sweet centre. Orange zest. Rum takes charge from the middle onwards.
**Finish:** Smooths into tropical fruits.

### DALMORE 11 YEARS OLD, ADELPHI 57.2%
Single Malt - Highland

**7¾** **Michael: A big, rich bottling, but some of the Dalmore character has been overpowered.**
**Nose:** Fragrant peat, then toffee.
**Palate:** Toffee. Orange zest.
**Finish:** Caramel dryness (suspiciously dark odour for its age). Syrupy and rich. Very faintly medicinal.

**6½** **Jim: This is not Dalmore at anything like its best. A miss, I'm afraid, for all its short-lived riches.**
**Nose:** Very ordinary sherry cask: off-key and unimpressive despite a toffeed sweetness.
**Palate:** Massively chewy and a little smoky. That off note persists throughout but is little more than a background screen against the delicious demerara sweetness.
**Finish:** Drier, still smoking, but some bitter tones.

### DALMORE 13 YEARS OLD, CADENHEAD'S 59.9%
Single Malt - Highland

**7½** **Michael: Extraordinarily sweet-but an engaging curiosity. This pale, golden Dalmore, without the sherry, has an especially characteristic touch of amontillado.**
**Nose:** Almondy.
**Palate:** Sweet. Creamy. Buttery. Faint orange coming through.
**Finish:** Very late smokiness brings some balancing dryness.

**9¼** **Jim: Unquestionably the finest Dalmore I have ever tasted bottled. A classic.**
**Nose:** Fresh and fruity. A briny edge that fits with the sweetest of malts. Invigorating.
**Palate:** A fanfare of sweet malt makes a brilliant arrival. Possible to detect deliciously burnt fudge, roast chestnuts and much more besides.
**Finish:** Amazingly long and dry. A more peppery version of what went before.

### DALMORE 15 YEARS OLD, CADENHEAD'S 57.5%
Single Malt - Highland

**7¼** **Martine: Quite a light character for a Highland malt. Water helps but still a bit rough. Even on a frosty morning!**
**Nose:** Tangy, vibrant. Summery. Green wood. Freesia.
**Palate:** Sweet. Flowing. A bit sharp. Minty. Dill. Touch of coconut milk.
**Finish:** Dry, spicy. Burning.

**7¼** **Dave: The fruit goes one way the oak the other.**
**Nose:** Suede, with ripe berry fruits. A slightly earthy note.
**Palate:** Lifted to start, violet. Slightly fizzy with gentle sweetness. Begins to deepen and broaden in the mouth. Good presence. Sweet and dry (earthy) together.
**Finish:** Light white fruits and oak.

### THE DALMORE 12 YEARS OLD 40%
Single Malt - Highland

**8** **Michael: Said to be married in sherry butts. In this instance, marriage certainly works.**
**Nose:** Beautiful balance of tempting aromas. Gently fragrant peat-smoke. Orange marmalade, malt and sherry.
**Palate:** Orange. Cream. Distinct aniseed. Honey. A very complex malt, with wonderfully combined flavours.
**Finish:** Almost chewy. Faint citrus zest. Smoky dryness. The faintest hint of the sea.

**8½** **Jim: Genuinely classy stuff from the 24 carat jewel in JBB's Scottish crown.**
**Nose:** Outwardly flattish, but time and patience reveals life beyond the sherry-hints of cherry and oak.
**Palate:** Mouth-filling and chewy. Lots of cream toffee. All the time there's a delicate, malty spice buzz.
**Finish:** Very long and still milky, silky toffee with malt and vanilla arriving. A wave or two of sweet liquorice adds further richness.

### THE DALMORE 12 YEARS OLD, BLACK PEARL 40%
Single Malt - Highland

**7½** **Martine: Good balance. A fruity profile. To be enjoyed with a lemon-meringue pie or a syllabub.**
**Nose:** Malty and nutty with a grassy note. Basil. Lemon balm. Redcurrant jelly. An unpleasant sulphury hint at times.
**Palate:** Sweet with a sharper core. Citrussy. Grapefuit peel.
**Finish:** Fruity and mellow. Rhubarb jam.

**7¾** **Dave: A rich sweet and fairly deep dram.**
**Nose:** Lightly caramelised notes, yoghurt-covered nuts, raisin/burnt cakes. Brioche, jammy.
**Palate:** Firmer than the 21 Years Old with more obvious nutty oak over the top of Wine Gums and tayberry.
**Finish:** Becomes sweet. Plump dates.

### THE DALMORE 1973, CABERNET SAUVIGNON FINISH 53%
Single Malt - Highland

**8** **Martine: A charming old lady with her pockets full of candies. Who can resist?**
**Nose:** Perfumy. Floral and fruity. Rose syrup, wine gums (blackcurrant). Marzipan in the back. Entrancing. Evokes the tender world of a candy shop. Then more of oak. Polished old floor.
**Palate:** Lively but smooth. Velvety, lusciously flowing. More oak than fruit but all is well integrated. A pleasant spicy tickle at mid-palate.
**Finish:** Drying, spicy, nutty. Lingering.

**7¾** **Ian: A medley of fruit conveniently assembled in a glass rather than a bowl.**
**Nose:** Rich and composed, toffee, apricot, cherries, underlying hints of vanilla and chocolate.
**Palate:** Creamy crème caramel is soon overlain by a rich fruit sauce with cherries, prunes and apricots, followed by orange marmalade, lightly spicy oak and malty notes emerging.
**Finish:** Fruit recedes while chocolate, caramel maltiness opens up.

### THE DALMORE 1991, MADEIRA FINISH 60%
Single Malt - Highland

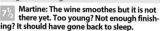

**7½ Martine: The wine smoothes but it is not there yet. Too young? Not enough finishing? It should have gone back to sleep.**
**Nose:** Buttery, biscuity. A slight rancid touch. Distant lemon curd. Pears poached in vanilla.
**Palate:** Mellow for such a strength. Quite rich and creamy. Almond milk, stewed sweet apples. Getting spicier and spicier.
**Finish:** Spicy, warm and tangy. Sweetened by a pleasant marzipan caress.

**8½ Ian: Like a passionate rendez-vous between a chocolatier and a distiller.**
**Nose:** Rich crème brûlée and butterscotch lead apricots, citrus and creamy vanilla trifle, with a final dusting of chocolate.
**Palate:** Creamy crème brûlée with a chocolate fest mid-way, extending with luscious apricots, oranges and grapefruit and lemon zest, culminating in creamy cappuccino.
**Finish:** Fruity with a chocolate flourish.

### THE DALMORE 21 YEARS OLD 43%
Single Malt - Highland

**8¼ Michael: Seductive, but it is all done with great finesse.**
**Nose:** Perfumy sherry. Walnuts. Apricots.
**Palate:** Rich, rummy. Dark chocolate with fruit and nuts.
**Finish:** Satisfying. Lingering smokiness.

**7¾ Dave: Charms on the nose but a bit too oaky.**
**Nose:** Initially quite dry, then juicy malt and overripe pulpy fruit begins to take over. Muscovado sugar, chocolate, a light winey/black fruit, then orange fruit pastilles. Juicy!
**Palate:** Good start mixing sweet malty weight with those black fruits within a fairly firm oak frame. Medium-bodied and rich with a soft feel.
**Finish:** Oakiness increases, then smoke. A bit short?

### THE DALMORE 21 YEARS OLD 43%
Single Malt - Highland

**8 Martine: An assertive character, with a pleasant crisp feel on the palate. The dram to take on long forest walk. Invigorating.**
**Nose:** Rich and fruity. Floral. Carnation. Baked peaches. Hazelnuts. Polished oak floor. A touch of blackcurrant.
**Palate:** Crisp, tangy. Lingering fruit. Blackcurrant jam. Gingerbread. Chocolate fudge.
**Finish:** Dry. Nutmeg. Liquorice.

**8½ Dave: Structure and softness in perfect harmony. A must drink.**
**Nose:** Mature. Candied peels, melted white chocolate, fresh fruit salad. The oak takes things into the sauna (pine). With water becomes deeper: honeydew melon, currant, heather.
**Palate:** A seamless flow of all the flavours on the nose. Beautifully balanced.
**Finish:** Fantastic length.

### THE DALMORE 30 YEARS OLD, GONZALEZ BYPASS 42%
Single Malt - Highland

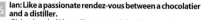

**8¼ Martine: A beautiful and complex nose, palate starts right then the elegant spiciness.**
**Nose:** Cherry compote. Green walnut. Touch of tar. Tobacco leaf. Hot coffee. Sweeter aromas slowly emerge. Shortcrust pastry. Vanilla biscuit.
**Palate:** Sherry reveals heavy fruit: prunes, plums, cherries. Pleasant sourness. Spicy, tickling.
**Finish:** Very spicy. Really numbing tastebuds. Bitter chocolate aftertaste.

**8½ Dave: An exotic dram with an extra dimension and complexity. Sensual.**
**Nose:** Amber in colour and fruity, almost winey nose of black fruits, Ribena, chocolate and in time resin. Water brings out wood oils, sandalwood.
**Palate:** Rich oak tones, well structured and complex. Cigar box, berry fruits, walnut. Very sweet, very deep with good tannic structure.
**Finish:** Long, sweet and savoury. Tea leaf.

### THE DALMORE CIGAR MALT 43%
Single Malt - Highland

**8¼ Michael: Beautifully constructed, very distinctive.**
**Nose:** Gentle smokiness like chestnuts roasting on an open fire. Emphatic 'box of chocolates' aroma: Orange cream pralines in black chocolate.
**Palate:** Texture and flavour of chocolate mousse cake. Powdered cocoa. Then juicy maltiness and understated vanilla-pod dryness.
**Finish:** Biscotti: chocolate and plain. A hint of toast. Charcoal, oak.

**7¾ Dave: A bling-bling dram. Goes wonderfully with cigars! (and fur coats and gold jewellery).**
**Nose:** Big, sweet, concentrated. Chocolate orange, cocoa, raisins, sticky toffee pudding, black fruits, Madeira-like, bitter-sweet. Needs water to calm it and show balanced oak clearly.
**Palate:** Big, fat, rich. Rum, raisin, kumquat peel/marmalade. Chocolate, dried peel, vanilla.
**Finish:** Bitter chocolate.

### THE DALMORE CIGAR MALT 43%
Single Malt - Highland

**7¾ Martine: Oak calls the tune but does not drown out the choir. A classic afterdinner dram.**
**Nose:** Buttery. Gingerbread. Plum jam. Raisins dipped in chocolate. Prunes and dates. White pepper. Butterscotch.
**Palate:** Enticing. Lovely oily mouthfeel. Spicy plum chutney. Cinnamon, nutmeg.
**Finish:** Oaky, spicy, warm and long.

**7¾ Dave: This is a Rubens nude, waving as she flies past in a flash car.**
**Nose:** Weighty, stewed fruits, cocoa (Green and Blacks) bramble jelly, flambéed pineapple, clotted cream, blackberry.
**Palate:** Rich fat and sweet. Dried fruits, Dundee cake, pecan, cherry, plum/pruneaux. Chocolate.
**Finish:** Sweet, long, mixing dried and hedgerow fruits. Molasses.

### DALWHINNIE 1981, DISTILLERS EDITION, OLOROSO SHERRY 43%
Single Malt - Highland

**8 Michael: Beautiful interplay and balance.**
**Nose:** Oloroso, liquorice, rooty, grassy.
**Palate:** Very sweet, toffeeish start. Honey. Very distinct lemony notes. Long flavour development to peatiness, cut-grass, vanilla and fresh oak.
**Finish:** Very long. Cut-grass, peat, smoke, oak.

**7 Doug: More complex than the 15 Years Old but somehow lacks the balance and lingering charm.**
**Nose:** Soft and honeyed with gentle traces of liquorice and stronger peat emerging through sherry notes.
**Palate:** Light, honeyed and playfully viscous; leading eventually to more liquorice and peat.
**Finish:** Disappointingly short. Perhaps over-sherried for such a delicate malt. The peat cuts in sharply to dominate the finish.

### DALWHINNIE 20 YEARS OLD 57%
Single Malt - Highland

**7¾ Dave: A soft hearted beauty. Cuddle up to it.**
**Nose:** Showing maturity. Rich and sweet with a touch of fireworks (sulphur). Then honey, banana loaf, sticky toffee pudding, baked/caramelised soft fruits, fudge and varnish.
**Palate:** Very rounded and plump. Supemely soft and gentle. Light chestnut then a surge of spice, light grip. All those sweet fruits re-emerge...
**Finish:** .. but then die a little quickly.

**7½ Arthur: Try to get the dilution right.**
**Nose:** Vanilla ice cream and nuts initially, then a sourness came through, like fresh grapefruit juice. This, combined with a saltiness gives it a margarita style. Wafts of barley sugar sweets there with a raisiny, bready character too.
**Palate:** Abroad dried fruit texture, with honeyed porridge giving way to a drying, tingling spice.
**Finish:** Dry.

## DALWHINNIE 29 YEARS OLD 57.8%
Single Malt - Highland

**8** **Michael: Seems to have become more lively with age.**
**Nose:** Restrained peat. Some grassy, moorland, aromas. New-mown hay.
**Palate:** Lemon grass. A suggestion of dried banana. Dessert apples, against a cereal-grain background.
**Finish:** Scenty. Minty. Appetising.

**7¼** **Dave: Seems reluctant to open.**
**Nose:** Slightly dumb with hints of cream, honey, cut flowers and sweet oak.
**Palate:** Soft fruits, vanilla, clover. Fairly woody with a dry mid-palate. A slightly bitter note.
**Finish:** Honeycomb, cream toffee.

## DEANSTON 12 YEARS OLD 40%
Single Malt - Highland

**7** **Michael: More of a Lowland style. If Deanston were regarded as a Lowland distillery, it would score higher.**
**Nose:** Dry. Light peat. Grass. Linseed, leather.
**Palate:** Lightly oily. Sweet. Lemon-zest. Lemongrass. Lightly malty.
**Finish:** Sherbet. Lemon-zest again. Grass. Appetising nutty dryness.

**6¼** **Jim: Oops. Nothing like the lovely dram at this age I normally come across. Pleasant enough, but too thin and lacklustre to be true.**
**Nose:** Delicate intertwining of honey and butterscotch with a bite of dry oak. Redeemed, rather unusually, by a sprinkling of crushed rose petals.
**Palate:** A thin, insipid, start then a roar of spice, malt and oak in one mad rush.
**Finish:** Bitter at first then softening oak.

## DEANSTON 17 YEARS OLD 40%
Single Malt - Highland

**7¼** **Michael: Gentle, but quite succulent.**
**Nose:** Hint of lemon marmalade.
**Palate:** Light but creamy. Lightly nutty. Then oily perfuminess.
**Finish:** Oily. Nutty. Orange peel.

**8** **Jim: An improvement from the 17 Years Old of old, which doesn't even begin to show its big age.**
**Nose:** Fabulously bitter sweet nose, breakfast time stuff with marmalade and honey. Thrilling complexity.
**Palate:** Again, a peculiarly thin mouthfeel. Begins oaky dry and then a surge of malt helps sweeten things a little. And a delightful spice buzz forms a permanent, lively strata.
**Finish:** A milky oakiness with dry coconut nuttiness.

## DEANSTON 30 YEARS OLD LIMITED EDITION 46.7%
Single Malt - Highland

**7½** **Dave: An old malty number just about holding its own, but it hasn't gained hugely in terms of complexity.**
**Nose:** Dry, with some raisin, toasted tea cake, wholemeal flour. A slight lactic touch goes with the addition of water, while the nuts turn into Ovaltine.
**Palate:** Pretty firm, though given a sugared almond sweetness. Soft-centred.
**Finish:** Clean and nutty.

**7¾** **Arthur: A very dry palate, but a pleasant drop none-theless.**
**Nose:** Tasty warm flapjacks, and orange muffins. Sweet orange blossom and good milk chocolate.
**Palate:** Orange, a green oakiness and lots of dryness.
**Finish:** Sulphurous, like roast pork crackling.

## DEWAR'S 15 YEARS OLD 43%
Blended - Scotland

**7½** **Martine: Wood bosses around. Lacks subtlety and complexity. Leaves a burning sensation.**
**Nose:** Tangy, oak speaks out. Earthy, damp cellar. Mushrooms. Pine cones. Opens up on creamy notes. Apples cooked in butter.
**Palate:** Sweet at start then oak quickly comes on stage. Slight astringency. Mixed spices.
**Finish:** Dry, nutty with a touch of milk chocolate. A spicy hint.

**7¾** **Dave: A palatable whisky which comes as some relief after the initially alarming nose.**
**Nose:** Start slightly sulphury with hints of ripe soft cheese. Pretty funky and leathery. With water out comes a mix of wax, moss and sandalwood.
**Palate:** Much better than the nose. A hot paprika burn which starts in the middle of the palate and runs to the finish.
**Finish:** Mossy.

## DEWAR'S FOUNDER'S RESERVE 18 YEARS OLD 43%
Blended - Scotland

**7¾** **Martine: Attractive nose but a wee more restrained palate than expected.**
**Nose:** Perfumed. Ripe pear. Delicate nuttiness. Lemony. Freshly varnished wood. Pleasant fruity bouquet. Releases more citrus fruit with water.
**Palate:** Smooth to start with then quickly drying on spices. Slightly austere.
**Finish:** Minty and spicy. Lingering with a dry edge.

**8½** **Dave: A very classy blend. Recommended.**
**Nose:** Stylish and mature. Lemon zest, dried pear, cereal, cream, pie crust honeycomb, sealing wax, parma violet. Deepens and mellows in time. Lightly oily with a touch of smoke.
**Palate:** Soft and gentle, with raspberry notes and a creamy edge. Crisps up nicely in the mid-palate.
**Finish:** Creamy and soft.

## DEWAR'S SIGNATURE 43%
Blended - Scotland

**7½** **Michael: Seems restrained at first, but needs time to open up, at which point it becomes quite loqacious.**
**Nose:** Softly fragrant. Toasted marshmallows and chocolate.
**Palate:** Spritzy freshness. Seville oranges. Toast.
**Finish:** Hearty interplay of heather, gentle peat and pine-log smoke.

**8** **Dave: A very sound, approachable and pretty classy blend.**
**Nose:** Sweet. Vanilla, raspberry ripple, soft grain. Floral (daffodil). Attractive.
**Palate:** Fragrant and soft-centred with blossom, dry hay, juicy apricot notes, vanilla. Rounded. Good balance.
**Finish:** Nutmeg. Long, gentle.

## DEWAR'S SIGNATURE 43%
Blended - Scotland

**7** **Martine: Quite ordinary. Surprisingly firey for the strength. Lacks delicacy.**
**Nose:** Heady. Artificially flavoured sweets. Fresh paint. Then much better. Drying hay. Freshly squeezed orange. Marzipan. Milk chocolate bar.
**Palate:** Creamy, chewy. Fresh oak. Pear and almond pie. Eau-de-vie cherries.
**Finish:** Hot, dry, slightly bitter.

**8½** **Dave: Broader than most. Great blending of old, mature whiskies.**
**Nose:** Chewy with some complexity: stewed fruits (apricot), barley sugar, sealing wax, sultana, coconut, light sweet spices and crystallised fruit.
**Palate:** Perfumed start, dried apple and a hint of smoke. Bitter chocolate. Layered, honeyed.
**Finish:** Oaky, mature.

## DEWAR'S WHITE LABEL 40%
Blended - Scotland

**8** **Michael: Decisive, cleansing and refreshing. A civilised apéritif before oysters Rockefeller and a New York strip steak.**
**Nose:** New leather upholstery. Polished oak. Beeswax. Hint of pine.
**Palate:** Firm body. Fresh, crisp, toast. Very spicy. Ginger-dusted melon.
**Finish:** Vanilla. Oak. Slightly piney again. Resiny.

**5** **Paul: Answers the question: why single malts?**
**Nose:** Sickly sweet, meek, and a bit too metallic and old holding tank-like to my liking: mildly heathery. The few scents pass by so fleetingly it's difficult to pin them down. Generally nondescript.
**Palate:** Flavours of sweet malt, sweet corn greet the taste buds at palate entry. The mid-palate stage, in a fit of overcompensation, displays lumpily sweet tastes of sugary grain.
**Finish:** The sweet-o-rama continues in the overblown, medium long aftertaste.

## DISTILLERY SELECT LOCH LOMOND, ORGANIC SINGLE HIGHLAND GRAIN 45%
Single Grain - Scotland

**7¼ Martine: Unusual profile for a grain whisky. More reminiscent of a calvados. Oak is too blatant. Water wipes it out.**
**Nose:** Resiny, earthy. Sour fruit like cider apples. The cereal character is not obvious at first.
**Palate:** Sweet, oaky. Cider notes. Caramelised apples. With water, a mushroom touch.
**Finish:** Dry, spicy, slightly astringent.

**7 Dave: Split into spirit on one side and wood on the other.**
**Nose:** Pinkish hue and an aroma of rhubarb, red apple, fruit compote, pomegranate juice but all of them teetering on the edge of mouldiness.
**Palate:** Rich with an assertive oiliness from the supporting oak. Rich and spicy: cinnamon stick. Slick and tongue-coating.
**Finish:** Short and overly dry.

## DRAM HOUSE VATTED MALT, 12 YEARS OLD, MILROY'S 46%
Blended Malt - Scotland

**7¼ Martine: Conclusion: A true and easy-going mariner. Straight forwardness takes the place of complexity. Is Caol Ila a major player in the vatting?**
**Nose:** Marine smokiness, Islay tinged. Cooked plums. Creosote. Smoked ham. Oyster chowder.
**Palate:** Assertive. Malty sweetness. Distinctively peaty with a sea-spray freshness.
**Finish:** Warm, spicy and dry.

**7½ Dave: Briefly this reminded me of the smell in the old Glasgow subway. Well put together.**
**Nose:** Biscuity, quite dry lifted by sugar puff sweetness, mandarine peel, heather. Hint of turfy smoke, stewed tea.
**Palate:** Smoke, then nutty malt, light oak, coconut. Crisp and firm. A little disappointing after the nose.
**Finish:** Firm. Light peat.

## DRAMBUIE BLACK RIBBON, 15 YEARS OLD 40%
Whisky Liqueur - Scotland

**7½ Michael: Substantially darker, bigger, fruitier, drier, firmer, more structured and less syrupy than the Drambuie without the ribbon.**
**Nose:** Sweet and honeyish, but with hints of malt and smoke.
**Palate:** Orangey at first, then lemon peel and aniseed.
**Finish:** Delicately whiskyish. Suggestions of Speyside.

**3 Jim: Sorry, not my cup of tea. The 15 Years Old whisky wasted in this has become an irrelevance against the surging sweetness.**
**Nose:** A heady dose of mixed herbs and spices, with aniseed, juniper and cloves sticking to a cloying, vaguely honeyed sweetness. Hello? Where's the whisky?
**Palate:** Massively sweet and, for me, unbearable.
**Finish:** Sugar, sugar, sugar, then a vague, almost pleasant bitterness on the very finish.

## DRUMGUISH HIGHLAND SCOTCH WHISKY 40%
Single Malt - Highland

**7¼ Michael: A newish distillery, so this whisky is still on the young side, but I like its old-fashioned grassy-peaty flavours.**
**Nose:** Nutty. Cereal grain. Light, fresh, peat.
**Palate:** Creamy richness. Some toffee. Sweetish dried grass.
**Finish:** Grassy. Toasted marshmallows. Faintly Kirsch-like fruitiness.

**7½ Jim:** Slightly feinty but much cleaner than some recent bottlings. Distinct barley sugar sweetness and caramel soften the blow and even make for an attractive aroma.
**Palate:** Extremely sweet and rich at first. There is a form of refined pepperiness new to the proceedings which compliments an intense, brown sugared maltiness. Enjoyably chewy.
**Finish:** Rather more bitter with some vanilla oakiness. Still malty and latterly toasty.

## DUFFTOWN 15 YEARS OLD 43%
Single Malt - Speyside

**7 Michael: An excellent aperitif malt.**
**Nose:** Assertively aromatic.

**Palate:** Starts syrupily malty, becoming drier and flowery, with a hint of late dusty peat.
**Finish:** Light but lingering.

**5 Jim: Pretty unpleasant.**
**Nose:** A flawed, musty, sulphury aroma.
**Palate:** Fish-oily, sweet and shapeless.
**Finish:** Some maltiness survives at the inelegant finale.

## DUFFTOWN 15 YEARS OLD 43%
Single Malt - Speyside

**7 Martine: To be served with an apple and hazelnut crumble. Classic, nothing really exciting, but a good Speyside character.**
**Nose:** Flowery, light and scented. Distinctive nuttiness. Juicy apples. Restrained spices (nutmeg).
**Palate:** Smooth and mellow. Good balance. Lots of marzipan.
**Finish:** Unexpectedly dry, rather short. Crisp, slightly bitter. Warms up with spicy notes.

**7¾ Dave: A good, mid-weight nutty style.**
**Nose:** A real nut-bowl aroma: almond, hazelnut and some creamy brazil, as well as a hint of marzipan and wholemeal maltiness. In time a toffee note. Mid-weight.
**Palate:** Lovely weight and feel with a spicy nuttiness. Softens as it moves in the mouth.
**Finish:** Nutty with decent length.

## DUFFTOWN 1975, 29 YEARS OLD, DEWAR RATTRAY 46%
Single Malt - Speyside

**8½ Gavin: With some Dufftowns you are glad when you've had enough. This is a well-made example which has been matched by very good bourbon wood.**
**Nose:** Very floral and elegant, lemon tea, then some darker, more smoky aromas emerging.
**Palate:** Lively, vanilla, ice cream soda, honey.
**Finish:** Agreeably citric, surprisingly zestful. Dries out more when reduced – the only real hint at its age.

**7½ Dave: Interesting, but without the overriding character to make it great.**
**Nose:** Nutty (brazil, cob) but rounded with dry oak, vanilla/coconut and mint. Fresh apple juice/cider, stewed fruits. Mature. Fading a little. A dusty edge.
**Palate:** Putty drying to maltiness. Light nut oil feel. Crisp and light with decent balance.
**Finish:** Dry and oaky.

## DUFFTOWN 30 YEARS OLD 1977, OLD MALT CASK 50%
Single Malt - Speyside

**7 Dave: Has a cleanliness and delicacy but lacking in impact overall. You expect complexity from old whiskies.**
**Nose:** Butterscotch and bounty bars mixed with marzipan. Crisp toasty oak, bread crust. With water become grassy, tweedy with a whiff of juniper.
**Palate:** Fat, but slightly flat. The middle is floral (damp lily petals). Thins badly with water which is surprising at 50%.
**Finish:** Short.

**8¼ Martine: A clean spirit, well matured and combining balance and smoothness. Very satisfying.**
**Nose:** Deep, rich. Cooked fruit. Lemon marmalade. Dried fruit (apricot). Shortcake.
**Palate:** Smooth, rich, mouth-coating. Wood is perfectly integrated. Citrussy and refreshing with a touch of liquorice. Nicely polished.
**Finish:** Warm and gentle. Hint of candied ginger. Honeyish aftertaste.

## DUFFTOWN-GLENLIVET 1975, 21 YEARS OLD, RARE MALTS 54.8%
Single Malt - Speyside

**7½ Michael: Pale in colour but by no means anaemic in flavour. Has matured a lot since it was 15.**
**Nose:** Honey and honeydew melon; glacé cherries, waxy; lipstick.
**Palate:** Remarkably fudgy. Treacle toffee.
**Finish:** Very gingery. Sweet, leafy bonfires smokiness.

**8½ Jim: Brilliant balance of barley sweetness and spice. A joy.**
**Nose:** Banana and bourbon, sweet and clean. A slight smoky, peppery note.
**Palate:** Intensely sweet with rich demerara sugar and spicy malt.
**Finish:** Barley sugar and caramel; chewy malt; spice, toastiness.

## DUMBARTON (INVERLEVEN STILLS) 18 YEARS OLD, CADENHEAD'S 57.9%
Single Grain - Scotland

**7½ Martine:** A great delicacy but the strength needs to be put down by a good dash of water. But it is not enough to cut all the edges off. *WHISKY Magazine Recommended*
**Nose:** Delicate and subtle. Bakewell tart. Tablet. Lots of sweety notes. Grassy. Aniseed. Getting spirity as it opens.
**Palate:** Light and silky. Lovely herbal sweetness. Lemon and ginger ale. Alcohol is not tamed.
**Finish:** Medium. Almondy. A bitter edge.

**9 Michael:** Hides its 57.9% completely on the nose; delivers it to knockout effect in the palate. Gorgeously light and summery with (lots of) water.
**Nose:** Pineapple, peach perhaps with some strawberry sweetness. Clean, smoothie-like freshness with water.
**Palate:** Hot and winey. Sugary, but surprisingly clean; fruity and refreshing with water.
**Finish:** Sweet, sharp, cleansing.

## DUMBARTON 1969, SHERRY WOOD, CADENHEAD'S 51.2%
Single Grain - Scotland

**8 Martine:** Bossily buoyant. Loses in delicacy what it gains in flavour and texture. Miles away from the Lowlands.
**Nose:** Heady and ample sherry notes. Morello cherry. Loads of vanilla. Old furniture.
**Palate:** Incredibly sprightly for its age. Speaks out. Trifle, toasted coffee, hint of smoke.
**Finish:** Very spicy. Cinnamon, ginger, hot paprika.

**8¼ Dave:** What a contrast!
**Nose:** Big and sweet with oily qualities and soft sherry notes: moist sultana cake, cherry/red berries. Wood-derived aromas.
**Palate:** Huge and powerful with incense, walnut, chocolate and ripe rich fruity notes. Honeyed warmth.
**Finish:** Long big and nutty, with spice.

## DUN BHEAGAN 8 YEARS OLD ISLAY SINGLE MALT 43%
Single Malt - Islay

**7¾ Michael:** A promising middleweight. Could be a contender in two or three years.
**Nose:** Burnt grass.
**Palate:** Light. Sandy. Peat. Fruit – lots of it. Iron. Plenty of flavour development.
**Finish:** Long, smoky, warming.

**7¾ Dave:** Eminently drinkable, direct and simple.
**Nose:** Dry with notes of heather, fishboxes, cigar ash and dried seaweed.
**Palate:** Dry malty (kiln-like) with good positive attack.
**Finish:** Ash like with a peppery lift.

## DUN BHEAGAN LOWLAND 8 YEARS OLD 43%
Single Malt - Lowland

**8½ Arthur:** A pretty face with muddy feet. *WHISKY Magazine Recommended*
**Nose:** Damp earth, kiwi, lemon Jif, tangerine. Pretty.
**Palate:** Citric, then woody and a touch buttery.
**Finish:** Crisp grassiness, with a little earthiness attached. Chocolate milk.

**7½ Dave:** OK, but lacks impact and definition.
**Nose:** Back to the bready template again: digestive biscuits, vanilla, melon, coconut matting with some sweetness behind. Pine needles.
**Palate:** Better than the nose and fills out with a splash of water shifting it into fruit smoothie territory. Soft and gentle.
**Finish:** Cocoa butter.

## DUNGLAS 1967, THE WHISKY EXCHANGE 46%
Single Malt - Lowland

**7½ Michael:** The fresh, charming bouquet was a revelation, but the palate was a little careworn.
**Nose:** Perfumy. Crème caramel. Crème brûlée. Then slightly acidic.
**Palate:** A hint of black chocolate. Dry. Cider apples. Cedary. Slightly woody. Astringent.
**Finish:** Slightly bitter.

**6½ Dave:** Either the sample bottle was not rinsed out or this is just plain weird.
**Nose:** Sweet and fruity. Mealy with kumquat, passion fruit and marzipan.

**Palate:** Oily with some fruitiness but a carbolic soap flavour begins to dominate.
**Finish:** Short.

## EDRADOUR 10 YEARS OLD 40%
Single Malt - Highland

**8 Michael:** Much more sherried than the previous 10 Years Old distillery bottling. The new version is very elegant, but the earlier one had more distillery character.
**Nose:** Dried apricots. Oloroso sherry. Faintly spicy smokiness.
**Palate:** Creamy. Minty. Nutty. Almondy dryness.
**Finish:** Firm. Grippy. A touch of peaty bitterness.

**8¾ Jim:** Massive whisky from a pint-sized distillery and massively impressive.
**Nose:** Usual heavyweight aroma associated with this distillery. Oloroso is evident. A very slight sulphur note spoils the harmony a little.
**Palate:** Enormously rich mouth feel, with roasted barley and then a wave of grapey fruit.
**Finish:** Deliciously oily and sprinkled with soft spices, vanilla, caramel and oak.

## EDRADOUR 11 YEARS OLD, MADEIRA FINISH, SIGNATORY STRAIGHT FROM THE CASK 59.6%
Single Malt - Highland

**7½ Arthur:** Bags of cask character, and fine if you find finishes fun.
**Nose:** Buttercups, grass, currants and Turkish Delight. Metal and bubblebath notes became more apparent with water.
**Palate:** Christmas cake, with raisins and glacé cherries.
**Finish:** A light meatiness, like baked gammon.

**7¾ Dave:** Well balanced and with more weight and substance than you might normally expect from this distillery. A good dram.
**Nose:** Quite sweet. Barley sugar, then sultana/fruit loaf, hay, spices being sauteed in butter, crisp oak.
**Palate:** Medium-bodied and fairly intense, high concentration of sweet fruits, yet slightly firmer than you expect from the nose. Well balanced.
**Finish:** Fine length. Dried peels/fruits. Tingling.

## EDRADOUR 1976, SIGNATORY 53.1%
Single Malt - Highland

**7¾ Michael:** Still a hint of the typical creaminess. Although its flavours are on the light side, Edradour is quite rich in body. It stands up well to age, but this is not the best '76 I have tasted.
**Nose:** Fresh, "green". Pronounced garden mint?
**Palate:** Herbal. Spicy. Lightly syrupy.
**Finish:** Sawn wood. Dry. Drying.

**7¾ Jim:** Past its best with one or two off-key notes, but otherwise still holds out well.
**Nose:** A perfectly-shaped layer of honey. A hint of lavender and peppermint add to the complexity.
**Palate:** Fat and explosive on the palate, the spiced oiliness is infused with acacia honey richness which gives way to biscuity maltiness.
**Finish:** Dries fast as the oak takes hold, though a sweetness lingers.

## EDRADOUR BURGUNDY FINISH, SIGNATORY 57%
Single Malt - Highland

**5½ Arthur:** Not to my taste.
**Nose:** Butyric, peach air freshener and a queasy cakiness. Like some showdown between two gateaux: as if a Battenburg attempted to outnancy a French Fancy.
**Palate:** Incredibly sweet, sugary and then nothing of merit. Better than the nose.
**Finish:** Pass!

**7¾ Owen:** Somewhat lighter on the palate than the nose suggests. But still a firm, chewy, whisky for after dinner.
**Nose:** Waxy at first, then apples, pears, cider, perry, calvados...Richer, crumbly chocolate cake undertones.
**Palate:** Creamy toffees. Egg custard. It is smoother and shows greater finesse with water.
**Finish:** Creamy, mint toffee richness. Some milk chocolate.

## EDRADOUR BURGUNDY MATURED, BALLECHIN 46%
Single Malt - Highland

**7¼ Dave: It is young and showing great promise. Keep watching this with interest.**
**Nose:** A pinkish cast to it. Chimney smoke, with a hint of burning wool. Cleaning peat ashes out of the hearth, then sweet fruit comes in over the top.
**Palate:** Positive palate, wine gums mixed with coal dust, a light cereal note. Some rubber (sulphur) which might be a sign of youth.
**Finish:** Fruity.

**8½ Arthur: Youthful, fun, smoked food character. A lack of the complexities that are brought on by aging can sometimes mean clarity. Has the clarity of a bell and is an immensely promising spirit.**
**Nose:** Sour fruits and floor polish. Wet wood smoke, fennel and an underlying chalkiness. A dry, smoky and medical nose.
**Palate:** Chicory, fennel and sweet, smoked ham.
**Finish:** Drying smoke.

## FAMOUS GROUSE 40%
Blended - Scotland

**8 Michael: Creates the illusion of being massively more malty than it really is. Very good extraction of flavours from the wood seems to be the secret (or part of it). I am in awe of the dexterity of the blender, though the result is a little soft and sweet for my personal tastes.**
**Nose:** Apricots. Sherry. Juicy fresh oak.
**Palate:** Calvados. Slight butter. Flowering currant. Crystallised ginger.
**Finish:** Faint suggestion of garden bonfires.

**7 Paul: Agreeable Saturday afternoon blend that doesn't feign profundity or complexity, it just gets down to the business of being a completely satisfying dram.**
**Nose:** The user-friendly bouquet offers delicate aromatic hints of fruit, very soft peat, and linseed oil. Quiet, calm, approachable.
**Palate:** On the palate, this easy blend travels the course from entry to throat in fine form, offering along the way uncomplicated flavours of moderately sweet grain, mild spice, and even a dash of oak. Medium-bodied.
**Finish:** Long, caramel-like, and as comforting as an old familiar friend.

## FAMOUS GROUSE 1987 VINTAGE MALT WHISKY 40%
Blended Malt - Scotland

**8¼ Michael: The Grouse at its most graceful.**
**Nose:** Very aromatic, minty, spicy, heather fragrance.
**Palate:** Silky. Gently sweetish start. Creamy. Nutty.
**Finish:** Toasty dryness. Slight juicy grassiness. Late, light, fragrant distinct, peat smokiness and hint of the sea (very late, on the front of the tongue).

*WHISKY Magazine Recommended*

**8¾ Jim: Vatted malts are notoriously disappointing. At last, one to take your breath away.**
**Nose:** A clean, malty aroma brimming with a salad bowl of banana, orange, grape and figs.
**Palate:** Teasing yet lush malt in cloud of smoke.
**Finish:** Soft oak, vanilla intermingle.

## FAMOUS GROUSE 1989 VINTAGE MALT 40%
Blended Malt - Scotland

**8¼ Michael: The Grouse enthusiast who tastes this vatted version will be seduced by it.**
**The aromas and flavours suggest malts from the company's own distilleries – and perhaps a little more Highland Park than last year?**
**Nose:** Evocative. Sweetshops. Mint. Liquorice.
**Palate:** Sherryish. Smooth Malty. Nutty. Creamy. Very gentle oily smokiness.
**Finish:** Firm. Toasty balancing dryness. Hint of salty coastal whisky. Again, all very restrained.

*WHISKY Magazine Recommended*

**8¼ Dave: Discreetly complex but go easy on the water. It's easily drowned.**
**Nose:** Attractive, fragrant with honeyed depth: notes of heather, gorse/coconut, madeira cake, honey, cinnamon and some grassy and smoky touches.
**Palate:** Slightly dry start then it softens mid-palate where all that honeyed, cakey, ripe fruitiness reappears. Good mouthfeel and balance.
**Finish:** Ripe silky and sweet.

## FAMOUS GROUSE CASK STRENGTH 56%
Blended - Scotland

**8½ Michael: Like the regular Grouse, it tastes maltier and bigger than it really is. An excellent justification of cask strength.**
**Nose:** Surprisingly powerful. Lovely clean, appetising aromas. Freshly peeled oranges. Dried apricots.
**Palate:** Thick-cut marmalade on well-buttered toast. Liquorice. Lots of flavour development in the glass.
**Finish:** A hint of burnt toast. A whiff of smoke, from the direction of Orkney.

**7½ Dave: The strength gives it greater weight than the standard bottling and a bottle will last three times as long!**
**Nose:** Generous with soft grain, vanilla, fruit, orange, treacle scones and smoke. Alcoholic.
**Palate:** Good weight but there's a hard note running all the way through. Smooth, sweet and fruity to start, then tightens.
**Finish:** Punchy.

## FAMOUS GROUSE FINEST 40%
Blended - Scotland

**7½ Martine: A beautifully mingled aromatic palate. But this whisky would have delivered more character if bottled at a higher strength.**
**Nose:** Harmonious. Butterscotch. Polished floor. Fruit cake. Oak and fruit combine.
**Palate:** Smooth, velvety. Pears poached in white port and vanilla. Oak is kept under control. A bit flat though.
**Finish:** Medium. Nutty with a touch of spice.

**7¼ Dave: This has breadth, but just lacks the depth of the others.**
**Nose:** Dry yet full with aromas of melting chocolate, hay loft, clover honey on toast. Dry sacking. Firm.
**Palate:** Stewed prunes, dark chocolate, earth, caramel toffee and light smoke.
**Finish:** Dried fruits.

## FAMOUS GROUSE GOLD RESERVE 43%
Blended - Scotland

**8½ Michael: A superb job of blending. When I tasted this whisky on its own, I found it was good, but not especially distinctive. Tasted among its competitors, it was one of the standouts.**
**Nose:** Soft, rounded. Dry Oloroso sherry. Juicy oak.
**Palate:** Syrup maltiness. Flavours develop. Vanilla. Fresh, sweet, lemon. Spiciness. Aniseed. Ginger.
**Finish:** Incredibly long. Tobacco? Underpinning of peaty dryness.

**8 Dave: A cracking juicy dram.**
**Nose:** Clean and spicy unreduced with roasted toasty notes, citrus fruit/honey. Water brings out a wet grass, sandalwood edge. Good soft grain. Rich with some complexity.
**Palate:** Well-weighted in the mouth opening into a silky mix of toffee, runny honey, dry spices and a marshmallow-like-mid-palate.
**Finish:** Well balanced, with unobtrusive dry wood.

## FAMOUS GROUSE ISLAY CASK FINISH 40%
Blended - Scotland

**8¼ Michael: To reconcile the style of the regular Grouse with Islay is an achievement, but a dubious one.**
**Nose:** Polished oak. Peat smoke. Sooty.
**Palate:** Bigger than the regular Grouse. Firm, biscuity maltiness. Hint of grassiness, rootiness, liquorice.
**Finish:** Dry and peaty – with some saltiness.

**7¾ Dave: Good.**
**Nose:** Immediate smoke/burnt matches, heather, soft fruits/honey. Dry yet soft.
**Palate:** Softly fruited: sultana, hazelnut with puffs of scented heathery smoke.
**Finish:** Dry long and slightly austere. Smoky.

## FAMOUS GROUSE PORT WOOD FINISH 40%
Blended - Scotland

**8 Michael:** Port wood can add toffeeish and spicy flavours, rounding out a whisky without adding an obvious wine flavour. That is what happens here.
**Nose:** Fragrant. Dried apricots. Some syrupy notes. Butter. Treacle toffee. Slight burnt grass, peat.
**Palate:** Starts dry. Toasted almonds. Very nutty. Creamy sweetness in middle. Clean toffee. Lemon.
**Finish:** Restrained spiciness. Ginger. White pepper.

**7 Dave: Doesn't like water. Is it Grouse – or something new?**
**Nose:** Sweet and silky. Hint of honey, nut and bracken along with red fruits, raisin and plum pudding. Light smoke.
**Palate:** A sweet start. Very fruity/winey, redcurrant jelly.
**Finish:** Sweet. Wine gums.

## FAMOUS GROUSE SCOTTISH OAK 45%
Blended - Scotland

**8 Dave: Seamlessly put together. Best drunk neat.**

WHISKY *Magazine* *Recommended*

**Nose:** A bit shy to start. Mossy with touches of pear, wine gums, apple juice. Gentle, smooth.
**Palate:** Mint chocolate, light cocoa and a crunchy texture which softens and is given a lift by tangerine, fruit jelly and berries. Balanced by a clove/cinnamon spiciness.
**Finish:** Berries. Quite short and a light, oaky grip.

**7 Arthur: Is this Scotch I thought? Yes, but not as we are used to it. Interesting.**
**Nose:** Pow! Lots of oaky lemons, and American oak-like character. Vanilla and pine wood sap. Some soft fruits and a little heather smoke too.
**Palate:** Boff! Again more of these bourbon-like oak tannins but some malt character hiding underneath.
**Finish:** More sappy woodiness.

## FEIS ISLE 2006 LAPHROAIG 94
Single Malt - Islay

**8¼ Dave: The reserved nose is compensated by a lively, palate. Laphroaig is bang on form.**
**Nose:** Wood embers/charcoal then a lift of fennel tops. Malt increases the smoke but reveals a stony heart: drying seaweed, bleached bones and tar.
**Palate:** A huge hit of smoke deepening into hot roads. Water spreads flavours, bringing out a fishy oiliness balancing the dry smoke.
**Finish:** Oatcake crunch, smoked red pepper.

**8½ Arthur: A foody whisky that is lip-smacking and moreish. Almost Thai at times.**
**Nose:** Lemon syllabub and antiseptic mouthwash. Ash, in the grate of a dead fire. Blackcurrant and aniseed. A little limey sourness with water, lemon pepper and maybe coriander. Barbecue sauce and coriander.
**Palate:** Oily, ashy and peppery.
**Finish:** Drying and peppery.

## FINLAGGAN 15 YEARS OLD 43%
Single Malt - Islay

**7½ Michael:** As a single, it must come from one of the Islay distilleries. Reminds me of Port Ellen, but there is surely not enough stock of that?
**Nose:** Sharp, firm, peaty, dryness.
**Palate:** Assertively seaweed start, almost immediately sliding into a slippery, oily, leaner maltiness then equally suddenly rising to a spicy crescendo.
**Finish:** Peppery, but with a complexity of other spices.

**9¼ Jim: If you love Islay whisky, especially the south-east coast variety, this is an absolute must.**
**Nose:** Sweet peat and dried dates add untold riches to the clean malt and oak. High quality stuff.
**Palate:** The oak arrives to confront the peat. Result is a complex, spicy battle. Huge intensity with molassed depth countered by seaweedy, briny dryness.
**Finish:** Remains massive and long with countless layers of peaty iodine and oak ramming the tastebuds.

## FINLAGGAN 17 YEARS OLD 46%
Single Malt - Islay

**7¾ Michael:** Sweeter than some Finlaggans I have tasted, but quite delicious.

**Nose:** Lightly smoky. More like wood smoke. A honey-maple barbecue.
**Palate:** Firm, malty. Lightly peaty.
**Finish:** At length, some peppery, seaweedy Islay phenol.

**8¼ Martine:** Not as pungent as younger versions, but retains Islay character. Lovely fruit/smoke interplay.
**Nose:** Not very intense, but enticingly perfumed. Citrus fruit. Bog myrtle. Lilac notes. Pear drops. Sooty echo mingled with brine. Gingerbread notes.
**Palate:** Well-balanced. Round and sweet with drying background smokiness. Pear poached in a minty syrup. Slightly fizzy on the tongue.
**Finish:** Sweetness, spicy lift. Smoke, cold ashes.

## FINLAGGAN 21 YEARS OLD ISLAY MALT 46%
Single Malt - Islay

**7½ Michael:** Has mellowed with the extra years, but, as is sometimes the case with island malts, it seemed happier with the vigour of youth.
**Nose:** More assertively smoky.
**Palate:** Smoother, richer, sweeter.
**Finish:** Spicier. More peppery. Seaweed more iron-like.

**7¾ Martine:** Same sweetness as the 17, but coastal aromas fade quickly. Distinct woodiness.
**Nose:** Intense, smooth. Shellfish, wet seaweed. Sea aromas soon give way to biscuity notes. Vanilla, honey, marzipan. Toasted almonds.
**Palate:** Round, velvety. Sweet mouthfeel like creamy fudge. Coconut milk. The smokiness drifts away very quickly. Becomes syrupy with water.
**Finish:** Long; drier, spicier than the 17 Years Old.

## FORMIDABLE JOCK 8 YEARS OLD 40%
Blended - Scotland

**6¾ Michael: Smooth and pleasant.**
**Nose:** Toffee. Honey. Then peat
**Palate:** Lightly smooth. Silky. Somewhat empty.
**Finish:** Lemongrass. Lemon sherbet. Quite long.

**6½ Dave: A decent enough dram, though not as formidable as the name suggests.**
**Nose:** Gold. Richer than the standard with a hint of honey, fair maltiness, hay/biscuit and some oak.
**Palate:** A silky start with plenty of ripe soft fruit. Light and slightly frotht-like butterscotch Instant Whip.
**Finish:** Medium length, quite chewy though a little hot.

## FORMIDABLE JOCK BLENDED SCOTCH WHISKY 40%
Blended - Scotland

**6 Michael: Overwhelmed by sugary sweetness.**
**Nose:** Very sweet, syrupy. Hints of burnt sugar.
**Palate:** Boiled sweets. Seaside rock.
**Finish:** Cry. Grass. Gorse.

**5½ Dave: I'm not convinced about the potential of any whisky named after a cow...(or a cliched term for a Scotsman.)**
**Nose:** Light gold. Hay, cereal, crisp nuttiness with some young grain and a light whiff of chimney smoke.
**Palate:** Starts fairly sweet then dries swiftly. Pretty thin with some peanut brittle and light fruit.
**Finish:** Short, nutty and very dry.

## FRISKY WHISKY MILROY'S 40%
Blended - Scotland

**7¼ Martine: Frisky to say the least! The palate is much more talkative and pleasant than the nose. Would be great in a granite with strawberries.**
**Nose:** Tangy, quite spirity. Water releases tender fruity notes of ripe pear. Hint of fresh oak.
**Palate:** Very fruity. Reminds me of a pear eau-de-vie. Juicy. Vanilla. Unexpectedly soft on the palate.
**Finish:** Quickly fades, a slight bitterness.

**7¼ Dave: Has firm and sweet elements but they're not linked.**
**Nose:** Young and clean. Light lemon, orange zest, cocoa, apricot. Harder edge with water (fishmonger's slab?).
**Palate:** Very citric with a smooth fruit syrup mouthfeel. Dries as it moves becoming bracken-like.
**Finish:** Dry. A little hot, even when dilute.

## GIRVAN 15 YEARS OLD, CASK 110636, OLD MASTERS 60.4%
Single Grain - Scotland

**7¾ Michael: Astonishingly full in both body and flavour for a grain whisky.**
**Nose:** Lemon grass. Banana leaves. Coconut ice-cream.
**Palate:** Big flavours. Sweet, then vegetal, then creamy, then hot. A suggestion of chilli peppers.
**Finish:** Stinging. Bring on the Thai food.

*WHISKY Recommended*

**7¾ Dave: Light and smooth and balanced. A crowd pleaser.**
**Nose:** Very soft and sweet. Some tinned pineapple, then menthol. With water there's banana, tropical fruit (passion fruit) and pear. High-toned and sweet.
**Palate:** Tightly focussed on to the front and centre of the palate. Menthol returns along with high citrus tones. Plenty of vanilla.
**Finish:** Clean and short.

## GIRVAN 16 YEARS OLD, OLD MASTERS 58%
Single Grain - Scotland

**7 Martine: Unrefined wood spoils the aromatic display. It does not leave a clean feel. A rather grumpy character.**
**Nose:** Buttery with a butyric/lactic edge. Floral (honeysuckle?) Sour fruit. Gooseberry. Sour yoghurt.
**Palate:** Oaky, far too oaky. A cardboardy tinge as well. Not very exciting.
**Finish:** Dry, with a bitter grip.

**7 Dave: A volatile, pale-faced wee dram that suddenly turns on you.**
**Nose:** Hay. A distinct cereal note, old cereal bags, hint of grappa-like twigginess, fennel. Thin.
**Palate:** Starts very soft and quiet (lemon barley water) then lashes out, snarling. Lemon juice and heat. Would give zest and energy to a blend, but lacks finesse and quality when on its own.
**Finish:** Hard cereal.

## GIRVAN 1989, BERRY'S OWN SELECTION 46%
Single Grain - Scotland

**8¾ Martine: An excellent refreshing dram. Well balanced, rich and light at the same time. Very enjoyable with chilled water.**
**Nose:** Fresh, lively, clean. A rich toffee creaminess teased by grassy and floral notes. Like breathing in a meadow field on a crisp September morning.
**Palate:** Sweet, smooth and caressing. Nutty flavours enhanced by a luscious mintiness (like minty fudges).
**Finish:** Long and dry. Clean also.

*WHISKY Recommended*

**7½ Dave: A clean session drink.**
**Nose:** Fresh, with light notes of chaff, acetone and a whiff of hot plastic. Improves no end with water: dolly mixtures, lime blossom, muscat and lots of sweet American oak.
**Palate:** Soft and gentle with a lightly fizzy quality that opens up into crisp apple and light toffee.
**Finish:** Medium. Smooth.

## GIRVAN SINGLE GRAIN 1964 48%
Single Grain - Scotland

**7½ Michael: I've always had a soft spot for this distillery's Black Barrel, and I like this version even more. Not very complex – but it is a grain whisky.**
**Nose:** Quick spiciness, then linseed and leather. Cedar. Body very rich for a grain whisky.
**Palate:** Smooth. Sweetish. Emphatic, lingering, milk chocolate. Developing a gentle, toasted-almond, dryness.
**Finish:** Firm. Soothing.

**9 Dave: Superb. Let's have more quality grain like this.**
**Nose:** Great legs. Intense and quite oily, this marries sweet and savoury beautifully. Spice galore. with soft caramelised fruit, plum/prune and treacle.
**Palate:** Elegant and smooth. A woody start then a luscious, spicy mid-palate like cinnamon buns slathered with butter.
**Finish:** Clove, all spice, cinnamon. Spicy!

## GIRVAN SINGLE GRAIN 1964 48%
Single Grain - Scotland

**8 Michael: Black Barrel with more age, more wood.**
**Nose:** Cedar. Leather. Linseed.
**Palate:** Buttery, nutty. Emphatic milk chocolate. Developing a gentle, toasted-almond dryness.
**Finish:** Firm. Soothing.

**8½ Dave: A very elegant dram which demonstrates (as do many of the others) just how great grain whisky can be.**
**Nose:** Lush with vanilla, sweet nuts and caramelised fruits: baked banana, orange, fenugreek leaves. Water brings out complex, spicy oak-derived tones; plum, coffee, butterscotch Angel Delight.
**Palate:** Rich, soft and chewy. Cream toffee, berry fruits, spiced oaky flavours.
**Finish:** Big and rounded.

## GLEN ALBYN 1965, KINGSBURY 49.1%
Single Malt - Highland

**7½ Michael: No distillery deserves to be knocked down to accommodate a strip mall, but Glen Albyn just did not have the muscle to defend itself (as Tom Wait might have put it).**
**Nose:** Oaky. Vanilla. Sweet apple. Acetyl. Pear drops. Cloves.
**Palate:** Light. Dry. Water wakes it up a little.
**Finish:** Dry herbal, clovey, slightly musty.

**9 Jim: Truly brilliant example of how an old malt should be: seriously big, full of complexity and minimum oak interference.**
**Nose:** A charming mixture of mealy malt, almost exotic fruitiness and a hint of smoke.
**Palate:** Deliciously oily and sweet with an early arrival of gentle peat and gathering spices.
**Finish:** Outstanding: with soft coffee, toffee and cocoa clinging to the waxy oak and lingering spice.

## GLEN ALBYN 1974, 28 YEARS OLD, COOPER'S CHOICE 46%
Single Malt - Highland

**7½ Michael: Fuller in flavours, and sweeter, than I remember Glen Albyn.**
**Nose:** Smoke. Char. Earthy. Rose bay willow herb.
**Palate:** The floweriness of Glen Albyn is dominated by musty cellar character. There is a fine line between Maderisation, positive oxidation, and stainless.
**Finish:** Just when I was swinging into criticism, the whisky emerged fresh, sweet, lively and delicious. Calvados? Coffee pralines. Mint creams.

**7¼ Dave: Attractive.**
**Nose:** Quite light and pleasant: toasted nut, dried grass, sandalwood.
**Palate:** Attractive but not a mouth filler, instead it runs down the middle of the tongue. Well balanced though with spice, soft sweet fruit and a little toffee.
**Finish:** Short.

## GLEN CALDER, GORDON & MACPHAIL 40%
Blended - Scotland

**7½ Martine: On the sweet side, although the finish brings out a more assertive note. A good winter warmer.**
**Nose:** Sweet and fragrant. Demerara sugar. Melon. Grapefruit. A touch exotic fruit. Pineapple. Then develops on fresh oak and cedar.
**Palate:** Mellow. Velvety. Releases more wood notes than on the nose. Resin.
**Finish:** A little biting. Long. After Eight mint chocolate.

**7½ Dave: A delicious rounded session blend.**
**Nose:** Creamily sweet and lush. Bread and butter pudding, grass/straw, custard Tokaji, clootie dumpling. Good grain notes.
**Palate:** Slick and soft, well matured. Spices, peach and a touch of almost burnt treacle underneath. Soft, toffee-ed.
**Finish:** Nutty, chocolate.

## GLEN DARBACH 12 YEARS OLD 40%
Single Malt - Speyside

**7¼ Michael: Approachable – even amiable – but with some substance. Wintery flavours that are warming without being challenging.**
**Nose:** A hint of fruit (apricot?), then creamy, with some peaty dryness. Appetising. Fresh.
**Palate:** Lightly fudgy and nutty.
**Finish:** A late balancing dryness and a surprising surge of spiciness. Reminiscent of cinnamon, then gingery.

**7½ Dave: Well-made, attractive. Lacks complexity but a decent dram.**
**Nose:** Fruity and lightly honeyed. A mix of butterscotch, fruit scone, heather, hazelnut with a wisp of smoke. Slight greenish note.
**Palate:** Light to medium bodied that starts with spices and orange peel then some honeyed fruit and a little smoke.
**Finish:** Dry and biscuity.

## GLEN DEVERON 10 YEARS OLD 40%
Single Malt - Speyside

**6 Martine: Too monolithic. No variety. The nose opens up after a while though.**
**Nose:** Intense. Wood dominates. Resin. Sawdust. Overripe pear, hazelnut.
**Palate:** Firm, assertive malty notes. A touch of orange peel but not much to deliver.
**Finish:** Did you say finish? It vanishes in a flash.

**7 Dave: Decent run-of-the-mill style.**
**Nose:** Very malty (malt loaf spread thickly with butter) with a slightly slick caramel/peanut brittle note. Water brings out floor wax and honey.
**Palate:** Juicy red grapes to start then it's nuts (yet again!), some spice. Soft and slightly sweet mid-palate.
**Finish:** A little short.

## GLEN DEVERON 1987, 10 YEARS OLD 40%
Single Malt - Speyside

**7½ Michael: Slightly less richness and wood-extract than in the 12, with which I am more familiar.**
**Nose:** Appetisingly fresh, both in its characteristic maltiness and its faint peat.
**Palate:** Creamy. Condensed milk. Horlicks. Malt.
**Finish:** Nice balance of estery, lemony fruitiness and a drying touch of peat.

**6½ Jim: I am sure this is a wood problem: nearly two full marks down on its score from three years ago. What a massive disappointment.**
**Nose:** Disappointingly closed and missing that rich, slightly honeyed magic of old. A dull oakiness is OTT.
**Palate:** Closer to its lovely old self, but still clouded by a chalky oakiness which dulls the richer, ultra-malty, notes.
**Finish:** Still out of sync. The oak seems to contain something too austere.

## GLEN ELGIN 19 YEARS OLD, CENTENARY BOTTLING 60%
Single Malt - Speyside

**8¼ Michael: For me, the classic example of Speyside heather-honey character. A beautifully rounded, characterful, elegant, whisky.** *WHISKY Magazine Recommended*
**Nose:** Flowery heather-honey, with spicy, creamy notes.
**Palate:** Very long. Lots of honey. Flowery. Orange blossom. Seville orange. A hint of cloves. Pepper.
**Finish:** Fragrant. Delicate smokiness.

**8¾ Dave: One of the great ignored classics of Speyside.**
**Nose:** Generous and rich: stewed peach/apricot, honey, heather, moist buttered sultana cake, some sulphur/burnt matches and even some smoke.
**Palate:** Medium to full-bodied. Ripe, sweet fruits with excellent honeyed concentration which slowly becomes nuttier and a little smoky. Big and powerful with great balance.
**Finish:** Liquorice and vanilla.

## GLEN ELGIN 1975, BERRY'S OWN SELECTION 46%
Single Malt - Speyside

**8½ Michael: By today's standards, an unusually peaty Speysider.** *WHISKY Magazine Recommended*
**Nose:** Brassy.

**Palate:** Lightly peaty smokiness.
**Finish:** Dry maltiness. Toasty. Some phenol.

**7½ Dave: Visions of cowled monks. It is Lent I suppose.**
**Nose:** Malty with dusty oak and a whiff of barley sugar then sacking, cinders and smoke.
**Palate:** A smoky start, wood embers, dried fruits behind. The sacking cloaks the sweet fruit.
**Finish:** Dry.

## GLEN ELGIN 32 YEARS OLD 58.3%
Single Malt - Speyside

**8¼ Michael: A lovely example of a honeyish Speyside whisky.** *WHISKY Magazine Recommended*
**Nose:** Fragrant. Cedary. Honeyed. Seductive.
**Palate:** Soft, rich, tongue-coating. Clean, sweet. A hint of Seville orange. Intense heather-honey. Cereal-grain. Crunchy.
**Finish:** Gently drying. Shortbread.

**8¾ Dave: A classic from one of Speyside's forgotten greats.**
**Nose:** Mature, elegant and complex. Rancio, mulch, toasty wood, hazelnut, mango, black cherry, clootie dumpling, light smoke.
**Palate:** Fragrant but pretty firm. Needs water to soften the oak and reveal peach, chestnut honey, dried fruit and a hint of smoke. Balanced.
**Finish:** Cocoa, beech nut. Cognac like.

## GLEN FLAGLER 1973 46%
Single Malt - Lowland

**7 Michael: Better than it sounds. Rather odd, but I liked it. With cheese?**
**Nose:** Pronounced aroma of new leather. Floral.
**Palate:** Light, slippery. Oily, creamy. Smoked cheese.
**Finish:** Dry. Strong, muscular.

**7½ Dave: And another one bites the dust. Shame to see it go.**
**Nose:** Light and toasty with notes of fizzy orange drink, as well as some malt and floral notes.
**Palate:** Gentle and nutty. Fine boned with decent grip.
**Finish:** Medium length. Nutty.

## GLEN GARIOCH 10 YEARS OLD 40%
Single Malt - Highland

**7¾ Michael: I have always enjoyed Glen Garioch as one of the few peaty whiskies still made in the Highlands. I hope this peaty character does not totally vanish.**
**Nose:** Flowery. Roses. Darjeeling tea. Peat.
**Palate:** Firm maltiness. Cake-like. Slightly honeyed.
**Finish:** Surge of spiciness. White pepper.

**7¼ Dave: An everyday, mid-weight malt.**
**Nose:** Clean, cereal-dominated nose: nutty wholemeal toast with some butter. In time a soft toffee note/apple sponge. Water crisps it up. Fresh and quite light.
**Palate:** Soft and mealy with pleasant light tangerine notes. Clean. Medium dry.
**Finish:** Light, clean. Floury.

## GLEN GARIOCH 12 YEARS OLD, NATIONAL TRUST FOR SCOTLAND BOTTLING 47.4%
Single Malt - Highland

**7¾ Michael: Approachable and enjoyable, but a little mild-mannered for me. Bring back the peat … please!**
**Nose:** Earthy. The aroma of the maltings. Toasty. Brown sugar.
**Palate:** Nutty. Sweet. Cereal grain. Slightly grassy.
**Finish:** Gently silky dryness.

**7½ Dave: The nicest GG I've tried for a while. Very, very drinkable.**
**Nose:** Straight-ahead and malty: white pudding, malt bins, turned earth, dried grasses, orange. Mouth watering.
**Palate:** Light, clean and malty with a soft juicy texture. Orange opal fruits and light spice.
**Finish:** Clean and fairly short.

## GLEN GARIOCH 14 YEARS OLD, SIGNATORY 50%
Single Malt - Highland

**7¼ Martine: The cask was too tired to give roundness to that elegantly grassy malt. Alcohol needs to be tamed by water but still …**
**Nose:** Prickly, even a bit spirity. Herbal, yellow Chartreuse. Angelica, lemon balm, star anis. Develops delicate pudding notes. Vanilla custard.

**Palate:** Surprisingly sweet. Very herbal. Verbena, lime tea. With a citrus appetising freshness.
**Finish:** Drier than at start. Slightly spicy and fizzy.

**7 Dave: Has better weight than the Bladnoch.**
**Nose:** White fruits clean and floral with touches of jasmine. Water shows a hard oak note before everything collapses.
**Palate:** Another very delicate dram. Apple blossom.
**Finish:** Clean. Very light, floral.

## GLEN GARIOCH 15 YEARS OLD 43%
Single Malt - Highland

**8 Michael: Less robust, more rounded. It is one of those choices that depends on the mood.**
**Nose:** Incense-like. Perfumy. Parma violets. Heather.
**Palate:** Quite rich. Starts malty, but becomes drier. More spicy. Spanish root. The flavour just keeps on developing.
**Finish:** More emphatic spiciness and peat.

**6¾ Jim: Disappointing, with one or two delicious moments.**
**Nose:** Slightly salty, a sprinkling of smoke, mint, sage and other herbal notes. Not harmonious or attractive.
**Palate:** Sweet arrival of peated malt and then becomes hot, jagged, yet somewhat unbalanced and thin.
**Finish:** A thick layer of peat and pepperiness softens the earlier blow. A biscuity maltiness adds charm, but it's a bit too late.

## GLEN GARIOCH 15 YEARS OLD, MWBH 52.3%
Single Malt - Highland

**8 Michael: A refreshing young whisky that would make a great aperitif when neat, or mixed in a classic Manhattan.**
**Nose:** Young and spirity. Faintly citric freshness above a malty, biscuity base.
**Palate:** Crisp. Sweet. Minty.
**Finish:** Eucalyptus. Fresh and appetising.

**6¾ Arthur: I was put off by that sour/acidic vinegar note that seemed like a clear fault.**
**Nose:** Estery, with melon, pear drops and ripe bananas. Meadow flower, varnish and something lightly chemical (sorry, couldn't put my finger on it). With water it turns like hot, dusty radiators, and turned a little acidic with a distinct whiff of vinegar.
**Palate:** Fruity, slightly peaty and woody. A little thin.
**Finish:** More woody bitterness.

## GLEN GARIOCH 18 YEARS OLD, OLD MASTERS 53.9%
Single Malt - Highland

**8¾ Martine: A rich aromatic profile and a soft texture give that whisky a sensuous feel. The perfect after dinner dram to enjoy a moment of calm and of solitude maybe …**
**Nose:** Intense. Lovely fragrances of freshly baked pastries. Very fruity. Apple cake. Sweet cider. Fresh hazelnuts. Coconut sherbet.
**Palate:** Almost syrupy. Lively and fresh. In total harmony with the nose. Fruit, fruit, fruit …
**Finish:** Drying out on ginger and cinnamon.

**8 Dave: Real weight and character.**
**Nose:** Dry. Burnt toast crumbs then some crème brûlée notes followed by orange and baked fruits. Sweet with some nutmeg. Water turns it into a spice cupboard fairly exotic with pot pourri. Dry.
**Palate:** Sandalwood, incense. Very perfumed in a slightly oily fashion shifting to light leather bruised peach green walnut. Good presence.
**Finish:** Long, fruity.

## GLEN GARIOCH 1968, 29 YEARS OLD 56.3%
Single Malt - Highland

**8 Michael: With its chestnut colour and highly distinctive flavours, this is a wonderfully wintery whisky.**
**Nose:** Smoky. Charred Oak. Earthy saltiness. Peat.
**Palate:** Black and white mint humbugs. Pronounced black treacle. Molasses. Pepper.
**Finish:** Cough sweets. Chlorodyne.

**9¼ Jim: A monster of a malt, fully underlining what truly magnificent distillery this once was when the peating levels were traditional and unrestrained.**
**Nose:** Enormous battle between the fattest, cleanest juiciest sherry you can imagine and chunky peat.
**Palate:** Every bit as mouth filling and chewy as the nose suggest.
**Finish:** Ladles of molten chocolate and sweet peat plus cherries and vanilla.

## GLEN GARIOCH 1979, 24 YEARS OLD 52.1%
Single Malt - Highland

**8¾ Gavin: Some Glen Garioch are sometimes dismissed on account of their 'tartan and stag' packaging, but this is a serious whisky and deserves to be treated as such.**
**Nose:** Scented, violets and plums. Soft and gentle.
**Palate:** Heather and toffee, oaky notes well held in the background by a complex floral and honey combination.
**Finish:** The honey lingers well, and there are a few negative signs of age from the wood.

**7½ Dave: A great nose, but let down on the palate.**
**Nose:** Exotic. Olde English marmalade, allspice, fresh grated nutmeg (spiced rum?). With water there's macaroon bars and afterdinner mints.
**Palate:** Perfumed attack, then the aromatics become slightly artificial and essence like. Mint and lavender again. Essential oil.
**Finish:** Perfumed. Some smoke.

## GLEN GARIOCH 1985, 16 YEARS OLD, SHERRY BUTT 51.9%
Single Malt - Highland

**8 Michael: I have always had a quiet fancy for this malt. It has a lot character: demonstrated here in the way it stands up to such heavy sherry.**
**Nose:** Assertive, rounded, appetising, smokiness. Some maltiness, reminiscent of Darjeeling tea.
**Palate:** Silky-smooth treacle toffee.
**Finish:** Chewy. Rooty. Anis. Liquorice.

**6 Dave: Robust but the cask is in charge.**
**Nose:** Dates, treacle, leather, fruit cake, smoke and a perfumed note.
**Palate:** That perfumed character runs against the figgy, rich spirit unbalancing the whisky.
**Finish:** Smoky. Dry and slightly tannic.

## GLEN GARIOCH 1986 54.4%
Single Malt - Highland

**8 Michael: A big, robust whisky from the days when Glen Garioch made its own peated malt. I love the idea of a smoky whisky from the edge of Speyside, but I find this slightly astringent.**
**Nose:** Forest floor. Rooty. Sappy. Brown sugar.
**Palate:** Lightly creamy. Nutty. Slightly bitter.
**Finish:** Robust. Smoky. A hint of ash.

**7½ Dave: It has weight, but it just lacks balance.**
**Nose:** Another with big cask influence – dunnage warehouse, varnish, black pepper, treacle, liquorice, dried fruits and smoke (smoked cheese?). A big boy.
**Palate:** Those big, rich, fruity, figgy, raisined flavours dominate, then comes a light perfumed note that just knocks the balance a bit.
**Finish:** Dry, smoky.

## GLEN GARIOCH 1988, 16 YEARS OLD, DUNCAN TAYLOR 56.1%
Single Malt - Highland

**8¼ Michael: Very sweet but the classic heather honey is balanced by the gently peaty, smoky dryness that has vanished from most Highland malts.**
**Nose:** Slight smokiness. Beeswax. Honey. Floral. Heathery.
**Palate:** Honey cake. Ginger. Spicy complexity.
**Finish:** Long. Gently warming. Lemony dryness. Rounded with a hint of peat.

**8¼ Marcin: Great balance and brilliantly structured. More please.**
**Nose:** Very rounded and attractive. Warm enveloping custard. Créme anglais. Smells like whisky!
**Palate:** Bursts into life. Still assertive, still attacking. Tastes like whisky!
**Finish:** Long and very bright. Consistent. Repeat to fade.

## GLEN GARIOCH 1988, 18 YEARS OLD, OLD MASTERS 53.9%
Single Malt - Highland

**8¼ Dave: A big warming dram whose generosity of flavour comes as a relief after a couple of meanies.**
**Nose:** Slightly muted with light cereal, trail mix, energy bar and dried cherry. Rounded and moving into maturity. Shows complexity.
**Palate:** A gentle, subtle smoked paprika flavour along with jammy fruit, then musky shiitake funkiness.
**Finish:** Touch of pine with a little bitterness.

**7½ Arthur: Elements of many of the flavour groups creates a balanced, Highland-style malt.**
**Nose:** Cherry liqueur, hay, grappa, and some sour fruitiness. A smoking gun barrel. Some floral mossiness and a little damp peat.
**Palate:** Stewed fruits and raisins, and more of that moss.
**Finish:** A gentle bitterness.

## GLEN GARIOCH 1988, DUNCAN TAYLOR 54.6%
Single Malt - Highland

WHISKY
Editor's choice

**8½ Dave: Has the X factor.**
**Nose:** Complex mix of ripe peachy fruit, baked banana, fruit smoothie, orange peel/blossom. Light nuttiness/malt, cream. Water adds weight and brings out extra maturity and depth.
**Palate:** Rich with good impact, slightly dry, then tingling spices. Heavy and quite explosive. Once again, it deepens (and dries slightly) with water.
**Finish:** Long, rich, cooked peach.

**8¾ Arthur: Right in so many ways: balanced but stimulating, challenging but comforting. It reminded me of Clynelish.**
**Nose:** Fizzy orangeness, steamed apple pudding, furniture polish, sherbert and mixed peel. Comb honey, fresh and perfectly ripe pears.
**Palate:** Complex.
**Finish:** Christmas pudding with flaming alcohol, and burnt twigs.

## GLEN GARIOCH 21 YEARS OLD 43%
Single Malt - Highland

**8 Michael: A very sophisticated bottling. Perfect after a fine dinner.**
**Nose:** Fresh leather. Attractive blend of sherry and peat.
**Palate:** Creamier. Raisiny. At this stage the sherry seems to find common cause with sweet, juicy oak. The peat emerges when water is added.
**Finish:** Teasing. Smoky, smooth.

**8 Jim: A lovely malt more delicious for its effect than its complexity.**
**Nose:** Surprisingly etheric for a malt this age with a peculiar plasticene like waxiness. A light brushing of smoke balances the vanilla.
**Palate:** Big, fat start with an oily peatiness undulating in intensity as a leathery, beeswax like maltiness offers a wonderfully restrained sweetness.
**Finish:** Lengthy, a build up of vanilla tapers the dryness.

## GLEN GARIOCH 21 YEARS OLD 43%
Single Malt - Highland

**8 Michael: A reminder that a distillery with its own maltings gains a layer of character. So long as the maltings is working.**
**Nose:** Sun-scorched grass. A hint of peat. Fragrant.
**Palate:** Surprisingly fat. Sweet, clean, cereal grain maltiness. Slightly syrupy. Developing minty notes. Peppermint patties.
**Finish:** Strong. Some phenol. Slight bitterness.

**6¾ Dave: Did someone throw a bunch of dried lavender in the kiln? There's something about this intense fragrance in old Glen Gariochs which spoils the balance for me.**
**Nose:** Minty! Quite smoky with clean malt, an earthy aroma. An intense heather/lavender lift. This highly-scented smoke intensifies with water. And time.
**Palate:** The perfumed smoke emerges fairly quickly. It's sweet but there's something unbalanced about it.
**Finish:** Oak grips slightly.

## GLEN GARIOCH 35 YEARS OLD, OLD & RARE PLATINUM 56%
Single Malt - Highland

WHISKY
Recommended

**9 Gavin: This has lasted superbly for its age, proof that Glen Garioch is a seriously impressive malt, one that improves with lengthy maturation.**
**Nose:** Floral, scented, Lily of the Valley, with some tinned peaches and a whiff of smoke when reduced.
**Palate:** Initially very sweet, some delicate peat and marmalade. The complexity develops. Big and firm.
**Finish:** Dries steadily, but the oak is well in check here.

**8¼ Dave: Old brocade, velvet curtains, tweed.**
**Nose:** Mature with good intensity. Slightly fungal, leaf mulch, hessian, powdered nut, old apricots, chestnut mushroom, peat smoke, treacle toffee, old cupboards.
**Palate:** Slightly earthy. Rum and raisin, with a hazelnut shell character acting like a filter for the softer more liquorous elements. Balanced.
**Finish:** Peat smoke comes through, giving extra depth.

## GLEN GARIOCH 8 YEARS OLD 40%
Single Malt - Highland

**7¾ Michael: I love the peaty, burnt notes notes in this robustly malty whisky.**
**Nose:** Autumn leaves. Grass. Peat smoke.
**Palate:** Picnic flapjack, slightly burnt at the edges. Nutty. Gingery. Lively flavours.
**Finish:** Honey. Cream. Some peat.

**8¾ Jim: Easily one of the best 8 Years Old on the market: very, very impressive and enjoyable.**
**Nose:** Light, despite a charming smokiness. Incredibly clean. A soft citric background reveals young age.
**Palate:** Intensely malty, fresh with increasing sweetness as the kippery peatiness gathers.
**Finish:** Echoing smoke and a delicious build up of cocoa notes. Long. Toasty. Highly satisfying with almost perfect bittersweet balance.

## GLEN GARIOCH, DEWAR RATTRAY 52.5%
Single Malt - Highland

**8 Dave: A quirky little number. Well worth a look.**
**Nose:** It's green! It might be the colour, but there's a green olive brine/feta cheese note alongside creosote covered twine. Minty oily with some smoke.
**Palate:** Improves on the palate, oily and rich with fair grip. There's light coal smoke and the cheesy note doesn't intrude. Good length and balance.
**Finish:** Juniper and little smoke.

**6 Martine: That baby needed to be cradled in oak a few more years. It can hardly mutter a few aromas. Or is it just a maturation in a tired cask?**
**Nose:** Spirity. Seems very young. Grassy. Freshly cut lawn. Lemon grass.
**Palate:** Sweet with a cheesy back note.
**Finish:** Tangy, not revealing much.

## GLEN GRANT 12 YEARS OLD WINE FINISH, OLD MALT CASK 50%
Single Malt - Speyside

**6 Dave: Seems cobbled together.**
**Nose:** An odd pewter-like colour. Light to the point of neutrality. Asparagus, grass and green apple.
**Palate:** The grassiness continues then is abruptly replaced by a confected rosehip syrup note. A garden centre in the rain.
**Finish:** Fades but with a slight greasy quality.

**7½ Arthur: Very light, easy going dram, slips down easy enough.**
**Nose:** Gala melon, wheat, some floral notes and some Satsuma pith. A light meaty note was present, but was not enough to put you off.
**Palate:** Sweet and fruity in a peach slice kind of way. Vanilla.
**Finish:** Light sweetness.

## GLEN GRANT 14 YEARS OLD, CASK STRENGTH 55.3%
Single Malt - Speyside

**8 Martine: A midsummer's night dream dram. So delicate, so rich but without ostentation.**
**Nose:** Delicately perfumey. Herbal and floral. Dry hay. Orange honey. Grapefruit. Cinnamon.

**Palate:** Light bodied. Silky and sweet. Perfectly balanced.
**Finish:** Long and whispering on sweet malty notes. Almond milk.

7½ **Dave: Pleasant enough but a little hollow and lacking in complexity.**
**Nose:** Firm and quite light. Dry grasses, coal dust. Slightly metallic. Malt bins.
**Palate:** Clean, sweet and attractive. Fibre (bran, rather than moral), toasted cereal. Attractive.
**Finish:** Light. Sweet.

### GLEN GRANT 1948, GORDON & MACPHAIL 40%
Single Malt - Speyside

WHISKY Magazine Recommended

8½ **Dave: 1948? Amazing. Has retained a refined almost raffish air and though frail is not overwooded.**
**Nose:** Whisky rancio to the fore: mints, furniture polish, and a powdery fragrance and behind some sooty smoke. Ethereal. Needs time to open.
**Palate:** Mature, but has intensity, a lively prickle. Slightly feral, nutty, and elegant. Do not water.
**Finish:** Short and ever so slightly smoky.

8½ **Arthur: A little too drying and old on the palate for me, but that bouquet was absolutely stunning.**
**Nose:** Musty boxes, and a luxurious and rich explosion of fruits. Undercurrents of varnish and a chestnut nuttiness too.
**Palate:** Tinned peaches, apricots and dark chocolate. This complexity is spanked into touch with a lot of wood character, and a little creosote.
**Finish:** Bitter woodiness and star anise spice.

### GLEN GRANT 1964, LOMBARD 46%
Single Malt - Speyside

8 **Michael: I usually find delicate old Glen Grants to be overwhelmed by oak. This example makes for a mature dram with considerable complexity.**
**Nose:** Winey. Treacle toffee.
**Palate:** Despite hefty oak and sherry, the distillery character survives. The characteristic hazelnut dryness extends into a maltiness reminiscent of hard cookies. Like drinking a Bath Oliver biscuit.
**Finish:** Some cedary oak.

7¾ **Dave: Interesting and while not overly woody (given its age) one for sherried malt lovers only.**
**Nose:** Oily, dried fruits, hint of rancio and Marmite. Burnt orange, allspice, nutmeg and clove.
**Palate:** Soft start builds nicely good weight. Rich and sherried, tannic but a chocolate/coffee richness and depth to it.
**Finish:** Woody and a bit short.

### GLEN GRANT 1968, GORDON & MACPHAIL 40%
Single Malt - Speyside

WHISKY Magazine Recommended

7¾ **Dave: A ghost-like dram almost too elusive to grasp.**
**Nose:** Very light and scented. Citrus, beeswax, coconut powder, coumarin/herbs/pot pourri. Barely seems anchored.
**Palate:** Fragrant, floral and delicate. Rather fragile and slightly thinner than 16.
**Finish:** Smoke.

8¾ **Arthur: Another nose that produces involuntary smugness.**
**Nose:** Lots of ripe fruits: banana, kiwi, pink grapefruit and melon. Cutting through this are other notes of grappa, sappy wood, fennel and tomato stalks.
**Palate:** Sweet peach, a little peat and sweet vanilla.
**Finish:** Grapefruit and drying woodiness.

### GLEN GRANT 1969, ADELPHI 52.9%
Single Malt - Speyside

WHISKY Magazine Recommended

7¾ **Michael: Holds up very well in the middle but the woodiness at the end is overpowering.**
**Nose:** Fudge. Raisins. Toasted nuts. Soft peatiness.
**Palate:** Smooth. Juicy oak. Richly nutty. Caramel.
**Finish:** Peat and woodiness combine in a very bitter departure. Somewhat astringent.

9¼ **Jim: Clean, complex and complete. Brilliant.**
**Nose:** Big, big sherry. Bursting with grape and cherry.
**Palate:** Richest, cleanest and naturally sweetest arrival of sherry notes you could ever encounter.
**Finish:** A dash of fresh malt and honeycomb keeps the vanilla in check.

### GLEN GRANT 1969, ADELPHI 53.9%
Single Malt - Speyside

7¾ **Michael: Glen Grant is a delicate whisky and does not always benefit from long maturation. This bottling is on the cusp. The distillery character can still be discerned, but only just.**
**Nose:** Peaty. I could almost smell the burn that flows through the distillery garden.
**Palate:** Syrupy. Surprisingly big and malty. Nutty. Dry toffee. A hint of liquorice. Rooty. Slight astringency.
**Finish:** Firm, peaty.

9¼ **Jim: The best Glen Grant of the last 20 years? Unquestionably. Near prefect stuff to the old school.**
**Nose:** The subtlest hint of medium roast Kenyan coffee and intertwines beautifully with the thick sherry.
**Palate:** Glorious array of sweet, demerara-style toffee sugars. Silky sherry and busy peppers, panning out into a raging sea of malty complexity.
**Finish:** Soft yet enormously long and playful.

### GLEN GRANT 1969, MURRAY MCDAVID MISSION II 46%
Single Malt - Speyside

7¾ **Michael: This delicate malt in unusually full flavour.**
**Nose:** New leather. Pigskin.
**Palate:** Slightly oily. Roast pork. Red apples. Hazelnuts.
**Finish:** Char. Oak.

8½ **Dave: Evidence of this still's ability to age superbly well.**
**Nose:** Very perfumed. Turkish delight, wood oils, leather, pine forest. With water: amaretto, dried flowers, orange peel. Complex.
**Palate:** Good weight and firm structure with an interesting sooty note. Allspice, orange pekoe tea and dry nuts. Very good balance.
**Finish:** Strawberry and marzipan.

### GLEN GRANT 1970, 27 YEARS OLD, CASK 7638, ADELPHI 56.9%
Single Malt - Speyside

8 **Michael: Enough character and complexity to withstand the heavy oakiness, but beginning to show its age.**
**Nose:** Hazelnuts. The skin of the nut. Papery. Toasty.
**Palate:** Smooth as polished oak. Treacle-toffee. Walnuts.
**Finish:** Sappy. Slightly sour.

6½ **Dave: A lot of wood...a lot of sherry wood but not a lot of Glen Grant.**
**Nose:** Treacle and molasses, almost fungal. Nut bowl, leather and bitter chocolate, even cold tea.
**Palate:** Thick to start then increasingly bitter and tannic.
**Finish:** Dry and bitter.

### GLEN GRANT 1970, 31 YEARS OLD, CASK 1036, ADELPHI 55.4%
Single Malt - Speyside

8¼ **Michael: The better balanced of these two Glen Grants. The more integrated flavours. Seems to have matured better.**
**Nose:** Peat fires.
**Palate:** Smooth. Estery. Cooked morello cherries. A hint of creamy nougat. Nutty. Late spiciness.
**Finish:** Smoky. Peaty.

7 **Dave: Old, venerable even, but only of historical interest.**
**Nose:** Oloroso wood with some fragrant/nutty notes some heavily roasted coriander/cumin seed, coffee and treacle. Water brings out chocolate, singed wool and walnut whip.
**Palate:** Chocolatey, tannic and smoky.
**Finish:** Dry and slightly bitter from wood tannins.

## GLEN GRANT 1970, SPEYSIDE REGION SELECTION NO 2, DUNCAN TAYLOR 51.7%
Single Malt - Speyside

**7¾ Dave: A lot of cask here but strangely subtle for such a heavy beast.**
**Nose:** High cask influence: walnut whip, caramelised fruit sugars, ginger buns, woodsmoke. Deep, resinous with clove and a little cardamom.
**Palate:** Immediate tannic grip with quite substantial spirit cutting through the oak: fungal, dark chocolate, chestnut purée. Not too tannic.
**Finish:** Ripe, old, cassis.

**7¼ Arthur: Too woody for me, but some people will adore its obvious 'old-ness'.**
**Nose:** Earthy mossiness and a fruit; oranges or raisins. Liquorice bark and furniture polish. Pine and some mustiness.
**Palate:** Viscous then drying. Some cognac-like fruitiness and aniseed.
**Finish:** Tannins by the ton. Tree bark.

## GLEN GRANT 1972, 29 YEARS OLD SHERRYWOOD, HART BROTHERS 53.6%
Single Malt - Speyside

**7¾ Michael: Glen Grant was one of the first malts to be bottled as a single malt, in the days when light-tasting spirits were often filled into heavy sherry casks. I have always felt that this overwhelms the spirit. This example is better balanced than most.**
**Nose:** Dates. Brown sugar. Caramel.
**Palate:** Rich. Smooth. Moist fruitcake, slightly burnt on the outside.
**Finish:** Slight woody bitterness.

**8 Dave: Here's a rarity: an old Glen Grant in which the spirit hasn't been drowned by the cask.**
**Nose:** Heady with an exotic lift. Chocolate, walnut whip, roasted nut. Oaky, but has some style. Water shows nutty, sherried notes.
**Palate:** A good weight of spirit. Rich and malty with a hint of soot. Pretty thick in the mouth and quite firm in structure. A complex range of flavours.
**Finish:** Dry and maybe just a little short.

## GLEN GRANT 1972, 33 YEARS OLD, BERRY'S OWN SELECTION 46%
Single Malt - Speyside

**7½ Dave: After a nose that can only be described as "hairy" it rather loses focus.**
**Nose:** Forceful and pungent. Fresh fruits. Seems to have good age and a certain exoticism. Water accentuates this sandalwood note.
**Palate:** Great intensity of flavour and pretty hot without water, the addition of which calms things, shows some nuttiness but also exposing a little too much grippy wood. Lacks flavour impact.
**Finish:** A little nutty bitterness.

**8 Arthur: The oak borders on intrusive at times, but just managed to restrain itself.**
**Nose:** Mandarin, varnished oak and marzipan. Chocolate orange and some pear. With a little time some musty, damp vegetation notes appear which are not unpleasant. Mint toffee too.
**Palate:** Lots of orange, milk chocolate and some sappy oak. The texture begins sweet and syrupy but is quickly dried out by the wood.
**Finish:** Mouth-drying, slightly astringent oakiness.

## GLEN GRANT 1972, BERRY'S OWN SELECTION 51%
Single Malt - Speyside

**8 Martine: A well matured and well balanced malt. The sherry notes tend to muzzle the distillery character. An iron hand in a velvet glove!**
**Nose:** A generous sherry character. Crème brûlée. Amaretto. Rhubarb jam. Quite an exotic profile. Sandalwood, vetiver.
**Palate:** Sweet mellow toffee.
**Finish:** Muscular. Cinnamon, liquorice.

**8 Dave: Brooding and slow to develop. Classic European oak but the spirit has enough weight to cope with the chunky wood.**
**Nose:** Deep and powerful. Burnt raisin and cinnamon. Date loaf, dried fig.
**Palate:** Leathery and deep, fine tannins and light meatiness. Savoury and intense. Chicory, rose.
**Finish:** Coffee bean.

## GLEN GRANT 1976, SIGNATORY 58.2%
Single Malt - Speyside

**9 Martine: So like an armagnac. Sherry at its best. At its peak. Why not with foie gras and a fig compote?**
**Nose:** Complex, rich, opulent. Prunes, ceder, Vanilla burnt caramel, liquorice, rancio.
**Palate:** Sweet Oloroso. Sultanas, toasted walnuts, dark chocolate. Lusciously sophisticated flavours. Please, no water!
**Finish:** Teasing, enveloping, lingering.

**8 Dave: Extremely well balanced for such a venerable creature. Still, you have to love sherried malts to love this.**
**Nose:** Big, sherried nose: chocolate, charred fruits, that exotic rancio note, prune, beech, but cracked pepper, even some red berries, and a hint of smoke.
**Palate:** Fairly dry and slightly tannic, bitter chocolate and nuts. Like a palo cortado in intensity. Attractive floral notes save it from being swamped by sherry.
**Finish:** Dry, nutty with a bit of smoke.

## GLEN GRANT 1977 27 YEARS OLD, SHERRY CASK, COOPER'S CHOICE 46%
Single Malt - Speyside

**8¼ Michael: A Speysider with a rich chestnut colour, plenty of aroma and lots of flavour. Makes a change from the dumbed-down and the terminally delicate.**
**Nose:** Polished oak.
**Palate:** Malty. Darjeeling tea. Leafy. Tobacco.
**Finish:** Liquorice. Cough sweets. Assertive spiciness.

**7¾ Dave: Fascinating, but the oak is having the greater say.**
**Nose:** Quite deep with oxidised notes. Dark chocolate, prune, black fruits, black cherry, walnut, polished leather, autumn earth.
**Palate:** Medium-bodied. Soft start but grips quite early showing real figgy age. Tannins begin to clamp down.
**Finish:** Dry, tannic.

## GLEN GRANT 1985 19 YEARS OLD, DEWAR RATTRAY 58.4%
Single Malt - Speyside

**7½ Martine: A definite sharpness which hides a sweeter character. Water does not help much, enhancing the pepperiness. For those who like it hot.**
**Nose:** Assertive, intense. A bit spirity. Citrus fruit salad with mint. Nutmeg and cinnamon.
**Palate:** Velvety, unctuous at start. A spicy outburst tones down the fruit. Black pepper; oak shines through.
**Finish:** Tangy, spicy. A nutty hint.

**8½ Dave: Voluptuous. A big bruiser at the perfect point of integration.**
**Nose:** Concentrated. Some mash tun notes to start, sooty phenols and a hint of sulphur. Allow it to open and it picks up: deck oil/resin, mixed nuts, dried fruit, dried plum but also key lime pie.
**Palate:** Very rich, sweet and caramelised. Flows well on the palate with light dry-roasted spices, dried fruits, burnt sugar, raisin.
**Finish:** Tingling, long, good.

## GLEN GRANT 1988, 15 YEARS OLD, PORTWOOD, COOPER'S CHOICE 46%
Single Malt - Speyside

**8 Michael: The delicacy of the Glen Grant survives here.**
**Nose:** Hints of winey fruit.
**Palate:** Hazelnut. Good flavour development. Nutty, marshmallow, toffee, cookie-like maltiness.
**Finish:** A hint of coconut. Elusive spiciness (nutmeg perhaps?).

**6¾ Dave: The port is trying to give this some life, but ends up dominating.**
**Nose:** Perfumed (almost artificially so): pot pourri, strawberry chews. Flattens with water, also rings out a cereal character.
**Palate:** Dry, almost papery feel, sweetened by the berries in the middle of the palate.
**Finish:** Sweet and winey.

## GLEN GRANT 31 YEARS OLD, DUNCAN TAYLOR 42.4%
Single Malt - Speyside

**6¾ Michael: A reticent nose is completely eclipsed by a huge but uncomplicated palate. Benefits greatly from water.**

**Nose:** Has to be coaxed out, but eventually ripe red apples, followed by gentle red fruit tartness.
**Palate:** Assaults the palate. Creamy but bitter. Everton mints. Sweeter with water. Popcorn?
**Finish:** Oily, alcoholic, with fennel or even aniseed notes. Slightly phenolic with water.

**8¾ Arthur: A typical and classic aged Speyside, which still has balance between spirit and wood.**
**Nose:** Fruity, with apples and fresh peaches. Something vaguely minty, like Mojo sweets or mint toffees. Grassy, with vanilla in the background too.
**Palate:** Was expecting more sweetness, but there is a balancing bitterness along with the toffee, mint and grass.
**Finish:** Brown toast and biscuits.

### GLEN GRANT 31 YEARS OLD, THE WHISKY EXCHANGE 56.9%
Single Malt - Speyside

**7 Michael: With water, more toffeish malt notes emerge in the middle, but the wood is very dominating.**
**Nose:** Nutty, leafy. Toasted. Charred oak.
**Palate:** Medicinal. Syrupy. Still some sweetness and juicy nuttiness, but quickly overwhelmed by the oak.
**Finish:** Long and warming, but some burnt astringency.

**8½ Dave: An espresso coffee going straight into the veins. Astonishing, but for sherry freaks only.**
**Nose:** Sulphur/coal gas, rubber, prune, walnut, clove, Christmas cake, cold tea, fig, coffee, chicory, dark chocolate and autumn bonfires.
**Palate:** An immediate hit of bitter chocolate, dried fig then some rich, powerful dried fruit. Good texture.
**Finish:** Slightly bitter.

### GLEN GRANT 5 YEARS OLD 40%
Single Malt - Speyside

**7 Michael: Hadn't tasted the 5 Years Old for a while. Cleaner, drier and less fruity than I remember.**
**Nose:** Fragrant. Heathery.
**Palate:** Very lightly malty. Creamy. Nutty. Interplay of sweetness and dryness.
**Finish:** A hint of fruity acidity.

**7 Dave: Made to be drunk long but even so needs to have a little more character.**
**Nose:** Very light. Muscadet, green grapes, fresh flowers. Hint of immaturity. Nutty.
**Palate:** Light and grassy floral. With water it becomes insubstantial.
**Finish:** Simply disappears.

### GLEN GRANT C3490 CASK STRENGTH RARE AULD SCOTCH WHISKY, DUNCAN TAYLOR 49.7%
Single Malt - Speyside

**8¾ Dave: Elegant and sophisticated.**
**Nose:** All spice and candied peel and the suggestion of an old whisky that has matured very gently. Very zesty and lively with tingling spice and a heavy floral note like lilies.
**Palate:** Sweet with caramelised sugars and a touch of rosewood. Balanced and discreet. Slightly less direct with water, but has a real subtle depth.
**Finish:** Long with gentle spice.

**8 Martine: A wonderful nose, a dash of water cuts the edges. Complex and harmonious.**
**Nose:** Elegant oaky fragrances. Floor polish, beeswax, sunheated pine cones. Fruity notes slowly emerge. Pears in custard. Greengage.
**Palate:** Rich, smooth at start then becoming crisp. With a spicy outburst and a sherbety feel. Oak is present. Custard and liquorice.
**Finish:** Spicy with an oaky bite.

### GLEN KEITH 1967, MACKILLOP'S CHOICE 41.4%
Single Malt - Speyside

**7½ Michael: A peatier expression of Glen Keith than I have tasted before.**
**Nose:** Flowery. Distinctly peaty. Straw. Fresh wood.
**Palate:** Oily. Cereal grain. Cakey. Wholegrain bread. Toast.
**Finish:** Peaty. Leafy. Dock Leaves. Slight tartness.

**7¼ Dave: Is this one of those GK peated experiments? Or made soon after? Shame it wasn't bottled five years ago when it had more life.**

**Nose:** A little flat. Smoky bonfires.
**Palate:** Sweet and fragrant with pretty fruit but with little energy.
**Finish:** Juicy but short.

### GLEN KEITH 1971 33 YEARS OLD, CASK 8066, DUNCAN TAYLOR 50.8%
Single Malt - Speyside

**8½ Martine: An old fellow on the edge of declining but with attractive sweet richness. No water, please!**
**Nose:** Intensely sherried. A huge aromatic array. Burnt caramel. Overcooked plum jam. Prunes. Dates, dried figs. Burning log.
**Palate:** Intensely sherried. Burnt caramel. Plum jam. Prunes. Dates, dried figs. Burning log.
**Finish:** Rather compact, less lingering than expected.

**7 Dave: Overwooded.**
**Nose:** Tomato leaf, moving into balsamic. Fruit cake. Dry and woody. Oak, oak and more oak.
**Palate:** Casky deep and very tannic. Like chewing your way out of a wardrobe.
**Finish:** Tannin.

### GLEN KIRK 8 YEARS OLD 40%
Single Malt - Speyside

**6½ Michael: Flavours do not combine. Lack roundness.**
**Nose:** Leafy. Some grassy peat. Hint of phenol.
**Palate:** Suggestion of charcoal. Some malty sweetness and peat, but thin. Drying on the tongue.
**Finish:** Medicinal. Eucalyptus.

**7¾ Jim: Uncomplicated, attractively fresh.**
**Nose:** A youthful, grassy clean aroma with dank barley in abundance.
**Palate:** Fresh and mouth-watering with an intense and delicious barley richness from the very start.
**Finish:** Slightly spicy with a touch of oak.

### GLEN MHOR 1976 28 YEARS OLD, RARE MALTS 51.9%
Single Malt - Speyside

**7¾ Michael: A straight-ahead, fruity, creamy, Speysider.**
**Nose:** Faint peaty dryness.
**Palate:** Fruity boiled sweets. Slight pear drops, but well rounded.
**Finish:** Sweet lemons. Gently appetising. Warming.

**8 Ian: Waltzes across the palate with grace and impeccable timing, even when the tempo rises.**
**Nose:** Lashings of vanilla, with citrus, figs and apricots followed by dark chocolate and maltiness.
**Palate:** Soft, creamy vanilla soon extends with dark chocolate, luscious orange marmalade and apricots, seasoned with spice, becoming richer.
**Finish:** Luscious, juicy fruit subsides to make way for chocolate maltiness.

### GLEN MHOR 1979, 22 YEARS OLD, RARE MALTS 61%
Single Malt - Speyside

**8¾ Michael: A rare delight.**
**Nose:** Surprisingly fresh, minty and herbal.
**Palate:** Lightly syrupy. Texture reminiscent of whipped cream. Rosewater. Sherbet. Meringue on a shortbread base.
**Finish:** Distinctly leafy and grassy.

**7½ Dave: Good but not quite balanced.**
**Nose:** Dry nose with a slight dirty/earthy note before toffee cream, wholemeal biscuit and a hint of cigar smoke.
**Palate:** Rich with pear, peach and some toffee. Dries very quickly.
**Finish:** Some smoke. Dry.

### GLEN MHOR 1979, GORDON & MACPHAIL 43%
Single Malt - Highland

**7¾ Martine: A hearty fellow, warming and expressive. A hip flask dram for a wet day.**
**Nose:** Forestry bouquet. Polished pinefloor. Mushroom quiche. Peppermint. A chalky touch.
**Palate:** Mouthcoating. Rich and warm. Stewed apples. Earthy root.
**Finish:** Long, minty. Ginger.

**7½ Dave: Good, but needs some oomph.**
**Nose:** Sweet yet slightly earthy. Hot bracken. New trainers, old cobbler's shop, peat. More intensity with water, light oak, apricot. Fresh chestnut mushroom.
**Palate:** Light smoke uncoiling over syrupy fruit, grass, spent fires. Quite ethereal.
**Finish:** Crisp and dry.

## GLEN MORAY 12 YEARS OLD 40%
Single Malt - Speyside

**7 ¼ Martine: A sweet, soft and mellow fruitiness. Too much is too much sometimes.**
**Nose:** Wood reluctantly gives way to fruity aromas. Wet cellar notes. Apricot skin, grape. Vanilla sweetness follows. Beeswax. Roasted coffee beans.
**Palate:** Round, leafy, malty. Sweetness all the way through.
**Finish:** Neat, rather dry and crisp. A touch of leaf bitterness.

**6 ¾ Dave: Approachable and pleasant but a tad bland.**
**Nose:** Light, malty and gentle with colour, honey and a bit of damp earth.
**Palate:** Well-balanced and on the soft light side with a soft vanilla undertow and that hint of light honey.
**Finish:** Short.

## GLEN MORAY 12 YEARS OLD 40%
Single Malt - Speyside

**8 ¼ Michael: So beautifully composed that it left me craving some imperfection.**
**Nose:** Pear drops, but no harshness. Clean, delicious. Fresh dessert apple. Calvados.
**Palate:** Crème Anglaise? Non! Ecossaise. Sweetish. Coconut ice. Toothsome.
**Finish:** Firm but gentle. Seductive. Fragrant.

**7 ½ Dave: Creamy soft and easy to drink. A good everyday drinker.**
**Nose:** Attractive and gentle. Very creamy. Double cream in fact. Light, oaty/ovaltine notes. Fairly sweet. Reminds me of Old-Fashioned lemonade. Time brings out a touch of parmesan.
**Palate:** Soft vanilla, light crisp oak. Slightly muted with dried banana. Decent balance.
**Finish:** Gentle and smooth.

## GLEN MORAY 12 YEARS OLD, CHENIN BLANC FINISH 40%
Single Malt - Speyside

**7 ½ Michael: Smooth body, beeswax-like. The wine adds an element, but many loyalists will miss the previous version.**
**Nose:** Pears, walnuts, fresh oak.
**Palate:** Pears in cream; late, lively, peachy fruitiness. Garden mint
**Finish:** Raisiny, also resiny. Fresh oak, soothing warmth.

**8 Jim: Glen Moray 12 Years Old used to be a bastion of ultra-malty simplicity. No more. Chenin Blanc barrels have added a delightful dimension.**
**Nose:** Altogether richer, more strident and confident. The wine effect is astonishing: sweet, overripe grapes balanced by a fabulous malty echo. Intriguingly smoky, too.
**Palate:** Soft and velvety on the palate. Charming spicy notes add to a complexity unusual for a Glen Moray.
**Finish:** Soft cocoa notes and some drying oak. The winey effect seems to linger while the spice battles to the end.

## GLEN MORAY 16 YEARS OLD 40%
Single Malt - Speyside

**8 Michael: Not quite as complex as the previous 16 Years Old, but delicious.**
**Nose:** Rich. Expressive. Notably banana-like.
**Palate:** Smooth. Substantial. Restrained banana. A hint of dessert apple. A dash of Calvados. Shortbread. Malty. Toffeeish.
**Finish:** Creamy. Soothing.

**8 Dave: Of more interest than the Classic simply due to its extra dimensions.**
**Nose:** Light maltiness alongside maturity: stewed fruits, crème brûlée, barley sugar, red apple. Rounded. Develops notes of chocolate eclair and peach.
**Palate:** Silky mid-palate. Custard-like. Cooked soft fruit, toasted almond, tea bread and a little cedar.
**Finish:** Soft, quite short.

## GLEN MORAY 16 YEARS OLD, CHENIN BLANC FINISH 40%
Single Malt - Speyside

**7 ¾ Michael: Less delicate and scenty, but more satisfying. More wine, but more of everything else.**
**Nose:** Very scented. Musky. Hint of cloves.
**Palate:** Smooth and firm. More assertive. Toffee, apple, oak.
**Finish:** Long. Hints of peat. Grassy. Leafy. Resiny oak.

**8 ½ Doug: Greater dimensions than the original 16 Years Old.**
**Nose:** Ripe melon, orange peel, violets, banana skins and vanilla.
**Palate:** Very smooth, almost buttery but with a prickling warming spice.
**Finish:** Lingering, spicy and oaky with a gentle smoky dryness.

## GLEN MORAY 16 YEARS OLD, CHENIN BLANC FINISH 40%
Single Malt - Speyside

**7 ½ Michael: Firmer and more assertive.**
**Nose:** Very aromatic, with a hint of cloves and apples. Tannin.
**Palate:** Toffee, apples and oak.
**Finish:** Long, with hints of peat, grass and leaves. Resiny, peppery.

**8 ½ Jim: Wow. This is not how Glen Moray used to be. A dram just brimming with complexity and threatening to explode.**
**Nose:** Big and massively complex. Healthy honey glow weaves in and out of the trademark Glen Moray malt intensity, weighted by a dash of peat. The wineyness is restricted to a fruit cocktail of apple and sultana.
**Palate:** Sublime mouthfeel: slightly oily and wonderfully lush. Sweet malt and lighter grapey notes go hand-in-hand at the start, though the middle sees the malt intensify.
**Finish:** Lovely coffee and vanilla mix with a drying oakiness fitting a 16 Years Old. Dries impressively.

## GLEN MORAY 1962, ED DODSON'S LAST MANAGER'S CHOICE 51%
Single Malt - Speyside

**8 ½ Martine: As appealing and intriguing as a cupboard full of granny's jams for a young pilferer (I was one!). You just can't resist!**
**Nose:** Tangy, estery. Sour fruit. Hint of nail varnish. Burnt wood. Develops intense fruit: red plum, apricot, sherry notes lusciously underline without overpowering.
**Palate:** Silky, crisp and firm. A beautiful array of Oloroso notes: plum jam, cherries, figs, coffee beans.
**Finish:** Long, lingering. Marzipan and oak.

**8 ½ Dave: We're looking at big interaction between oak and spirit, but has balance and complexity.**
**Nose:** Light wood oil notes, chocolate/hazelnut, bracken, frangipan, lemon. A hint of rancio. Mature.
**Palate:** Surprisingly soft. Caramel. Light tannic grip, into Terry's Chocolate Orange, dried cherries, firm oak.
**Finish:** Marzipan.

## GLEN MORAY 1971 VINTAGE 43%
Single Malt - Speyside

**8 Michael: Glen Moray has never been seen as a glamorous malt, but it gains mystery with maturity.**
**Nose:** Clean malty sweetness, but also peatiness.
**Palate:** Light, fir, dry. Opens up with some luscious sweetness, but with a background of graininess, a hint of black chocolate, and delicately fragrant peatiness.
**Finish:** A firm, grainy, almost stony, finish, but leaving a lingering peaty fragrance.

**9 Doug: Remarkably rich, smooth and refined. A classic Speyside.**
**Nose:** Rich deep honeyed and raisiny; ripe bananas, nutty and creamy.
**Palate:** Creamily smooth, sherryish, nutty and salty.
**Finish:** Very long, beautifully textured, gently warming with a little pepper and smoke at the tail.

## GLEN MORAY 1974, DISTILLERY MANAGER'S CHOICE 53.4%
Single Malt - Speyside

**7 ¾ Michael: The aromas remind me of a young woman I tried to bed in the early 1970s. She bit my tongue when I did something to offend her feminist ethic.**
**Nose:** Perfumed candles. Wax. Smoke. Joss sticks. Spicy.
**Palate:** Oily, creamy, malty. Develops the typical cereal-grain character of Glen Moray. Drying.
**Finish:** Slightly sharp. Provocative.

**8 ½ Dave: Rounded and elegant, this is one hell of a dram from a hell of a manager.**

**Nose:** Rich and mellow. Honey, toffee, sultana alongside walnut, nutmeg and dry, biscuity malt. Succulent and spicy, gentle yet complex.
**Palate:** Very sweet to start but immediately balanced by ginger and nutmeg spiciness, soft fruit (apricot, banana) and dried fruit (date). Superb balance.
**Finish:** Soft, tobacco.

## GLEN MORAY 1981 SINGLE SHERRY BUTT 57.7%
Single Malt - Speyside

**8¼ Michael: The richness of the whisky more than balances the slight woodiness. This is delicious. Glen Moray with maturity-and dimension-than we can usually experience.**
**Nose:** Honeydew melon. A hint of garden mint. Milk pudding. Caramel. Cedar.
**Palate:** Creamy. Rich. Spicy. Sultanas. Plum cake. Nougat. Some toffeeish chewiness.
**Finish:** Slightly burnt. Slightly rooty and woody.

**6¾ Dave: Sherry but(t) no Glen Moray.**
**Nose:** Full-on sherried notes: bitter chocolate, hot water bottle, cold tea, fig, smoke, autumn bonfires.
**Palate:** Big, thick and mouthcoating. A hint of sulphur. Oily and soft.
**Finish:** Thick and long. Some spice and rancid butter on finish.

## GLEN MORAY 1986 COMMEMORATIVE BOTTLING 64.4%
Single Malt - Speyside

**7¾ Michael: Robust. Complex. After dinner.**
**Nose:** Perfumes candles. A brief hint of sulphury smoke, quickly dissipating. Cinder toffee. Cereal grain.
**Palate:** Creamy. Nougat. Exotic fruit.
**Finish:** Slightly sharp.

**7¼ Marcin: Reminiscent of a slightly flabby Australian chardonnay.**
**Nose:** Sophisticated and subtle. Créme caramel.
**Palate:** Far more assertive and flame-grilled than expected from the nose.
**Finish:** Water knocks out the mid-palate and the whisky loses its nuts and bolts. A fader.

## GLEN MORAY 1989 SIGNATURE MALT 16 YEARS OLD 57.6%
Single Malt - Speyside

**7¼ Dave: It's hard to get excited about.**
**Nose:** Stewed apple, estery coffee grounds, planed wood. Hints of complexity.
**Palate:** Sweet and highly concentrated. A battle between fruit and oak. Lacks personality. Dislikes water.
**Finish:** Hot and feisty.

**7 Arthur: A little sour for me.**
**Nose:** Fudge, wet grass, lemon, peach and white breadcrumbs. There was a grubbiness to this nose that didn't appeal.
**Palate:** Some astringent citrus, jelly babies and a little yeasty, breadiness.
**Finish:** Sourness with a little spice.

## GLEN MORAY 20 YEARS OLD 54.5%
Single Malt - Speyside

**8 Michael: Bonus points for knowing its own mind.**
**Nose:** Fresh apple pie. The English type, not the American.
**Palate:** Firm. Muscular. Extraordinarily quick hit. Knocked out my gumshield. A right hook and a straight left, so fast that I backed on to the ropes. Between rounds, my second has sprayed something medicinal into my mouth.
**Finish:** I am embraced with syrupy sweetness.

**7¾ Dave: Decent but lacks definition.**
**Nose:** Creamy again with notes of grass clippings. Quite subtle but a little one dimensional. Alcohol is a little abrasive.
**Palate:** Intense and zesty with a sugary quality and soft creamy oak. Green grass, lemon mousse, pear.
**Finish:** Green chilli.

## GLEN MORAY CHARDONNAY FINISH 40%
Single Malt - Speyside

**8 Michael: Pale and soft, but textured.**
**Nose:** Fresh, scented, fruity, like an unpeeled dessert grape. Perhaps a suggestion of banana.
**Palate:** Water melon, banana, white chocolate. Lightly creamy. Shortbread.

**Finish:** Grape skins and apple cores, hay and cereal grains. Lightly dry and very crisp.

**6½ Jim: Hmmm. Not quite as well structured as I might have wished. I prefer the old Glen Moray to this, which has its moments, but tends to be a little awkward.**
**Nose:** Dry and less overtly malty than the usual Glen Moray; comes to life only when well warmed. Then slightly buttery and marshmallow-sweet.
**Palate:** Tangy fruit, unquestionably grapey, but fails to marry with the intense malt which offers some much needed sweetness.
**Finish:** Dry, vanilla, lacking depth, save some toasty cocoa notes. Short.

## GLEN MORAY CLASSIC 40%
Single Malt - Speyside

**7¾ Michael: Seems rather neutral at first, but develops engaging subtleties.**
**Nose:** Fresh. Dusty. Nutty. Slightly acidic. Dessert grapes.
**Palate:** Starts soft and light; then develops a chalky, gritty, cereal-grain dryness; opening into an appetising malty sweetness.
**Finish:** Spicy. A hint of cloves. Slightly sour.

**7¼ Dave: So light you should have it for elevenses.**
**Nose:** Light and floral. Powdered almond, hay loft. Attractive. Water accentuates youth. Delicate and very pleasant.
**Palate:** Light-bodied though with a firm, nutty structure (almond, cereal.) Sweet and lemon like. A dusting of icing sugar.
**Finish:** Medium. Fizzy. Nuts again.

## GLEN MORAY MANAGER'S CHOICE MOUNTAIN OAK MALT 60%
Single Malt - Speyside

**7¾ Michael: A robust rendition. One for mountaineers?**
**Nose:** Instant hit of the breezy peat-smoke that I remember in Speyside malts. Did Glen Moray have this smokiness a dozen years ago?
**Palate:** The characteristic cereal-grain character is surprisingly assertive, almost husky, but it soon calms to biscuity shortbread and buttery notes.
**Finish:** Vegetal, rooty. Liquorice.

**8¼ Dave: Fascinating-single malt aged in new US oak-resulting in a half-way house between bourbon and malt. A cracking drink.**
**Nose:** Vibrant/zesty. Vanilla, citrus. Spices: cinnamon powder. With water, hot cross buns and marzipan.
**Palate:** Fairly firm structure but fizzing with life. Thick cream, soft fruits and a light malty cereal note. Sweet.
**Finish:** Oak and orange Spangles.

## GLEN MORAY MOUNTAIN OAK THE FINAL RELEASE 58.6%
Single Malt - Speyside

**7¾ Dave: More of a whisky spread than a drink. For those with a sweet tooth.**
**Nose:** Huge, butter-fat oaky notes. Sweet with caramelised fruit sugars, plum jam. Water brings out a candied peel note. Perfumed and slightly minty.
**Palate:** Lots of oak lactone and just enough grip to give structure and interest. Nutty malt and in time a strangely exotic rose petal/angelica flavour.
**Finish:** Floral.

**7¾ Martine: Quite enticing and heady but so dressed up, and reminiscent of a rum. The cask has knocked the maltiness down.**
**Nose:** Fruity. Pineapple juice. Spicy. Allspice, cloves. Orange peel. Medicinal like a rum grand arôme. Sandalwood. Very fragrant.
**Palate:** Sweet at start then displaying a sensuous spicy palette. Rum again! Demerara custard.
**Finish:** Tangy, spicy. Lingering.

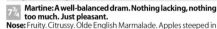

### GLEN ORD 43%
Single Malt - Highland

**7¾ Martine: A well-balanced dram. Nothing lacking, nothing too much. Just pleasant.**
**Nose:** Fruity. Citrussy. Olde English Marmalade. Apples steeped in caramel. Star fruit.
**Palate:** Silky. Slowly opening on pastry flavours. Watermelon. Almond cake. Beautiful mouthfeel.
**Finish:** Long, spicy. Ginger and chilli. A soothing almond milk aftertaste.

**7½ Dave: Another good session dram.**
**Nose:** Malty, cereal, lightly honeyed. Light with toasted almond, nougat, wholemeal bread, light earth, cut grass.
**Palate:** Round but firm, a surge of initial maltiness softens into green pear, green walnut, mandarin.
**Finish:** Dry and clean.

### GLEN ORD 12 YEARS OLD 40%
Single Malt - Highland

**7¾ Michael: Anyone not quite understanding the term "malt" should try this whisky. All will then be clear.**
**Nose:** Nice touch of sherry to round its big maltiness – and a subtle hint of peat.
**Palate:** Luscious, clean, maltiness and barley-sugar sweetness. Moving to drier maltiness and, again, gentle peating.
**Finish:** Firm, smooth. Orange zest. Cinnamon. Late, light ginger.

**6½ Jim: Zzzzzzzzzzz.**
**Nose:** Seriously unimpressive: sub-standard sherry notes topped only by a hint of smoke. Pretty grim.
**Palate:** Silky but otherwise bland. Very little emerges beyond the flavourless sherry except a brief, malty, smoky peat.
**Finish:** Caramel and vanilla. Otherwise dead.

### GLEN ORD 12 YEARS OLD 43%
Single Malt - Highland

**7¾ Michael: I have long had a sneaking feeling that this malt was underrated. It is: based on my first tasting of the day, in April, 2003.**
**Nose:** Rich maltiness. Some sherry.
**Palate:** Clean, firm, nutty, toasty. Becoming marshmallowy. A hint of ginger.
**Finish:** Silky. Smoky. A well-judged touch of peaty dryness.

**7 Dave: A good, solid all-rounder.**
**Nose:** Very malty (Weetabix) medium-bodied with light oak and a mossiness/fresh-turned sod note. With water, there's coconut pulp, orange, nougat.
**Palate:** Dry, crisp and quite oaky. Some light honey, and orange again alongside maltiness.
**Finish:** Dry, short but appetising.

### GLEN ORD 19 YEARS OLD, CADENHEAD'S 57%
Single Malt - Highland

**7¾ Michael: 'Born on' dates are not a big issue when John Barleycorn must die, yet this whisky seems to have an especially fresh maltiness. A refreshing dram for the sultry suns of summer.**
**Nose:** A waft of clean, crisp peat. Grassiness?
**Palate:** Malty sweetnesss. Barley sugar. Shortbread. Quick balancing dryness, with some estery fruitiness and acidity. Gooseberries.
**Finish:** Fruity, lively, almost effervescent.

**7¼ Dave: A good aperitif whisky. Great drinking.**
**Nose:** Fresh and clean, mixing green grass, lime, buttery malt/shortbread and bourbon biscuit. Grassier with water.
**Palate:** Sweet (honey, apple, orange) and then dries (malt, nuts). Very clean, but slightly rigid in structure.
**Finish:** Apple, dried, quite short.

### GLEN ORD 1974, 23 YEARS OLD, RARE MALTS 60.8%
Single Malt - Highland

**8 Michael: Far paler and less sherried than the main version from this distillery. I would like at least some sherry to round the gingery spiciness, but I like the way that rose character comes through in this one.**
**Nose:** Very fresh, assertive. Leafy, lightly peaty. Fragrant smoke.
**Palate:** Big, slightly syrupy and very malty, with nuts, raisins, ginger, lemon peel and roses.
**Finish:** Spicy, flowery, peaty.

**8 Jim: Extremely high quality expression from an ill-served distillery.**
**Nose:** Orangey and very faintly peaty, yet light and slightly ethereal.
**Palate:** Tangy and sweetly malted. Rich, slightly oily body; biscuity, chewy. Gentle smokiness.
**Finish:** Very clean and soft with the malt managing to outweigh the oak. Impressive.

### GLEN ORD 30 YEARS OLD, SPECIAL RESERVE 58.7%
Single Malt - Highland

WHISKY Magazine Recommended

**8¼ Dave: A successful and intriguing balance between fragrance and dryness. Worth a look.**
**Nose:** Light almost lean, grassy nose: baled hay, light lemon, light peat. Has a mashy note with a subtle undertow of cucumber, sweet oak, earth. Water wakes it up.
**Palate:** These flavours are delivered best on the palate. Crisp and direct to start then softening into light toffee, ginger and a mouth-filling softness.
**Finish:** Hint of malt. Fresh.

**8¾ Arthur: A real fruit bomb, dusted with spice. Deserves to be popular.**
**Nose:** Mint sirop and an aromatic fragrant fruit, like guava. A good shake of spice, indicating a fair amount of age. With more time and water, lots of melon.
**Palate:** Intense mouthfilling fruit: oranges, apples and quince jelly.
**Finish:** Drying woodiness with a creosoted edge.

### GLEN SCOTIA 1974 30 YEARS OLD, CHIEFTAIN'S CHOICE 42.2%
Single Malt - Campbeltown

WHISKY Magazine Editor's choice

**9 Martine: What a lovely nectar. Great fruit and cream combination.**
**Nose:** Delicate, floral. Orange blossom. Apricot and almond pie cooking in the oven. Develops on toffee. A peat echo.
**Palate:** Caressing, luscious, rich. Peach melba. Floral honey. Pear drop.
**Finish:** Smooth, sensuous, deliciously lingering. Spicy dryness.

**8 Dave: Fantastic balance, but uncompromising.**
**Nose:** Buttery yet oily. Complex notes of car mechanic workshop, coconut oil, black olives in brine. With water, goats' cheese, smoke and candied peel.
**Palate:** The oiliness shows best here giving a mouth coating texture. Lemon, light spices. Ever so slightly salty. Pure flavours.
**Finish:** That salty cheese again.

### GLEN SCOTIA 1992 CASK STRENGTH, GORDON & MACPHAIL 62.1%
Single Malt - Campbeltown

**7 Michael: Far from the best Glen Scotia, but I have always entertained a sneaky respect for this distillery.**
**Nose:** Waterfront. Slight tar-like smokiness.
**Palate:** Syrupy maltiness with suggestions of stewed fruit. Seems suddenly to slim down, becoming firm and slightly metallic. Then takes on a surge of saltiness.
**Finish:** Dusty. Slightly woody.

**7¼ Dave: I try to like Glen Scotia, really I do, but I simply can't.**
**Nose:** Great start: clotted cream, banana split. Oily. Then inner tube, peat shed in the rain, damp tweeds. The rubber intensifies with water. Old wellies/neoprene.
**Palate:** Peaty, nut oil, earth. Reminiscent of a back-street garage. Long and oily.
**Finish:** Grubby.

### WHISKY FAIR GLEN SCOTIA 'HEAVILY PEATED' 52.7%
Single Malt - Campbeltown

**7½ Dave: This is just too odd.**
**Nose:** A plain nose whose smokiness mingles with coumarin. In fact it's almost like salt drying on the clothes. In time, wet barns, fishing nets and burning orange crates.
**Palate:** Intense if a little narrow, it expands into a very odd flavour which brings to mind cow pats, then a burst of citrus.
**Finish:** Biscuity, then sweet.

**8 Arthur: A little pongy at points, but with youthful charm. A tyke with a grubby face.**
**Nose:** Blackberries and stables (hay and dung). Ashy. Compost and farmyards.
**Palate:** Ashy, silagey, and dark chocolate.
**Finish:** Berries and wet grass.

## GLEN SPEY 11 YEARS OLD, DEWAR RATTRAY 59%
Single Malt - Speyside

**7¾** **Dave: It's a cad pursuing an innocent girl. The big bad wolf after little Red Riding Hood.**
**Nose:** Peculiar. Damp horse blankets, wet wood, light smoke, slightly fungal.
**Palate:** Better than the nose with light grip. Sandalwood, old apples and tobacco, malt extract. Then it becomes light and fragrant before the darkness of the woods creeps back in.
**Finish:** Lit cigar.

**8** **Martine: Wood, wood, wood … And this cheesy note does not improve the aromatic profile. Water enhances the bitterness.**
**Nose:** Woody. Fresh pine sawdust. Spirity with a faint cheesy note. Goat cheese in olive oil and thyme. Wet dog.
**Palate:** Sweet and oaky. Quite tangy. Chilli and the bitter taste of pepper.
**Finish:** Dry, bitter, warm.

## GLEN SPEY 12 YEARS OLD 43%
Single Malt - Speyside

**7½** **Martine: Definitely Speyside. Elegant interplay between fruit and malt.**
**Nose:** Expressive, grassy. Dry hay. Huge puff of black pepper followed by sweeter notes. Cider apples cooked in honey. Beeswax. Touch of cedar.
**Palate:** Round, oily, sweet and malty. Toasted nuts. Stewed apples. Less spicy than the nose. Good balance.
**Finish:** A bit evanescent but enjoyable.

**7¼** **Dave: A good, solid, bone-dry malt.**
**Nose:** Very light and grassy to start. In time becoming more sappy, like a pine forest in the summer. Some creamy nuttiness as well.
**Palate:** Heathery. Very light, dry and nutty with that light sappy note returning. Well-balanced.
**Finish:** Soft then fades quickly.

## GLEN SPEY 12 YEARS OLD, DISTILLERY MALT 43%
Single Malt - Speyside

**7½** **Michael: Richer and more expressive than any version I have tasted previously. Extraordinary sweetness.**
**Nose:** Herbal. Fruity.
**Palate:** Intensely sweet. Creamy-tasting. Ice-cream (or perhaps the Indian equivalent, kulfi).
**Finish:** Lively. Zesty lemon peel. Candied angelica. Cilantro.

**7** **Dave: Simple, pleasant but a little one-dimensional.**
**Nose:** Like an Italian delicatessen: dry and slightly dusty with hints of spice, coffee, bran, vanilla pod and nut.
**Palate:** Sweeter than the nose suggests. Estery and floral with sweet grass.
**Finish:** Short and a little dry.

## GLENALLACHIE 15 YEARS OLD, CASK STRENGTH EDITION, CHIVAS BROTHERS 58%
Single Malt - Speyside

*WHISKY Recommended*

**8½** **Michael: Perhaps too sweet for some malt lovers but packed with flavour. Bland it ain't.**
**Nose:** Perfumy. Luxury soap. A country house hotel. Polished oak. Beeswax.
**Palate:** Nutty. Honeyed. Suggests baclava, but not quite so sweet. Belgian wafers, interleaved with chocolate.
**Finish:** Liqueur-ish. Concentrated. Intense. Serve it with the petit-fours.

**7¾** **Dave: Well balanced, just decays a little over time in the glass.**
**Nose:** Intriguing mix of sweet and dry. Raisin, some carbonised notes. Dried tangerine peel, chocolate, fruit loaf and some earth. Development shows a slight falling off.
**Palate:** Sweet start, some clove, treacle toffee. Has sufficient weight to cope with the oak. Has some light tannins.
**Finish:** Fruit peels, bitter chocolate.

## GLENCADAM 13 YEARS OLD, BERRY'S OWN SELECTION 46%
Single Malt - Highland

**8** **Martine: A pleasant freshener. Delivers a lot. To be enjoyed on a warm day with raw fish and salad.**
**Nose:** Young in style. Herbal. Garden mint, lemon grass. Bread dough. A light floral touch (meadow flowers). Distant marine echo.
**Palate:** Oily, thick. Mouth coating. Vivid and fresh. Mustardy. Very clean. Sweet maltiness in the back.
**Finish:** Surprisingly long for the young age. Grassy.

**7¼** **Dave: A fine enough dram, but insubstantial compared to the others in this company.**
**Nose:** Lifted floral and fruity notes: lilac, conference pear, lemon zest. With water there's ginger and camomile tea but also slightly plain oak.
**Palate:** Alcohol burn even at this strength. Water needed to bring out vanilla syrup and blossom. Light, yet firm and unyielding.
**Finish:** Slightly bitter.

## GLENCADAM 15 YEARS OLD, ANGUS DUNDEE 40%
Single Malt - Highland

**8** **Michael: A very unusual whisky. I liked it, but it would benefit from a firmer malty middle to support the interesting component flavours.**
**Nose:** Powerful. Spicy. Cinnamon. Dry.
**Palate:** Cereal, coconut, toffee, raisins. Winey.
**Finish:** Rummy. Medicinal.

**7½** **Dave: Well put together.**
**Nose:** Clean and quite big-boned. Putty, bruised peach, pencil shavings, fruit tea, a light waxiness.
**Palate:** Medium-bodied. Good weight and very, very soft. Fine texture with light, spicy oak tones.
**Finish:** A tart lift which picks interest up.

## GLENCADAM 1971, 28 YEARS OLD, KINGSBURY 55.6%
Single Malt - Highland

**7** **Michael: Lacks roundness, structure, balance. I was sorry to hear that this distillery has been closed. Temporarily?**
**Nose:** An almost papery, fruit-skin, dryness.
**Palate:** Starts like the layer of soft caramel in a Mars bar. Remarkably creamy. Astonishingly peach-like.
**Finish:** Very lively. Almost effervescent.

**7¾** **Jim: A charming malt, though rather shy. Easily among the top Glencadams yet bottled.**
**Nose:** Sweet, gristy and fresh for age.
**Palate:** Melt in the mouth despite strength with oak and malt battling out for honours.
**Finish:** A very late almost subliminal hint of peat.

## GLENCADAM 1973, BERRY'S OWN SELECTION 46%
Single Malt - Highland

**7½** **Dave: A ripe dram which seems to have headed across to Kentucky. Big and lush.**
**Nose:** Rich, mature wooded notes. Coconut and cocoa overlaying some tropical fruits. With water a sweaty saddle note.
**Palate:** Rounded and silky. Cherry stone. Good length and feel. Plenty of wood on show here. Bourbon like.
**Finish:** Sweet spices and oak.

**8¼** **Arthur: Lip-smackingly mature.**
**Nose:** A very fruity nose: ripe melon, bananas and kiwis. Milk chocolate, digestive biscuits, and pear drops.
**Palate:** Lots of bourbon character, with vanilla, refresher sweets and some mint.
**Finish:** Milk chocolate, and a trace of sulphur.

## GLENCADAM 1974, CASK 10, MACKILLOP'S CHOICE 59.9%
Single Malt - Highland

**7** **Michael: Showing its age, but still with the distillery character. Glencadam has its devotees and, with the distillery's future uncertain, supplies are finite.**
**Nose:** Smoky, dry.
**Palate:** At first, the sensation of soft spring water. Then the development of the creaminess that is the house character, with fruity and peppery notes gradually emerging.
**Finish:** Woody. Orange boxes.

**7½** **Dave: Fuller and yet somehow crisper than the 16 Years Old.**
**Nose:** Oaky notes dominate along with butter, toffee, Nutella and tangerine. Water brings out sweet butter, cooked fruits, peach and syrup. A woodier note as it develops.
**Palate:** Pretty dry. Lots of spice and vanilla. Rounded and silky.
**Finish:** Vanilla and black fruits.

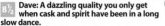

## GLENCADAM 1975 30 YEARS OLD, DEWAR RATTRAY 54.4%
Single Malt - Highland

**8½ Dave: A dazzling quality you only get when cask and spirit have been in a long slow dance.**
**Nose:** Layered and complex. Murray mint, stewed fruit. Water brings toffee, scented wood, vanilla pod. Deepens to treacle toffee, a lift of ginger biscuits, and dried peach. Palate.
**Palate:** Everything on the nose plus an added spiciness dried flower, Turkish delight, hot pine.
**Finish:** Long slightly oaked but still fresh.

**8½ Arthur: Elegant, complex and satisfying.**
**Nose:** Ripe melons and sultanas. Sawdust and a lightly antiseptic Savlon note. With a little more time mango, white chocolate and a lemon butter icing.
**Palate:** Raisins, lemon biscuits and a toasty oakiness that is almost lightly medicinal.
**Finish:** Spicy oak.

## GLENCADAM 1985, 16 YEARS OLD, CHIEFTAIN'S CHOICE 43%
Single Malt - Highland

**9½ Martine: Graceful and characterful. To be sipped on a midsummer starlit night. A true dancing dram.**
**Nose:** Subtlety in action. Perfumes, dried apricot, aniseed, jasmine tea, dried spring flowers, green grape, marzipan.
**Palate:** Smooth, silky and creamy. A caress of mingled flavours. All nose promises are delivered.
**Finish:** Dry, spice-festooned.

**7¾ Dave: Attractive rather than complex, but very attractive at that.**
**Nose:** Medium-bodied and slightly floral but with a rich malty core. Water reveals a buttery richness with honeyed fruits, hot cross buns and spices.
**Palate:** A dry-ish start with light spice and nut, then citrus oils, hazelnut and an overall pleasant texture. Well balanced.
**Finish:** Dry with a touch of smoke.

## GLENCADAM 1991, BERRY'S OWN SELECTION 40%
Single Malt - Highland

**7½ Martine: A dram for a sweet tooth. Nearly sugary. Unbalanced.**
**Nose:** Buttery. Herbal. Meadow flowers. Lemonade.
**Palate:** Very sweet. Pear nectar. Aniseed lollipop.
**Finish:** Sweet, sweet and then a touch of biting oak.

**7½ Dave: Fresh and zesty. A good aperitif.**
**Nose:** High toned. Pear drops, fresh carnation, lightly floral, mango. After water, chalk dust, lychee.
**Palate:** Sherbet lemons and vanilla. Water brings out pears, spice, white chocolate and sawn oak.
**Finish:** Clean and zingy.

## GLENCADAM 21 YEARS OLD 1985, OLD MALT CASK 50%
Single Malt - Highland

**7¾ Dave: Well balanced and with real charm and some complexity.**
**Nose:** Fragrant. Custard and crème brûlée, quince, baked apple (almost the pastry of an apple pie as well). Hint of vetiver. Balanced oak.
**Palate:** Gentle and soft in feel. Lightly sugary with a hint of mint and plenty of floral character. Balanced.
**Finish:** Long, quite sweet.

**7¾ Martine: Mature, balanced, elegant.**
**Nose:** Sweet, clean bouquet of autumn fruit. Ripe apples, cooking pears, a touch of grape. All framed by an elegant oakiness. In the back, a hint of toasted bun. A citrussy note.
**Palate:** Beautifully balanced. Smooth and velvety. The flavours open like a blossoming flower: gently, displaying interlaced fruit and oak.
**Finish:** Creamy, toffeish, with just a dry spicy punctuation.

## GLENCADAM 29 YEARS OLD, SIGNATORY SILENT STILLS 52.5%
Single Malt - Highland

**7 Michael: This whisky used to remind me of strawberry shortcake. This bottling turns me toward tiramisu.**
**Nose:** Coffee.
**Palate:** Creamy. Chocolate. Toasted nuts.
**Finish:** Pleasant nutty dryness.

**8 Dave: The spiciest of this selection … and just to show there's still hope, Glencadam has just been bought! And rightly so if this is anything to go by.**
**Nose:** Quite aromatic and spicy. Hints of honey, apple, treacle toffee, malt.
**Palate:** Venerable, but has life. Spiky and lively with gentle softness underneath: cinnamon, toasted marshmallow. Good balance.
**Finish:** Crisp. Rose.

## GLENCOE 8 YEARS OLD 58%
Single Malt - Highland

**7¾ Michael: That simple one-two of sweetness and dryness is not especially complex, but the flavours are delicious. Very wholesome and appetising.**
**Nose:** Lightly peaty. Dry. Clean.
**Palate:** Big-bodied. Lightly syrupy. Malty. Sweet.
**Finish:** Long. Almost stingingly peaty. Warming. Soothing.

**8 Jim: A vatted malt that has comprehensively changed shape in the last year.**
**Nose:** Much cleaner and uncluttered than of old. Light and quite alluring.
**Palate:** Impressive malt-fruit ratio with some playful young grassy tones standing up well to the bigger grapey notes. Mouth-watering all round.
**Finish:** Shorter than before with more emphasis on the fresh malt.

## GLENCRAIG 1981, 21 YEARS OLD, CADENHEAD'S 56.2%
Single Malt - Speyside

**7 Michael: Pleasant, sociable. With mint tea and Moroccan food?**
**Nose:** Lemony, oily.
**Palate:** Sweet green tea. A hint of mint.
**Finish:** Peppery.

**7¾ Dave: Quite decadent. A whisky from Lomond stills for fruity types.**
**Nose:** Fairly dry and slightly smoky to start. There's a lush fruitiness behind which is brought out with a combination of water and time.
**Palate:** Very sweet to start, that overripe tropical fruit/tinned apricots in syrup again. Good energy.
**Finish:** A bit short.

## GLENDRONACH 13 YEARS OLD, CADENHEAD'S 55.4%
Single Malt - Speyside

**7¾ Michael: Drier and less rich than the distillery bottlings.**
**Nose:** Fresh dessert apples. Apricot jam. Vanilla.
**Palate:** Fresh. Sweet. Cookies. Shortbread and caramel.
**Finish:** Spicy. Dry. A hint of salt.

**7¼ Dave: Well balanced and gentle.**
**Nose:** Cereal with earthy notes: dunnage warehouses, soggy rich tea biscuits. A mealy note with water: muesli and rope. Vanilla custard.
**Palate:** Light to medium bodied. Brazil nut, crunchy malty mid-palate becoming creamier.
**Finish:** Soft malt and a hint of currant leaf on the back palate.

## GLENDRONACH 1976 CASK STRENGTH, SIGNATORY 53.1%
Single Malt - Speyside

**7½ Michael: An enjoyable malt, but Glendronach is capable of more.**
**Nose:** Aromatic. Light, clean. Flowery. Nutty maltiness. Restrained peat.
**Palate:** Lightly malty, syrupy. Very sweet.
**Finish:** Drying. Faintly peaty. Very leafy. Fruity sourness. Like eating a kumquat.

**7¾ Dave: Attractive if light. At least someone's bottling it! Allied how about you?**
**Nose:** Light. Undiluted it's vegetal and grassy with hints of putty and soot. Water brings out a sweeter mash tun/soggy shredded wheat note, almond, dried grass with some melon.
**Palate:** Gentle, clean and pretty. Vanilla, smoke and a spiky citric lift.
**Finish:** Grassy and soft.

### GLENDRONACH 33 YEARS OLD 40%
Single Malt - Speyside

7¾ **Martine: To be enjoyed like a glass of port. Bring walnuts and blue cheese.**
**Nose:** Leather, sheepskin. Sherried oak. Quickly develops on fruit. Sour apples. Stewed summer fruit. Redcurrants and raspberry.
**Palate:** Sweet, winey. Slightly watery at mid-palate. Becomes oaky.
**Finish:** Oaky but not dry. Rather short.

8¾ **Dave: Has hidden depths. Doesn't like water.**
**Nose:** Roast chestnut, treacle, Old English marmalade. Becomes incense like/resinous with water. Briary notes, Turkish Delight, gingerbread and raisin, parma violet, hint of peat. Antique shop.
**Palate:** Quite firm, black fruits, raisin. Good grip but not too tannic. Runny toffee. Rich.
**Finish:** Lightly tannic autumn leaves.

### GLENDRONACH ORIGINAL, 12 YEARS OLD 40%
Single Malt - Speyside

7¾ **Michael: A very enjoyable whisky, but somewhat lacking in liveliness.**
**Nose:** Heather. Vanilla. Scented cream toffee. Lots of bourbon.
**Palate:** Silky smooth. Clean, creamy. Shortbread.
**Finish:** Crisp, with balancing nutty dryness from winey sherry notes.

7¾ **Dave: A welcome return.**
**Nose:** Oak, Autumn fruits: medlar, pear, orange crates, vanilla pod, butter toffee. In time a nuttiness takes over.
**Palate:** A silky feel, pecan pie, soft fruits, nutty maltiness (pecan). Becomes almost vinous with water.
**Finish:** Firm. Nut bowl.

### GLENDULLAN 12 YEARS OLD 43%
Single Malt - Speyside

7½ **Michael: Very pale indeed. Wood a little worse for wear. Has a hard edge, but becomes silky and disrobes quite sexily.**
**Nose:** Light, dry maltiness; hint of fruit.
**Palate:** Dry start, becoming buttery, malty, nutty and lightly fruity.
**Finish:** Extraordinarily perfumy and long.

9 **Jim: A malt which has changed direction in recent years, probably because of the new stillhouse. It's nothing like as oily as of yore. The charm and delicacy more than make amends.**
**Nose:** Intriguingly complex: kiwi and peach, pansies, peat and gentle oak.
**Palate:** Fuller and richer than the nose suggests.
**Finish:** Dark chocolate and malt.

### GLENDULLAN 12 YEARS OLD 43%
Single Malt - Speyside

7¾ **Michael: A son of the soil. I would like to pit its spicy flavours against a good haggis.**
**Nose:** Hay. Grass. Vegetal. Oily. Waxy, perfumy.
**Palate:** Firm and smooth. Seems unyielding, then begins to develop surprising complexity, with moments of intense grassy sweetness and herbal dryness.
**Finish:** Peppery. Chillis? Stinging. Tenacious.

7½ **Dave: A very attractive, highly drinkable malt.**
**Nose:** A dry nose with crisp malt, attractive notes of flowers, fruit (lemon/quince/dried fruit) oil and a hint of smoke.
**Palate:** Dry and clean to start, then opens nicely with mid-palate sweetness balancing a firm structure.
**Finish:** Soft and gentle.

### GLENDULLAN 12 YEARS OLD 43%
Single Malt - Speyside

7¾ **Michael: Big in both body and flavours, but restrained and controlled throughout.**
**Nose:** Fragrant. Linen, flax. Moorlands.
**Palate:** Firm, smooth, oily, cereal grains. Dry maltiness.
**Finish:** Heather. Honey. Lemon. Estery.

7½ **Dave: Very well made. Mid-weight, attractive and very drinkable.**
**Nose:** Clean, perfumed and lifted with good intensity and a suggestion of some weight. Linseed oil/dubbin/mink oil.
**Palate:** More smoky than the nose suggests. That oily quality fills the mouth well.
**Finish:** Just a little short.

### GLENDULLAN 1978 26 YEARS OLD, RARE MALTS 56.5%
Single Malt - Speyside

8¼ **Michael: In the crush bar at the opera?**
**Nose:** Silks and satins. The aromas of a coutourier's salon.
**Palate:** Generous. Bordering on voluptuous. Perfumy, fruity. Sweet limes.
**Finish:** Aromatic. Full. Fleshy.

8¼ **Ian: Sit back and enjoy the ride, it's full of great surprises.**
**Nose:** Dried fruit, pear drops, citrus zest, toffee apples then a thick slice of gingerbread, garnished with caramel sauce and spicy oak.
**Palate:** Delicate créme caramel and digestive biscuit sweetness with fresh citrus, orange marmalade, creamy cappuccino and nutmeg.
**Finish:** Fruity, ripe sweetness with drier maltyness.

### GLENFARCLAS 105 60%
Single Malt - Speyside

7¾ **Martine: A bold character. Rich, sherry-armoured. Dangerously palatable even without water.**
**Nose:** Definitely on the sherry side. Caramelised nuts, almost praline. Old leather. Sweet bakery notes: crème caramel, marmalade. A distant bacon echo.
**Palate:** Velvety, sweet at start then spices and chocolate burst. Ginger, red chilli. Marzipan.
**Finish:** Long, sweet and nutty.

8¼ **Dave: Fine mix of dry and savoury. A grower.**
**Nose:** Robust. Starts with cream toffee, honey, light cereal/hay. Then stewed autumn fruits, cake mix, toasted almond, raisins, maple syrup.
**Palate:** Tongue-coating. Deep. Dried fruits. A good attack with a sweet concentrated start. Good balance. Cognac like.
**Finish:** Spicy. Tingling and dry.

### GLENFARCLAS 12 YEARS OLD 43%
Single Malt - Speyside

8½ **Michael: Confident. Straightforward. A first-class whisky. Well-rounded. No-nonsense.**
**Nose:** Deceptive. Seems restrained, but at close quarters is quite powerful. Nutty, with a splash of lemony sourness.
**Palate:** Big, firm. Hard toffee. Burnt, peat-smoke notes.
**Finish:** Spicy. Ginger snaps. Shortbread. Long, lingering.

7¾ **Dave: A powerful bugger and a great introduction to the distillery style, but you feel you'd get much more in a couple of years.**
**Nose:** Big, rich, appetising nose: Dundee cake, oak, sherry, ripe fruits, fern/bracken and the greenish edge you seem to get with many 12 Years Olds.
**Palate:** Robust, deep and fruity with lovely rich oaky notes.
**Finish:** A little short.

### GLENFARCLAS 15 YEARS OLD 46%
Single Malt - Speyside

8¼ **Michael: Judging from the colour, as well as aroma and flavour, this is Glenfarclas without its dressing of sherry. Having removed its jacket and necktie, it appears more muscular and aggressive.**
**Nose:** Earthy. Autumnal. Rain on the forest floor. A smoky peat fire somewhere in the distance.
**Palate:** Big, firm, cereal-grain nuttiness. Develops a lot of sweetness, then a balance of floweriness.
**Finish:** Intense. Honey, shrubs and reeds. Mustardy.

6½ **Dave: Another that seems too young. Pent-up energy but no integration. Not the Glenfarclas 15 I know.**
**Nose:** Very pale. Touch of flowers, baked banana and some leather (pigskin). Seems immature.
**Palate:** Starts dry. The mid-palate is very concentrated with a dry nuttiness. Pretty tight.
**Finish:** Crisp.

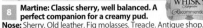

## GLENFARCLAS 15 YEARS OLD 46%
Single Malt - Speyside

**8** **Martine: Classic sherry, well balanced. A perfect companion for a creamy pud.**
**Nose:** Sherry. Old leather. Fig molasses. Treacle. Antique shop. Orange marmalade. Crème brûlée.
**Palate:** Sweet. Sherry shines through. Polished oak. Raisins. Dark chocolate.
**Finish:** Long, nutty and spicy.

**8** **Dave: The most fragrant on show. Slightly OTT, but has the weight to cope. George Melly in a glass.**
**Nose:** Outrageously flagrant in its perfume, like a gentleman's cologne kept in a rosewood casket.
**Palate:** Turkish delight, fresh timber, barley sugar sweetness, rum-like notes. Rich and sweet. Doesn't take water too well.
**Finish:** Dense, creamy/oily. Very powerful with good tannic balance. Supple power.

## GLENFARCLAS 17 YEARS OLD 43%
Single Malt - Speyside

**8¼** **Martine: A bunch of interesting flavours displayed in an elegant oak frame.**
**Nose:** Floral. Heather. Lots of herbal notes. Fresh coriander, dill, parsley.
**Palate:** Lovely fresh feel. Soothing sweetness. Fresh pulpy fruit. Peaches, pears. Develops on bakery notes. Oak keeps its grip but without overdoing it.
**Finish:** Long, oaky, spicy.

**8** **Dave: A good example of a whisky at the start of its mature phase.**
**Nose:** Clean, rich, dried fruit, stewed rhubarb, raffia. Weighty, concentrated, slightly fungal, deep. Dries a little with water.
**Palate:** Instead of a blast of weight this spreads discreetly across the tongue. Good complexity and fine balance. Plenty of black fruits. Best neat, though water shows how deep the flavours are.
**Finish:** Nutty and slightly astringent.

## GLENFARCLAS 1955 44.6%
Single Malt - Speyside

**7¼** **Michael: The russet colour promised something more luxurious, but this whisky is not as rich as it was.**
**Nose:** Perfumy. Rosewater. Pruney.
**Palate:** Starts sweet. Rather thin. Soft, gentle. Falling apart somewhat.
**Finish:** Slight woody astringency.

**9** **Dave: A fantastic dram. Overlook this at your peril.**
**Nose:** Thick, resinous and richly scented with a drift of smoke overlaid by a beautiful perfume. Water pulls out a silky soft note with grilled nut, fig jam and with time honey. Layered and complex.
**Palate:** Sweet start. Light, tea-like tannins, hard toffee, chestnut, ginger spiciness. Silky feel.
**Finish:** Embers, oak, Dundee cake. Very long. Becomes a little tight with time.

## GLENFARCLAS 1974 30 YEARS OLD, BOTTLE FOR THE WHISKY EXCHANGE, THE WHISKY EXCHANGE 50.5%
Single Malt - Speyside

**7½** **Martine: A lot of elegance and distinction but as if it has lost health. Surprisingly enough, waters boosts it.**
**Nose:** Creamy, slightly restrained. Coffee toffee. Tiramisu. Polished floor. Old library. Orange peel. All well integrated and mingled. Elegant. Attractive.
**Palate:** Sweet and soft, a bit too soft. Watery at mid-palate. Marmalade. Nutmeg. Hint of cinnamon.
**Finish:** Long, gentle, a bit tired. Almondy.

**7¾** **Dave: Seems older. A little fragile.**
**Nose:** Rich in weight yet slightly dry. Spearmint, treacle, walnut. Mature.
**Palate:** Slightly oily. Sponge pudding, cocoa. Oak is quite firm but there's enough sweetness to balance.
**Finish:** Leaf mulch.

## GLENFARCLAS 2001 SINGLE CASK BOTTLING, CRAIGELLACHIE HOTEL OF SPEYSIDE 51.2%
Single Malt - Speyside

**8¾** **Michael: In each corner, a fighter rather than a boxer. Not much refinement, but plenty of punch.**
**Nose:** Very powerful and seductive. Polished oak. Marzipan. Black chocolate. Candied orange peel.
**Palate:** Treacle-toffee richness versus burnt-grass peatiness. Big flavours, locked together like boxers punching their way out of a clinch. Long, muscular interplay; one seems to dominate, and then the other.
**Finish:** Smoky. Oaky. Very spicy.

**7¾** **Dave: Good stuff with plenty of rich distillery character. Balance. That's what it is all about.**
**Nose:** Robust and cakey: date, prune, cooked fruits, treacle, Dundee cake. Resinous with a little smoke.
**Palate:** Big and powerful. A balanced mix of (European) oak and rich, sweet spirit.
**Finish:** Rich and long.

## GLENFARCLAS 21 YEARS OLD 43%
Single Malt - Speyside

**8¾** **Michael: A straightforward Speyside classic. Also big enough to benefit from considerable age.**
**Nose:** Sherryish, nutty aromas predominate. Then malt (slightly buttery), and peat. Each seems to manifest itself as a separate hit.
**Palate:** Lively expression of classic Speyside flavours: sherry, malt and slight smokiness.
**Finish:** Lightly peaty. Appetising.

**8¼** **Dave: Excellent, has great balance.**
**Nose:** Takes time to open, and once some water is added, there's a wall of aromas: rich, fruity with some toffee, vanilla, caramelised apple, barley sugar, coconut, dried fruit and hints of peat and banana.
**Palate:** Dry, quite heathery overall. A firm body with rich and ripe mid-palate. A whisky that demands to be chewed.
**Finish:** Powerful, heather and bracken. Moreish.

## GLENFARCLAS 40 YEARS OLD, MILLENNIUM EDITION 54.7%
Single Malt - Speyside

**8¾** **Michael: Some of the voluptuousness has sagged with age.**
**Nose:** Oaky.
**Palate:** Medium to full. Very firm. Oaky start, with nutty maltiness and raisiny sweetness fighting through. Tightly locked flavours open with a dash of water.
**Finish:** Peat. Log fires. Oak.

**9¼** **Jim: An almost immaculate portrayal of an old-fashioned, high quality malt. Quite outstanding for its age.**
**Nose:** Beautifully defined oak; almost chestnut sweet with clean sherry, softly peated and bourbony.
**Palate:** Oak again, teasingly spicy with sweetness and intense malt. Hint of liquorice.
**Finish:** Long, chewy, smoky and initially sweet with the liquorice continuing, dries slowly to an oaky encore.

## GLENFIDDICH 12 YEARS OLD, SPECIAL RESERVE 40%
Single Malt - Speyside

**7** **Martine: Easy-going, fresh and fruity, but the palate does not reflect the liveliness of the nose.**
**Nose:** Light and delicate. A mouth-watering full basket of fruit. Pear, cherry, plum. Honey.
**Palate:** Does not deliver the delicacy of the nose. Sweetness ends up in softness. Pears in honey. A hint of toasted nuts.
**Finish:** Pleasantly dry. Soothing freshness.

**7¼** **Dave: Very clean, well-made and attractive.**
**Nose:** Light and malty/mealy. Some citric notes (lemon/orange peel). Water opens up the nutty crackerbread maltiness alongside some dry grass and dried apple.
**Palate:** Soft with vanilla, malt, a light nuttiness and a soft mid-palate.
**Finish:** Soft and lightly fruity with a hint of chocolate.

## GLENFIDDICH 12 YEARS OLD, SPECIAL RESERVE 40%
Single Malt - Speyside

**7¾** **Michael: Glenfiddich has much more roundness of flavour since it switched from 'no age statement' to 12 years.**
**Nose:** Faint peat. Underlying fruit. Pears, but very restrained. Fresh, appetising.
**Palate:** Light, lean, firm. A dryish, oily, matiness. Hints of white chocolate coming through.
**Finish:** White chocolate. Toasted nuts. Bitter black chocolate.

**7¼ Dave: A young, light, uncomplicated dram. Drink over ice.**
**Nose:** Cereal once again with some citric light. Some cracker-bread/biscuit and light wood notes. Everything in the upper register.
**Palate:** A bit creamier than you'd think with a chewy maltiness, whisper of orange and some chocolate. Discreet.
**Finish:** Soft.

## GLENFIDDICH 12 YEARS OLD, TOASTED OAK 40%
Single Malt - Speyside

**7½ Dave: A bit of a let down after such a great nose. A very pretty whisky but higher alcohol might have given it better impact in the mouth.**
**Nose:** Pine sap, aromatic woods, beech nut. In time a sweeter note of kumquat, then pan drop/minty sweets. Oak driven, sweetly so.
**Palate:** Slightly thin after such an impressive nose. Plenty of wood and a touch of crème brûlée.
**Finish:** Soft, pillow-like.

**7½ Arthur: A pretty nose but fairly uneventful on the palate. Pleasant.**
**Nose:** Satsuma segments, nail polish, apricot cream and papaya. Then a doughy, pumice-like element, that borders on soapy.
**Palate:** Sweet, with vanilla and almonds and a lightly bitter oakiness.
**Finish:** Pretty short, but a delicate US oakiness.

## GLENFIDDICH 15 YEARS OLD, SOLERA RESERVE 40%
Single Malt - Speyside

WHISKY Magazine Recommended

**8 Michael: Light but very smooth. Scores points for its suave smoothness and sweetness.**
**Nose:** Chocolate. Toast. Hint of peat.
**Palate:** Suave and silky; white chocolate, pears in cream, cardamom.
**Finish:** Cream and a hint of ginger.

**9½ Jim: A classic.**
**Nose:** The most complex nose in the Glenfiddich stable: fruit, spice, oak, honey
**Palate:** A brilliantly balanced array of honey, spice and intense malt.
**Finish:** The delicate sherry works well with the oaky, cocoa notes.

## GLENFIDDICH 18 YEARS OLD, ANCIENT RESERVE 43%
Single Malt - Speyside

**8 Michael: Scores points for sophistication and sherry character.**
**Nose:** Very rich.
**Palate:** More mellow and rounded, soft and restrained, with very soft body.
**Finish:** Nutty with a flowery hint of peat.

**8½ Jim: A wonderfully elegant whisky.**
**Nose:** Blood oranges, apples, gentle smoke and oaky saltiness. Delicate and enormously sexy.
**Palate:** Melts in the mouth: sherry, sultanas, honeyed maltiness, spice.
**Finish:** Medium length but extremely clean, chewy and well defined.

## GLENFIDDICH 1965 VINTAGE RESERVE 47.8%
Single Malt - Speyside

WHISKY Magazine Editor's choice

**9 Michael: A playful whisky for one of such maturity. Starting very sweetly, but reluctant to reveal its secrets. Give it time to reveal its complexity.**
**Nose:** Light, fresh, almond-blossom. Hard butterscotch. Nutty. A hint of grassy peatiness.
**Palate:** Slowly reveals white chocolate flavours. Fondant-like, peppermint. Then spicy, herbal notes.
**Finish:** Restrained. Lightly gingery. Warming.

**8¼ Dave: Vibrant but not quite balanced between the sharp citrus notes, wood and fruit.**
**Nose:** Intense, perfumed almost sharp nose with lemon zest, fresh flowers, cereal/Shredded Wheat, light vanilla, pine forest/resin and a touch of candlewax.
**Palate:** Light and quite acidic. There's some vanilla mid-palate but overall crisp, penetrating and zesty.
**Finish:** The lemon notes stay with it all the way.

## GLENFIDDICH 1967, VINTAGE RESERVE 43%
Single Malt - Speyside

**8½ Michael: On the light side among older Glenfiddichs, but delicate and appetising.**
**Nose:** Pears, grass, heather.
**Palate:** Soft, delicate, sweetish. The characteristic white-chocolate note of the older Glenfiddichs.
**Finish:** Light, fresh. Orange-honey. Light spicy dryness.

**8 Jim: Delicious but rare. Every bottle has already been sold.**
**Nose:** Sensuous, softly spiced and boasting a subtle, maple sweetness. Brilliantly delicate.
**Palate:** Early oak and then a surge of sweet, deliciously textured malt. Soft peppers and a balancing fudge.
**Finish:** Dry and oaky but with barley-sweetness. Late chocolate and ageing liquorice.

## GLENFIDDICH 1973 VINTAGE 48.1%
Single Malt - Speyside

WHISKY Magazine Recommended

**8½ Dave: Beautifully calm and seamless.**
**Nose:** A glossy kind of nose: ripe fruits, polished oak, oolong tea, roasted cereal and cocoa nibs. With water a delicious deep fruit cake note.
**Palate:** Soft, slow, silky with a slightly syrupy quality and firm oak. Water smooths things. Manages to be sweet with treacle toffee weight.
**Finish:** Shifts to chocolate and fades. Elegance.

**8¾ Arthur: A sophisticated, spicy dram with oodles of class.**
**Nose:** Sultanas and mixed peel. Prune juice, and a hint of smokiness. Blackberry and apple cumble, with some stem ginger. Liebkuchen and christmas cake spices.
**Palate:** Apricot jam, dark chocolate and a good shake of gingery spice. Bath Oliver biscuits.
**Finish:** More of that smoky woodiness.

## GLENFIDDICH 1973 VINTAGE RESERVE 49.5%
Single Malt - Speyside

WHISKY Magazine Recommended

**8¾ Michael: Luxurious and sweet, but background is gently dry. Deftly balanced and sophisticated, as ever.**
**Nose:** Flapjack made with treacle. French toast dusted with cinnamon. Ginger. Clean, appetising.
**Palate:** Dusty. Spicy, then dark chocolate. Developing white chocolate. Vanilla ice-cream. Rum and raisin.
**Finish:** Crisp. Belgian wafers.

**8¼ Dave: All very precise with a polite procession of flavours. "No please, you go first. " "Why thank you old boy. "**
**Nose:** Great charm and complexity: apple, malt, flowers, bracken, spice, sawn oak, dunnage. More sweet oak with water. Sophisticated stuff.
**Palate:** Nutty to start, then bursts into life with chocolate, cut flowers, cinnamon and mandarin.
**Finish:** Crisp, biscuity.

## GLENFIDDICH 1974 50TH ANNIVERSARY OF THE QUEEN'S CORONATION, THE WHISKY EXCHANGE 48.9%
Single Malt - Speyside

WHISKY Magazine Recommended

**8¼ Michael: Despite the rich descriptors, I found this slightly sharp with some vintage Glenfiddichs.**
**Nose:** Pastry out of a hot oven. Slightly smoky. Fresh pears in butterscotch sauce.
**Palate:** Light to medium body. Like exploring a box of chocolates. Milk chocolate first, then dark. Chocolate limes (perhaps the odd kumquat), then mint creams.
**Finish:** Liqueur-ish. Soothing.

**8¾ Dave: All very elegant and sophisticated.**
**Nose:** Aromatic. Hyacinth, raisin, dried apple, chocolate cake, preserved plum. Good depth and complexity.
**Palate:** Soft with a good steady flow. Chocolate ganash, orange, tobacco. Flattens a little towards the finish. Good grip.
**Finish:** Fragrant. Spiced oranges. Grand Champagne Cognac.

## GLENFIDDICH 1991 VINTAGE RESERVE 40%
Single Malt - Speyside

**7¾ Michael: Gentle. Accessible. Enjoyable.**
**Nose:** Fresh bread being toasted by an open fire.
**Palate:** Light but firm. Hard toffee. Creamy.
**Finish:** Sweet spiciness.

**8½ Dave: No water needed here. Good, complex.**
**Nose:** Heavy, extractive nose, rich and mature. Dry with oak, Dundee cake, liquorice. Firm oak. Becomes more assertive with water.
**Palate:** Sweet and syrupy. Dried fruits, red fruits, almond croissant, but with sufficient dry, coconut oak to balance. Shifts into honeycomb.
**Finish:** Quite dry.

## GLENFIDDICH 21 YEARS OLD, GRAN RESERVA 40%
Single Malt - Speyside

**7¾ Martine: Delivers more than expected. Seems a bit bland at start but it displays an attractive array of aromas and flavours on time. The rum influence is under control.**
**Nose:** Shy. A grassy note. Quite perfumy and enticing in time. Water chestnut. Very elegant.
**Palate:** Smooth, satisfying. Oak is well integrated. Pear. Orange and almond tart. Spices burst out after the sweet release.
**Finish:** Medium, refreshing. Slightly nutty.

**8¼ Dave: Great balance. An exemplary finish.**
**Nose:** Mature. Malty with dark chocolate-covered strawberries, some prune. With water becomes musky with hints of cedar and a gentle relaxed sweetness held in check by quite firm oak.
**Palate:** Softer than the nose suggests and significantly sweeter. Layers of fruits, cocoa, syrup, demerara sugar, coffee.
**Finish:** Cigar-like then softens and sweetens.

## GLENFIDDICH 21 YEARS OLD, MILLENNIUM RESERVE 43%
Single Malt - Speyside

**8 Michael: Lighter and more delicate than the 21 Years Old that appeared in a Wedgwood decanter in years past.**
**Nose:** Marshmallow and toasted coconut.
**Palate:** Oily and chewy. Bitter chocolate, becoming extraordinarily fruity, then sweetish.
**Finish:** Gentle, fruity. Reminiscent of lemon peels.

**8½ Jim: A charming, almost shy malt that must be drunk at full strength to appreciate its guile and complexity.**
**Nose:** Light, vaguely doughy and suet-like, with an understated oaky backbone.
**Palate:** Warming and very sweet from the start with some prime bourbony characteristics.
**Finish:** Very soft smoke, a hint of toffee and vanilla.

## GLENFIDDICH 30 YEARS OLD 40%
Single Malt - Speyside

**8½ Michael: Luxurious, but in a restrained, understated way.**
**Nose:** Sweetish. Beeswax. White chocolate. Hint of ginger.
**Palate:** Satiny. Sweeter, more honeyed than most versions, with the characteristic pears-in-cream offering.
**Finish:** Apple wood flavours and light smokiness in a gently rounded conclusion.

**7¾ Jim: Rarely does Glenfiddich pass 21 years unscathed by time, but this has done much better than most.**
**Nose:** "Quality Street" dark chocolate sweet with soft lemon inside with kumquats and nuts.
**Palate:** Delicate malt notes followed by a prickly spice and then a menthol backwash revealing great age.
**Finish:** Simple and clean. Vanilla at first and then bourbon-style oak notes.

## GLENFIDDICH 30 YEARS OLD 40%
Single Malt - Speyside

**8½ Michael: Salient house characteristics, especially the chocolate, at their boldest and most sustained.**
**Nose:** Notes of sherry, fruit, chocolate, and ginger.
**Palate:** Sherry, raisins, chocolate, ginger. Quite luxurious.
**Finish:** Unhurried, with chocolatey notes and gingery dryness.

**7½ Dave:** Another where the nose promises a lot, but the palate doesn't quite deliver.
**Nose:** Autumnal. Damp leaves, turned earth, chocolate truffle, hint of rancio. Barley sugar, privet.
**Palate:** Very smooth and silky. Good maturity. Cereal notes. Crisp, woody texture.
**Finish:** Short.

## GLENFIDDICH 40 YEARS OLD 43.6%
Single Malt - Speyside

**9¼ Michael: This is an urbane whisky that will not easily reveal itself. Take your time with it. Enjoy its company.**
**Nose:** Burnt-heather smokiness. Sappy oak.
**Palate:** Very luxurious. Beeswax and honey. Bitter black chocolate. Treacle toffee. Anise.
**Finish:** Spicy. satisfying. Long.

**9 Jim: Anyone who reckons Glenfiddich is not a top-rate distillery should sample this.**
**Nose:** Wild blackberries add some fruity lustre to an otherwise oaky yet understated aroma.
**Palate:** An explosion of grape and spice.
**Finish:** Long, continually fruity yet still smoky.

## GLENFIDDICH 40 YEARS OLD, RARE COLLECTION 44%
Single Malt - Speyside

**9¼ Michael: Extraordinary flavour development. An astonishingly complex whisky.**
**Nose:** A depth of honey aromas. Beeswax. Finally, a balancing flowery dryness and faint smokiness.
**Palate:** Very slow emergence of flavours. Firm, dryish, honey. Biscuity maltiness. A hint of bitter chocolate. A surge of soft, smokiness, with peat.
**Finish:** Hint of anis. Satisfying. Long.

**8½ Dave: Has the extra dimension which sets the finest old whiskies apart.**
**Nose:** Slow to open. Elegant and mature. Blue cheese, church halls/hassocks. Light smoke and hint of chocolate.
**Palate:** Old, but still with a fresh and youthful centre. Good balance.
**Finish:** Woody, bung cloth.

## GLENFIDDICH CAORAN RESERVE, 12 YEARS OLD 40%
Single Malt - Speyside

**7½ Michael: A more sprightly Glenfiddich than the standard 12. Thirst-quenching. Peatiness and the smoked finish aren't as 'distinct' as the label suggests.**
**Nose:** Aromatic. Damp cellars. Earthy and rooty. Dundee cake. A touch of orange peel and pot pourri. A distant smoky note.
**Palate:** Sweet but vivid. Refreshing. Barley sugar.
**Finish:** Lingering, warm. Leafy, becomes bitter with water added.

**7½ Dave: An interesting experiment...but why not just peat some Glenfiddich and see what happens? You'd have a genuine peated Speyside malt.**
**Nose:** Soft malty, cereal notes: ground hazelnuts, vanilla, oak and light smoke.
**Palate:** Sweet, malty and lightly fruity. A slight woody catch on the tongue then the smoke builds up.
**Finish:** Perfumed smoke then a medicinal note.

## GLENFIDDICH HAVANA RESERVE, 21 YEARS OLD 40%
Single Malt - Speyside

**8 Michael: When you cook, do you want the herbs and spices to announce themselves individually, or to be part of the blend of flavours? David Stewart seems usually to opt for the latter, and does so with great deftness and sophistication.**
**Nose:** Toasty. Biscuity. Petits fours.
**Palate:** Vanilla flan. Sweet Cuban coffee.
**Finish:** Juicy. A hint of dried tropical fruits.

**8 Dave: Good balance with the rum at no point overwhelming the whisky. American readers will have to smuggle it into the country along with their Cohibas.**
**Nose:** Rich and rounded with clean malty notes. Chocolate, caramelised banana, some citric notes, orange pulp, toffee and spice.
**Palate:** The chocolate comes back giving a sweet, balanced dram. Good mature malt character.
**Finish:** Chocolate, coffee and orange peel.

## GLENFIDDICH MALT WHISKY LIQUEUR
Whisky Liqueur - Scotland

**7½ Michael: A mid-evening treat when the open fire is glowing and the family gathered.**
**Nose:** Honey, lemons, pears and brown sugar.
**Palate:** Starts honeyish, becomes malty, developing to a heathery, faintly peaty, balancing dryness.
**Finish:** Warming, soothing.

## GLENFIDDICH SPECIAL RESERVE 40%
Single Malt - Speyside

**7½ Michael: Lean, smooth and appetising.**
**Nose:** Light, fresh but sweet, appetising, fruity, pear-like.
**Palate:** Dryish, pear-like, more fruitiness as flavour develops. A dash of water releases a hint of smokiness and some sweet, malty notes.
**Finish:** Restrained, aromatic.

**7 Jim: Rather simple, but very enjoyable – except for the slightly duff nose.**
**Nose:** Youthful and slightly fat. Quite underripe.
**Palate:** Fat and full, lots of malt concentrate. Initially sweet then some drier banana notes . Refreshing.
**Finish:** Some oaky notes.

## GLENGLASSAUGH 1976 29 YEARS OLD, DEWAR RATTRAY 53%
Single Malt - Speyside

**7¼ Dave: Of interest, but not great.**
**Nose:** Estery. Acetone then almond, lemon verbena, green tea, lime blossom moving to cut grass. Sharp and firm.
**Palate:** Better than the nose. Fragrant though with surprising depth. Direct and sweet. Good grip and decent balance.
**Finish:** A little bitter.

**6¾ Arthur: A strange cask, which has produced an unusual malt whisky. Could be to some people's tastes but not mine.**
**Nose:** Behind fruitiness is a curious earthy and mechanical character, exhaust fumes and rusty cans, and maybe even a little tarriness.
**Palate:** Some stewed fruit and some oaky, cinnamon spice suggesting age.
**Finish:** Drying, tingling oak leaving a lasting bitterness.

## GLENGLASSAUGH 1976, DORMANT DISTILLERY CO. 47.4%
Single Malt - Speyside

**7¼ Michael: A distinctive malt, but now slightly past its best.**
**Nose:** Linen. Lemon grass. Gorse. Coconut. Fruity.
**Palate:** Grassy. Spicy. Peppery. Drying on the tongue.
**Finish:** Medicinal. Slightly astringent.

**8 Dave: Not the most complex, but a bloody good drink.**
**Nose:** On the edgy side of fragrant: sweet apple, green pear, quince. With water becomes more like a freshly peeled apple.
**Palate:** Another light and fresh dram. Orange Spangles, very lively, light fruits Good balance and real charm.
**Finish:** Odd fellows (that's the sweet, not the staff of RMW...then again...).

## GLENGLASSAUGH 21 YEARS OLD 1986, DEWAR RATTRAY 53.4%
Single Malt - Speyside

**6¾ Dave: "Sweet and sulphury" now, there's a catchy brand name.**
**Nose:** Lurid colour. Toffee, nutella and cereal dryness to start, then becomes increasingly sulphury.
**Palate:** More tannic than you expect, the sulphur like a firework on the palate. Lacks elegance and balance.
**Finish:** Bitter.

**6¼ Martine: A good example of cask tyranny. The sherry acts like a tsunami. Makes no quarter!**
**Nose:** Sulphury, woody. Walnut stain. A hint of date. The sherry cask chokes the whisky.
**Palate:** Dry, sour, astringent. Oak juice, and not much more.
**Finish:** Of the same metal as we say in French! Wood, wood, wood...

## GLENGLASSAUGH 25 YEARS OLD, CADENHEAD'S 45.2%
Single Malt - Speyside

**7¾ Michael: Glenglassaugh can be malty, and this one is. It stands up very well for it's age. With an apricot colour that suggests sherry, very much a dessert whisky.**
**Nose:** Starfruit. Caramel sauce. Candied lemon peel.
**Palate:** Smooth. Dark chocolate souffle.
**Finish:** Chocolate Olivers. Slightly woody.

**7¾ Dave: A spiky mix of apple and grass. Intriguing.**
**Nose:** Apples: flesh, skin, core and pips, in fact. Water gives straw, grass with herbs and nuts.
**Palate:** Medium bodied. Pear, toffee apple and herbs. Goes down the middle of the tongue rather than filling the mouth. Smoky oak late on.
**Finish:** Firm, dry, little short.

## GLENGLASSAUGH 26 YEARS OLD, CADENHEAD'S 51.1%
Single Malt - Speyside

**6¾ Michael: This has dried out to a point where it is aggressive and unbalanced.**
**Nose:** Freshly cut wood. Sawdust.
**Palate:** Gorse. Flowering currant.
**Finish:** Medicinal. Bitter.

**7½ Dave: Another which wears its age lightly, just a bit woody and sharp.**
**Nose:** Acidic. Some bracken, kumquat, dry oak. Water softens it and brings out pine and coconut.
**Palate:** Dry and fairly firm with a fine texture. Some sweet malt in the centre. Grips again towards the finish.
**Finish:** Light and fresh.

## GLENGLASSAUGH 30 YEARS OLD, OLD MALT CASK 45.6%
Single Malt - Speyside

**7½ Dave: Another whose palate runs counter to its nose.**
**Nose:** Acetone, a hint of glue, bubblegum. Is your name Ester by any chance? Very grassy. After the volatiles fly off you're left with (cloudy) apple juice, marzipan, gooseberry jam and light oak.
**Palate:** Good layering of fruits. You can almost feel the velvet skin of the apricot as it slides over the tongue. Creamy.
**Finish:** Soft with a slight tart note.

**7 Arthur: Some delightful fruity elements but ultimately dominated by woodiness. Don't attempt if you don't like dry whisky!**
**Nose:** Gala melon, struck flint and warm bread. Watermelon and pear drops. Borders on that over-chemically esters board-marker note.
**Palate:** Fruity (melons and pears), fruit salad chews, then bone dry.
**Finish:** Bourbon-like woodiness, and more dryness.

## GLENGOYNE 12 YEARS OLD 57.2%
Single Malt - Highland

**7 Martine: Lacks elegance and complexity. Oak dominates, with a bitter grip. Water does not help.**
**Nose:** Oaky, sappy. An unpleasant cheesy aroma. Opens on nicer toffeeish notes.
**Palate:** Mellow. Sweet maltiness. But bitterness soon becomes insistent. Hot spices.
**Finish:** Warm. Dry, slightly astringent.

**8¼ Dave: Greater depth and apparent maturity than you'd expect from a 12 Years Old.**
**Nose:** A little faded with touches of autumn leaves, bung cloth, unripe mango, (bread crust on a Scottish plain loaf). Alcohol in balance. With water there's more overt oak and a hint of condensed milk.
**Palate:** Dense and full but a balance struck between sweet and sour flavours: grape syrup, sugared almond, red apple. Smooth with good grip.
**Finish:** Spice, chestnut, overripe pear.

## GLENGOYNE 17 YEARS OLD 43%
Single Malt - Highland

**8** **Michael: A lovely, complex, sophisticated malt.**
**Nose:** Clean linen. Cedar. Fresh oak. Palo cortado sherry.
**Palate:** Remarkably smooth. Sweet. Hints of brazil nut and apple.
**Finish:** Creamy. Hint of lemon pith dryness. Very delicate touch of sherry.

**7¾** **Jim: By no means the most complex whisky on the market, but unquestionably one of the most elegant and charming.**
**Nose:** Very clean nose: the oak is minimal with honeyed-grassy malt. Beguiling.
**Palate:** A fabulous, honey-sweet infusion of tender malty notes do take on a waxy middle.
**Finish:** Bitter-sweet and still waxy with mounting vanilla and even a late hint of cocoa.

## GLENGOYNE 17 YEARS OLD 43%
Single Malt - Highland

**7¾** **Martine: Quite a complex character for its age. The palate is well-structured, just a little too woodframed.**
**Nose:** Elegant, mouthwatering. Praline ice cream. Turkish delight. A hint of exotic fruit. Mango. Spicy carrot cake.
**Palate:** Rich, fruity at start. A certain austerity. Oak is more present than on the nose.
**Finish:** Fades away slowly. Retains a delicate fruitiness.

**8** **Dave: There's masses of oak here, but it has real sweet-hearted charm.**
**Nose:** Masses of sweet oak: cocoa, hot butter, taffy, chocolate ganash and some light cherry notes. Some cereal alongside polished oak and nuts.
**Palate:** Excellent layering effect. Flows across the palate: creamy and smooth, hot gorse and very chewy.
**Finish:** Red and black fruits.

## GLENGOYNE 19 YEARS OLD 55.8%
Single Malt - Highland

**7½** **Martine: A nice fresh feel. But alcohol is not tamed. Water cools it down but takes the zesty kick away.**
**Nose:** Perfumy. Citrus fruit. Tangerine and seville orange. Flower honey. Oatcakes.
**Palate:** Tangy. Alcohol dominates. Sherbety. Spices dance on the tongue. Smoother with water.
**Finish:** Very spicy, keeps spirity.

**7¾** **Dave: Very good, but not quite the great balance of the last three.**
**Nose:** Sweet and luscious, creamy. Some sultana, some toasted malt, pine nut, bread and a charred note. Shows maturity.
**Palate:** Surprisingly firm, grippy backbone after such a soft appealing nose. Shows some age along with orange, honey. Soft, long and full.
**Finish:** Sweet spices.

## GLENGOYNE 1972 46%
Single Malt - Highland

**7¾** **Dave: Amazingly fresh for such an oldie. Much prefer this style of Glengoyne to the sherried monsters which tend to drown the distillery character.**
**Nose:** Fresh, sweet and quite light with cream, coconut, baked banana. Water brings out clover honey, jasmine, cucumber and very light ginger.
**Palate:** Sweet and light. Very clean and lifted with enough going on in the centre to give it good balance and feel.
**Finish:** Minty.

**7¼** **Martine: The nose promised smoothness, the palate delivered dry oakiness. Water cuts the edges but enhances bitterness and spices.**
**Nose:** Perfumy. Starts with cereal notes entwined with fruit and oak. Barley sugar, peardrop, gooseberry, polished floor. Then herbal notes break through. Linden tree.
**Palate:** Good velvety feel stiffened by grippy oak.
**Finish:** Dry, spicy, oaky.

## GLENGOYNE 2000 AD 43%
Single Malt - Highland

**8½** **Michael: Delicious example of maltiness in a whisky. I always enjoy Glengoynes very much, but they invariably leave me wanting a little more.**
**Nose:** Very aromatic, appetising and softly spicy.

*WHISKY Recommended*

**Palate:** Very malty. Long and unfolding. Clean. Sweet start. Creamy flavours, becoming cookie-like and nutty.
**Finish:** Chewy, malty. Very soft, restrained, dessert apple.

**9½** **Jim: This single bottling places Glengoyne in the super-league status; the finest expression from this distillery.**
**Nose:** A glorious mixture of malt, sweet pipe smoke subtle grape and leather and a sprinkling of peat.
**Palate:** An absolute flavour explosion of sweet and dry malt, cherries, vanilla and a fruit cocktail.
**Finish:** Heaps of vanilla and other subtle oaky tones and lashings of sweet malt.

## GLENGOYNE 21 YEARS OLD 43%
Single Malt - Highland

**8** **Michael: If this were a Lowland malt, it would be a star. As a Highlander, it gets lost.**
**Nose:** Lively. Light earthiness. Faint hint of smoke.
**Palate:** Smooth and firm. Dryish, cedary. Tannin. Apples. Oranges. Then creamy and sweet.
**Finish:** Spicy. Cinnamon. Ginger. Long, warm.

**7½** **Dave: Subtle. A wee charmer.**
**Nose:** Soft and attractive with good weight. Light honey, buttered scones, orange, grass and balanced toasty oak. Water brings out a fresh spiciness, but reduces the interest a bit.
**Palate:** Slightly drier than the nose suggests. A good mix of spicy oak, mid-palate weight and smooth texture.
**Finish:** A little short. Light honey, then biscuit.

## GLENGOYNE 32 YEARS OLD, SINGLE CASK 48.7%
Single Malt - Highland

**8½** **Arthur: Complex, old, not perfect, but good darned fun!**
**Nose:** Fragrant, like a guava or kushi pear. Floor polish, mint syrup, artificial cherry flavour and a whiff of wood glue.
**Palate:** Orange, raisins, gooseberries and a balsa woodiness indicating a good bit of age.
**Finish:** A light burnt character, and possibly some rose. Relatively subtle, whispering of its age.

*WHISKY Magazine Editor's choice*

**9** **Dave: This is a stunningly great whisky, subtle and profound...**
**Nose:** Intense, mature and complex. Fruit coulis made from slightly tart hedgerow fruits and mint. Raspberry leaf, light cream, beech nut, patisserie.
**Palate:** Layers of flavour with a zesty, citric quality. Balanced oak, Seville orange, mulled wine. Firm and nutty structure but has sweetness to balance.
**Finish:** Long, generous, complex.

## GLENGOYNE 37 YEARS OLD, SHERRY BUTT 47.6%
Single Malt - Highland

**8¼** **Arthur: Sweet, filling, rich and satisfying. An impressive after-dinner drop.**
**Nose:** Ripe fruit bowl, marker pens and parsnips! With water more woodiness appears along with Peach Schnapps and marzipan.
**Palate:** Apricot jam, treacle toffee and lots of European oak. With water a light mintiness and camphor character.
**Finish:** Malty, with blood pudding, and European tannins.

**9** **Owen: Luxuriant without decadence. Aristocratic.**
**Nose:** Sweet, ripe red apples. Pears. Blackcurrants. Summer fruits. Lemon zest. Honey. Chocolate cake.
**Palate:** Big, rich, firm, confident. Pears, first poached in port, then coated in a Valrhona sauce.
**Finish:** Long, urbane, elegant. Organic chocolate coated ginger. Toasted coconut.

## GLENGOYNE SCOTTISH OAK FINISH 53.5%
Single Malt - Highland

**8** **Michael: A rather eccentric version of Glengoyne. Very distinctive. A digestive after Thai food or even a curry?**
**Nose:** Very aromatic. Smells like a freshly cut tree. Resiny. Lemon skins.
**Palate:** Dry creaminess. Vanilla pods. Cinnamon. Tropical fruits. Paw-paw.
**Finish:** Like biting into a tree bark. Hot, spicy, flavours. Cloves?

**7¼** **Dave: Scottish oak veneer? A fascinating experiment, but the really interesting malt, Glengoyne matured in Scottish oak refill, is yet to come.**

**Nose:** Sweet, honeyed and woody. Water brings out honey nut cornflakes, fruit and nut, oak, clover and a whiff of sap and the farmyard.
**Palate:** Soft and quite honeyed. Toasted almonds, rose, dolly mixtures. Sweeter than standard Glengoyne.
**Finish:** Sweet, but oak takes charge.

## GLENKINCHIE 10 YEARS OLD 43%
Single Malt - Lowland

**7½** **Michael: I always enjoy this whisky, even though it is not the most typical of Lowlanders.**
**Nose:** Freshly aromatic: grassy, spicy and lemongrassy.
**Palate:** Soft, spicy: cinnamon and, ginger. Beautiful balance of sweetness and dryness.
**Finish:** Fragrant spicy dryness.

**7** **Jim: One of the better samples I've tasted recently. This malt can be temperamental. Delightfully intense but a lack of complexity through the middle disappoints.**
**Nose:** Thin and spirity. Exceptionally malty and reminiscent of boiled barley-sugar candy.
**Palate:** Sweet, grassy-sharp and mouthwatering. Dominant malt, a hint of banana and custard.
**Finish:** Intense vanilla and caramel with rich oaky tones and a delicate hint of smoke. Slightly bitter at finish.

## GLENKINCHIE 10 YEARS OLD 43%
Single Malt - Lowland

**7** **Arthur: Very much in its regional style, but lacks finesse or genuine interest.**
**Nose:** Plasticene, wet grass, spearmint.
**Palate:** Light, then dry and grassy.
**Finish:** Bran, malt and a little soapy.

**7½** **Dave: A charming everyday drinking malt.**
**Nose:** Estery. Orange oil/zest, freesia, stewed rhubarb, cinnamon, dry grasses, raisin bread.
**Palate:** Delicate and lightly floral, raspberry yoghurt and a crisp nuttiness alongside light vanilla.
**Finish:** Tea leaves, then mango.

## GLENKINCHIE 12 YEARS OLD 43%
Single Malt - Lowland

**7½** **Dave: A huge leap in quality from the old 10 Years Old.**
**Nose:** Mealy with some sweet grassiness. Apple purée, wet fern and a floral character (lilac). Some toasty oak below. Good creamy sweetness.
**Palate:** Intense and focused with real lemon tartness to start. Mellows into clotted cream, tangerine and a crisp oak giving balancing grip.
**Finish:** Surprisingly dry.

**7½** **Martine: A very linear aromatic display. No surprise. Just pleasant.**
**Nose:** Refreshing, fragrant. Fruit cake, crystallised violets. Candy-floss. Liquorice toffee. Very confectionery-like.
**Palate:** Very much in tune with the nose. Smooth, round and fresh. With water, malt extract.
**Finish:** Carrying on the same aromatic path. Minty and aniseed lozenges. Oat in the back.

## GLENKINCHIE 1986 AMONTILLADO CASK FINISH 43%
Single Malt - Lowland

**8** **Michael: As a relatively restrained whisky, Glenkinchie stands up well to the amontillado finish.**
**Nose:** Light, polished oak. Lemon, cinnamon and ginger.
**Palate:** Assertive flavours. Sweet then suddenly dry, salty, and nutty.
**Finish:** Long, echoing interplay of crystal-sugar sweetness and oaky dryness. Soothing.

**8½** **Jim: Far more complex than the standard Glenkinchie. Quite intriguing stuff, not least because it is best very slightly chilled.**
**Nose:** Roast chestnut, malty, sherryish. Brisk and brittle, impressive.
**Palate:** Shows at first a biscuity-sweetness. Big and malty while the sherry remains slightly subdued.
**Finish:** Quite long but now oaky as the malt and sherry seem played out.

## GLENKINCHIE 1988 DISTILLER'S EDITION 43%
Single Malt - Lowland

**8** **Michael: Glenkinchie was always robust for a lowlander, and this expression is more so. Again, it works: the typical grassy sweetness brought out by a touch of sherry.**
**Nose:** Perfumy. Floral. Slightly oily. Seedcake?
**Palate:** Beautifully rounded. Nutty. Grainy. Grassy. Sweet.
**Finish:** Brown sugar. Rum butter. Remarkably long.

**7¾** **Dave: The finish gives a subtle extra layer of flavour rather than dominating.**
**Nose:** Sweet, soft and inviting: hot fruit scones, honey, orange, barley sugar and a hint of struck match.
**Palate:** Good balance between sweet cooked fruits and dried nuttiness. Good texture with a sweet malty centre.
**Finish:** Clean and soft.

## GLENKINCHIE SPECIAL EDITION, FRIENDS OF THE CLASSIC MALTS, CLASSIC MALTS 58.7%
Single Malt - Lowland

**8** **Michael: Only two Years Older than the regular Glenkinchie, but much richer. A very good cask.**
**Nose:** Grass. Straw. Marshmallow. Lime jelly.
**Palate:** Custard. Finely grated lemon peel. Lemongrass. Root ginger. Nutmeg. Cinnamon.
**Finish:** Spicy. Big. Long. Dryish.

**7¾** **Dave: Bigger and more robust than you might expect.**
**Nose:** Big and fairly dry. A whiff of sulphur mixed in with bran flakes, grass and dried banana.
**Palate:** Medium-bodied though with good texture. Soft fruits and dry malty notes.
**Finish:** Long and soft vanilla mixed with with light nuttiness.

## GLENLIVET 1943, PRIVATE COLLECTION 45%
Single Malt - Speyside

**9** **Michael: The Glenlivet is another whisky that I have encountered at great ages, often past their best. This shows its age only in its raffish, extrovert, confidence.**
**Nose:** Astonishingly fresh fruitiness and peatiness.
**Palate:** What remarkable freshness, in the maltiness of flavour. Like malted milk, thickening into cream toffee. Then mint toffee. Apricot-ish fruitiness.
**Finish:** A hint of spice, sherry and cedary oakiness.

**7¾** **Dave: Incredible for a whisky this age to have retained such charm and elegance. A faded beauty.**
**Nose:** Perfumed, initially dominated by intense menthol/peppermint aromas. There's exotic spices, flowers: allspice, dried leather, beech nuts, oak/applewood. A smokiness dominates as it develops.
**Palate:** Spice and peat smoke. Woody yet somehow graceful.
**Finish:** Woody dry.

## GLENLIVET 1971, 32 YEARS OLD, SHERRY CASK, COOPER'S CHOICE 46%
Single Malt - Speyside

**8½** **Gavin: This example has stood up to its 32 years in the cask very well. A good example of how supple an old Glenlivet can be.**
**Nose:** Big sherry nose, toffee, stewed fruits.
**Palate:** Lively sherry, mixed spices, caramel, a hint of ginger. Nimble for its age.
**Finish:** Lingering caramel; not overly long, but lacking the pepperiness that could be a peril here.

**8¼** **Dave: A fine whisky, just lacking the finesse and balance of the 1974.**
**Nose:** Rich. Cooked plum, Christmas cake, then tomato soup, balsamic notes. With water, tomato leaf, fig. Has balance and richness. Intriguing.
**Palate:** Good weight but not too tannic. A hint of smoke, violet, chicory and rotten fruits.
**Finish:** Ripe, oaky. Some smoke?

## GLENLIVET 1972, 30 YEARS OLD, COOPER'S CHOICE 46%
Single Malt - Speyside

**8½ Michael: Lovely glowing colour. A big Glenlivet, more robust than complex.**
**Nose:** Very fruity. Cherries. Peaches.
**Palate:** Syrupy-sweet. Firm. Fruit and nuts in bitter chocolate. Toasted nuts.
**Finish:** Slight woody bitterness. Enough to balance the sweetness, but too little to offend.

**7¾ Dave: The cask overwhelms things slightly.**
**Nose:** Dense. Tobacco leaf, apple bowl/dried apple, stewed fruit, rum and raisin, cold tea.
**Palate:** Chewy, concentrated and sweet, (cream sherry?). Treacle. Big sherry influence and firm grip.
**Finish:** Dry bracken.

## GLENLIVET 1972, BERRY'S OWN SELECTION 46%
Single Malt - Speyside

**8½ Michael: Lots of flavour but restrained and well balanced. Very confident. If there is a** *WHISKY Recommended* **Speyside style, surely this is it.**
**Nose:** Sugared almonds. Fudge. Chocolates in a box.
**Palate:** Honeyed dryness. Dark liquid honey. Flavours gradually emerging. Restrained citrus, orange, then lemon.
**Finish:** Mixed spices. Slight ginger.

**7¾ Ian: Fruit-driven with spice and oak extending the spectrum and adding gravitas.**
**Nose:** Spicy, fruity overture, then caramel sauce and fruit syrup, with fudge and butterscotch.
**Palate:** Smooth, mellow, subtle baked apples with spicy gingerbread, citrus, pear drops, some underlying dry oakyness and clove.
**Finish:** Subtle poached fruit sweetness and dry, spicy oak.

## GLENLIVET 1973 CASK STRENGTH, GORDON & MACPHAIL 55.9%
Single Malt - Speyside

**8½ Michael: Some of the older Smith's Glenlivets are too woody for me, but this one is a delight.**
**Nose:** Peaches. Dessert grapes.
**Palate:** A box of dark chocolate pralines with creamy fillings: fudge, apricot, mint. All of these flavours in a glass of whisky.
**Finish:** Concentrated sweetness, balanced by fruity acidity. As though raisins give way to fresh grapes.

**7½ Martine: Surprisingly vibrant for its age. There is a gap between the sharp nose and soothingly smooth palate. Water reconciles both. Would go well with a pear and almond pie.**
**Nose:** Tangy, ethereal. A full basket of orchard fruit. Pear poached in vanilla. Distant almond notes.
**Palate:** Sweet and fruity (mango, pear). Quite oily. Velvety mouthfeel. Becomes spicy (white pepper).
**Finish:** Leafy, dry but lingering. Finishes with walnut peel bitterness.

## GLENLIVET 1973, GORDON & MACPHAIL 55.9%
Single Malt - Speyside

**8 Martine: A dash of water is perfect. Skip the pudding and enjoy your dram with a shortbread.**
**Nose:** Rich biscuity notes. Honey and toffee. Shoe polish. Greengage. Vanilla ice cream. A distant touch of wet cellar. Water releases lighter floral notes.
**Palate:** Lovely velvet feel. Rich, oily. Complex. Oak and age give a bold structure to the palate.
**Finish:** Spicy, dry. Slightly bitter. Like gentian root.

**7¾ Dave: Has maturity and some elegance.**
**Nose:** Clean and spicy. Lightly fragrant, dried apple, cinnamon toast, ripe citric notes, toffee, wholemeal. Becomes woodpile like.
**Palate:** Soft and smooth. Menthol. Light, with some flowers.
**Finish:** Toasty oak.

## GLENLIVET 1974, BERRY'S OWN SELECTION 46%
Single Malt - Speyside

**7¾ Martine: Very elegant and balanced on the nose. Oak tends to show off but the dram keeps its charm though.**
**Nose:** Malty and nutty. Oak is well integrated. Cooked plums, marzipan. Apples drying in the attic. Mustiness and earth. Oak comes back.

**Palate:** Smooth and crisp too. Oak is more prominent but flavours are nicely intertwined. A touch of milk chocolate.
**Finish:** Dry, with a refreshing sour/bitter touch.

**8 Dave: Charming and well balanced.**
**Nose:** Dried lemon peel. Fresh and floral, daffodil/iris and touches of dry malt. Shifts into tisane, straw and apple.
**Palate:** Very soft with good flow. This has more of a juicy guava like softness. Silky and almost wine like. Well integrated oak which adds a lightly spiced element.
**Finish:** White pepper.

## GLENLIVET 1974, MURRAY MCDAVID MISSION 46%
Single Malt - Speyside

*WHISKY Editor's choice*

**8¾ Michael: The most feminine Glenlivet I have encountered.**
**Nose:** Flowery. Camomile.
**Palate:** Creamy Flowery. Pollen-like. Dusty. Perfumy.
**Finish:** Sweet lemons.

**8½ Dave: Softness and subtlety is underrated these days, but can be more complex as any big old bruiser.**
**Nose:** Gentle and floral, apple (fruit/blossom), heather, pear, raspberry, chocolate. Sweet oak.
**Palate:** Soft start, a burst of sweetness with gentle waves of flavour: flowers, nutty oak, malt, dried grasses and orchard fruits. Subtle and balanced.
**Finish:** Complex, nutty.

## GLENLIVET 1975, BERRY'S OWN SELECTION 54%
Single Malt - Speyside

**7¼ Dave: This is a big mean mother whose youthful charms have been lashed into submission by oak.**
**Nose:** Ripe apples, treacle, leaf mulch, shifting slightly into linseed along with a flick of a leather. Water brings out a whiff of turps and dusty spices.
**Palate:** Real concentration, then napthalene. The leather comes back...as do tannins.
**Finish:** Dries significantly and reveals smoke.

**8 Arthur: Very pleasant aged whisky.**
**Nose:** Refresher sweeties, lavender and demerara rum. Leafy, floral and something slightly silagey.
**Palate:** Floral, with a bourbon-like character with lots of vanilla oak and some piney sap.
**Finish:** Demerara, rum-like sweetness.

## GLENLIVET 24 YEARS OLD, 2.35, SCOTCH MALT WHISKY SOCIETY 61%
Single Malt - Speyside

**8½ Michael: A heavily sherried whisky that is nonetheless surprisingly lively for its age.**
**Nose:** Peach jam. Crème brûlée. Some fragrant smokiness.
**Palate:** Smooth. Soothing. Very spicy. Scottish tablet. Dusty. A little oaky, but not excessively so.
**Finish:** Smoky. Long, warming.

**7¼ Dave: Full-on but distillery character is obliterated.**
**Nose:** A rich slippery nose. Gives little away without water. When added there's butter tablet mixed with dried fruit, burning leaves and walnut whip.
**Palate:** Big European oak cask influence making it a pretty tannic experience. The impression is of a bowl of nuts and overripe fruit/dates.
**Finish:** Dry and a little smoky.

## IMPERIAL GLENLIVET 1977, 24 YEARS OLD, CADENHEAD'S 57.6%
Single Malt - Speyside

**7¾ Michael: A robust whisky that deserves more exposure.**
**Nose:** Soft, sooty smoke. Not pronounced, but it is definitely there.
**Palate:** A big, malty, whisky. Dry maltiness at first, like pastry, but it gradually sweetens: shortbread, a scattering of sugar; then raisins. Black bun?
**Finish:** A hint of sherry. Soothing.

**7½ Dave: It wears its heart on its sleeve, and its big heart.**
**Nose:** Rich, toffee apple. Ripe and dried fruits: sultana and date. With water more overt sherried notes along with boot polish.
**Palate:** Sweet and quite sherried. Rich and soft with good weight.
**Finish:** Gentle.

## RARE VINTAGE SMITH'S, GLENLIVET 1974, GORDON & MACPHAIL 40%
Single Malt - Speyside

**7¼ Gavin: Somewhat lifeless and one-dimensional. Not the best old Glenlivet I've tasted.**
**Nose:** Spice and old leather sofas, caramel. Water releases more expansive floral and marzipan notes.
**Palate:** More spice, fudge, dry sherry, then peppery old oak.
**Finish:** Shorter than one might hope, quite flat, dry oak.

**9 Dave: A fantastic old Speyside which hits a perfect balance between cask and spirit.**
**Nose:** Gentle and slow to open. Rich tea biscuits, Madeira, nuts, peach juice, apple core, flowers and dried peels. A light oiliness. Complex and balanced.
**Palate:** Restrained, with sweet honeyed notes. Great width on the palate, lovely soft feel. Water shatters it.
**Finish:** Long, aromatic.

## THE GLENLIVET 12 YEARS OLD 40%
Single Malt - Speyside

**7½ Martine: A pleasant anytime dram. Very refreshing.**
**Nose:** Floral and malty. Ivy. Sweet cereals. Fresh paint. Cedar. Polished floors. A touch of marzipan. Apples in puff pastry. Buttery.
**Palate:** Fresh and minty. Quite chewy. Spices emerge but not excessively so. A splash of water brings out flavours.
**Finish:** Satisfying, warm and spicy.

**8 Dave: Right back on form. Is some more mature stock being blended in?**
**Nose:** Lifted. Apple wood, heather, baked soft fruits mixed with cereal, citrus and pear. In time there's notes of freshly-sawn wood, freesia and dried orange peel. Complex but light as well.
**Palate:** Light and fragrant. All the notes on the nose come through. Medium-bodied and gentle.
**Finish:** Dry and clean.

## THE GLENLIVET 12 YEARS OLD AMERICAN OAK FINISH 40%
Single Malt - Speyside

**8½ Michael: Lacks the subtlety of a more conventional Glenlivet, but will charm some consumers with a richer, creamier, style. Very drinkable indeed.**
**Nose:** Very perfumy. The typically peachy bouquet of The Glenlivet seems to be accentuated.
**Palate:** Firm, medium to full, body. Very smooth. Rich and fruity, with slightly more peat than usual.
**Finish:** Silky, creamy tastes. Vanilla. Some, very restrained, burnt grass, dryness.

**7 Dave: Unbalanced, the high-impact of new cask sits uncomfortably with the distillery character.**
**Nose:** Candy floss, dry spices, the smell of the woodshed. In time overripe banana, cherries, coconut and orange appear.
**Palate:** Very sweet start with ripe fruits, then wood starts to dominate.
**Finish:** The wood takes over making it a pretty dry experience.

## THE GLENLIVET 12 YEARS OLD FIRST FILL SHERRY CASK 40%
Single Malt - Speyside

**7½ Michael: Not much middle palate. Lacks roundness.**
**Nose:** Slightly vegetal. Olives?
**Palate:** Syrupy but very light. Becoming dry. Peaty, smoky, bitterness.
**Finish:** Late explosion of spiciness. Lemon grass. Ginger. Cinnamon.

**8 Dave: Attractive, versatile.**
**Nose:** Lightly malty/dusty. Dried grasses, yew. Becomes perfumed with water: floral (hyacinth, almost frangipani).
**Palate:** Soft and clean. Blossom-like. Gentle grip. Very clean and quite light.
**Finish:** Medium length, a soft fade.

## THE GLENLIVET 12 YEARS OLD, FRENCH OAK FINISH 40%
Single Malt - Speyside

**8¾ Michael: The oak does not dominate, but is quite powerful for such an elegant malt.**
**Nose:** Lots of fruity, fresh-apple, oak extract.
**Palate:** Firm, rich, rounded. Dessert apples, peaches, honey.
**Finish:** Crisp, clean, oakiness.

**8 Jim: It's The Glenlivet. But not as we know it. The oak is extraordinary, but the bitter-sweet sync impresses most.**
**Nose:** Heady stuff for a Glenlivet this age; almost perfumed in style but it is oak that pulls the strings.
**Palate:** Walloping oakiness produces a prickly spice and chewy, spectacularly beautiful sweet malt.
**Finish:** Big toffee and spice with countless oak rings.

## THE GLENLIVET 15 YEARS OLD 40%
Single Malt - Speyside

**7½ Martine: A very pleasant summery dram. Quite fragile though. Water tends to wipe out flavours.**
**Nose:** Cheery, full summer fruit basket. ripe apricot, juicy peaches. Honeyed custard. Butterscotch. On the sweet side.
**Palate:** Soft and tender. Stewed fruit. Vanilla syrup. Spices gently emerge. Flavours lose their charm with water.
**Finish:** Soft and mellow with a nutty tinge.

**7½ Dave: This is more about oak than the whisky. Seems forced: trying to fit a square peg into a round hole.**
**Nose:** Rich and heavily spiced. Aromatic, exotic, some varnish, mint, Puy lentil, sweet polished oak. Good intensity.
**Palate:** More interesting to start: apple purée, flowers then the oak grips. Sappy.
**Finish:** Spiced, slightly tannic.

## THE GLENLIVET 15 YEARS OLD FRENCH OAK RESERVE 40%
Single Malt - Speyside

**8¾ Michael: Complex. Entrancing.**
**Nose:** Strawberries and cream. Vanilla. Heady.
**Palate:** Firm, Slippery-smooth, cookie-like maltiness, spicy middle. Lots of flavour development.
**Finish:** Creamy, fruity. Like a Slavic sour cream pancake laced with Maraschino cherry brandy.

**7¾ Dave: Has good energy, but just grips slightly on the finish.**
**Nose:** Incense. Lightly oily (wood oil), russet apples and buttery notes. Quite firm. Some pineapple and then floral notes.
**Palate:** Medium bodied. Light cinnamon spiciness, then apple and a sparkling feel.
**Finish:** Fades, leaving a slightly bitter note.

## THE GLENLIVET 16 YEARS OLD, CASK STRENGTH 56.6%
Single Malt - Speyside

**8¼ Martine: The rich fruity profile of Glenlivet blossoms at cask strength. So well balanced.**
**Nose:** Unmistakably Glenlivet. Appetising. Full basket of summer fruit. Becomes custardy in time.
**Palate:** Smooth and mellow. Melts in mouth like a ripe fruit. Generous sweetness. Ends drily and elegantly with nutty notes.
**Finish:** Medium long, spicy, slightly tangy and dry.

**9 Dave: Has the wow factor that separates the very good from the truly great.**
**Nose:** Gentle, but complex. Sultana cake, baked fruits, wild flowers, melting milk chocolate truffle. Rich, mellow and gorgeous!
**Palate:** Lively and exciting. Complex nose: sweet spices, apple juice. Good depth and mouthfeel.
**Finish:** Macaroon bars and light fruits.

## THE GLENLIVET 1959 CELLAR COLLECTION 41.7%
Single Malt - Speyside

**8½ Michael: Vivid descriptors, but the flavours are very restrained. A most elegant whisky.**
WHISKY *Editor's choice*
**Nose:** Fresh bread, well-toasted, buttered, and spread with grapefruit marmalade. A vase of flowers: orange blossom, surely?
**Palate:** Complex citrus and apricot flavours, very tightly combined, as though anxious not to seem showy. Discretion in the British tradition.
**Finish:** Orange oil. Perfumy. Bittersweet.

**9 Dave: No woodiness at 43 Years Old, instead incredible intensity and freshness. Truly remarkable.**
**Nose:** Heady, aromatic and beautifully intense with floral notes, heather, a little smoke, fudge, sultana, honey, pot pourri and a sweetly subtle polished oak.
**Palate:** Sweet, rounded and honeyed with macadamia nut. The slightly heathery smoke hits mid-palate. Complex, subtle and rewarding.
**Finish:** A hint of smoke, fresh, a touch of oak dryness.

## THE GLENLIVET 1964 CELLAR COLLECTION 45.1%
Single Malt - Speyside

**7¼ Michael: After that sensuous aroma, the palate is subtle to the point of reticence. Still interesting.**
**Nose:** Powerful. Sliced blood oranges in Maraschino liqueur.
**Palate:** Fruity. Cherryish. Sappy. Falls away somewhat.
**Finish:** Late resurgence of fruity flavours. Cream soda.

**8½ Dave: An excellent mature spirit.**
**Nose:** Fat and unctuous with some resinous notes moving into Worcester sauce. Light smoke, Iced Gems, cedar, fig, stewed tea, caramelised fruits.
**Palate:** Very slow and soft showing real maturity. Fungal. Structure and grip. Good age, with a nutty oaky start which grows and opens beautifully.
**Finish:** Fades into chocolate, dust and velvet.

## THE GLENLIVET 1967 CELLAR COLLECTION 46%
Single Malt - Speyside

**9 Michael: The Glenlivet is the fruitiest, most flowery and most delicate.**
WHISKY *Recommended*
**Nose:** Fruity. Sweetly flowery. Hay. Hint of peat.
**Palate:** Firm, lively. Sweet peaches, marshmallow, biscuity malt. Shortbread.
**Finish:** Spicy (cinnamon), appetising. Very long.

**9 Jim: Jim Cryle has done a wonderful job picking these casks.**
**Nose:** Fabulously delicate. Soft vanilla, flickering malt, fruit salad with a smoke/oak combination.
**Palate:** Very even with a non-specific fruitness.
**Finish:** Light and softly oaked. Sensual spiciness.

## THE GLENLIVET 1967 VINTAGE 53.32%
Single Malt - Speyside

**9 Michael: Lots of flavour development. I enjoyed this one.**
WHISKY *Recommended*
**Nose:** Very aromatic; hay, grass and peat.
**Palate:** Lovely balance of sugared almonds, syrup, a hint of orange-zest, grass and peat.
**Finish:** Light, soft, warming. Deceptively long.

**8 Jim: Astonishing for a Speysider of such antiquity. First class complexity with no over-ageing.**
**Nose:** Deep sweetish sherry, just a hint of smoke and old leather; and a very healthy, rich maltiness.
**Palate:** An awesome, oily wave of sweet sherry-malt intensity. Fabulous complexity.
**Finish:** Rich chocolate notes, lightly metallic finale.

## THE GLENLIVET 1968 VINTAGE 52.75%
Single Malt - Speyside

**9 Michael: Has the complexity I expect from The Glenlivet.**
**Nose:** Polished oak.
**Palate:** Sugared almonds, spicy; flowery, fresh herbs. A dash of herbal, leafy, flowery peatiness.
**Finish:** Sweet, flowery, long, smooth.

**7 Jim: Excellent character, though the oak has taken a firmer grip than on the 1967; this is never quite so rich.**
**Nose:** Ripe figs amidst oak and malt. Deliciously fruity.

## THE GLENLIVET 1969 CELLAR COLLECTION 50.8%
Single Malt - Speyside

**9¼ Dave: Magnificent, but I hate to think of the price!**
**Nose:** Mature and elegant with a beautiful exotic fragrance. Light resin, date, ginger, Turkish Delight.
**Palate:** Unctuous with a slow release of flavours. Allspice and cinnamon all the way. Baked pineapple, mint. Superb balance.
**Finish:** A dusting of rose petals.

**8½ Martine: A very satisfying afterdinner dram.**
**Nose:** Intense. Rich. Toffee apple, sticky toffee pudding. Oak is well integrated. Dates and figs.
**Palate:** Satin like. Oily but not cloying. Toffee, chocolate, cappuccino parfait. Outburst on spices. Minty liquorice at the back.
**Finish:** Long, drying on oaky tones. A touch of brazil nut.

## THE GLENLIVET 1969 VINTAGE 52.2%
Single Malt - Speyside

**8 Michael: A little woody.**
**Nose:** Peaty, leafy, sappy, oaky.
**Palate:** Nutty, toffeeish, creamy flavours. Lacks development and complexity.
**Finish:** Dry.

**8½ Jim: Brilliant whisky with great age.**
**Nose:** Sherry again, but this time fabulously clean and precise. Deftly smoked.
**Palate:** Dry, oaky start; malty; saltiness shows quite early. Fruit-cake richness.
**Finish:** Lots of oak and intense malt: bittersweet and chewy finale.

## THE GLENLIVET 1970 VINTAGE 56.58%
Single Malt - Speyside

**8 Michael: Enjoyable, but I expected a little more.**
WHISKY *Recommended*
**Nose:** Peat.
**Palate:** Sweet, syrupy. raisins. Cinnamon. Oak.
**Finish:** Firm; some cream flavours. Raisins and oak.

**9½ Jim: Outstanding. The finest and probably most delicate Glenlivet I have ever tasted.**
**Nose:** The most honeyed and least sherried; tangerines, salty oak and coconut milk.
**Palate:** Oily and intense with honey richness. Perfectly balanced with roast malt and oak.
**Finish:** Stunning bittersweet, oaky dry, honeysweet.

## THE GLENLIVET 1972 VINTAGE 54.29%
Single Malt - Speyside

**8 Michael: A little woody. Choice of cask?**
**Nose:** Peaty. Lightly phenolic.
**Palate:** Sweet, syrupy. Lightly creamy. Developing light floweriness and sugared almonds.
**Finish:** Peach-stone notes. Attenuated. Dry.

**8½ Jim: A big whisky which shows not all Speysiders are shrinking violets. Beautifully weighted throughout; breathtaking complexity.**
**Nose:** Dry sherry and lots of natural caramel.
**Palate:** Big mouthfeel with lots of ripe fruit. Sweet throughout, like sugared plums and custard.
**Finish:** The longest, most full-bodied finale of all; rich saline oakiness and toasty malt. The rich fruit is never far away.

## THE GLENLIVET 1983 CELLAR COLLECTION FRENCH OAK FINISH 46%
Single Malt - Speyside

**8½ Michael: The oak does not totally dominate, but is powerful for such an elegant malt.**
**Nose:** Lots of floral, tannic, oak extract. Heady. Hypnotic.
**Palate:** Peaches, honey, anis.
**Finish:** Crisp, dry oakiness.

**7¾ Dave: Balances sweet and savoury. Next time though make it unchillfiltered!**
**Nose:** Tight, fragrant nose: cinnamon, clove, apple and heather. Firmer and more malty with water.

**Palate:** A fairly tight structure with root ginger, heather, dry grass, dried apple. Good maturity, well balanced and a spicy, exotic overtone.
**Finish:** Clean, good length.

## THE GLENLIVET 21 YEARS OLD ARCHIVE
Single Malt - Speyside

**6¾ Michael: Slightly sweeter, fuller and more structured than an earlier (younger) version with no age statement.**
**Nose:** Very fresh in both its heathery peatiness and its juicy, sweet, sherry. Appetising.
**Palate:** Sweet, flowery, honey-syrup, butter, toast and butter.
**Finish:** Cinnamon. Lightly spicy dryness. Well-done toast. Gently sustaining.

**8 Jim: A substantial malt, which on the palate does not match the complexity of outstanding nose.**
**Nose:** Stunning: oak and hint of marzipan and cherries. The malt is sweet and multi-layered.
**Palate:** Initially light with sweet cereal notes and then the oak kicks in to add a drier dimension.
**Finish:** Toasty with hints of hickory and chocolate fudge. Quite long.

## THE GLENLIVET 21 YEARS OLD ARCHIVE 43%
Single Malt - Speyside

**8½ Michael: A first-class malt, but I would like a little more structure and style.**
**Nose:** Lively. Fruity. Peaty.
**Palate:** Light, clean, cereal grain maltiness. Very firm and smooth. Developing toastier, nuttier flavours. Orange oil. Some macaroon-like sweetness, too.
**Finish:** Sweet grass. Smoky fragrance.

**8 Dave: A powerful spicy malt.**
**Nose:** Lifted and mellow. Good, complex mix of floral, bracken top notes with plenty of spicy oak, malt and sweet fruit.
**Palate:** A sweet, rounded start with some honey and soft fruit, then it's given a kick from the oak: tobacco, hazelnut and a whiff of smoke. Good feel. The oak comes to the fore as it develops.
**Finish:** Maybe just a little woody.

## THE GLENLIVET 25 YEARS OLD 43%
Single Malt - Speyside

WHISKY
Recommended

**8 Dave: Just needs a little more in the middle.**
**Nose:** Mature and deep. Stewed tea, dried cherry, fig, madeira cake mix alongside some tomato/balsamic rancio notes.
**Palate:** Slightly tannic grip think hard toffee dried blossom rich with substance. Light to medium fruits lovely balance.
**Finish:** XXX (triple x-ED)

**8¼ Martine: A classic sherry. Oak is perfectly integrated. So elegantly balanced.**
**Nose:** Sherry leaves its mark. Rubber, dried currants, damp cellar.
**Palate:** Smooth and sweet. Elegant display of sherried notes: deep toffee, chocolate, candied chestnuts, figs. Touch of sulphur. Soft spices.
**Finish:** Lingering, chocolatey. Liquorice. Delicate spiciness (nutmeg). Tobacco leaves.

## THE GLENLIVET 30 YEARS OLD AMERICAN OAK FINISH 48%
Single Malt - Speyside

**8¾ Michael: Who would have thought that finishing in American oak could add so much? The Glenlivet character is showcased not overwhelmed.**
**Nose:** Peach cobbler, being cooked. Warm aroma. Fruity and sweet, with a suggestion of burnt pastry.
**Palate:** Like biting into a good praline, the biggest, roundest one in the box. Black chocolate on the outside, fudge, syrupy alcohol and raisins inside.
**Finish:** Crunchy. Belgian wafers.

**7¾ Dave: Good, if you like this in-yer-face style but why do you need to 'finish' a 30 Years Old malt? To give a lift to a malt that lacked complexity?**
**Nose:** Rich, sweet oak tones: gingerbread and raisins, orange honey, coconut, polished oak table. Water brings out butterscotch, spice, menthol, apples.
**Palate:** Upfront, ripe and sweet: gingery, toffee, very sweet oak, custard cream, apricot.
**Finish:** Sweet.

## THE GLENLIVET NADURRA 48%
Single Malt - Speyside

**7¼ Michael: Delicate to the point of reticence.**
**Nose:** Sugary mint sauce. Garden mint. Bay leaves.
**Palate:** Smooth. Dryish. Light but firm maltiness. Slight earthiness. Porcini mushrooms.
**Finish:** Honeyish. Flowery dryness. Hop pillows.

**7¾ Dave: Firm, but with enough sweet notes to balance.**
**Nose:** Floral (bluebell), some malty notes, lemon/tangerine marmalade, lychee. Oakier than the 12 Years Old.
**Palate:** Slightly fizzy (orange spacedust) cinnamon balls, odd-fellows. Some sweet nuttiness towards the finish. Good flow and softly textured.
**Finish:** Oak, then candy floss.

## GLENLOCHY 1965, RARE OLD 40%
Single Malt - Highland

**7 Michael: A breakfast whisky?**
**Nose:** Rich. Sweet orange marmalade. Vanilla pods.
**Palate:** Firm but silky-smooth. Waxed orange skins. Nutty. Grainy. Suggestion of coffee.
**Finish:** Peppery. Bison grass. Peaty, smoky. Some bitterness.

**7¼ Martine: The unpleasant rancid aromas on the nose are not perceptible on the palate. Doesn't fulfill the expectations of age.**
**Nose:** Rancid notes at first which give way to elegant oakiness. Passion fruit, honeyed apples.
**Palate:** Very smooth and syrupy like a liqueur. Wood does its stuff. A pleasant creaminess.
**Finish:** Dry, oaky with a hint of burnt wood. Almond milk. Quickly dries out with spices.

## GLENLOSSIE 10 YEARS OLD 45%
Single Malt - Speyside

**7¼ Martine: Doesn't deliver the promise of the nose. Surprisingly smooth for a fairly high alcohol strength.**
**Nose:** Sweet and intense. Almond cake. A hint of varnish. Barley sugar. Waxed floors. Plum compote. Rich sherry notes. Raisins, a touch of marmalade.
**Palate:** Fat, creamy, velvety, fruity. Stays on the sweet side. Stewed plums with ginger.
**Finish:** Not very assertive. Aromas quickly dwindle. Becomes sappy and somewhat astringent.

**6¾ Dave: Attractive enough but hardly complex.**
**Nose:** Clean and light. Red apple, sweet hay, vanilla, buttered popcorn/rice cakes.
**Palate:** A sweet and soft start. All very gentle and pretty much straight down the middle.
**Finish:** Light.

## GLENLOSSIE 1975, CONNOISSEUR'S CHOICE 40%
Single Malt - Speyside

**7¼ Michael: Again, rather dried out. Lacks roundness and structure.**
**Nose:** Very aromatic. Peaches and pears. Fruit tea.
**Palate:** Lightly viscous. Assam tea. Burnt grass. Brown sugar.
**Finish:** Gingery. Spicy. Dusty.

**7½ Dave: Has some faded elegance.**
**Nose:** A catalogue of mature notes: wax floor polish, antique shop, hemp rope, light smoke, mushroom, hay bales and a hint of citrus peel.
**Palate:** Lightly tannic, old nutbowl, mulch. Gentle and smooth, just a little faded.
**Finish:** Bitter chocolate/espresso.

## GLENLOSSIE 1975, MURRAY MCDAVID MISSION II 46%
Single Malt - Speyside

**7½ Michael: A rare chance to taste Glenlossie but, again, the wood gets in the way.**
**Nose:** Grassy. Herbal. Spicy.
**Palate:** Oily. Perfumy Lively.
**Finish:** Oaty, bitter, woody.

**7½ Dave: Decent balance, just a little too long in wood for me.**
**Nose:** Mature. Nutty, powdered hazelnut, cashew. Fresh timber. Limeade and oak with water.
**Palate:** Caramelised nut. Sweet but the oaky frame is pretty sturdy. Some black fruit (cherry).
**Finish:** Nuts.

## GLENLOSSIE 1980, SIGNATORY 43%
Single Malt - Speyside

**7½ Michael: Delicate, appetising and refreshing, but falls away in the middle.**
**Nose:** Sweet maltiness. Cereal grains. Sandalwood. Musk. Light smoke. Light on the tongue, very smooth.
**Palate:** Sweet. Malty but light and refreshing.
**Finish:** Oily. Creamy.

**8 Jim: A much busier, more complex malt than the nose suggests. Entertaining stuff.**
**Nose:** Subdued slightly. Surprisingly fresh.
**Palate:** Mouth-watering. A fine flush of intense malt tops the middle. Excellent bittersweet ratio.
**Finish:** Now the oak kicks in, but gently so.

## GLENLOSSIE 1981, ADELPHI 59%
Single Malt - Speyside

**7¾ Michael:** Seville orange peel. A hint of tamarind (suggested by the colour?). Pronounced cloves. Cough sweets. Slight phenol.
**Palate:** The aroma is carried through in the palate. Very fruity and spicy. Attenuated maltiness. Firm.
**Finish:** Drying. Strong sandalwood or cedar flavours.

**9 Jim: Simply the best rendition.**
**Nose:** A heavyweight that wallows in its oaky resonance and malty sweetness. Really pleasing.
**Palate:** Awesome display of toffee apple, chocolate fudge and demerara sugar.
**Finish:** Sweet vanilla, late wisp of peat.

## GLENMORANGIE 10 YEARS OLD 40%
Single Malt - Highland

**7¾ Michael: Slightly sweeter on the nose, and less complex, than the best bottlings I have tasted.**
**Nose:** Walnuts. Vanilla. Green herbs. Some flowery sweetness.
**Palate:** Flowery, herbal, salty.
**Finish:** Slightly resiny. Very salty.

**9 Jim: A great single malt: beautifully uncompromising from the first sniff to the last gulp.**
**Nose:** Perhaps the most enigmatic aroma of them all: delicate yet assertive, sweet yet dry, young yet oaky. A malty tone poem.
**Palate:** Flaky oakiness with a complex toastiness to the barley suggesting the lightest hint of smoke.
**Finish:** Amazingly long, drying from the initial sweetness but with flaked almonds amid the oakier notes.

## GLENMORANGIE 12 YEARS OLD, MILLENNIUM MALT 43%
Single Malt - Highland

**8 Michael: Very evident first-fill Bourbon character.**
**Nose:** Lightly oaky. Sandalwood. Hint of brown sugar.
**Palate:** Butterscotch, lots of vanilla and honey.
**Finish:** Light, refreshing. An almost spritzy, crunchy, toasty, dryness.

**8 Jim: A charming and excellent single malt offering untold complexity in the layers of flavours.**
**Nose:** Fabulously complex with malt in varying degrees of sweetness and intensity giving an almost three-dimensional feel. Apples and kumquats offer a mixed fruitiness that lightens it a little. The oak offers vanilla and polished leather.
**Palate:** Big dry oak start which sweetens as the malt gathers pace. Brilliant balance of drier vanilla and sweeter toffee.
**Finish:** Extremely long and malty with the heavier, silky tones clinging, unusually for a Glenmorangie, to the roof of the mouth. The oak returns to add extra dryness and weight.

## GLENMORANGIE 12 YEARS OLD, MILLENNIUM MALT 43%
Single Malt - Highland

**8 Michael: The earlier, and less expensive, of two millennium bottlings. In this one, the** *WHISKY Magazine Recommended* **emphasis is on first-fill bourbon barrels.**
**Nose:** Lightly oaky. Hint of brown sugar.
**Palate:** Slightly syrupy. Honey. Butterscotch. Butter. Vanilla. Crème brûlée.
**Finish:** An almost spritzy, crunchy, toasty dryness.

**9 Jim: A charming and excellent single malt offering untold complexity in the layers of flavours.**
**Nose:** Fabulously complex with malt in varying degrees of sweetness and intensity. Apples and kumquats offer a mixed and fruitiness that lightens it.
**Palate:** Dry and oak start. Sweetens as the malt kicks in.
**Finish:** Long and malty with the heavier, silky tones clinging to the roof of the mouth. The oak returns to add extra dryness and weight.

## GLENMORANGIE 15 YEARS OLD 40%
Single Malt - Highland

**8 Michael: If you like the classic flavours of the 10 Years Old but find it a bit light, this range-filler is for you.**
**Nose:** Fresh. Sea air.
**Palate:** Smooth, sweet, slightly syrupy. Lovely balance of sweet creaminess and herbal notes.
**Finish:** Appetisingly spicy. Clean hit of salt.

**8¼ Jim: Rich by Glenmorangie standards and very warming.**
**Nose:** Fruitier with dense grapey tones: malty yet nothing like as complex as the 10 Years Old.
**Palate:** A silky feel followed by a delicious explosion of peppery notes around the palate. Clean fruit, including the juiciest of plums, balance nicely.
**Finish:** Remains warm and lingering with more emphasis on simple vanilla and malt.

## GLENMORANGIE 15 YEARS OLD 43%
Single Malt - Highland

**8 Michael: If you like the classic flavours of the 10 Years Old but find it a bit light, this range-filler is for you.**
**Nose:** Cinnamon. Spiciness. Sea air.
**Palate:** Smooth, sweet, slightly syrupy. Walnuts.
**Finish:** Appetisingly spicy. Some salt.

**8 Jim: A belter beside last embers of a log fire.**
**Nose:** Delicate malt-wood style, highly concentrated form. Butterscotch, apples, vanilla.
**Palate:** Big with immediate dry oakiness that is softened only by the flowering of the malt.
**Finish:** Bourbony notes towards finish, which remains dry and delicately spiced.

## GLENMORANGIE 18 YEARS OLD 43%
Single Malt - Highland

**8 Michael: While the middle brother in this range seems best to capture the Glenmorangie house character, this older version is a richer whisky. I could like them equally, according to my mood.**
**Nose:** Some oak. More vanilla. Lots of walnuts. Touch of peppermint.
**Palate:** Fleshier. Good wood-extract and esters. Some peatiness emerging. The whole potpourri of spiciness.
**Finish:** Firm, dry, rounded. Nutty. Hint of peat.

**8 Jim: A rich, mouth-filling dram that offers surprising length and depth to the finish.**
**Nose:** Not as clean as usual. A distant sulphur note where the sherry should be. Sweet and pollen encrusted.
**Palate:** A short, sweet introduction fans out into a mixture of sherry and spice. Levels off with peppery maltiness.
**Finish:** A soft smokiness lingers endlessly as does the chocolate malt.

## GLENMORANGIE 1977 43%
Single Malt - Highland

**7½ Michael: Very juicy wood, but just too much of it?**
**Nose:** A hit of oaky vanilla toffee, then an unfamiliar hint of peat and a surprisingly emphatic sea note. A very long aroma.
**Palate:** Surprisingly sweet and juicy. The fresh oak character combines with the typical walnut, but somewhat overpowers the usual spiciness.
**Finish:** That very slight peat again, adding an appetising full stop.

## GLENMORANGIE 1991, SAUTERNES WOOD FINISH 46%
Single Malt - Highland

**7¼ Michael: Not easy to evaluate what sauternes casks have brought in. An extra sweetness maybe but no particular sauternes aromas. Appreciable bottling strength.**
**Nose:** Biscuity. Shortbread. Dundee cake. Cellar.
**Palate:** Buttery and nutty. Crushed apples, cider. Vanilla. A sweet note of peach marmalade.
**Finish:** Too much softness. Gentle spiciness.

**8** Dave: This works as a finish. The slight woodiness just knocks it down a mark or two and it doesn't like water.
**Nose:** Thick, creamy yet malty nose with concentrated fruits: apricot, orange peel, tarte tatin, vanilla pod.
**Palate:** Real presence in the mouth. Ripe and well-rounded with banana/orange.
**Finish:** Rich, with woody notes.

## GLENMORANGIE 1995 ARTISAN CASK 45%
Single Malt - Highland

**8¼** Michael: This is a substantially richer style of Glenmorangie, but not overwhelmingly sweet. The balancing spices and herbs are all present and correct.
**Nose:** Custard. Tropical fruits.
**Palate:** Fruit salad. Tangerines. Peaches. Trifle with milk chocolate chips.
**Finish:** Belgian wafers. The cinnamon scattered on a cappuccino.

**8** Dave: Zesty and well made. Good aperitif.
**Nose:** Light acetone notes on an intense nose: pencil shavings, lychee, lightly floral perfumed (vetiver). Seems young.
**Palate:** Light and sweet with lively citric character. Fragrant/floral: jasmine flowers, very light. Fizzes with life and sweet spices.
**Finish:** Short, fresh and very lively.

## GLENMORANGIE 25 YEARS OLD 43%
Single Malt - Highland

**8¼** Michael: A confident, handsome whisky.
**Nose:** An old shop, with fittings in polished oak, leather and brass. A ship's chandlers', perhaps?
**Palate:** Big. Cakey. Oily. Beeswax.
**Finish:** Late gingery spiciness with some saltiness.

**8½** Dave: Seems much younger than it is. Has real charm.
**Nose:** Light and spicy. Toasted pine nuts, citrus fruits, cereal. Stewed orange, jasmine, almond.
**Palate:** Mulled, spicy warmth. Fragrant and exciting. Tangerine, banana, lemon. Well-balanced with soft, sweet oak.
**Finish:** Those spices again. Tangerine jelly and cream.

## GLENMORANGIE 30 YEARS OLD 44.3%
Single Malt - Highland

**8** Martine: Sherry wood is undoubtedly invasive but yet, here's a complex one. To be softened by chocolate pralines or almond biscuits.
**Nose:** Woody, musty. Sherry. Walnut oil. Cappuccino then wet ground coffee. More sherry. Liquorice lozenges. Hint of praline.
**Palate:** Sweet and sour. Coffee toffee. Gripping.
**Finish:** Lingering, spicy and dry. Liquorice.

**9** Dave: A classic complex mature whisky where the wood has not taken over.
**Nose:** Complex. Starts with bung cloth and concentrated fruits; then cereal, a hint of smoke, and floral notes (Cognac) citrus, pine wood, light chocolate, freshly charred wood, orange zest.
**Palate:** Intense. The oak has grip but sufficient caramelised flavours to carry.
**Finish:** Long, tingling, elegant.

## GLENMORANGIE ARTISAN 46%
Single Malt - Highland

**8¼** Martine: A malt to make peace with the whole world. Soothing, graceful, satisfying.
**Nose:** Estery. Floral (flowering currant, gorse). Delicate creaminess. Tangerine juice followed by vanilla toffee and warm waffle.
**Palate:** Mellow, velvety, caressing but firm. Keeps floral all the way. And fruity too. Pear drop.
**Finish:** Long lasting, lots of flowering currant. Crystallised ginger in the back.

**8** Dave: Attractive nose, but it is on the palate where this really delivers.
**Nose:** Smooth, soft, vanilla-like, American oak fruitiness with some mango, orange spangles, mixed citrus peels. Perfumed and lightly herbal.
**Palate:** Good flow. Really spicy, coconut, passion fruit, nutmeg. Everything in balance.
**Finish:** Lightly nutty, sweet and long.

## GLENMORANGIE BURGUNDY WOOD FINISH 43%
Single Malt - Highland

**8½** Michael: Seems simple at first, but then develops stylishly.
**Nose:** Toasty.
**Palate:** Big. Soft. Syrupy. Sweetish. Very fruity. Winey. Easily drinkable.
**Finish:** Lurking behind, and emerging gradually, restrained balancing dryness of toast and oak.

**8** Dave: Decent balance means the finish isn't dominating. Just a bit blowsy?
**Nose:** An overwhelming array of aromas: vanilla, orange blossom, poached pear, cooked plum, membrillo, overripe fruit, maple syrup.
**Palate:** Sweet with a soft, full texture. Victoria plum, citrus oil and a malty core. Good structure.
**Finish:** Black fruits. Soft.

## GLENMORANGIE BURR OAK 56.3%
Single Malt - Highland

**8¾** Martine: A malt disguised in rum! Very surprising but not less exciting for that.
**Nose:** Luscious, exotic, floral. Demerara sugar. Cloves. Old Jamaican rum. Verbena. Vanilla.
**Palate:** A sweet start followed by a salute of spices and exotic flavours. Coconut, cloves, cane sugar. Alcohol never bites, even without water.
**Finish:** Medium long, with lots of toffee and vanilla. Stem ginger.

**8¼** Dave: A wonderful rum...sorry, whisky! You can feel the calories piling on when you drink this.
**Nose:** HUGE oak impact. Starts like an ice cream float (on cherry cola), then becomes even sweeter: sponge cake, banana loaf. Add water and there's a lightly singed note from the wood.
**Palate:** Slow and sweet. Tropical fruits all mushed together with vanilla, but still has a balancing grip.
**Finish:** Long and rounded.

## GLENMORANGIE COGNAC MATURED 43%
Single Malt - Highland

**8** Michael: Crisp, but not as characterful as might be hoped.
**Nose:** Perfumy, lemony, clean, crisp.
**Palate:** Hint of soft, dusty, lemon, then lots of typical Glenmorangie spiciness.
**Finish:** Hint of icing sugar, then very light and dry. Slightly weak.

**7½** Jim: One of the sweetest Glenmorangies of all time.
**Nose:** Sweet and thin, sugary; subtle smoke and grassy malt.
**Palate:** At once malty and spicy with an immediate powerful oak arrival. Very sweet throughout.
**Finish:** More brown sugary, custardy sweetness. An oaky thrust adds a welcome dryness.

## GLENMORANGIE CÔTE DE BEAUNE 46%
Single Malt - Highland

**8½** Michael: As the glass sits on my desk, aromas and flavours slowly emerge, I like it more and more, but I suspect it will always be overshadowed by last year's Côte de Nuits.
**Nose:** Sweetish, creamy, herbal, winey.
**Palate:** Smooth, sweet. Soft berry fruits. Prunes. Lots of flavour development. Becoming spicy, with cinnamon and later ginger.
**Finish:** Figs and honey. Green peppercorns. Very long.

**8** Dave: Liqueur style. Good balance.
**Nose:** Sweet and softly elegant. Fresh herbs (thyme), orange, bread with a hint of charred wood in background.
**Palate:** Quite dry. Plenty of wood with soft fruit mid-palate. Char.
**Finish:** Soft.

## GLENMORANGIE COTE D'OR BURGUNDY WOOD CASK 43%
Single Malt - Highland

**7¾ Martine:** A beautifully balanced Highlander. Serious, reliable, pleasantly displaying a good array of flavours. Maybe the wine cask has imparted more intensity.
**Nose:** Intense, balsamic. Pine needle. Dry Sylvester herbs. Pear nectar. Honeycomb.
**Palate:** Bitter/sweet. Crushed hazelnuts, touch of liquorice. A dry and clean freshness.
**Finish:** Clean and fresh with a pleasant spicy bite.

**7½ Ian:** Opens up with a measured pace, but also takes some unexpected turns.
**Nose:** Initial toffee with spicy pungency, settles down with chocolate, crème brûlée and fruitcake.
**Palate:** Soft, silky with a subtle range of sweet crème brûlée, poached fruit, citrus freshness, before butterscotch and light cappuccino creamyness with underlying spicy oak.
**Finish:** Poached fruit and caramel sauce lead to distinct maltiness.

## GLENMORANGIE FINO SHERRY WOOD FINISH
Single Malt - Highland

**9 Michael:** A marriage made in heaven.
**Nose:** Gentle sea fragrance. Very appetising.
**Palate:** Cinnamon toast, then rhubarby fruitiness and wineyness. Appetisingly sourish acidity.
**Finish:** The coastal whisky and near-coastal sherry combine in a clinching hug of saltiness and oakiness.

**9 Doug:** A wonderfully teasing complex and balanced creation.
**Nose:** Lightly caramel and winey, cream crackers, soft brine.
**Palate:** Fuller, creamy textures, chocolate liqueurs?
**Finish:** Long, chocolatey, gently smoky, salty, prickling finale.

## GLENMORANGIE FINO SHERRY WOOD FINISH
Single Malt - Highland

**9 Michael:** The light saltiness in a coastal whisky and near-coastal sherry make this a delight.
**Nose:** Gentle sea fragrance. Very appetising.
**Palate:** Very delicate and teasing. Lightly toasty. Cinnamon toast. Faintly rhubarby fruitiness and wineyness, tinge of sourish acidity.
**Finish:** Very salty.

**8½ Jim:** Outstanding stuff from Glenmorangie, and for my money their most delicate expression yet.
**Nose:** Crisp and dry with an enticing hint of smoke. This sherry is wonderfully delicate.
**Palate:** Clean and dry with complex spices. Brilliantly balanced.
**Finish:** Long oaky finale that lingers over the Fino influence.

## GLENMORANGIE MADEIRA FINISH
Single Malt - Highland

**8½ Michael:** The madeira almost overwhelms the whisky, but the Glenmorangie saltiness finally sings.
**Nose:** Sweet. Very spicy. honey-cake. Baclava?
**Palate:** Unusually buttery. Barley-sugar sweetness at first: toffeeish, chewy, cakey. Then nutty, seed-like and grainy as it dries. Cinnamon and spices.
**Finish:** Short and sweet. Salty, oaky, rummy.

**8½ Doug:** Glenmorangie in spite of its lightish origins can walk the wood finish tight rope with majestic balance.
**Nose:** Fresh and lively with grassy, oaky, vanilla notes and salty extremes.
**Palate:** Teasing sweet and sour balance of nuts and raisins, chocolate orange and brine.
**Finish:** Very warming, still teasingly raisiny until a faintly peaty dryness finally prevails.

## GLENMORANGIE MADEIRA MATURED 56.6%
Single Malt - Highland

**8¾ Michael:** One of the most expressive 'Morangies.
**Nose:** Rich, buttery. Yes, Madeira.
**Palate:** Luscious and toffeeish, then sudden explosion of sand, salt and oak.
**Finish:** Stinging saltiness.

**8¼ Dave:** Exotic and strangely appealing. More intensity and better grip than the Burgundy finish.

**Nose:** Exotic. Burnt notes: toffee, dry tea, citrus, walnut, raisin bread. A hint of dust with water.
**Palate:** Rounded with a sweet burnt note old apple barrels. Good concentration with a savoury edge over a light, raisined core.
**Finish:** Prickly with attractive spiky oak.

## GLENMORANGIE MALAGA WOOD FINISH, 25 YEARS OLD 43%
Single Malt - Highland

**8½ Michael:** Reminiscent of the port finish but slightly gutsier and less sophisticated. I would love to try it, tapas-style, with Manchego, or perhaps Grazelema, cheese.
**Nose:** Distinctive, complex, rich, sweet, slightly winey.
**Palate:** Cedary. Very nutty indeed. The more raisiny notes of Malaga seem to play hide-and-seek in the background. Creamy. Nutty.
**Finish:** The characteristic Glenmorangie salt comes through very late.

**8¾ Jim:** Eye-catching, complex and downright deliciously unusual.
**Nose:** Delicious infusion of sweet, perfumed notes of the candy shop dusted with a sprinkling of oak.
**Palate:** That sweetness is evident early on but soon diminishes as a fruity lustre gives way to a significan't build-up of spices.
**Finish:** Extremely long. Peppery, then fine malt interacts with oak and just a little smoke.

## GLENMORANGIE MANAGER'S CHOICE PORT WOOD 57.2%
Single Malt - Highland

**8¾ Michael:** Very port-tasting and curiously unrefined. Having robust tastes in food and drink, I loved it. Some might find it lacking in sophistication.
**Nose:** 'Rough', fresh, fruity. Brought to mind fruit skins and almondy cherry pits.
**Palate:** Big, smooth, fruity, earthy. Becoming marshmallow-like and malty.
**Finish:** Sandalwood, walnut, salt … all the Glenmorangie flavours come powering through.

**6¾ Dave:** More of a cocktail than a malt as if some wine has been left in the glass and Glenmorangie poured on top of it. Help! I'm confused!
**Nose:** Soft. Raspberry fool, cranberry sauce, custard, stewed apple/apple skin, fennel seed, dry wood.
**Palate:** Sweet and soft, apples in red wine, red fruit and cream.
**Finish:** Very soft. Wine gums.

## GLENMORANGIE MARGAUX CASK FINISH VINTAGE 1987 46%
Single Malt - Highland

**7¼ Dave:** This starts so promisingly, but the soapiness knocks it for me.
**Nose:** Another pinkish one. Nougat, flower stems when neat, fruity and juicy with water when there's melon, strawberry, cassis and baked banana. Good.
**Palate:** A slightly soapy start. The fruitiness which lies behind slightly hidden and the spirit seems a little covered.
**Finish:** Cloying.

**7 Arthur:** Disappointing to drink given the price tag and all the fancy fripery that goes with a bottling like this. I much prefer the 10 Years Old and Artisan cask!
**Nose:** Orange squash, sugar soap and wet grass. A bit thin on the nose, with a confected cakiness.
**Palate:** Fairy liquid, with some buttery, fruit pastry.
**Finish:** More of those dishwater suds.

## GLENMORANGIE ORIGINAL 43%
Single Malt - Highland

**8 Michael:** Made when the distillery had its own maltings, and an eloquent advocate for such an arrangement.
**Nose:** Very distinctive, clean, oaky peatiness. This character is in the background throughout.
**Palate:** Flowery. Fudgy. Toffeeish. Nutty. Very soft, strained spiciness. Then toasty and peaty.
**Finish:** Firm, clean (almost crisp), peatiness. Then long, very soft, spicy and remarkably warming.

9 **Jim: For my money the best Glenmorangie I have yet come across: complexity beyond belief. Truly outstanding.**
**Nose:** A lighter, more flowery aroma but still not lacking in mixed fruit. There is an ethereal quality to the vanilla-malt complexity.
**Palate:** Sweet and delightfully spicy at first, then becomes richer and oilier. Barley sugar sweetness and some creeping oak.
**Finish:** Wave upon wave of brilliant malt carresses the tastebuds: sometimes sweet, sometimes a little drier.

## GLENMORANGIE ORIGINAL 43%
Single Malt - Highland

WHISKY Magazine Recommended

8¾ **Michael: Illustrates the extra dimension in whiskies when most distilleries did their own malting.**
**Nose:** Very distinctive, clean, oaky peatiness. This character is in the background throughout.
**Palate:** Flowery. Fudgy. Toffeeish. Nutty. Very soft, restrained, spiciness. Then toasty and peaty.
**Finish:** Firm, clean (almost crisp), peatiness. Then long, very soft, spicy and remarkably warming.

9 **Jim: For my money the best Glenmorangie. I have yet come across: complexity beyond belief. Truly outstanding.**
**Nose:** A lighter, more flowery aroma with mixed fruit. Ethereal quality to the vanilla-malt complexity.
**Palate:** Sweet and delightfully spicy at first, then becomes richer and oilier.
**Finish:** Brilliant malt caresses the tastebuds: some times sweet, sometimes a little drier.

## GLENMORANGIE PORT WOOD FINISH 43%
Single Malt - Highland

8¾ **Michael: Do you smoke after sex? No I have a port finish.**
**Nose:** Pronouncedly fruity (raisins, cherries?) and winey.
**Palate:** The sweetness and smoothness could obtrude at first, enwrapping the delicate dimensions of Glenmorangie, but eventually the two elements blend in sensuous fashion.
**Finish:** Soothing, soporific, relaxing.

8 **Doug: The best behaved of the trio. Most would expect the portwood to be the big gun.**
**Nose:** Delicate orange blossom at first then soft brine seeping through.
**Palate:** Soft gentle, barley sugars with occasional salty and sherbety highlights.
**Finish:** Reasonably long, some lingering sweetness and late spice.

## GLENMORANGIE SHERRY FINISH 43%
Single Malt - Highland

8½ **Michael: Quite heavily sherried, but the distillery character turns out to be surprisingly resilient.**
**Nose:** Dry, nutty, sherry notes, but the saltiness still comes through.
**Palate:** Much more voluptuous than the more familiar bourbon versions. Long, sustained, flavour development. Sherryish richness almost overpowers the distillery character.
**Finish:** Liquorice. rooty. Late, restrained, saltiness.

8¼ **Doug: Interesting and complex with some characteristics reminiscent of Scotland's other national drink.**
**Nose:** Deep and enticing, peaches and cream and a little added salt and sour.
**Palate:** Rounded and nutty while the cocoa and sherry are paraded.
**Finish:** Warm and lingering giving way to salt and oak.

## GLENMORANGIE SPEAKEASY 58.4%
Single Malt - Highland

7¼ **Martine: A pretty, refreshing malt. The high strength is more noticeable on the nose than on the palate. But it does need water.**
**Nose:** Prickly. Mustard. Angelica. Lemon grass. Hint of carnation. Condensed milk. Ice cream.
**Palate:** Quite smooth for the strength. Light bodied but syrupy with water. A full burst of pear drops. Sweet cereal. Touch of aniseed.
**Finish:** Drying. Slightly fizzy. Ends abruptly.

7¾ **Dave: A frisky wee beastie.**
**Nose:** Some nose burn. Behind that there's custard, cooking apple, banana chips, lemon. Touch of Turkish delight, icing sugar. With water a carpenter's workbench. Bounty bar.
**Palate:** Lively. A little perfumed, slight tongueclinging quality, lightly nutty. Tingling, orange fondant and milk chocolate.
**Finish:** Mustard leaves.

## GLENMORANGIE TAIN L'HERMITAGE 46%
Single Malt - Highland

WHISKY Magazine Editor's choice

8¾ **Michael: Perhaps more robust, less elegant, than the previous bottling, but full of flavour and soundly structured.**
**Nose:** Deep, fruity, toffeeish.
**Palate:** Clotted cream. Cinnamon. Spicy. Liquorice. Rooty. Nutty. Developing dry fruitiness. Very long.
**Finish:** Yet further length. The flavours concentrate in a winey, spicy, warming "cough syrup".

8¾ **Dave: A resounding success. Would make a great, if expensive, Rob Roy.**
**Nose:** Sweet, fruity and estery: brown sugar, mashed banana, orange peel, maraschino cherry juice, dried mango. Oak-softening with water.
**Palate:** Thick, sweet, chewy and liquorous. Cooked fruits, creamy custard. Complex and teasing.
**Finish:** Sweet. Rosehip.

## GLENMORANGIE THREE CASK MATURED 40%
Single Malt - Highland

8 **Michael: A very unusual vatting (bourbon, plain charred oak and Rioja) has produced equally strange flavours. Less oaky vanilla and more Rioja than I would have expected. I like its eccentricity, but it loses points for lack of whisky character.**
**Nose:** Blackberry pie dusted with icing sugar.
**Palate:** Scented, dryish. A first bite of the fruits.
**Finish:** The juice, with some acidity and bitterness.

7 **Dave: Doesn't quite hold together on palate.**
**Nose:** Fragrant and lifted: apple, strawberry, orange blossom, vanilla, chocolate, spice. In time, Irn Bru.
**Palate:** Starts soft, but is lightly tannic with an acidic edge. Soft fruits, plum skin, chocolate.
**Finish:** Creamy and fruity, peach apricot, Opal Fruits (aka Starburst).

## GLENMORANGIE TRADITIONAL 57.2%
Single Malt - Highland

8¼ **Michael: A surprisingly robust expression of Glenmorangie.**
**Nose:** Very aromatic. Very spicy.
**Palate:** Slightly fuller-bodied than the 10 Years Old. Firm, smooth, slippery. Raspberry syrup over vanilla ice cream, eaten on the beach.
**Finish:** Creamy and soothing, then salty. Very long.

8½ **Dave: The nose lets it down a little, but what a fantastic palate. The higher alcohol really brings this to life – delicate doesn't mean one-dimensional.**
**Nose:** Very light and estery: citrus fruits, vanilla, wet grass/gorse, floral, subtle oak tones.
**Palate:** Charming, sweet, summery. Lemon, orange, coconut, vanilla, dried apple and beautifully-balanced light oak. Gentle, with stunning balance.
**Finish:** Soft, oak, spices.

## GLENMORANGIE TRUFFLE OAK 60.5%
Single Malt - Highland

WHISKY Magazine Recommended

8¾ **Martine: A superb fruity expression, with a summery aromatic profile. Water makes it even more sensuous. Definitely morish.**
**Nose:** Perfumy, fruity. Like being in a sun-exposed orchard on a scorcher. Ripe juicy peaches. Apricot blossom. A touch of minty freshener. Appetising.
**Palate:** Mellow and round at start. Oily feel. Sweet maltiness, followed by a burst of spicy flavours.
**Finish:** Lingering and spicy. Beautifully dovetailing.

8¾ **Dave: Multilayered with hidden depths and subtle sweetness. A marvellous addition to a fascinating and groundbreaking, innovative range.**
**Nose:** Buttery, intense and lightly oily, then a blast of exotic herbs and spices (fresh fenugreek, pepper tree leaves). Then comes porcini mushroom, passionfruit, syrup, caramel and vanilla.
**Palate:** Great balance here between cask and spirit. Peachy, then a light grip, sweet fruits.
**Finish:** Crushed black fruits.

## THE GLENROTHES 13 YEARS OLD, PROVENANCE 46%
Single Malt - Speyside

**9** **Gavin: Large, yet complex. A lovely example of this outstanding Speyside whisky which still has far too low a profile.**
**Nose:** Heather and malt, cooked plums; notably sophisticated. Makes you want to keep nosing it.
**Palate:** Lovely big, malty dram, buttery and sweet, background ginger, with later claret notes creeping in.
**Finish:** Long, drying, very stylish.

**7½** **Dave: Good, but lacks a little sweetness.**
**Nose:** Rich, sweet and rounded. Cake mix, malted loaf. In time burnt notes, treacle scone then Worcestershire sauce. Light peat, pecan.
**Palate:** Dried fruits. Rich fruit cake. Plum. Soft and deep to start then like the nose becomes grippy, charred and tannic.
**Finish:** Dry. Fruit cake again.

## THE GLENROTHES 1965, GORDON & MACPHAIL 43%
Single Malt - Speyside

**8¼** **Michael: Classic Speyside. Confident. Aristocratic.**
**Nose:** Evokes grand houses, polished oak and elegant living.
**Palate:** Buttery, toasty. Slight burnt toast. Lime marmalade. A touch of ginger.
**Finish:** Bittersweet. A hint of black coffee.

**8½** **Dave: A venerable and complex beast that's just holding on. Don't add water.**
**Nose:** Pine needles, Badedas bath, light citrus oil/dried tangerine peel, some bitter herbs/bark, light vanilla. Settles down into butterscotch, pine wood mulch. Seems fragile. Raspberry leaf. Layered. In time fruit cake, raisin, light peat.
**Palate:** Surprisingly soft, quite fragile with a lacy feel. Flavours shift into peppermint. Complex.
**Finish:** Firm becoming dry.

## THE GLENROTHES 1968 32 YEARS OLD, SIGNATORY 50.5%%
Single Malt - Speyside

**8** **Michael: Less soft than the younger expression. A drier, more robust, expression.**
**Nose:** Less aromatic than the 1987. Less spicy, too. A hint of peat.
**Palate:** Quite syrupy and lively. Icing sugar. Mince pies in front of a log fire.
**Finish:** Cough sweets. Dusty spiciness. Warming.

**8½** **Jim: An amazingly relaxed malt for such great age; delicate and understated. Impressive.**
**Nose:** Mildly citrussy and herbal. The minty malt is lovingly tendered by some delightful oak. Very well balanced.
**Palate:** A wave of sweet malt is retained by a waxy body; mouth-watering and amazingly fresh for its age.
**Finish:** Deft vanilla oak slowly dries the sweet malt. Lots of cream toffee to finish.

## THE GLENROTHES 1971 43%
Single Malt - Speyside

**8½** **Michael: I have always felt that Glenrothes deserved to be more widely appreciated** and this bottling confirms that opinion. It is on the sweet side, but beautifully rounded. A sophisticated after-dinner malt.
**Nose:** Waxy orange-skins. Spices. Liquorice root.
**Palate:** Oily but firm. Dried apricots. Dates. Anise. Nougat.
**Finish:** Lightly dry, dusty, spiciness. Gently warming. Log fires. Good oak.

**8¾** **Jim: An improbably well-balanced and deliciously layered malt for it's age. An outstanding Speysider.**
**Nose:** Extraordinary malt concentrate tempered with intense vanilla. Brooding and fabulously balanced.
**Palate:** A curious but enormously delicious amalgam of rich barley, toffee and liquorice. Extremely sweet throughout and with the softest of bodies.
**Finish:** Long, melt-in-the-mouth, with a hint of honeycomb and countering spice.

## THE GLENROTHES 1985, BERRY BROS. & RUDD 43%
Single Malt - Speyside

**9¼** **Dave: This is head and shoulders above everything else in this tasting. Fills all the senses.**

**Nose:** Immensely complex and mature with great breadth of aromas. Weighty but with fragrant spice. In time polished oak giving it balancing dryness.
**Palate:** Layers of complexity with honeyed rich fruits cut through with citrus and spice. Concentrated, luscious, a slow-motion explosion.
**Finish:** Long, elegant, balanced.

**7¾** **Arthur: Slight spiciness adds some zing to an otherwise pleasingly sweet dram.**
**Nose:** Raisins, cumin, butter, pot pourri, warm bread. Peshwari Naan filling.
**Palate:** Raisins and peach syrup. Some European tannins.
**Finish:** Sweet malt and some grassiness.

## THE GLENROTHES 1987, 13 YEARS OLD 40%
Single Malt - Speyside

**8¼** **Michael: The flavour metaphors evoke childhood, but this is a very adult, sophisticated malt.**
**Nose:** Sweetshops. Icing sugar. Liquorice. Very delicate hint of rooty peatiness.
**Palate:** Silky-smooth. Nougat. Dried apricots. Anis.
**Finish:** A suggestion of orange. Teasing delicate, gently soothing.

**8** **Jim: A well-sculpted malt with a restrained richness and limited complexity. Lovely weight throughout.**
**Nose:** Charming acacia honey and demerara sugar within a floral theme of pansies and violets.
**Palate:** Initially enclosed and oaky. Pans out to allow a richer, toffee-cream and intensely malty middle.
**Finish:** Medium length, simple mixture of oak and barley.

## THE GLENROTHES 1988, JAMES MACARTHUR 53.5%
Single Malt - Speyside

**8** **Michael: Sophisticated flavours in a delicate structure. Like elaborate petits-fours.**
**Nose:** Set honey. Fragrant.
**Palate:** Minty. First peppermint creams, then leafy garden mint.
**Finish:** Bitter chocolate.

**7½** **Ian: A mellow character with integrated flavours rather than an individual sequence.**
**Nose:** Creamy porridge with honey, then baked apples and apricots take over.
**Palate:** Luscious, syrupy texture with nuances of digestive biscuits, thick set honey, crème brûlée, gingerbread and dried fruit.
**Finish:** Digestive biscuit dryness and crème brûlée sweetness, with a final flourish of dried fruit.

## THE GLENROTHES 1989 43%
Single Malt - Speyside

**8** **Michael: A whisky for a reverie. Daydream of childhood and the local sweet-shop.**
**Nose:** A subtle suggestion of soft liquorice, as in Pontefract cakes.
**Palate:** Light, soft, syrupy. The liquorice more emphatic now. Spanish root. Develops juicy, mouth-watering flavours. Aniseed. Coconut.
**Finish:** Soothing, relaxing.

**8** **Dave: A very elegant, superbly balanced middle-weight dram.**
**Nose:** Sweet spices with toffee, banana, cream, dried pear and fruit cake (sultana, raisin and cherry). Complex and delicious.
**Palate:** The spiciness comes right through from the start giving a subtle lift to the rich fruits, light sherry and ginger loaf.
**Finish:** Long and soft.

## THE GLENROTHES 1990, SIGNATORY 46%
Single Malt - Speyside

**8¼** **Michael: An elegant and luxurious malt. Glenrothes. This is an elegant and luxurious interpretation of it.**
**Nose:** Hard toffee. Peanut brittle. Fruitier (cherries?) when water is added.
**Palate:** Long development of sweet and nutty flavours. Nougat. Coconut ice.
**Finish:** Hard liquorice. Medicinal. Soothing.

**7½** **Dave: Good, but not as good as the distillery bottlings.**
**Nose:** Ripe and deep with dried fruits: sultana, apricot then (with water) burnt wholemeal bread crust.
**Palate:** Smoky/sulphur. Burnt but with soft concentrated dried fruit. Like liquid pannetone.
**Finish:** A little short.

## THE GLENROTHES 1991 43%
Single Malt - Speyside

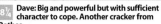

**8¼ Dave:** Big and powerful but with sufficient character to cope. Another cracker from Rothes.
**Nose:** Weighty and rich: cumin powder, sweet orange peel (and pulp), bitter chocolate torte. Water melts the chocolate and orange together.
**Palate:** Very dense and fungal, suggesting maturity. Lightly smoked with tannins and a citric/marmalade fruitiness. Balanced and complex.
**Finish:** Long, soft and raisined.

**8½ Arthur:** Impressive, complex Speyside with a pleasing body.
**Nose:** Fennel, stewed plums and rhubarb, Juicy Fruit chewing gum, and blackcurrant.
**Palate:** Complex combination of maltiness (brown toast), wet grass, toffee and cooked fruit.
**Finish:** Tannins and even a little woodsmoke.

## THE GLENROTHES 1992, 10 YEARS OLD, PORT FINISH, CHIEFTAIN'S CHOICE 43%
Single Malt - Speyside

**8¼ Michael:** More mature than its 10 years would suggest. Fruitier than the conventional distillery bottlings. Refreshing. Like sorbet between courses.
**Nose:** Creamy. Hint of ground almonds.
**Palate:** Medium to full body. Firm, smooth. Apples and pears, freshly peeled and cut. Fruit salad.
**Finish:** Quick touch of caramel dryness. Oranges in caramel.

**7 Dave:** The nose suggests this was in sherry before being in Port. Has Glenrothes character but a bit dry.
**Nose:** An interesting nose: red fruits, (redcurrant, raspberry) then sultana and other dried fruit, struck matches, rubber, mushroom, oak.
**Palate:** Sweet and malty to start. Cherry and sultana cake with sloe, black fruits and raisin.
**Finish:** A little hard.

## THE GLENROTHES 1994 43%
Single Malt - Speyside

**7¾ Dave:** A teasing mix of aromas and flavours.
**Nose:** Fleshily ripe. Dried pear, clotted cream with scented estery notes. With water there's wholemeal bread, a touch of orange. Quite zippy.
**Palate:** A slightly strange mix of stewed fruit and dry malt tussling together. Hint of sulphur. Seems young suggesting greater things to come.
**Finish:** Long rich, lightly spiced slightly citric.

**8 Arthur:** A full-on, after dinner style and a bold, characterful spirit.
**Nose:** Orange: pith and rind. Lemon Jif and geraniums.
**Palate:** Dark chocolate, baked apples, hazelnuts and something sweet yet savoury like black bean sauce.
**Finish:** Dry roasted peanuts.

## THE GLENROTHES 35 YEARS OLD, DUNCAN TAYLOR 40.2%
Single Malt - Speyside

**7¾ Dave:** Old with a certain sexy, slinky quality.
**Nose:** Sweet and very pure. There's touches of wet clay, cowgum, apple sponge, bran, pecan, orange zest and apple. Seems young, but touches of varnish and wood oil suggests it's older than it appears.
**Palate:** Clean though a little soapy. Light citrus and crisp oak. Decent balance. Nutty power and good length.
**Finish:** Slightly malty.

**7¾ Arthur:** One of those drams with a nose which is quite different to the palate. I worried that the bitterness might get too much after a few drams, but adored that confected, cute and fluffy nose.
**Nose:** Rose (Turkish Delight), strawberry tart, and marshmallow. Pear drops and milk chocolate.
**Palate:** Wood dominated, with a lime pickle and a barky bitterness.
**Finish:** More bark, and a herby dryness.

## THE GLENROTHES SELECT RESERVE, BERRY BROS. & RUDD 43%
Single Malt - Speyside

**7½ Arthur:** Youthful, but without the lip-smacking class of the older vintages.
**Nose:** Spice, spirit and citrus. Fruitiness too, with a combination of pale sultanas and sharp woodland berries.
**Palate:** Slightly spirity, spicy and with mixed peel character.
**Finish:** Biscuity.

**7½ Dave:** It's a perfectly decent dram but not a patch on the great 'vintage' bottlings.
**Nose:** Crisp oak, malt bins/shredded wheat, estery. Hot bracken, patisserie (almond, vanilla) kumquat, praline. Seems young.
**Palate:** Spicy and fresh. Decent depth in the centre. Good flow. Light milk chocolate, clootie dumpling mix, citrus peels, hazelnut shell.
**Finish:** Dry cereal, nutty, young.

## GLENTAUCHERS 1990 14 YEARS OLD, OLD MASTERS 58.8%
Single Malt - Speyside

**8 Michael:** Serve as an aperitif. Chilled?
**Nose:** Fresh. Leafy. A hint of citrus.
**Palate:** Light, firm, drying. Lemon zest. Sweet limes. Remarkably fruity.
**Finish:** Peppery. Slightly hot. Aggressive.

**6 Dave:** No maturation.
**Nose:** Plain nose, some sulphur, biscuit crumbs, marsh gas. Immature.
**Palate:** A mix of overripe fruits, pineapple essence, pear drops, then oak. Tart.
**Finish:** Hard.

## GLENTAUCHERS 1990, 13 YEARS OLD, JAMES MA-CARTHUR 59.2%
Single Malt - Speyside

**7 Martine:** Pleasant fruitiness on the nose but the palate is somewhat dour and one dimensional.
**Nose:** Floral and fruity. Wild rose, apple blossom. Barley sugar. Sweet apple compote. Slightly spirity. Hint of toffee.
**Palate:** Light bodied. A bit sharp. Overripe medlar. A cheesy touch.
**Finish:** Tangy and dry, soothing almondy notes.

**7½ Dave:** A good aperitif dram.
**Nose:** Gentle and delicate. Apple pie, banana, cooked brown sugar. A little buzzy with alcohol.
**Palate:** Needs water which improves it considerably. Fruit kernel, orchard fruit. Lively with a hint of flowers.
**Finish:** Short and clean. Oak.

## GLENTAUCHERS 1990, GORDON & MACPHAIL 40%
Single Malt - Speyside

**6½ Martine:** Sherry influence calls the tune. Water calms the flavours down.
**Nose:** Sherry. Rubbery. Lilac.
**Palate:** Sherry prevails. Burnt oak. Slightly sulphurous. Touch of chestnut.
**Finish:** Surprisingly discreet for what could be expected from a sherried malt.

**6½ Dave:** Easy-going, but nothing to get too excited about.
**Nose:** Gold. Dry spices, garam masala/coriander powder. Reminds me of an old trunk in the loft. There's some chocolate/biscuit notes, burnt orange and spent matches. Undemanding stuff.
**Palate:** Clean and lightly malty. Slightly dry with a little bitterness on the side of the mouth.
**Finish:** Nuts.

## GLENTURRET 12 YEARS OLD 40%
Single Malt - Highland

**7½ Michael: Crisp. Earthy. After a walk in the forest?**
**Nose:** Light, fresh and very flowery.
**Palate:** Fresh dessert apple. Nutty. Cereal-grain. Faint peat.
**Finish:** Perfumy. Dry. Refreshing.

**6¾ Jim: Bizarre. The sweetest Glenturret I've come across and a must for liqueur lovers.**
**Nose:** Mildly butyric. Some redeeming honey notes can't quite set the aroma back on track.
**Palate:** Incredibly sweet opening and middle, lashings of cane juice to dampen the malt.
**Finish:** Some hint of normality as a little vanilla tries to calm things a little by offering some balance.

## GLENTURRET 14 YEARS OLD 59.7%
Single Malt - Highland

**8¾ Dave: Only 14. I'm amazed. A must try.**
**Nose:** Date, light resin, liquorice black fruits, treacle pudding, malt extract. Water brings out tomato ketchup, as if it's heading into balsamic territory. Great weight and complexity.
**Palate:** Rich fruits, plum jam, parma violet. This amazing concentrated sweetness means it needs time for everything to be teased out and a fair bit of water to cut the heat. Complex.
**Finish:** Long, silky.

**7¾ Arthur: Limited depth and complexity, but the dimensions this offers are bold and pleasing without particular off-notes.**
**Nose:** Treacle and molasses with some floral notes. This treacle character is prevalent. A bit of fennel, some earthy peatiness.
**Palate:** Sweet, simple with orange and aniseed.
**Finish:** An exhaust-like smokiness, and I couldn't quite work out if it was just the sherry cask maturation or a peatiness underneath.

## GLENTURRET 15 YEARS OLD 40%
Single Malt - Highland

**8 Michael: More luscious, but beautifully balanced. Aperitif?**
**Nose:** Fruitier, with more obvious malt and oak.
**Palate:** Creamier, maltier, deeper.
**Finish:** Rounder. More soothing. Hint of peat.

**8¾ Jim: A sma' still style with loads of body and massive Perthshire honey.**
**Nose:** Back to its old complex self. Even a hint of cherry tomato in a wonderfully fruity sub-strata.
**Palate:** Excellent balance from the off. As the malt intensifies, so does the oiliness which sweetens dramatically.
**Finish:** Echoes of honey and wax with a developing bitterness and faint spice bite.

## GLENTURRET 15 YEARS OLD 55.3%
Single Malt - Highland

**8 Dave: The balance is just tipping in favour of the cask. Glad this was bottled now.**
**Nose:** Mellow and heavily sherried. Calf leather, tarragon, spice cupboard and then an oxidised nuttiness cut with scented fruit. Palo cortado. Dried fruits, cooked dates. Care for a sherry vicar?
**Palate:** Dense and tannic with lots of sherried notes. Fairly tannic but there's a sweet undertow and a hint of malt. Big and chewy.
**Finish:** Long, slightly perfumed.

**7¾ Arthur: This must have been a very fresh cask, as the woody tannins are very prevalent for one so young.**
**Nose:** Wedding cake, hicory and some rubbery sulphur. With a little time and water ginger, barley wine and some more woody notes come out.
**Palate:** An oily texture, with sweet ginger flavours, aniseed and dried apricot but drying out very quickly with lots of wood.
**Finish:** Tannic and drying.

## GLENTURRET 18 YEARS OLD 40%
Single Malt - Highland

**8 Michael: Liqueur-ish. With dessert?**
**Nose:** More honeyed. Spicier.
**Palate:** Firm maltiness. Vanilla pods.
**Finish:** Very fragrant. Hint of peat. Long. Glowing.

**8¼ Jim: A thought-provoking, complex and enjoyable whisky.**
**Nose:** Genuine depth and weight here. The nose depends on clean oak, lavender and a sprig of mint. An aroma captured from a summer garden.
**Palate:** Firm mouthfeel then an explosion of acacia honey controlled, somewhat, by soft oak.
**Finish:** Long, cream toffee, then bitter coffee and orange peel, finale. But with honey in the middle.

## GLENTURRET 1965, KINGSBURY 46.2%
Single Malt - Highland

**7½ Michael: Very much the house style. Has not gained, or lost, much by such a long maturation.**
**Nose:** Peat, then flowery, with cinnamon and apples.
**Palate:** Firmly malty. Nutty. Grassy. Herbal.
**Finish:** Dry. Peaty and warming.

**6 Jim: The result of a stillman's very worst nightmare.**
**Nose:** A tale of an out-of-control wash still and bars of soap. Some honey still filters through. Amazing!
**Palate:** The oak takes command and though the vanilla-honey-malt combination tries to hold sway the balance has been lost a little.
**Finish:** Waxed honey, slightly strained oak but ultimately very soapy.

## GLENTURRET 1972 LIMITED EDITION 47%
Single Malt - Highland

**8¼ Michael: More robust and less finessed than I remember.**
**Nose:** Peachy, fruity. Coconut oil. Slight cereal grain oiliness.
**Palate:** Light but creamy. Grassy, sweet graininess, maltiness. Flapjack.
**Finish:** Powerful and soothing. Spiciness and smokiness.

**5¾ Dave: I tried two samples and five glasses. The soap was still there.**
**Nose:** Resin. Spearmint/toothpaste to start then more cake like as it opens, fig rolls. Soft and juicy.
**Palate:** Soft texture with sweet nuttiness then a soapy flavour begins to dominate.
**Finish:** Soapy. Off-putting.

## GLENTURRET 1973, SIGNATORY 55.5%
Single Malt - Highland

**7¾ Michael: Distillery bottlings of Glenturret from this era tend to be quite sherryish, but this Signatory edition is not. The absence of sherry reveals the use of a truly peaty malt in the 1970s.**
**Nose:** Decidedly more peaty.
**Palate:** Smooth. Fragrant peat-smoke throughout. Very distinctive, but lacks complexity.
**Finish:** A late interplay between intense malty sweetness and peat-smoke.

**8¼ Jim: Brinkmanship at its bravest and best: another summer would have done this one in.**
**Nose:** Pretty oaky stuff: wood notes succeed in dampening the honey onslaught. A puff of smoke?
**Palate:** Early honey-malt in the true Glenturret tradition, then a wave of pretty big oak that suggests the end was just about nigh when bottled.
**Finish:** Burnt honeycomb and toffee blends well with the softening oak and that opaque trail of smoke.

## GLENTURRET 1980 LIMITED EDITION 55.2%
Single Malt - Highland

**8½ Michael: More rounded, and longer, than the 1972.**
**Nose:** Coconut oil.
**Palate:** Marshmallow maltiness. Nutty. Condensed mllk. Cinder toffee.
**Finish:** Gentle, long, warming. Some soft, restrained, peaty notes.

**8½ Dave: Round, soft and gentle. A charmer.**
**Nose:** Clean, oaky and nutty (acorn/hazelnut/ground almond). Behind that there's soft creamy fruits, nutmeg, orange, cereal, juniper and dried grass. Very attractive.
**Palate:** Sweet nut to start. Well balanced with a fine-boned structure and a soft, fruity mid palate.
**Finish:** Lightly spiced.

## GLENTURRET 1985, SIGNATORY 58.4%
Single Malt - Highland

**8 Martine: Original bunch of flavours that Towser and her descendants would have enjoyed.**
**Nose:** Surprising. White chocolate, nougat, lemon curd. Coffee and cream liquor.
**Palate:** Viscous, milky. Cappuccino. Good balance between palate and nose.
**Finish:** Quite dry. Sappy, slightly astringent.

**7½ Dave: Big, gentle and attractive if you are a fan of old-style Aussie Chardonnay.**
**Nose:** Creamy. A pat of butter melting over wholemeal toast. OTT. Water brings out tangerine, lemon and spring flowers.
**Palate:** Crisper than the nose suggests. The flowers are hanging in there along with some spiciness but all locked into the soft embrace of the butter.
**Finish:** Quite light.

## GLENTURRET 1986, 15 YEARS OLD, CADENHEAD'S 54%
Single Malt - Highland

**8 Michael: A charming whisky, and a reminder that Glenturret is a place, not an experience.**
**Nose:** Fresh. Minty boiled sweets.
**Palate:** Concentrated sweetness. Scottish tablet. Nuts.
**Finish:** Gingery. Spicy. Lively. Dry. Long.

**6¾ Martine: One-dimensional with a butyric aroma which is far from exciting.**
**Nose:** A definite sour, unpleasant milky aroma. Varnish-like fresh paint scent. Cedar notes behind.
**Palate:** Lots of liquorice and aniseed (like Liquorice Allsorts). Nothing much else.
**Finish:** Liquorice again. Turning slightly bitter.

## GLENTURRET 1986, OLD MASTERS 51.3%
Single Malt - Highland

**8 Martine: As refreshing as a herbal tea but much more rewarding and fulfilling. Would suit a leg of lamb with mint sauce.**
**Nose:** Light and fragrant. Grassy. Herbal. Straw. Garden mint. Elegant spices. Paprika, touch of curry.
**Palate:** Incredibly fresh and clean. Enticing, fresh herb flavours. Luscious sherbety mouthfeel.
**Finish:** Not very long but keeps the taste profile high. Tender bitterness.

**6¾ Dave: Sadly it's just unbalanced.**
**Nose:** Delicate and floral with hints of boiled milk and dry malt. Seems to have quite a subtle richness.
**Palate:** Fragrant blossoms: orange/jasmine and a chewy start, but a sour note spoils things.
**Finish:** Dry and soft then that milky note again.

## GLENTURRET 1990, 12 YEARS OLD, PORT FINISH, CHIEFTAIN'S CHOICE 43%
Single Malt - Highland

**7¾ Michael: Refreshing, appetising.**
**Nose:** Earthy. Forest floor, resiny, sweet, malty. Cereal grain, becoming nuttier and sweeter.
**Palate:** Starts with dessert apples, moving to raspberry.
**Finish:** This is where the Port finally comes through, and does so very assertively. "Better late than never, " it seems to say.

**6¾ Dave: A cocktail rather than a finish.**
**Nose:** An onion skin colour. Sweet, floral notes: apple purée, raspberryade, cherry, jam. Becomes firmer with water.
**Palate:** A mix of light dry maltiness alongside sloe, strawberry. Very sweet. Like wine and whisky shaken together.
**Finish:** Somehow sticky but thin.

## GLENTURRET 21 YEARS OLD 40%
Single Malt - Highland

**8½ Michael: After dinner.**
**Nose:** Sherry. Peaches and cream.
**Palate:** Sherryish nuttiness and sweetness at first, but the drier distillery character gradually emerges. Lots of flavour development.
**Finish:** Rounded, spicy (aniseed?) with a lovely peaty warmth.

*WHISKY Magazine Recommended*

**8¾ Jim: A restrained malt for all its massive complexity and depth.**

**Nose:** Absolute class! A cluster of berry-fruits add to the complexity.
**Palate:** Sexy, voluptuous mouthfeel with the honey taking off early then a more estery fruitiness and a big build up of malt.
**Finish:** Hints of cocoa underline the age and the bitter/sweet honey oak finish lasts forever.

## GLENTURRET 29 YEARS OLD 55.6%
Single Malt - Highland

**9 Dave: An underrated distillery which, when on form, is up there with the best. More please!**
**Nose:** Bready, freesia, hyacinth. Needs ages to open fully then a honeyed complexity, some semidried fruits, wax, tablet. Hint of herbs. Elegant.
**Palate:** Subtle. Spices lining up and giving it a zing. Excellent balance. This is in the space where wood and spirit are so integrated that the flavours have been taken into a new dimension.
**Finish:** Long, sweet, fizzing with energy.

*WHISKY Magazine Recommended*

**8¾ Arthur: A classic all-round drinking malt in the Highland style. Good to see another bottling from this distillery.**
**Nose:** Mature, with baked apple and orange mixed with a grainy fudge. With water, fruits leap to the fore and the sweet creaminess of evaporated milk.
**Palate:** A great balance between spirit and cask. Tinned fruit, watermelon and grass. Wonderful honeyed, syrupy sweetness.
**Finish:** Fresh, wet grass.

## GLENTURRET, 10 YEARS OLD, CHIEFTAIN'S CHOICE 43%
Single Malt - Highland

**7½ Michael: Pleasant, but I have had more complex bottlings from this distillery.**
**Nose:** Flowery. Marshmallow.
**Palate:** Light but smooth. Clean. Spun sugar. Creamy.
**Finish:** Vanilla. Crème brûlée.

**7¾ Dave: Crunchy! Attractive.**
**Nose:** Malty (bran flakes) and nutty with a floral note. Water brings out apple, lemon, honey, toffee and coconut.
**Palate:** Crisp, almost friable, nutty and crunchy with good mid-palate weight.
**Finish:** Soft fruit, coffee, then crisps up.

## GLENUGIE 1968, 43 YEARS OLD, GORDON & MACPHAIL
Single Malt - Highland

**7¾ Martine: Oak is not as prevailing on the nose as on the palate. An exotic profile. Reminds me of Irish whiskey. Interesting richness. Avoid water.**
**Nose:** Malty. Cereal. Toasted bread. Very farmlike. Hay loft. Wet dog. Some floral notes coming through like after a gentle rain in a garden. Dried fruit. Raisins and apricot. Dried apples.
**Palate:** Thick, rich. An explosion of exotic fruit. Passion fruit, guava. Dark chocolate.
**Finish:** Drying on oak. A bitter edge.

**8 Michael: Like kissing your lover after they've finished off an entire family pack of Liquorice Allsorts.**
**Nose:** Tart fruitiness balanced with Rye-like notes. Dusty, grainy, cereals.
**Palate:** Full and sweet. Peppery. Aniseed top notes. Vaguely smoky?
**Finish:** Hot. Fennel. Imps. Bertie Bassett's hat. More manageable with water.

## GLENURY ROYAL 28 YEARS OLD, RARE MALTS 58.4%
Single Malt - Highland

**8** **Michael: An elegant middleweight after the oak-fisted heavyweight 23 Years Old in the same series.**
**Nose:** Nutty, almondy, Oloroso sherry.
**Palate:** Very firm, rounded. Honey, lemons, pistachio nuts, angelica, garden mint.
**Finish:** Like biting into a green leaf. Tree-bark woodiness. Cinnamon. Fragrant. Long.

**8½** **Jim: Unquestionably the finest Glenury I have tasted in 20 years and extraordinary for its age. Among the best low-peated Rare Malt bottlings of all time.**
**Nose:** Fresh and briny, younger than its great age. A delicate hint of sherry adds extra weight, as does a wisp of smoke.
**Palate:** Fat and fabulously textured: acacia honey and fruity maltiness. A subtle peatiness adds an extra, unexpected dimension.
**Finish:** Enormously long and increasingly spicy. Great complexity of vanilla, peat and enormous malt richness.

## GLENURY ROYAL 50 YEARS OLD 42.8%
Single Malt - Highland

**9** **Michael: A stunning farewell performance.**
**Nose:** Soft smoke. The burnt skin of some chestnuts roasting.
**Palate:** Rich, smooth, luxurious. A whole box of liqueur chocolates concentrated into my tasting glass. Dark chocolate, variously filled with coffee and cherry liqueurs. Perhaps even peppermint.
**Finish:** Sappy, oaky, dryness.

**7¾** **Dave: A wonderful nose but too woody for me.**
**Nose:** Fragrant wood (rosewood?) incense/musk, rancio, cheese rind, sweet and rum-like, toffee apple. Perfumed.
**Palate:** Starts very concentrated and sweet. Treacle scones, bung cloth, humidor, then firm wood starts to dominate. Grippy.
**Finish:** Treacle toffee, tannic.

## GRAND OLD PARR 12 YEARS OLD 43%
Blended Malt - Scotland

**8½** **Michael: If you want to taste barley in a blend, look no further than this muscular heavyweight.**
**Nose:** Malty, sweet scented, cake-like. Linseed.
**Palate:** Big. Notably firm-bodied. Malty. Cereal grains. Toasted sesame seeds. Demerara sugar and raisins. Honey. There even seems to be a hint of chilli in there somewhere.
**Finish:** Soothing. Long. Developing slight lemon grass and peatiness.

**8** **Dave: A fine, well-weighted pretty lush blend.**
**Nose:** Well-balanced nose with sherried notes of orange, nutmeg, wine gums and vanilla. Water introduces a heathery/earthy smoke note.
**Palate:** Chewy. It's well balanced and juicy but with little jabs of citrus to keep you interested.
**Finish:** Long and mellow, starts cakey then comes pepper.

## GRAND OLD PARR 18 YEARS OLD, CLASSIC 46%
Blended Malt - Scotland

**8** **Michael: Is this a vatted malt? Glendullan-plus?**
**Nose:** Assertive. Rich, honeyed. Malty. Also fruity. Peach cobbler?
**Palate:** Big, textured. Perfumy. Passion fruit, peaches, maraschino cherry brandy, almonds.
**Finish:** Very firm, perfumy and long, with a balancing ginger dryness.

**7¾** **Dave: The balance tips things to the oaky side. Good on the palate, but only for lovers of old whisky.**
**Nose:** Mature. A light fingal note: cep, roasted meat, dry oak. Old cupboards, antique shops.
**Palate:** Delivers on the palate. Old and quite rich: leather, nut bowl, black fruits, oaky and firm, a hint of smoke. Just enough sweetness to carry.
**Finish:** Woodland walk in autumn.

## GREENWICH MERIDIAN 2000 BLENDED SCOTCH 40%
Blended - Scotland

**7¼** **Michael: Seems like an attempt at an old-fashioned blend, but a bit two-dimensional.**
**Nose:** Some fresh peatiness.
**Palate:** Starts very sweet and syrupy, with some maltiness. Becomes rather bland.
**Finish:** Weak. Late warmth.

**9** **Jim: Excellent classic blend from the old school: brilliantly firm grain guarantees class and complexity. If they dropped the colour – which affects the taste towards the middle – it would hit amazing heights.**
**Nose:** Finely tuned and impressive, an intriguing hint of juniper and liquorice co-ordinate with a firm grain.
**Palate:** Remains firm and here the complexity takes hold with fabulous cocoa, grassy malt and spices.
**Finish:** Long and simple; malt glow lingers.

## HARRIS WHISKY NO ORDINARY 16 YEARS OLD 53.1%
Single Malt - Speyside

**7¾** **Martine: A wake up call dram for those who like action on the tongue. A classic bourbon maturation which outlines a buoyant character.**
**Nose:** Creamy, fragrant. White peaches, mirabelles. Vanilla flan. Crushed rush. Aniseed lollipop. Develops on mint toffee notes.
**Palate:** Brisk, fizzy. Entices tastebuds in the most active way. Mint toffee again and a major spicy outburst.
**Finish:** Dry, spicy, nutty.

**6** **Dave: At least the name is accurate.**
**Nose:** There's nothing here. Watery in colour, watery in aroma. Maybe some peanut?
**Palate:** Guess what? Light. The only thing to tell you it's not water is the heat of the alcohol.
**Finish:** Huh?

## HART BROTHERS BEN NEVIS 35 YEARS OLD, SHERRY WOOD 50.1%
Single Malt - Highland

**8¼** **Michael: The best Ben Nevis I have tasted.**
**Nose:** Tightly combined, and balanced, fragrant smoke, oak and hard toffee maltiness.
**Palate:** Chewy. Malty honeycomb in dark chocolate. As though the Belgians had upgraded the British Crunchie bar. Tropical fruits.
**Finish:** Clinging. Bittersweet. Firm. Intense black chocolate, but avoids astringency.

**6½** **Dave: Of interest certainly, but is it a pleasurable experience? Not really.**
**Nose:** Woody and earthy (dunnage warehouses) with notes of stewed tea. Water brings out a muscular, toffeed note.
**Palate:** Big, very dry and tannic with some mushroomy, rancio notes but no great complexity.
**Finish:** Dry and tannic with some lively spiciness.

## HAZELBURN 8 YEARS OLD 46%
Single Malt - Campbeltown

**8** **Dave: Good impact for a 'light' whisky. Highly recommended.**
**Nose:** Very sweet with lots of estery notes: lemon, apple, bubblegum, iris. American cream soda, orange smarties.
**Palate:** A clean, sweet, start. Barley sugar, banana, lightly floral/chestnut blossom. Water shows a touch of honey. Lovely feel.
**Finish:** Glides away. Great length.

**7¾** **Arthur: An ideal first dram of the day, and a good example of how younger malt can offer a livelier, fat texture in the mouth.**
**Nose:** Fresh plums, green wine gums and green fresh pears. Grass and hay, a hot, dry meadow.
**Palate:** Full and sweet, with a grassy, floral flavour and some green maltiness. A pleasing oily body.
**Finish:** More cereal character and a bit of earthiness.

## HIGHLAND HARVEST ORGANIC SCOTCH WHISKY 40%
Blended - Scotland

**7¾** **Dave: Well put together. Not hugely complex, but a pleasant dram.**
**Nose:** Highly spiced. Old apple skin, raisins soaked in water, fig rolls, stewed Earl Grey tea.
**Palate:** Raisined sweetness on the front of the mouth, very light smoke and a touch of menthol. Gentle juicy grain carries flavours across the tongue well. Clean with decent balance.
**Finish:** Wheat chaff, chocolate digestive crumbs.

**6¾** **Arthur: Fine, but no dandy.**
**Nose:** Granny Smith apples, lemon peel, and a delicate minerally graininess. Fudge, lime and Shredded Wheat.
**Palate:** Pleasant sweet fruitiness and a medium viscosity.
**Finish:** Short, sweet with a bit of burnt caramel too.

## HIGHLAND PARK 10 YEARS OLD, OLD MALT CASK 50%
Single Malt - Island (non Islay)

**8** **Michael: Utterly delicious, but the sherry masks the peat and salt.**
**Nose:** Fragrant smoke and polished oak.
**Palate:** Rich. Hugely voluptuous sherry. Golden Syrup.
**Finish:** Some spicy esters emerging. Soothing. Warming.

**7½** **Jim: Only the fabulous honey-peat core saves this from being something of a disappointment. I have always felt the Highland Park is a malt that suffers at the hands of a sherry cask and this sample, while having one or two fabulous moments, rather proves the point.**
**Nose:** A surprisingly oaky start for a young Highland Park; spicy and subdued peat as well. Lacks the usual distillery balance.
**Palate:** Massively spicy start, though once the big honey-peat middle kicks in, this soon fades. Some sherry fruitiness makes itself evident, but succeeds only in flattening the palate.
**Finish:** Quite long and peaty but otherwise featureless.

## HIGHLAND PARK 12 YEARS OLD
Single Malt - Island (non Islay)

**8½** **Michael: A beautifully balance classic islander.**
**Nose:** Smoky, "garden bonfire" sweetness, heathery, malty, hint of sherry.
**Palate:** Exceptionally smooth. Succulent, with smoky dryness, heathery-honey sweetness and maltiness.
**Finish:** Teasing, heathery, delicious.

**9** **Jim: This malt changes shape slightly from vatting to vatting, with the smokiness, honey, malt and heather each having turns at domination. A 12 Years Old classic.**
**Nose:** One of the world's most subtle and teasing noses: delicate wafts of smoke mingle effortlessly with sweet malt, a hint of oaky salt, apples, old polished leather and trademark heather.
**Palate:** Intensely malty and fresh at first, and then a lingering smoky depth adds weight. Fabulous bitter-sweet balance which pans out on the sweet side with a gentle build-up of honey.
**Finish:** Long, smoky with a heathers dryness and spice.

## HIGHLAND PARK 12 YEARS OLD, ADELPHI 60.9%
Single Malt - Island (non Islay)

**8** **Michael: I like the richness but lacks the balance, roundness and complexity of a great Highland Park.**
**Nose:** Fresh toast, spread with Nutella.
**Palate:** Firm, smooth. Sweet, sherryish. Juicy oak. Salt.
**Finish:** Salt. Wind-blown heather.

**8¾** **Jim: One of the least smoky renditions you are likely to find, compensated by the honey presence.**
**Nose:** Lashings of sweet honey and nectar and some drier heather and oak. Sublime.
**Palate:** Rich in toffee apples, melt-in-the-mouth malt.
**Finish:** Long, Slightly waxy but big oak pressure.

## HIGHLAND PARK 15 YEARS OLD 40%
Single Malt - Island (non Islay)

**7¼** **Martine: Oak is present all the way. A bit dull. Lacks vividness.**
**Nose:** Fresh saw. Pine resin. Nutty. Hazelnut milk chocolate. A mineral touch. Wet pebble.
**Palate:** Mild and round. Vanilla toffee, with a distinct bitter oakiness.
**Finish:** Medium, salty feel, nutty.

**7½** **Dave: Balanced, as whiskies of this age should be but just too sweet for this palate.**
**Nose:** Light peat smoke gives a perfume to a sweet nose: tablet, demerara sugar, dried fruits (mango as well as grape). Water makes it more phenolic.
**Palate:** Hot with sweet treacle, black banana, raisin, firm oak and that delicate smoke. Very sweet and honeyed.
**Finish:** Gentle, long. Good balance.

## HIGHLAND PARK 16 YEARS OLD 40%
Single Malt - Island (non Islay)

**7½** **Arthur: Pleasant but undramatic. I was a little disappointed to find out it was Highland Park ... surely we can do better than this?**
**Nose:** Burnt orange and vanilla.
**Palate:** Rounded, with soft fruits, burnt toast and sherry cask maturation in evidence.

**Finish:** Dry leaves and woodsmoke.

**7¼** **Owen: I find Port and even Madeira characteristics here. Complex enough, but probably not to everyone's liking.**
**Nose:** Malty, nutty, biscuity, mixed dried fruit (apricots?). Some creamy toffee and the faintest whiff of smoke.
**Palate:** More dried fruit – tea loaf? Sweet and bitter. Vaguely winey, too.
**Finish:** On the short side and somewhat tannic. Oxidisation? Faint smoke?

## HIGHLAND PARK 16 YEARS OLD, ADELPHI 57.9%
Single Malt - Island (non Islay)

**8** **Martine: This bottling does not have the heathery profile of the official bottlings. Drink with water.**
**Nose:** Fragrant. Sweet honey, crushed almonds. Grapefruit. Marzipan. Porridge. A touch of peat.
**Palate:** Smooth, silky. Mouthcoating. Sweetness with spice. Hint of nuttiness. Beautifully balanced.
**Finish:** Reasonably warm, peters off with pleasant spicy notes. Candied ginger.

**8¼** **Dave: All you'd expect. A little less sweet than the proprietary bottlings but none the worse for that.**
**Nose:** Dry and heathery. Light perfumed smoke, cumin, fudge/tablet, and with water rhubarb sweets.
**Palate:** Rich and soft, the high heathery phenols balanced by soft fudgey fruit. A good spread of flavours. It grows and softens then dries before …
**Finish:** … honey.

## HIGHLAND PARK 16 YEARS OLD, DOUGLAS LAING 50%
Single Malt - Island (non Islay)

**9** **Michael: For the end of the evening. Of considerable complexity and will require several attempts before it's cracked. Not for everyone.**
**Nose:** A little woody dryness then chocolate, coconut, marzipan. Some glueiness and menthol.
**Palate:** Thin and drying. Cough candy. Cinnamon. Cloves. Toasted coconut. Sandalwood.
**Finish:** Seemingly short, but, just when you think it's all over, a long, lingering, Fino infused finish.

**7½** **Arthur: A pleasant and balanced malt with a definite island character, but given the choice available from this great distillery, it pales.**
**Nose:** Estery, salty and fruity (peach slices and baked apples). With water up comes fennel, satsuma and melon. Also a husky, gristy character.
**Palate:** Fruity, tingly and lightly peaty.
**Finish:** Dry and biscuity.

## HIGHLAND PARK 16 YEARS OLD, THE WHISKY EXCHANGE 46%
Single Malt - Island (non Islay)

**7** **Dave: No better than average HP.**
**Nose:** Very plain with light smoke. Slightly flinty, firm and a little exposed and lacking integration.
**Palate:** A mineral quality which teases into dried grass. Water brings out a perfumed quality, some smoke, chilli flakes and a slight weight pressing into the middle of the tongue.
**Finish:** Short and clean.

**8** **Martine: A cheeky character, uplifting, cheery and vibrant. For an outdoor meal, with shellfish maybe. Water gives it depth.**
**Nose:** Herbal, sweet. Honey, lemon balm. Light juicy fruit. White currant. Rhubarb juice. A touch of lemon drop.
**Palate:** Quite fizzy on the tongue. Spices unveil immediately. Teasing.
**Finish:** Dry, spicy, with a touch of burnt wood.

### HIGHLAND PARK 17 YEARS OLD, CASK 2903, ADELPHI 55.3%
Single Malt - Island (non Islay)

**9** **Michael: That dance might have been led by Fred Astaire. The great all-rounder in lean and energetic mood. Makes it look easy. Try it with a late-night movie.**
**Nose:** Smoke, shading into oak and sherry.
**Palate:** Notably creamy. Distinctively fruity. Honeyed. Very spicy. Herbal. Faint hint of seaweed.
**Finish:** Lively. As though all the flavours had come on stage to dance a finale.

**9¼** **Dave: Gorgeous, one of the best I've ever tried.**
**Nose:** Rich, soft. Gorgeous: fudge with peaches in syrup, honey, baklava, star anise and caraway spice. Heathery smoke. You could nose this forever
**Palate:** Big, sweet, silky. A beautiful, elegant mix of heathery smoke, Moroccan spices, ripe fruit and a hint of chocolate. Perfect harmony.
**Finish:** Chewy, long.

### HIGHLAND PARK 18 YEARS OLD 1989, DEWAR RATTRAY 53.5%
Single Malt - Island (non Islay)

**7½** **Dave: Couldn't be more different from the other Highland Park. That's casks for you!**
**Nose:** Odd, slightly sweaty start then berries, banana, green grapes. Vanilla to the fore but seems fragile.
**Palate:** Starts spicy(cinnamon and allspice) with a slight soapiness, but gets sweeter and juicier as it progresses. Lightly perfumed.
**Finish:** Gentle light, floral.

**7¾** **Martine: A lively character, delivering more than the first nose lets you expect. The alcohol is perfectly mastered.**
**Nose:** At first, a distinctive fudgy note, closer to tablets. Then becomes malty with a grassy note. Wet hay.
**Palate:** Sweeter than expected. A smooth but vivid texture. More fruit than on the nose. Cooked plums in a gingery syrup.
**Finish:** Dry, warm and spicy. Slightly sherbety.

### HIGHLAND PARK 18 YEARS OLD 43%
Single Malt - Island (non Islay)

**9** **Michael: If I smoked I would have a cigar with this one.**
**Nose:** Warm, notably flowery. Heather-honey, fresh oak, sap, peat, smoky fragrance. Very aromatic and appetising.
**Palate:** Remarkably smooth, firm, rounded. Lightly salty. Leafy (vine leaves?), pine nuts. Lots of flavour development: nuts, honey, cinnamon, dryish ginger.
**Finish:** Spicy, very dry, oaky, smoky, hot.

**9½** **Jim: This has to be my favourite Highland Park of them all, and each new bottle I taste (this was my sixth sample) seems to underline the overall class and consistency of this distillery. Brilliant.**
**Nose:** An empty honey jar which once held peaty embers. An enormous nose which seems to improve with each bottle I sample, though the characteristic salted butter is always present. Fabulous.
**Palate:** Beautifully sweet: even sweeter than the 12 Years Old with peat on the back of the palate. Beautifully chewy, oily and substantial.
**Finish:** Still peaty and now a little oaky. Cocoa and toffee cream compexity.

### HIGHLAND PARK 1958 44%
Single Malt - Island (non Islay)

**9** **Michael: Some drinkers might perfer this great whisky slightly younger and fresher. Those who like a touch of oak will find this very elegant.**
**Nose:** Sweet tobacco. Scented: sandalwood, walnuts.
**Palate:** Sultanas, lemons, vanilla, butterscotch, toasted almonds. Very restrained sweetness.
**Finish:** Long and soothing. Late hint of spicy, heathery smoke.

**7** **Jim: This would never have survived another summer. Impressive brinkmanship, though still over-aged.**
**Nose:** Powering bourbon sweetness. Lashings of oak and vanilla with liquorice and plummy fruit. Tired, but hanging on.
**Palate:** Creamy and spicy with a large smoky, oaky background. Just enough honey comes through to give a Highland Park signature.
**Finish:** Dry, chalky and some late sensuous peat lift this from a weary start. Lovely salty sea tang lingers, too.

### HIGHLAND PARK 1967, CELTIC HEARTLANDS 40.1%
Single Malt - Island (non Islay)

**8½** **Michael: The more heavily-sherried expressions of Highland Park seem more open in displaying their charms.**
**Nose:** Flapjack, warm from the oven. Cooked morello cherries.
**Palate:** Sweetly smoky. Flavours well integrated and contained. Slow, disciplined, development.
**Finish:** Firm, powerful, straight-ahead. Rounded with a suggestion of mint toffee.

**8¼** **Dave: A beauty-but what else would you expect from HP?**
**Nose:** Full and rich. Dry grass, light peat, lanolin. Touch of perfume, (heather bells) fudge, kumquat. Fine-framed oak.
**Palate:** Excellent weight. More fruity than nose suggests with good balance between firm oak and sweet, butter tablet mid-palate. Complex.
**Finish:** Fragrant smoke.

### HIGHLAND PARK 1970, 4.73, SCOTCH MALT WHISKY SOCIETY 52.5%
Single Malt - Island (non Islay)

**8¾** **Michael: Not as sophisticated as the distillery bottlings, but robustly salty, earthy and peaty. Good characteristics, but in this bottling they mask the maltiness and sherry character. I wonder whether all island whiskies once tasted like this?**
**Nose:** Oaky. Smoky, earthy, salty.
**Palate:** Big layered. Sooty, oily.
**Finish:** More peat. Almost abrasive.

**9¼** **Jim: Looking for a 30 Years Old sherry cask malt that is just about blemish free and boasting a mind boggling complexity? I've found one here...**
**Nose:** Voluptuous and bulging at the sporran with the richest, ripest sherry you will find.
**Palate:** Enormous dexterity: despite the massive sherry start there are many layers of malt.
**Finish:** Almost endless with further honey-peat riches hanging on to the silky malt-sherry body.

### HIGHLAND PARK 1970, RARE OLD 40%
Single Malt - Island (non Islay)

**7¾** **Michael: Disappointing. Where is the richness, and especially the island character?**
**Nose:** Lightly grassy, leafy, earthy.
**Palate:** Textured body. Honeyed. Rummy. Bitter chocolate. Ginger. Spicy. White pepper.
**Finish:** Salty. Rooty.

**9¼** **Martine: A cheering malt with a rich array of aromas and flavours. Enjoy with good company.**
**Nose:** Rich yet subtle. Minty freshness. Pear drops and pineapple. Floral notes and a hint of honey.
**Palate:** Sweet and mellow. Mouth-coating. Biscuity and buttery (lemon cake). Fresh crushed almonds with a touch of aniseed. White chocolate. Ginger.
**Finish:** Long, warm, whispering out a luscious combination of mixed spices.

### HIGHLAND PARK 1977 BICENTENARY VINTAGE RESERVE 46%
Single Malt - Island (non Islay)

**9¼** **Michael: My favourite expression of whisky's greatest all rounder. Sets an incredibly high standard for Highland Park to maintain.**
**Nose:** Sherry. Toast. Polished oak.
**Palate:** Rich. Very creamy. Freshly peeled Satsumas. Very bitter black chocolate. Astonishing length.
**Finish:** Violets. Lingering, scented, fragrant, smokiness.

**9½** **Jim: Distilled during one of the best periods in HP's recent history. If only they had bottled at 46!! One of all time greats, for all that.**
**Nose:** One of the most herbal noses around. Exceptional.
**Palate:** Perhaps the most melt-in-the mouth malt of all time. A hint of something fruity moistens the mouth.
**Finish:** Lazy and light; smoky barley and mildly kippery oiliness.

## HIGHLAND PARK 1979, MURRAY MCDAVID 46%
Single Malt - Island (non Islay)

**8½ Michael: Very good indeed as a lightish, delicate, interpretation of Highland Park.**
*WHISKY Magazine Recommended*
**Nose:** Fragrantly peaty.
**Palate:** Good flavour development, beautifully balanced as it unfolds. Fragrantly smoky, then nutty, becoming flowery, and finally honeyish.
**Finish:** Late, clean, appetising, smokiness.

**8½ Jim: A pretty old and slightly tired malt but the richness of the peat and malt, and the harmony they create, makes this a delicious dram. Big stuff.**
**Nose:** A big, slightly brawny, oaky nose with diffused peaty notes.
**Palate:** Immediately dry as the oak bites hard, but the peat and honey offer traditional Orcadian riches.
**Finish:** Long, with vanilla and a rich grapey fruitiness. The peat hangs on to the very end.

## HIGHLAND PARK 1988, SIGNATORY 46%
Single Malt - Island (non Islay)

**9 Michael: A lovely whisky. A sweetish bottling. More complex and elegant than**
*WHISKY Magazine Editor's choice*
the 'official' 12 Years Old, but not quite as expressive as the 18.
**Nose:** Fresh burnt grass. Garden bonfires.
**Palate:** Honey. Heather. Sherryish, nutty, buttery. Marshmallow.
**Finish:** Gradual emergence of smoky warmth. Like sitting in front of a log fire.

**8½ Dave: A Norse nose, concentrated and delicious with more smoke than you normally find, though maybe a little woody.**
**Nose:** Dense, concentrated nose: mead/metheglin, spiced apple, singed orange peel, peat smoke. Beerenauslese with peat on top.
**Palate:** As you'd expect, thick with a good feel. Quite phenolic, subtle and elegant.
**Finish:** Medium smoky.

## HIGHLAND PARK 1989, LOMBARD 50%
Single Malt - Island (non Islay)

**8¾ Michael: Very slow, long, flavour development. Gets up to speed at the very end.**
**Nose:** Smoky. Some phenol.
**Palate:** Silky. Sweetish. Sherryish. Syrupy.
**Finish:** Quite assertive. Late crisp oakiness. Some peatiness. Some warming alcohol. Long.

**7½ Dave: Vivacious but no great depth.**
**Nose:** Clean and quite creamy. Seems young. There's a hint of smoke. Not overly complex.
**Palate:** Medium-bodied with a clean honeyed palate and some peat smoke lurking in the background. Good-ish balance.
**Finish:** Long sweet and honeyed. A tickle of smoke.

## HIGHLAND PARK 21 YEARS OLD, AMBASSADORS CASK 56.1%
Single Malt - Island (non Islay)

**7¾ Arthur: A touch astringent for my tastes, but respectable. Ambassador, surely you should be really spoiling us?**
**Nose:** Quince jelly, cereal husk, wine gums and papaya. Warm apple turnover with almonds on top. A smear of engine oil.
**Palate:** Sherry, unripe apples, mixed spice and oak.
**Finish:** A chewed pencil, flaking paint and all.

**7¼ Owen: Don't be tempted to take it neat, it's way too big and unbalanced. Senescent?**
**Nose:** Big and smooth. Linseed oil with a creamy vanilla toffee background. Pears.
**Palate:** Sweet and oily, then tannic and woody. Charred. Sun dried fruits. Attains balance and elegance with water. Tropical fruit characteristics develop.
**Finish:** Oily, yet astringent. Fruity.

## HIGHLAND PARK 24 YEARS OLD SINGLE CASK, DEWAR RATTRAY 52.3%
Single Malt - Island (non Islay)

**7½ Dave: Decent enough, and the palate is lovely, but somehow you expect more**
*WHISKY Magazine Recommended*
after 24 years in the cask.
**Nose:** Toothpaste/spearmint, macadamia nut but with slightly harsh alcohol behind. Water brings out a waxy note.
**Palate:** Sweet, with a lovely peach jam quality which impresses after a let-down of a nose.

**Finish:** Gentle smooth hint of smoke.

**8¾ Arthur: A great body wearing flattering clothes, the oak showing off the spirit's considerable curves in a classy way.**
**Nose:** Orange, mixed peel, dried papaya and ginger. Subtle swirling smoke and some sweet medicinal character, like Pink Dettol. Some malty, nutty cereal character.
**Palate:** Lime starbursts, marmalade and fruit syrup. A great malty body.
**Finish:** Sweet, oaky and a little smoky.

## HIGHLAND PARK 25 YEARS OLD
Single Malt - Island (non Islay)

**9½ Michael: Have this one with dessert.**
*WHISKY Magazine Recommended*
**Nose:** Full, rounded. Fudge, white chocolate, Oloroso sherry, honey, melon, lemon. Fruity .
**Palate:** More honey, slightly chewy. Nutty toffee. Nougat. Pistachio nuts. Turkish delight. Cedar.
**Finish:** Lemon, honey, roses. Fragrant, smooth. Balancing dryness.

**8½ Jim: Still haven't come across a 25 Years Old which quite matches the 18 Years Old, but this is a lovely whisky nonetheless and holds its shape and character briliantly for such an old lady. Charming.**
**Nose:** Here the heather returns and the expense of the silkier honey. The peat also plays a big part, but fails to keep the emerging oak under a tight enough leash.
**Palate:** An unusually oaky dryness makes way for a steady build-up of sweetening honey. Still beautifully peated.
**Finish:** A much drier finish than the 18 Years Old but smouldering peat adds charm and stability. Some late honey gives a degree of complexity.

## HIGHLAND PARK 25 YEARS OLD, HART BROTHERS 43%
Single Malt - Island (non Islay)

**8½ Michael: Needs water to open it and release some of the drier flavours. A gentle expression of Highland Park. I missed the bigger dimensions of the distillery bottlings.**
**Nose:** Smoke very restrained. Fragrant, spicy.
**Palate:** Lightly syrupy. Clean. Teasing, gentle, dexterous interplay of sweetness and smokiness.
**Finish:** Slightly starchy. Musty.

**7½ Dave: A pretty phenolic example. Lacks the complexity and harmony of the Adelphi bottling.**
**Nose:** Dry, lean and woody. Fairly phenolic. Water shows the wood, but also sugared almond, cigar smoke/cedar.
**Palate:** Has honeyed sweetness and good weight. The smoke dominates the back palate. Perfumed but dry.
**Finish:** Smoky.

## HIGHLAND PARK 29 YEARS OLD 1978, OLD & RARE 56.7%
Single Malt - Island (non Islay)

**8½ Dave: Old, slightly grumbly but fascinating. Highly recommended.**
*WHISKY Magazine Editor's choice*
**Nose:** The slightly fungal note of maturity – mushroom compost, late autumn leaves, antique shops. Then a beautiful smouldering peaty note. Sweetness too: both oak and a concentrated black fruit, toffee, then nuts. Old but fresh.
**Palate:** Explosive palate. Light smoke, nutty wood, coconut, brambles, shifting to nutmeg and then the peat begins to creep through. Rooty with great length.
**Finish:** Rooty and smoky with a fungal note.

**8½ Martine: Obviously sherried with a perfect integration of malt and wood. Incredibly smooth given the strength. Bring the chocolates, please!**
**Nose:** Aromatic. With an antique fragrance. Old library. Cloved orange, cedar. Then a mouth-watering pastry note. Dundee cake. But the maltiness is not covered.
**Palate:** Satin-like. Splendid display of sherry flavours. Dates, candied orange, toasted hazelnuts, sultanas. Suple oakiness.
**Finish:** Dry, lingering. Raisins, oak.

## HIGHLAND PARK 30 YEARS OLD, MACPHAIL'S COLLECTION 43%
Single Malt - Island (non Islay)

**9** **Michael: More robust and less sophisticated than the distillery bottlings.**
**Nose:** Malty, heathery, oaky.
**Palate:** Malty. Brown sugar. Ginger. Oak. Body is smooth and creamy.
**Finish:** Crisp treacle toffee.

**8** **Dave: An old bugger, but the character still shines through the sherry.**
**Nose:** "Sherried" notes: date, dried fruits, walnut/chestnut, heading to rancio. There's a rich, generous spirit as well: burnt orange, rooty, honey.
**Palate:** Smoke under the rounded nutty dried figgy notes. Honey and soft malt.
**Finish:** Slightly tannic.

## HIGHLAND PARK 36 YEARS OLD, CASK 10252, THE WHISKY EXCHANGE 49.7%
Single Malt - Island (non Islay)

**8¾** **Michael: Enough tannic bite to suggest considerable age, but a remarkably youthful freshness.**
**Nose:** Restrained sootiness. Good oak extract.
**Palate:** Spun sugar. Vanilla. Raspberry and apple pie.
**Finish:** Crisp, refreshing.

**7½** **Dave: The oak has enveloped what was there before.**
**Nose:** Oak essence. Lightly perfumed with some boot oil, mint, varnish, waxed twine. Hint of tablet, smoke, a maritime breeze but seems faded.
**Palate:** Very intense, very oily. Some soft fruit in the peaty ashes. Fragile.
**Finish:** Heather root and ash.

## HIGHLAND PARK 8 YEARS OLD, MACPHAIL'S COLLECTION 40%
Single Malt - Island (non Islay)

**8½** **Michael: Only 8 Years Old, but a seasoned sea-salt. A return to form for the independent youngster.**
**Nose:** Strong sea aromas.
**Palate:** Salt. Ground white pepper sandy. Waterlogged driftwood. Sulphury notes.
**Finish:** Stinging.

**8¼** **Dave: All you expect from this always classy performer.**
**Nose:** Furniture polish. Waxy and quite perfumed. Kumquat, honey, malt, bracken, tea and honey.
**Palate:** Soft, gentle and creamy. Light smoke. Floral with apricot jam and light fruit. Soft-centred sweetness.
**Finish:** Tickle of smoke. Fresh.

## HIGHLAND PARK SINGLE CASK BOTTLE FOR PARK AVENUE LIQUORS 1980 58%
Single Malt - Island (non Islay)

**8½** **Michael: Very satisfying flavours.**
**Nose:** Sherry. Christmas cake. Some of the dried fruit has burned in the oven.
**Palate:** Malty. Buttery. A slice of Wensleydale cheese. On top of the cake.
**Finish:** Slightly woody bitterness. Late saltiness.

**8** **Dave: Seems like a very old whisky with strange exotic flavours.**
**Nose:** Late autumn. Dry oak, firm and quite earthy with rooty/smouldering peat calf. Tweed. Has good depth and a slightly obscured sweetness. Seems old.
**Palate:** A peaty start, then the smoke lifts and allows some honey and fudge in along with old dried peels. Becomes progressively oaky.
**Finish:** A bit tannic.

## ILEACH SINGLE MALT 40%
Single Malt - Islay

**7½** **Michael: Like Finlaggan, this must come from one of the Islay distilleries. It seems bigger, more rounded, but less assertive, than Finlaggan.**
**Nose:** Fino sherry? Saltiness. Grassy peatiness.
**Palate:** Silky, malty. Herbal fruitiness and bitterness, and some pepper.

**Finish:** Grassy and peaty again. Oily. Very late seaweedy medicinal touch.

**7½** **Jim: This is fun stuff, a rare chance to taste a high-quality peaty malt at a relatively young age.**
**Nose:** Like Tobermory, another dram offering pre-pubescent peatiness; green and raw.
**Palate:** The type of peaty malt usually seen only in blends. The intensity is overwhelming, with only limited oak to offer complexity. Big malt.
**Finish:** Peaty. Hasn't extracted sweetness from the oak so gristy greenness is unchecked.

## IMPERIAL 1976, BERRY'S OWN SELECTION 46%
Single Malt - Speyside

**7¾** **Martine: A classic malty malt. Good balance, interesting dry spiciness. Well structured, hexagonal like Bach music. For those who don't like the unexpected. I don't mean boring though.**
**Nose:** Malty. Cereals. Dry hay. Vanilla creeps in. Belgian waffle. Roasted pinenuts. Lemon pie.
**Palate:** Sweet and syrupy. Malt extract, honey. Building up into a spicy bouquet.
**Finish:** Dry, spicy. A slight astringency.

**6¾** **Dave: A real shame. Imperial's rather fine spirit has always been bedevilled by poor casks.**
**Nose:** Fermenting grass/compost. A thick sweetness, violet and some sulphur. Becomes slightly grubby.
**Palate:** Strangely flat and that mustiness comes through. There's a light fragrant floral quality trying to break free.
**Finish:** Musty.

## IMPERIAL 1990 CALVADOS FINISH, PRIVATE COLLECTION 40%
Single Malt - Speyside

**7¾** **Michael: As with the Caol Ila wood finishes, the calvados is a powerful influence but the whisky does fight back- makes for an interesting combination.**
**Nose:** Fresh apple aroma. Grass. Touch of peat.
**Palate:** Firm. Fresh, fruity, apple, combining well with the vanilla, cereal character of the whisky.
**Finish:** Fruity. Dry. Lively, Some length.

**5** **Jim: Remind me never to put Imperial into a calvados cask.**
**Nose:** Thin, tinny, cabbage water: awfully off-beam and unattractive.
**Palate:** Sweet and shapeless, quite sugary.
**Finish:** Bitter and unwieldy.

## IMPERIAL 1990 CLARET FINISH, PRIVATE COLLECTION 40%
Single Malt - Speyside

**7½** **Michael: The wine seems to have made common cause with the juicy sweetness, and the two have overwhelmed the cereal-grain and peat smoke that usually make this a more robust malt. This version would be a good dessert though.**
**Nose:** Very sweet. Citrus. Passion fruit. Winey.
**Palate:** Butterscotch. Peaches. Brambles.
**Finish:** Still fruity and sweetish, with some balancing spicy dryness.

**8½** **Jim: A superb offering. Just wish G and M would be braver and go with a 43 or 46 rather than the standard 40.**
**Nose:** Quite heady; bittersweet Turkish delight. Firm with clean oak. Exceptional.
**Palate:** Maintains the bittersweet style suggested by the nose with chewy maltiness replaced by lazy spice.
**Finish:** A rare dryness that fits in with the deft oak. The spice continues to buzz.

## IMPERIAL 1990 COGNAC FINISH, PRIVATE COLLECTION 40%
Single Malt - Speyside

**7¼** **Michael: Cognac finishes seem to have achieved results that are, at best, mixed. In this instance, the contribution is less than obvious.**
**Nose:** Raisins and lemon peel. Possibly a hint of lime.
**Palate:** Creamy, nutty. Vanilla pod.
**Finish:** A faint suggestion of violets, then a crisp farewell. Perhaps both hint at the influence of cognac?

**9** **Jim: Don't bother looking for cognac – you won't find it, just a delightful imperial.**

**Nose:** Malty and elegant. Rather simple and one-dimensional, but delightfully so.
**Palate:** Beautifully complex from the very start with delightful interplay between varying layers of malt and oak. Quite oaty and mealy.
**Finish:** Remains charmingly bittersweet with very soft vanilla.

## IMPERIAL 1990 SHERRY FINISH, PRIVATE COLLECTION 40%
Single Malt - Speyside

7¼ **Michael: The flavours hang together better in this version, and I favour it over the port finish but by too narrow a margin to score.**
**Nose:** More distillery character in that touch of smokiness. Slightly vegetal.
**Palate:** Creamier. Apricot. Seville orange peels. Orange-and-ginger marmalade. Very expressive.
**Finish:** Spicy. Dusty. Like powdered nutmeg or cinnamon.

6¾ **Dave: Drier and nuttier than the port but again the finish is in charge.**
**Nose:** Full sherry notes: roasted almond/dry amontillado. Rich and generous with fruity malt behind smoky wood.
**Palate:** Nutty, raisined, sultana flavours dominate. Sweet and chewy yet nutty.
**Finish:** The sherry softens slightly.

## IMPERIAL 1991 PORT WOOD FINISH, PRIVATE COLLECTION 43%
Single Malt - Speyside

7¾ **Michael: More Imperial than Port. With or without Port, I would like to see more Imperial.**
**Nose:** Sweet smokiness. A breakfast malt, with sweetcure bacon?
**Palate:** Seems empty at first. Flavours take a very long time to emerge. Creamy malt; long, lingering sweetness. Late, very restrained oak.
**Finish:** Restrained spiciness. Lingering warmth.

7 **Dave: Decent, but only for those with a sweet tooth.**
**Nose:** Sweet (hey, there's a theme here) and even sweeter with water. Butterscotch, stewed rhubarb, macaroon bar/coconut and a light crisp nuttiness.
**Palate:** Rounded. Toffee and malt, macadamia nuts playing against concentrated red fruits.
**Finish:** Sweet and soft.

## IMPERIAL 25 YEARS OLD, SIGNATORY SILENT STILLS 59.2%
Single Malt - Speyside

7¼ **Michael: A little less eccentric, and more rounded than other bottlings I have tried recently.**
**Nose:** Fruity, sherbety. Strawberries.
**Palate:** Oily. Waxy. Fruity. Fresh limes.
**Finish:** Dry. Leafy. Peppery.

7¼ **Dave: Not as generous as some Imperials, but has some style.**
**Nose:** To start with there's roasted malt, a hint of draff, then there's fruit, vanilla, and, as water is added, smoke and then oak. An intriguing combination.
**Palate:** Concentrated and packed with dried fruit, baked apple. Sweet with turfy smoke.
**Finish:** Long, slightly smoky.

## IMPERIAL, NC2 46%
Single Malt - Speyside

7¼ **Dave: An aperitif dram.**
**Nose:** Lightly herbal with a sweet and silky undertow. In the estery world: fresh pineapple green grape, Vibrant.
**Palate:** Very sweet. White fruits, pear and stewed apple, ginger beer/old-fashioned lemonade. Sweet centre. Heats up a little to the end. Easily drowned.
**Finish:** Creamy, but quick.

8¼ **Arthur: Stood up well in a tasting with lots of old whisky. Another of the un-sung distilleries that made an engaging spirit.**
**Nose:** Waxy appleskins, mango lassi and pineapple cubes. Watermelon sweets. Hot summer fields, and sun-baked wood.
**Palate:** Toffeeish, fruity and oaky. That watermelon seemed to come back.
**Finish:** Dry grassiness.

## INCHGOWER 14 YEARS OLD 43%
Single Malt - Speyside

7¾ **Martine: A bit restrained initially, then unveils a charming vibrant sweetness. Well-balanced.**
**Nose:** Light and shy to start with. A bit sharp. Lemon zest. Then moves to sweet, delicate fruit. Lemon meringue pie. A whiff of sea-breeze.
**Palate:** Grassy, dessert-like with a contrasting note of pleasant sourness. Chewy. Spices burst out quite energetically. Ginger.
**Finish:** Long-lasting. Spicy dryness.

7¼ **Dave: The freshest malt you could wish for. Perfume and appetising.**
**Nose:** Light and very fresh, almost a sea breeze nose. With water, a delicious perfume: cut grass, daffodil, green apple. Delicate with a whisper (Wispa?) of chocolate.
**Palate:** Delicate with jasmine, tangerine and a lightly liquorous texture. Slightly acidic.
**Finish:** Tart and clean. A little short.

## INCHGOWER 1974, BERRY'S OWN SELECTION 46%
Single Malt - Speyside

WHISKY
Magazine
℞recommended

7¾ **Dave: A great wee aperitif. Fresh and fun.**
**Nose:** Light, fresh and very clean start, with delicate cereal notes and some wax crayons. Then it suddenly becomes sweet. Very pretty and lifted. Baked apple and lemon meringue pie.
**Palate:** Macaroon bars and dessicated coconut. The high alcohol obscures things, but things improve enormously with a drop of water. Delicious, light and zesty.
**Finish:** Short and clean.

8½ **Arthur: A ray of sunshine.**
**Nose:** Estery with very ripe pineapples, sweet sawdust and banana yoghurt. Rum-like sweetness with plenty of vanilla from bourbon casks and fresh orange.
**Palate:** Rum-enflamed bananas, demerara sugar raisins and pears.
**Finish:** Oak and perhaps a little spiciness.

## INCHGOWER 1980, BERRY'S OWN SELECTION 46%
Single Malt - Speyside

WHISKY
Magazine
℞recommended

7¾ **Dave: A big powerful bruiser.**
**Nose:** Deeply sherried. Like being plunged into a deep, dank, autumn wood. Liquorice and cold Darjeeling tea coupled with wet wool/leather. More sulphur with water. Funky and mature.
**Palate:** Rich and not as tannic as the nose suggests. Nutty, rich and mellow. Good depth.
**Finish:** Treacle toffee.

8½ **Arthur: Cracking whisky led by an intense relationship with its sherry cask.**
**Nose:** Fruit cake mix with cherries, ginger, prune syrup, tangerine and treacle toffee. Coffee and demerara sugar.
**Palate:** Gingerbread, smoked venison, prunes in Armagnac. Nice, broad mouth-coating texture on the tongue.
**Finish:** Traces of burnt, pork crackling.

## INCHGOWER 1980, BERRY'S OWN SELECTION 46%
Single Malt - Speyside

7¾ **Dave: Just lacks a little length. Not as pure as the 74, but I like its weirdness.**
**Nose:** Plenty of stone fruit and vanilla. A Viognier like fleshy peachiness as well as a certain oiliness, but it's peaches from a parallel universe. Fruit, Jim, but not quite as we know it. Mature, with a flor-like nuttiness. Yeasty. It's all intriguingly odd.
**Palate:** Great age on show here, manages to balance the oak with a toffee-ed depth.
**Finish:** Nut shell.

7¼ **Arthur: Choose the 1974 over this one, although if you are a fan of sherry cask led malt this may be your thing.**
**Nose:** Both jammy and meaty, think of venison and redcurrant jelly. Water turned it a bit grubby, but this note settled to become like an earthy, forest floor. Some sweet, wine-like fruitness is there too.
**Palate:** Sweet and jammy, then drying.
**Finish:** Tannic, with a dry and husky, aftertaste like you get when you chew peated barley.

### INCHGOWER 1980, SHERRY CASK, COOPER'S CHOICE 46%
Single Malt - Speyside

**8¼ Michael:** Mature. Complex. A little woody for sure, but plenty of pleasant things going on elsewhere in this contemplative dram.
**Nose:** Instant complexity. Ginger cake, ripe fruit, dessert wine. Dried figs. Honey? Later, some acetone. A faint, savoury undertone. Smoke?
**Palate:** Rich, creamy. Dried fruits. Woody. Yorkshire Parkin. Treacle pudding.
**Finish:** Rich and dark. Burnt treacle tart, liquorice.

**7¼ Arthur:** I enjoyed it, but I am sensitive to that sulphur/ meaty character of certain sherry casks. That finish is a hindrance to the drink, not a help.
**Nose:** Cola bottles, plum pudding and autumn leaves. Maraschino cherries, venison with a berry sauce. More dried floral character with water.
**Palate:** More of that cola bottle note, with dark fruits too and some sulphur.
**Finish:** More sulphur: roast beef and peanuts.

### INCHMURRIN 10 YEARS OLD 40%
Single Malt - Highland

**7 Michael:** Very scenty and sweet. A restorative. Perhaps after a bath or swim?
**Nose:** Tropical fruit. Water melons. Orange flower water.
**Palate:** Pleasantly oily. Very light-tasting at first, but with some flavour development. Honeydew melon with ginger.
**Finish:** Spicy, warming, long, soothing.

**7½ Jim:** Interesting stuff. Hardly glorious but unlike any other single malt around with an astonishing array of flavours and mood changes.
**Nose:** Typically heady and sweet. Soft ginger and mint make for a complex and attractive nose.
**Palate:** Surprisingly light at first, then fattens with a malty, slightly bitter oiliness.
**Finish:** A better balance of oak and malt as the vanilla punches in.

### INCHMURRIN 1973, RARE OLD 40%
Single Malt - Highland

**7 Michael:** Maturity improves it. Still needs rounding out, but less gauche than the distillery bottling.
**Nose:** Fresh. Fruity. Lemon zest.
**Palate:** Flowery. Perfumy. Gin-like.
**Finish:** Spicy. Hint of clove. Some astringency.

**7¼ Martine:** More refreshing and expressive with water. A fairly pleasant classic malt for an apéritif with oatcakes and smoked salmon.
**Nose:** Intense and sharp. Grassy, becomes waxy. Distant hints of fruit. With water, opens up with cereal notes. A touch of coconut milk.
**Palate:** Starts smooth but quickly turns crisp and dry. With water, pleasant spicy flavours and less dryness.
**Finish:** Firm and very dry.

### INVEREY 12 YEARS OLD 40%
Single Malt - Highland

**7 Michael:** On the bland side. The overall impression is of lightness and sweetness, but a nice touch of balancing dryness in the finish.
**Nose:** Sweet. Pastry. Confectioner's custard. Vanilla slices.
**Palate:** Lightly malty. Cereal grain. Green. Slightly vegetal. Melony. A bit empty.
**Finish:** Candied angelica. Faintly rooty, earthy, dryness. Very slight hint of peat. Dry.

**7¼ Dave:** Light. A breakfast malt.
**Nose:** Fresh, apparently young, light and malty (bran) with some lemon and dry woody notes and a little coconut.
**Palate:** Light bodied. Attractive, mealy. All malt, citrus and flowers.
**Finish:** Floury.

### INVERGORDON 12 YEARS OLD, WHISKIES OF THE WORLD, CADENHEAD'S 65.3%
Single Grain - Scotland

**7 Martine:** The sweetness on the palate can't tame the alcohol harshness. It has not benefited from the casks as its pale colour confirms.
**Nose:** Spirity, restrained. Herbal and lemony notes. Very tangy. In time, a nutty touch. Fresh crushed almonds.
**Palate:** Far sweeter than expected. Unexpected earthy notes. Crystallised parma violets. Harsh fizziness. A demerara sweet flavour at mid-palate.
**Finish:** Dry, tangy.

**6¼ Dave:** Has bags of intensity, but lacks quality, balance and integration.
**Nose:** Dry, with a metallic edge: hot tin cans, balloons, play-doh. Water doesn't improve things. Dry and spiritous.
**Palate:** Hot! There's also a strange vegetal note (cabbage/garden compost) and then sugar puffs. It's better than the nose, but the fermenting grass is a touch off-putting.
**Finish:** Light.

### INVERGORDON 13 YEARS OLD, CADENHEAD'S 67.8%
Single Grain - Scotland

**7¼ Michael:** Paler than the Royal Mile version, and drier, too.
**Nose:** Hint of fresh limes.
**Palate:** Perfumy sweetness. This characteristic is quite emphatic, and lingers for quite some time. Complex fruity flavours. Passion fruit.
**Finish:** Fresh lime juice. Citrus peels. Hit of alcohol. Dry, long.

**7¼ Dave:** A sound mix of power and weight with lifted top notes.
**Nose:** Very creamy (American cream soda) with some perfumed notes. A lean edge gives it some interest.
**Palate:** Excellent presence in the mouth. Slightly oily with citrus sweetness and grainy juiciness, yet firm.
**Finish:** Just a touch metallic.

### INVERGORDON 1964, ADELPHI 47.1%
Single Grain - Scotland

**8 Martine:** A rich grain whisky on the fruity side. Interesting.
**Nose:** Fruity sourness. Cider apple. Ripe apricot. Vanilla cream biscuits. Fresh saw. Sappy. Beeswax. A floral touch. Gillyflower.
**Palate:** Round and mellow. Oak frames the fruity flavours. Light spices. Enticing.
**Finish:** Medium, sweet with a fresh bitter edge. Nutty.

**7¾ Dave:** Best on its own or one cube of ice.
**Nose:** Appealing, complex and broad becoming honeyed with fudge/tablet, cream and BIG vanilla toffee notes. Herbal as well, with some fresh pineapple and pear. Water firms the oak up.
**Palate:** Very smooth and rounded but given balancing grip from the oak. Fudge, tangerine, zest. Touch of firm grain on the sides. It then drifts into smooth toffee once more.
**Finish:** Lush long and ripe. Macaroon bars.

### INVERGORDON 1964, DEWAR RATTRAY 51.3%
Single Grain - Scotland

**7¾ Arthur:** A pretty bundle of US oak, slathered in silky creaminess. Impossible not to like.
**Nose:** Vanilla, fudge, face cream, dry twigs, and some floral character. Slightly hot.
**Palate:** Vanilla, lavender, milk chews and kindling wood.
**Finish:** Vanilla ice cream and a light, fragrant grassiness.

**7¾ Dave:** Ridiculously over the top. Great!
**Nose:** Sweet luscious and fat. High coconut factor, sun-tan lotion (high UV factor), butterscotch, golden syrup on a hot crumpet. Water brings out a light spiciness. Rum-like.
**Palate:** Very smooth and unctuous. Coconut ice cream, black banana. Becomes drier with crisp oak giving much needed structure. Good length.
**Finish:** Spice, light leather.

### INVERGORDON 1964, DEWAR RATTRAY 52.1%
Single Grain - Scotland

**8¼ Martine:** Shy at first but cheering up on cake aromas. A liquid pudding.
**Nose:** Restrained. Flowery. Mint cream. Fudge. Opens up on balsamic touch. Cedar.
**Palate:** Very creamy and soft. Crème brûlée. Cherry flan. Stewed apricots with almonds. Very Cognac-like. Oak is present but beautifully integrated, interlaced with fruit.
**Finish:** Good length, spices and fruit nicely proportioned.

**8 Dave:** While it might not have the complexity of the best malts here it's a cracking example of a mature grain.

**Nose:** Another sweetie, this time with barley sugar, apple, fondant icing, tangerine and lemon. Creamy with a tropical fruit edge. Good depth.
**Palate:** A lovely sweet layered effect. Orange peel, banana split. Water brings out coconut cream and a nutty oak along with an explosion of spices.
**Finish:** Full, ripe, long.

### INVERGORDON 1965 38 YEARS OLD, DUNCAN TAYLOR 50.1%
Single Grain - Scotland

**7¾ Michael: Such a long ageing has made the bourbon wood very dominating. The crisp, cleansing, hint of pine in the distillery bottling better suited a single grain.**
**Nose:** Lightly smoky. Tequila-like. Lime. Slightly musty.
**Palate:** Light. Sugary. Icing sugar. Citrus oil.
**Finish:** Key lime pie. Pastry.

**6¾ Marcin: I wasn't surprised to learn this was a single grain whisky.**
**Nose:** Rich and silky. Luxurious nose with a threat of alcohol to come.
**Palate:** Mouth-watering spice but otherwise little of distinction.
**Finish:** Shorter than expected. Finishes on a high but loses flavours along the way.

### INVERGORDON 22 YEARS OLD, ROYAL MILE WHISKIES 45%
Single Grain - Scotland

**7¼ Michael: Appetising. Some length and complexity.**
**Nose:** Scenty, sweetly piney. An exotic dessert from the Eastern Mediterranean.
**Palate:** Creamy-tasting. Long sweetness. Intense.
**Finish:** Piney. Fragrant. Drying slightly.

**6½ Dave: Well-made, just lacks some complexity.**
**Nose:** Gentle yet crisp. Some leather, marzipan and rounded fruits: apple/apple wood, banana. Water makes it slightly harder and woodier.
**Palate:** Crisp, clean and slightly grassy. A bit immature.
**Finish:** Good length with some spiciness.

### INVERGORDON 40 YEARS OLD, DEWAR RATTRAY 48.1%
Single Grain - Scotland

WHISKY *Magazine* Recommended

**8½ Michael: A strange, huge, dark and dense whisky. Try with Pecan pie or scallops seared in burnt butter. Surely a nod to the Ozarks?**
**Nose:** Artist's studio, linseed oil, distilled spirits of turpentine, quiet concentration. Then fruits: strawberries, melon, honey, sandalwood and pine resin against a biscuity background …
**Palate:** Oily. Oaky. Dense linseed notes. Creamy. Vanilla. Black butter sauce? Marshmallow?
**Finish:** Oily, burnt, minty, drying.

**7½ Dave: This isn't a bourbon? Shows how much oak has had its say. Throw some ice in and sip.**
**Nose:** Bourbon-like. Intensely spicy, bitter cherry, sap caramelised/waxy notes. This is all about oak. With water, rock candy and sticky Murray Mints.
**Palate:** Very sweet and direct. A sweet distillate with masses of oak around it. Tightens on the finish. Zesty and tingling then melting chocolate.
**Finish:** Dry and slightly acidic.

### INVERGORDON 40 YEARS OLD, DUNCAN TAYLOR 49%
Single Grain - Scotland

**7¾ Dave: Want to get bourbon drinkers into whisky, give 'em grain! Maybe not 40 Years Old grain but it could be the way in.**
**Nose:** Initially this is all fennel tops, then it deepens and sweetens: vanilla, maple syrup, spun sugar. Bourbon?
**Palate:** Immediate impact of spice: nutmeg, allspice and toasty grip. Good with water. Mature, woody, smooth.
**Finish:** Firms up nicely.

**8 Martine: Another classic sherry, especially on the palate. No water please.**
**Nose:** Pleasant tanginess. Fresh crushed white grapes (Italia). Cider cellar. Then freshly baked fruit cake. Hint of praline.
**Palate:** More sherried than on the nose. Rubbery. A smoky note (like a dying fire). Coffee toffee.
**Finish:** Long, liquoriced. Spicy dryness.

### INVERGORDON 40 YEARS OLD, DUNCAN TAYLOR 50.3%
Single Grain - Scotland

WHISKY *Magazine* Recommended

**7¾ Martine: An interesting profile. Well matured. The butyric note on the nose does not echo on the palate.**
**Nose:** Soft, creamy. Peaches in syrup. Lemon sherbet. A slight butyric touch.
**Palate:** Smooth, supple feel. Oak and fruit are elegantly combined. Liquorice.
**Finish:** Firm, flowing nicely. Liquoriced.

**8¼ Dave: Very smooth, but lacking definition due to the length of time in a very active cask.**
**Nose:** Lots of luscious wood on show here. Cocoa butter, hazelnut, nutmeg, tablet. Behind the sweetness is raspberry and toasted marshmallow.
**Palate:** Similar to the nose. Water gives it a smooth creaminess. Big, generous and broad with rich silky tropical fruitiness.
**Finish:** Long. Silky.

### INVERLEVEN 1985, GORDON & MACPHAIL 40%
Single Malt - Lowland

**7½ Michael: Not much complexity, but an unusually summery whisky.**
**Nose:** Freshly cut ripe, sweet, pears. Scented.
**Palate:** Tastes of cream, nectarines, melons and pears. Soft, stalky and woody.
**Finish:** Refreshing.

**7½ Jim: Beyond the stark, disappointing nose, this is a genuinely fine dram. The star turn is the balance.**
**Nose:** Spirity and ethereally light. More malty and sweet when reduced.
**Palate:** A hot dram at first, but offers immediately a faultlessly clean maltiness.
**Finish:** More of the same. The final notes show a lush richness usually associated with small stills and lots of copper.

### INVERLEVEN 1986, GORDON & MACPHAIL 40%
Single Malt - Lowland

**8½ Martine: Light, straightforward. Delicacy without mannerism. Keep it for a romantic candlelit dinner.**
**Nose:** Scented garden aromas: wild rose, thyme, lemon grass. Muscat grape and orange peel.
**Palate:** Bracing mouthfeel yet almost syrupy. Redcurrant. A lovely blancmange aftertaste.
**Finish:** Slightly spicy (nutmeg), even warmer with water.

**5¼ Dave: Like drinking a ghost.**
**Nose:** Very pale suggesting a neutral cask. Light floral/apple blossom notes and some white fruit. Delicate to the point of ethereal. Water kills it stone dead, just the aroma of dead leaves.
**Palate:** More to it than the nose suggests but that's not saying a lot. Lightly floral, but no complexity, no drive.
**Finish:** What finish?

### INVERLEVEN 1990, 40 YEARS OLD, GORDON & MACPHAIL
Single Malt - Lowland

**7¼ Martine: The nose is appealing but the palate far tougher. Water eases the release of grassy notes. But the aromatic profile keeps shallow.**
**Nose:** Very herbal. Angelica, lemon grass. Like a chartreuse. Quite pleasant.
**Palate:** Smooth at start then getting assertively oaky and bitter. The herbal notes keep on.
**Finish:** Quite short, slightly biscuity.

**7½ Michael: Funky nose is compromised by a relatively straightforward palate. Still enjoyable enough, though.**
**Nose:** Lemonade/Lucozade. Spritzy-sweetsharp. Pink bubblegum. All this, yet well formed and not overpowering. (Japanese levels of complexity!)
**Palate:** Simple and somewhat winey at first. Then chocolate. A little nutty?
**Finish:** Oily perhaps and a little toasty.

## INVERLEVEN 26 YEARS OLD, CASK 1873, DUNCAN TAYLOR 50.1%
Single Malt - Lowland

**7¾** **Martine: An interesting character. Much sweeter on the palate than expected from the nose. Water brings out an unpleasant cardboardy touch.**
**Nose:** Light, open. Outdoor fragrances: wet earth; a touch of moss and fern. Thyme, rosemary.
**Palate:** Velvety. Round and soft. Incredibly sweet given the strength. Greengage. Cooked peaches. Cherry stone. A subtle spicy rise.
**Finish:** Dry, spicy. Fresh almonds.

**8¾** **Michael: Opens up beautifully with water, developing sweet, vermouth-like herbal notes. Holds one's attention.**
**Nose:** Floral notes underpinned by icing sugar sweetness. Some balancing fruit acidity. Lemony with water.
**Palate:** Creamy at first, develops Crunchy bar, caramel notes. Herbal character with water.
**Finish:** Medium. Apple skins. Pithy dryness emerges. Develops slowly to a complex finish.

## ISLAY 1991, SMOKED SAUSAGES 46%
Single Malt - Islay

**6¾** **Dave: It's young and seems to have been too heavily reduced.**
**Nose:** High phenols. Intense. Seaweed mixed with lime, bog myrtle, wet fish. Seems young and slightly plain. Rubber emerges with water.
**Palate:** Very light. Alcohol, smoke and pork fat. Killed by water. That rubbery note returns suggesting youth (or immaturity).
**Finish:** Dilute and thin.

**7¾** **Martine: The smoke gives its full expression on the palate, overwhelming the fruit. An early morning dram. Possibly to be tried on your porridge!**
**Nose:** Grassy with a lingering distant smoke. Like a burnt off bonfire. Apple skin with a hint of yeast, reminding of a fermenting cider.
**Palate:** Smoke is far more distinctive. Sweet shellfish. A hint of roasted coffee beans.
**Finish:** Dry, smoky, slightly sooty.

## ISLAY MIST 12 YEARS OLD 40%
Blended - Scotland

**7** **Dave: Needs water to open the nose, but the palate is rather simple.**
**Nose:** Bready with a tickle of smoke. With water a herbal note (rosemary). With water more tarry notes appear. A little plain.
**Palate:** Clean, malty but surprisingly light. The smoke is a mere wisp in the background. Little hollow in the centre.
**Finish:** Dies a quick and painless death.

**8** **Martine: An interesting dram. Perfumy, dense on the palate though so sweet at first.**
**Nose:** Outdoor fragrances. Garrigue herbs (thyme, savory). Earthy with a floral touch (wet forest ground after a summer shower). A hint of curry. A distant far note.
**Palate:** Sweet, round, syrupy. Toffee, liquorice. A peated note. Oak is well integrated.
**Finish:** Dancing on tastebuds. Spicy. Thyme comes back.

## ISLAY MIST 17 YEARS OLD 40%
Blended - Scotland

**8¼** **Dave: Cutting this to 40% means it's lost some of its energy. Let's have a cask strength version!**
**Nose:** Peaty. Smouldering fish boxes, fish heads, heather, ink, meat. Mature and complex. Mixing the harbour and the beach. Good weight.
**Palate:** A lovely balance struck between dried soft fruits, damson like sweetness and the heathery smoke.
**Finish:** Long. slightly leathery.

**7¾** **Martine: A pleasant autumnal dram. Good balance, a bit tottering on the palate. But that can be forgiven.**
**Nose:** Rich, oaky. Chestnut, warm melted chocolate, ripe dates. Cedar. Tobacco leaf. Hint of mushroom.
**Palate:** Round, smooth. Slightly watery at midpalate but regaining life. Oak prevails in a gentle way. Dried fruit and stewed apples.
**Finish:** Medium, smooth. Liquorice.

## ISLAY MIST 17 YEARS OLD, PREMIUM 40%
Blended - Scotland

**8¼** **Michael: The Islay aromas and flavours seemed to have almost vanished among the heathery mainland notes in the blending. They were just hiding. I came back to the glass three or four hours later and they had emerged.**
**Nose:** Light "edible seaweed" salty sweetness.
**Palate:** Earthy, ground almonds. Nutty, syrupy, smooth. Some sherry.
**Finish:** Late salt. Some pepper.

**7½** **Dave: Not the full-on blast of peat reek you may expect, but a good, pretty dry dram.**
**Nose:** An intriguing smoky nose mixing hickory, citrus peel. The water brings out notes of charred wood on a beach bonfire, a blast of ozone with dried heather.
**Palate:** Gentle to start and quite dry. In fact it's pretty dry, nutty/spicy and rooty all the way with the occasional glimpse of soft fruit.
**Finish:** Light smoke.

## ISLAY MIST BLENDED SCOTCH WHISKY 40%
Blended - Scotland

**8½** **Michael: A distinctively Laphroaig-led blend, even though that distillery and this blend are now owned by separate companies.**
**Nose:** Big, seaweedy, medicinal, slightly sharp tang.
**Palate:** Firm, malty, grassy, with sweetness, spiciness and oily, olivey, bitterness.
**Finish:** A return to seaweed. Very appetising.

**9** **Jim: Classic blended whisky which lets the grain maximise the complexity of peated Islay malts.**
**Nose:** A subtle and seductive mixture of peat and seaweed. Mellow grain thins this out backed by a salty background and compelling sweet malt.
**Palate:** The peat is dominant but checked by a complex fusion of sweet malt, salt and oak.
**Finish:** The soft peats cling to the roof of the mouth as toffee and coffee ensure a bitter-sweet finish.

## ARRAN 1996 RAW CASK, BLACKADDER 56.8%
Single Malt - Island (non Islay)

**7¼** **Michael: Slightly gin-like. I have preferred bottlings that had more contribution from the wood. A touch of vanilla would round out the flavours.**
**Nose:** Some peat. Grassy.
**Palate:** Sweet and slightly rooty. Candied angelica. Starts smooth and sweet, then develops a curiously fibrous dryness.
**Finish:** Liquorice. Pepper.

**7** **Dave: Young but attractive. A distillery to watch.**
**Nose:** Crisp, malty and nutty with a light earthy note.
**Palate:** Sweet to start, but the wood stands slightly apart from the spirit. Young but has a delicate charm.
**Finish:** Lemon, then butter.

## ISLE OF ARRAN 10 YEARS OLD 46%
Single Malt - Island (non Islay)

**7½** **Dave: Have this before lunch and maybe chilled down.**
**Nose:** Drying grass, lawnmower box with light cereal and a sherbert like citric lift. Hints of green walnut and tangerine. Pretty...but young.
**Palate:** Real malty sweetness with soft fruits in the centre and balancing oak.
**Finish:** A little short. Seems young, but has decent balance. Good.

**8** **Arthur: A satisfying everyday malt. I can't think of a time when you wouldn't want one of these. Populist.**
**Nose:** Pear, lemon, crab apples and a raspberry coulis.
**Palate:** A little hot without water, but settles into a light plum sauce, dark chocolate and apples. Mouthfilling, complete and satisfying.
**Finish:** A short, tingling nutmeg.

## ISLE OF ARRAN 4 YEARS OLD 43%
Single Malt - Island (non Islay)

**7½** **Michael: A lovely whisky for one so young. What will it be like at two or three times this age?**
**Nose:** Creamy, flowery. Very faint fresh peat-smoke.
**Palate:** Clean and dryish and nutty at first. Then creamy and toffeeish, with hints of banana.
**Finish:** Surprisingly powerful sweet lime flavour. Flowery. Developing light dryness.

**7½ Jim:** Quite exceptional for its age and pretty complex too. But loses marks for the poor nose.
**Nose:** A trace of sulphur makes for a discordant opening, but there is a big malt character, clean and sweet, which makes amends.
**Palate:** Again, immediately malt-sweet and intense with soft, chewy cream toffee depth. A little grapey fruitiness also in evidence.
**Finish:** Very long; malty with delicate spice. Excellent sweet/dry balance.

## ISLE OF ARRAN 8 YEARS OLD, PROVENANCE 46%
Single Malt - Island (non Islay)

**8½ Gavin:** A delicate but satisfyingly complex dram. Arran has been getting better and better, perhaps this will be the optimum age.
**Nose:** Slightly feinty, cereal notes. 'Midget Gems'.
**Palate:** Quite sweet, with just a hint of oiliness. Weetabix. Perfume – lavender water? Develops, and peaches when reduced.
**Finish:** Satisfyingly long – the breakfast cereal lingers.

**6¾ Dave:** The spirit is still coming together. Would have been best kept in the cask for a few more years.
**Nose:** Light, intense. Quite tight and grassy with green grape. Still some new make character.
**Palate:** Light and clean with crisp sweet cereal (Frosties). Middleweight but slightly unformed.
**Finish:** Short.

## ISLE OF ARRAN 8 YEARS OLD, UNCHILLFILTERED, PROVENANCE 46%
Single Malt - Island (non Islay)

**8 Michael:** Uncomplicated but delicious.
**Nose:** Apricot jam being boiled.
**Palate:** Very full creamy, fruity flavours. Bananas. Sweet limes. Very sweet, without being cloying.
**Finish:** Bittersweet marmalade. Very spicy.

**7¾ Dave:** The rich oak and gentle distillery character in balance. The right time to bottle.
**Nose:** Uncomplicated but delicious.
**Palate:** Gentle and youthful. Cooked fruit, fungal, orange. Good intensity and feel.
**Finish:** Dried fruits. Raspberry.

## ISLE OF ARRAN BORDEAUX FINISH 59.6%
Single Malt - Island (non Islay)

**7¾ Michael:** Oddly distinctive. Curiously sweet and savoury.
**Nose:** Forest floor. Piney, resiny, tar-like.
**Palate:** Sweetish, hesitant, then really late surge of cooked fruit. Peach cobbler.
**Finish:** Slightly clovey. Peppery. Long.

**6¾ Dave:** Another finish. Why precisely?
**Nose:** Pale pink. Rhubarb and cream. Light berry fruit accents with dry notes. Dilute redcurrant juice, blackberry leaf, young spirit behind.
**Palate:** Sweetness sitting on top of dry cereal/dry grass spirit. Not knitted or balanced.
**Finish:** Fruit pastilles.

## ISLE OF ARRAN CALVADOS FINISH 62.1%
Single Malt - Island (non Islay)

**8 Michael:** Was the Calvados cask notably generous, or is Scotch whisky particularly receptive to the Norman spirit?
**Nose:** The clean, sweet, Arran whisky and a kiss of Calvados promise a romantic encounter.
**Palate:** Exciting interplay: creamy whisky, cinder toffee, Belgian wafers, chocolate, crisp Calvados.
**Finish:** Surprisingly hot, but this bottling is high in alcohol. Needs a little ministering from the angels.

**7¾ Dave:** Balanced. Arran is becoming pretty impressive.
**Nose:** Intense and spicy: cinnamon, green grass apple pie. With water reminiscent of a Martinique rum: vegetal, green banana, toasted oak.
**Palate:** Appley and intense. Fairly sweet and spicy. The grassy apple note continues.
**Finish:** Nutty.

## ISLE OF ARRAN FIRST 1995, LIMITED EDITION 46%
Single Malt - Island (non Islay)

**8 Michael:** The early releases were promising, and this one has matured well.
**Nose:** Warm. Sweet scenty. A hint of salt.
**Palate:** Clean. Toffee. Creamy. Bananas.
**Finish:** Cedary. Long, soothing.

**8¼ Dave:** Arran's coming of age – and it's doing so impressively.
**Nose:** Malty, concentrated and very toasty. Cheesecake base. Camomile flowers. Overripe apricot, with water peach syrup.
**Palate:** Medium bodied with a smooth texture. Sweet with flavours of cooked pear and light toffee notes.
**Finish:** Creamy and balanced.

## ISLE OF ARRAN MARSALA FINISH 56.9%
Single Malt - Island (non Islay)

**8½ Martine:** Not much connection between nose and palate. But the surprise is pleasant. A beautiful wake-up malt on rainy days.
**Nose:** Floral and fruity. Delicate touch of orange blossom. Overripe pear. Distinctive creamy nuttiness. Fresh walnut. Wood notes emerge slowly and softly.
**Palate:** More vibrant than nose announced. Fizzy. Develops on buttery notes. Plum pie.
**Finish:** Tangy, spicy, lingering. Fresh ginger. Peppery.

**7¾ Dave:** A well balanced 'finish'. Marsala suits it well.
**Nose:** Nutty. Burnt toast, llight rasin notes, cooked raspberry, almost jammy. Water releases top notes, tinned fruit salad.
**Palate:** Ripe and thick, dried fruits, raisin, light spices. Soft feel. Oak in balance.
**Finish:** Charred, almost smoky. Mushroom.

## ISLE OF ARRAN NON CHILL FILTERED 46%
Single Malt - Island (non Islay)

**7½ Martine:** More a summery malt than a warmer-up. Pleasant but not captivating. Mid-palate is a bit weak.
**Nose:** Herbal. Green tea. Tangerine sherbet. Biscuity. Red fruit. Hint of wet moss. Fragrant and light.
**Palate:** Sweet maltiness. Leafy. Peppermint. Touch of violet. Not very eloquent.
**Finish:** Short, crisp and dry. Pleasant mintiness followed by a harder bitter note.

**7½ Dave:** Slightly more weight and a little drier than the standard, but less defined.
**Nose:** Slightly citric, green apple, coconut. Good weight, soft summer fruits.
**Palate:** Medium weight. Malt/biscuit with a slightly floury quality. Sweet, limey.
**Finish:** Dry, malty.

## ISLE OF ARRAN PORT CASK 57.5%
Single Malt - Island (non Islay)

**8 Michael:** Sinful. Bonus points for shamelessness.
**Nose:** Spicy crème brûlée, perhaps with some berry fruits.
**Palate:** Brandy snaps. Rich flavours of cream. Cannoli, French style cheesecake.
**Finish:** Gingery balancing dryness. Like a biscuit base made of crushed ginger cookies.

**7¼ Dave:** Initially it's fine, but ends up more port rinse than finish.
**Nose:** Clean with light cereal and fruit notes: redcurrant, dilute raspberry cordial, sloe, mint, malt. In time becomes increasingly wine-like.
**Palate:** Sweet, tongue-coating. Hot and peppery when neat, red fruits and a sweet attack. Balanced.
**Finish:** Red fruits.

### ISLE OF ARRAN RUM CASK 58.5%
Single Malt - Island (non Islay)

7¼ **Michael: Rather cloying.**
**Nose:** Powerful, sweet almonds.
**Palate:** Buttery. Slightly sticky. Sweet, honeyed.
**Finish:** Spicy. Gingery.

8½ **Marcin: Extremely accomplished whisky. Isle of Arran continues to impress.**
**Nose:** Assertive attack of toffee, heather honey and cream giving impression of luxury to follow. More feminine when reduced; creamier and softer.
**Palate:** Vigorous. This whisky is making a statement. Allspice emerges.
**Finish:** Good length. Drying, warming and very moreish.

### ISLE OF ARRAN SINGLE MALT NON CHILL FILTERED 46%
Single Malt - Island (non Islay)

7¾ **Michael: A curious inversion. As though the whisky (rich and sweet, but without penetrating flavours) provides the background, while the sherry and wood are the highlights.**
**Nose:** Sun-scorched grass. Pistachio nuts. Dates.
**Palate:** Flowery. Fruity. Gingery. Sappy.
**Finish:** Powerful. Spicy. Oily. Becoming dry.

7¼ **Dave: Another interesting milestone in the evolution of what is obviously a fine distillery making good quality spirit.**
**Nose:** Fresh, young and lively. Green grapes, sour apple, crisp malt. Attractive but with a slight immaturity.
**Palate:** Softer than the nose suggests but full of the taut firmness of youth.
**Finish:** Clean. Malty.

### ISLE OF ARRAN THE ARRAN MALT 43%
Single Malt - Island (non Islay)

8 **Martine: A subtle yet characterful malt. Sweetness is teased up by dry spices. Beautiful structure. The proof that you can be young and accomplished.**
**Nose:** Delicately scented. Lemony. Semi-dried apricots. Peach in syrup. Hazelnuts. Quite an intricate aromatic build-up. Shortbread developing on creamier notes.
**Palate:** Smooth and sweet. Citrussy. Mandarin. Muesli.
**Finish:** Dry, crisp, spicy, chilli. Almondy notes.

7¾ **Dave: Well made, with good balance.**
**Nose:** Light. Green fruits, elderflower, cereal. Pure and sweet. Water makes it like an old-fashioned lemonade. Blossom-like.
**Palate:** Sweet to start, then a firm maltiness. Lively, light fruits. Effervescent.
**Finish:** Perks up nicely.

### ISLE OF JURA 10 YEARS OLD 40%
Single Malt - Island (non Islay)

7½ **Michael: A lovely aperitif.**
**Nose:** Oily, lightly piney, earthy, salty, dry.
**Palate:** Sweetish, soft, malty, oily, slowly developing a slight island dryness and saltiness.
**Finish:** A little malty sweetness and some saltiness.

7½ **Jim: Still a hit-and-miss dram, though this sample was simple and strictly middle of the road. Very quaffable all the same.**
**Nose:** Enormously fruity at first; a salad of under and overripe banana, raisin and apple. The malty notes are flat and lifeless by comparison, but offer balance.
**Palate:** Much more upfront, fresher malt than on the nose with a light, though chewy, oakiness. A spicy dryness offers some pizazz.
**Finish:** More oak and softer vanilla with a lingering maltiness.

### ISLE OF JURA 16 YEARS OLD 40%
Single Malt - Island (non Islay)

7¾ **Michael: For an islander Jura is often thought to be something of a lightweight, but it has hidden depths.**
**Nose:** Fragrant, piney, a hint of the sea.
**Palate:** Light but firm body. Lightly oily, creamy, malt background.
**Finish:** Delicate sweetness and salt.

8 **Jim: A delicious and sophisticated dram with impressive depth and almost perfect weight.**
**Nose:** A flighty aroma, sea-inspired yet slightly citric.
**Palate:** A backbone of firm oak guarantees a dry start and middle.
**Finish:** Softer and sweeter with waves of vanilla.

### ISLE OF JURA 16 YEARS OLD 40%
Single Malt - Island (non Islay)

7¾ **Michael: More wood-extract, or sherry, than I remember. I prefer a drier expression.**
**Nose:** Freshly chopped pine trees. Ferns. Forest floor.
**Palate:** Dryish. Vegetal. Ground coriander. Fiddlehead ferns. Rhubarb.
**Finish:** Sea tastes: sweetness and saltiness, with the latter overwhelmingly the winner. Long.

7¼ **Dave: Surprisingly young for a 16 year-old.**
**Nose:** Gutsy, citrus and oaky notes. Cracker bread/Ryvita. Water brings out orange and very malty qualities; some hessian. A touch metallic?
**Palate:** Medium sweet. There's good interplay between dry (wood/malt) and sweet fruits. Mid weight.
**Finish:** Mealy.

### ISLE OF JURA 16 YEARS OLD 40%
Single Malt - Island (non Islay)

8¼ **Martine: A very restorative and comforting dram.**
**Nose:** Cedary. Shoe polish. Wood speaks up first but elegantly gives way to fruity notes. Fruit cake. Marmalade. Raisin scones. Cinnamon.
**Palate:** Round and mellow. Mouth-coating. Rich and luscious. Candied chestnut. Resiny. Smooth.
**Finish:** Round, sweet, drying off on wood. Hint of chewed tobacco.

7½ **Dave: Clearly the 10 Years Old is much beefier, but soft-hearted brother.**
**Nose:** Cream, overripe fruits, light citrus, sugared almond, bletted fruits then shifts back to dryness.
**Palate:** Oloroso sweetness to start. Good oxidised notes, nutty. Soft...very soft.
**Finish:** Prune. Length.

### ISLE OF JURA 1988, BLACKADDER 59.4%
Single Malt - Island (non Islay)

6¾ **Martine: Nose better than palate. A tired cask?**
**Nose:** Very light but aromatic. New make fragrances. Herbal, floral. Dry hay. Sweet meadow flowers. Wild garlic. Water brings out briny garnish.
**Palate:** Sweeter than expected. Light-bodied. Sharp and tangy. Malty and herbal flavours. Toasted hazelnuts. Definitely needs water.
**Finish:** Warm, nutty, dry.

7 **Dave: A good, straightforward Jura.**
**Nose:** VERY heathery nose along with macadamia nut, biscuit, dry, hot bracken.
**Palate:** Clean and quite a sweet malty/nutty start. Good feel mid-palate. Very fresh and clean.
**Finish:** Heather. Biscuity.

### ISLE OF JURA 1999, 5 YEARS OLD, THE WHISKY EXCHANGE 63%
Single Malt - Island (non Islay)

WHISKY Magazine Recommended

8½ **Michael: Why wasn't this done years ago? More please. Captivating.**
**Nose:** Leafy bonfires in autumn. Pine logs.
**Palate:** Starts sweet and nutty. Development of oily, soothing, smoky flavours.
**Finish:** Firm, gripping, balsamic. Appetising.

8 **Dave: Jura's manager Michael Heads worked at Laphroaig. A coincidence? More please!**
**Nose:** Straw-like, then immensely smoky; chimney sweep's sack, engine oil. Water calms it down, brings out lentil, sweetness, pine wood and a zestiness.
**Palate:** A fug of smoke. Thankfully there's a sweetness beneath and a bracken-like note to balance.
**Finish:** Smoke and more smoke. Tarry.

### ISLE OF JURA 21 YEARS OLD 40%
Single Malt - Island (non Islay)

8 **Michael: The sherry, and the balance of flavours, seem to work better in this version.**
**Nose:** Piney. Cedary. Oaky.
**Palate:** Nutty. Bittersweet orange marmalade. Sweet lemons.
**Finish:** A surprising, refreshing acidity. Tangy. Salty. Echoes of the sea.

7¾ **Dave: A good sipping dram that's not too demanding but has good weight and a supple body.**
**Nose:** Richly oaky with malt, bung cloth and dried fruits. Water brings the fruits to the fore. Very juicy, like semi-dried pears and apricots.
**Palate:** Soft, managing to be both succulently fruity and slightly wild in nature. Oak, spice and heather.
**Finish:** Slightly oaky.

## ISLE OF JURA 21 YEARS OLD 40%
Single Malt - Island (non Islay)

8 **Martine: The perfect dram to sip on Valentine's night but I am not sure I would spare some for my sweetheart. I wish it had been bottled at a higher strength though.**
**Nose:** Rich and luscious. Treacle. Raisins. Dates. Honey. Old furniture. White pepper. Walnut and coffee.
**Palate:** Voluptuously smooth. Thick, mouth coating. Chestnut purée. A touch of candied orange. Sherry.
**Finish:** Long, oaky, spicy and dry. Walnuts. Nutmeg.

8 **Dave: Jura needs time to open and this is a good example.**
**Nose:** Mature. Seville orange. Varnished oak. Good weight, dried fig, bitter chocolate, dried orange peel. Shows some complexity.
**Palate:** Caramelised sweetness. Demerara, ripe and honeyed. Chestnut, cooked black fruits. Doesn't like water.
**Finish:** Continues to soften into peachiness.

## ISLE OF JURA LEGACY, 10 YEARS OLD 40%
Single Malt - Island (non Islay)

7 **Martine: Not as enticing as the older versions. Lacks depth but it has nothing to do with youth. Water kills it down.**
**Nose:** Sweet. Restrained. Pine nut. Rice pudding and custard. Caramel. With a dash of water, stewed apples.
**Palate:** Sweet, a bit soft and watery in the middle. Toffee and honey.
**Finish:** Short, dry. Nutty.

7½ **Dave: Seems bulkier than I recall.**
**Nose:** Earthy, damp bracken, pine wood, grass. Firm cereal notes. Warm, woollen hiking socks. Ovaltine. Slightly milky. Young, beginning to come together.
**Palate:** Nutty, crunchy, hazelnut. Grass. Unctuous feel. Sweet in the centre.
**Finish:** Crisp. Dry grass.

## ISLE OF JURA SUPERSTITION 45%
Single Malt - Island (non Islay)

8 **Michael: It is good to have a more muscular Jura, but I find this a bit too smooth. I would prefer something less sophisticated and more sexy. Must be the size of those paps.**
**Nose:** Very light peat smoke, but also some sherryish sweetness.
**Palate:** Smooth. Waxy. Piney, honeyish. Developing sweet creaminess. Opens very slowly.
**Finish:** Salty, with a surprising sting.

7¾ **Dave: The smoke gives extra character to the often slightly rigid Jura style. Great price too!**
**Nose:** Heathery with hints of hard Highland toffee, wet bracken, smoke, date, chocolate-covered raisins. Water brings polished oak, nuts and heather blossom.
**Palate:** Soft, with an immediate puff of heathery smoke playing alongside toffee, crisp malt. Good balance and weight.
**Finish:** Lightly smoky.

## ISLE OF JURA SUPERSTITION 45%
Single Malt - Island (non Islay)

7¼ **Martine: The nose is lively but the palate is put to sleep by sweetness.**
**Nose:** Cider. Burnt apple tree. A rustic bouquet. Cow-shed. Distant smokiness. Earthy roots. Freshly baked multi-grain bread. Sultanas. A seashore echo.
**Palate:** Smooth and soft. Too soft. Sweetness thickens mouthfeel and taste. Nutty. Wood is there, not dominating but blurring the flavours.
**Finish:** Slightly spicy, sweet. Liquorice. Lacks elegance.

7¾ **Dave: This seems to have the peatiness more to the fore than in the past.**
**Nose:** Immediate peatiness. Turfy rather than marine. Phenolics, macadamia nut, horchata. Light meaty note. Sweet centre.
**Palate:** Light smoke lying above firm, young grassy, notes. Beech nuts, heather. Silky feel.
**Finish:** Good length. Drifting smoke.

## ISLE OF JURA WHISKY FAIR BOTTLING, CASK 144 61.3%
Single Malt - Island (non Islay)

8¼ **Michael: A lot happening. A very lively whisky.**
**Nose:** Grainy. Flour-like. Pastry fresh out of the oven.
**Palate:** Sweet spiciness. Cinnamon. Savoury and sweet. Meaty. Pine nuts. Moroccan pastilla.
**Finish:** Piney. Balsamic. Peppery.

7¼ **Dave: For serious peat freaks only. Would have been better if kept in cask for a few more years.**
**Nose:** Extremely peaty with cereal/dried grasses/brown bracken behind. Smoked fish/venison and tar. Becomes rubbery with water.
**Palate:** Good delivery with lots of smoke, then gymshoe soles. Young.
**Finish:** Smoke and oatcake.

## ISLE OF SKYE 12 YEARS OLD 40%
Blended - Scotland

8 **Michael: The aromas and flavours evoke breakfast, but in a farmhouse kitchen with an open fire, rused and dashed by the winds down the chimney.**
**Nose:** Fresh smokiness. The smell of burning hay. Earthy.
**Palate:** Sweet and salty. Firm, cereal-grain maltiness. Peanut butter on toast.
**Finish:** Orange and ginger marmalade. Satisfying. Sustaining.

8¼ **Dave: Very well balanced. A lovely blend.**
**Nose:** Ripe, fruity and well balanced. Sherry, dried fruits and a hint of smoke. Water brings out a buttery edge. A lot going on.
**Palate:** Overall, a little drier than the nose suggests but with excellent, soft, mid-palate weight. Light smoke all the way through.
**Finish:** Ripe and soft.

## ISLE OF SKYE 8 YEARS OLD 40%
Blended - Scotland

6¾ **Martine: Nose and palate seem to be flattened by excess of sickly sweetness.**
**Nose:** Grenadine. Biscuity. Shortbread. Becoming slightly nutty. Soft spices. Touch of cumin.
**Palate:** Sweet, too sweet. Syrupy. Barley sugar. Caramel. Coffee flavoured toffee.
**Finish:** Tightened up. Sweet all the way, then leaves a warm feel back in the throat. Rhubarb jam.

7 **Dave: Though it flows well and has balance it just lacks complexity and energy.**
**Nose:** Heathery, slightly splintery, very light smoke. Sweeter with water. Vanilla. Quite distant. Lacks life.
**Palate:** Soft and sweet. Flows well. Orange crates, light soot, nutty.
**Finish:** Pretty short.

## ISLE OF SKYE 8 YEARS OLD 40%
Blended - Scotland

8¼ **Michael: Tasty, satisfying. Linger over it. It opens up after a long time in the glass.**
**Nose:** Scorched earth. Brimstone and treacle.
**Palate:** Sweet. Firm, crunchy, maltiness. Hard cream toffee, then peanut brittle. Salted peanuts.
**Finish:** Salty. Peppery. Sweet mustard. Long, with repeated bursts of warmth.

7½ **Dave: A grumbly bass-note blend but it all seems slightly muted, as if the blanket of smoke has dampened things down.**
**Nose:** Needs lots of time to open in the glass. Maderia cake, oak, cigar smoke and rumbling peatness.
**Palate:** Starts with a mix of scented, but sooty peat smoke (like inside a kiln) dry wood, rooty flavours.
**Finish:** Long, smoky then softening.

# Scotch
## J - Johnnie

### J & B RARE 40%
Blended - Scotland

**7½ Michael: Some very enjoyable flavours, but lacking in dimension for me. I'll try it again at bedtime.**
**Nose:** Toasted almonds, raspberries, limes, lemongrass.
**Palate:** Light, but firm. Sweet, like biting into a raspberry-jam tart. Then blackberries and passion-fruit (Bowmore?).
**Finish:** Seems slightly sharp and stinging at first, then a gradually unfolding potpourri dryness.

**5 Paul: Okay, okay, so you can mix with it. Do I hear any other useful applications?...I'm waiting...Is this that famous sound of one hand clapping?**
**Nose:** The ethereal bouquet is delicately fruity at the opening. With aeration, there are hints of rubber (pencil eraser) and cotton fabric. Deflates in the glass after one minute.
**Palate:** Sweet at palate entry, sweet at mid-palate. So wan in flavour and paper-thin in texture that I consider screaming, "Give me some meat". Manufactured. Light-bodied. Doesn't quite do it justice in terms of texture.
**Finish:** Candy sweet. Watery. Brief.

### JAMES MACARTHUR 14 YEARS OLD ISLAY BLENDED MALT 58.3%
Blended - Scotland

**8¼ Martine: Alcohol is so well tamed. A fully Islay vatted malt. Vatted, really? More a single than a vatted. Or an Ardbeg vatted with a Laphroaig?**
**Nose:** Grassy, peaty, citrussy. Thick smoke wraps up seashells and green seaweeds Coal tar.
**Palate:** Sweet to start even at full strength. Milk chocolate, lemon pulp released in a wave of freshness. Water enhances a bitter edge.
**Finish:** Dry, chewed rush.

**7¾ Dave: A big playfight on Port Ellen beach after closing time.**
**Nose:** Immediately smoky. Fish boxes and brine. Higher alcohol increases the feeling of rigidity, but it needs water to soften things.
**Palate:** Oily phenols hit home. Quite tarry. Without water its rather dusty and dry, with it though there's caramelised scallops.
**Finish:** Long, a little metallic.

### JAMES MARTIN'S DELUXE BLEND 20 YEARS OLD 40%
Blended - Scotland

**7¾ Michael: Very sweet. A mid afternoon pick me up? A dessert whisky?**
**Nose:** Very fresh, appetising fruitiness.
**Palate:** Quite mouth-filling. Malty. Butter. Shortbread.
**Finish:** Lively. Gingery.

**7½ Dave: It's a lovely whisky, but somehow I expect more from a 20 Years Old.**
**Nose:** Pretty high-toned with lemon, honey nut loops, vanilla and mead. Water brings out coconut, vanilla. All very clean and pretty.
**Palate:** Very soft grain to start. There's plenty going on with a nice contrast between tingling spice and soft sweet grain. Well balanced. Flows across the palate.
**Finish:** Very soft.

### JOHNNIE WALKER 15 YEARS OLD, PURE MALT 43%
Blended Malt - Scotland

**8½ Martine: Neat, characterful and witty. Keeps the woody tones in the back.**
**Nose:** Fragrant, inspired. Mango and guava. Beeswax. Toffee. Peppercorn. A whiff of sea-breeze.
**Palate:** Smooth, mellow. Honeyish. Then sailing off with dainty sea flavours. Cinnamon and coffee fudge. Toasted almond.
**Finish:** Spicy, long, warming. Walnut stain. An echo of peat smoke.

**8 Dave: Subtle and beautifully balanced. A sophisticated drink which will ease blend drinkers into malts – and vice-versa.**
**Nose:** Full, mellow and elegant. It starts quite restrained. Tangerine, soft chewy fruitiness with apricot jam. Smoky seaside aromas and a custard creaminess and baked apple/ginger with water. Phew.
**Palate:** Soft with good silky/waxy mouthfeel. Cooked apple then heathery smoke. Superb balance.
**Finish:** Heathery.

### JOHNNIE WALKER BLACK LABEL 40%
Blended - Scotland

**9 Michael: Is Black Label a great whisky? Was Dizzy Gillespie a great musician?**
*WHISKY Magazine Editor's choice*
**Nose:** Rich. Maple syrup, spices and mustard. Can a whisky have a hint of acidity on the nose? Yes, but rather the acidity of a Lenny Bruce rather than of vinegar.
**Palate:** Marijuana. Big interplay of smoky dryness, spicy heat and sweetly malty, creamy vanilla.
**Finish:** Rounded with raisiny sherry. At length, mellow.

**8 Paul: A blend that I like more every time I evaluate it.**
**Nose:** The salty thumbprint of Talisker is identifiable from the moment of pouring. Mature, moderately oaked and oily in a nutty manner. A lovely and textured bouquet.
**Palate:** Medium-to-full bodied. Leaps far past the Red Label in terms of grip on the tongue as grainy flavours start out dry at entry, then go pedal-to-the-metal at mid-palate with tangy, vivid tastes of peat, tobacco leaf, malt, and ripe apple.
**Finish:** The malt becomes sweet and zesty in the aftertaste.

### JOHNNIE WALKER BLACK LABEL 40%
Blended - Scotland

**8¾ Michael: Deceptively gentle at first. I have on occasion been completely led astray by what seems to be mildness of this whisky, then taken on a journey of rediscovery. I find new flavours every time.**
*WHISKY Magazine Editor's choice*
**Nose:** Leather armchairs. Sherry. Spices. Mustard.
**Palate:** At first, sweeter than I remember. Then maltiness and vanilla. Then smoky dryness.
**Finish:** An eruption of pepper, ginger and allspice.

**9½ Dave: The benchmark. Unconvinced by blends? Try this.**
**Nose:** Complex, rich and fruity nose: peat, nutmeg, vanilla, baked apple and raisin over a peat fire. Water brings out peach, heather and a crisp maltiness.
**Palate:** Sweet to start, syrup, white pepper, orange blossom honey, peaty bass note. Very ripe and chewy. Moves silkily into every part of the mouth.
**Finish:** Long rich smoky

### JOHNNIE WALKER BLUE LABEL 40%
Blended - Scotland

**9¼ Michael: A lovely, luxurious whisky. I imagine a restaurant called café Opera. First, a little foie gras, then a couple of Maine lobsters, Marron glacé....and Blue Label?**
*WHISKY Magazine Editor's choice*
**Nose:** Perfumy. Lime skins. Juniper. Slightly sweet spiciness. Tobacco? Juicy oak.
**Palate:** Beautifully rounded. Voluptuous. Ginger cake. Marzipan. Nuts. Pears in chocolate.
**Finish:** Flowery dryness. Roses. Long, lingering.

**9 Dave: This needs time. Right enough at this price, you're hardly going to shark it back.**
**Nose:** Opens very slowly to reveal a mass of aromas: lanolin, smoke, hessian, dried fruit, polished wood floors, oak, liquorice, cake, silky red fruits, cream.
**Palate:** Hold it in the mouth and there's allspice, sultana cake, crisp malt, bung cloth, turfy smoke which builds in intensity as the whisky opens.
**Finish:** Long, smoky, but also fruit pastilles.

### JOHNNIE WALKER GOLD LABEL 40%
Blended - Scotland

**8½ Michael: Stylish and cool. Supper club whisky.**
*WHISKY Magazine Recommended*
**Nose:** Fruit-unpeeled apricot? Fragrant. Hint of creamy pepper-mint.
**Palate:** Silky. Delicate. Scottish tablet. Kendal mint cake. Very subtle fruitness.
**Finish:** More delicate minty dryness.

**9 Dave: Voluptuous and deeply sexy. More of a cousin to Black than a brother.**
**Nose:** Big, soft-hearted nose: honeycomb, mead, exotic spice, rose petal, butter, light wood and ozone.
**Palate:** Hugely silky and ripe: a whiff of smoke, peach, mango. All very rich, waxy and long.
**Finish:** Soft, honeyed and gentle with some light smoke.

## JOHNNIE WALKER RED LABEL 40%
Blended - Scotland

**8½** **Michael: Full of youthful daring, but with enough stamina to last all night (this means that you and your buddy will probably drink the whole bottle).**
**Nose:** Very aromatic, indeed. Sexily earthy. Peaty, junipery, fruity.
**Palate:** Robust malt and grain. Very lively. Scenty spiciness. Gingery. Comes on hot and strong.
**Finish:** Island smokiness and saltiness emerging: lingering and insistent.

**6** **Paul: I liked this blend more than the last time I sampled it blind several years ago.**
**Nose:** Feathery wisps of dry grain emerge after a few moments of air contact. Beyond that are coy notes of holiday spice and dark caramel. Washes out after only three minutes.
**Palate:** Runs the risk of being too sugary-sweet at palate entry as the brown sugar taste and medium-bodied texture coat the tongue like a wool blanket. The mid-palate is better behaved, offering subtler tastes of toasted walnut, pine-nut, and ripe red fruit.
**Finish:** The aftertaste is very extended, a tad fiery, and exhibits a quick flash of brine/peat.

## JON, MARK AND ROBBO'S THE FRESH FRUITY ONE 40%
Blended - Scotland

**7½** **Dave: Best drunk – and meant to be drunk – mixed. Try with ginger ale, it really works!**
**Nose:** Light and clean. Hint of butter. Mostly green fruits: melon, pear, unripe banana, lawnmower box. Some sweetness. Seems young.
**Palate:** Much softer (and better) than the nose: tinned fruit, firm grainy grip in the middle then easing into Opal Fruit juiciness.
**Finish:** Sweet melon balls.

**6½** **Arthur: A very clean spirit, but I was left with a sense of absence.**
**Nose:** A curious lack of 'whiskiness'. Alcohol, a gin-like citrus, juniper even. Fizzy kiwis, and a mineral-like quality. Very light.
**Palate:** Slightly toffeeish, some melon then a slight bitterness like paracetemol.
**Finish:** The sound of one hand clapping.

## JON, MARK AND ROBBO'S THE RICH SPICY ONE 40%
Blended - Scotland

**8** **Michael: The best of the three. A hint of The Macallan?**
**Nose:** Nutty. Sherryish, clean. Attractive.
**Palate:** Syrupy. Full of flavour. Good oak extract, sherry, malt, fruit.
**Finish:** Ginger. Bitter chocolate.

**7¾** **Dave: Substantial, weighty and easy drinking!**
**Nose:** Chewy and thick. Crème brûlée, nuts, pecan pie, dried peels. With water it's like a just-baked fruit cake. Sultana, buttered muffin, clootie dumpling.
**Palate:** Rounded and honeyed. Balanced grip mid-palate walnuts and caramelised fruits. Chewy.
**Finish:** Mix of dried fruits and caramel.

## JON, MARK AND ROBBO'S THE SMOKY PEATY ONE 40%
Blended - Scotland

**7** **Michael: Good as far as it goes, but pulls its punches.**
**Nose:** Cedary. Logs on the fire. Embers.
**Palate:** Cedary. Sweet grass. Vegetal. Vanilla.
**Finish:** Ginger ale.

**7½** **Dave: All very well knitted together.**
**Nose:** Malty, bran. Water brings out a whiff of smoke drifting above Dundee cake and nuts.
**Palate:** Soft start. Well rounded with good weight. Fragrant heathery smoke carrying through. Malt and balanced oak.
**Finish:** Clean.

## JON, MARK AND ROBBO'S THE SMOOTH SWEETER ONE 40%
Blended - Scotland

**7½** **Michael: A curious whisky. Not sure where it's coming from, or going to.**
**Nose:** Somewhat dry and dusty at first, it eventually permits me some sharp green fruits (gooseberries?) with an almost candyfloss-like top note. Then furniture polish? Beeswax? Resin?
**Palate:** Medium. Balanced. Some burnt pastry. Vanilla? Young oak. A hint of menthol.
**Finish:** Surprisingly soft with some green, vegetal notes.

**7¼** **Dave: Water splits it. Oak not quite integrated. A good session dram.**
**Nose:** Light and young. Floral (gladioli) and a hint of cereal with a nodule of sweetness. Cooking marmalade, citrus peels, flour.
**Palate:** Liquorous. Sweet and slightly dusty (sawdust and malt). Raisins, coconut, muesli then a soft floral quality. Smooth and rounded, poached fruits to finish.
**Finish:** Charred. Short.

## KILLYLOCH 1967 40%
Single Malt - Lowland

**6¾** **Michael: Astonishingly fresh and youthful. Not complex, but an enjoyable drink. A lamented Lowlander.**
**Nose:** Very aromatic. Sourness remarkably like fresh lemon juice.
**Palate:** Light but smooth. Lemon sweets. Sherbet. Sweet vanilla.
**Finish:** Spicy dryness. Crisp. Refreshing.

**7½** **Dave: Clean and lively despite its age. Just lacks body.**
**Nose:** Soft. Ginger ale, peach nectar, Tokaji, papaya.
**Palate:** Not as full as the fruity nose suggests. A slightly hollow centre. Light and drinkable.
**Finish:** Short, peachy, bland.

## KINGSBURY ISLAY 1973, 27 YEARS OLD 47.4%
Single Malt - Islay

WHISKY
Recommended

**8** **Michael: Has this cask slept so long that it cannot completely wake up?**
**Nose:** Very restrained. Where has the seashore gone?
**Palate:** Lightly syrupy. Bafflingly thin flavours at first, then developing the earthy Ardbeg character, with a nice splash of mustard.
**Finish:** Finally the phenolic, tar-like, rope flavours come through.

**9½** **Jim: Every connoisseur should get his hands on this at any cost. A classic among classics.**
**Nose:** Truly awesome complexity. Sprig of mint with peat, malt, iodine and oak.
**Palate:** Ultra-rich and dense at first, then actually thinned out by the vanilla oakiness. Unbelievable.
**Finish:** Soooo long...with some chocolate adding to the tapestry.

## KNOCKANDO 1980, 23 YEARS OLD, CASK 1913, DUNCAN TAYLOR 47%
Single Malt - Speyside

**7½** **Gavin: Knockando is always a well-mannered whisky, although this expression seems a tad tired.**
**Nose:** Gentle. Peardrops, butterscotch, a hint of lemon.
**Palate:** Initial apples and sherbet, hard toffee. Some woody notes ultimately predominate.
**Finish:** Quite short, more toffee, oak.

**7¾** **Dave: The first clotted cream finish? Amazing freshness for this age. A great cask – quick use it again!**
**Nose:** Malt bin, lime and orange, passion fruit, coffee ice cream becoming hugely, almost alarmingly creamy: fudge, butter.
**Palate:** Creaminess seems to hide. Direct and nutty with a crisp centre. Pigskin leather. Dry and malty.
**Finish:** Dusty.*

## KNOCKANDO 1990 40%
Single Malt - Speyside

**6¼** **Martine: Too mild to hold its own against the wood.**
**Nose:** Intense. Freshly sawn oak. Hint of resin. Malty notes hardly break through. Touch of fruit, syrupy peaches. Becomes soapy with water added.
**Palate:** Smooth and gentle. Maybe a bit too much. Could be more energetic with a higher alcohol content. Fruitier and nuttier than the nose.
**Finish:** Soft and pleasant almondy flavours with a touch of dryness.

**6¾** **Dave: Simple, attractive and easy-drinking.**
**Nose:** Light and nutty/malty with some green pear, straw, dry spices. Estery and crisp.
**Palate:** Equally light and nutty with a touch of milk chocolate in the mid-palate. Soft, easy and ultra-clean.
**Finish:** Crisp, short and dry.

## KNOCKDHU 1989, 12 YEARS OLD, CASK 286, ADELPHI 56.6%
Single Malt - Speyside

**7¾ Michael: Delicious. Perilously drinkable. Drink it with dessert. No, pour it all over the ice-cream.**
**Nose:** Mint toffee.
**Palate:** Butterscotch sauce. Oat cookies with raisins. Ginger snaps.
**Finish:** Long, warming.

**7¾ Dave: Best with only a splash of water.**
**Nose:** Very viscous. A big, quite robust, and, in time, toasty nose filled with cooked fruits, nutmeg, chestnut with a lift of mustard leaves and ginger.
**Palate:** Thick and quite exotic to start with hints of wild herbs. Slightly lacking in definition.
**Finish:** Nutty with some peach stone. Some smoke.

## KNOCKDHU 23 YEARS OLD LIMITED EDITION 57.4%
Single Malt - Speyside

**8¼ Martine: A classic friendly Speyside, well balanced and enjoying its maturity.**
**Nose:** Grassy and fruity. Red apples, star anis. A touch of cedar. Hint of smoke.
**Palate:** Delightfully creamy and smooth. Fizzy feel without water. Summery.
**Finish:** Warm and spicy.

**8 Dave: Uncomplicated but at the same time rather charming and no hint of its age.**
**Nose:** Clean, gentle and lifted. Grassy with citric notes and a very faint hint of smoke.
**Palate:** Soft, quite sweet, almost sherbety start with a pleasing lemon and lime tingle. Creamy mid-palate with grass, apple/pear, mirabelle. Delicate and attractive.
**Finish:** Soft and fruity.

## LADYBURN 1973, 27 YEARS OLD 50.4%
Single Malt - Lowland

**6 Michael: I am pleased that this very rare malt has been made available. Ladyburn is a product about which I am frequently asked. Sad to say, its greatest appeal is as a collector's item.**
**Nose:** Powerfully earthy-fruity perfumes. Fruit skins. Fruit boxes at a market.
**Palate:** Smooth and syrupy. Sweet. Peachy, orangey.
**Finish:** Assertive. Dry. Peach stones. Rind-like. Woody.

**6½ Jim: This has lost all trace of shape and form. Pretty one-dimensional yet easily drinkable thanks to a singular malty sweetness, especially towards the very end. Don't bother opening.**
**Nose:** Varying shades of light oak have not entirely dimmed the malt. Just a tad spirity but pleasant with minimum complexity.
**Palate:** Oak, oak and more (spicy) oak.
**Finish:** Oak.

## LAGAVULIN 12 YEARS OLD 57.7%
Single Malt - Islay

**8¼ Dave: You can see into this like a rockpool. Clean and pristine. Complexity building.**
**Nose:** Intense, fresh. Marine notes, salty seaweed, fresh fish. The smoke begins to charge out: smokehouse chimney. Sweet all the way.
**Palate:** Sweet start then it snags on the palate and starts to flow. The scented smoke rises to the top of the mouth the sweetness dips onto the tongue. Succulent, intense and marine.
**Finish:** Long and sweetly smoky.

**8¾ Arthur: Typical of this great distillery: satisfying and sophisticated.**
**Nose:** Obviously phenolic but also with sugared almonds, green tea and green peppercorns. Gooseberries, soot and wood smoke. Chinese restaurant seaweed. At times a pink dettol note.
**Palate:** More of that green tea, smoky almonds and some jalapeno spice.
**Finish:** Coal tar. Very dry.

## LAGAVULIN 12 YEARS OLD 57.8%
Single Malt - Islay

**9 Gavin: Complex, sophisticated heavy-weight. The one they all have to beat.**
**Nose:** Big, with Lapsang Souchon and newly-tarred roads.
**Palate:** Warming and full, with lots of peat smoke and wet seaweed.
**Finish:** Dominant peat lingers all the way.

**9 Dave: Excellent. Lagavulin isn't as peaty as it used to be? Pull the other one.**
**Nose:** Pungent, complex. Smoked eel, coal tar, applewood, smoked cheese, bitumen. Frisky.
**Palate:** Intensely peaty. Rounded with big kick: marine character, fragrant smoke, touch of black pepper, but balanced by sufficient sweetness.
**Finish:** Smoke belch.

## LAGAVULIN 16 YEARS OLD 43%
Single Malt - Islay

**9½ Michael: The driest of Islay malts, and an established classic.**
**Nose:** Lapsang Souchong and fruity sherry.
**Palate:** The dryness is at first offset by the sweetness of the sherry character. As the palate develops, oily, grassy, and, in particular, salty notes emerge in a long, sustained, aggressive, attack.
**Finish:** A huge, powerful, bear-hug of peat.

**9¾ Jim: A true classic in every sense that offers breathtaking depth.**
**Nose:** Massive peat. Ultra-intense iodine carries a shade more spice than of old. The fruity-sherry notes are clean, vanilla is much deeper. Beautifully layered.
**Palate:** Peat so thick you could stand a spoon in it. Chewy iodine bolstered by sherry and big oak.
**Finish:** A little spice lightens the grip of the peat and vanilla. Dries off with malt, dried dates...and iodine.

## LAGAVULIN 1979 DISTILLERS EDITION, PEDRO XIMENEZ FINISH 43%
Single Malt - Islay

**9½ Michael: The wrestling match between distillery character and Pedro Ximinez finish ends, at length, in a draw.**
**Nose:** Fresh attack, with hits of peat, tar, sulphur and salt, soothed with beeswax.
**Palate:** Rich and extremely sweet, then smoky, becoming medicinal and eventually seaweedy.
**Finish:** Pepper, salt, sand.

**9 Jim: A big improvement on the first version with much more fruit, body and intensity. Beautiful.**
**Nose:** Extraordinary fruit: cherries mainly but some fresh grape, too. Very winey and this drifts in and out of the peat gathering in intensity.
**Palate:** Immediately spicy, but the peat arrives with a beautifully clean grape. Peat dominates over coffee.
**Finish:** Some salty notes are added to the coffee and the fabulously lingering peat. Long and satisfying.

## LAGAVULIN 1979, MURRAY MCDAVID 46%
Single Malt - Islay

**8¼ Michael: An opportunity to taste another version of Lagavulin. Subtle and complex, but I missed the instant punch of peat.**
**Nose:** Restrained for a Lagavulin. Surprisingly sweet. Perfumy. Bog myrtle. Peat bogs before cutting.
**Palate:** Begins with herbal, grassy sweetness and develops a firm, malty, background.
**Finish:** Finally, the peatiness and smokiness sneak up, with embarrassed grins on their faces.

**8½ Dave: Fishier than many Lagavulins, but has the distillery's complexity and range.**
**Nose:** Immediate hit of antiseptic, then seaweed, smoked fish. With water, like hot stones on the beach, some bog myrtle. Sweetly fruity as well.
**Palate:** Tense start, fragrant smoke all the way. Heather, marine characters. Subtle and balanced.
**Finish:** Smoky.

## LAGAVULIN DISTILLERS EDITION, PEDRO XIMENEZ FINISH 43%
Single Malt - Islay

**9½ Michael: What it loses in character it gains in a different dimension of distinctiveness.**
**Nose:** Fresh attack, with a barrel of tar and punches of peat, sulphur and salt. The victim, enjoying being a masochist, is then soothed with beeswax.

**Palate:** Rich and extremely sweet, then smoky becoming medicinal and eventually seaweedy.
**Finish:** Pepper, salt, sand.

**9½ Doug: A more lingering, classic Lagavulin with some of the corners knocked off and some subtle depths added.**
**Nose:** Deep fragrant sherry slightly burnt and winey notes, followed by salt and seaweed.
**Palate:** Lightness subsides to reveal a chewy, dancingly oily body which resurges before releasing the sooty medicinal saviours.
**Finish:** Long, smoky, medicinal, smoky, salty, smoky.

## LANGS SELECT 12 YEARS OLD 40%
Blended - Scotland

**7½ Martine: A light, refreshing and aromatic blend. To be enjoyed with light food such as seafood salad or trifle. No water please.**
**Nose:** Starts on creamy aromas then opens up to a springtime bouquet. Hazelnut toffee. William pear. Lemon drops. Freesia. Touch of pepper. Echo of peat.
**Palate:** Flowing. Mellow. Pears stewed in vanilla. Lemon syllabub. Virginia tobacco. Salty sensation.
**Finish:** Quickly vanishing but pleasant.

**7¼ Dave: Slightly too firm a grip.**
**Nose:** Soft and spicy. Citrus (lemon, tangerine), vanilla, mint/basil, then soft toffee spices.
**Palate:** Rounded and silky with good top notes. Turmeric with light honey and planed wood.
**Finish:** Short and clean.

## LAPHROAIG 10 YEARS OLD 43%
Single Malt - Islay

**8½ Michael: The most medicinal of Islay malts. I love it.**
**Nose:** Phenolic, seaweedy, with a hint of estery, melony, sweetness.
**Palate:** Seaweedy, salty, oily.
**Finish:** Round, dry, iodine-like.

*WHISKY Recommended*

**9 Jim: A gentle giant.**
**Nose:** A thick coating of peat isn't enough to cover a soft, oaky background. Iodine appears alongside a pear-fruity sweetness. Delicate for a whisky so big.
**Palate:** Continuous gentle waves of dry peat lap upon the tastebuds but are balanced by a sweet malt middle and the most hesitant of vanillas.
**Finish:** Long and peaty, the shy vanilla now begins to show as the oak adds a certain dryness.

## LAPHROAIG 10 YEARS OLD, CASK STRENGTH 55.7%
Single Malt - Islay

**4 Martine: The tough guy. Medicine man? Muscular, solidly built. Dominated by camphor.**
**Nose:** Intense. Prickly. Enormous. Highly medicinal. Hospital emergency service. Scents enveloped by a light veil of smoke. Oak is soaked in camphor. Fruit rise up later.
**Palate:** Assertive and pungent. Smoke lingers on tastebuds. Medicinal flavours in the front stage.
**Finish:** Dry, spicy, with a touch of earthy peat. Nutty as well.

**4 Dave: Overall, the combination of peat smoke and overt cereal notes makes this a very dry whisky.**
**Nose:** Robust. Scented candles, cough medicine, hospitals, peat bog, kipper, always a cereal note.
**Palate:** Immediate peat and cereal mixing (with water) a light fruity note with a peatiness which clings to the palate. Still tarry and deep.
**Finish:** Light pepper, oatcake and, finally, lingering smoke.
*Peat rating out of 5*

## LAPHROAIG 10 YEARS OLD, CASK STRENGTH 57.3%
Single Malt - Islay

**8¾ Gavin: A fine robust dram with lots happening. Laphroaig at its best.**
**Nose:** Fresh, mild antiseptic, subtle peat smoke.
**Palate:** Complex. Smoked haddock, cut plug tobacco, burnt newspapers, but buttery, sweeter cooked fruit notes predominate.
**Finish:** Chewy toffee drying out to oak.

**7¾ Dave: Sweeter and more oaky than I remember.**
**Nose:** Sweet. Tarry with stewing citrus fruits (like making marmalade). Bere meal, varnish and tar. Like fence posts in the sun/caulked wood.

**Palate:** Big blast of smoke, then oak, malt, with sweetness and orangey fruit. The phenols lurk...
**Finish:** ...then reappear with a crunchy oatcake.

## LAPHROAIG 11 YEARS OLD, PORT FINISH, SIGNATORY STRAIGHT FROM THE CASK 60%
Single Malt - Islay

**7½ Gavin: Intriguing, but a little too much imposed sweetness for my taste.**
**Nose:** Red wine, stewed fruit, delicate wood smoke.
**Palate:** Initially very dry and intense, but soon becomes remarkably sweet, even reminiscent of a hot toddy for a few seconds.
**Finish:** More of the dryness returns, but still sweet-cherry-flavoured cough lozenges dominates.

**7¾ Dave: Good, but seems to come in different sections rather than a complete package.**
**Nose:** The colour of onion skin. Fragrant perfumed smoke. Quite light. Cigar smoke mixing with sea shell, sloe, strawberry, travel sweets, a floral note.
**Palate:** Bone dry (oak and soot). A touch of seaweed. A fizzy fruitiness in the middle.
**Finish:** Great: sweet red fruits balance dry smoke.

## LAPHROAIG 12 YEARS OLD, CHIEFTAIN'S CHOICE 46%
Single Malt - Islay

**7¾ Dave: A good, clean Laphroaig. Not exceptional, but true to character.**
**Nose:** Very pale and prickly. Seems young and edgy with big seashore aromas. Drying fishing nets with a certain sweetness behind raffia, peat fire, oyster shells. Water adds a little depth and brings out a bitumen/freshly laid road note.
**Palate:** Softer than the nose suggests. Light oiliness and robust smokiness.
**Finish:** Oats.

**8 Arthur: Good young Islay, with an enticing nose.**
**Nose:** Creamy, medical peatiness, like lint bandages or plasters. There's a good sweetness behind, with lemon bonbons and sponge cake. A bit of spice.
**Palate:** Coal tar soap, and that vanilla creaminess is there, but cut through by a light creosote and some wood.
**Finish:** A little smoke, but relatively light and short.

## LAPHROAIG 15 YEARS OLD 43%
Single Malt - Islay

**9 Michael: Lively. Full of flavours. Multi-faceted.**
**Nose:** Phenol, tar, sulphur.
**Palate:** A deceptive moment of peppermint sweetness and grassiness, then an explosion of sulphur, burning peat and Islay intensity.
**Finish:** Round, dry, long, warming.

*WHISKY Recommended*

**8 Jim: I do enjoy the big peat, but something is out of sync here. Enjoyable but ultimately disappointing.**
**Nose:** Fruitier than the 10 and in some ways more intense, though not as far as the peat is concerned.
**Palate:** Chewy and intense, but a feeling there is something missing. The oaky middle is slightly nutty.
**Finish:** Long, chocolatey and peaty. Lots of vanilla. Also a slightly off-putting tang that I can't recognise.

## LAPHROAIG 15 YEARS OLD, 1987, DOUGLAS LAING 50%
Single Malt - Islay

**8¾ Michael: A lean and lively Laphroaig, more smoky than seaweedy. The flavours are long and persistent. Enjoyable, more-ish and appetising.**
**Nose:** Peaty, burnt grass.
**Palate:** Cracker-like crisp maltiness. Leafy, herbal flavours. A hint of seaweed.
**Finish:** Smoky. Both appetising and warming. Very distinctive.

*WHISKY Recommended*

**8¾ Dave: The colour indicates a second/third fill cask: it's spirit not cask in charge.**
**Nose:** Strangely pale. Immediate hot blast of iodine, toasting sea shell, tar and driftwood burning. Sooty, a touch of smoky paprika. In time lanolin and TCP.
**Palate:** Seems young. Bone dry. Very smoky, tarry neat. Water coaxes out a sweet fruitiness.
**Finish:** Dry.

# Scotch Laphroaig

## LAPHROAIG 16 YEARS OLD, LIMBURG WHISKY FAIR BOTTLING, DOUGLAS LAING 56.1%
Single Malt - Islay

**8½** **Michael: At first, I did not recognise this as a Laphroaig. Then I thought that age must have muted its attack, but 16 is scarcely venerable. Can a whisky be an old fogey?**
**Nose:** More like wood smoke than peat. Gradually, beach aromas emerge. Barbecued scallops?
**Palate:** Oily sweetness. Cereal grain. Toast. Buttery vanilla.
**Finish:** Peppery, lemony.

*WHISKY Magazine Recommended*

**9** **Dave: A classic Laphroaig. Allied? Beat this.**
**Nose:** Incredibly pungent, room-filling phenolics. Fishboxes, hot tar, engine rooms. With water, biscuity malt, wet rope, salt spray, dried fruits.
**Palate:** Very dry. Smoked paprika and balancing sweet maltiness.
**Finish:** Fish oil.

## LAPHROAIG 16 YEARS OLD, OLD MALT CASK 50%
Single Malt - Islay

**8¼** **Gavin: Good all-round Laphroaig. Sound stuff.**
**Nose:** Lots of smoke, molasses, coal-tar soap. Very focused.
**Palate:** Increasingly dry. Bladderwrack and machine oil.
**Finish:** Smoke and oak plus brine, but also sweeter notes trying to come through.

**8** **Dave: Good balance between sweet/soft and dry/peat.**
**Nose:** Peat reek and deck oil, toasty oak, then a sweet cereal: Sugar Puffs. Fruit, dried orange peel. Begins to dry and smoke: wet canvas, iodine.
**Palate:** Supple with a sweet, generous mid palate balanced by crisp malt/oak. Smoke on the back palate: tar, peppered mackerel, light salt.
**Finish:** Lightly oily. Liquorice and smoke.

## LAPHROAIG 17 YEARS OLD, DOUGLAS LAING 50%
Single Malt - Islay

**3½** **Martine: An unusual Laphroaig. No trace of the medicinal character. Water brings out sweet malty notes and more smoke. Why such a difference? Cask influence? Different peating level in the malt? Puzzling.**
**Nose:** Sharp, slightly spirity. A fresh marine breeze but no expected medicinal notes. Rather turfy.
**Palate:** Starts sweet then fizzy and tickling. Getting peatier on smoked spices, burnt caramel.
**Finish:** Dry, fizzy, spicy. Smoked nuts.

**3** **Dave: Atypical, though not really when you think of the old 15 Years Old. Where has the peat gone? It's not been overwhelmed by oak.**
**Nose:** 'Plain' charred nose. Phenolics are reminiscent of dry lumps of tar on the beach, some TCP. Malty still, toasted oak and roasted malt, in time marzipan.
**Palate:** Sweet. Amaretti biscuit. Smoke hangs like a cloud, makes its boldest statement on the finish.
**Finish:** Malty, crisp, some smoke.

*Peat rating out of 5*

## LAPHROAIG 17 YEARS OLD, FEIS ILE 2004, CASK STRENGTH 55.2%
Single Malt - Islay

**8¾** **Michael: A touch sophisticated for the likes of me. Where are those stinging iodine notes? They are in there somewhere, but beautifully balanced and rounded.**
**Nose:** Soft. Lemongrass. Orange flower water. Very restrained phenols.
**Palate:** Rich oiliness. Linseed. Lemon zest. A martini with a twist.
**Finish:** Soothing, appetising.

*WHISKY Magazine Editor's choice*

**9** **Dave: Available via the website. A classic Laphroaig – much better than the 15 Years Old.**
**Nose:** Intriguing mix of smoke and cream. Coal tar soap, deck oil, dried seaweed, tar. Sugared almond and vanilla. Great balance.
**Palate:** A slow starter. Quite sweet then the peat ramps up into Germoline iodine. A silky feel.
**Finish:** Medicinal and dry.

## LAPHROAIG 17 YEARS OLD, RUM FINISH, OLD MALT CASK 50%
Single Malt - Islay

**8½** **Michael: Confident. Slightly austere.**
**Nose:** Very dry smoky phenols.
**Palate:** Lightly oily. Firm. Then exploding with dry, peppery flavours.
**Finish:** Warming, digestif.

**7** **Marcin: Good complexity, weight and mouthfeel but lacking balance.**
**Nose:** Attractive and harmonious. Lavender. More bed linen when reduced. Creamy.
**Palate:** Peanuts (with skin on), soft mocha and chocolate. Pistachio nuts.
**Finish:** Pistachio ice cream. Good length.

## LAPHROAIG 18 YEARS OLD, OLD MALT CASK 50%
Single Malt - Islay

**8** **Dave: This has balance. Like it.**
**Nose:** Melting butter and smoke. A smouldering bonfire. Smoked ham. Complex with notes of date and a touch of wood.
**Palate:** Interesting interplay between toasted nut, caramel, apple wood smoke. Great length and complexity though it is better neat.
**Finish:** Sweet oak and long.

**7¾** **Arthur: Intensely flavoured, but while it shouted very loud I didn't necessarily enjoy everything it had to say.**
**Nose:** Sappy tannins, crystallised ginger, and a fruit cake. A lint medical note and some smoke. Water brings up some new sawn oak, a raisiny sweetness and more spice.
**Palate:** A big, sappy, woody palate with barley sugars, smoke and ginger wine.
**Finish:** Tannic and smoky.

## LAPHROAIG 1960 VINTAGE RESERVE 42.4%
Single Malt - Islay

**7¾** **Michael: There is something getting in the way. Woodiness?**
**Nose:** Sea air. Driftwood. Seaweed on the beach. Not as medicinal as I expect from Laproaig. Some sulphur.
**Palate:** Again, less iodine than usual. Flowery. Peppery.
**Finish:** Firm, long. More of the typical Laphroaig flavours emerge, especially when water is added.

**9** **Dave: Complex, graceful and fascinating.**
**Nose:** Complex, intense yet graceful. Apples, tar, a beach slathered in seaweed. A tiny drop of water brings out rose hip, anise, lanolin and an intense high balsamic note.
**Palate:** Very dry to start, it hits the palate with charred embers from a beach bonfire, then mellows into an apple-laden mid-palate...
**Finish:** ...and smokes its way to the finish.

## LAPHROAIG 1985 17 YEARS OLD, OLD MALT CASK 50%
Single Malt - Islay

**8½** **Michael: This seems far less lively and rounded than the 1987 whisky bottled in 1992.**
**Nose:** Seaweedy. Vegetal. Only slightly medicinal. Musty. Woody.
**Palate:** Sweet. Spun sugar. Marshmallowish maltiness. Edible seaweed.
**Finish:** Musky, leafy. At first, seems a little dried-out and tired, then a leafy and peppery late rally.

**7¾** **Dave: A good example that harks back to the cask strength 10 Years Old but with extra weight (and tarry smoke!).**
**Nose:** Intense with a clean sharp character. Tarry notes, engine oil, dried seaweed and a weird cabbagey note. Peat/smoked tea.
**Palate:** Surprisingly soft given the nose nutty with great crisp maltiness. Smoke.
**Finish:** Long and smoky.

## LAPHROAIG 1988 UNCHILLFILTERED, SIGNATORY 46%
Single Malt - Islay

**8¾** **Michael: I enjoyed this very much, but it does not add a great deal to the canon.**
**Nose:** Peppery. Seaweed. The sea. Some iron-like notes.
**Palate:** Very oily. Sweet, but also salty. Long flavour development. Seems a mature, restrained, rounded, expression of Laphroaig; and then …
**Finish:** Sudden explosion of salt and pepper.

*WHISKY Magazine Editor's choice*

**8¾ Dave: A huge, rich and strangely elegant Laphroaig. Miles better than the official 15 Years Old.**
**Nose:** Immediate: smoked haddock, creosote/tar, hessian, peat smoke with lovely sweet fruitiness behind. In time, leather. Great.
**Palate:** Smouldering peat fires, heather, violet. Dry oak balanced by lovely toffee sweetness in the middle of the palate. Complex.
**Finish:** Long, peaty, tarry.

## LAPHROAIG 25 YEARS OLD 40%
Single Malt - Islay

**6½ Dave: All the aromas are working against each other and it's incredibly muted. Why bottle this at 40%?**
**Nose:** Light, lactic and slightly grubby. Milking a cow in a mucky byre. In time, suet pudding, slightly rotting fish and butter. Very odd.
**Palate:** Very light. Ashes, spent fire, then butter, then Savlon. Claggy. Unbalanced.
**Finish:** Very thin.

**6 Martine: So shy (apart from the dairy aromas) that it is hard to describe.**
**Nose:** Lactic. Dairy floor. Emerging sourness. Gooseberry. A hint of clover honey. Then a floral note. Meadow sweet maybe. A very faint marine touch.
**Palate:** Sweet but weak. Watery. Not delivering much. A cardboard note.
**Finish:** Did you say finish? Nearly missing here.

## LAPHROAIG 27 YEARS OLD VINTAGE 1980 51%
Single Malt - Islay

**7¾ Dave: An acquired taste. Some will like it, but it's too woody and nothing on the 1974 bottling by la Maison du Whisky.**
**Nose:** Sherry central. Bitter chocolate, coffee grounds, treacle, liquorice, tinned prunes in syrup. A leathery/shoe polish note suggestive of age. Smoke emerges but in a savoury way.
**Palate:** The nose shouts: "here be tannins" and it's not wrong. Grippy, stewed Earl Grey tea. Still savoury with a sweetness in the centre. Better with water where the smoke comes through but aggressive and unbalanced.
**Finish:** Tarry and nutty malt.

**7½ Martine: A "wyniwyg"(what you nose is what you get) whisky. You have got to be a sherry cask fan. I'd like to perceive more distillery character.**
**Nose:** A sherry cask, for sure. Dark wood. Humus in a wet underwood. Sultanas, dried dates. Liquorice. All concentrated aromas.
**Palate:** Just the same. With assertive wood prevailing. Quite refined though.
**Finish:** Oaky with a burnt wood note. Nutty aftertaste.

## LAPHROAIG 30 YEARS OLD 43%
Single Malt - Islay

**3½ Martine: Age acts as a melting pot. All the distinctive Laphroaig features are there but combined into oak. Interesting.**
**Nose:** Big, rich, intimidating, sherried. Resolutely by the shore. The medicinal touch mingled with oaky tones. Burning applewood log.
**Palate:** Sweet and silky. Sherry elegantly balanced by peat. Camphor is integrated in oak, giving way to a complex range of flavours.
**Finish:** Dry, spicy, light smoke.

**3½ Dave: Laphroaig's tarry phenols seem the hardest to break down and reluctant to change.**
**Nose:** Rich and powerful with hanging smoke: applewood, smoked nuts, lightly tarry, wet leaves. Water brings out hessian, walnut and a sweet soft fruitiness, cider, wax. Perfumed.
**Palate:** This is dried fruits and a hint of melon. The phenols reduced to fish oil, Vick's inhaler, tar. Becomes drier to the finish.
**Finish:** Emerges like the engine of a fishing boat.

*Peat rating out of 5*

## LAPHROAIG QUARTER CASK 48%
Single Malt - Islay

**8½ Martine: Seems to hesitate between sweetness and dryness. Give it time to open, you will not regret it.**
WHISKY *Editor's choice*
**Nose:** Rich heavy nose with a vague floral touch (lilac?). Chestnut purée, white chocolate. A huge whiff of smoke emerges. Develops on toffee.

**Palate:** Smooth for the strength. Good grip. Water rounds it up. Creamy with an ashy dryness. Smoky.
**Finish:** Toffeish with a spicy burst. Smoke lingers.

**8½ Dave: Expansive and complex. The balance and complexity gives it the edge over the other Islay.**
**Nose:** Maritime. Kipper-like, orange peel thrown on a barbecue, peat oil, tar, slightly sooty. Ever changing mix of dry, perfumed and sweet.
**Palate:** Starts soft and fruity, then peat. Medicinal peatiness balanced by caramelised sweetness.
**Finish:** Oatcake.

## LAPHROAIG VINTAGE, 17 YEARS OLD 50.3%
Single Malt - Islay

**9 Dave: An excellent mix of the rich, the sweet and the smoky. Mouthfilling and complex.**
**Nose:** Tarry with some liquorice, becoming increasingly medicinal alongside pipe smoke, smoked meats and burning yew branches.
**Palate:** An immediate sackful of soot, but then the layers slowly reveal themselves. A cracker.
**Finish:** Long smoky, slightly oily.

**8¾ Martine: A perfect example of the "tough guy with a tender heart". Sitting on the dock of an Islay bay, what would one ask for more?**
**Nose:** Medicinal. Obvious TCP. Bold but the alcohol is well mastered. Light smoke. Boat tar. Fishing nets. Drying seaweeds.
**Palate:** Sweet, tender and yet, pungent. Oily feel. Perfect balance of iodine and malt.
**Finish:** Iodine, tarry warm but not fiery.

## LAPHROAIG, RARE CASK, QUEEN OF THE MOORLANDS 54.7%
Single Malt - Islay
WHISKY *Recommended*

**8 Michael: A deft, attractive, dram.**
**Nose:** Peaty. Dry. Smoky.
**Palate:** Begins with crisp, toasted (slightly burnt) hazelnuts. Develops a passion-fruit bitterness. Rounded out by a lemony, spicy, background.

**8½ Ian: A cross between a trapeze artist and a tightrope walker: performs dazzling routines while retaining poise and balance.**
**Nose:** Chargrilled notes, barbecue embers, peppery extra-virgin olive oil, then a vanilla garnish.
**Palate:** Ultra-delicate with smoky vanilla, earthy, chargrilled notes opening up, while baked apples, vanilla sauce, juicy lemon and maltines.
**Finish:** Earthy, barbecued flourish with lightly luscious sweetness.

## LEAPFROG 1987, MURRAY MCDAVID 40%
Single Malt - Islay
WHISKY *Recommended*

**8 Michael: Both the name and the medicinal character suggests the distillery of origin.**
**Nose:** Fruity seaweed.
**Palate:** Freshly medicinal. Salty. Rooty, liquorice-like, maltiness.
**Finish:** Iron. Iodine. Pepper.

**9 Jim: One of the finest, intense and complex single cask Islay has bottled in the last five years.**
**Nose:** At first glance soft and aloof but revealing a complex array of iodiney-salty smoky notes, sweet malt and drier oak. All very laid-back.
**Palate:** Sweet malt then a tidal wave of massive peat. Toffee-vanilla oak follows before more peat.
**Finish:** Long, lip-smacking and spicy. There is a toasty dryness and coffee-chocolate afterglow.

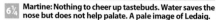

### LEDAIG 42%
Single Malt - Island (non Islay)

6¼ **Martine: Nothing to cheer up tastebuds. Water saves the nose but does not help palate. A pale image of Ledaig.**
**Nose:** Fresh sawdust. Butyric. Slightly rancid. Varnish. Vanilla comes through with difficulty. Citrussy touch. Much nicer with water.
**Palate:** Sweet and round. Peppermint. Wood. A bit watery on mid-palate.
**Finish:** Short, very dry. Tangy.

7½ **Dave: The nose doesn't promise much but the palate delivers well.**
**Nose:** Seems very young. Tarry rope, sacking. Understated.
**Palate:** Gentle peatiness covering crisp malt. Decent structure. A sweet start. The peat is light and sits in the centre of the mouth.
**Finish:** Short.

### LEDAIG 10 YEARS OLD 43%
Single Malt - Island (non Islay)

7½ **Dave: Another that's growing in character. I'm looking forward to the 12 Years Old.**
**Nose:** Slightly edgy. Young and lightly floral before smoke is ignited with a drop of water. Some vanilla.
**Palate:** Quite dusty, then the smoke builds but balanced by a fragrant lift. It's like a florist's shop with a peat fire blazing in the corner.
**Finish:** Slightly rubbery.

7¾ **Arthur: No complexity, but a pleasant peaty dram. A definite step up from the old bottlings with no age statement.**
**Nose:** Sweet egginess, like a custard tart. Some juniper, and cigar smoke. It feels youthful and vibrant, although a little clumsy at full strength but seemed to settle down with water.
**Palate:** Sweet, smokiness and some tinned peaches.
**Finish:** Dry smoke and ash.

### LEDAIG 14 YEARS OLD, OLD MASTERS 56.1%
Single Malt - Island (non Islay)

7 **Michael: The aroma promises more than the whisky delivers.**
**Nose:** Sherbety, fruity, perfumy.
**Palate:** Grassy. Some sweet perfuminess.
**Finish:** Firm. Slightly sharp. Hot.

7½ **Dave: A needle of flavour. Flies straight down the middle.**
**Nose:** Intense. Lightly estery (banana), limeade and nougat. Quite lean with some cumin seed and a tickle of smoke.
**Palate:** Fizzy and direct. Compressed. Blanched almond, flowers. Sugar puffs.
**Finish:** Short. Slightly nutty.

### LEDAIG 7 YEARS OLD 42%
Single Malt - Island (non Islay)

7½ **Martine: Quite an unusual profile. A comforting malt to enjoy while camping in the wilderness.**
**Nose:** Cold ashes. Burnt toast. Sour milk. Damp cellar in a musty atmosphere. Then a strange combination of floral and phenolic notes. Charcoal.
**Palate:** Very floral and light with phenolic undertones. Cereal flakes. Smoked barley.
**Finish:** Short, dusty. Liquorice root. A hint of ginger.

7¾ **Dave: Direct. One to watch.**
**Nose:** Young and firm. Hot roads, peat fire ashes. A touch of fish oil then firms up into burning leaves and wood smoke.
**Palate:** Good feel. Fills the palate well. Light spiciness, engine oil. Young and lively. A great blast of smokiness. Well-balanced.
**Finish:** Dry and smoky. Touch of nut.

### LEDAIG 7 YEARS OLD 43%
Single Malt - Island (non Islay)

8 **Michael: That wasn't breakfast toast after all. It was melba toast, with a game pate. Or better still, a mousseline.**
**Nose:** Distinct burning grass. Maillard reaction. Caramelised onions.
**Palate:** The morning toast overdone, and burned at the edges, but still appetising.
**Finish:** Onion marmalade.

8 **Dave: A cheeky wee monkey. Lively.**
**Nose:** Germoline, hot bitumen (two-lane blacktop), smoked meat. With water the smoke becomes more subtle and a creamy maltiness appears.
**Palate:** Soft and pretty sweet, ripe pear, malt and understated smokiness. Good balance.
**Finish:** Smoky, medium length.

### LEDAIG SHERRY FINISH 42%
Single Malt - Island (non Islay)

7¾ **Martine: Quite a rich and complex malt. Needs a long aeration to release it all.**
**Nose:** Oaky at start then fruity notes. Pinewood forest. Humus, bracken. Dates and apricots. Marmalade. Biscuity notes. Madeira cake. Toffee.
**Palate:** Velvety and round. Sweet fruit. Blancmange. Stem ginger. With water, becomes herbal and malty.
**Finish:** Medium, nutty with soft spices. Liquorice.

7½ **Dave: The finish swamps the whisky a little.**
**Nose:** Like eating a sultana cake next to a peat fire. Becomes medicinal, Savlon. Has a certain buttery sweetness.
**Palate:** Soft with dried fruits and a mix of nut and peat. Rounded and soft. The peat seems suppressed.
**Finish:** Dried fruit. Ash.

### LINDORES ABBEY 'ANGELS SHARE' 40%
Blended - Scotland

7¼ **Michael: Lots of cereal-grain character. Seemed dry at first, but developed dessert sweetness – especially with water.**
**Nose:** Aromatic. Dried flowers. Buttercups. Grated lemon zest.
**Palate:** Lemon meringue pie, but fairly tart.
**Finish:** Slightly dusty and gritty.

7¼ **Dave: Promises plenty on the nose, but doesn't deliver fully on the palate.**
**Nose:** Very sweet. Macaroon bar, marzipan, box, oak, caramel shortcake. Pink marshmallow.
**Palate:** Fragrant. Starts sweetly then wood clenches up. Slightly insubstantial.
**Finish:** Sweet creamy, light lemon.

### LINKWOOD 11 YEARS OLD, DUN BHEAGAN 46%
Single Malt - Speyside

7¼ **Dave: Insubstantial.**
**Nose:** A little closed. Light with some fruity sweetness rosehip syrup? But also a dusty attic mustiness.
**Palate:** Better than the nose, quite liquorice. Smooth with decent balance.
**Finish:** Cranberry jelly.

7½ **Arthur: Pleasant, sweet and light in character despite its deep colour.**
**Nose:** A sweet, perfumed cakiness, like a Battenburg or a sweet sponge. Treacle. Sweet egginess, like a custard tart or scambled egg even. Stewed plums or stewed rhubarb.
**Palate:** Very sweet and then grassy.
**Finish:** A little burnt caramel.

### LINKWOOD 12 YEARS OLD 43%
Single Malt - Speyside

8 **Michael: Linkwood always evokes thoughts of sweet-meats. This one seems a particularly sweet interpetation.**
**Nose:** Extremely fragrant, floral, rose-like.
**Palate:** Angelica. Indian desserts. Condensed milk.
**Finish:** Balancing almondy dryness. Spicy, becoming quite hot. Extraordinarily long.

7¾ **Dave: Malts which waft delicately about are deeply unfashionable in these blockbuster times but this is the perfect aperitif.**
**Nose:** Lifted, intense and perfumed: jasmine/muscat grapes, cut grass and apple blossom with hints of crisp malt.
**Palate:** A light aromatic mouthful with a silky quality that keeps it rooted in the mouth. Even a hint of pepper.
**Finish:** Perfumed.

### LINKWOOD 12 YEARS OLD 43%
Single Malt - Speyside

7½ **Martine: A strange fellow. As if all was delivered in a dash. Then the finish seems to never end.**

**Nose:** Delicate, a bit shy. Gingerbread. Parma violet. Sweet potato. Hay, dry flowers. Water brings out a touch of varnish.
**Palate:** Fresh and straightforward. A malty touch then seems to rush through to a very spicy end.
**Finish:** Gingery, dry. Hefty.

**7¼ Dave: A wee charmer.**
**Nose:** Young and crisp. Green apple, green plum/plum stone, wet grass, cut flowers. A firm oaky counterpoint with hints of porridgy malt.
**Palate:** Medium-bodied. Peppery, vibrant. Good weight filling it out. Sweet and well balanced. Spreads well on the palate. Good grip.
**Finish:** Clean, soft grassiness.

## LINKWOOD 15 YEARS OLD, GORDON & MACPHAIL 43%
Single Malt - Speyside

**7½ Martine: That malt could easily be thrown in a calvados blind tasting, with aged oaky individuals.**
**Nose:** Sylvestry. Pine needles. Wet cider cellar walls. Cooked apples in oven with cinnamon and honey. A touch of beeswax.
**Palate:** Very smooth if not too soft. Sweet oakiness giving way to a drier edge with some astringency at mid-palate. Ripe hazelnuts.
**Finish:** A bit grippy. Oak never gives up.

**7½ Dave: Decent balance. Worth a look.**
**Nose:** Soreen malt loaf, candlewax light sultana. Hint of varnish shows some maturity plum. Ripe and broad with raisin and light sweet spices. Balanced.
**Palate:** Light start then grips well in the centre. Cedar. Fairly tannic in time.
**Finish:** Orange peel nut and light smoke.

## LINKWOOD 16 YEARS OLD, DOUGLAS LAING 50%
Single Malt - Speyside

**7¾ Martine: A classic malty beast. Well balanced. A winter warmer to enjoy with nuts and crispy nibbles.**
**Nose:** Toffee and fudge. Malty. Barley sugar. Fresh mash. Apple skin. White chocolate.
**Palate:** Round. Alcohol is perfectly integrated. Sweet maltiness developing on fruity flavours. Ripe bananas. Tickling spices. Ginger, a hint of tabasco.
**Finish:** Spicy, nutty.

**7¼ Dave: An aperitif best taken by 10am. Has identifiable Linkwood character but it's all rather muted.**
**Nose:** Slighty oily, cut grass powdered almond. A discreet vetiver like scent develops but that turpentine note never quite disappears.
**Palate:** Oily in texure, clinging to the tongue mandarin. Light creaminess. Delicate.
**Finish:** Rice crispies.

## LINKWOOD 17 YEARS OLD, ADELPHI 64.2%
Single Malt - Speyside

**8½ Michael: Linkwood always evokes thoughts of sweetmeats, sometimes delicate, on other occasions more robust. This is in the latter mood: down-to-earth sweetness.**
**Nose:** Roses. Floral. Creamy.
**Palate:** Creamy, soft. Treacle tart. Flapjack. Fruity. (cherries?). Slightly spicy (ginger?).
**Finish:** Lemony. Lively.

**9 Dave: Tremendous stuff-with lots of water**
**Nose:** Straw/gold. Once water has been added, a fragrant aroma emerges-freesia, cherry, iced gems, rose petals, pears in syrup behind.
**Palate:** Round, silky mouthfeel. The high alcohol propels it across the palate with fragrant floral flavours, light oak and sweet fruit all playing off each other.
**Finish:** Syrupy and sweet.

## LINKWOOD 1969, GORDON & MACPHAIL 40%
Single Malt - Speyside

**8½ Michael: Linkwood is a lovely whisky, especially in its older incarnations.**
**Nose:** Fudge. Creamy oriental desserts.
**Palate:** Teasing balance of rosewater, marzipan sweetness and cedary dryness. Beautifully combined flavours.
**Finish:** Big, almondy. Like chewing on halva. Long, lingering soothing.

**6¼ Jim: Old and awaiting the grim reaper.**
**Nose:** Slightly tired with fading malt supplemented by ripe cherry.
**Palate:** A spicy start only tends to disguise the over eager oak.
**Finish:** Dry and oaky.

## LINKWOOD 1972, GORDON & MACPHAIL 40%
Single Malt - Speyside

**8¼ Michael: A luxurious afterdinner malt.**
**Nose:** Honey. Turkish delight. Cedary dryness.
**Palate:** Firm. Smooth. Creamy Oriental desserts. Roses. Flowery dryness.
**Finish:** Coffee fudge. Almonds. Pistachio nuts. Dryish. Long.

**7½ Martine: Hard to find Linkwood delicacy and elegance in this version. Probably not from outstanding sherry casks.**
**Nose:** Pear drop. Sherry notes (fruit cake and chocolate). Oxtail consommé, toffee, beeswax. Slightly sulphury. Hides its complexity.
**Palate:** Sherry. Sour apple and orange peel with a balsamic touch (eucalyptus). Dry and oaky.
**Finish:** Oaky, coffee beans, bitter chocolate.

## LINKWOOD 1973, MURRAY MCDAVID MISSION II 46%
Single Malt - Speyside

**8¼ Michael: Very sophisticated bittersweet flavours. Adults only.**
**Nose:** Tarte au citron.
**Palate:** Nutty. Almonds. Drying to become slightly bitter.
**Finish:** Spicy dryness. Especially nutmeg.

**9 Dave: Why isn't Linkwood rated as a top-class distillery? I feel another campaign coming on.**
**Nose:** Complex with good weight. Apple (dried), light spice, hard toffee, dried pear, raspberry. Elegant.
**Palate:** Medium to full-bodied with a sweet centre of summer fruits. Cooked apple, poached pear.
**Finish:** Long. Creamy.

## LINKWOOD 1974, RARE MALTS 54.9%
Single Malt - Speyside

**7 Arthur: I couldn't decide if this lacked a little, or was just subtle. Pleasing enough, aging with prettiness, but didn't do enough for me.**
**Nose:** Ham and green apples with a minerally quality. Plums, lemon rind and exhaust pipes. With water a little thyme, meadow flowers and phenols.
**Palate:** Sweet then sour and a little bitter. Gooseberries and raspberries.
**Finish:** Light bitterness and American oak tannins.

**7½ Dave: Good, but a tad reserved.**
**Nose:** Rather dumb nose. Green rhubarb, ripe apple, turned earth, cream toffee. With water there's soft white fruit, green apple, pear drops.
**Palate:** High alcohol with a light caramelised quality. Ripe pear and apple. Cocoa powder. Crisps up, with a firm. Cognac-like grip. Perfumed with a silky feel.
**Finish:** Very light, clean, hint of mint.

## LINKWOOD 1993, SHERRY BUTT, CASK 3517, SINGLE MALTS OF SCOTLAND 59.1%
Single Malt - Speyside

**7½ Arthur: Big cask character, with spirit style just poking through. The spirit seemed at odds with the cask.**
**Nose:** Immediate sherry character. Floral and muddy, like river mud perhaps, and lots of dark fruits. A little sourness, like green Bramley apples.
**Palate:** Raisins, cherry liqueur chocolates, and fermenting grass.
**Finish:** Rich, and slightly burnt fruitcake.

**8 Owen: More than a nod to fine sherry wood. Elegant and self assured.**
**Nose:** Solvent and beeswax. Then ripe red apples. Custard and pastry. Some menthol in there, too. With water, linseed oil.
**Palate:** Oily. Dark toffee. Burnt pastry. A really expensive pain au chocolate. With water, more cocoa and some ginger. Nuttiness?
**Finish:** Rich, sustained, dark, again faintly charred. Slightly burnt brandy snaps?

## LINLITHGOW 1975, SIGNATORY 51.5%
Single Malt - Lowland

**7½ Michael: Good for its age, but I preferred it two or three years ago.**
**Nose:** Very flowery. Lemony. A touch of sulphur.
**Palate:** Starts quietly, with gradual flavour development. Dry. Cereal grain. Grassy. Burnt grass.
**Finish:** Slightly astringent.

**7½ Dave: Attractive, but just a touch insubstantial, lacking the texture and flavour range to make it great.**
**Nose:** Light, then a suggestion of lawnmower box, wet grass and fresh green herbs. A sugary sweetness alongside a charred, phenolic note whick develops.
**Palate:** Seems light, but has a good weight mid-palate with those burn, smoky notes balanced by raspberry and lemon.
**Finish:** Dies a little quickly.

## LINLITHGOW 1982, CASK 1336, MACKILLOP'S CHOICE 62.6%
Single Malt - Lowland

**7½ Michael: Very pungent and powerful for a Lowlander. Tending toward harshness. This seems typical of these last Linlithgows.**
**Nose:** Hugely powerful. Linseed. Leather.
**Palate:** Big. Grassy. Sweet lemons.
**Finish:** Syrupy. Anis. Medicinal. Hot.

**7½ Dave: Lovely weight and carries its age well (though dies a bit quickly in the glass).**
**Nose:** Grassy/sappy with greengage, hazelnut and sesame oil/olive oil? It has good weight though.
**Palate:** Full, spicy, slightly smoky palate. It's a whisky you feel as much as taste or nose.
**Finish:** Clover and nut.

## LITTLEMILL 12 YEARS OLD 40%
Single Malt - Lowland

**6½ Arthur: Marked down for that cabbagey character – right back to school dinners.**
**Nose:** Pencil erasers, a faint peat, tropical fruit, and a little chalkiness. A slightly vegetal note crept in, almost cabbagey.
**Palate:** A pleasing rounded maltiness, followed by a crisp mineral-like character.
**Finish:** Slightly sicky.

**6 Dave: The oak trying to cover a very poor spirit.**
**Nose:** Fat and buttery to start, then a weird vegetal note emerges alongside something akin to a flat sports drink (Lucozade/Pokari Sweat?) then sulphur, heavily chlorinated swimming pools, cheese and sour baby vomit (ie butyric). Mmmm!!
**Palate:** Oily and a little rubbery coconut.
**Finish:** Sadly long.

## LITTLEMILL 1984, 18 YEARS OLD RUM FINISH, CHIEF-TAIN'S CHOICE 46%
Single Malt - Lowland

**7¾ Michael: I have always rated Littlemill more highly than most tasters do, but stocks are getting past their best.**
**Nose:** Turkish delight. In a small wooden box, as favoured by posh shops.
**Palate:** Scenty, oily. Marshmallows. Rosewater.
**Finish:** Toasted coconut. Dusty icing sugar.

**7½ Dave: Pretty woody but has a certain rough-hewn charm.**
**Nose:** Malty, leathery (the smell of a new wallet), soft fruit, and with water, increasing wood. A love or hate aroma.
**Palate:** Juicy, almost Irish in style: peaches, orange juice, crisp oak and malt. Still leathery.
**Finish:** Cigar and sweet fruits.

## LITTLEMILL 1984, 18 YEARS OLD, CHIEFTAIN'S CHOICE 46%
Single Malt - Lowland

**7¾ Michael: The rum finish is very sympathetic towards the natural flavours of Littlemill, but the combination never quite delivers what it promises.**
**Nose:** Very fruity. Pineapple. Luscious. Appetising.
**Palate:** Syrupy smooth. Cream soda. Coconut.
**Finish:** Rounded. Sweetish. A splash of orange.

**7½ Dave: A gentle, appealing drink.**
**Nose:** An attractive, sleek, oaky frame. Sweet wood and fruity soft malt.
**Palate:** Soft and pretty. A silky feel with some peachy fruit. Soft, round and chewy. The wood's in balance.
**Finish:** Soft and malty.

## LITTLEMILL 1990, 11 YEARS OLD, CADENHEAD'S 60.6%
Single Malt - Lowland

**7¾ Michael: Littlemill has never been a favourite with critics – or blenders – but I have always thought it a good example of a Lowland malt.**
**Nose:** Light, lemony.
**Palate:** Creamy. Condensed milk. Becoming flowery and drying.
**Finish:** Surprisingly hot.

**7 Dave: Seems sweet, but just isn't quite balanced, as if the cask has yet to interact fully with the spirit.**
**Nose:** Sweet and slightly confected, but has depth. Orange squash/opal fruit and almond. In time a note like lead pipe. A bit immature?
**Palate:** Light and very sweet to start, then a promising creamy maltiness, but a certain hardness remains.
**Finish:** Fast.

## LITTLEMILL 21 YEARS OLD, SHERRY FINISH, DUN BHEAGAN 46%
Single Malt - Lowland

**7½ Michael: Full flavours but slightly tired. A Lowlander for Christmas? Well, perhaps for Boxing Day.**
**Nose:** Mint crème chocolates. Stem ginger. Liqueur chocolates.
**Palate:** Caramel, rum, crystallised ginger.
**Finish:** Roasted chestnuts, slightly scorched.

*WHISKY Magazine Recommended*

**7¾ Dave: Eminently drinkable.**
**Nose:** Rounded and toasty warm. Light bran, sweet digestive biscuit, choc ice. With water there's dried grass balanced by soft fleshy fruits.
**Palate:** Sweet start then crisp nutty varnished oak in the middle, then apricot juice towards the back.
**Finish:** Slightly bitter. Black butter.

## LIVING CASK VOLUME XI 57%
Blended - Scotland

**7 Martine: A loud lad whose tone needs softening.**
**Nose:** Fruit wrestling with oak. Caramelised pineapple. Vanilla toffee. Cider cellar, rooty peat and mushroom.
**Palate:** Unexpected sharpness. Very peppery. Surprisingly dainty kippery smokiness. Gets a little smoother with water.
**Finish:** Sergeant Pepper in control. Slowly losing ground to a milder tone.

**8¼ Dave: Difficult to mark as the next sample will be totally different. A thing of fascination and warped genius.**
**Nose:** Ever-changing. Intense, seaside aromas and dense peaty chimney-like smokiness. Dry bracken, hazelnut, sugared almond with lifted fragrant notes: Orange/kumquat, lemon zest.
**Palate:** Immediate smoke. Vibrant and intense, the peat balancing citrus oils and spiciness. Savoury note.
**Finish:** Smoky with a little orange muscat.

## LOCH LOMOND 1974, 29 YEARS OLD, CHAIRMANS STOCK, CADENHEAD'S 54.4%
Single Malt - Highland

**7 Michael: The brilliant greeny-gold colour sets a summery mood. Remarkably fresh. Drier than other Inchmurrins I have tasted. Green salad rather than the more usual tropical fruit salad.**
**Nose:** Sliced cucumbers on buttered brown bread.
**Palate:** Fresh. Vegetal. Grassy. Sweetness.
**Finish:** Mustardy.

**7½ Dave: Not complex, but very drinkable.**
**Nose:** Starts all fluffy and light (marshmallow, floury baps, icing sugar on apple sponge), then stiffens. Reminiscent of tarmac on a hot summer day, with hints of dry bracken, green fern.
**Palate:** Sweet, malty start and soft mid-palate. The hardness on the nose disappears.
**Finish:** Okay, clean, short.

## LOCH LOMOND SINGLE MALT SCOTCH WHISKY 40%
Single Malt - Highland

**7** **Michael: Very sweet. Definitely a dessert whisky.**
**Nose:** Freshly-made toast. Brandy snap.
**Palate:** Candyfloss (cotton-candy). Powdered sugar. Turkish delight. Pistachio nuts. Banana.
**Finish:** Light but long. Lemony balancing dryness.

**7** **Jim: Not the greatest malt I have tasted from this distillery but the finish saves it.**
**Nose:** Feintiness on the nose which gives a fat and oily shape to the aroma. A sprig of mint and a dash of menthol combine with soft oak.
**Palate:** Dry, oily, feinty start with a surge of rich malt.
**Finish:** Sugared almonds and toast combine with the softest hint of cocoa. Long and oily but the highlight of the experience.

## LOCHNAGAR, 33 YEARS OLD, OLD & RARE 57.2%
Single Malt - Highland

**8¼** **Dave: Full but very well balanced for such an ancient character.**
**Nose:** Cooked/dried fruits appear first, then there's some olive oil and cracked pepper. Peachy. In time a waxy/paraffin note which isn't as unpleasant as it reads.
**Palate:** More lifted and aromatic than you expect with a light zestiness. Good balance.
**Finish:** Light smoke. Layered fruits.

**7½** **Arthur: A heavy old malt which seemed a bit flabby in places.**
**Nose:** A meaty note mixes with sherbet-like element. Water brings out some lighter fruity notes, like tinned peaches and possibly a little floral element. Some mint sirop.
**Palate:** Bready and malty, with sweet Hob Nob biscuits. A little orange too.
**Finish:** Oak.

## LOCHSIDE 19 YEARS OLD, CADENHEAD'S 60.9%
Single Malt - Highland

**7** **Michael: Never a great distillery but it made some perfectly pleasant whiskies and its loss is to be regretted. This bottling is past its best but obviously has rarity value.**
**Nose:** Beeswax. Honey. Lemongrass. Peat.
**Palate:** Starts rich. Lemon. Blackcurrant. Menthol. Becoming dry and astringent.
**Finish:** Cedary. Woody. Abrupt.

**9** **Jim: Is it too late to transport this dead distillery brick by brick to Ireland? The most Irish Scotch of all time! Astounding.**
**Nose:** Wine gums and salt: breezy and quite polished.
**Palate:** Hard as nails: another that shows Irish pot still characteristics – and how. The barley is hard enough to break your teeth on but brilliantly mouth-watering.
**Finish:** The oak is subdued by the barley concentrate, which continues to overwhelm the taste buds. Fantastic.

## LOCHSIDE 1981, LOMBARD 50%
Single Malt - Highland

**7½** **Michael: Lochside was a capricious malt, but it is missed nonetheless.**
**Nose:** Lemon curd in a wooden tub. Some cooked notes. Smoky.
**Palate:** Slippery-smooth. Astonishingly sugary. A real sugar-rush. Then buttery. Like eating breakfast pancakes with fruit.
**Finish:** Hot, fruity. Himbergeist.

**7¼** **Dave: Vibrant, sure wakes you up.**
**Nose:** Fresh with light fruits, preserved lemon, green grapes. Water tames it a little but those high-toned fruity/floral aromas dominate.
**Palate:** Incredibly sweet to start and also slightly fizzy. It's a lemon sherbet dab! Water doesn't manage to kill this zippiness though there is a slight woody edge.
**Finish:** Toasty and a little tannic.

## LOCHSIDE 1991, BERRY'S OWN SELECTION 40%
Single Malt - Highland

**8** **Martine: Well balanced, fresh and plea-sant. The finish lacks some depth maybe. But that does not take the pleasure away.**
**Nose:** Fragrant. Almondy. Dry hay. Tinned peaches. Honey. Becomes biscuity. Ginger oatcakes.
**Palate:** Mellow. Sweet maltiness. Honey biscuits.

*WHISKY Magazine Recommended*

**Finish:** Rather shy. Fades away softly. A hint of spices.

**8½** **Dave: Mature interactive character.**
**Nose:** Malty and sweet. Light coconut, Jaffa cake, banana chips, pine, musk. Layered flavours, balanced oak. Shows substance.
**Palate:** Sweet (especially in the centre) and peachy. Tongue coating. Lush and ripe with lightly gripping oak. Good length and depth.
**Finish:** Bung cloth moving to nuttiness.

## LOCHSIDE 1991, CONNOISSEUR'S CHOICE 43%
Single Malt - Highland

**7** **Michael: Never a classic, but the closure of a distillery is a loss. Lochside was a pleasant whisky, and now it is a collector's item.**
**Nose:** Very light saltiness. A hint of pastry-like maltiness.
**Palate:** Creamy, oily and oaty. Then pollen-like.
**Finish:** Dry. A hint of citrus. Not very long.

**7** **Martine: A refined and pleasant dram, perfect for a summer tea-time. Less attractive and aromatic when diluted.**
**Nose:** Light, floral and fruity. A hint of mint toffee. Mandarin freshness. A butyric touch with water.
**Palate:** Smooth and fresh. Good balance. A certain delicacy in the way flavours mingle.
**Finish:** Dry and spicy. What it gains in intensity it loses in elegance.

## LOMBARD ANCHOR BAY 40%
Blended Malt - Scotland

**7½** **Martine: A satisfying, nourishing, clean malt. But where is the bay?**
**Nose:** Fragrant. Leafy and grassy with meadow flower scents. Mash-tun atmosphere.
**Palate:** Aniseed. Rich maltiness reminiscent of hayloft. Nutty and creamy.
**Finish:** Quiet and soothing with an appetising liquoriced profile.

**7¼** **Dave: Drink neat.**
**Nose:** Very pretty, lifted nose all apple blossom, icing sugar, light honey and reminiscent of those crystallised fruits filled with fruit syrup.
**Palate:** Light, (as you'd expect) maybe just a little too light. Some lemon/icing sugar mid-palate but it doesn't quite carry to the finish.
**Finish:** Short. Fades quickly.

## LOMBARD GOLDEN HARVEST 40%
Blended Malt - Scotland

**6¾** **Martine: Too young? Or a restricted vatting? Not very exciting.**
**Nose:** Earthy. Wet leaves. Vanilla comes out with time. A hint of peat.
**Palate:** Very close to a pear spirit. Whereas wood is present on the nose, the palate stands on distillation ground. Pear and crushed fresh almond.
**Finish:** Short, melting into vanilla syrup.

**6¼** **Dave: Lacks energy.**
**Nose:** Medium-bodied nose with some cakey/malty notes. There's caramel toffee/butterscotch and caramelised fruits. Some oakiness. Water seems to pull it apart slightly.
**Palate:** Drier than you'd expect from the creamy nose, a hint of prune, a little walnut and chocolate but it's all rather flat with the wood in charge.
**Finish:** Short.

## LOMBARD SMOKING EMBER 40%
Blended Malt - Scotland

**9** Martine: A 'love it or hate it' islander. Bold and uncompromising. And so charming.
**Nose:** Straight from the kiln. Sooty. Haddock. Sea spray. Bog myrtle. Apples cooked under ashes. Seductive.
**Palate:** You get what you nose but in a tame manner. Smoked sea-scallops, salted buttered fudge.
**Finish:** Firm and crisp, reluctantly fading away like the sun sinking into the sea.

**7** Dave: The name says it all. Big and bold but it's all smoke and no trousers.
**Nose:** Immediate robust peatiness: tar, creosote, spent barbecue, sand dunes, tarry twine and a smokehouse jammed full of herring.
**Palate:** Everything the nose suggests but water dissipates its flavours rather than bringing them out, showing a lack of mid-palate richness.
**Finish:** Rooty, smoky with some nice oily qualities.

## LONGMORN 15 YEARS OLD 45%
Single Malt - Speyside

**8¾** Michael: I had never noticed the rose water note before, I also find it in Linkwood – from the same valley.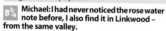
**Nose:** Fresh, marshmallow, maltiness.
**Palate:** Smooth, sweetish, delicious, clean. Spun sugar. Never cloying, though. Crunchy dryness.
**Finish:** Flowery. Rose water. Briar-like dryness.

**8½** Dave: A cracker. Now Pernod will you please do what Seagram refused to do and start selling it (and Strathisla)?
**Nose:** Soft, with those baked fruits again (peach, apple) with caramel, sticky toffee pudding and a hint of damp chamois leather.
**Palate:** Substantial and well built, the soft fruits sitting within a firm structure, and a lovely Murray mint note.
**Finish:** Nutty.

## LONGMORN 15 YEARS OLD 45%
Single Malt - Speyside

**8½** Martine: That frisky Speysider judiciously bottled at 45% has a lot to deliver. Will certainly light up a zen moment.
**Nose:** Silvestry, wet moss, fern. A heady floral note. Gillyflower? Marshmallow. Slowly developing on fudgy aromas. A real complexity.
**Palate:** Velvety, appetising smoothness. Fudge, evaporated milk. Lovely spicy tang.
**Finish:** Dry, spicy. Toasted almonds. A hint of marzipan.

**8¾** Dave: This has fantastic complexity and balance. Subtle yet powerful. Seamless. Very good.
**Nose:** Smooth, rich and elegant. Fruity weight: semi-dried soft fruits (peach), fresh cherry, toffee, tea leaf, pecan, toasted nut. Superb balance.
**Palate:** Ripe. Clootie dumpling mix, damson, cinnamon dusted on top of rich honeyed soft fruit. Light wood oils. Packed with flavour.
**Finish:** Long, ripe, dark fruits.

## LONGMORN 16 YEARS OLD 45%
Single Malt - Speyside

**8¼** Dave: Great balance and depth. At last! Longmorn gets the bottling it deserves.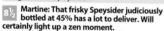
**Nose:** Very honeyed with sweet dried fruits (peach). In time a sweet malty note (malt loaf) alongside a light waxiness (spent candle) and brazil nut. Layered.
**Palate:** Clean, spicy with a fragrant (freesia?) note on top. Honeyed, very soft and deep in the centre. Raisin, custard, malt.
**Finish:** Long with returning spices.

**8½** Martine: A "sunny" dram. So satisfying. Beautiful example of a well managed bourbon cask maturation.
**Nose:** A sweet tempting almost heady coconut fragrance. Like walking among gorses on a summer day. Opens on biscuity aromas.
**Palate:** Smooth, silky. Enticing. Marzipan, macaroon, chocolate and cereal bar.
**Finish:** Drying on pleasant oaky notes. And chewed grass.

## LONGMORN 17 YEARS OLD, CASK STRENGTH 58.2%
Single Malt - Speyside

**8** Martine: Maybe not as balanced as the classic 15 year-old. But who would turn one's nose up to a Longmorn? So rare, so satisfying. Yummy.
**Nose:** Fragrant. Clover, honey. Buttery and fruity. A touch of pepper and saddle leather, then vanilla.
**Palate:** Sweet, then a burst of spices. Ginger, oak, nutmeg. Fizzy mouthfeel. A distant smoky note.
**Finish:** Long, warm and dry.

**8¼** Dave: The Longmorn bandwagon rolls on. Good to see Chivas coming to its senses – but we want more!
**Nose:** Rich, rounded and fruity: stone fruits, dried apricot, sponge cake, sultana, coconut, privet blossom. In time a firmer note. Honey.
**Palate:** Gentle start. Great width and mouthfeel. Complex, hints of dried fruit, firm mature oak notes.
**Finish:** Zesty, complex.

## LONGMORN 1973, BLACKADDER 56.9%
Single Malt - Speyside

**8** Michael: This mahogany dram looks like a winter warmer, and that is how I would use it.
**Nose:** Dried figs.
**Palate:** Figgy.
**Finish:** Minty. Warming, soothing. Late bitterness.

**7** Dave: A beast of a dram. Another case of Longmorn versus wood which has been won by the latter.
**Nose:** A dense, nutty, heavily sherried nose with touches of chocolate and, in time, a fungal and mulch note.
**Palate:** Dense again: figgy, chocolate cake, dried Pedro Ximénez/muscatel. Some sulphur. Tannic.
**Finish:** Tarry.

## LONGMORN 1975, 27 YEARS OLD, COOPER'S CHOICE 46%
Single Malt - Speyside

**8** Michael: Complex, as Longmorn always is, but I wonder about the cask.
**Nose:** Chocolate biscuits. Coffee grounds. At the bottom of the cup. Someone smoking a cigar. Leather armchairs. The smell of newspapers.
**Palate:** We are in a coffee house in Cracow. The cakes are slightly stale, but we love being here.
**Finish:** Slight acidic dryness. Like a fruit vodka.

**8¼** Dave: Another fine Longmorn. Chivas, please do something with this gem.
**Nose:** Some dunnage warehouse notes with fruit cake, sultana, clove, mandarin, a hint of smoke.
**Palate:** Ripe, full and fruity. A sweet mid-palate: soft fruits, tinned peach. The wood is firm wood, but there's sufficient sweetness.
**Finish:** Orange pekoe tea.

## LONGMORN 1984 20 YEARS OLD, DEWAR RATTRAY 54%
Single Malt - Speyside

**8** Arthur: Very pretty and summery. A good antidote if you feel you might be turning into a phenol-guzzling loony.
**Nose:** Conference pears in butter and lemon. Lemon toffees. With water citrus remains, toffee diminishes, and meadow flowers bob in the sun.
**Palate:** Tangy, with a fun balance between citric and sweet. Floral too.
**Finish:** Floral and lightly drying.

**7** Owen: More appealing in the mouth than the nose would suggest, and benefits from water.
**Nose:** Caramel; milk chocolate. Some vanilla or fudge. Underlying spirity sharpness points to youth. Menthol.
**Palate:** Big and fat. Sweet. Buttery and creamy. Then tangy. Becomes more streamlined with water. Pears and custard?
**Finish:** Some late aniseed-like bitterness. Fennel?

## LONGMORN 1988, BERRY'S OWN SELECTION 46%
Single Malt - Speyside

**7½** Dave: Well balanced. A real wee sweetie.
**Nose:** Pannetone with candied peel. As it opens, it softens and turns into custard trifle. Drier with water, maybe leftover trifle sponges.

**Palate:** Barley-sugar sweetness cut with a light hay-like quality. Decent depth, but with an apple and pear lightness.
**Finish:** Clotted cream.

**8¼ Arthur:** Not overly-complex, and I had thought this one was a bit younger. Packed with enthusiastic personality and delicious.
**Nose:** Sweet pizza dough with a light yeastiness and sparkly Limoncello citrus.
**Palate:** Lemon toffee and high quality lemon biscuits. Along with all this citrus (there's lime too) it is mouth-coating with an intense sweetness that is very seductive.
**Finish:** Lemon balm.

## LONGMORN 1990 14 YEARS OLD, DEWAR RATTRAY 55.3%
Single Malt - Speyside

**8½ Michael:** I loved the aroma. After that the stern, impenetrable palate was frustrating but in keeping with the mood. A good, old-fashioned Speysider.
**Nose:** Delicately flavoured peat. Even more delicate sweet malt background.
**Palate:** Austere. Cereal grain. Dry. Passion fruit. Bittersweet.
**Finish:** Glowing. Long.

**7¼ Dave:** More about feel than flavour. Seems pent up.
**Nose:** Juicy and rather pretty. Orange, lime, malt. Becomes fruitier in time: pear juice/fresh pineapple. Quite tense.
**Palate:** Hint of mustiness but good weight. Fruit syrup. Seems to dry and tighten from mid-palate back.
**Finish:** Dry, grassy.

## LONGMORN 1990 MARSALA FINISH, WILSON & MORGAN 46%
Single Malt - Speyside

**8½ Michael:** This highly respected whisky lives a blamelessly quiet life near Elgin. One little drink of Marsala and the Lossie goes all Mediterranean.
**Nose:** Sesame toast. Sweet oranges. Marsala wine.
**Palate:** Fresh. Oily. Light and lively on the tongue. More sesame toast – an exotic transformation of the whisky's typical cereal grain character.
**Finish:** Fresh tangerines, pistachio nuts, then peppercorns. Very big and very long.

**7 Dave:** One way to get people to rediscover Marsala, but what we need is to get them to discover Longmorn. More Sicilian than Speyside.
**Nose:** A charred wood note, date, quite nutty in an oxidised wine fashion. Water brings out fruit cake.
**Palate:** Soft and smooth with a rich fruity core. That charred note comes through in a slightly jarring manner.
**Finish:** Long and quite dry.

## LONGMORN 1990, BERRY'S OWN SELECTION 46%
Single Malt - Speyside

**7½ Dave:** A perfectly pretty dram but it is almost too light. Even delicate whiskies need backbone.
**Nose:** Fresh and estery (acetone, pear, cooking apple, linoleum?) with light floral and citric notes. Some barley sugar sweetness. Better with water.
**Palate:** Sweet and direct. Flowers an intense sweetness: banana with brown sugar. Light structure, decent balance.
**Finish:** Sugary almond biscuits.

**8 Arthur:** Very pleasant youngish malt whisky. Not groundbreaking but a credit to any cabinet.
**Nose:** Lovely combination of crystallised orange, a little toffee and some lemon zest. Some fresh cut grass.
**Palate:** Fruit, toffee and a bold maltiness.
**Finish:** Drying and long-lasting malt character.

## LONGMORN 1992, BERRY'S OWN SELECTION 46%
Single Malt - Speyside

**7¼ Dave:** What a bizarre bottle...musty nose and fragrant palate.
**Nose:** Prickly. Immature? Slight metallic note, raw peanut, polished school corridors. Slightly musty carpet underlay.
**Palate:** Fresh and jasmine like. Lifted and fragrant but overall dilute. Grippy oak.
**Finish:** Spicy, dusty.

**7 Arthur:** Pleasant enough malt, but a little unexciting.
**Nose:** Daffodils, flint, limestone, honey lockets, vanilla and chocolate. Coconut. Liquorice in places, but slightly sour in others.
**Palate:** More of those honey lockets and chocolate. Although clearly a malt there was again this liquerish quality.
**Finish:** Light sweetness.

## LONGMORN 31 YEARS OLD BOTTLE FOR THE WHISKY FAIR 49.8%
Single Malt - Speyside

*WHISKY Magazine Recommended*

**8½ Michael:** An extremely complex – and for me, pleasant – nose is matched by a dense and demanding palate.
**Nose:** At first, turpentine spirit and linseed oil – studio aromas – punctuated by spearmint? Menthol? Juicy fruit gum? Cointreau?
**Palate:** Astringent and a little salty. Cough mixtures. Dense treacle toffee.
**Finish:** Burnt pastry. Not quite as oily as one might have expected. Eucalyptus notes with water.

**8½ Arthur:** A complex, aged and vibrantly mature Speyside. Very good.
**Nose:** Succulent esters, with pear drops and crêpe suzette. Also strawberry, violet, lime and sherbert. Some luscious coffee fudge, ginger and vanilla.
**Palate:** Chocolate, bourbon, oak and perhaps a little ashy peat.
**Finish:** Dry and subtly spicy.

## LONGMORN-GLENLIVET 12 YEARS OLD, GORDON & MACPHAIL 40%
Single Malt - Speyside

**8½ Michael:** The most honeyed Longmorn I have tasted. A breakfast malt.
**Nose:** Beeswax. Intense honey. Mead-like as it opens.
**Palate:** Tongue-coating. Dark honey. Cereal grain. Cream.
**Finish:** Explosion of intense sweetness.

**8¼ Martine:** Straightforward, well-balanced, pleasant anytime. Should go perfectly with a summer dessert (fruit pie, trifle or sherbet).
**Nose:** Floral and fruity. Geranium. Stewed apricots with vanilla. Fresh oak. A touch of varnish.
**Palate:** Smooth and silky. Pleasant creamy maltiness with fruity tones in the back (muësli).
**Finish:** Medium, soothing and nutty (toasted almonds).

## LONGROW 10 YEARS OLD 46%
Single Malt - Campbeltown

*WHISKY Magazine Recommended*

**9 Michael:** A beautifully composed whisky. Classic intense, Scottish flavours.
**Nose:** Resiny. Piney. Peaty.
**Palate:** Piney. Stunningly fresh peat flavours.
**Finish:** Sweet, salty and peppery. Astonishingly long.

**7½ Jim:** Enjoyable, but ideally needs another five years to smooth the rough edges.
**Nose:** Smoky, but not overly so. The peat is soothing.
**Palate:** Pretty young for a Springbank and there is a slight coarseness amid the malt.
**Finish:** Remains peppery and peaty.

## LONGROW 10 YEARS OLD, SHERRYWOOD 46%
Single Malt - Campbeltown

*WHISKY Magazine Recommended*

**9 Michael:** Many blenders feel that second-fill sherry casks give a more balanced result than first-fill. This whisky is a lesson in that technique.
**Nose:** Very restrained, nutty, sherry, with sea air.
**Palate:** Slightly sweeter, creamier, more rounded.
**Finish:** Almost a shadow of the nose.

**8½ Jim:** Superb harmony in spite of the youth. Much, much better.
**Nose:** Soft, strangely neutral aroma.
**Palate:** Excellent sherry thrust perfectly countered by the peat. Massive depth.
**Finish:** Medium length and Turkish delight sweet.

## LONGROW 14 YEARS OLD 46%
Single Malt - Campbeltown

**8¼** **Martine:** Far more interesting than the 10 Years Old versions. It has the freshness and vibrancy of a crisp cold and rainy morning.
**Nose:** Medicinal and peaty. Fresh asphalt. Creosote. Smoked salmon. Shortbread pastry. Mint chocolates.
**Palate:** Smooth at start then warming up with a spicy burst of ginger and chilli. Stewed pears. A hint of toffee.
**Finish:** Minty, quickly fading with a smoky sweetness.

**8¼** **Dave:** You feel this is old fashioned, coal-fired, steam driven kind of whisky and its none the worse for that.
**Nose:** A big sooty, briny, phenolic nose. Liquorice, stove blacking, hot roads in the sun. Long and phenolic. Big phenols, but balanced.
**Palate:** Drives down hard onto the palate. Coal-like slightly salty. Generous and powerful.
**Finish:** Coal tar.

## THE MACALLAN (RUM FINISH), 12 YEARS OLD, OLD MALT CASK 50%
Single Malt - Speyside

**7¼** **Dave:** All rather insubstantial but attractive enough though.
**Nose:** Green grapes, moscato, blossom. Hot gorse with water. Green tea and grapefruit. Simple but attractive.
**Palate:** All that fragrance along with a slight thickening quality in the centre of the tongue. Light malt. Falls apart with water.
**Finish:** Whipped cream.

**7½** **Martine:** A monochromatic dram. The nose is more interesting than the palate.
**Nose:** Fruity. Pear Williams and peach nectars and hardly anything else. A touch of dry hay in the back maybe. No alcoholic sensation.
**Palate:** Sweet. Still fruity but without the juicy feel of the fruit. The palate does not have the appetising zing of the nose.
**Finish:** And the pear goes on …

## THE MACALLAN 10 YEARS OLD 40%
Single Malt - Speyside

**8¾** **Michael:** Very satisfying.
**Nose:** Apricot-like sherry and buttery, honeyish, malt character. Lots of roundness and depth, even at this young age.
**Palate:** Lots of sherry, without being rich. Plenty of malt. Sweetish. Very faint hints of flowering currant and Calvados. Tightly combined flavours.
**Finish:** Satisfying, malty, gingery, becoming dry, with a hint of smoke.

*WHISKY Magazine Recommended*

**9** **Doug:** A king-pin malt which never disappoints.
**Nose:** Bewitching balance of heady sherry, spice and wood. Subtle rhubarb and smoky suggestions.
**Palate:** Big, creamy nutty and spicy. An obvious rich sherry character prevails.
**Finish:** Lingering and soothing with wood spices and soft peat.

## THE MACALLAN 10 YEARS OLD 40%
Single Malt - Speyside

**8¾** **Michael:** Modern-day Macallan. Full of flavour but neither cloying nor overwhelming.
**Nose:** Darjeeling tea. Dry Oloroso sherry.
**Palate:** Rich and smooth, but supple. Emphatically malty. Cookie flavours. Butter. Distinctly fruity. Sweet red apple. Flowering currant.
**Finish:** Toast and ginger marmalade. A hint of smoke.

**7½** **Dave:** Good strong spirit that's in balance with the wood. Young but beginning to hit its stride.
**Nose:** Slightly oily/resinous with good soft malty notes, orange (pulp and peel) tea leaf and cream.
**Palate:** Soft with good palate weight. Some prune-like fruit, olive stone, treacle and crisp malt. Good feel.
**Finish:** Long fruity/malty. Liquorice.

## THE MACALLAN 10 YEARS OLD, CASK STRENGTH 58.8%
Single Malt - Speyside

**9** **Michael:** With its distinctly reddish chestnut colour, this is clearly well sherried. An uncomplicated, robust, Macallan. Simply delicious.
**Nose:** Earthy, nutty, sherry.
**Palate:** Rich, big. Orange toffee. Lively.
**Finish:** Long, peppery, spicy. All spice.

**7¾** **Dave:** Fiery. Alcohol dominates too much for me.
**Nose:** A little slick undiluted: apple, resin and orange. Water brings out rubber, fruits, nuts, orange peel and treacle. Autumnal.
**Palate:** Slightly slick sweet note. Youth and high alcohol combined makes it a pretty lively mouthful.
**Finish:** Lemon balm, pepper and sherry notes, then alcohol heat. After the fires die there's dry wood, liquorice and soot.

## THE MACALLAN 10 YEARS OLD, FINE OAK
Single Malt - Speyside

**8** **Gavin:** The extra two years have made this a little drier, and it still lacks complexity. Improvement to come here.
**Nose:** More zest than the eight Years Old, fresh lemon, then it begins to veer towards sticky buns.
**Palate:** Dry, with resin notes. Dried fruits.
**Finish:** Appreciably longer than the 8 Years Old. Quite astringent.

**8** **Dave:** Best neat. Clean, crisp attack.
**Nose:** Broad. Buttery and soft. Ripe fruits, demerara. Dusty and malty underneath, with some floral notes.
**Palate:** Soft and creamy but still young. A plump palate with brioche, light red fruits and crisp cereal.
**Finish:** Clean, refreshing, apple mint. Hard butterscotch, rhubarb.

## THE MACALLAN 11 YEARS OLD, 24.48, SCOTCH MALT WHISKY SOCIETY 57.8%
Single Malt - Speyside

**7¾** **Michael:** It is always interesting to taste a Macallan that is less sherried than usual. This one could have been rounder.
**Nose:** Very faint sulphur. Some peat smoke. As the whisky opens, nutty malt and flowering currant emerge.
**Palate:** Smooth. Malty, condensed milk. Nougat. Pistachio nuts.
**Finish:** Nut-skins. Slightly grainy. Crisp dryness.

**8** **Dave:** An apparently contradictory package, dry yet sweet, that just manages to hold together.
**Nose:** Intense, weighty and quite oaky: brown butter, coriander powder, chocolate/mocha. With water: gorse, toffee, light turfy smoke, lemon.
**Palate:** Sweet yet dry: soft fruit, rich tea biscuits, herbs and roasted spices, almond/hazelnut dryness.
**Finish:** Medium length, some juiciness and a woody grip.

## THE MACALLAN 12 YEARS OLD 40%
Single Malt - Speyside

**8½** **Michael:** Can a malt be both popular and good? Of course, but not if your taste is determined by elitism. (The same applies to musicians, writers, etc).
**Nose:** Creamy. Butter. Sherry.
**Palate:** Firm. Glazed cookies.
**Finish:** Depth of tastiness. Both appetising and satisfying. Maltiness, estery spiciness (ginger?) and just a hint of smoke (I could take more).

*WHISKY Magazine Recommended*

**8½** **Dave:** Great balance between whisky and wood. To be honest I think this is a better Macallan than the Exceptional Cask.
**Nose:** Big, with well-balanced sherried notes. Juicy malt, dried fruit (date/fig) Madeira cake. Water brings the sherry notes forward: tea, rubber, oak, but it hasn't taken over.
**Palate:** Rich, weighty. Elegant. Orange and light wood.
**Finish:** Long, oaky and winey.

## THE MACALLAN 12 YEARS OLD, FINE OAK
Single Malt - Speyside

**8½** **Gavin:** Starting to get there now. The qualitative jump from 10 to 12 is exactly parallel to that in sherried expressions. I'd buy this one!
**Nose:** Perfume notes that were not in the younger ones. Marzipan. More complex.
**Palate:** Expansive fruit, oranges and marmalade: notes more typical of a Macallan.
**Finish:** Longer and sweeter, much more balanced.

**8½** **Dave:** The best balanced of the youngsters. Everything is beginning to fill out. A 'Drink Me' malt!
**Nose:** Rounded, some complexity. Fresh malt, hemp rope, burnt grass. Sweetens into toffee, sultana, soft fruits. Hint of smoke, oak and white pepper.
**Palate:** Mouthfilling. Banana split, milk chocolate and juicy fruits but sufficient crisp oak and malt to balance.
**Finish:** Medium length. Creamed coconut, popcorn.

## THE MACALLAN 14 YEARS OLD, DEWAR RATTRAY 57.6%
Single Malt - Speyside

**7¼ Michael: A very odd Macallan. Perhaps a very odd cask.**
**Nose:** Warm, malted milk. Bitter chocolate. Slightly smoky.
**Palate:** Dry. Liquorice. Rooty. Sappy. Woody.
**Finish:** A suggestion of quinine. Iron tonic. Medicinal. Astringent.

**7¾ Dave: Though a little short has more substance than the rest of the range.**
**Nose:** Direct and malty. Fresh and light. Seems young. In time a summery mix of cut watermelon, cucumber, grass. Hint of smoke. Clean.
**Palate:** Medium bodied with good feel. Honey, malt, peat and balanced oak.
**Finish:** Dry. Hay-like.

## THE MACALLAN 15 YEARS OLD, FINE OAK
Single Malt - Speyside

**8¼ Gavin: This is getting difficult, but the 12 Years Old still just edges it for me.**
WHISKY Magazine Editor's choice
**Nose:** Perhaps a touch more vanilla sweetness than the 12 Years Old.
**Palate:** Altogether 'bigger' in the mouth than its younger stablemates, but slightly more citric and winey.
**Finish:** Mellow, cooked fruits.

**9¼ Dave: Takes time to open but worth the wait. The complete package and arguably the best.**
**Nose:** Orange peel and ripe melon, mango, vanilla pod. Hot sawdust, coconut/hazelnut, wax polish.
**Palate:** Honey, nutty oak, cooked orchard fruits (Crème de pêche, black banana). Caramel toffee, oak, bracken, malt, dark chocolate. Superb balance.
**Finish:** Very complex fruits with a spicy tingle.

## THE MACALLAN 16 YEARS OLD, BURGUNDY FINISH, THE VINTAGE HOUSE, DOUGLAS LAING
Single Malt - Speyside

**8 Martine: A real finesse, some thinness too. But Twiggy was a popular model in her time, wasn't she?**
**Nose:** Luscious fruitiness. Apricot jam, trifle, marzipan, almond and pear tart. A winey note hovering over that tempting bakery selection. Orange blossom.
**Palate:** Malty and fruity. Lightbodied. Raisins, scones. Cherry jam. Red apple. Muscat grape.
**Finish:** Soothing, fruity. Rather short.

**7¾ Dave: Fair balance.**
**Nose:** Slightly indistinct without water. Soft, gentle and nutty.
**Palate:** Delivers much more than on the distant nose. Quite a thick feel balanced by fragrant top notes, balanced oak and a Nutella like crispness. Balanced oak.
**Finish:** Dark chocolate.

## THE MACALLAN 16 YEARS OLD, DEWAR RATTRAY 51.3%
Single Malt - Speyside

**7½ Michael: Puts me in mind of an aged Tequila, with a big splash of lime.**
**Nose:** Green fruit crispness. Slight acidity. Dusty, chalky top notes. Faint turpentine and resin notes? Balsam? More rounded, toffee notes with water.
**Palate:** Tart. Peppery. Dusty dryness. (Lemon juice?). Fresher with water.
**Finish:** Drying and quite abrupt, but not unpleasant. Artichokes. Faintly smoky.

**7½ Arthur: A pleasant summery kind of dram.**
**Nose:** Almond pastries dusted with icing sugar. Very raisiny, with butterscotch and lemon peel too. With time more citrus/sour notes appear, along with more floral character.
**Palate:** Very drinkable at cask strength, with a corn-like character, grassy and citric (orange perhaps).
**Finish:** Medium length and dryish.

## THE MACALLAN 17 YEARS OLD, DEWAR RATTRAY 58.4%
Single Malt - Speyside

**8¾ Martine: A beautifully combined aromatic display with a caressing texture. Delicious.**
WHISKY Magazine Editor's choice
**Nose:** Fruity and flowery. Strawberry jam. Muscat grapes.

**Palate:** Smooth, round. Velvety. Sweet fruitiness balanced by a refreshing sourness. Very pleasant and refined. Fruit gums. Blackcurrant. Liquorice.
**Finish:** Long, balanced, pleasantly spicy.

**8½ Dave: Plump. A pudding whisky. Excellent.**
**Nose:** Deep and mature. Tarte tatin cinnamon stick. Fleshy and ripe with peaches, quince, cedar and complex. Sweet and rich.
**Palate:** Totallly different to the nose. Here it is all about suede leather fragrant pipe smoke and ripe soft fruits. A teasing whisky with great length. Oddly exotic.
**Finish:** Liquorice and treacle, then sweet.

## THE MACALLAN 18 YEARS OLD 40%
Single Malt - Speyside

**9 Michael: A lovely whisky in its own right, but not quite as layered as the best vintages.**
WHISKY Magazine Recommended
**Nose:** Sherried of course, but also a little more peat in this vintage.
**Palate:** Pale sherryish, with late peat. A harmonic segue, but less fruity than I remember.
**Finish:** Very smooth, with some good wood-extract.

**9½ Doug: An aristocratic and balanced Macallan, though drier than some recent 18 year releases.**
**Nose:** Deeply attractive, honeyed with prickling wood spice and brandy butter.
**Palate:** Rich and lingering, yielding warm raisiny, sherried and oaky notes.
**Finish:** Long, oaky-peppery, distinguished. Smoky at the last.

## THE MACALLAN 18 YEARS OLD, FINE OAK
Single Malt - Speyside

**7¾ Gavin: A lovely, elegant yet large whisky. Why would you ever use sherry wood?**
**Nose:** Spices, barley, subtle floral perfume.
**Palate:** Firm and confident. More spices, ginger, some trademark Macallan honey and malt.
**Finish:** Honey lingers, angelica.

**8½ Dave: Good weight. Ripe.**
**Nose:** Drier. Robust and oily: earthy, seasoned oak, hazelnut, dry spices. Cherry stone, dried apricot, ripe pineapple, melon, peels, then into coconut and cocoa.
**Palate:** Mouthcoating. Peaches cut with toasted nuts, ginger powder, cherry stone, burnt grass.
**Finish:** Dry, a little fresh malt.

## THE MACALLAN 1926, 60 YEARS OLD
Single Malt - Speyside

**8 Michael: A privilege to taste such an old whisky but I just cannot handle such woody astringency.**
WHISKY Magazine Recommended
**Nose:** Medicinal, fig-like, peaty, oaky.
**Palate:** Dried fruits, very dry and concentrated. Rooty, liquorice-like. Treacle-toffee. Molasses.
**Finish:** Liquorice-toffee. Cedar. Oak. Heavy wood.

**9¼ David: For a 60 Years Old whisky it still displays fresh vigorous vitality.**
**Nose:** Very rich dried fruits, resinous spice. Complex.
**Palate:** Woody. Dried fruit. Deep resinous spice. Mouth feel is viscous, syrupy and oily.
**Finish:** Rich wood with resinous spice.

## THE MACALLAN 1937, 36 YEARS OLD 43%
Single Malt - Speyside

**8½ Michael: Blindfold, I am not sure I would not recognise this as a Macallan until that familiar finish.**
WHISKY Magazine Recommended
**Nose:** Hint of mint. Restrained spices. Very subtle, complex and attractive.
**Palate:** Extremely syrupy. Herbal. Lightly nutty.
**Finish:** Familiar sweet, smoky notes and emerging.

**8½ David: Macallan was a peaty whisky from the mid 1930's through to the late 1940s.**
**Nose:** Wood with hints of dried fruits, peat smoke and cinnamon spice.
**Palate:** Appley, lemons and peat smoke.
**Finish:** Richly phenolic with fresh lemons.

## THE MACALLAN 1937, 37 YEARS OLD, VINTAGE 43%
Single Malt - Speyside

**9** | **Michael:** With a colour close to that of today's product and a bright clarity, this visually recalled some of the yet-older Macallans that have inspired replica editions.
**Nose:** Malt. Vanilla.
**Palate:** Nice syrupy, malty middle. Creamy. Sweetshop flavours. Sufficiently soothing to calm the palate before the abrupt termination.
**Finish:** Spicy. Hot. Late smokiness, and astringency.

**8½** | **Martine:** A rich, smooth expression of The Macallan. Relatively light in colour. Seems stronger than it really is.
**Nose:** Fruity, intense. Pear drops, lemon curd. Orangey notes, halfway between flowers and fruit. Quince jam.
**Palate:** Smooth. Citrus fruits. Orange sherbet, candied orange peel. Nougat. Wood easily dominates.
**Finish:** Quite dry, but fresh with a delicate mintiness.

## THE MACALLAN 1940, 35 YEARS OLD
Single Malt - Speyside

**9** | **Michael:** Not quite the complexity of the 1946 and 1948. Oaky woodiness begins to intrude.
**Nose:** Fragrant smoke, with dryish maltiness.
**Palate:** Quite full and syrupy, oaky and smoky.
**Finish:** Remarkable emergence of mint toffee.

**8¾** | **David:** The 1937 and 1940 are currently fetching between £250 and £500 per bottle at auction.
**Nose:** Cooked apple and lemon citrus, some wood.
**Palate:** Richer apples, lemons and peat smoke.
**Finish:** Richly phenolic with fresh lemons and cooked apples.

## THE MACALLAN 1945, 56 YEARS OLD, VINTAGE 51.5%
Single Malt - Speyside

**8** | **Michael:** Very lively, but ill-tempered. I kept expecting it to propose the return of military service, or demand that I had my hair cut.
**Nose:** Fresh. Minty. Spicy.
**Palate:** A clear, bright orange colour suggests sherry, which duly emerges. The whisky nonetheless seems thin; then intensely sweet; those green fruits again.
**Finish:** Suddenly peppery, hot and aggressive.

**8** | **Martine:** More of a spicy tendency than other versions.
**Nose:** Rich, fruity. Very biscuity. Butter shortbread or warm apple crumble. A hint of peat. Some delicate forest aromas (fern, moss).
**Palate:** Smooth, sweet and very spicy. All fruit cake aromas. Candied grapefruit. Oak tends to hold back fruity flavours. Ginger and paprika.
**Finish:** Crisp, dry and long.

## THE MACALLAN 1946, 52 YEARS OLD
Single Malt - Speyside

**9¾** | **Michael:** A whisky of seductive charm.
**Nose:** Restrained, dry, smokiness.
**Palate:** So smooth as to be elusive. Soft, delicate, elegant. Sweet limes and lemons.
**Finish:** Bitter orange. The peat and smoke returns, with sugared-almond sweetness gradually emerging.

**8¾** | **David:** A very unusual expression of The Macallan. Unquestionably a classic.
**Nose:** Floral and fragrant. Hints of wood and spice.
**Palate:** Richly phenolic with lemon and apples.
**Finish:** Mouth coating oiliness delivers a long lasting phenolic and lemony aftertaste.

## THE MACALLAN 1948 SELECT RESERVE 43%
Single Malt - Speyside

**9** | **Michael:** Paler in colour and lighter in body, but what a palate...great Speyside whiskies once tasted like this.
**Nose:** Sherry not obvious – Fino? Leafy, peaty, woody.
**Palate:** An altogether more elegant, wistful, style than today's Macallans. Some sweetness and floweriness, but the outstanding feature is an astonishingly fresh peat-smoke flavour.
**Finish:** Gentle but lingering and warming, leaving smoky memories.

**7** | **Jim:** This is just a shade over-aged unlike the 1946. Even so, the intense, complex middle does offer certain riches. The nose is exceptional.
**Nose:** A subtle hint of sandalwood, polished oak and sweet pipe smoke is no match for the extraordinary, ripe plum fruitiness and crystal-clear sweet malt. Quite exhilarating.
**Palate:** Deep and spiced with aged oak from the off. Massively dry through the middle but there are some richer, digestive biscuity malt notes which ensure stability.
**Finish:** Bitter-sweet, slightly salty, waxily honied and smoky. The oaky notes are the ones which last longest.

## THE MACALLAN 1948, 51 YEARS OLD
Single Malt - Speyside

**9¾** | **Michael:** Drink it and travel back in time. It is one of the finest malts I have ever tasted.
**Nose:** Fragrant. Fino sherry. Sacks of spices.
**Palate:** Wistful. Restrained. Fresh, peat-smoke.
**Finish:** Wonderfully appetising interplay of juicy sweetness and clean, light, smokiness.

**9¼** | **David:** Spicier than the 1946 Macallan with the peatiness less pronounced.
**Nose:** Sweet ripe apples, lemon and orange.
**Palate:** Strongly phenolic with citrus fruit.
**Finish:** Rich, oily and viscous on the palate with a long citrus and phenolic aftertaste.

## THE MACALLAN 1949, 50 YEARS OLD, MILLENNIUM 46%
Single Malt - Speyside

**9¾** | **Michael:** A beautifully composed, luxurious whisky.
**Nose:** Peaty, smoky, almost sooty.
**Palate:** Firm, slippery. Treacly, oaky. The oak is big but never overpowering.
**Finish:** Like eating hard butterscotch flavoured with root ginger, while indulging the odd post-prandial burp of Christmas pudding.

**9¼** | **Jim:** Magnificent finesse and charm makes this a Macallan to die for.
**Nose:** Toffee and sherry hand in hand, alongside ripe apples and grape. Sweet and sexy.
**Palate:** Mouth-filling and malty, sandwiched by some fine and extremely clean sherry notes.
**Finish:** Lingering Oloroso and liquorice; good age but light enough for the malt, spice and smoke finish.

## THE MACALLAN 1949, 52 YEARS OLD, VINTAGE 41.1%
Single Malt - Speyside

**8¼** | **Michael:** Not much evidence of alcohol. Elegant but frail. Doesn't approach the 1948 I tasted a few years ago.
**Nose:** Fruity (cherryish? Or am I being suggestible? It does have a dark amber colour).
**Palate:** Malty but thin. Tastes like fruity herb bitters.
**Finish:** Very slight. Cough sweets.

**7¾** | **Martine:** Very unusual but interesting. Wood leaves a heavy imprint on malty aromas. Water is a real killer with this one.
**Nose:** Very unusual. Almost animal. Beefy, oxtail soup aromas. After a while, becomes earthy and musty, and later on, some sweet aromas break through (toffee, a touch of vanilla).
**Palate:** Sour and tangy citrus fruit notes. Overripe pear. Passion fruit. Nice chocomint taste behind.
**Finish:** Dry, warm and bitter.

## THE MACALLAN 1951 VINTAGE 49.6%
Single Malt - Speyside

**8¼** | **Michael:** I am a great devotee of the older Macallans, but this one is too woody for me.
**Nose:** An evocative sootiness over oaky Calvados aromas.
**Palate:** Sweet, treacly, start. Quickly moves to peppery, earthy, peaty and burnt flavours. Phenol. Some sulphur.
**Finish:** Oaky, woody.

**9½** | **Dave:** A bit scary. A 50 Years Old malt with stunning balance and vivaciousness...but I can't afford it on my wages.
**Nose:** Clove, incense, coffee grounds, raisin, date, liquorice, rubber and a hint of rancio.

**Palate:** There's gunky earth tones, coal fires/soot but also a lovely bramble fruitiness. Spicy, figgy clove.
**Finish:** Bone dry, cigar smoke, dried malt.

## THE MACALLAN 1961 VINTAGE 54.7%
Single Malt - Speyside

9½ **Michael: This one I loved. The flavours have melded beautifully, in what must have been an excellent cask.**
**Nose:** Moist Dundee cake topped with toasted almonds. Candied peel. Lemony.
**Palate:** Astonishing fresh, spicy, sweet, toffeeish, buttery, vanilla, charred oak, peaty dryness.
**Finish:** Honey, cinnamon and ginger.

9 **Dave: Fascinating. A very different style of Macallan. If you buy for your unopened collection, get a miniature as well so you can at least try it.**
**Nose:** Biscuity start to the nose. Preserved lemon, ginger, cumin, allspice.
**Palate:** A soft start to the nose. A juicily soft centre.
**Finish:** Long with a tickle of smoke.

## THE MACALLAN 1964, 37 YEARS OLD, VINTAGE 58.6%
Single Malt - Speyside

7¼ **Michael: Interesting in its own right. Hard to envisage as a Macallan, especially with its pale, greeny-gold colour.**
**Nose:** Fruity. Creamy. Vanilla. Some woody dryness.
**Palate:** Syrupy. Sweet. Green fruits – or chillies.
**Finish:** Burning sensation of having bitten into a chilli pepper.

7 **Martine: An odd Macallan. Light in colour. Quite aggressive, a spicy bite. Where is the elegance and roundness? Macallan on the dark side of the moon!**
**Nose:** Rooty, leafy and spicy. Fresh ginger root, bitter orange. White chocolate. Dill. A slight butyric note. Not the usual sherry nose.
**Palate:** Sweet and spicy. Very oaky. Spices burn the tongue even with water added. Fresh ginger root.
**Finish:** Very warm, a touch of smoke (burnt wood).

## THE MACALLAN 1967, 35 YEARS OLD, VINTAGE 56.3%
Single Malt - Speyside

8¾ **Michael: The dark mahogany colour speaks of wood. The cask itself had more to give than the 1970.**
**Nose:** Lots of sherry. Malt.
**Palate:** Very sweet and toffeeish. Creamy. Good wood extract. Spicy. Dusty.
**Finish:** Spicy, lively, long.

8 **Martine: Quite a robust Macallan. Less delicate than the 1970 but in tune with the Macallan style.**
**Nose:** Less intense than the 1970 but in the same vein. Vanilla fudge. Flowering currant. Sultanas. A hint of yeast.
**Palate:** Bitter-sweet. Slightly tangy. More spices and more wood than the 1970. Takes more time to open up.
**Finish:** Long and spicy.

## THE MACALLAN 1968, CELTIC HEARTLANDS 40.2%
Single Malt - Speyside

7¾ **Michael: Dry Oloroso is a very good idea.**
**Nose:** Powerful flowering currant.
**Palate:** Good malt background, but the esters seem to have vanished. Add water and they come out of hiding; not the usual fruit, but peppermint.
**Finish:** White pepper. Dry.

7½ **Dave: Light but attractive.**
**Nose:** Pretty crisp. Corn, mouthwatering malt, clean wood with a wisp of smoke.
**Palate:** Good balance. Juicy fruits, curry leaves, cumin and earth. Fairly light.
**Finish:** Biscuity, dry.

## THE MACALLAN 1970, 32 YEARS OLD, VINTAGE 54.9%
Single Malt - Speyside

8½ **Michael: Still recognisably Macallan, but the dark claret colour sounded a wood warning. I am forgiving of woodiness, but this approached my limits. Other malt-lovers may be more tolerant.**
**Nose:** Very oaky, but Macallan spiciness and apple esters come through.

**Palate:** Chewy, malty, sweet, rum butter flavours. Sherryish. Some woody astringency.
**Finish:** Peppery. Powerful. Very long. Warming.

9 **Martine: A classic, classy Macallan with added richness. A splendid autumnal dram. Perfect match for dark chocolate cake.**
**Nose:** Rich, luscious. Candied chestnut (marron glacé). Crème brûlée. A liquid dessert menu. Cigar box. Mushrooms.
**Palate:** Sweet and nutty. Wood prevails, but with a high standard of elegance. Port flavours (chocolate, eucalyptus, touch of cherry).
**Finish:** Long, lingering and refined.

## THE MACALLAN 1977 27 YEARS OLD, OLD & RARE PLATINUM 51%
Single Malt - Speyside

8½ **Gavin: This is a very decent example of an independent bottling.**
**Nose:** Fresh fruit and some mild acetone notes. Bright and inviting, more scented when reduced.
**Palate:** Rich, mouth-coating, plums and thick-cut marmalade, with a whiff of smoke.
**Finish:** Becoming astringent as the old oak comes to the fore.

7½ **Dave: Good balance, but not the weight or maturity you want from such an old malt.**
**Nose:** Light and nutty/malty. Crisp red apple, hints of spice and orange zest. Polished oak, burnt grass, waxed jacket. Seems youthful.
**Palate:** Light. Soft texture, good balance. Some floral notes. No great concentration. Sulphur.
**Finish:** Very long with attractive crunchy malt.

## THE MACALLAN 1977, 25 YEARS OLD, CHRISTOPHER'S QUEEN'S JUBILEE MAGNUM
Single Malt - Speyside

8¾ **Michael: Lighter-bodied and drier than the others. I found it a little thin in the middle.**
**Nose:** Smoky, earthy, sensuous.
**Palate:** Light, lively, smoky, toffeeish.
**Finish:** A suggestion of salt. How on earth did that get into the bottle?

9¼ **David: Its wood smoke is the richest and easiest character to recognise.**
**Nose:** Rich wood smoke, wild mountain thyme with hints of cloves and cinnamon.
**Palate:** Richly woody with floral and citrus orange.
**Finish:** Woody dryness. Warming cinnamon spice.

## THE MACALLAN 1979 18 YEARS OLD, GRAN RESERVA 40%
Single Malt - Speyside

9½ **Michael: Strictly for lovers of powerfully oaked whiskies.**
**Nose:** Rich sherry at first. Then malty nuttiness. Cottage pudding. Finally floweriness.
**Palate:** Big and oily but very dry. Thick-cut bitter-orange and ginger marmalade on well-done toast. Then buttery, syrupy maltiness, developing to nutty sherry sweetness.
**Finish:** Richly fruity. Raisiny. Warming.

9½ **Doug: A formidable dram with enough about it to scrum down with any heavyweight.**
**Nose:** Deep and rich, raisins, beeswax and toffee, then a greener edge of toffee apples and wood sap.
**Palate:** Dark, luxurious, treacle toffeeish and lingering with fresher notes of apples; oranges and spice.
**Finish:** Long, rewarding rich chocolatey and smoky.

## THE MACALLAN 1981, UNFILTERED CASK STRENGTH 57%
Single Malt - Speyside

WHISKY *Editor's choice*

**9 Michael:** When I tasted this bottling, I was shocked by its spiciness. When I had recovered my composure, I gradually began to find it very more-ish.
**Nose:** Fino sherry, with that typical hint of dry acidity. Earthy. Mushroom-like. White peppercorns. Cumin seeds.
**Palate:** Very firm, nutty, maltiness. Dry. Oaky, resiny. Extraordinarily intense.
**Finish:** Big. Herbal. Pepper. Salt. Surprisingly peaty.

**9¼ Jim:** This is simplified summary of a breathlessly complex Macallan. Their finest bottling in years. Magnificent.
**Nose:** Fresh, moist dates, toffee apple, herbs and spices. Crystal clear Fino, perfectly sculpted oak.
**Palate:** An immediate caress of sherry then wave of broiling spices pop against the taste buds.
**Finish:** Much more restrained with bigger oaky notes but long and very chewy.

## THE MACALLAN 1988, ADELPHI 57.5%
Single Malt - Speyside

**8 Michael:** I prefer my Macallan with its typical sherry character.
**Nose:** Toffee. Cedar. Slight peat.
**Palate:** Rich. Cream toffee. Fudge.
**Finish:** Typical Macallan 'Calvados' and flowering currant.

**6½ Jim:** Oh what might have been...
**Nose:** Musty and sulphur-sour. Heavy sherry but not particularly of the clean kind.
**Palate:** Good bittersweet balance. The sherry side doesn't gel though.
**Finish:** A late arrival of something orangey.

## THE MACALLAN 1989 SINGLE CASK, MONTGOMERIE'S 46%
Single Malt - Speyside

**8¼ Martine:** Macallan in disguise. Impossible to recognise blind. So unusual but really attractive.
**Nose:** Light, scented. A herbalist's shop. Waxed furniture, dried herbs. Refreshing. Mint. Lemon. Peat.
**Palate:** Surprisingly sweet and velvety. Rich, sweet barley notes. Close to medicinal (the herbalist again). Citrus fruit salad. A hint of peat.
**Finish:** Warm, leaving a fizzy sensation in the mouth then fading quickly.

**7½ Dave:** This is Macallan?? Either a peated experiment at the distillery or it's been filled into an ex-Caol Ila cask.
**Nose:** Light and slightly neutral when naked. In time there's smoke, lemon, fresh fruit. Becomes increasingly phenolic.
**Palate:** An oily texture. Powerfully phenolic, very dry with a chewy centre.
**Finish:** Smoke … and lots of it.

## THE MACALLAN 1989, EXCEPTIONAL CASK V 59.2%
Single Malt - Speyside

WHISKY *Recommended*

**9 Michael:** Lovely pinkish mahogany colour. Big esters, together with alcohol, balance a surprising degree of woodiness. Drinks older than it is. Another fogeyish bottling.
**Nose:** Mint chocolates. Fudge. Calvados. Oak.
**Palate:** Packed with flavour. Cocoa. Demerara sugar. Ginger.
**Finish:** Coffeeish dryness. Bittersweet.

**8½ Dave:** A big boy, but has sufficient sweetness to balance the oak.
**Nose:** Complex and meaty: cooked fruits, polished oak, incense, coffee grounds, medlar, wet tea leaves, dry amontillado, flamed orange peel.
**Palate:** Perfumed, almost oily start. Good balance. Wood gives grip but there's sweet centre with notes of heather blossom and maraschino cherry.
**Finish:** Lightly peaty.

## THE MACALLAN 1990, MARSALA FINISH, WILSON & MORGAN 46%
Single Malt - Speyside

**8¾ Michael:** The estery Macallan notes are as brassy as the Basie band on top form.
**Nose:** Fresh peat. Smells of the kiln. These aromas quickly diminish. Lemony and malty notes emerge.
**Palate:** Slippery smooth. Sweet, rich maltiness. A crescendo of citrussy, estery, liqueur-ish, flavours.
**Finish:** Only now do I detect a hint of caramel-like flavour from the wine cask. Sherry? Madeira? When the blindfold is removed, it turns out to be Marsala.

**7 Dave:** It doesn't quite hang together, but hits the mouth in three totally separate sections. I can understand the underlying idea, it just hasn't been pulled off.
**Nose:** Slightly buttery malt and a strange (non-peaty) smokiness like heavily roasted nuts.
**Palate:** This burnt/roasted quality hits you immediately, then comes the soft sweet buttery/oily centre, then a slight bitterness.
**Finish:** Soft and long.

## THE MACALLAN 1993 SPEYMALT, GORDON & MAC-PHAIL 40%
Single Malt - Speyside

**7¾ Martine:** Another unusual Macallan. Well-balanced. No sherry overload. Second-or third-fill maybe. Or a Fino cask?
**Nose:** Intense. Fresh paint. Nutty. Almond milk. Green peas boiling. Crushed walnut. Beeswax in the background.
**Palate:** Silky, smooth. Wood (pine cone). Freshly baked loaf. Distant fruitiness. Perry. Cinnamon.
**Finish:** Fairly rich. On the bitter side.

**7¾ Dave:** A lovely and quite complex range of flavours and textures. A palate whisky.
**Nose:** Rich, soft and malty with cream, soft fruit, sultana (bread and butter pudding) alongside light turfy/heathery notes.
**Palate:** Generous and soft. Quite oily on the palate with some charred wood notes. Chewy, fruity and gentle.
**Finish:** Light smoke. Drying.

## THE MACALLAN 21 YEARS OLD, FINE OAK
Single Malt - Speyside

WHISKY *Recommended*

**8¼ Gavin:** Fine if you're a bourbon fan, but this is perhaps a little too far for me.
**Nose:** Fewer floral notes, more vanilla and toffee.
**Palate:** The bourbon cask is beginning to assert its influence here. Vanilla and toffee on top of still lively malt and spice.
**Finish:** Lengthy and complex, malt and vanilla nicely in harmony.

**9 Dave:** A cracker, typical of old (and older style) Speyside.
**Nose:** Rich, heavy, shows maturity. Floral notes (violet/pot pourri) and spices (ginger, allspice, nutmeg, candied peels). Oily; floor polish, sandalwood.
**Palate:** Lively. Fruit, sweet spices and oak pool in the centre. Big with a silky/oily mouthfeel.
**Finish:** Cocoa butter. Long.

## THE MACALLAN 25 YEARS OLD, FINE OAK
Single Malt - Speyside

**7¾ Gavin:** No further, I think.
**Nose:** Vanilla and caramel, but undercut by something smoky and slightly bitter. A raked over bonfire of autumn leaves.
**Palate:** Cloves, marmalade and smoky malt are in here, but so is old wood. Spices and honey, brittle toffee.
**Finish:** The cask is just about held in check by the integrity of The Macallan. A creamy character lingers.

**9 Dave:** Maturity, refined rather than OTT. Great to see distillery character retained at this age.
**Nose:** More concentrated. Citrus peels, overripe fruit, polished oak. Intense and exotic: rose petals, Turkish Delight, parma violet, nutmeg and cinnamon.
**Palate:** Tobacco notes, chocolate and coconut. Coffee, heather. A good back-palate whisky.
**Finish:** White pepper, crystalline ginger. Elegant.

## THE MACALLAN 30 YEARS OLD 43%
Single Malt - Speyside

**7½ Jim:** The finish does have the same effortless charm as the '46 or the 25 Years Old. Sensational nose.
**Nose:** Fiendishly spiced, exceedingly complex. Excellent Oloroso presence, much more intense than the standard 18 or 25 Years Old. Distinct orange peel; zesty.
**Palate:** A prickly malt, with the sherry taking the lazy route, allowing some lovely peaty notes through.
**Finish:** Dry, too dry. Some deep roasted Columbian coffee tries to rescue it, but a little disappointing.

### THE MACALLAN 30 YEARS OLD, FINE OAK
Single Malt - Speyside

9 **Gavin: I was wrong! This is infinitely better.**
**Nose:** Keeps to itself initially, then fudge and candyfloss notes prevail, with fresh floor polish.
**Palate:** Austere, quite dry for an instant, then lots of life bursts though. Bubble gum, lemon, brittle toffee.
**Finish:** Lengthy and sophisticated. Less bourbon influence and fewer negative wood factors here.

8¼ **Dave: Great nose, firm palate. Wood dominating a little.**
**Nose:** A 'chewy', spicy nose with some cocoa, orchard fruits and a hint of flowers (lily), crème brûlée and dried leaves.
**Palate:** A sweet start, then caramel, but the tannins and grippy oak. The driest of the range. Some peat, earth.
**Finish:** Softens for a second and gets a spark of juicy youth pop out.

### THE MACALLAN 50 YEARS OLD, MILLENNIUM DECANTER
Single Malt - Speyside

8¾ **Michael: This is on the woody side. A little too woody for me in its late astringency, but it is always a privilege to taste such old whiskies.**
**Nose:** Smoky. Toasting almonds. Crème brûlée.
**Palate:** Firm, smoky, oaky, slightly astringent.
**Finish:** Smokiness. Sweetness. Hot peppermints.

9¾ **David: A classic example of well-aged Spanish.**
**Nose:** Rich phenolic nose with oranges, lemons.
**Palate:** Smoky phenols, sherry with spices.
**Finish:** Richly phenolic with classic Macallan resinous spice and sherry.

### THE MACALLAN 8 YEARS OLD, FINE OAK
Single Malt - Speyside

7¾ **Gavin: I'm not a fan of younger Macallans, but this is a drinkable, if somewhat undemanding, 8 Years Old.**
**Nose:** Initially yeasty, then wine gum. Fresh sawdust. More floral when reduced.
**Palate:** Dry, quite tight and one-dimensional. Some cereal notes.
**Finish:** Comparitively short. Raisins linger.

7¾ **Dave: Fresh and young, but balanced with good feel. Have it long.**
**Nose:** Young, clean and lovely. Slightly sappy with touches of balsa wood, cereal (malt bins/sugar puffs), vanilla white chocolate and turned earth.
**Palate:** Crisp but with a super-sweet and soft mid-palate. Fizzy and young.
**Finish:** Quite hot, peppery and short. Malty.

### THE MACALLAN EASTER ELCHIES SEASONAL CASK SELECTION SUMMER 2007 60.2%
Single Malt - Speyside

7¼ **Dave: All about power, show and bravado and misses out on elegance depth and nuance. Some will love it.**
**Nose:** High alcohol. Robust. Orange, dried fruits, Dundee cake. Big, resinous with lacquer-like notes. Some sulphur.
**Palate:** Very aggressive, even brutal, when neat. Water brings out a scented quality, glacé cherries, tobacco. Much better with water.
**Finish:** Tight. Resin.

7½ **Martine: There is more on the nose than on the palate. Fairly young maybe?**
**Nose:** Very balsamic. Eucalyptus, cedar. Praline, caramelised pecan nuts. Overcooked plum pudding. In the back, a meaty note like Oxo cubes. Séville orange peel. The alcohol is well mastered.
**Palate:** Surprisingly sweet. Cooked plums, orange marmalade. A hint of liquorice.
**Finish:** Dry, lingering oak but still gentle. A rubbery echo.

### THE MACALLAN ELEGANCIA 40%
Single Malt - Speyside

8 **Michael: Macallan Lite? Because I dislike the idea, I don't want to like the whisky, but it is a pleasant, easily drinkable dram.**
**Nose:** Crisp. Spicy. Ginger ice cream.
**Palate:** Restrained start. Gentle flavour development. Lean. Lightly creamy. A suggestion of malted milk. Some concentrated sweetness.
**Finish:** Now the ice cream is rum and raisin.

7¾ **Dave: A (deliberately) lighter style of Macallan. Wonder how the purists will take it?**
**Nose:** Light, spicy and quite citric. Malt, orange peel, almond, caramelised peach and baked apple.
**Palate:** Soft and light with an attractive juiciness from those fruits. Delicate and well balanced.
**Finish:** A little rapid.

### THE MACALLAN EXCEPTIONAL CASK IV 57.4%
Single Malt - Speyside

8¾ **Michael: Not so much a winter whisky as a bear-hug. Or do the Grampians have a Mac Yeti?**
**Nose:** Sooty. Smoky. Burnt. Crème brûlée. Sweetish. Very malty.
**Palate:** Toffeeish, but in an interplay of soft sweetness and harder, smokier, more burnt flavours. Sticky toffee pudding meets hard treacle toffee.
**Finish:** Buttery. Spicy. Hot rum butter.

9 **Dave: A great example of European oak and Macallan in harmony. Exceptional indeed.**
**Nose:** Concentrated, complex, resin, seville orange, prune, varnish, roasted nuts. Almost Armagnac-like: earthy weight, savoury density.
**Palate:** Powerful, rich, mouth-coating; dark fruit, cocoa. Almost meaty. Great balance. Lighter tannins than you'd think.
**Finish:** Long, sweet and soft.

### THE MACALLAN EXCEPTIONAL SINGLE CASK 59.3%
Single Malt - Speyside

9 **Michael: I like oak, but this was a bit too much for me.**
**Nose:** Mint chocolate. Sherry. Slightly vinous. Oak.
**Palate:** Firm, smooth. Thick. Demerara sugar. Crispy malt. Chocolate wafers. Toffee. Forest berries. Oak. Some earthy notes.
**Finish:** Rummy. Warming.

7½ **Dave: Delicate, light and simple.**
**Nose:** Delicate. Nuts, sultana, honey. Hint of linoleum and oily rag.
**Palate:** Gently pleasant. A chewy mid-palate, with a little liquorice bitterness.
**Finish:** Banana, toffee. Short.

### THE MACALLAN FIFTIES 40%
Single Malt - Speyside

9¼ **Michael: Closest to The Macallan of today, appropriately enough.**
**Nose:** Sherried. Raisiny. Toasted nuts.
**Palate:** Rich. Smooth. Toffeeish. Port-like.
**Finish:** Spicy. Liquorice. Mint, late warming.

8½ **Dave: Dry Oloroso.**
**Nose:** Sweetest of the range and the most 'classically' Macallan: toffee (Rolos), crème brûlée, chestnut honey, spice, rubber. Figgy and resinous.
**Palate:** Rich slippery texture that coats the mouth. Rich and ripe with spikes of dry spices (nutmeg/cinnamon).
**Finish:** Good length sulphur, oil/resin, chocolate and bitter orange.

### THE MACALLAN FINE OAK 'WHISKY MAKER'S SELECTION' 42.8%
Single Malt - Speyside

7½ **Dave: Fine, not a lot of oak.**
**Nose:** Malty: combine harvester, green malt, grilled nuts, wholemeal flour. In time some raisin bread, earthy. Like a handful of barley with the soil attached.
**Palate:** As nose but with added clootie dumpling dried fruit notes. Hazelnut spread on wholemeal toast. Gingery.
**Finish:** Baked apple. Hot.

7 **Arthur: Just didn't hang together for me.**
**Nose:** A fruity breadiness, like banana bread or a Chelsea bun. Toffee, orange juice, ginger and parma violets. A herbaceous element too, along with a compost-like whiff of vegetable peelings.
**Palate:** A creamy sweetness, with peach slices and chocolate coated raisins. Ginger biscuits.
**Finish:** Drying, sulphurous, in an over-bearing way.

# Scotch Macallan - Macduff

## THE MACALLAN FORTIES 40%
Single Malt - Speyside

**9¼ Michael: A similar style to 30s but less delicate and more robust.**
**Nose:** Light. Fragrant. Herbal. Grassy. Some smokiness.
**Palate:** Lively. Leafy. Flowery. Dry.
**Finish:** More peat. Late lemongrass and mustard. Warming. Hot.

**8½ Dave: Manzanilla pasada. The pre-lunch member.**
**Nose:** More oak on show. Slightly austere and grassy (dry bracken). Some sulphur.
**Palate:** Light, dry, quite friable but still with that oily maltiness.
**Finish:** Medium length. Fresh.

## THE MACALLAN REPLICA 1874
Single Malt - Speyside

**9½ Michael: A deft re-creation. This version is notably estery.**
**Nose:** Smokier than I remember. Quick, soft, with a hit of smoke – then juicy wood.
**Palate:** Citrus. Toffee. Nutty. Toasty. Smoky.
**Finish:** Mesquite.

**9 David: We attempted to recreate the whisky's character launching it in 1996 at £65 per bottle.**
**Nose:** Fresh citrus. Hints of nuttiness and wood.
**Palate:** Richly citric with oranges easy to recognise.
**Finish:** Warming citrus with drying wood. Its freshness dances on the tongue.

## THE MACALLAN REPLICA 1876 40.6%
Single Malt - Speyside

**9¼ Michael: Similar to the 1841, but not quite as sophisticated.**
**Nose:** Very spicy and dusty. Honeyed.
**Palate:** Firm. Intense sweetness at first. Then perfumy. Lemony. Anis. A hint of quinine dryness.
**Finish:** A touch of oakiness.

**6¼ Dave: A bit young and one-dimensional. Quite disappointing.**
**Nose:** Light and malty with light pear and an earthy note. Hay-like, wholemeal flour, yeasty, slightly immature (greengage).
**Palate:** A softer slightly oilier texture than the nose suggests. Light and cereal-driven. No breadth or complexity.
**Finish:** Crisp and fairly short.

## THE MACALLAN REPLICA, 1841 41.7%
Single Malt - Speyside

**9½ Michael: Delicious whisky, of true sophistication and style. Tasted blindfold, it seems a perfect whisky for today, not an evocation of the past. I would re-package it as 2041.**
**Nose:** Incongruously, very fresh. Fudge with vanilla essence and pistachio nuts.
**Palate:** Silky. Fresh, appetising. Sweet but not cloying. Light, fresh, delicate, notes of orange-blossom honey.
**Finish:** Very gentle acidity gives balancing dryness.

**7¾ Dave: Controlled. A very drinkable young Macallan.**
**Nose:** Light to medium-bodied. Attractive earthy notes with some smoke, a hint of bashed neeps. Gentle, subtle and malty.
**Palate:** Soft and rounded, with butterscotch, light pepperiness, then the earthy, lightly smoky character reappears. Well balanced.
**Finish:** Light, short, earthy.

## THE MACALLAN REPLICA, 1861 42.7%
Single Malt - Speyside

**9 Michael: Quite an achievement. Like the previous 'replica' edition, this is more delicate than the robustly sherried Macallans of today.**
**Nose:** Potpourri. Spice cupboard. Flapjack. Syrup. Rosewater. Custard.
**Palate:** Slippery-smooth. Very sweet. Perfumy. Anis. Restrained fruitiness. Candied orange peel. Delicious sherry character. Great depth of flavour.
**Finish:** Toasty dryness. Long, soothing.

**8½ Dave: Like the touch of peat-when's that batch getting bottled?**
**Nose:** Citric yet soft and juicy: zabaglione, cereal (Weetabix), orange (Seville), heather blossom, smoke.

---

**Palate:** Perfumed and juicily soft with some sweetness. Dried apricot, orange peel, clove-like notes, walnut. Light peat. Dries as you hold it in the mouth. Good weight.
**Finish:** Sultana cake, coriander powder, hint of smoke.

## THE MACALLAN SPECIAL RESERVE
Single Malt - Speyside

**9¼ Michael: This is true of several of the older Macallans, suggesting that the sherry casks had contained styles other than dry Oloroso.**
**Nose:** Immediate clean, dry, peat smoke.
**Palate:** Big, firm. Peaty, grassy, lively.
**Finish:** Sweet, gingery. Treacly. Astonishingly long.

**9½ David: Classic example of The Macallan.**
**Nose:** Clove spice, cinnamon, citrus orange, some dried fruits.
**Palate:** Powerful rich clove spice with dried fruit.
**Finish:** Viscous and rich in the mouth it has a long and lingering spicy clove finish.

## THE MACALLAN THIRTIES 40%
Single Malt - Speyside

**9½ Michael: With its floweriness and a hint of peat, this seems to me a classic old-style Speysider.**
**Nose:** Seville orange. Fresh leather. Lemongrass. Peat.
**Palate:** Smooth, sweet. The fruitiest and most estery of the set.
**Finish:** Sweet grass. Juicy.

**8¾ Dave: The dry amontillado.**
**Nose:** Finer nose, crisp with toasted almonds and a leaf mulch/earthy richness. Lightly peaty but in time a crème anglaise note mellows things slightly.
**Palate:** Firm and malty but that ripe apricot fleshiness fills out the mid-palate.
**Finish:** Chewy yet dry.

## THE MACALLAN TWENTIES 40%
Single Malt - Speyside

**9¼ Michael: Despite a relatively full colour, suggesting plenty of sherry, the Macallan flavours shine through. The driest of these bottlings.**
**Nose:** Syrupy. Flowering currant. Apricot. Lemon. Sweet and dry. Spicy.
**Palate:** Firm but creamy. Honeyed.
**Finish:** Sweet grass. Some peatiness and late sappy oak.

**8¼ Dave: The palo cortado of the range.**
**Nose:** Juicy: madeira cake, white peach, currant, cocoa, brazil nut – all with a turfy/smoky, pipe tobacco/resin/pitch undertow.
**Palate:** Medium dry yet with a pleasant oiliness.
**Finish:** Good length with hints of citrus, plump sultanas and smoke.

## THE MACALLAN, 28 YEARS OLD, OLD & RARE PLATINUM 48.2%
Single Malt - Speyside

**7¾ Dave: Have this without water. Hinting at complexity.**
**Nose:** Mature. Ever so slightly musty. Cognac-like nuttiness, some saddle soap, still a malty edge (draff).
**Palate:** Expands well in the mouth with light grip on the sides and almost blackcurrant sweetness in the middle before a bonfire smoke emerges. Dusty and slightly nutty.
**Finish:** Fresh and malty.

**8¼ Arthur: A quality spirit standing up to a long maturation.**
**Nose:** Crispy basil, nectarines, those foamy banana sweets, vanilla cream. Damp grass. Smoke from a fire made with damp logs. Lemon juice, peaches and Madeira cake.
**Palate:** More peaches and cream, toast and a wisp of woodsmoke.
**Finish:** Woody bitterness, like chewing a pencil.

## MACDUFF 14 YEARS OLD, HARRIS WHISKY 58.7%
Single Malt - Speyside

**7 Dave: No great complexity and a little green.**
**Nose:** Sugary sweet and delicate. Some crystallised fruits, lemon with cut flower, quince, but also a sharp note.
**Palate:** Light, but hot with a touch of spice. Lilac.
**Finish:** Flour and flowers.

**7¼ Arthur: A strange, floaty dram suited to summer drinking.**

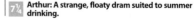

**Nose:** Pear and lemon peel. Dough, damp cloths and white pepper. Tinned pears.
**Palate:** Pear and smoked meats, but it seems to exist at the top of the mouth, without any malty undercarriage.
**Finish:** Chalky.

## MACLEODS 8 YEARS OLD HIGHLAND SINGLE MALT 40%
Single Malt - Highland

**7¾** **Michael: Bold flavours. "Take me as I am, " it seems to say. I will. Let's live dangerously.**
**Nose:** Sesame toast. Seaweed. Japanese breakfast.
**Palate:** Gritty. Grainy, nutty, salty.
**Finish:** Pepper. Salt. Iron. Minerally.

**7** **Dave: Pleasant enough. Undemanding.**
**Nose:** Farmyard. Wet grass, fresh mushroom. Wisp of woodsmoke. Becomes oakier (and maltier) with water.
**Palate:** Firm structure. Nut bowl. Malty.
**Finish:** Dry. Melting chocolate.

## MACLEODS 8 YEARS OLD LOWLAND 40%
Single Malt - Lowland

**7¾** **Arthur: A pleasing balance of spirit and wood, but lacked complexity. Young spirit in active oak?**
**Nose:** A pencil case: wood shavings, lead and crayons. Some orange and biscuity character. With water an intriguing aromatic herbal note – perhaps kaffir lime leaves?
**Palate:** Mouthfilling, fruity, and a little rubbery.
**Finish:** Lightly bitter and drying.

**7** **Dave: This just doesn't have the guts to deliver. A wee, coo'rin, timrous beastie.**
**Nose:** Round and crisp. Toasty oak, wood shavings, sacking, raffia. Slightly oily as is that a hint of smoke? Baked apple/pie crust, then green pear (immaturity).
**Palate:** Slightly thin and a bit flabby. Fern, then cream.
**Finish:** Zesty.

## MANNOCHMORE 12 YEARS OLD 43%
Single Malt - Speyside

**8¼** **Martine: Rich, bonnie and complex. Not showing off, just beaming.**
**Nose:** Very delicate and fragrant. Wild rose, honeysuckle. Hint of mint. Marshmallow. Earth and grass after summer rain. A spring walk in the country.
**Palate:** Appetising, rich, fresh. Smooth to begin with. Blossoms with an array of spices. Candied ginger. Mint, liquorice. Vanilla cookies.
**Finish:** Satisfying, lingering and luscious. Ends on an almond milk note.

**7½** **Dave: A lovely sweet, frothy, summery dram.**
**Nose:** Sweet, light and perfumed: dried flowers, lemon, soft fruits, hazelnut and syrup. Reminiscent somehow of crunchy nut cornflakes.
**Palate:** Still floral and attractive. There's a hint of lemon meringue pie in the middle, and all very light, sweet and fragrant.
**Finish:** A little short, but you don't want this style of malt to last forever.

## MATISSE 12 YEARS OLD 40%
Blended - Scotland

**7½** **Martine: Quite a complex blend but it takes time to deliver. Well-balanced. Again it would have displayed more at a higher strength.**
**Nose:** A bit restrained at the start. Floral. Lilac. Creamy. Grand Marnier sauce. Pine needles. Touch of smoke.
**Palate:** Smooth. Fruity. Exotic fruit salad. Pineapple, banana, guava.
**Finish:** Lasting. Nutty. Orange peel. Spicy.

**7¾** **Dave: Well made and worth trying.**
**Nose:** Exotic and soft. Milk chocolate, tight spice. Cherry, nutmeg, black banana. Concentrated, overripe/bruised fruits. Has good balance.
**Palate:** Very soft start, then tingling sweet spices and light soft fruits: pear, coconut and a tickle of smoke. Balanced.
**Finish:** Short, fresh. Oaky grip.

## MATISSE 12 YEARS OLD 40%
Blended - Scotland

**7¾** **Michael: Enjoyable. More-ish. Perfect for lacunae in a busy schedule. Those leather sofa moments in hotel lobbies. Sip it while munching cocktail snacks.**
**Nose:** Scenty.
**Palate:** Starts clean and refreshing. Slowly develops marshmallow maltiness, becoming nutty and sweet, with a touch of roasted nuts.
**Finish:** Sugared almonds.

**7½** **Dave: Decent balance. A light session dram.**
**Nose:** Supple. Vanilla and lemon with sweet barley sugar/honeycomb. A touch of green plum and in time a nutty, wheaty, cereal. Lawnmower box.
**Palate:** Light syrupy feel with toasty coconut, some citrus, butterscotch and chocolate-coated Brazil.
**Finish:** Quite short fresh.

## MILLBURN 1969 35 YEARS OLD, RARE MALTS 51.2%
Single Malt - Highland

**WHISKY** **Magazine** **Recommended**

**8¼** **Dave: The mental picture is of an old library filled with leather bound volumes and someone smoking a pipe in the distance.**
**Nose:** Broad, mature, with light turfy smoke and a sweet crispness like cheesecake base. Hint of sourdough, grass, autumn leaves, dry oak.
**Palate:** Very upfront despite obvious age. Another which is slow to open once it sinks onto the tongue: caramelised black fruit, toffee, brazil nut.
**Finish:** Surprisingly fresh and almost zesty.

**8½** **Arthur: Enjoyable and distinctive. Like an eccentric old aunt.**
**Nose:** Lime, underripe mangos and slight sour bready note, like brioche. Spritzy and slightly grassier with water. With more time there are distinct chocolate limes and marzipan.
**Palate:** Lime marmalade on brown toast. Viscous, then dries out with a little woodiness.
**Finish:** Complex citrus fruits and woodiness. Candied lemons.

## MILLBURN 1975, 25 YEARS OLD, RARE MALTS 61.9%
Single Malt - Highland

**7½** **Michael: A grizzled old character, but gains points for resilience.**
**Nose:** Vegetal. Peppery. Aromatic.
**Palate:** Dry, firm, chewiness. Lots of flavour development. Sooty. Smoky. Oaky. Sappy. Orange pith and zest.
**Finish:** Surprisingly lively, spicy. Faintly medicinal.

**8** **Dave: Very well balanced.**
**Nose:** Full: clootie dumpling mix, chocolate, toffee then nut, coal/smoke.
**Palate:** Medium rich. The smoke clings to everything: soft cakey fruit and apple and as it dries walnut bread.
**Finish:** Smoky.

## MILLBURN 1983, SIGNATORY 46%
Single Malt - Highland

**7½** **Michael: Confusing aroma, but otherwise the most enjoyable Millburn I have tasted.**
**Nose:** Perfumy. A suggestion of phenol. Somewhere between mothballs and tar-like peat.
**Palate:** Surprisingly rich. Sweetish. Emphatic sugared almonds. Hazelnuts.
**Finish:** Pistachios this time? Nutty dryness rounds out the palate. Very soothing and warming.

**7½** **Dave: Nice but could do with more in the middle.**
**Nose:** Intense and malty, mixing smoke, cake mix and coconut. Water dries it: biscuity, toasted wood, soot.
**Palate:** Surprisingly sweet to start. Dry but slightly woolly texture. Biscuity.
**Finish:** Smoke, hay, dry.

### MILLBURN 31 YEARS OLD, CADENHEAD'S 52.3%
Single Malt - Highland

**7¼ Martine:** Not a great aromatic display. A cardboardy touch on the palate. Water soothes alcohol a little while underlining the unidimensional aniseed/minty profile.
**Nose:** Herbal, grassy. Green fruit. Granny Smith. Lemon sherbet. Refreshing.
**Palate:** Sweet aniseed infusion. Touch of lime tea and cardboard.
**Finish:** Warm, tangy.

**9½ Michael:** Unusual and beautiful wine-like nose is backed up by solid malt character-rich palate.
**Nose:** Instant, rich, sweet Sauterne-like notes. Honey and honey dew melon. Strawberries?
**Palate:** Oily. Cereals. Some smoke, perhaps. Chocolate chip? Orange zest.
**Finish:** Full and firm. Beautifully structured (toasted?) graininess gives way to faint, aromatic, astringency. Sandalwood? Tobacco?

### MILLBURN 34 YEARS OLD, OLD & RARE PLATINUM 50.9%
Single Malt - Highland

**8¼ Michael:** Luxurious. An adult taste.
**Nose:** Malty sweetness. Icing sugar. Candied orange peel.
**Palate:** Lightly oily. Halva. Turkish delight in a cedarwood box.
**Finish:** Balancing bitter spiciness. Nutmeg. Ginger.

**7¼ Dave:** Has the austerity of age but not the sweetness to balance.
**Nose:** Mature. Rich tea biscuit, toasted oak, bung cloth, sawdust. Some smoke moving into wood ash. Dry oak.
**Palate:** Sweet start with a good feel. Fudge like. Good balance, but disappointing with water.
**Finish:** Short. Dry.

### MILTONDUFF 1968, GORDON & MACPHAIL 40%
Single Malt - Speyside

**7¾ Michael:** Remarkably scenty. Very clean indeed. Delicate for my tastes but if you like an elegant malt.....
**Nose:** A suggestion of sherry. Buttercup-like. Very faint peat.
**Palate:** Fresh, flowers, oily, nutty. A hint of vanilla lightly clean maltiness.
**Finish:** Fragrant. Just a hint of smoke.

**7¾ Jim:** An easy-going and well preserved oldie with reasonable complexity.
**Nose:** Crushed leaves and apricot: an unusual, lively combination but dulled by some vanilla.
**Palate:** Lively on the palate with an intensely sweet maltiness pitted against some starker, spicier oaky notes. First-rate balance.
**Finish:** The bitter-sweet style plays out a long finale with some hints of java coffee creeping in.

### MILTONDUFF 1993, GORDON & MACPHAIL 61.8%
Single Malt - Speyside

**7¾ Michael:** Lusty, voluptuous. Finishes with a bang.
**Nose:** Treacle toffee.
**Palate:** Smooth, marshmallow, middle. Dairy toffee. Scottish tablet.
**Finish:** After all that comfort confectionery, a late, loud, explosion.

**8 Dave:** Has a punchy refreshing quality. Worth a look.
**Nose:** Greenish tinge. A little musty to start, bleated fruit with plenty of cask influence (bung cloth) alongside marzipan and green plum. Intense. Water brings out a floral perfume.
**Palate:** Sweeter than the nose and a slight vegetal quality reminiscent of agave. Piercing.
**Finish:** Fairly hot.

### MONKEY SHOULDER BATCH 27 40%
Blended Malt - Scotland

**7½ Martine:** An elegant dram, dominated by orange and spices. For a Christmas treat? Water is not needed.
**Nose:** Elegant, refined. Orange crème brûlée. Chocolate slowly shines through. Beeswax.
**Palate:** Silky, very sensuously coating the mouth. Slightly clinging to the palate. Candied orange. Marmalade. Cloves and cinnamon. Very rich.
**Finish:** Drier, Seville oranges, a touch of liquorice.

**8¼ Dave:** Exuberant, sweet and extremely well balanced. A great introduction to whisky.
**Nose:** Ripe, very sweet and long. Toasted/polished oak, light resin notes, nutmeg.
**Palate:** Still sweet: a soft start, vanilla custard, a hint of dried fruit, baked banana, cinnamon, vanilla. Honeyed centre. Toasted, indeed roasted, wood gives much needed grip.
**Finish:** Membrillo.

### MORTLACH 10 YEARS OLD, COOPER'S CHOICE 43%
Single Malt - Speyside

**8½ Michael:** A good bottling of this lovely malt. Mortlach has such complexity that I find new aromas and flavours every time I raise the glass.
**Nose:** Fruity. Lemon curd. Sweet limes. Grassy notes. Fragrant smokiness emerges.
**Palate:** Smooth. Light toastiness. Cookie-like maltiness. Restrained sweetness. Nectar-like.
**Finish:** Delicate balance of firm, rounded dryness. Clean, appetising smokiness. Heathery.

**8¼ Jim:** A superb single cask boasting outstanding complexity. Marked down only by a slightly blemished nose.
**Nose:** Vaguely sulphury but enough sweet maltiness and delicate smoke to make for a winning aroma.
**Palate:** Highly spiced and warming, then a rich vein of sweet sherry and coffee makes for a superb middle.
**Finish:** Loads of grapey notes with firm oaky depth. Fantastic bittersweet balance.

### MORTLACH 10 YEARS OLD, PORT FINISH, DUN BHEAGAN 55%
Single Malt - Speyside

**7½ Michael:** Mortlach is usually a supple, muscular malt. At ten years, this already seems a trifle tired.
**Nose:** Sweet nuttiness. Almonds. Fresh figs.
**Palate:** Slow start. Heavy footed. Black treacle.
**Finish:** Crisp. Ginger biscuits.

**7¾ Dave:** The Port gives a sweetness you don't usually encounter in Mortlach. This has balance.
**Nose:** Some sweetness. A BIG nose: brambles and summer fruits, loganberry, roast chestnut, chocolate, treacle toffee, Lea and Perrins, smoke.
**Palate:** Rich with good depth of flavour. That treacle toffee again alongside roasted nuts. Stewed tea.
**Finish:** Hedgerow fruits.

### MORTLACH 12 YEARS OLD, THE WEE DRAM 43%
Single Malt - Speyside

**7¾ Michael:** The first bottling from The Wee Dram. A promising debut.
**Nose:** Gently spicy.
**Palate:** Sweet. Seems rather simple at first, but gently reveals a complex of spicy flavours.
**Finish:** Big, sweet, barley-sugar rush.

**8¾ Dave:** Great balance, the distillery character not dominated by the cask. Slightly more restrained than the Signatory example.
**Nose:** Big and grumbly, hitting a balance between roasted notes, meat, walnut and butter, heather and lilac.
**Palate:** Rich, with good weight. Chestnut, toffee, marmite. Dries towards the finish.
**Finish:** Dry and nutty.

### MORTLACH 15 YEARS OLD, DEWAR RATTRAY 55.44%
Single Malt - Speyside

**7¼ Dave:** The lack of interaction between oak and spirit makes this hard to get excited about.
**Nose:** Closed and quite distant aromas: lemon barley water, bitter lemon, light oak, alcohol. Water doesn't improve it but does reveal some sulphury notes akin to a gym changing room.
**Palate:** Showing more weight. Candied fruits. Becomes tart and acidic after a sweet start. Fizzy.
**Finish:** Light malt, sherbert.

**7¾ Arthur:** Balanced, attractive and a rightdown-the-middle Speysider. An anytime dram.
**Nose:** Poached pears, melon and lychees, along with vanilla. Attractive. With water there is more floral character, like standing in a florists trying to choose what to get her.

**Palate:** Lightly toffeeish, with melon and Jelly Babies.
**Finish:** Brown bread maltiness.

## MORTLACH 16 YEARS OLD 43%
Single Malt - Speyside

**8¼ Michael: A great malt that is enigmatic and sometimes seems reclusive.**
**Nose:** Flowery. A suggestion of peppermint. Black chocolate? Mint crisp?
**Palate:** Memorable for its challenging complexity and subtlety. Flavours beautifully combined. A touch of sherry. Dances on the tongue.
**Finish:** Smooth, dry smokiness. Very long.

**7¾ Dave: Tell me this and Knockando share similar characteristics. A single Speyside style? I think not.**
**Nose:** Huge, meaty (Bovril, roasting tin, oxtail soup) treacle, singed, hint of smoke. Massive concentration.
**Palate:** Robust and powerful with an almost earthy power. A massive grumbly malt which might not have the complexity of others in its weight division but which delivers a mighty punch.
**Finish:** Long.

## MORTLACH 1938, 60 YEARS OLD, GORDON & MAC-PHAIL 40%
Single Malt - Speyside

**8¾ Michael: A great age, but it has matured beautifully.**
**Nose:** Fragrant. Lightly smoky. Oaky. Slightly musty.
**Palate:** Soft for its age. Fresh, fruit. Some sweetness in the middle. Mint creams. Oaky woodiness.
**Finish:** Kirschwasser, Cherry brandy. Almondy.

**8¾ Martine: A rich, luscious, venerable malt although time and sherry have silenced the distillery character. A real piece of history. No water, thanks!**
**Nose:** Sherry with leather and smoke. Powerful, complex, resiny. Polished old furniture. Dried fruit, cider and cinnamon slowly emerge. Custardy notes.
**Palate:** Slight apple sourness with burnt wood and dark chocolate. Candied chestnuts.
**Finish:** Lingering but dry and slightly bitter.

## MORTLACH 1951, GORDON & MACPHAIL 42%
Single Malt - Speyside

**8 Michael: After dinner. Or with a re-run of Inspector Morse.**
**Nose:** Aromas as dark as the colour. Prunes in Armagnac.
**Palate:** Soft. Fruity. Spicy. Cinnamon.
**Finish:** Dusty. Venerable.

**5 Dave: For all the interest on the nose this is not a great drinking experience.**
**Nose:** Big, intense, 'sherried'. Black cherry, raisin, wet leather, blackstrap, resinous, rancio. Dark and funky with some sweet notes. Promises a lot...
**Palate:** ...then the tannins clamp onto your tongue like a pack of terriers.
**Finish:** Bitter (cubed).

## MORTLACH 1980, 17 YEARS OLD, CASK STRENGTH 63.1%
Single Malt - Speyside

**9 Michael: A big, rich interpretation; an outstanding digestif.**
**Nose:** Distinct peat character; stalky. Lime skins.
**Palate:** Flowery: buttercups. Syrupy, with rich sherry notes. Very big in the middle, with lots of flavour development. Soft mint humbugs.
**Finish:** More mint, becoming drier.

**6½ Jim: Not very well balanced.**
**Nose:** A sulphury sherry note. Alas, still present when reduced.
**Palate:** Malt and fruit richness, dry oakiness. The off-notes vanish leaving a big maltiness.
**Finish:** Smoky, slightly peaty and chocolatey.

## MORTLACH 1980, GORDON & MACPHAIL 63.8%
Single Malt - Speyside

**8½ Michael: A lovely digestif whisky.**
**Nose:** Sherry. Ripe red fruit. Smoke.
**Palate:** Winey. Body is sweetish and creamy. Nougat. Port-like.
**Finish:** Huge fruit. Cherry brandy.

**7 Martine: The unusually high strength of this 23 Years Old malt makes it taste younger. Water tames the spirit but heightens woodiness. Lacks delicacy.**
**Nose:** Tangy, spirity. Creamy when aerated. Dates, figs. Marzipan. Black pepper.
**Palate:** Biting, fizzy mouthfeel. A lot of toffee and dark chocolate.
**Finish:** Dry, liquoriced and peppery. Turns quite bitter. Wood is blatantly overpowering.

## MORTLACH 1988, CASK STRENGTH, WHISKY GALORE 57.9%
Single Malt - Speyside

**8 Dave: Good weight of spirit, but needs more from the cask to make it great.**
**Nose:** Dried fruits, little musty, tinned prune, damp earth, hint of meat stock. The lurking sweetness is brought out by water.
**Palate:** Quite concentrated, orange Spangles, nougat. A slight fizzy quality which leads into (pink) marshmallow. Shows finesse and good balance.
**Finish:** Long, clean hint of smoke.

**7½ Arthur: Speyside style.**
**Nose:** Tinned pears, parma ham, aniseed, lemon balm, grass and a little earthiness. Lime juice.
**Palate:** Lemon sorbet, biscuits and a sweet meatiness.
**Finish:** A light toffeeness.

## MORTLACH 1989 SPIRIT SAFE & CASK SELECTION, CELTIQUE CONNEXION 43%
Single Malt - Speyside

**6¾ Michael: Lacks contribution from wood. Lacks complexity.**
**Nose:** Light, fresh. Dessert apples. Hint of smoke.
**Palate:** Almost as light as the colour (eau de nil). Flowery. Apple blossom. Honey.
**Finish:** Fresh pears.

**7 Dave: A simple, drinkable but average glass.**
**Nose:** Light. Burnt grass, apple, raw chestnut, dry forests, earth. Young? Retreats in time.
**Palate:** Very light and quite sweet. Lacking in complexity.
**Finish:** Short, clean.

## MORTLACH 1989 UNCHILLFILTERED, SIGNATORY 46%
Single Malt - Speyside

**8½ Michael: The most complex and structured of the Mortlachs in this tasting.**
**Nose:** Freshly baked bread, straight out of the oven. That Mortlach aroma gets me every time.
**Palate:** Very nutty. Barley sugar. Spicy complexity.
**Finish:** A hint of passion fruit. Big, expressive and long.

**8¾ Dave: As robust a Mortlach as you could wish for.**
**Nose:** Powerful. Meaty: roasting tin, Bovril, roasted chestnut, black butter, treacle toffee, struck match. With water: charred, rich and smoky-campfire/burnt rope.
**Palate:** Thick and powerful. Meaty again: water makes it sweeter, bringing out dried fruits over the smoky dry notes of char and roasted coffee.
**Finish:** Campfire ashes.

## MORTLACH 1989, BLACKADDER 60.5%
Single Malt - Speyside

**8 Michael: Enjoyable, with an appropriate touch of earthy rawness, but not as statuesque as this elegant whisky can be.**
**Nose:** Leafy. Green. Slightly spirity.
**Palate:** Nutty. Chewy. Mint humbugs.
**Finish:** Minty. Fragrant. Smoky oaky.

**8½ Dave: Considerably less concentrated than other Mortlachs on the market.**
**Nose:** Typical Mortlach meatiness with soft ripe banana, bourbon creams, burnt toffee and smoke. In time a sulphury note and some mustiness.
**Palate:** Starts lightly honeyed then deepens into those roasting tin/meat reduction flavours with a peaty drive. Wood is slightly abrasive.
**Finish:** Hot, chewy then smoke.

## MORTLACH 1990 16 YEARS OLD, SHERRY CASK, COOPER'S CHOICE 46%
Single Malt - Speyside

**WHISKY** *Magazine* Recommended

**8** Dave: Yup, it's Mortlach alright. Every bit as good as the OB.
**Nose:** Mortlach? Silky sweet with raisin, malt extract, hard treacle toffee and prunes in syrup. With water a burnt, nutty, roasted character. Rich.
**Palate:** Blackstrap molasses and roasted meat. Manages to be sweet and grumbling at the same time.
**Finish:** Long, slightly dry and tannic but there's enough richness to balance.

**8¼** Arthur: An afterdinner tongue-lasher.
**Nose:** A gruff Christmassy nose with an enticing mix of fruit and spice. Fig rolls, a clove-studded orange, stewed plums and cloudy apple juice. Treacle toffee. With time a more meaty, herbaceous character barges in.
**Palate:** Sulphury with marmalade on brown toast.
**Finish:** The mouth-piece of a snorkelling mask.

## MORTLACH 1990, LOMBARD 50%
Single Malt - Speyside

**6½** Michael: Extraordinarily pale colour. The floweriness was perhaps a hint at Mortlach but, if I were served this out of context, would I recognise it as whisky? I might guess at aquavit rather than usquebaugh.
**Nose:** Flowery, vegetal, piney.
**Palate:** Green flavours. Refreshing. Tingly.
**Finish:** Tingly. Warming.

**6** Dave: Poor.
**Nose:** There's some alcohol, but the whisky's gone missing.
**Palate:** Sweet and some heat from alcohol. If you look hard enough there's some meaty notes.
**Finish:** Quick.

## MORTLACH 1992 12 YEARS OLD, SHERRY FINISH, DOUGLAS LAING 50%
Single Malt - Speyside

**7¾** Michael: Urbane. Austere.
**Nose:** Fresh, flowery, perfumy.
**Palate:** Slippery smooth. Nutty. Passion fruit. Steely.
**Finish:** Dry. Leafy bitterness. A hint of peat.

**7** Dave: Little interaction going on here.
**Nose:** High impact. Alcoholic without water. Firm, young and estery. Sulphur, lemon, banana.
**Palate:** Hot and sweet without water, but very light with it. Lacks weight and substance.
**Finish:** Light.

## MOSSTOWIE 1975 30 YEARS OLD, RAREST OF THE RARE 48.1%
Single Malt - Speyside

**7½** Martine: Tempting nose, the palate is somewhat tougher. A good example of classic bourbon maturation. Pleasant.
**Nose:** Fragrant. Creamy. Apricot flan. Vanilla syrup. Caramelised almonds. Gets sweeter and sweeter. Warm bakewell tart.
**Palate:** Rich and smooth. Clinging on the palate. Rich fruit (stewed apples seared in butter). Sylvestry flavours. Liquorice toffee. Fennel.
**Finish:** Dry with a slight astringency.

**7½** Michael: A difficult whisky to pin down. A tricky nose shouldn't distract from a pleasant enough palate.
**Nose:** Tricky. Not unpleasant but tends to dryness. Packaging materials? Polystyrene cups?
**Palate:** Sweeter than the nose would suggest. A touch of maltiness.
**Finish:** Now drying. Warming. Ginger biscuits and cloves. Lemon grass? Thai herbs? Bok choi?

## MOSSTOWIE 1979, CONNOISSEUR'S CHOICE 40%
Single Malt - Speyside

**7¼** Michael: A nostalgic reminder of the Lomond still, though I had forgotten it could produce such sweet whisky.
**Nose:** Beeswax. Flowery.
**Palate:** Orange flower water. Jaffa Cakes. Good malt background.
**Finish:** Cocoa powder.

**8** Dave: It ain't subtle, but it's well worth trying.
**Nose:** Fragrant to start, then becomes increasingly oily and rich: cloutie dumpling, cooked fruits, spices, syrup; then saddle soap, coffee, nut and light camphor.
**Palate:** Generous, thick and smooth with an oily feel and overall sweetness. Golden syrup.
**Finish:** Nutty and oily. Empire biscuits, almond.

## NORTH BRITISH 1974, SCOTT'S SELECTION 53.1%
Single Grain - Scotland

**7¼** Michael: A pleasant summer whisky.
**Nose:** Sweetish. Aromatic.
**Palate:** Smooth, firm, slippery. Candy floss and some berry fruits.
**Finish:** Clotted cream.

**7** Dave: Attractive and quite assertive. Good.
**Nose:** Light honeyed notes, sandalwood, crisp oak. Reminds me of a young Cognac. Some banana in time.
**Palate:** Sweet and honeyed with some good concentration. Some nuttiness and slightly oaky. Sweet with subtle weight.
**Finish:** Oaky.

## NORTH BRITISH 21 YEARS OLD, CADENHEAD'S 57.8%
Single Grain - Scotland

**7** Michael: Somewhat one-dimensional.
**Nose:** Dryish, grainy. Much drier than the Scott's version. Longer in the wood, of course.
**Palate:** Firm, smooth. Citrussy, orangey.
**Finish:** Marmalade-like bitterness.

**7¾** Dave: Great balance and great character.
**Nose:** Weighty and substantial, mixing dry and soft notes: light toffee, sugared almond, vanilla, honey. Attractive.
**Palate:** Sweet, concentrated and very long and soft. Spicy and fruity with a firm body giving it drive and some complexity.
**Finish:** Big and generous.

## NORTH BRITISH 27 YEARS OLD, DUNCAN TAYLOR 52.8%
Single Grain - Scotland

**7¼** Martine: The palate does not have the refreshing appeal of the nose. Water tames it but not enough to make it really palatable.
**Nose:** Vibrant. Citrussy. Lemon curd. A touch of exotic fruit. Passion fruit maybe. Verbena; light and fragrant.
**Palate:** Oak shows more than expected. A slight cardboardy note. With a phenolic hint.
**Finish:** Tangy, peppery.

**7** Dave: More in line with the first two. The most 'grainy' on show.
**Nose:** Edgy with a light metallic note: aluminium, green grass, geranium, whiff of sulphur.
**Palate:** Surprisingly sweet start with a firm grip and a very dry mid palate that carries a light phenolic note from the cask.
**Finish:** Short and slightly hard.

## NORTH OF SCOTLAND, 1963, SCOTT'S SELECTION 46.8%
Single Grain - Scotland

**7** Michael: Very rich for a grain whisky. Not much dimension. No flavour peaks.
**Nose:** Sweet. Aromatic.
**Palate:** Surprisingly heavy-bodied. Creamy-tasting. Vanilla.
**Finish:** Soothing. Late medicinal note.

**7¾** Dave: This has personality, weight and is the most tightly focused of the bunch.
**Nose:** Firm 'grainy', grassy with some roast almond. Water accentuates the firmness and brings out some juicy/oily qualities. Gets bigger in time but always dry.
**Palate:** Dry and sweet at the same time. The soft gentle grain does play its part, but overall this is a big whisky with a firm structure.
**Finish:** Surprisingly sweet.

## NORTH PORT 19 YEARS OLD, RARE MALTS 61%
Single Malt - Highland

**6** Michael: Some malts are deservedly rare, but full marks to United for at least giving us the chance to taste them.
**Nose:** Dry, lightly smoky, grassy. Dry fruitiness.
**Palate:** Light. Leafy. Dried apricot. Dried banana. Toasted marshmallow.
**Finish:** Dry, spirity, sharp. Cedary.

**6** **Jim: The weaknesses which made North Port one of the poorer distilleries come to the fore at first. Completely loses direction and balance for a while but recovers in the finish thanks to some calming oak influence. The nose is very impressive though.**
**Nose:** Soft and finely balanced; almonds and mint and freshly cut grass.
**Palate:** Hot with a short, unbalanced burst of burnt barley and OTT oak; for an ungainly ride.
**Finish:** Lots of age; some cocoa notes. Toasty and dry. Lingers quite well.

### NORTH PORT 36 YEARS OLD, OLD MALT CASK 49.3%
Single Malt - Highland

**6¾** **Michael: Of interest to collectors, historians and the likes of me, but this Brechin brew, staunched in 1983, never made a great whisky.**
**Nose:** Cedary. Newly sawn wood. Resin. Oil of peppermint.
**Palate:** Oily. Black chocolate. Bitter.
**Finish:** Drying. Musty. Woody.

**7½** **Martine: It's my first taste of North Port so I can't decide if the distillery character has been blurred or not by sherry. Like a bulldozer after an earthquake.**
**Nose:** Big and pungent. Fruit and wood. Cider apple, damson plums, honey. Dark chocolate.
**Palate:** Sour fruitiness. The spices and biting alcohol is hardly tolerable, even with water. Wood dominates maltiness. Reminiscent of a rye whiskey.
**Finish:** Robust, warm, biting.

### OBAN 14 YEARS OLD 43%
Single Malt - Highland

**7¾** **Martine: Classic, gentle and pleasing. A consensual malt. Good match with salmon and light seafood dishes.**
**Nose:** Refreshing and gentle. Summer fruit. Melon. Vanilla pod. Touch of new leather. Developing on cooked fruit notes. Pear pie. Stewed peaches. Yeasty.
**Palate:** Delivers nose promises. Smooth and silky.
**Finish:** Fruity, gentle and slightly nutty.

**8** **Dave: Good energy, balance with surprising weight.**
**Nose:** Spicy. Hot sawdust, fresh ginger, citrus zest. Crisp. With water fragrant oak, allspice, shortbread with sugar. Summery.
**Palate:** Dried apricot, tingling. Slightly sweet with good balance in the mid-palate. Hint of menthol.
**Finish:** Tingling ginger. Short but fresh.

### OBAN 20 YEARS OLD 57.9%
Single Malt - Highland

**7¾** **Martine: The nose is very distinguished and floaty. The palate is a bit too assertive because of the high strength. Requires oxygenation and water.**
**Nose:** Shy, delicate. Spring garden. Grassy. Orange sherbet. Raspberry. Mint lollipop. A briny echo.
**Palate:** Smooth, gentle at start. Then the alcohol strength breaks out. Iced mint sweets.
**Finish:** Tangy (even with water), dry. Herbal.

**8¼** **Dave: Excellent balance given the age – wood hasn't overpowered it.**
**Nose:** Mature. Crystallised ginger, lemon drizzle cake, chalk, spicy marmalade. Subtle. Needs a drop of water to open into polished oak. Linseed.
**Palate:** Clean and soft with dried peels. An interesting, strangely exotic quality. Deep.
**Finish:** Long and spicy.

### OBAN DISTILLERS EDITION, MONTILLA 43%
Single Malt - Highland

**8** **Michael: Demonstrably an evocative whisky. Salty and winey, but neither as overt as in the comparable Glenmorangie Fino.**
**Nose:** Fragrant. Edible seaweed, sweetish, restrained fruit. Aroma of white, uncut peaches.
**Palate:** Smooth, scenty. Developing notes of tobacco.
**Finish:** Sitting in a leather armchair, reading Masefield, before a log fire, listening to the tide with a whiff of brine under the weather-warped door.

**9½** **Doug: Much enhanced Oban. Perfect with after coffee and brazils.**
**Nose:** Succulent honeyed traits with a briny background.

**Palate:** Rich nutty, malty and full-bodied with dark chocolate and spice emerging.
**Finish:** Very lingering, chocolatey and warming. With a late peaty finesse.

### OLD BALLANTRUAN 50%
Single Malt - Speyside

**8** **Martine: A charming nose with a less delicate palate but altogether a refreshing dram.**
**Nose:** Citrussy, very aromatic. A distant dry smokiness swirling up. A mineral touch (wet pebble). Then a fruity whiff of ripe peaches and pears. All is wrapped in a delicate honeyed veil.
**Palate:** Rich, silky, enticing. Oily, getting drier on the tongue as spices burst out. Some green gage flavours mingling with spices.
**Finish:** Lemony, drying on ginger.

**6½** **Dave: If you are going to drink it do it neat.**
**Nose:** Very sweet start with light smoke. Clover honey and woodsmoke. With water becomes dramatically drier and then a rubbery note.
**Palate:** Very sweet when neat then the smoke charges onto your tongue. The diluted palate is better than the nose to start.
**Finish:** Phenolic.

### OLD BALLANTRUAN THE PEATED MALT 50%
Single Malt - Speyside

**8** **Michael: A number of surprising, and perhaps contra-dictory, characteristics that actually come together quite nicely in the end.**
**Nose:** Acetic. Coffee icing. Then creamy toffee, caramel notes combining with pear drops remind me of Elastoplast. Herbal.
**Palate:** Cereal grains. Newsprint. Faintly smoky. Creamy toffee and vanilla develop with water.
**Finish:** Oily, burnt croissant. Wood ash.

**8** **Arthur: I was reminded of the time I met a German loon who claimed to sprinkle heavily peated barley on his muesli. This is 30ppm Ready Brek.**
**Nose:** Malt loaf, dark chocolate sauce, vanilla, warm tar and peat. With water more eucalyptus/tea tree, and Limoncello.
**Palate:** Like crunching peated barley malt. Porridge and peat, with lemon rind.
**Finish:** More youthful peatiness.

### OLD COURSE HOTEL 12 YEARS OLD SPEYSIDE MALT 43%
Single Malt - Speyside

**6¾** **Dave: The sweetness fails to mask a whisky that hasn't matured. All rather flat and plain.**
**Nose:** Creamy and rounded if quite simple nose. Water brings out elderflower sweetness, but also a note akin to balloons.
**Palate:** Sweeter than the nose with cereal, oak, rubber and a confected sweetness. Thin and quite hot. Not quite knitted together.
**Finish:** Short, syrup, crisp oak.

**6¾** **Arthur: OK, but given that there are so many wonderful whiskies around, this gets lost.**
**Nose:** Bran, cereal husk, pear drops and daffodils. Freeze-dried raspberries and peach slices.
**Palate:** Oily texture which dries out and becomes astringent. Baked pears then dried flowers.
**Finish:** Dry and biscuity.

### OLD FETTERCAIRN, 37 YEARS OLD, 94.3, SCOTCH MALT WHISKY SOCIETY 50.1%
Single Malt - Highland

**8** **Michael: An elegant, elderly chatelaine.**
**Nose:** Delicate peat. Clean with an almondy nuttiness.
**Palate:** Lightly oily. Minty. Chlorophyll. Starched clothing in a linen press. Perfumy. Orange flower water.
**Finish:** It wells up in the finish like a surge of memories.

**8¾** **Jim: Outstanding for any malt this age. As fresh as a daisy and a must to experience. Fettercairn really does come into its own at 30 plus!**
**Nose:** Typically rich and floral for a Fettercairn of antiquity. Lush yet complex enough for primroses to abound.
**Palate:** Brilliantly fresh and teeming in cut grass and mouth-watering malt. A lovely butterscotch plateau.
**Finish:** Restrained peppers and more malt. The oak is no more than a shadow.

WHISKY Magazine Recommended

## OLD ISLAY SINGLE MALT BUNNAHABHAIN 33 YEARS OLD SELECTED BY ROYAL MILE WHISKIES 45.5%
Single Malt - Islay

**7¼ Michael: Caramel and creamy notes dominate this whisky, which could be boring were it not for the intriguing hints or ripe fruit and Calvados.**
**Nose:** Treacle toffee, cream toffee, toffee apples? Ripe red apples. Calvados. Pears? Milk chocolate. Illusive smoke.
**Palate:** Light but well structured. Caramel and burnt toffee top notes with a slight tart and savoury undercurrent. (Flaumkuchen?)
**Finish:** Creamy and rounded.

**8¼ Dave: Balanced, mature. Recommended.**
**Nose:** Big and fruity. Cherry, overripe melon, tinned apricot, old apple. Mulled cider, black banana, confiture. Plenty of oak with water.
**Palate:** Immediate spice. Another forest-like dram. Fairly dry and grippy some dried herbs, fine oak. Much better with with water which allows chocolate and nutmeg to come out along with maraschino, vanilla slice and orange peel.
**Finish:** Long and biscuity with light spice.

## OLD MALT CASK DIRECTOR'S TACTICAL SELECTION, 18 YEARS OLD 50%
Single Malt - Scotland

**8¼ Dave: This has it all but goes about it in an unflashy manner. Good.** WHISKY *Recommended*
**Nose:** Peaty and slightly briny. Oily notes once more. Dry leaves lanolin mint and ginger beer.
**Palate:** Medicinal. Chocolate orange. Smoke returns to balance things on the finish. Very interesting.
**Finish:** Fruity and sweet.

**8¾ Arthur: Good complexity, structure and balance of smoke, spice and sweetness.**
**Nose:** Sweet mint, some basil and creamy vanilla. Some cereal husk. Apples and lime and an elegant smoke. A little linseed.
**Palate:** More sweet mint, some dark chocolate and lots of vanilla. Bright yellow vanilla ice cream.
**Finish:** Gentle smoke and some wood-spice.

## OLD MAN OF HOY SINGLE ORCADIAN SCOTCH MALT WHISKY, BLACKADDER 58%
Single Malt - Island (non Islay)

**7 Michael: Weak in the middle. Lacks roundness.**
**Nose:** Faintly sulphury peat. Burnt grass. Lemon grass.
**Palate:** Syrupy and remarkably lemony.
**Finish:** Sherbert lemons. Sweet red peppers.

**8½ Jim: There is no mention as to whether this is Scapa or Highland Park, but this cannot be anything other than the elder statesman of the two. This is uncompromising, ultra-rich from the old school. A real stunner.**
**Nose:** Winey and rich, softly oaked with an almost oily peatiness. Fabulous heathery depth with an almost flower-scented sweetness, this is the kind of malt that would send bees into a frenzy.
**Palate:** Fabulously fat and oily and then a massive wave of intensely sweet malt followed by wave upon wave of the most gentle peat. Thick, intense, uncompromising and chewy.
**Finish:** Long, peaty and intense with heather and oak. Some late cocoa adds further depth.

## OLD PULTENEY 12 YEARS OLD 40%
Single Malt - Highland

**7¾ Michael: A complex and distinctive malt.**
**Nose:** Gunmetal. Passion fruit. Sweet broom.
**Palate:** Honeydew melon. Orange syrup. Honey roast peanuts.
**Finish:** Salty but oily and soothing.

**8½ Jim: Pretty impressive and singular in style. First-rate bittersweet balance.**
**Nose:** Attractively floral with significan't oak input. Polished floorboards and a scattering of crushed hazelnut: firm to the point of being rock hard.
**Palate:** Hard and bullet-like from the off with an almost Irish pot still firmness.
**Finish:** Medium length and remains pretty sharp and crisp.

## OLD PULTENEY 12 YEARS OLD 40%
Single Malt - Highland

**7¾ Martine: Forget about the first nose and enjoy that luscious exotic profile. But no water, thank you.** WHISKY *Recommended*
**Nose:** A sour note at start. Cow milking station. Then exotic fruit. Caramelised pineapple, dry coconut. Tamarind juice.
**Palate:** Syrupy. Mouth-coating. Sweet but with a good balance between sweet and sour. Coconut flan. Fresh ginger
**Finish:** Balanced. Sappy. Hint of mint and ginger.

**8½ Dave: Seems like a younger whisky, if so it has held its own very well in some pretty extraordinary company.**
**Nose:** Oily, big and peachy (and come to think of it, beachy). Whisky-saturated barrels. A strangely appetising mix of apricot, ripe fruit and wet oilskins.
**Palate:** Lush and rounded with a rich, deep almost leathery structure. Unctuous and fruity. Balanced.
**Finish:** Big, long and oily.

## OLD PULTENEY 15 YEARS OLD MILLENNIUM EDITION
Single Malt - Highland

**8 Michael: More distillery character than a 15 Years Old identified as "sherry-aged" I tasted some months ago.**
**Nose:** Nutty. Broom. Vanilla.
**Palate:** Clean, sweet, nutty, sherry, honey. Oily.
**Finish:** Peat-smoke and salt. Very long. Therapeutic.

**7 Jim: Tastes a lot older than its 15 years and has lost a lot of character due to slight over maturation.**
**Nose:** Highly perfumed, a heady infusion of sweet bourbony drier herbal notes.
**Palate:** Big oak kick dominates over roast malt and spices.
**Finish:** Sweet vanilla towards finish, some hickory lingers with the oak.

## OLD PULTENEY 15 YEARS OLD, CASK STRENGTH 57.8%
Single Malt - Highland

**8 Dave: A slightly odd melange of flavours and textures...but it works.** WHISKY *Recommended*
**Nose:** Full and lightly nutty, then a heavy floral fragrance, spiced bun, stewed peaches, apricot stone and then an oily/fruity mix.
**Palate:** Concentrated semi-caramelised fruits, cocoa butter, then ground nutmeg. Reminds you of waxed fruit. Water helps to smooth things.
**Finish:** Fruit smoothie.

**8½ Arthur: Complex and changeable in the glass. Not only very tasty, but interesting.**
**Nose:** Mouth-watering strawberries, Chewitts and lime juice, hot hay and a little dusty, mustiness. Blossom. Real rope, such as is found on Tall Ships. Liquorice.
**Palate:** Lots of fruit, with strawberries and peaches particularly, squished over an oaky background.
**Finish:** That lingering, grippy oak.

## OLD PULTENEY 15 YEARS OLD, SHERRY CASK 40%
Single Malt - Highland

**8 Michael: If you like whisky on your therapeutic porridge (and who doesn't?) this is the salty one.**
**Nose:** Peach cobbler. Raisins.
**Palate:** Sherry-soaked sponge. Fudge. Cookies. Sweet at first and then dry. Chocolate digestive?
**Finish:** Suddenly the salt is back.

**8 Jim: A genuinely delightful malt that shows great charisma beyond the so-so nose.**
**Nose:** Tainted mildly by sulphur. Fruitcake rich, nonetheless, and pretty sweet despite the drier oaky tones.
**Palate:** Big, irrespective of the strength. Quite peppery, smoky and enticingly sweet with hickory? A gently salty edge with subtle build up of malty complexity.
**Finish:** Lingering peat. Vanilla oak guarantees a soft finale than might be expected.

## OLD PULTENEY 17 YEARS OLD 46%
Single Malt - Highland

**9 Martine: A great combination of complexity and simplicity. A liquid fruit basket. Yummy.** WHISKY *Recommended*
**Nose:** Enticing, elegantly fruity. Apple and quince jelly. Barley sugar. Honey syrup. Strawberry shortcake. Sawdust. Oak notes unwind lazily.
**Palate:** Crisp and clean. Warm straw. Wood and fruit well integrated. Stewed apples and pears, a soft wave of black pepper. Perfectly balanced.
**Finish:** Drier. Spicy. Sticking to the palate.

**8¼ Dave: A complex, paradoxical individual for complex individuals.**
**Nose:** Cooked pear/apple, peach, quince, light vanilla pod. Some spice. Slight oilskin note. Fresh.
**Palate:** Distinct salt spray tingle, lightly nutty. Fresh, chalky but with depth. Very rich central weight. Liqueur Tokay. Plump pulp fruits.
**Finish:** Tingling, dare I say salty freshness, then spice and the fruit comes back.

### OLD PULTENEY 18 YEARS OLD, SHERRYWOOD, CASK 1498 59.9%
Single Malt - Highland

**8 Michael: I hope the new owners value this distillery. Its location, stillhouse design and – most important – its whisky, bring something special to the far north.**
**Nose:** Hint of peat. Nutty. Earthy.
**Palate:** Oily. Distinctly nutty. Toasted nuts. Peanut brittle.
**Finish:** Now salted nuts. Intense salt on the tip of the tongue. That distinctly maritime Manzanilla character.

**8¾ Dave: Like all Pulteneys this is all about texture and weight. A lovely big hairy bear of a dram.**
**Nose:** Rich with honey/wax, dried fruit and a savoury/sulphury note. There's damp chamois leather and oilskins. Some oak as well.
**Palate:** Big, (make that BIG) thick and oily. Coats the mouth with robust savoury/sweet flavours, chestnut honey, wax and layered fruit/fruitcake.
**Finish:** Tingling, long with treacle toffee and oak.

### OLD PULTENEY 1990 CASK STRENGTH, GORDON & MACPHAIL 58.8%
Single Malt - Highland

**7½ Martine: So sherry ... Dark Oloroso wipes out all maltiness. Unbalanced but sherry fanatics will love it.**
**Nose:** Sherry, sherry and sherry again. Bovrils, Marmite, burnt tyre. Date molasses. Musty cellar. Hint of earthy mushroom. Dry walnuts.
**Palate:** Heavily sherried. Currants marinated in a spicy syrup. Dates and figs, with a touch of dried apricot. Walnut peel. Bittersweet.
**Finish:** Rich and spicy. Sweet oak.

**7½ Dave: A grumbly kind of cove.**
**Nose:** Grunty but mellow. Ripe fruits, pot pourri, cold coffee, kicking up wet leaves in the winter. Lightly waxy with a hint of phenol and furniture polish.
**Palate:** Silky, moving into fruit compote, peaches in red wine, sultana. Fine tannins. Has depth.
**Finish:** Tingling. Bitter chocolate, honeycomb, light smoke.

### OLD PULTENEY 1990, GORDON & MACPHAIL 59.4%
Single Malt - Highland

**8 Michael: The hug of sherry is soporific; the saltiness a stinging reviver. A morning run in Wick; a gale in John O'Groats.**
**Nose:** Raisins, citrus peel, smoke. Mince pies in front of a log fire. Black bun.
**Palate:** Marshmallow maltiness. Treacle toffee. Long, slow flavour development.
**Finish:** Hefty sherry.

**7 Dave: A shame. Pulteney is a weighty enough spirit to cope with European oak. Not this time though!**
**Nose:** Filled with wood-derived aromas. Sherried, oaky, sulphur, singed wool. Meaty, oily.
**Palate:** Sherried(!). Some sweet, oily spirit struggling to free itself from the oaky clamp. Water loosens the grip a little.
**Finish:** Oak.

### OLD PULTENEY 8 YEARS OLD, GORDON & MACPHAIL 40%
Single Malt - Highland

**8 Michael: Tastes like Manzanilla to me. I don't speak for anyone else.**
**Nose:** A walk on sun-warmed sands that Wick might have difficulty in delivering. Tropical trees. Orange blossom.
**Palate:** Delicate. A hint of resin. Vanilla. Slightly winey.
**Finish:** Very salty. Very appetising.

**7½ Dave: All the elements are there but haven't knitted. Better with a couple more years in the cask.**
**Nose:** Dusty warehouse. Hint of marine character and soft fruits. A little musty.

**Palate:** Good oily feel (typical of the distillery) apricot, Juicy Fruit chewing gum. Touch of smoke, dry oak.
**Finish:** Short.

### PITTYVAICH 12 YEARS OLD 43%
Single Malt - Speyside

**6 Michael: Pittyvaich has always seemed a bit spirity to me, like a Scottish grappa. This version is softened slightly by the sherry.**
**Nose:** Sherryish, perfumy, pear-skins.
**Palate:** Very sherryish; assertive. Some malty chewiness. Vanilla. Soft, sweet, pear-like fruitiness, moving to a spicy dryness.
**Finish:** Spicy, perfumy, intensely dry.

**6½ Jim: A weird whisky all round. Pleasing character, but just doesn't feel right.**
**Nose:** Caramel, pulped fruit and oak. Not unpleasant, but curiously artificial. Almost brandy-like.
**Palate:** Fat and fruity, some sweet malt.
**Finish:** Coffee-biscuit sweetness and mealiness; not bad, but doesn't seem to hang right.

### PITTYVAICH 12 YEARS OLD 43%
Single Malt - Speyside

**5¾ Martine: You need to be sherry-mad to love this. Water releases more pleasant fruitcake notes on the nose but more harshness on the palate.**
**Nose:** Big brutal sherry. Winey. Quite beefy. Marmite. Over-powering sherrywood. Tobacco.
**Palate:** Toffee but with rancid butter notes. Cardboard. No subtlety in that sherry first-fill. Where has the malt gone?
**Finish:** Long but bitter. Smoky burnt wood.

**7¼ Dave: The richest by far, but all of it wood-driven.**
**Nose:** The colour suggests European oak and the nose is a classic dry amontillado: resin, clove, savoury notes-roasted almond, flamed orange peel, smoked tea, some toffee.
**Palate:** Heavy sherry flavours, almond especially. A slightly oily but tannic feel. There's perfumed smoke but the spirit is beefed up by heavy oak flavours.
**Finish:** Smoked cheese.

### PORT DUNDAS 34 YEARS OLD 57.9%
Single Grain - Scotland

**8 Dave: Lush and sexy. A truly delicious hedonistic dram.**
**Nose:** A glossy hue. Massively sweet, voluptuous even, chocolate fruit and nut bar melting in the coat packet, black banana, black grapes. Lots of mint. Huge!
**Palate:** Corn like sweetness but wood gives balance and stops it becoming flabby. Thick and chewy. Mature.
**Finish:** Long. Coconut.

**8¾ Arthur: A really, really good grain whisky. I'd like to try making an adult milkshake with this!**
**Nose:** Vanilla ice cream, Fry's orange cream, Refresher sweets and bourbon. The sweet note found in demerara rum. Some deep fruits, wet grass and coffee crème chocolates.
**Palate:** A great bourbony palate with sweetness balanced with oak, leaves and chocolate milk.
**Finish:** The sweet, sugary bottom of an expresso cup.

### PORT ELLEN 1975, 24 YEARS OLD, ADELPHI 59%
Single Malt - Islay

**7½ Michael: Seems to have faded slightly with age.**
**Nose:** Flowery. Very herbal. Bay leaves. Fragrant.
**Palate:** Peppercorns, but also some creamy sweetness. Parsley.
**Finish:** More parsley, and very peppery.

**8½ Jim: A malt lacking in complexity perhaps but certainly not in class.**
**Nose:** A rich tapestry of subtle but confident peat and oak interwoven with a sexy malty sweetness.
**Palate:** The peat rises early to state the dram's style. A fine iodiney stratum manages to stay the course, offering a peaty pulse as sweeter malt notes arrive.
**Finish:** Quite long with echoes of peat and roast Columbian coffee but a very well controlled vanilla.

## PORT ELLEN 1978 20 YEARS OLD, RARE MALTS 60.9%
Single Malt - Islay

**8½** **Michael: An expressive, arousing, version of this fine malt.**

**WHISKY** *Magazine* **Recommended**

**Nose:** Appetising. Bay trees. Seaweed.
**Palate:** Fruity olive oil. Parsley. Edible seaweed.
**Finish:** Salty. Smoky. Oaky. Extremely peppery.

**9** **Jim: This is a very big whisky which has withstood the test of time. Top rate and memorable.**

**Nose:** A crisp, lively nose with gentle spice to the peat-reek. Salty and nutty, chunky iodine, ripe pears.
**Palate:** Explosive stuff with heavy, chewy peat. Nothing like as complex as the nose but the vanilla does offer a calming diversion.
**Finish:** Good age with intense vanilla lingering on a higher layer than the deeper, yet sweeter peat.

## PORT ELLEN 1978 22 YEARS OLD, RARE MALTS 60.5%
Single Malt - Islay

**8½** **Michael: Pungent, powerful and appetising. A dram for the Islay-lover and connoisseur. This distillery should be revived.**

**Nose:** Fruity, seaweed, bay leaves, and olive oil.
**Palate:** Big bodied. Slightly sticky. Chewy. Edible seaweed. Parsley.
**Finish:** Hugely salty and equally peppery.

**9½** **Jim: This is whisky for the true connoisseur; exactly how a great old Islay should be. But why, oh why, did this distillery have to die?**

**Nose:** Almost kippery in its style of smokiness. Beguiling!!
**Palate:** The sweet coating of malt is defenceless against the pulsing peat.
**Finish:** Magnificently long. The balance is exemplary with the oak confined to bitter chocolate amid the intensifying malt.

## PORT ELLEN 1978 24 YEARS OLD, OLD MALT CASK 50%
Single Malt - Islay

**8¾** **Michael: This one blew up a storm for me.**
**Nose:** As though a sea breeze were gusting across the glass, and promising to blow a gale.
**Palate:** Firm, oily but drying. Bay leaves. Parsley. Emphatic seaweed.
**Finish:** Powerful, peppery, warming.

**8** **Dave: Port Ellen has always struck me as the most Calvinist of Islay's malts.**
**Nose:** Initially old style Californian chardonnay, all butter, nut and wood, then the smoke starts and with water becomes pretty firm and severe.
**Palate:** Robust, firm, quite alcoholic, powerful. A nodule of sweetness in the middle.
**Finish:** Dry and austere.

## PORT ELLEN 1978 24 YEARS OLD, SHERRY BUTT, THE WHISKY SHOP 46%
Single Malt - Islay

**8¼** **Michael: Bring on the pizza Napoletana (or if you are in Naples, the Romana).**
**Nose:** Salt. Crusty bread. Well-done toast. Dusty malt. Warehouse aromas.
**Palate:** Sweet. Bay leaves. Ground black peppercorns. Sea salt. Seaweed. Iron.
**Finish:** Very long. Hugely powerful. Have I sipped whisky or eaten Gentleman's relish?

**8** **Dave: Needs more input from the cask. Still, another great selection for TWS.**
**Nose:** Needs time (and water) to open. When it does, there's olive oil, pepper, burned timbers on the beach.
**Palate:** Lean with a lightly oily feel, then a blast of smoke giving hints of seaweed, smoked fish, underpinned by a honeyed sweetness.
**Finish:** Dies a little.

## PORT ELLEN 1978 PORT WOOD, SIGNATORY 58%
Single Malt - Islay

**8¾** **Martine: Typical fragrant, alert Port Ellen, but the port finish lends more fruit and an amazing orangey-pinkish colour.**

**WHISKY** *Magazine* **Editor's choice**

**Nose:** A kitchen garden. Floral, herbal. Jasmine. Chervil. A garden after a summer shower. Juicy grapefruit pulp. Shellfish, smoked haddock. Tar.

**Palate:** Light and appetising. Sweet cherries. A much fruitier version than usual. Smoke is less distinct than on the nose. Distant seaweed notes.
**Finish:** Tangy. Sherbety. A fruity note.

**7¾** **Dave: Austere, pretty challenging. Finished, I suspect, to inject some fruity life into its dry bones.**
**Nose:** Another of those pink whiskies, yet it smells of iodine, tar and fish oil. Water brings out peat-smoked apricots. In time there's raspberry leaf and Spangles scattered over a stony beach. Weirdly interesting.
**Palate:** The smoke hits immediately, then some light but concentrated fruitiness. Still very tense and dry.
**Finish:** Wood and peat smoke. Singed wool.

## PORT ELLEN 1978, SIGNATORY 59%
Single Malt - Islay

**8¼** **Martine: More body and richness than the '79. Still not a great warrior but a hearty fisherman.**

**WHISKY** *Magazine* **Recommended**

**Nose:** Delicately phenolic. Summer shower on a bonfire. Shellfish. Sea-lettuce. Cinnamon. Thyme. Hint of leather.
**Palate:** Sweet maltiness and butterscotch balanced by the sharpness of the spirit. Herring in oatmeal.
**Finish:** Dryness. Fizzy pepperiness.

**8¾** **Dave: Classy. A top-notch Port Ellen which manages to be austere yet filled with texture and rich flavours.**
**Nose:** Quite austere, linseed oil, pepper, olive with phenolic notes of tar/creosote, sea shells, a light kippery note, pipe smoke.
**Palate:** Great savoury start. Bursts in the mouth. Still austere, the olive and tarry smoke is there but spice as well. Huge presence.
**Finish:** Long, powerful.

## PORT ELLEN 1979 SHERRY CASK 21 YEARS OLD, OLD MALT CASK 50%
Single Malt - Islay

**8** **Michael: Port Ellen had such a distinctive character. This seems to be one of the less robust bottlings, yet has some character.**
**Nose:** Clean, appetising smokiness and seaweed.
**Palate:** Oily, olivey. Bay leaves. A hint of cedar, but a bit empty.
**Finish:** Very distinctive. Flowery. Leafy, aromatic, smooth, soothing.

**8¾** **Dave: Classic depth but like all Port Ellen it needs time to open.**
**Nose:** Seaweed/high water mark notes with pipe smoke, tar and hessian mixed with sherried notes.
**Palate:** Rich, big and silky. Quite sherried, mixing winey flavours with a rich Islay character.
**Finish:** As much happens after you've swallowed as goes on in the mouth.

## PORT ELLEN 1979, 22 YEARS OLD 56.2%
Single Malt - Islay

**8½** **Michael: From a sadly silent still: a great malt that is too good to chill, but wonderful with smoked salmon or scallops. Or, deservedly, caviar. You serve vodka? Shame on you!**
**Nose:** Very aromatic. Bison-grass. A hint of smokiness.
**Palate:** Earthy. Peppery. Sandy. Austere.
**Finish:** Fruity. Seaweed, pronounced salt. Very appetising.

**8** **Dave: Takes time to get to know. One to sip.**
**Nose:** Intense and haughty. There's oils at work along with fresh bay leaf and an austere, flinty smokiness. Maritime.
**Palate:** Dry and austere initially but manages to coat the mouth leaving lingering smoke in every corner.
**Finish:** Long dry with some oiliness.

## PORT ELLEN 1979, 25 YEARS OLD, 5TH RELEASE 57.4%
Single Malt - Islay

**7¾** **Martine: A very good balance between nose and palate. An island character with a pleasant earthy background.**
**Nose:** Peaty and spicy. Curry. Quite zesty. Créosote.
**Palate:** Smooth at first, gently flowing down. Gets spicier but keeps a delicate malty sweetness. Smokier than on the nose. Hint of thyme. Spices keep the word.
**Finish:** Dry, smoky. Liquorice root.

**9¼** **Michael: Beautifully composed. Focused. Elegant, mature structure belies the inherent strength of this malt.**

**Nose:** Calm and understated. Faint phenols hover over modestly smoky, grainy base notes.
**Palate:** Exquisite fruity malt character. Clootie dumpling? Becomes sharper with water.
**Finish:** More indulgent than the nose would suggest, and only slightly smoky.

## PORT ELLEN 1979, SIGNATORY 43%
Single Malt - Islay

7½ **Martine:** A rather pleasant dram but a paler version of Port Ellen.
**Nose:** Faint sea echo. Distant peat. Sea-scallop. Vanilla. Custard. Orange sherbet. Touch of lavender.
**Palate:** Light, sweet and gentle. Maltier, then marine.
**Finish:** Warm, dry, open-hearted. Water brings back peaty flavour.

7¾ **Dave:** The smokier of the two, but doesn't have the roundness and complexity of the '78.
**Nose:** Lean, green olive/sap with a belch of kiln smoke behind. Water shows immense smokiness: tarry ropes, sea thrift, fishermen's jumpers and a little burst of citrus.
**Palate:** Direct, dry. More of the kiln than the seashore. Oily.
**Finish:** Smoky, dry.

## PORT ELLEN 1982 21 YEARS OLD, OLD MALT CASK 50%
Single Malt - Islay

8¾ **Gavin:** A big beast of a Port Ellen, nicely caught before the sherry-wood tipped it over the edge.
**Nose:** Dried fruits, some rubber, sherry, lacquer, warm putty.
**Palate:** Burning timber, peat, dry sherry, mouth-coating oiliness.
**Finish:** Long and quite pungent, more smoke.

7¾ **Dave:** Big European oak influence. A little dry but good.
**Nose:** Aromas of roasted nuts, pickled walnuts, cordite, cracked leather. Touches of resin and rubber.
**Palate:** Smoked nuts, oil, leather. Generous. Fairly tannic but has enough sweetness to carry.
**Finish:** Coffee and smoke.

## PORT ELLEN 1982, GORDON & MACPHAIL 40%
Single Malt - Islay

8¼ **Michael:** A restrained example of this fine malt, but the silent still is almost out of stock. There will be few further opportunities to buy.
**Nose:** Fresh, maritime. Harbour-front.
**Palate:** A complex mix of flavours, emerging one after the other, in clean hits: Oily, seaweedy, green, leafy. Garden mint. Flowery.
**Finish:** Herbal. Salt. Very long indeed. Waves lapping on the palate.

7¾ **Martine:** A gentle Port Ellen, with the sea influencing the nose more than the palate. Would have proved a heftier guy at a higher strength.
**Nose:** A real mariner (fishnet, seaweed). Smoke mingled with sea spray. Grassy. Watermelon. A touch of wild mint.
**Palate:** Sweet and minty. Caressing mouthfeel. Very refreshing and appetising. Quite simple.
**Finish:** Warm, drying on liquorice and soft spices.

## PORT ELLEN 20 YEARS OLD, RARE MALTS 60.9%
Single Malt - Islay

8½ **Michael:** Bring on the caeser salad.
**Nose:** Appetising. Bay trees. Seaweed.
**Palate:** Lightly oily. Fruity olive oil. Parsley. Edible seaweed.
**Finish:** Salty. Smoky. Oaky. Extremely peppery.

9½ **Jim:** This particular distillation seems actually to have exceeded the 35 ppm that were the norm for Port Ellen. A stunningly peaty dram; an absolute must for Islayphiles.
**Nose:** Surprisingly light for a big Islay. The peat is delicate, nothing like as seaweedy or intense as the other Islay malts from the south-eastern shore. Briny, malty.
**Palate:** Contrary to the nose, the peat arrives by the wheelbarrow-full. Sweet and heathery with gentle spice.
**Finish:** This trademark clean but dusty maltiness of Port Ellen. Very, very long.

## PORT ELLEN 23 YEARS OLD, PROVENANCE, MCGIB-BON'S 46%
Single Malt - Islay

7½ **Martine:** Reminded me of old Calvados. Oak tends to overwhelm fruit but a wee dash of water tones it down. Very unpeated for a Port Ellen!

**Nose:** Fruity. A declension of apple fragrances. Cider, oven roasted apples with cinnamon. Apple blossom. All framed in burning applewood.
**Palate:** Firm, slightly tangy. Getting sweeter in time but oak keeps a spicy grip on the fruit.
**Finish:** Dry, spicy and almondy.

7¾ **Michael:** A nose, rich in dessert character, is balanced by charcoal-like dryness.
**Nose:** Rich with ripe, red fruits. Some pear and Calvados notes. Pain au chocolate. Chocolate and caramel.
**Palate:** Sweet, then charcoal. Fresher with water.
**Finish:** Peppery. Charred. Becomes pleasantly astringent. Water reveals wood smoke.

## PORT ELLEN 24 YEARS OLD 57.3%
Single Malt - Islay

8¾ **Gavin:** Very well balanced, this expression has enjoyed a great relationship with its cask. *WHISKY Recommended*
**Nose:** Sea salt, floor polish, mild antiseptic, and subtle oak.
**Palate:** Waxy, full, with pepper and light smoke.
**Finish:** Long and dry, sea-spray.

8¾ **Dave:** Has all of Port Ellen's great length, oiliness (and reserve).
**Nose:** Pungent. Acetone, linseed oil/putty, olive oil, canvas, squid ink even apple. Briny (scallop shell, fishmonger) Quite oaky.
**Palate:** Mouth-coating and smooth. Beeswax, lanolin, pepper, dry smoke. Needs time.
**Finish:** Rich and tight.

## PORT ELLEN 24 YEARS OLD, BURGUNDY FINISH, SIGNATORY STRAIGHT FROM THE CASK 58.8%
Single Malt - Islay

8½ **Gavin:** Lots happening here. A complex and highly unusual expression of Port Ellen. *WHISKY Recommended*
**Nose:** Sweet and perfumed, plums followed by smoke and cigar boxes.
**Palate:** Short sweetness, stewed prunes, then dry note of damped-down bonfire.
**Finish:** Plums and a faint whiff of peat smoke.

9 **Dave:** Audacious but it works. Brilliantly.
**Nose:** Concentrated. Fruit compote, baked fruits, tinned raspberry, cooked plum but with phenolics acting as a counter-point: tobacco leaf, coal.
**Palate:** A sweet, winey start then it dries allowing the peat to emerge before relaxing and letting raspberry fruitiness to return. Layered, complex.
**Finish:** Mellow, winey, a hint of fragrant smoke.

## PORT ELLEN 24 YEARS OLD, CHIEFTAIN'S CHOICE 59.4%
Single Malt - Islay

8½ **Dave:** Complex stuff going on here. A really rewarding Port Ellen. *WHISKY Editor's choice*
**Nose:** An immediate and huge hit of phenols combined with rich fruit cake. Dubbin and peat oil. Cocoa powder with water there's a hint of petrol and saltiness.
**Palate:** Eruption of smoke just held in check by crisp oakiness. The peat then wriggles back like a smoked eel bringing with it a gentle fruit.
**Finish:** Salty. Yes SALTY!

9 **Arthur:** Confidentially and quietly smoky, this is a lovely example of this elegant old Islay.
**Nose:** A combination of baked pear and pineapple fruitiness, with old and complex phenols rumbling beneath. More apparent with water, with tinned fish and some smoked meat. Lemon biscuits.
**Palate:** Fruit syrup, raisins and a little sulphur. Phenolic too, with dentist's mouthwash and a little of that canned brine. Some dry oak.
**Finish:** Salty and drying.

## PORT ELLEN 25 YEARS OLD, DOUGLAS LAING 50%
Single Malt - Islay

**9** **Martine: Forget your herbal tea. Go for this fantastic Islay potion!**
**Nose:** Perfumy, floral. Clover. Elderflower. A touch of acacia honey. Frangipani flower. Touch of malt syrup. Gets biscuity. All very appetising.
**Palate:** Sweet, intriguing. Flavours coil up in a sensuous herbal aromatic display.
**Finish:** Warm and tender, gingery, with a sweet touch of liquorice. Water reveals peat and smoke.

**7¼** **Michael: Somehow, fails to progress into anything really characterful.**
**Nose:** Green bananas. Tending to dryness with some icing sugar and menthol.
**Palate:** Tart. Good balance between initial sweetness and later sharp notes. Water releases some fruitiness.
**Finish:** Soft and slightly papery. Some very late fennel-like bitterness.

## PORT ELLEN 25 YEARS OLD, SPECIAL RELEASE 2005 57.4%
Single Malt - Islay

**9¼** **Arthur: Old, intense and busting for an olfactory fight. Complex and grizzly, like Clint Eastwood in The Unforgiven.**
**Nose:** Germolene, whiteboard marker pens, tarry rope, and blackberries. Undiluted there is a light vegetal note that becomes silagey with water.
**Palate:** A lovely viscious texture at cask strength, with dark chocolate melting in pools of sweet, peaty butter.
**Finish:** Incessant phenols that cling till breakfast.

**8½** **Owen: Well balanced and well structured. Instantly appetising.**
**Nose:** A dry smokiness with toffee and biscuit undertones. Maybe the brief tang of tropical fruits at the end? Pineapple?
**Palate:** Sweet at first, then drying. Honey and lemon. Salty mango lassie?
**Finish:** Oily and warming. Well structured phenols lead to a delightful wood smoke conclusion.

## PORT ELLEN 6TH RELEASE 54.2%
Single Malt - Islay

**7½** **Dave: Takes no prisoners.**
**Nose:** Restrained and salty linseed. Slightly skeletal and needs time to open which puts some flesh on the bones, as does a decent splash of water. Cod liver oil, juniper/pine. Medicinal. Deep Heat rub.
**Palate:** Oily and smoky. Direct and open faced. Feisty and slightly aggressive. Hot reminiscent of wasabi on sashimi.
**Finish:** Seashell, prickly.

**8¾** **Arthur: Took a while and a bit of water to open up so don't rush it.**
**Nose:** Watermelon, lemon pith and rind. Hot sauna wood, dry haystacks and wet woodsmoke. Coastal, with the smell of fish on the breeze.
**Palate:** Sweet, smoky with wood cutting through a thick texture. Apple sauce, tar and lemon notes are over-lain but a persistent smoky undercurrent.
**Finish:** A complex and long-lasting finish that is a combination of fizzy, earthy and spicy.

## PRIDE OF ISLAY 12 YEARS OLD, GORDON & MACPHAIL 40%
Blended Malt - Scotland

**7½** **Martine: More Islay character on the nose than on the palate. A good appetite-teaser.**
**Nose:** Melon, cucumber. Fresh almond. Develops smokiness and tarred wood.
**Palate:** Thirst-quenching. Cucumber juice. Smoky aftertaste.
**Finish:** Harmonious and gentle.

**7½** **Dave: A great, light introduction for Islay virgins but best sipped neat.**
**Nose:** On the more perfumed/aromatic side of smokiness: herring, heather blossom, baked apple, orange. Quite delicate. With a drop of water there's biscuits, lemon and some maritime notes.
**Palate:** Soft with a rounded mid-palate. Good balance: the gingery/heather tingle rounded out by soft fruit.
**Finish:** Dry, soft.

## PRIDE OF ORKNEY 12 YEARS OLD, GORDON & MACPHAIL 40%
Blended Malt - Scotland

**7¼** **Martine: Very fragrant on the nose but more restrained in the mouth. Needs time to perk up.**
**Nose:** Green apple. Garden mint. Orchard flowers. Honey. A hint of white chocolate.
**Palate:** Very clean. Surprisingly austere on the palate. A hint of smokiness in the background.
**Finish:** Dry spiciness. Slightly rooty. Softens to almond milk and porridge notes.

**7½** **Dave: Good balance and nice weight if a little woody.**
**Nose:** Gold. Juicy fruits (in fact, Juicy Fruit chewing gum) and some ripe strawberry. Water dries it slightly; malty, with coke (the fuel) and soft creamy fruits and cream. Charming.
**Palate:** Soft and well-fruited (peach/caramelised apple), then it dries up.
**Finish:** Dry, quite biscuity.

## PRIDE OF STRATHSPEY 12 YEARS OLD, GORDON & MACPHAIL 40%
Blended Malt - Scotland

**8** **Martine: Good introduction to Speyside's generosity. Especially if served with a crème brûlée.**
**Nose:** Toffeish. Candied orange. Heather. Delectable fruitiness (pears and apricots).
**Palate:** Velvety, smooth. Full, custardy. Pudding-like.
**Finish:** Delicately lingering, rolling out with toasted malt notes.

**8** **Dave: Very attractive, approachable and charming.**
**Nose:** Scented, lifted, estery with some coconut matting, vanilla, with hints of citrus. Water brings out a lovely floral edge (lily/freesia), some orange and poached pear.
**Palate:** Though subtle it has good weight and a great balance between honey, cream and dry nuttiness.
**Finish:** A tickly cough of smoke.

## PRIDE OF THE LOWLANDS 12 YEARS OLD, GORDON & MACPHAIL 40%
Blended Malt - Scotland

**7** **Martine: Disappointingly on the wood side. For those who like it oaky!**
**Nose:** Fragrant. Sandalwood. Gorse, bracken. Develops caramelised walnut and buttery notes.
**Palate:** Medium, sweetness muzzled by oak. Gingered rhubarb. More wood flavours as it opens up.
**Finish:** Pleasantly spiced but becomes bitter when water added.

**7** **Dave: Lovely soft, vanilla nose obliterated by wood. Shame.**
**Nose:** A light, gentle nose with custard creams, lemon and with water some wood and a fruity jammy element.
**Palate:** Dry and very woody. Overpoweringly so. There's some citric, perfumed/lavender stuff trying to come out but the wood batters it over the head.
**Finish:** Dry and woody with that jammy flavour at the very end.

## PROVENANCE BRAEVAL 1996, 8 YEARS OLD, SHERRY FINISH 46%
Single Malt - Speyside

**7½** **Martine: More attractive on the nose than on the palate. Water spreads it thin.**
**Nose:** Warm and sweet. Barley sugar, butterscotch, creamy strawberries. A hint of straw and cow's breath. Young bracken. Touch of floor polish.
**Palate:** Satin-like. Oily. Extreme smoothness, close to softness. In harmony with the nose but less intense.
**Finish:** Soothing. Light spices. Almond skin.

**7½** **Dave: A fragile dram. Interesting.**
**Nose:** Concentrated baked fruit with an exotic note. Raisin, damp chamois leather and in time pineapple and earthen warehouse floors. Slightly fungal with a burnt note.
**Palate:** Full-bodied. Black cherry juice, overripe fruit, some crisp oak. Has an aversion to water.
**Finish:** Dry and oaky. Fortified wine.

## PURE ISLAND MALT, IAN MACLEOD 43%
Blended Malt - Scotland

**7½** **Michael: Light but enjoyable flavours. A lively, attractive, feminine whisky, but the island character is scarcely evident: an omission for which a half point is deducted.**

**Nose:** Fresh. Fruit salad.
**Palate:** Long, fruity, dusty. Sweet shop flavours. Children's sweet. Dolly mixtures.
**Finish:** Soft liquorice. Some liquorice root. A hint of phenol smokiness.

8 **Dave: A young, punchy vatting. For beginners and peat lovers.**
**Nose:** Clean and light with precise phenolic notes, citrus, vanilla yellow haddock. All quite restrained...in a peaty way. Like standing on a high, rainy moor.
**Palate:** Immediate smoke, but with a balancing sweetness that runs the length of the palate. Great drive and energy.
**Finish:** Phenolic, dry. Medium length.

## PURE ISLAND MALT, IAN MACLEOD 43%
Blended Malt - Scotland

7½ **Martine: Definitely an Islander, tastes young. Could have more finesse.**
**Nose:** Intensely marine, briny, invigorating. Creosote, wet pebble. Dying bonfire by the shore.
**Palate:** The sweet maltiness followed by a phenolic dryness. Water brings out more sweetness and smoke. Garden mint.
**Finish:** Dry, quite lingering, slight bitterness. Chewed herbs coming back.

8 **Dave: Well put together, but not as smoky as I recall.**
**Nose:** Fresh with light creamy notes, scented, crisp oak, bracken, cut grass. In time a dry smokiness.
**Palate:** A good match between this delicate, slightly floral quality, a crunchy palate and light smoke. Balanced and restrained.
**Finish:** Creamy.

## QUEEN OF THE MOORLANDS 12 YEARS OLD 40%
Single Malt - Speyside

7¼ **Michael: Has nothing to be ashamed of, but could do with more action at the front end.**
**Nose:** Compact cereals at first: develops a background of summer fruits in the local greengrocers shop. A trace of lemony freshness. Perhaps some menthol?
**Palate:** Light, but a little creamy. Jammy? Cream cakes? Still menthol in there.
**Finish:** Fairly short and quite sharp.

6¾ **Dave: There's just not a lot happening.**
**Nose:** Flat, dull oak. Reminds me of school blackboards (chalk dust, oak). In time a light hay/cereal note. Lot of cask.
**Palate:** As light as a feather. Some sweetness, some light fruit.
**Finish:** Short.

## ROSEBANK 12 YEARS OLD 43%
Single Malt - Lowland

7¾ **Michael: Relatively young, but beginning to weary nonetheless. Perhaps this tiredness is caused by worry about the future. A feminine whisky that has lost the first bloom of youth. Snatch a kiss while you can.**
**Nose:** Rosebank's typical camomile.
**Palate:** Lightly creamy. Flowery sweetness.
**Finish:** Mint imperials.

7¾ **Dave: This remains a cracking dram. Shame the distillery is being bulldozed. No, make that a disgrace.**
**Nose:** Fragrant. Light fruits, fresh pear, creamy and zingy-ginger beer? There's smoke and a hint of green, sappy sticks.
**Palate:** It rolls nicely in the mouth. Elegant, with little spikes of flavour: nut, grass and flowers laid on top. Light and delicate. Soft, clean and quite floral.
**Finish:** It all zips into life at the end.

## ROSEBANK 15 YEARS OLD, DOUGLAS LAING 50%
Single Malt - Lowland

8 **Martine: A straightforward refreshing dram. To be sipped on a summer afternoon. I would easily drop one or two ice cubes in my glass.**
**Nose:** Light but tangy. Lemon zest, dry hay. Lemon grass. Fresh and lively.
**Palate:** Malty, sweet. Cereal bowl. Grassy. Garden mint. White peaches. Pleasant mouthfeel.
**Finish:** Rather short but clean.

7¾ **Michael: Uninspiring nose more than compensated for by challenging and surprising palate. Appetising.**
**Nose:** Not especially forthcoming. Tends to flat, dusty caramel notes. Waxy and minty.
**Palate:** Sweet and salty. Warming and gingery. Unexpected but definite coastal touches – iodine?
**Finish:** Firm, chewy and ever so slightly phenolic.

## ROSEBANK 15 YEARS OLD, THE WEE DRAM 40%
Single Malt - Lowland

7¾ **Michael: Once a vamp. Now a trouper. She is a little astringent, but I am blind to her faults. I could fall for her all over again.**
**Nose:** Dry, Lemony. Flowery. Camomile.
**Palate:** Seemed watery for a moment, then opened to delicate, very light, oiliness. Walnut oil. Perhaps even olive oil. A hint of sweet red peppers. Lightly toasted ciabbata bread.
**Finish:** Oiliness smooths warming alcohol.

7¾ **Ian: A delicate texture releases growing richness, with a sip turning into a rewarding mouthful.**
**Nose:** Créme brûlée, violet floral notes, raisins and pear drops, leading to shortbread and a waft of maltiness.
**Palate:** Rich sweetness, pear drops, baked apples, raisins, and underlying honey.
**Finish:** Creamy, sweet, malty flourish with a hint of dry oak.

## ROSEBANK 1974 20 YEARS OLD, THE WHISKY FAIR, DOUGLAS LAING 55.8%
Single Malt - Lowland

7¾ **Michael: Who needs afternoon tea?**
**Nose:** Floral. Like a clean, invigorating, bath soap.
**Palate:** Quite big for a Lowlander. Sugared almonds. Cake decorations that look like slices of orange and lemon but are made from jelly, sprayed with sugar. Scones with rhubarb jam.
**Finish:** Drier. More almonds, glazed this time.

7½ **Dave: Some will love the combination of a cult malt, alcohol, great age and smoke but I'm not so convinced.**
**Nose:** Smoky. Has weight and touches of complexity. Wood ash, spent campfire, fig, coffee. Peat-dominant.
**Palate:** Very peaty (certainly when compared to everything else on show) and powdery peat at that. Sweet and light with firm oak. A bit confused.
**Finish:** Oak and smoke.

## ROSEBANK 1988, GORDON AND MACPHAIL, CONNOISSEUR'S CHOICE 40%
Single Malt - Lowland

8 **Michael: A deft balance between the whisky's own character and the sherry.**
**Nose:** Buttercups, clover, sweet grass, honey and a tender touch of sherry.
**Palate:** Flowers softened and sweetened by sherry. Honey, junket, very lightly nutty dryness.
**Finish:** Candied angelica, honey-coated nuts.

8 **Jim: Fabulous whisky, though never quite living up to the expectation built by the astonishing nose.**
**Nose:** A hint of smoke and plethora of other delicate aromas. Primroses and sandalwood, faint marzipan and passion fruit. Stunning.
**Palate:** Delicate, with very firm malt and gentle spice.
**Finish:** Relatively flat, dependent on a burnt mallow and vanilla oakiness.

## ROSEBANK 1989, 9 YEARS OLD, CADENHEAD'S 43%
Single Malt - Lowland

8½ **Michael: All of the characteristic floweriness of Rosebank, but with some roundness.**
**Nose:** Assertively flowery. Fragrant and dry. Light body.
**Palate:** Flowery, soft, grassily sweet, moving to a very gentle dry finish.
**Finish:** Flowery, very lightly nutty, nougat-like.

9 **Jim: Despite the worrying nose, to taste this has a bit of everything, in just the right amounts. A real collector's item. And don't add water.**
**Nose:** Young and still immature with fresh cut grass and the faintest waxy honey giving a lift above the alcohol.
**Palate:** The tell-tale signs of youth: citrus zest and barley concentrate. Yet the middle is magnificent with acacia honey and oak and some salty, tangy slightly peaty notes.
**Finish:** Long, chocolatey, a hint of oranges and warm spices. The balance is pretty nearly perfect.

## ROSEBANK 1989, LOMBARD 50%
Single Malt - Lowland

**8¼ Michael: A good example. Such a love potion, from a distillery that no one loved enough to keep alive.**
**Nose:** Dryish, floral, camomile, buttercups. Typical Rosebank.
**Palate:** Lightly creamy. A nectar of flower petals. A love potion from a Shakespeare play.
**Finish:** Drier again. Herbal. Tickling. Arousing, appetising.

**7¾ Dave: Ethereal. It seems to fill the mouth with perfume.**
**Nose:** A lifted, perfumed, slightly floral nose. Intense. Lemon sherbet.
**Palate:** Very light and sweet all the way. Like drinking a meadow. All very delicate and almost fragile. A sweet, pure, lemon-like quality.
**Finish:** Sweet.

## ROSEBANK 1989, SIGNATORY 43%
Single Malt - Lowland

**6 Michael: With its curiously greeny-white colour, this one actually looks like a ghost. A shadow of a great malt.**
**Nose:** Faint spearmint. Papery.
**Palate:** Thin, empty, drying. Tastes like exhausted chewing gum.
**Finish:** Papery, woody.

**6½ Dave: All very light with no interplay between cask and whisky. Disappointing.**
**Nose:** Very, very pale. There's a wisp of smoke, a touch of light blossom and a hint of the smell that you get inside a new welly boot (not a bad thing in my opinion).
**Palate:** Very light with central sweetness and that light smoke again.
**Finish:** Just disappears.

## ROSEBANK 1990, BERRY'S OWN SELECTION 46%
Single Malt - Lowland

**7½ Michael: A teasing early freshness is the overture to a richer, modestly structured, conclusion.**
**Nose:** Youthfully fresh and clean. Slight cleansing acidity – sparkling lemonade?
**Palate:** Lemon sharpness, balanced by a barley sugar sweetness.
**Finish:** First warming lemon ginger, then, later, a hint of dark organic chocolate.

**7¼ Dave: An attractive summery aperitif. Just lacks a middle.**
**Nose:** Clean, sweet and quite delicate. Light sappy notes: chewing on a leaf of grass, gooseberry jam, raffia. Becomes floral with a hint of flat ginger beer.
**Palate:** Light and fragrant becoming very sugary (gomme) with good delivery. Hay, coriander seed. A little hollow.
**Finish:** Drying slightly, surprisingly long

## ROSEBANK 1990, BERRY'S OWN SELECTION 46%
Single Malt - Lowland

**8¼ Arthur: Cute as a button.**
*WHISKY Magazine Editor's choice*
**Nose:** Raspberry sweeties, a little yeastiness and a whole bag of lemon sherberts.
**Palate:** Citric, malty round texture and a grassy finish.
**Finish:** Utterly cleansing dryness with a grassy bitterness.

**8½ Dave: Another which manages to be both delicate but complex. The best balanced on show.**
**Nose:** Fragrant. Stewed fruits, daffodil, yellow fruit pastille, orange pith, pineapple cubes, barley sugar, cut grass. Blackboard dusters, powdered ginger/ginger beer (a whisky mule?). A little sappy.
**Palate:** This is where it delivers, the sappiness mellows into late spring blossom and white fruits. Like sticking your head into a bouquet of flowers.
**Finish:** Gentle fruit.

## ROSEBANK 1990, MURRAY MCDAVID 40%
Single Malt - Lowland

**8 Michael: Rosebank is a delicate whisky, but just a touch more wood-extract would hold together its flavours.**
**Nose:** Lightly fragrant, with grass, camomile and mint.
**Palate:** Light, flowery and dry. Camomile and spearmint. Very distinctive, but slightly spirity.
**Finish:** Potpourri, flowery, slightly sharp.

**5 Jim: The label quotes my devotion to Rosebank at 8 years. I'm not devoted to it in this form. The cask this malt was filled into must have been exhausted as the whisky is closer to a 2 Years Old in character. The only good point is that there are no off notes.**
**Nose:** Horribly unbalanced mixture of new make and sappy oak. The malt is merely incidental.
**Palate:** Sweet, malty and, er, that's it .
**Finish:** Almost sickly sweet. The oak remains off-key.

## ROSEBANK 1990, SHERRY CASK, MURRAY MCDAVID 40%
Single Malt - Lowland

**8 Michael: The flowery youth of the whisky and the freshness of the sherry cask achieve an interesting harmony.**
**Nose:** Sherry, honey, lemons, buttercups.
**Palate:** Seductively soft and honeyed, with flowery lemon and camomile emerging.
**Finish:** Smooth, appetising. A teasing balance of sweetness and dryness.

**Jim: This is the sublime to the other's ridiculous.**
**Nose:** Elegant and fluting, the soft grapes mingle in faultless harmony with the deeper malts and gentle oak. Understated and effortlessly complex.
**Palate:** Immediately embracing and surprisingly spicy, there is a surge of roasty malt which never succumbs to the succulent grape. Fabulous mouthfeel: slightly oily and viscous.
**Finish:** A buzzing of soft spices and some cocoa-vanilla notes complete an impressive act.

## ROSEBANK 1991 SHERRY FINISH, 11 YEARS OLD, CHIEFTAIN'S CHOICE 43%
Single Malt - Lowland

**8 Martine: An attractive medium-bodied Rosebank. The sherry finish has added complexity to delicacy. Some exotic notes which makes it really appetising.**
**Nose:** Floral and fruity. Bluebells. Pears poached in vanilla syrup. Exotic wood. Toasted bread.
**Palate:** Flowery. Chocolate toffee. Coconut. Burnt cream. Sandalwood.
**Finish:** Quite delicate, crisp and dry, vanishing on a bitter note. Walnut peel.

**7¼ Dave: Straight down the middle of the palate. A nice drink.**
**Nose:** Fresh and appetising if slightly hard to get at. Pear drops, lemon leaf and a hint of smoke.
**Palate:** Very soft and light. Reminds me, somehow, of fern cakes. Light and lemony.
**Finish:** Light and soft.

## ROSEBANK 1992, 12 YEARS OLD, COOPER'S CHOICE 46%
Single Malt - Lowland

**7½ Gavin: Perhaps 12 years in the cask is slightly too long for most Rosebanks. This does not seem a particularly well-behaved example.**
**Nose:** Insistent pepper and some malt.
**Palate:** Some initial smoke, unexpected weightiness, quite mouthcoating and malty. Pears, mixed spice, and melon – especially when reduced.
**Finish:** Hot, salt, with oak notes lingering.

**7½ Dave: Like lace on the palate. Treat carefully.**
**Nose:** Floral. American cream soda, fizzy sherbet, lemonade. A little water concentrates the aroma well. Has delicate complexity and a dry edge.
**Palate:** Fragrant. Icing sugar, elderflower, polished wood. Light and rather fragile.
**Finish:** Sweet. Grapes dusted with icing sugar.

## ROSEBANK 1992, 9 YEARS OLD, ADELPHI 61%
Single Malt - Lowland

**7½ Michael: The aroma promised much, but the palate is curiously drying. Rosebank was never peaty, and this is too young to be woody, so I don't know the origin of that harshness.**
**Nose:** That distinct camomile character of Rosebank.
**Palate:** Some creaminess, but becomes gritty and peppery. A little more flowery when water is added.
**Finish:** Astringent.

**8½ Dave: Only nine? A child prodigy of Mozartian standards.**
**Nose:** Very pale. Floral with some apple blossom, pear, lemon butter icing.
**Palate:** Needs water. When added there's an immediate puff of peat, then a tingling exciting explosion of freesia, apples, orange blossom.
**Finish:** Dry.

## ROSEBANK 1992, BLACKADDER 60%
Single Malt - Lowland

**6 Martine: Far from Rosebank at its best. Fiery.**
**Nose:** Highly spirity, almost nostril-burning. Light cereal notes. Bread dough.
**Palate:** Much sweeter. Velvety mouthfeel. Pleasant fruity notes. Apple jelly. Walnuts.
**Finish:** Hot and nothing more. Like swallowing a teaspoonful of tabasco sauce.

**8 Dave: A lovely ethereal dram.**
**Nose:** A burst of fragrant top notes: lemon (zest, icing, leaf), blossom/fresh flowers, vanilla/cream soda. Almost rye-like. Water brings out mint, anise/basil.
**Palate:** Delicate, fragrant and almost sherbety. There's some smoke lurking in the background alongside violet. Gorgeous.
**Finish:** Complex with a hint of smoke.

## ROSEBANK 1992, COOPER'S CHOICE 40%
Single Malt - Lowland

**7¾ Michael: A reminder of a great Lowland malt lost.**
**Nose:** Flowery-fruity. Dry. Camomile. Lemon grass.
**Palate:** Firm, smooth, lightly creamy. Delicately sweet in the middle. Icing sugar. Wonderfully subtle, complex and teasing. Becoming dry.
**Finish:** Hint of burnt sugar and sulphur.

**8¾ Jim: A flawless example of the most luscious and complex Lowlander of them all. Should be bottled at least 43% abv, though, to highlight the full complexity.**
**Nose:** Wonderfully complex with a maltiness punctuated by a series of grassy, spicy and coal-smoky notes. Fabulously delicate.
**Palate:** Mouth watering at first; a wonderful display of light and heavy malt tones.
**Finish:** Drying with some soft vanilla-caramel notes.

## ROSEBANK 20 YEARS OLD, RARE MALTS 62.3%
Single Malt - Lowland

**8¼ Michael: This is how Lowlanders used to be: drier, more herbal, more complex. Buy now, while stocks last.**

WHISKY
Editor's choice

**Nose:** Perfumy. Herbal. Vegetal.
**Palate:** Starts softly and sweetly, then explodes with flavours. Camomile, lemon grass, anise, fennel. Very spicy.
**Finish:** Very dry. Intense.

**8¼ Dave: You don't have to have masses of peat or sherry to make a malt interesting. The best of these Lowlanders show that. Try them!**
**Nose:** Touches of tobacco, waxed floors, hessian, then brazil nut, cooked fruit and tinned peach. Mature.
**Palate:** Sweet, rounded, mixing a silky feel with light fruits, flowers and some fresh nuttiness. It hits a perfect balance between delicacy and substance.
**Finish:** A hint of smoke.

## ROYAL BRACKLA 10 YEARS OLD 43%
Single Malt - Highland

**7¼ Michael: A pleasant malt, but this bottling has less structure than I remember. It is to be hoped that new owners Dewar's give more prominence to this distillery.**
**Nose:** Sweet but slightly burnt. Reminiscent of treacle toffee. Perhaps even molasses.
**Palate:** Starts sweet, almost icing-sugar, then quickly dries to grassier, herbal, oily notes.
**Finish:** Light peat. Cedar.

**8½ Jim: An impressively balanced, stylish dram that deserves far better recognition.**
**Nose:** Delicate and floral, the oak input from the bourbon barrel is in perfect harmony with the gently sweet malt.
**Palate:** Less compelling than the aroma. Offers mouth-watering malt before a burst of peat dries it out.
**Finish:** Bittersweet, oaky-smoky affair that lasts longer than expected.

## ROYAL BRACKLA 15 YEARS OLD, CADENHEAD'S 58.2%
Single Malt - Highland

**7¾ Michael: Hardly elegant but a muscular malt of a style that is sadly vanishing from the Highlands. I greatly enjoyed it.**
**Nose:** Fruitier. Lemon grass. Honeydew melon.
**Palate:** Much richer. Syrup, vanilla, ginger, then spicy smokiness.
**Finish:** Deliciously smoky, lively and warming. Quite aggressive.

**8 Jim: Shows some signs of deterioration but, like many a good oldie, tells an interesting tale.**
**Nose:** A massive custard-vanilla theme and gentle, mildly peated malt. Oaky, mildly complex but always attractive and effective.
**Palate:** Mouth-watering. Strong waves of sweet malt. Spicy. Waxier and fuller bodied.
**Finish:** Excellent length with trademark sweet vanilla recognisable through the wrinkles of oaky old age.

## ROYAL BRACKLA 1975, MURRAY MCDAVID MISSION 46%
Single Malt - Highland

**7¾ Michael: An especially rich sherryish bottling. Voluptuous. With the afterdinner chocs.**
**Nose:** Creamy. Leafy.
**Palate:** Rich, dark flavours. Lots of sherry. The body is light, soft and smooth.
**Finish:** Big, warming, soothing.

**8 Dave: The same underlying fruity character as the distillery bottling but this is more structured and spicy. Take your pick, they're both very fine.**
**Nose:** Firm, spicy and oaky. Night stocks, black fruits, cinnamon and nutmeg. Walking in the pines after rain.
**Palate:** A floral start with some soft fruits. Firm structure, toffee, oak/pine. Good balance.
**Finish:** Firms up. Lots of spice.

## ROYAL BRACKLA 25 YEARS OLD 43%
Single Malt - Highland

**7¾ Michael: More typical of the unusual hot, dry, cleansing character of this distinctive whisky.**
**Nose:** Warm. Sweet.
**Palate:** Lean and spicy. Very lively flavours. Immediate anise. Herbal, Tobacco-like.
**Finish:** Firm, gripping. Took me by the scruff of the neck and sent me to work.

**8¼ Dave: A well built and delicious dram.**
**Nose:** Fresh wood (sandalwood) sweet malt, cherry, spices and peanut shells with a lovely vanilla pod/custardy note.
**Palate:** Sweet fruits (melon, apricot). That sweet vanilla custard takes charge, but there's a nutty undertow balancing things. Oak is fairly firm.
**Finish:** Dry and nutty.

## ROYAL BRACKLA 27 YEARS OLD, CASK 5467, ADELPHI 59.5%
Single Malt - Highland

**7¾ Michael: The best Brackla I have tasted. Night-cap?**
**Nose:** Rich heavy sherry. Butter. Rum. Moist fruit cake.
**Palate:** Chewy. Mint toffee. Treacle toffee.
**Finish:** A small explosion of spiciness. Ginger, allspice. Hot, dry. Very long.

**7½ Dave: Big and aromatic. There's bags of oaky character and not a lot of the distillery's. One to sip and ponder over.**
**Nose:** Rich, sweet wood-derived aromas of coconut flesh, cumin, Old English marmalade.
**Palate:** Immediate woodiness at the side of the mouth. There's a lovely rose petal/raspberry coulis fragrance and massive spiciness.
**Finish:** Soft then a bit woody.

## LOCHNAGAR 1994, PROVENANCE 46%
Single Malt - Highland

**8** **Martine: That guy hides a tender heart under a reserved manner. Give it time and a dash of fresh water. Definitely an outdoor dram.**
**Nose:** Buttery with a faint butyric note. A thin veil of smoke hoovers over poached pears. Wet rush. Aeration brings a delicate fresh citrus breath.
**Palate:** Smooth, silky, sweet at start. An earthy dryness pleasantly invades the palate while spices tingle tastebuds.
**Finish:** Fruity, spicy, dry. Fresh almond aftertaste.

**7¼** **Dave: Better weight but ultimately this is still fragile.**
**Nose:** Malty/Ovaltine with hazelnut, wood shavings red grapes and candied peel. Becomes hard with water.
**Palate:** A dry slightly charred start before deepening moving through hazelnut into stewed fruit decent balance.
**Finish:** Sudden raisin.

## ROYAL LOCHNAGAR 12 YEARS OLD 40%
Single Malt - Highland

**8** **Michael: Complex, beautifully rounded and soothing.**
**Nose:** Fruitcake. Faint burnt currants.
**Palate:** Cakey, sherryish, sultanas with a malty, grassy, sweetness.
**Finish:** Peatier than I remember but becomes rich and spicy.

**6¾** **Jim: Not a patch on the old style Lochnagar when the bourbon cask was king.**
**Nose:** The sherry is not quite as clean as it might be: also cuts out the more intricate malt notes. Quite doughy.
**Palate:** Good bitter-sweet balance from the off but rather hot and spirity. Again some sherry, fruity notes but not quite as in harmony as you'd expect.
**Finish:** Very dry and slightly bitter. Too much vanilla.

## ROYAL LOCHNAGAR SELECTED RESERVE 43%
Single Malt - Highland

**7½** **Michael: Too firm and well proportioned to be deemed voluptuous – but it's a delightfully close call.**
**Nose:** Lovely balance of sherry, malt and peat.
**Palate:** Fruitcake, ginger cake, spiced bread. Sambuca.
**Finish:** Luscious and smoky.

**7¼** **Jim: A quality malt that restores the faith.**
**Nose:** Toffee apples and Blue Mountain coffee: clean and fruit cake rich, complete with toasted almonds. An aroma worth passing a few malts for.
**Palate:** Drier than the nose suggests, but no less rich. Quite fat and fudgy, though, with a very malty middle despite the spicy fruit.
**Finish:** Not as long as some previous renditions, but continues the toffee-apple theme.

## ROYAL SALUTE 100 CASK 40%
Blended - Scotland

**7½** **Michael: Robust, rather than complex. A sustaining, sweetish, restorative.**
**Nose:** Condensed milk.
**Palate:** Creamy toffee. Burnt sugar. Treacle toffee.
**Finish:** Flapjack and black coffee.

**8** **Dave: Sumptuous, soft and sultry.**
**Nose:** Big and rich. Fruit and nut, black cherry, olde english marmalade, peat, touch of moss/fern, dried peels, black banana and caramel, some smoke.
**Palate:** Fruit cake sweetness. A thick feel and a broad mid-palate which tapers into a dry spicy finish. Water brings out milk chocolate.
**Finish:** Nutty and long.

## ROYAL SALUTE 21 YEARS OLD 40%
Blended - Scotland

**8½** **Michael: After dinner, I would usually think of a malt, but have long enjoyed the unashamed luxuriousness of this blend. This example seems fractionally less voluptuous than I remember, but my memories may be teasing me.**
**Nose:** Poached apricots in crème anglaise. Then dark chocolate pralines, with hazelnuts.
**Palate:** Gingery. Lively. Creamy. Very sherryish.
**Finish:** Fragrant smokiness, and oakiness.

WHISKY *Magazine* Editor's choice

**9** **Dave: A stunningly good blend.**
**Nose:** A mellow, softly complex nose, mixing sweet fruits, dried grassy notes, sandalwood, bourbon, biscuits, beech nut and with water a fungal/mushroom note along with cinnamon, vanilla, apple and sultana.
**Palate:** As smooth as silk, rich and elegant with a huge range of rich flavours and a light nuttiness which counterbalances the soft fruits.
**Finish:** Spicy, long.

## ROYAL SALUTE 21 YEARS OLD 40%
Blended - Scotland

**8¾** **Michael: In the rich, luxurious style, this is a long established favourite of mine.**
**Nose:** An expensive sweet-shop, with parma violets, pralines and cream toffees.
**Palate:** Big, silky. Juicy oak. Very sherryish. Developing peaty notes. Very complex.
**Finish:** Big with drier oakiness, more sherry, spicy esters, and fragrant smokiness.

WHISKY *Magazine* Recommended

**8** **Dave: A huge mouthful that takes blended whisky onto a new level of exoticism. Shame about the packaging. Velvet pouches are so very camp.**
**Nose:** An unreduced nose that starts with freshly turned earth. Exotic aromas emerge: Moroccan spices. Water reveals old apples in a fruit bowl.
**Palate:** Silky, soft and mouthfilling with rich fruit cake. All those exotic aromas return.
**Finish:** Long, warming, perfumed: cinnamon/nutmeg.

## ROYAL SALUTE 21 YEARS OLD 43%
Blended - Scotland

**8½** **Martine: Antique shop aromas. Oak and fruit locked in a sensual embrace.**
**Nose:** Distinguished. Old library. Pot pourri. Dundee cake. Orange flan. Pepper. Fresh almond.
**Palate:** Smooth and silky. Dried apricot. Raisins in rum. Walnut and date biscuit.
**Finish:** Everlasting. Spicy. Ginger. Slowly vanishing on a luscious praline note.

WHISKY *Magazine* Recommended

**8¾** **Dave: A classic example of the understated, elegant approach of the old Chivas blends.**
**Nose:** Understated and takes time to open. Almond skin, dried peels, honeycomb, light smoke, bruised apple, nut bowl, wax. Mature.
**Palate:** Lemon, lime, then marzipan, coconut, hay, nutmeg deepening into honey, cooked raspberry.
**Finish:** Anise/basil. Expansive and complex.

## ROYAL SALUTE 50 YEARS OLD 40%
Blended - Scotland

**9** **Michael: A work of craftsmanship, elegance and its own style.**
**Nose:** Perfumy maltiness. Fragrant smoke. What the nose promises, the palate delivers.
**Palate:** Silky. Very full flavours, but very light on their feet. It is the interplay and dexterity that captivates. Fred Astaire and Ginger Rogers? Billie Holiday and Lester Young?
**Finish:** Dry, oaky, more-ish.

WHISKY *Magazine* Editor's choice

**8¾** **Dave: Fragile but fascinating.**
**Nose:** Slightly shy to start. Subtle notes of dried mushroom (cep), casks, dried flowers, graphite, bitter orange, tea caddy tobacco leaf. Ever-changing and mature.
**Palate:** Dry and elegant. Seems fragile and old but with real character, then a startling orange lift and a tickle of smoke.
**Finish:** Dried peels and nuts.

## ROYAL SILK RARE SCOTCH WHISKY 40%
Blended - Scotland

**7½** **Michael: Pleasant, though real character emerges only in the finish.**
**Nose:** Sweetish, creamy, maltiness. Late touch of peat.
**Palate:** Clean, sweetish, creamy, marshmallow-like.
**Finish:** Lightly dry. Leafy. Grain mustard. Long.

**6½** **Dave: Easy going and light.**
**Nose:** Very light, young, slightly floral with touches of pigskin leather, lemon puffs and vanilla.
**Palate:** Very sweet light syrup start, plenty of good grain.
**Finish:** Medium sugar candy touch of spirit on the very end.

## SCAPA 12 YEARS OLD 43%
Single Malt - Island (non Islay)

**8** **Michael: Scapa can seem a delicate whisky, but it is full of flavours, and deserves its growing following.**
**Nose:** Soft. Hay, with a hint of oily chocolate and vanilla. Warm.
**Palate:** Smooth. Chocolate, vanilla, nuts. Very lively and appetising.
**Finish:** Late salt and pepper, with a hint of rooty peat.

**9** **Jim: An essay in elegance with a delicate honey note attached to the malt and heather. The smokelessness and resulting lack of weight easily distinguishes it from a Highland Park, despite the honey-heather.**
**Palate:** Immediately malty and rich with a delicious spicy tingling of old oak. The honey holds the middle and interplays with the drier oak notes and juicier malt. Wonderfully complex.
**Finish:** Cocoa-rich notes and biscuity maltiness makes for a quite weighty finale, and some curious smoke even wafts in from somewhere.

## SCAPA 13 YEARS OLD, DUN BHEAGAN 43%
Single Malt - Island (non Islay)

**7¾** **Michael: A very light, clean expression. Scapa deserves to be in regular production.**
**Nose:** Faint whiff of peat.
**Palate:** Starts fresh and soft as spring water. Then develops delicate flavours, but plenty of them: flowery; a hint of cereal-grain sweetness, the faintest hint of peat.
**Finish:** Refreshing. Very late saltiness.

**6** **Dave: Lacks the energy and the lusciousness you expect from Scapa.**
**Nose:** Light and earthy: some banana, but pretty lean and woody.
**Palate:** Very sweet with light tropical fruit (lemon and orange Opal fruits). Spiky alcohol. Wood is quite firm.
**Finish:** Heathery.

## SCAPA 13 YEARS OLD, OLD MALT CASK 50%
Single Malt - Island (non Islay)

**7½** **Dave: Light and discreet. Perfectly pleasant but not exactly exciting.**
**Nose:** Back to oiliness again. This time oilskins along with cream, light smoke and an earthy quality. Cherry and pear.
**Palate:** Fragrant fruitiness. Very lifted and charming. Tinned cling peaches...
**Finish:** Pears topped with tinned cream.

**8** **Arthur: Not overly complex but very pleasant flavour and well textured. A sunny dram.**
**Nose:** Candied lemon, some smoke, and a slightly sulphury in the background. Fruit salad and some dry grassiness.
**Palate:** Sweet malt, fruit cocktail and vanilla custard, with a lightly syrupy texture.
**Finish:** Custard cream biscuits.

## SCAPA 14 YEARS OLD 40%
Single Malt - Island (non Islay)

**7¾** **Martine: Good integration of wood and malt. A very decent dram.**
**Nose:** Spicy and fruity. Half dried apricots in cinnamon. Hazelnuts.
**Palate:** Round and sweet. Fruit gives way to a nutty spiciness.
**Finish:** Rather short. Cinnamon lingers on.

**8½** **Dave: Fantastic balance. One for sweet-toothed drinkers.**
**Nose:** Heathery. Oak, light peat, damson jam. Lavender honey dripping off hot buttered toast. Water brings out sweet almond, orange and cumin.
**Palate:** Sweet and honeyed with balancing oak and a long unctuous feel. Leather and caramelised notes.
**Finish:** Tablet and a tickle of smoke.

## SCAPA 1985, 16 YEARS OLD, CHIEFTAIN'S CHOICE 43%
Single Malt - Island (non Islay)

**8** **Martine: Rich and generous. Again, overwhelming distillery character.**
**Nose:** Sherry wood indeed. Slightly winey. Stewed quinces with cinnamon. Buttered apples. Beeswax.
**Palate:** Thick mouthfeel. Malty flavours break through oak. Spices emerging.
**Finish:** Strong. Liquoriced and spicy. Black pepper.

---

**7½** **Dave: A northern monster in which Scapa's lusciousness is left as texture with the sherry having a greater impact.**
**Nose:** Fat, sherried aromas: walnut/pecan, date, treacle toffee, leather with oily/honeyed notes behind.
**Palate:** Thick, sweet and very juicy. Ripe and full with dry nuttiness around it. Robust and a bit slick.
**Finish:** Soft.

## SCAPA 1987, GORDON & MACPHAIL 43%
Single Malt - Island (non Islay)

**8** **Michael: A complex, delicate, well-balanced vintage.**
**Nose:** Leafy. Slightly sour, herbal note. Peat. Salt.
**Palate:** Lightly syrupy, nutty, salty.
**Finish:** Nutty, salty, very long. Appetising.

**7½** **Jim: Gordon and MacPhail has been the purveyor of Scapa's excellent malt far longer than owners Allied, which was slow to wake up to its allure. However, this is not its finest bottling and lacks that lovely cocoa depth of yore.**
**Nose:** Stunningly fresh and clean with gristy, grassy malt, a lovely thread of orange and honey and the very faintest echo of smoke. As mouth-watering as any nose could be.
**Palate:** Immediately dry with a zesty fruitiness. Deep malty notes do water the mouth but the development seems arrested by a non-specific flat fruitiness.
**Finish:** Slightly spicy; rather lacking in complexity.

## SCAPA 1988, GORDON & MACPHAIL 43%
Single Malt - Island (non Islay)

**7¼** **Michael: I am not sure about that sulphur. Is it from the cask, or is it seaweedy? I usually like seaweed, but am not convinced by this bottling.**
**Nose:** Salty, rooty, seaweed.
**Palate:** Salty. Grainy. Some wood-pulp, sulphury, notes.
**Finish:** New mown hay. Sweetness. Slight peatiness, saltiness.

**6** **Doug: Fairly gentle for a Scapa and a little drier throughout than expected.**
**Nose:** Clean, soft fruity, pears, whiffs of carbolic soap and smoke.
**Palate:** Medium-full bodied, slightly viscous, nutty, malty, toasty.
**Finish:** Sweet to salty. Dry with a gently smoked character.

## SCOTCH MALT WHISKY SOCIETY 1972 BIRTHDAY BOTTLE 54.6%
Single Malt - Speyside

**8¼** **Michael: Lovely chestnut colour. Soothing. After dinner and in front of a log fire. A touch woody, but I enjoyed it nonetheless.**
**Nose:** Malty. Treacle toffee. Appetising, juicy, sherryish, oak. Poire Williams.
**Palate:** Layers of malty, nutty, flavours.
**Finish:** Intense raisiny sweetness, then drying on the tongue, with a suggestion of char. A hint of cough sweets.

**8½** **Dave: A big gentle well-balanced dram. Deep and old.**
**Nose:** Aged sherry (dry Oloroso) walnut, chicory, fig rolls, chocolate, wrinkly Cox's, tarragon. Water makes it smokier/meatier, leather, raisin, date and coal smoke.
**Palate:** Soft yet savoury: chocolate with a whiff of coal smoke, coffee cake.
**Finish:** Big soft and gentle. Liquorice and soot.

## SCOTCH MALT WHISKY SOCIETY 9 YEARS OLD MILLENNIUM MALT 58.1%
Single Malt - Campbeltown

**9½** **Michael: Frighteningly good. Godzilla is alive and well and living in Campbeltown.**
**Nose:** Pungent, piney, tar-like, intensely smoky, earthy, darkly sherried.
**Palate:** Coconut oiliness. Resiny. Fruity and phenolic.
**Finish:** Oaky and very salty. Immensely powerful, tenacious.

**9¼** **Jim: A cask well worth keeping back to see in the new century. And, as a 9 Years Old, proves that youth can conquer over age. Spectacular.**
**Nose:** An extraordinarily delicate smokiness, boasting soft, plummy fruit and a gristy maltiness.
**Palate:** Bigger than the nose suggests: peat runs before everything else in between sweet maltiness.
**Finish:** Chewy, vanilla-rich, kippery, buttery, still gristy and a little young but wonderfully long.

## SCOTCH MALT WHISKY SOCIETY 9 YEARS OLD, BRIM-STONE & TREACLE
Single Malt - Island (non Islay)

**8** **Michael:** Light, fragrant, peat, smoke and salt.
**Palate:** Light, dry, leafy, with vanilla-pod and creamy, syrupy, malt emerging.
**Finish:** Late gust of salty warmth.

**7½** **Jim:** A light-coloured young malt which thanks to the peat notes suggests Highland Park or maybe Ledaig. The sweetness tends to point the Orkneys. Unusual, very tasty and great fun. Don't know about the 'Brimstone and Treacle', though.
**Nose:** Light, delicately peated, freshly ground malt with a young, ammonia note. Beautiful and very clean honey more than compensates.
**Palate:** Big alcohol kick, very mouthwatering and delightfully peated.
**Finish:** Some oaky notes which soften the peaty spice and malty sweetness.

## SCOTTISH LEADER 12 YEARS OLD 40%
Blended - Scotland

**7½** **Michael:** Very mild, but a blend assembled with great skill and subtlety.
**Nose:** Perfumy, spicy, musky.
**Palate:** Rounded, slippery-smooth. Very malty indeed. Creamy. Sweet. Some orangey notes.
**Finish:** Spicy. Minty.

**7½** **Dave:** LOTS of sherry and fat, rich flavours. One for those who like their whiskies well covered.
**Nose:** Fat, sweet and a little slick. Creamy toffee, sponge cake, stewed apple, date and gingerbread.
**Palate:** Quite thick and slightly syrupy with a mix of dried and stewed soft fruits.
**Finish:** Fruity!

## SCOTTISH LEADER 15 YEARS OLD 40%
Blended - Scotland

**8** **Michael:** More subtlety sophistication and elegance than the Platinum.
**Nose:** Still decidedly orangey, but much more restrained. Very nutty and malty. A touch of sherry and oak.
**Palate:** Gentle. Lightly oily. Orangey, perfumy. Creamy, oaty, malty notes. Well rounded.
**Finish:** Firm but light. Flowery. Heathery. Hint of peat.

**7½** **Dave:** A soft, gentle, labrador of a dram.
**Nose:** An unreduced nose of smoked cheese, toasty wood, rich fruits, rubber and crème brûlée. With water added: honey, fresh sawdust and bran.
**Palate:** Sweet, concentrated red fruits along with toffee, caramelised fruit and a soft grainy mid-palate.
**Finish:** Clean and dry with a hint of lemon.

## SCOTTISH LEADER PLATINUM SEAL 40%
Blended - Scotland

**7¾** **Michael:** Remarkably fruity, but in a lively interplay with all the other elements.
**Nose:** Fruity, orangey, musky-spicy. Hint of leafy peatiness. A rich, complex aroma.
**Palate:** Silky, enwrapping. Powerful orange-peel, but also maltiness and nuttiness, and some underlying dryness from a touch of peat.
**Finish:** Light, clean, dry.

**8** **Dave:** Obviously old but still very well balanced. Sean Connery.
**Nose:** There's some sulphur notes when unreduced but water pulls out incense, lapsang souchong tea, dried apricot. An 'old' aroma: all walnut, cedar and orange honey.
**Palate:** Sweet start with toffee and cream. The wood is a little grippy, but not overpowering.
**Finish:** Dry, long and lively.

## SILVER BARLEY MILROY'S 40%
Blended - Scotland

**6½** **Martine:** A very young, new-make like whisky. On the bitter side. A fresh nose isn't enough.
**Nose:** Very young, drying hay. Quite refreshing with a minty whiff. A hint of butterscotch.

**Palate:** Smooth and sweet at start. Leafy. Green wood takes over, developing on bitter notes.
**Finish:** Quite short, not especially elegant. Nutty flavours cheer up a somewhat astringent aftertaste.

**6½** **Dave: Is this whisky? I know the industry needs to 'convert' vodka drinkers but this is ridiculous.**
**Nose:** For starters, it's clear. Very light and clean, verging on neutral. Hint of vanilla. Flat ginger ale. Water brings out a sulphury, new make note.
**Palate:** Very sweet and smooth-almost too sugary and slick.
**Finish:** Huh?

## SINGLE MALTS OF SCOTLAND ROSEBANK 14 YEARS OLD, BOURBON BARREL 46%
Single Malt - Lowland

**7½** **Martine:** A surprising character. A light aromatic profile with a heavy mouthfeel. A touch of water keeps the balance right.
**Nose:** Restrained but subtle. New leather. A floral delicacy. A touch of orange blossom honey.
**Palate:** Thick, sweet. Very oily. Lemon pulp. Not a great range of flavours but a pleasant citrussy profile. A hint of ginger.
**Finish:** Nutty. Smoked almonds.

**7¾** **Michael: Simple, well structured malt.**
**Nose:** Light, simply structured. Some cereal notes behind slightly drier fruit.
**Palate:** Delicate. Sweet. Slightly chewy cereals. Malty, buttery cookies. Some chocolate.
**Finish:** Simple, well structured, perhaps slightly salty? Liquorice toffee. Appetising.

## SINGLETON OF DUFFTOWN 12 YEARS OLD 43%
Single Malt - Speyside

**7½** **Dave:** A perfectly pleasant dram, but lacking the finesse and complexity of the best on show here.
**Nose:** Straightforward nuttiness/nut shell, slightly bitter. Opens into yew, sawn oak, draff, then marshmallow and a touch of apple and fig relish.
**Palate:** Nut oils. Quite biscuity and rich. Leafy.
**Finish:** Crisp short.

**7½** **Arthur:** Has that balanced character that makes for an ideal gift whisky, but lacked drama.
**Nose:** Malt extract, chocolate mint, melted cheese, honeysuckle, brown bread with lots of butter. Background grassiness.
**Palate:** Citric, with orange juice and lime. Stewed fruits and toasted oak.
**Finish:** Malty and citric.

## SMOKEHEAD 43%
Single Malt - Islay

**7¾** **Dave: Not subtle, but is it meant to be? Just needs a little sweet oak to round the edges off, but why is it called smackhead?**
**Nose:** Bang! Kipper paté with lemon served on an oatcake. Medicinal notes (Germoline) then: fish stock, cow shed, smoked meat. Seems young.
**Palate:** Instant dry smoke (suggesting youth) but calms down a little and mellows in the centre.
**Finish:** Crowdie cheese rolled in oats, hotsmoked salmon.

**9** **Arthur: That Lapsang Souchong character is distinctive. Attractive youth, resolutely smoky but with a class. Lauren Bacall before the wrinkles.**
**Nose:** Smoky tea, an ashiness like a fire grate the morning after.
**Palate:** A little fruitiness, like black grapes. Some sweetness too and a herb character (almost basil, but not quite).
**Finish:** Lots of smoke, masking a fruitiness.

## SPEYBURN 10 YEARS OLD 40%
Single Malt - Speyside

**7** **Martine:** Quite a pleasant pre-dinner dram, with light nibbles perhaps. A little shy though. Would yield more at a higher alcoholic strength or in a few years.
**Nose:** Elegant and light. Vibrant gingerbread. Spicy. Stewed apricot. A hint of toasted almonds.
**Palate:** Smooth and soothing. Liquorice. Develops into creamy custard flavours.
**Finish:** A bit too soft but later enhanced by a spicy note, releasing a slight bitterness. Chewed stalk.

7½ **Dave: There's plenty going on here. Not big, but has real charm.**
**Nose:** Soft and malty. In time there's heather honey, orange and that nutty spicy note which keeps recurring. Water brings out sweet tobacco.
**Palate:** A light, dry, malty start then a really spicy mid-palate. Medium-bodied with a lovely balance struck between spice, dry nut and sweetness.
**Finish:** Spicy, slightly dry.

### SPEYBURN 16 YEARS OLD 46%
Single Malt - Speyside

7¾ **Michael: One of the most assertive, flavoursome examples of Speyburn I have tasted. A pretty whisky from a pretty distillery.**
**Nose:** Herbal notes, becoming sweeter. Heather honey.
**Palate:** Blossoms first, then fruit. Apricot, orange, raspberry, strawberry.
**Finish:** Long and lingering, with echoes of all those flowers and fruits.

7¾ **Dave: Sweet and gentle.**
**Nose:** Clean and attractive with a light sweetness undiluted. Water brings out a deeper earthy/grassy note and a hint of violet.
**Palate:** Clean and again quite sweet. Heather. Gentle but with a subtle weight.
**Finish:** Medium weight. Sultana cake, orange. Juicy.

### SPEYBURN 1973 46%
Single Malt - Speyside

7¾ **Michael: Another light-tasting malt that blossoms with age. Its flavours belie the use of a malt that is scarcely peated.**
**Nose:** Very fruity, estery, leafy, spicy. Tea-like. Apples, cloves.
**Palate:** Firm, clean sweet. Pastry. Marzipan.
**Finish:** Fragrant, perfumy, flowery, herbal. Heathery, gently peaty, smoky.

7¾ **Jim: The nose lies. A classic example of a Speysider beyond its prime. Ultimately it fails to give full satisfaction.**
**Nose:** Astonishingly light: the malty grassiness is closer to it being an 8 Years Old!! Oak is apparent but almost apologetic.
**Palate:** At its height the intensity is a must for chocoholics.
**Finish:** Dry and jaded with the cocoa keeping a lid on the oaky excesses.

### SPEYBURN 21 YEARS OLD 58.5%
Single Malt - Speyside

WHISKY Magazine Recommended

7¾ **Michael: Full of flavour and interest, but the sherry and oak verge on being overwhelming.**
**Nose:** Heavy sherry. Bitter chocolate. Heathery. Leafy
**Palate:** Very firm. Slightly oily. Good malt background. Nutty. Spicy. Aniseed.
**Finish:** Peaty. Sappy. Oaky.

8¼ **Dave: Well-balanced. The spirit isn't drowned by the wood and sherry. Macallan fans will love this.**
**Nose:** Rich, powerful sherry notes: cake, nut and figgy, pruney fruits, raisin, butter and a charred meaty note.
**Palate:** Great powerful European oak punch: orange, sweet spices, treacle scones, with some sweet spirit well in evidence. The charred notes give it an intriguing balance. Big, rich and savoury.
**Finish:** Liquorice.

### SPEYBURN 21 YEARS OLD 60.2%
Single Malt - Speyside

7¾ **Michael: Very restrained, but lovely gentle peat smoke.**
**Nose:** Flowery, leafy, peaty.
**Palate:** Clean. Reticent at first, but develops a good long malt background, then fresh, herbal, heathery notes.
**Finish:** Nutty sweetness, becoming drier. Late peaty warmth.

8¼ **Jim: Highly impressive whisky, quite exceptional for a Speyburn. Only the over-firm finale stops this from being one of the top five Speyside expressions of the last five years.**
**Nose:** Marvellously rich and fruity. Unmistakable sherry influence but lifted in complexity by a hint of raspberry, apple and peat. The oaky vanilla is beautifully synchronised with a molasses sweetness, the sweet pipe tobacco.
**Palate:** An immediate explosion of spice and sweet Oloroso defuses slowly so the malt gains a firm and chewy hand. Very substantial.
**Finish:** Slightly hard and metallic with some smoke and malt still hanging on against the drying oak.

### SPEYSIDE 1990, COCONUT CREAM 46%
Single Malt - Speyside

7½ **Dave: Light, but a good aperitif. Have it with ice.**
**Nose:** Plain and lightly grassy. Touch of creamy mashed potato and light apricot. Slightly vinous. Water brings out Dolly Mixture like esters, bubblegum.
**Palate:** Delicate and slightly minty and an acetone-like note. High toned with banana, raspberry.
**Finish:** Coconut.

8 **Martine: A very well wrapped present! Fresh, cheery with a charming combination of fruity and floral flavours. Luscious.**
**Nose:** Delicate, sweet and caressing. Almondy. Blancmange. A floral note. Gorse.
**Palate:** Round, mellow. A creamy sweetness. Pear flan. A touch of marshmallow. Appetising.
**Finish:** Crisp, minty. Peppermint.

### SPEYSIDE 1991, APPLES AND PEARS 46%
Single Malt - Speyside

7 **Dave: A strange package that almost works.**
**Nose:** An odd oxidised note. Tinned pear and evaporated milk. Burning cigar, roasted nut and a signed note like burning hair. Glossy, but there's something not quite right behind.
**Palate:** Big hit with good length. Pretty, fresh and balanced though a touch of soapiness knocks it back.
**Finish:** Cereal.

7½ **Martine: Not so far from an aged calvados. Well balanced but the wood is not totally integrated.**
**Nose:** Cider apples, damp cellar. Dessert-like. Crème caramel. Pears in puff pastry.
**Palate:** Smooth, quite sweet. Caramelised apples. Tarte Tatin.
**Finish:** Medium, spicy (nutmeg and a touch of cinnamon).

### SPEYSIDE 1994, GLACE FRUITS 46%
Single Malt - Speyside

7¼ **Dave: There's a restrained quality about all of these. Amusing lunchtime companions.**
**Nose:** Clean and lifted. Old orange peel, geranium, custard then sesame and dried mango. Slightly too edgy oak.
**Palate:** More impact than you expect. Soft feel, fresh pineapple, cherry, light spice.
**Finish:** Clean quite short.

7¾ **Martine: Another well knitted dram. Obviously under bourbon influence. The exotic hint is "gourmande".**
**Nose:** Malty and fruity. Muësli. Lemon drops. Candyfloss. Poached rhubarb. Opens on herbal notes. Verbena, green tea.
**Palate:** Silky, gently flowing on the tongue. Lovely fresh feel. Light fruit. Hint of tangerine juice and pineapple juice. And possibly guava.
**Finish:** Delicate but reasonably long. Herbal notes.

### SPEYSIDE 1995, CHOCOLATE HEAVEN 46%
Single Malt - Speyside

7¼ **Dave: Slightly disappointing until the finish which is worth the entry price.**
**Nose:** Dry and malty with touches of hessian, malt bin and crisp oak. Some orchard fruit, cocoa, but a little musty.
**Palate:** Light again but fizzy giving an interest to a very soft and smooth mid-palate. White chocolate. Alcohol sticks out just a little.
**Finish:** Digestive biscuits, then chocolate, vanilla pod and cream all the way down the throat. It all comes together at the end.

8 **Martine: Another pleasant dram. Has this friendly, straightforward invite. To be served slightly chilled with a fruit dessert.**
**Nose:** Nutty, creamy. Apricots in mascarpone. A light touch of cappuccino. Honey syrup.
**Palate:** Smooth, mouthcoating. Toasted hazelnuts. Peach infused in basil.
**Finish:** Neat, a little too dry maybe.

## THE SPEYSIDE 10 YEARS OLD 40%
Single Malt - Speyside

**7½**
**Michael: Good to see one of the newest distilleries now offering a 10 Years Old. One to watch.**
**Nose:** Pronounced oily nuttiness.
**Palate:** Sweet, buttery, rich. Some cream toffee, cookies and caramel.
**Finish:** Faintly kirsch-like fruitiness.

**7½**
**Dave: A gentle warm-hearted glassful.**
**Nose:** There's half-melted cream toffee, yellow fruit gums, hay loft and an aroma that's like a freshly baked sponge cake.
**Palate:** Chewy, soft and silky with a moist coconut mid-palate and a lovely fresh maltiness.
**Finish:** Soft.

## THE SPEYSIDE MILLENNIUM
Single Malt - Speyside

**9¾**
**Michael: A fine malt, with great character for its relative youth. Greater ages are eagerly awaited.**
**Nose:** Some peaty grassiness. Oily, creamy, maltiness. Very nutty indeed.
**Palate:** Astonishingly nutty. Sliced almonds. Ripe cherries.
**Finish:** Kirsch-like.

**6½**
**Jim: Recovers well from disastrous nose. Never becomes complex on the palate but flavours are vivid and helped by a glossy sheen.**
**Nose:** Feinty, fat, young. Off-centre. Oily and sweet with some malty notes fighting through.
**Palate:** Immediately sweet and coats the mouth with a pleasant maltiness. A little spice towards the middle, alongside some sweet vanilla.
**Finish:** Sweet coffee and lingering oils.

## SPRINGBANK 10 YEARS OLD 40%
Single Malt - Campbeltown

**8¾**
**Michael: Scores extra points for complexity.** *WHISKY Recommended*
**Nose:** Fragrant, salty. The sea begins to emerge. Very fresh.
**Palate:** Powerful. Intense clean sweetness. Coconut. Mint.
**Finish:** Mint toffee. Hot peppermint. Late saltiness on the front of the tongue. Extraordinarily long.

**8½**
**Dave: A worthy replacement for the previous cask vatting, another complex Campbeltown beauty.**
**Nose:** Straw/gold. A good mix of spume, sweet fruit, leather, dried grass and light toffee.
**Palate:** A smooth sweet start then a blast of flavour dried herb, salt spray, smoke, moss, toffee apple.
**Finish:** Very long, some coconut.

## SPRINGBANK 10 YEARS OLD 46%
Single Malt - Campbeltown

**7¼**
**Martine: The nose is lighter and more subtle than the palate. A dash of water tones down the flavours. Disappointing.**
**Nose:** Fragrant. Balsamic, herbal. Touch of eucalyptus. Dry hay, meadow flowers. Creamy. Developing on buttery notes. Hint of marshmallows.
**Palate:** Chewy. Less sweet than expected from the nose. Sour apples with the astringency of the skin.
**Finish:** Spicy, slightly tangy. Drying on oaky notes.

**8½**
**Dave: Your starter for 10. A classic.**
**Nose:** Fresh. Black olive, hot gorse/coconut then a tickle of smoke and some lemon notes. Green oak, tangerine and a gently oily quality.
**Palate:** Silky soft feel. Coconut cream/milky coffee. Brine, oily but zesty with sooty smoke. Hits top gear half-way through. Subtle.
**Finish:** Lightly sooty.

## SPRINGBANK 12 YEARS OLD, RUM CASK 54.6%
Single Malt - Campbeltown

**9**
**Michael: More rounded and elegant than the earlier, 10 Years Old rum cask. I enjoy** *WHISKY Editor's choice*
**the Springbank rum cask whiskies very much, though even at the expense of the more traditional expressions.**
**Nose:** Sweetish. Fragrant. Smoky, with fruit behind. Like an applewood grill. Hint of salty sea air.
**Palate:** Soft. Marshmallowy. Sweet red apples. Pears. Hedgerow fruits.
**Finish:** Small explosion of spiciness. Peppermint.

**7½**
**Dave: The sweetness of the rum is never allowed to dominate the Springbank character. Well integrated.**
**Nose:** All quite sweet and light with banana, café au lait, dried fig, but as it opens out comes some sooty/peaty notes. An intriguing mix.
**Palate:** A very solid start with toffee/caramelised fruit in the centre held in check by a slightly austere grip.
**Finish:** Smoky with raisin, baked banana, spice.

## SPRINGBANK 1965, LOMBARD 46%
Single Malt - Campbeltown

**8**
**Michael: Robust, but lacks the delicacy and structure of the best Springbanks.**
**Nose:** Salty. Cookie-like maltiness. A hint of banana.
**Palate:** Medium-bodied. Firm. Oily. Some coconut. Some apricot-like sherry character. Winey, even.
**Finish:** Leafy. Vine leaves. Cedary, dry, slightly bitter. Some smokiness.

**8¼**
**Dave: Drink neat.**
**Nose:** A fascinating, oily mix of soot and perfume: smoke and lilies. White pepper, oak and sage leaves.
**Palate:** Rounded with bags of personality and citrus fruits giving it an acidic zestiness. Spice (ginger/nutmeg) and oak as well and an overall oily, briny quality.
**Finish:** Dies a little after the exciting nose.

## SPRINGBANK 1965, MURRAY MCDAVID 46%
Single Malt - Campbeltown

**8½**
**Michael: The characteristic salt and coconut characteristics of Springbank are very** *WHISKY Recommended*
**evident in this bottling, but perhaps overwhelmingly so. I may need more time to understand this one.**
**Nose:** Fresh brine. Coconut flesh. A suggestion of banana.
**Palate:** Sweet. Oily. Winey. Marsala? Vine leaves.
**Finish:** Dryish. Gently warming. Long. Very late smokiness and saltiness.

**9**
**Jim: Truly brilliant for a whisky of this age with not a single sign of deterioration.**
**Nose:** Midly sawdust like but enriched by a dazzling array of spicy, very faintly smoked fruit notes.
**Palate:** An outstanding tidal wave of spicy, oaky tones level out to reveal a multi-layered richness of malt. All supremely balanced.
**Finish:** Long, toasty and dries very slowly to offer further complexity.

## SPRINGBANK 1975 LIMBURG WHISKY FAIR 49.2%
Single Malt - Campbeltown

**8**
**Michael: Astonishingly citric.** *WHISKY Editor's choice*
**Nose:** Fresh. Briney. Lemony.
**Palate:** Creamy porridge with salt. Then pancakes with sugar and lemon juice.
**Finish:** Sherbet lemons.

**8¼**
**Dave: Contemplative.**
**Nose:** Complex. Coconut oil, oak, wood, basil, dried orange skin, hint of smoke. With water, sultana and a singed note.
**Palate:** Smoke again. Everything quite concentrated then leaps into life, broadening and coating the palate. Builds in complexity, then spice.
**Finish:** Tangerine and toast.

## SPRINGBANK 1989, LIMITED EDITION LIMBURG FESTIVAL BOTTLING 55.8%
Single Malt - Campbeltown

**9**
**Michael: Springbank in pyrotechnic form. The sherry doubles the flavours, but** *WHISKY Editor's choice*
**arguably also softens the Campbeltown character.**
**Nose:** Distinctly fruity. Peaches. Sherryish. Nutty.
**Palate:** Big flavours and it's packed with them. Liquorice. Salt. Spice merchants. Dusty.
**Finish:** Big, spicy explosion.

**9**
**Dave: The sweetest Springbank I've ever tried. Has the extra dimension that elevates great malts from good.**
**Nose:** Amazingly buttery; butterkist popcorn/crème caramel/tablet. Water opens it and rings out some dry smoke, sultana and charred oak.
**Palate:** Mouthfilling, complex. Sweet, then unfolds and dries: date loaf, black olive, smoke, caramelised fruits.
**Finish:** Leather, long, great balance.

## SPRINGBANK 1991, LOMBARD 50%
Single Malt - Campbeltown

**8** **Michael: Jumps and bites. This is the young Springbank, not yet the mature sophisticate.**
**Nose:** Citrus zest. Coconut. Salt.
**Palate:** Plenty of flavour development. Starts with coconut ice intense sweetness, moving to marshmallow-like maltiness, and then an astonishingly sudden rush of lemon juice.
**Finish:** Passion fruit. Hard and strong.

**8½** **Dave: A lovely young Springbank with all the distillery's classic attributes.**
**Nose:** Starts creamy/buttery, then sooty smoke and hints of oily weight. Water teases out a marine/medicinal note and malty core. Gains power as it develops but is subtle and complex, not overpowering.
**Palate:** A firm structure with briny character on show. Great rich, quite oily feel. Mouthfilling and complex.
**Finish:** Decent length.

## SPRINGBANK 1992, 7 YEARS OLD, DA MHILE ORGANIC 46%
Single Malt - Campbeltown

**8¼** **Michael: Lively and refreshing, but the flavours have not combined and fleshed out as probably they will in another six or seven years.**
**Nose:** Salt. Cucumber. Lettuce. Tobacco.
**Palate:** Sweet. Malt background. Angelica. Coconut.
**Finish:** Coconut. Sugar, but also salt.

**7** **Jim: Has an extraordinary finish, suggesting something twice the age.**
**Nose:** Fat and mildly feinty.
**Palate:** Lemon drop sharpness, fan tailing out for a beguilingly malty middle.
**Finish:** Chewy and tantalisingly spicy.

## SPRINGBANK 25 YEARS OLD, FRANK MCHARDY BOTTLING 46%
Single Malt - Campbeltown

**8¾** **Michael: Springbank can sound like a fruit salad, but the whisky has a lot of authority.**
**Nose:** Fresh, fruity. Red apples, lemons and coconut.
**Palate:** Sustained, teasing interplay of firm, malty, sweetness and dryness-and yet more fruit. Bananas, raspberries.
**Finish:** Shortbread, cookies. Like the base of a fruit pie.

**8** **Dave: Understated – a bit like Frank in fact.**
**Nose:** Neat it has a fresh spray of tangerine peel. With water, more oily and mature. Notes of strawberry, quince/medlar, pine and Maltesers. All quite reserved.
**Palate:** Great feel. A dram which fills the mouth. Good balance between sweet and almost savoury. Orange curaçao and a sooty note.
**Finish:** Very light smoke.

## SPRINGBANK 35 YEARS OLD SINGLE CASK SHERRY BUTT, CHIEFTAIN'S CHOICE 54.2%
Single Malt - Campbeltown

**8¼** **Michael: Springbank is a big whisky but the sherry here is even bigger, and wipes out some of the whisky's subtleties.**
**Nose:** Huge, mellow, buttery, sweetish, sherry.
**Palate:** Big-bodied and drying. Treacle toffee, coconut, rhubarb, vanilla.
**Finish:** Some bitterness and a late salty tang.

**7½** **Dave: Big and rich, but where's the whisky?**
**Nose:** Rich, Oloroso influenced. Dark, dried fruits, black olive tapenade. Whiff of fragrant smoke even a touch of tomato ketchup.
**Palate:** Very sherried (Bristol Milk) and thick. Spirit a little muted.
**Finish:** Sweet then becomes tannic.

## SPRINGBANK MARSALA, 9 YEARS OLD 58%
Single Malt - Campbeltown

**7¾** **Dave: These strange combinations make me think of an unconventionally beautiful model like Erin O'Connor.**
**Nose:** Thick and slightly oily. Boiled sweets, then a melange of fruit. Water increases the perfume and calms things down.
**Palate:** Starts dry then oily then fruity. Very silky with tinned fruit, smoke, charred wood and salt.
**Finish:** A little cloying.

**8¼** **Arthur: Bags of flavour and a good duel between cask and spirit.**
**Nose:** Chutney spices, like a good homemade tomato and onion chutney. Homemade plum jam. Marmalade on malt loaf. Wet peat. A box of dark chocolates.
**Palate:** More floral than the nose, with a little peat smoke.
**Finish:** Some meatiness and cloves.

## SPRINGBANK RUM WOOD, 16 YEARS OLD 54.2%
Single Malt - Campbeltown

**7** **Dave: Almost as if it is still coming together.**
**Nose:** Direct with notes of fennel, pine, green leaf and a tickle of smoke. Slight biscuity sweetness with water.
**Palate:** Delicate with hints of jasmine and elderflower and a tingle of alcohol. Very sweet with a decent feel, but seems strangely fragile.
**Finish:** Slightly lactic.

**8¾** **Martine: Mellows once the alcohol has evaporated, especially with water. A good summer refresher.**
**Nose:** Herbal. Aromatic. Fragrant but the alcohol bite masks the aromas at start. Then smooths on rich cream (Jersey clotted cream?) and freshly churned butter. Gooseberry fool.
**Palate:** Surprisingly sweet. Star anise. A hint of passion fruit. Sherbet dib-dabs.
**Finish:** Quite short, fading quickly.

## SPRINGBANK VINTAGE, 10 YEARS OLD 55.2%
Single Malt - Campbeltown

**9** **Dave: There's an uncompromising feral power to this. Magnificent.**
**Nose:** Big. Savoury. Black olive, bung cloth, bay leaf, and a little smoke. Lightly waxed notes mixing with coconut, trifle sponge, malt and sweet dried fruits. Substantial and complex.
**Palate:** Enjoyably thick and chewy palate with big, upfront flavours allowing the smoke to slide underneath. Good grip.
**Finish:** Slightly briny.

**7½** **Martine: A strange character. Hard to grab. The palate reveals an interesting sweetness but the finish disappoints.**
**Nose:** Sharp, tangy. Warm blackcurrant pie. A balsamic note of thyme oil. A hint of bogmyrtle maybe. Quite difficult to assess. Old furniture.
**Palate:** Sweet, less sharp than on the nose. Wood speaks up too. Bitter chocolate. Artichoke leaves.
**Finish:** Rather short. Does not leave a great impression. Slightly bitter.

## ST MAGADALENE 23 YEARS OLD, DOUGLAS LAING 50%
Single Malt - Lowland

**7¾** **Martine: Interesting but a sweet note too far maybe but the finish gets a grip on itself and leaves a clean minty freshness. Recommended for sweet tooth.**
**Nose:** Grassy, minty. Vanilla merges through in sweet waves, until flooding the lighter vegetal notes. Butterscotch. Develops on pudding notes.
**Palate:** Sweet, velvety. Lasciviously unfolding biscuity sweet flavours. Slightly over the top.
**Finish:** Dry mintiness with a gingery touch.

**7** **Dave: There's just nothing to get excited about here.**
**Nose:** Yet another light one. Hawthorn cream and with water wet cardboard.
**Palate:** Better than the nose with surprising grip more oak than you'd guess from that etheral nose.
**Finish:** Mouth drying. Cigarette smoke.

## ST MAGDALENE 1975, GORDON & MACPHAIL 43%
Single Malt - Lowland

**WHISKY** *Magazine* *Recommended*

**8½ Arthur:** Typically lowland, with a nice progression of sensation: sweet, malty then zingy.
**Nose:** Green apples, fresh paint and fruit syrup. Kiwis and brown bread. A little eucalyptus oil and mint choc chip later on.
**Palate:** Sweet, malty, earthy then dry. Maturity and complexity.
**Finish:** Chocolate with citric sourness.

**8 Dave:** Well balanced, though not quite the extra dimension of the very best on show.
**Nose:** Intense. Cooked marrow (cauliflower), yeasty start then opens into rose petal, Turkish delight, green apple/old apple. Grassy and shows some complexity. Lightly charred.
**Palate:** Very light, perfumed. Lacy texture. Sweet to start then comes a fresh stewed green plum flavour and red liquorice.
**Finish:** Vanilla essence.

## ST MAGDALENE 1982, RARE OLD 40%
Single Malt - Lowland

**7½ Michael:** Livelier, fresher, less "difficult" flavours than in most bottlings.
**Nose:** Faint smoky fragrance.
**Palate:** Still a lively interplay of exotic fruit sweetness and smoky dryness.
**Finish:** Fragrant again. Some woody bitterness but more restrained than in most St Magdalene.

**6¾ Dave:** Brings to mind those fragile Swiss white wines. All very delicate and ever so slightly faded.
**Nose:** Gentle and floral. Wet grass, green fruit, violet, coal bunkers. Water flattens it a bit.
**Palate:** Light and delicate. Pineapple, grass again. Seems a bit tired.
**Finish:** Short, watery.

## ST MAGDALENE 1998 19 YEARS OLD, RARE MALTS 63.8%
Single Malt - Lowland

**7¼ Michael:** For a ghost, quite aggressive.
**Nose:** Sweet. Burnt. Caramelised.
**Palate:** Brown sugar on porridge, followed by marmalade on toast.
**Finish:** Hot and drying.

**8 Dave:** I like its directness, there's nothing fussy or fancy about this, just a bloody good drink.
**Nose:** Assertive, nutty and malty with burnt stubble and rich bourbon oak. Dry but characterful. Good oakiness.
**Palate:** Lemon, vanilla with crisp red fruits and orange. Decent feel. Fills the front of the mouth then narrows and tightens. Very direct, as the nose suggests.
**Finish:** The memory of oak and grass. Appetising.

## ST MAGDALENE, 24 YEARS OLD, OLD MALT CASK 50%
Single Malt - Lowland

**5½ Dave:** If this was in a better cask it would have been a rather pleasant whisky.
**Nose:** Wet and slightly burnt grass. Daffodils that have stood in water for too long. Cereal. Wet wood. With water very plain with a light plastic note. Flowers underneath.
**Palate:** Very dry and austere...not letting anything out.
**Finish:** Grubby. An old cellar.

**6 Arthur:** Had potential, but a shame to see such a poor cask bottled.
**Nose:** This started curiously, like the underside of a sheepskin rug, mushrooms and a little wood-glue. It soon settled down and fruity notes appeared, freshly cut red grapes, lemon, and sweet warmed bread.
**Palate:** Lemony with malty breadiness.
**Finish:** Relatively short, and a little sweet soap.

## STRATHCLYDE 37 YEARS OLD 54.4%
Single Grain - Scotland

**8 Dave:** It's in the twilight of its autumn, but has subtle complexity and less of the overt sweetness that old grains usually exhibit.
**Nose:** Mature notes: dunnage warehouse, discreet nuttiness. Water brings out its real substance. Oily and strangely, funkily, sweet.

**Palate:** Extremely sweet: elderflower and icing sugar, milk chocolate. With water, orange Spangles, pink marshmallow. Light grip.
**Finish:** Medium, oaky.

**7 Martine:** The alcohol bite is assertive, on the nose as on the palate. And water does not make it much more palatable.
**Nose:** Grassy, herbal. Orange like in Cointreau. Candied angelica. Oatcakes. A touch of caramelised demerara sugar.
**Palate:** Very spirity and tangy. A note of corked spirit and must.
**Finish:** Spicy, liquoriced.

## STRATHISLA 12 YEARS OLD 43%
Single Malt - Speyside

**8 Michael:** A malt that dares to be truly oaky. Thank heavens for boldness and individuality in a world where blandness is always an easier option. This beautiful old distillery is Chivas' showpiece, but it is more than a pretty face.
**Nose:** A hint of (appetising) phenol. Polished oak.
**Palate:** Robust exchange of sweetness and dryness. Juicy flavours from the oak. Vanilla, violets, sherry.
**Finish:** Apricot. Prunes in Armagnac. Sappy.

**8¼ Dave:** Charming, subtle and gorgeous.
**Nose:** Fragrant with citrus (orange peel), flowers (freesia), spice, and a hint of cream-filled choux pastry. Juicy! Water pulls out more weighty malty notes.
**Palate:** Lovely mid-weight malt that's softer than the nose initially suggests. Great momentum in the mouth with cranachan, soft baked fruits, fruit cake, syrup, apricot and malt. It dances on the tongue.
**Finish:** Bursts into life.

## STRATHISLA 15 YEARS OLD, CASK STRENGTH 55.1%
Single Malt - Speyside

**8¾ Martine:** Make the effort to sample a cracking dram and to visit the bonniest distillery in Scotland.
**Nose:** Attractive, vivid. Lots of citrus fruit. Orange marmalade. Lemon meringue pie. Floral hint.
**Palate:** Ample. Velvety, mouth coating. Complex and tasty festoon of spices. Mint cream. Hazelnut toffee. Liquorice. Shortbread. Malty sweetness.
**Finish:** Warm, lasting, soothing on creamy notes.

**7¾ Dave:** Strathisla is a funny beast – rigid when young it takes a long time to come out of its shell. This is just starting to do so.
**Nose:** Milky. Light hazelnut, cocoa powder, haystacks, unmalted barley, popcorn, flour sacks.
**Palate:** Medium-bodied. Some complexity beneath a pretty firm structure. Flour, nutmeg.
**Finish:** Dry, nutty.

## STRATHISLA 1960, GORDON & MACPHAIL 40%
Single Malt - Speyside

**8 Michael:** Strathisla has its own distinct, rather dry style- and this is a good example.
**Nose:** Resiny. Sappy. Crème brûlée. Smoky.
**Palate:** Lightly syrupy, developing fruity dryness, then vanilla-pod nutty spiciness...
**Finish:** Sudden, surprising, surge of smokiness.

**8 Martine:** A rich expression of a venerable sherry maturation. Will delight sherry-cask aficionados.
**Nose:** Rich and intense. Unmistakeably Oloroso. Resiny. Plum marmalade. Clove orange, cinnamon.
**Palate:** Very complex and elegant, releasing waves of flavours. Mulled wine. Jaffa cake. Candied ginger. Spanish oak.
**Finish:** Lingering, dry, slightly astringent, spicy.

## STRATHISLA 1976, 27 YEARS OLD, COOPER'S CHOICE 46%
Single Malt - Speyside

**7¾ Michael:** Always a complex whisky, hard to pin down. This sample seems to have triggered an oriental mood.
**Nose:** Cedar. Boxes of dim sum.
**Palate:** Cereal grain. Egg fried rice. Macaroon on rice paper.
**Finish:** Sticky rice in banana leaf. Green tea.

**8¼ Dave:** A demonstration of how good this distillery can be.
**Nose:** Lightly oily note. Floral with soft fruits. Sandalwood, hint of compost, rhum shrub, mace. Succulent, sweet and aromatic.

**Palate:** A nutty shell which cracks open, giving up a burst of flavour, mandarin, sweet spices. Lively, energetic. Light oaky notes.
**Finish:** Juicy and long.

### STRATHISLA 1976, MURRAY MCDAVID MISSION II 46%
Single Malt - Speyside

8¼ **Michael: A good example of this distinctive and underrated malt.**
**Nose:** A hint of peat, and a robust suggestion of fresh oak.
**Palate:** Textured. Chewy blend of marzipan, jam and icing sugar. Like drinking a Bakewell tart.
**Finish:** Almondy dryness. Satisfying.

7¾ **Dave: Strathisla is always charming but can be a touch frosty. This is one of those.**
**Nose:** Intense, high-toned and tight. Floral with honeysuckle, vanilla, wood.
**Palate:** Complex mix of malt, ginger and nut. Fairly grippy though it broadens in middle.
**Finish:** Toasty, short.

### STRATHISLA 34 YEARS OLD, HART BROTHERS 43%
Single Malt - Speyside

8 **Michael: Classic Strathisla, in good shape for it's age.**
**Nose:** Very Spicy indeed. Violets. Almonds.
**Palate:** Creamy coffee. Espresso with a twist of lemon peel.
**Finish:** Twist of lemon peel. Woody but not musty. To me, that is a distinctive element of Strathisla. It reminds me of the taste of the wooden "spoon" provided with tubs of ice-cream.

6½ **Dave: Ah well.**
**Nose:** Dumb to start with. It needs time to build up hints of citrus, honey and then oak.
**Palate:** Soft and muscular but the wood starts drying things a bit too quickly for my liking.
**Finish:** Woody.

### STRATHISLA 37 YEARS OLD, CASK 1332, DUNCAN TAYLOR 47.6%
Single Malt - Speyside

7¾ **Martine: More complexity on the nose than on the palate. A pleasant whisky though. But quite disappointing for a Strathisla of that age.**
**Nose:** Hazelnuts. White pepper. An echo of fresh paint. Light fruit then fudge. Orange chocolate.
**Palate:** Tangy. Gingery. Quiet one-dimensional. Almond cake.
**Finish:** Spicy, slowly fading on creamy toffee.

7¾ **Dave: Highly attractive. Worth having a look at.**
**Nose:** Fragrant. Grass, bracken and lemon peel. In time mead-like, spiced apple cider, coconut. Deep but perfumed.
**Palate:** Sweet start, mixing syrup, spices, apple, glacé cherry and sweet grasses. Well-balanced.
**Finish:** Slightly bitter nuttiness.

### CASK COLLECTION STRATHMILL 15 YEARS OLD, DEWAR RATTRAY 63.5%
Single Malt - Speyside

7¾ **Michael: Whatever its age, this whisky is full of youthful vigour.**
**Nose:** Appetising. Delicate. Lightly malty sweetness blending into slight smokiness.
**Palate:** A rush of spring water, then sticky. Juicy. Fruity.
**Finish:** Lively. Explosion of spiciness. Hot.

7¾ **Dave: Shows good complexity, just tipped slightly into the oak camp.**
**Nose:** High oak notes. Starts tight and slightly citric and grassy then into fir and deepens to cooked fruits, plasticene and a heavy floral perfume (iris/lily).
**Palate:** Good depth. Sweet fruitiness-apple juice, nutty. Increasingly firm and oaky.
**Finish:** Dry, nutty.

### STRATHMILL 12 YEARS OLD 43%
Single Malt - Speyside

7 **Michael: A dessert malt, perhaps, but for that purpose I prefer sweeter bottlings.**
**Nose:** Lightly fragrant. Skins of dessert apples.
**Palate:** Smooth. Syrupy. A touch of vanilla-pod. Spicy (a hint of clove?). Lively.
**Finish:** Flowery dryness. Slightly stinging.

7¾ **Dave: Attractive and delicate.**
**Nose:** Dry, nutty and airy. Dried banana on muesli, green grassy notes, tea leaves, walnut.
**Palate:** Very soft and attractive and flows straight down the middle. Medium sweet with some vanilla and nut.
**Finish:** Soft.

### STRATHMILL 1975 31 YEARS OLD, DEWAR RATTRAY 49.3%
Single Malt - Speyside

7 **Dave: The wood has taken charge. Doesn't appear to have the character to carry extended aging.**
**Nose:** Mature. Jammy, stewed fruit but slightly flat. Some currant and shoe polish. In time a mash tun note.
**Palate:** Sweet and honeyed with good depth. Tongue-coating. Oak showing. Hates water.
**Finish:** Short.

7¾ **Arthur: Tannic but pleasant enough old malt.**
**Nose:** Red apples and dried fruits (apple, coconut and papaya). With water a mustiness comes out, although with a fine oatiness like muesli-dust. Floral too.
**Palate:** A complex mix of fruit, chocolate and lots of wood.
**Finish:** Drying tannins grip to the tongue.

### STRATHMILL 1992, JAMES MACARTHUR 64.2%
Single Malt - Speyside

7 **Michael: This bottling strongly manifests the woody dryness that seems to characterise the whiskies from the Islay valley. Water brings out Strathmill's muscat note.**
**Nose:** Dryish. Faintly peaty.
**Palate:** Spicy and fruity. Very pronounced dessert apples. Lemons. Cloves also very emphatic.
**Finish:** Still dry, but nicely rounded.

7 **Dave: Those decaying vegetables give this a really weird edge. Was the cask too close to the kitchen?**
**Nose:** Mandarin oranges with a note reminiscent of rotting vegetable matter. Citrus and turnip tops: it's like one of my mother's less successful soups.
**Palate:** Hot and peppery – this needs lots of water. A dusty/flour sack note and those neeps again.
**Finish:** Malty.

### STRATHMILL 31 YEARS OLD 1976 48.4%
Single Malt - Speyside

6¾ **Dave: All was going so well then the finish undoes all the good work. Ultimately unbalanced. Still at least my breath smells minty fresh.**
**Nose:** All sorts of interesting angles here. Mature, leathery, brown apples, dusty bready/yeasty, then a fudgey note mixed with black grape.
**Palate:** Sweet, then cardamom. Lightly perfumed and some woods then out of nowhere comes a toothpaste like mintiness.
**Finish:** Minty with some chocolate.

8¾ **Martine: A rich, complex character. Seems to have captured a full aromatic palette.**
**Nose:** Mature, fruity with honeyed tones. Beeswax, polished floor. Touch of new saddle. A fragrant herbal note in the back. Red fruit herbal tea. White pepper.
**Palate:** Round with a palatable oiliness. Honeyed fruit as well as on the nose. No oaky edges. Perfectly smooth.
**Finish:** Warm, spicy, uplifting.

### STRONACHIE 12 YEARS OLD 43%
Single Malt - Highland

7¾ **Michael: On principle, I have misgivings about private bottlings of unidentified malts, but this is an excellent dram.**
**Nose:** A heathery moorland.
**Palate:** Deft interplay of slightly syrupy, malty, sweetness and very restrained peaty dryness.
**Finish:** Warming, soothing.

7½ **Dave: I have a vague family connection with the original Stronachie Distillery. Good to see the name back. A good aperitif.**
**Nose:** Appealing: malty (green malt), dry bracken with sweet fruit and nut notes. Dry bracken.
**Palate:** Good, firm attack: toasted nuts, malt but with sufficient toffee sweetness to keep things interesting.
**Finish:** Medium length, pecan, fruit.

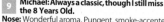

## TALISKER 10 YEARS OLD 45.8%
Single Malt - Island (non Islay)

**9** **Michael: Always a classic, though I still miss the 8 Years Old.**
**Nose:** Wonderful aroma. Pungent, smoke-accented, rounded.
**Palate:** Full maltiness, slightly syrupy, with sourness and a very big pepperiness developing.
**Finish:** Very peppery, huge, long.

**9½** **Jim: A dram to be savoured and celebrated.**
**Nose:** A razor-sharp spiciness lances through demerara sweetness and rich peat. Absolutely magnificent.
**Palate:** The enormous build up of spice adds to the multi-layered peat. The sweetness is almost like freshly crushed grist. Wave upon wave, layer upon layer of complexity.
**Finish:** Massively warming and still spicy. The peat lingers while the spice bristles.

## TALISKER 10 YEARS OLD 45.8%
Single Malt - Island (non Islay)

**7½** **Martine: Less peppery than in my memory. As if the spicy outburst on mid palate has been tamed. A bit harsh too.**
Seems to have lost its volcanic temper.
**Nose:** Beeswax. Old furniture. Black pepper. Boat rope. Wet sand. Touch of seaweed. Crisp bacon. Gooseberry.
**Palate:** Sweet at start then slightly bitter. Wood comes quickly through. Smoked meat. Smoked almonds.
**Finish:** Sweet and spicy. Dry.

**8¼** **Dave: Elemental. Another classic...**
**Nose:** Fishboxes, pier heads, light smoke. Somewhat reminiscent of a manzanilla pasada: green olive and saltiness (oh yes there is) albeit with smoke. Yeasty, vibrant, heathery, fresh.
**Palate:** Fresh. Marine notes. Immediate smoke, leading to a sweet, lightly oily centre. White pepper.
**Finish:** Vibrant, prickly. Turfy.

## TALISKER 18 YEARS OLD 45.8%
Single Malt - Island (non Islay)

**9¼** **Martine: Loch Harport on a winter's day, gale force eight! Less peppery than**
younger versions. Complex, endearing, balanced. 18 seems a perfect age for malts.
**Nose:** TCP, tarred boat, iodine-impregnated seaweeds. Peat. Wouahh! Then candied orange, trifle, milk chocolate.
**Palate:** And the beat goes on … iodine, tar pastilles, salty water. Ginger bread. Liquorice.
**Finish:** Warm, salty. Dry and nutty. Sooty touch.

**9** **Dave: Truly fantastic. All of Talisker's attack...and then some.**
**Nose:** Complex, burning heather, sweet tobacco, old warehouse, spent bonfire. Underneath is almond paste/nougat, butter biscuits and a lightly herbal note. Plenty of smoke. Rich and complex.
**Palate:** A slow start, then pepper, a light smoked fish note, fruit syrup. Builds to an explosive finish.
**Finish:** Red peppercorn.

## TALISKER 1975, 25 YEARS OLD, CASK STRENGTH 59.9%
Single Malt - Island (non Islay)

**9** **Michael: Less instantly explosive than the regular 10. The flavours in the 25 are more**
tightly combined and take longer to unfold. You pays your money...
**Nose:** Minerally. A hint of sulphur.
**Palate:** Quite rich. Nutty, with a suggestion of artichoke. A touch of salt, then a burst of freshly milled pepper.
**Finish:** Volcanic. Reverberating.

**9** **Dave: The distillery character sings out. A muscular, smoky yet rounded malt. Superb.**
**Nose:** Robust with plenty of scented smoke (burning heather) balanced by soft Dundee cake/singed orange peel aromas.
**Palate:** Full and ripe to start, plenty of mellow fruits (sultana, date, fig) then an explosion of dry smoke. A complex mouthful.
**Finish:** Long, complex, dry peppery heather root.

## TALISKER 1982, 20 YEARS OLD 58.8%
Single Malt - Island (non Islay)

**9¼** **Michael: Doesn't sound enjoyable? You bet it was.**
**Nose:** Scorched earth. Harbour aromas. Seaweed.

**Palate:** Distant thunder. Seems to rumble and reverberate as the volcanic heat builds ever so slowly. Hot, slightly sour, peppery. Very tightly combined flavours, reluctant to unfurl. When they did, the earth moved.
**Finish:** Quite quick and sharp. A thunderflash.

**8¾** **Dave: As subtle a Talisker as you'll come across.**
**Nose:** Light smoke. A complex, slightly restrained nose. Putty, macadamia, moorland, sooty chimney, wet seaweed.
**Palate:** Delivers all its complexities here. Soft mouthfeel, mixing gentle oak, heather, sweet pear-like fruits then a powerful dark smokiness.
**Finish:** Iodine. Long. sweet.

## TALISKER 1986, THE DISTILLER'S EDITION 45.8%
Single Malt - Island (non Islay)

**7½** **Michael: Not for Talisker purists, but a highly distinctive interplay of whisky and**
sherry.
**Nose:** Toffee, bitter chocolate and toasted nuts, with late salt and pepper.
**Palate:** Toffeeish, then toasty. The distracting richness of these flavours introduces a shock of contrast when the seaweed and pepper suddenly burst through.
**Finish:** Powerful salt and pepper.

**7½** **Jim: Wonderful whisky: a rare case where sherry cask doesn't spoil but merely offers a variation on a theme. No**
peat-lover should miss this one. But don't expect the usual explosiveness.
**Nose:** A much sweeter aroma than the standard 10 Years Old, with the peat playing a much more liberated role with less spiciness. Soft sherry with a suet/sultana pudding heaviness to the malt.
**Palate:** Big, rumbling peat, first crisp and hard, then much, much softer. Again the mouthwatering grape keeps the spiciness to a minimum.
**Finish:** Peat and cocoa combine and the sweet/dry ratio remains in perfect balance throughout. Really big malt, this time free of the peat with the vanilla topping it all off.

## TALISKER 20 YEARS OLD, DIRECTOR'S TACTICAL, OLD MALT CASK 50%
Single Malt - Island (non Islay)

**6** **Martine: The distillery character is buried far below the wood. One can hardly detect even a light puff of smoke.**
Water does not help.
**Nose:** Sherry from top to bottom. Nothing but wood.
**Palate:** Sweet and bitter. Wood, wood and wood again. Cigar box. Then, shyly emerging, a mix of fruity and earthy flavours. Hint of peat. Dried fruit.
**Finish:** Quite long, but soon turning dry and bitter.

**5¾** **Dave: What is the point of this other than to prove that leaving Talisker in first-fill sherry casks for 20 years leads to oblivion?**
**Nose:** Heavily sherried. Christmas cake, burnt raisin, cold stewed tea. Where's the whisky?
**Palate:** Very tannic, so woody that the spirit has been obliterated and you have to pick splinters out of your tongue.
**Finish:** Dry.

## TALISKER 25 YEARS OLD 56.9%
Single Malt - Island (non Islay)

**9** **Dave: Bold, subtle, sweet yet smoky. Class.**
**Nose:** Heather honey with smoke underneath. Salty again but everything softened by oak. Wet sails, oilskins, cough sweets, bitter orange peel, white peppercorn and Lochaber smoked cheese. Mature and rich. Complex.
**Palate:** Multifaceted, rounded and harmonious. Smoke is there but also a dense savoury fruitiness. Great balance.
**Finish:** Elegant and long with a little pepper.

**8¾** **Arthur: Certainly complex, and a phenolic element that wove slyly in and out of what was a coastal experience.**
**Nose:** Melon and sweetened, stewed rhubarb. Dark chocolate sauce, roast hazelnuts and some Dettol medicinal notes.
**Palate:** More of that chocolate, some quite astringent tannins and chilli spice.
**Finish:** Brooding smoke and a little salty chlorine. Possibly a light soapiness too.

## TALISKER 25 YEARS OLD 57.8%
Single Malt - Island (non Islay)

**8¾** **Martine: Rich and luscious. Needs a dash of water to cut spirit harshness. The marine** influence is overwhelmed by wood but in a charming way.
**Nose:** Herbal. Lemon balm. Humus. Wet leaves. Vanilla rises, custard and trifle aromas. Sea spray. Beautiful.
**Palate:** Sweet and lively. Then bursting out on liquorice and spices. Nutmeg. Hint of cinnamon. Distant smoke.
**Finish:** Lingering, dry. Nutty. Cinnamon.

*WHISKY Recommended*

**8½** **Dave: More subtle than the 18 but still feisty.**
**Nose:** Soft and creamy with perfumed smoke in the background. Tarry beaches, sandalwood. Danish oil. Wet rope. Marine. Balanced.
**Palate:** Thick, peach then a blast of peat, pepper, salt. Flows over the tongue. Tamed with water making it rounded and elegant. One to tease out.
**Finish:** The peat comes...and stays.

## TALISKER 25 YEARS OLD, SPECIAL RELEASE 2005 57.2%
Single Malt - Island (non Islay)

**8½** **Arthur: Excellent, although I was slightly put off by the fishiness. I think all fish are** stinking, slimey creatures however, so I am admittedly biased.
**Nose:** Greenhouses full of tomato plants, Seville oranges, putty and fish oil. With time, burnt driftwood and heather.
**Palate:** More Seville oranges, arrabbiata sauce, heather and creosoted wood.
**Finish:** Clove-spice.

*WHISKY Recommended*

**6¾** **Owen: Easier drinking with water, but for full effect...**
**Nose:** Delicate yet complex. Sweet yet savoury, with a salty earthiness in there somewhere. Faint linseed character at the end.
**Palate:** Confident. Firm. Sweet. Salty. Pronounced phenol development. Fiery. Burnt and burning peat.
**Finish:** Warming and medicinal. Reminiscent of the aroma of polished antique furniture.

## TALISKER 28 YEARS OLD 43.3%
Single Malt - Island (non Islay)

**8½** **Martine: More medicinal than other versions. If matched with oysters, add bar-** becued sausages as the French do in Marennes-Oléron.
**Nose:** By the shore undoubtedly. Fishing net. Seaweed bonfire. Tangerine. Vanilla.
**Palate:** Robust. Neat and open. Malty. Peaty. A lot to tell.
**Finish:** Pepper breaks through a veil of smoke. Totally Talisker.

*WHISKY Editor's choice*

**9** **Dave: Amazingly little wood impact for a whisky of this age. Not the most robust Talisker but a cracker none-** theless.
**Nose:** Fragrant, slow developing, complex nose: heather blossom, malt toast, hearth. Scented and slightly herbal: elegant and powerful at the same time.
**Palate:** Excellent texture and mouthfeel mixing rich oily malt with gentle fruit and all-embracing peat smoke. It has an elegant muscularity.
**Finish:** Long, smoky.

## TALISKER THE DISTILLER'S EDITION AMOROSO SHERRY
Single Malt - Island (non Islay)

**9** **Michael: Sensational (both literally and figuratively).**
**Nose:** Bitter chocolate and fudge pralines. Toasted nuts with late salt and pepper.
**Palate:** Astonishingly toffeeish, then toasty. The distracting richness of these flavours introduces a shock of contrast when the seaweed and characteristic volcanic flavours suddenly erupt.
**Finish:** An explosion in a gale.

*WHISKY Recommended*

**9** **Doug: Talisker bigger though slightly calmer than ever. And rather more-ish.**
**Nose:** Sulphury, deep and honeyed with a peppery character and traces of wet labrador.
**Palate:** Bursting with prickling sweetness and teasingly reticent to subside. Eventually the pepperiness allows an infusion of soft peatiness to infiltrate.
**Finish:** Gently and soothingly fades with all characteristic intact.

## TALISMAN BLENDED SCOTCH WHISKY 40%
Blended - Scotland

**7¾** **Michael: Bigger in body than flavour, but with more complexity and an excellent balance.**
**Nose:** Sweet, spicy. Lemon cake.
**Palate:** Rich, sweet, creamy, fudgy. Fruity. Lemon tea. Jasmine.
**Finish:** Appetising development of soft smokiness.

**8** **Dave: Attractive, well-balanced and harmonious. Good session blend.**
**Nose:** Clean and soft with vanilla, orange and very light smoke.
**Palate:** Young and fresh, but balancing mellow grain with ripe and fruity malt. Some heathery notes.
**Finish:** Medium. Soft.

## TAMBOWIE 12 YEARS OLD 40%
Single Malt - Highland

**7¾** **Michael: Starts interestingly, but doesn't seem to go anywhere.**
**Nose:** Apricots sautéed in butter.
**Palate:** Orangey. Malty. Light-bodied. On the thin side.
**Finish:** Slightly peaty.

**6¾** **Dave: Gentle and undemanding.**
**Nose:** Earthy and autumnal: nut, smoke, mulch, damp earth.
**Palate:** Better than the nose suggests with a sweet thread of fruity malt notes. Goes straight down the middle of the palate. Medium bodied.
**Finish:** Very soft.

## TAMDHU 14 YEARS OLD, HARRIS WHISKY 58.5%
Single Malt - Speyside

**7¾** **Martine: More interesting without water. But then, alcohol prevails. The nose is appealing.**
**Nose:** Sharp. Lively. Young oak. Rhubarb crumble. White pepper. Develops on spices. With water, more wood, damp cellar.
**Palate:** Crisp, clean. Flowing. A full spices outburst. In the back, a winey flavour (sweet grapes). Water cuts the edges off but it also trivializes the flavors.
**Finish:** Sweeter than midpalate. Almondy.

**7½** **Dave: At last something to get to grips with.**
**Nose:** Sugared almond, wood sap/pine resin back to estery notes. Pineapple, sulphur.
**Palate:** Concentrated and quite firm the alcohol giving heat to the sweet demerara sugar sweetness. Toffee with good weight.
**Finish:** Spicy. Good length.

## TAMDHU 1966, KINGSBURY 43%
Single Malt - Speyside

**7¾** **Michael: A welcome bottling of this neglected malt, and an interesting example.**
**Nose:** Light, fresh, fragrant, peat-smoke. Very attractive.
**Palate:** Firm, biscuity maltiness. Some barley sugar sweetness, developing suggestions of butter. A hint of black treacle. Some sherry.
**Finish:** Cereal grain oily dryness. Oat-like flavours. Sappy, smoky.

**8½** **Jim: This is big, bruising, uncompromising whisky of very high class.**
**Nose:** Stunning honey depth with a touch of mint and eucalyptus adding oaky firmness. Rare and glorious balance for is age.
**Palate:** A big honey-oak arrival that is waxy and chewy but filters out into more controlled deep.
**Finish:** A bitter-sweet honeyed saltiness, then thumping arrival of malt and oak in tandem.

## TAMDHU 1981 RESERVE, GORDON & MACPHAIL 43%
Single Malt - Speyside

**7¾** **Michael: No, I don't think I was being suggestible. An unusually complex Tamdhu.**
**Nose:** Sweet lime (am I being suggestible? The whisky is that colour).
**Palate:** Firm, smooth. Dry toffee. Flowery. Lemony.
**Finish:** Slightly resiny. Peppery.

**7** **Dave: Mild-mannered though some would say bland.**
**Nose:** Lightly perfumed, malty and dry with some clover, banana and lemon.
**Palate:** Soft, gentle, sweet and clean with typical Tamdhu juicy maltiness and a hint of clover honey.
**Finish:** Soft but short.

## TAMDHU 1985, ADELPHI 55.3%
Single Malt - Speyside

**7¼ Michael:** Judging from the very pale colour, the wood did not have much positive input. Hence, perhaps, the lack of Tamdhu's sometime elegance.
**Nose:** Peaty. Slightly woody. Cereal grain. Apples.
**Palate:** Oily. Sweet. Fruity. Pears in rich syrup.
**Finish:** Fruity. Perfumy. Spicy (cloves?). Drying.

**8¼ Jim:** Massive by Tamdhu standards. Brilliant and lingering interplay between cocoa and malt.
**Nose:** A full malty, slightly abrasive nose.
**Palate:** Initially hot as the nose suggests, then fades as a sumptuous wave of grassy, sweet malt.
**Finish:** Drier with some bitter chocolate notes.

## TAMDHU 30 YEARS OLD, MACPHAIL'S COLLECTION 43%
Single Malt - Speyside

**7¾ Michael:** Tamdhu is a pleasant, polite, whisky. Does it really have the stamina for such a marathon maturation?
**Nose:** Orange-flavoured boiled sweets. Citric but dry.
**Palate:** Orangey, resiny, but somehow constrained. Attenuated. Cork-like woodiness.
**Finish:** Musty. Quick.

**7¾ Dave:** Just enough oak for structure. A real surprise for a distillery which can often be pretty bland.
**Nose:** Lightly perfumed: fondant icing, sweet cereal, apricot jam, clove, almost like a light gold rum. Drier and grassier with water.
**Palate:** Silky. Nut and vanilla. Dries nicely in the middle. Flowers and spiciness on the back palate.
**Finish:** Soft and malty.

## TAMNAVULIN 12 YEARS OLD 40%
Single Malt - Speyside

**7¾ Michael:** Very much as I remember it. Fresh, attractive.
**Nose:** Distinctively aromatic. An oily perfume. Oil of peppermint? Very floral.
**Palate:** Clean, light, minty, very herbal.
**Finish:** Clean, dry, flowery. Vermouth-like. Gently appetising.

**6½ Dave:** Strangely the label says both "naturally light" and "rich and mellow."
**Nose:** The maltiest nose you'll ever experience: Weetabix with lots of milk. One-dimensional.
**Palate:** Light and soft.
**Finish:** Short.

## TEACHER'S HIGHLAND CREAM 43%
Blended - Scotland

*WHISKY Magazine Editor's choice*

**8½ Michael:** Malty, even creamy, but never cloying. Big and sustaining. The whisky world's answer to Kendal Mint Cake.
**Nose:** Oily, Fudge-like.
**Palate:** Big, rounded, yeasty. Full of crunchy maltiness. To drink this whisky is like biting into peanut brittle. Then toffee. Then liquorice flavours.
**Finish:** Rooty, oaky, smoky, these dry flavours providing a perfect balance.

**8½ Paul:** Cream is the appropriate moniker. Smoky, robust, vibrant.
**Nose:** The subtle notes of bittersweet chocolate, dark toffee, and bacon fat sneak up on you only after a couple of minutes of air exposure. One of the more complex and elegant bouquets in Scotch blends. Buttery, oily, luscious.
**Palate:** The sweet, wine-like, sherry imprint taste of the Glendronach Distillery malts is all over this poised, chewy thoroughbred.
**Finish:** Long. Oloroso sherry sweet and almost prune-like. Satiny. I think of the muscular, sinew, peaty side of Speyside malts.

## TEANINICH 43%
Single Malt - Highland

**7½ Martine:** This malt improves with oxygenation. Quite shy, it may appear insignificant at first, which it is not. Just pleasant.
**Nose:** Light and slightly restrained. Grassy. Minty. Touch of cardboard. Opening on green fruit notes.
**Palate:** Smooth and sweet. Very soft, flattening in the middle but nicely refreshing. Peaches in syrup.
**Finish:** Lacks length but clean with a pleasant nutty touch.

**8 Dave:** The opposite of its lush companions. A poet on a wobbly bicycle (Norman MacCaig?) I like its perversity. Regional style? Pah!
**Nose:** Austere and strange: lemon verbena, some smoke. Assertive, grassy, green tea, birch sap.
**Palate:** Lovely perfume. A delicate bone like structure. Grasses again. Flinty on first impressions but with a sweet heart.
**Finish:** Dry. teasing.

## TEANINICH 10 YEARS OLD 43%
Single Malt - Highland

**7½ Michael:** Teaninich seems to have become more fruity and herbal over the years. And thinner. Or is it me who has become fatter?
**Nose:** Aromatic. Fruity. Dry. Leafy.
**Palate:** Sweet-and-dry. Seems to warm up as flavours develop. Chocolate limes.
**Finish:** Cilantro. Leafy. Herbal.

**8 Dave:** A dram you admire first, then love.
**Nose:** Intriguing; green tea, dry grasses, floral. Sappy note, sandalwood, ginger snaps, lemon verbena. About to burst into life. Water softens it, but too much kills the spiky aromatics.
**Palate:** Seemingly light, but complex. Almost sugary start, solid mid-palate with a lovely oily feel. Slightly austere (which I like).
**Finish:** Dry, soft, oily, moreish.

## TEANINICH 1972 27 YEARS OLD, RARE MALTS 64.2%
Single Malt - Highland

**7½ Michael:** This little-known malt almost always surprises me with its robust flavours.
**Nose:** Big. Very perfumy. Incense. Sandalwood. Malt and vanilla.
**Palate:** Very assertive. Intense. Sugary. Nutty. Perfumy. Lots of depth.
**Finish:** Powerful. Very spicy indeed. Peppery. Gunpowder tea.

**8½ Jim:** Do whiskies get any sexier than this? An essay in balance and complexity for its age that teases and tantalises the taste buds mercilessly. Outstanding: truly awesome!!
**Nose:** A feather-light, deft aroma boasting a subtle but curious guava fruitiness.
**Palate:** A composed and delicious maltiness gains hold for the most intense of crescendos. The climax is almost erotic.
**Finish:** A long, oak-rich afterglow.

## TEANINICH 1973, BERRY'S OWN SELECTION 43%
Single Malt - Highland

**8 Martine:** Not a heavyweight nor a sophisticated lad. But a perfect companion for a plate of smokies or a fruit salad.
**Nose:** Deliciously refreshing. Malty and grassy. Dune herbs. Camomile. Linseed. Hint of mustard. Lemon pulp. A faint cheesy note.
**Palate:** Sweet and lively. The same fresh feel. Lemon sherbet. Can'taloup. Ripe peach.
**Finish:** Mint and aniseed. Soft pepperiness.

**6½ Dave:** Just seems a little unformed. Not holding all its parts together.
**Nose:** Slightly watery colour. Light with hint of Moscato grappa, perfumed but a little hard.
**Palate:** Light and sweet, quite grassy.
**Finish:** Hot. Acorn.

## TEANINICH 1983, GORDON & MACPHAIL 46%
Single Malt - Highland

**7½ Michael:** Well worth sampling, but don't expect anything fancy. This is a workaday malt.
**Nose:** Lightly minty. Kendal mint cake.
**Palate:** Firm, smooth. Hard toffee. Golden syrup. Buttercream filling in a sponge-cake.
**Finish:** Bamboo-like dryness.

**7 Martine:** Sherry tends to overwhelm the palate. Persistent dryness. A good companion for coffee.
**Nose:** Intense and robust. Earthy and rooty. Toffee, orange peel. Sandal wood. Wood polish. Restrained sherry notes.
**Palate:** Sweet but tangy too. Full expression of sherry: lots of oak, burnt wood, citrus fruit and spices. Gingerbread.
**Finish:** Dry, oaky and nutty. Slightly bitter.

## TEANINICH 21 YEARS OLD SHERRY BUTT, CHIEFTAIN'S CHOICE 46%
Single Malt - Highland

**7¾ Michael: Not much subtlety, but I always enjoy its big, confident, flavours.**
**Nose:** Lightly toasty. Slight smokiness. Fragrant. Very fresh.
**Palate:** Slightly chewy. And toffeeish. Distinctly fruity. Then peppery. Very lively.
**Finish:** Just a hint of appetising herbal bitterness. Gunpowder tea?

**7¾ Dave: A good Teaninich, austere, grassy yet with an extra dimension.**
**Nose:** Tense and austere despite some malty sherried notes. Lightly floral, slightly green and grassy with nut (young Hunter Valley Semillon) roasted almond and hint of sappy sawn timber.
**Palate:** Subtle dryness with light seashore aromas, moss and some sherry slickness mid-palate. Lean.
**Finish:** Decent weight if a little short.

## TEANINICH 30 YEARS OLD, DEWAR RATTRAY 60.8%
Single Malt - Highland

**7¼ Martine: The high strength makes it difficult to tame even with water. Some like it hot. But my palate waves a white flag.**
**Nose:** Fragrant. Almond milk. Orange pekoe tea. Some yeasty notes. Creamy toffee with water.
**Palate:** Sweet start, the alcohol bite tickles. Pleasant toffee flavours, a touch of candied lemon peel. Still burning with water.
**Finish:** Hot, spicy. Tabasco.

**7¾ Dave: Manages to corral a number of disparate flavours well.**
**Nose:** High alcohol. Limoncello light wood (ash) camomile/scented grass then guava and mandarin. Slightly vegetal.
**Palate:** Sweet and concentrated with clove, kumquat and a hint of clove.
**Finish:** Long and spicy.

## TEANINICH 31 YEARS OLD, ADELPHI 57.8%
Single Malt - Highland

**WHISKY** *Editor's choice*

**8½ Martine: Well-matured, amazing for its age.**
**Nose:** Intense, beautifully combined wood and fruit. Juicy apricot. Cedar. Beeswax, polished floors. Vanilla. Delicate gingerbread. A touch of peat.
**Palate:** Caressing, enveloping, oily. So well in tune with the nose. Fudgey. Nutmeg. Cinnamon.
**Finish:** Warm, lingering spiciness.

**8 Dave: Like a maiden aunt. It's hard to believe that after 31 years in cask it's still this strength!**
**Nose:** Austere, quite haughty. A wild grassy note with fresh tobacco/unlit cigar. With water there's vanilla, coconut, as well as Rich Tea biscuit. Rich but clean.
**Palate:** Very pure. Green tea. Good weight on the palate but held in check by a pretty firm structure.
**Finish:** Long, drying.

## TOBERMORY 40%
Single Malt - Island (non Islay)

**7 Michael: A surprising degree of continuity from the earlier vatted Tobermory, though this version has more individuality.**
**Nose:** Light but definite touch of peat. Some sweetness.
**Palate:** Faint peat. Enjoyable interplay of malty, nutty, dryness and toffeeish, faintly minty, sweetness. Slightly weak in the middle, but recovers well.
**Finish:** Light, soft, becoming sweeter.

**7½ Jim: A rare chance to taste a malt that is not so much youthful as pre-pubescent. Really pleasant and full-flavoured for all that.**
**Nose:** Deliciously fresh and malty, almost green though aroma-wise, this sample had nothing like the peat promised on the label. However, there is a delicate peat smoke that is gristy and sweet.
**Palate:** Young and underripe and magnificently mouth-watering. The peatiness begins to make itself felt towards the middle. Simple but effective.
**Finish:** Gently smoked; further highly intense malt.

## TOBERMORY 10 YEARS OLD 40%
Single Malt - Island (non Islay)

**7¾ Martine: Classic bourbon cask profile. Perfumy like Eau de cologne. Well balanced. Nuttier with water but it takes the freshness off.**
**Nose:** Refreshing, grassy. Aniseed. Citrus fruit. Stewed Bramley apples. Poached in syrup pears.
**Palate:** Velvety. Aniseed lozenge.
**Finish:** Gingery. A pleasant almondy come back with a bitter chocolate touch.

**7 Dave: The oak tries to kick it into life, but a little lacking in energy.**
**Nose:** Rolled oat and honey. Damp earth, orange pulp, melted fruit and nut chocolate bar, some mango.
**Palate:** Quite sweet. Sits in the centre, though fizzles out in the middle with a drying sensation.
**Finish:** Chocolate again.

## TOBERMORY 11 YEARS OLD, DEWAR RATTRAY 59.9%
Single Malt - Island (non Islay)

**5 Dave: This just hasn't been allowed to mature out. The result being it's harsh and all over the shop.**
**Nose:** Beeswax, then a powerful acetone note. This then becomes more chemical-like, akin to gloss paint. Was this distilled in a hardware superstore rather than a distillery?
**Palate:** Coconut to start but the effect is similar to drinking air freshener. Slightly dusty.
**Finish:** Glue.

**6¼ Ian: Falls apart with water.**
**Nose:** Some wood and sherry notes. Slightly artificial.
**Palate:** Wood dominates. Immature?
**Finish:** Short finish disappoints.

## TOMATIN 10 YEARS OLD 40%
Single Malt - Highland

**7½ Michael: Simple and straight forward but well composed and enjoyable. A reliable, solid, malt. I always enjoy it.**
**Nose:** Warm, sweet, malty. Then clean, soft, peatiness. Inviting.
**Palate:** Quite big and syrupy. Juicy maltiness. Suggestion of soft liquorice.
**Finish:** Spicy. Smoothly warming.

**7¼ Dave: No great complexity, but pleasant.**
**Nose:** Initially seems young and slightly agressive. Water brings out some honey, soft fruits, light woodiness, charred sticks.
**Palate:** Rounded and quite sweet. Honey and fruit with some menthol. Crisps up as it stays in the mouth.
**Finish:** Tingling and peppery.

## TOMATIN 12 YEARS OLD 40%
Single Malt - Highland

**7½ Michael: More delicate than I remember.**
**Nose:** Delicately spicy. Fresh. Aniseed. Sandalwood bath oil.
**Palate:** Sweet. Biscuity. Pistachios. Sweet lassi.
**Finish:** Créme de Menthe.

**7¼ Dave: A pretty straightforward malty malt. For comple-tists only.**
**Nose:** Mix of nut, bracken and an aroma that's like old slippers: rubber, inner tubes. A seed-like cereal note.
**Palate:** More on the body than the nose: burnt toffee, sugary, nutty. The rubbery note reappears.
**Finish:** Pink marshmallow.

## TOMATIN 18 YEARS OLD 43%
Single Malt - Highland

**7 Dave: Lacks balance.**
**Nose:** Mature but slightly greasy and a little soapy. Boiled sweets. Very buttery and slightly spicy (cumin).
**Palate:** Cognac like: dried peels, grilled nut and good grip. Long and quite full in body.
**Finish:** Burnt cake. Slightly bitter.

**6¾ Arthur: Not a great example.**
**Nose:** Tomato paste and hoi sin sauce. Melted chocolate.
**Palate:** Sweet and sickly yet astringent at the same time.
**Finish:** Cloying yet woody at the same time.

### TOMATIN 1962 42.2%
Single Malt - Highland

7½ **Dave: High maintenance. Beneath that sleek exterior beats a hard, one dimensional heart.**
**Nose:** Great maturity. Nail varnish, lacquer. Velvety with some nuttiness (walnut/cashew). Glossy.
**Palate:** Starts sweetly enough, then grips. Lacks complexity and breadth.
**Finish:** Firm. Hard.

7¾ **Arthur: Clearly old, and pleasant enough but slightly muted.**
**Nose:** Old, gingery mulling spices and an exotic musky spice. Spiced apple compote, honey and a background sherbety zip. Faint chlorine and vanilla.
**Palate:** Lemon, orange sherbet, nutmeg and dry spice. Slightly waxy.
**Finish:** Woody, dry/bitter complexity.

### TOMATIN 1975, CASK 4, MACKILLOP'S CHOICE 58.2%
Single Malt - Highland

7¾ **Michael: Perhaps because the distillery was built to make quantity, as a filler, the industry seems universally – but unfairly – to deny the possibility of Tomatin making a truly interesting single. I could certainly enjoy this one after dinner.**
**Nose:** Floral. Bergamot. Tobacco.
**Palate:** Well rounded. Fleshy. Voluptuous. Syrupy. Malty. Fudge-like.
**Finish:** Spicy. Cedary.

7¾ **Dave: Lovely, soft and sweet.**
**Nose:** Mature, slightly fungal, nose: chestnut, mushroom, then out comes milk chocolate, sticky toffee pudding and oak.
**Palate:** Big, fat, toffeeish, then coconut. Big and spicy: cinnamon, orange and vanilla.
**Finish:** Fruity and ripe.

### TOMINTOUL 10 YEARS OLD 40%
Single Malt - Speyside

7½ **Martine: Quite a muscular Speysider. The perfect dram to buck you up after a woodland walk mushroom-picking on a cold November day.**
**Nose:** Intense and sharp. Slightly spirity. Leafy. Fern. Cherry trifle. White pepper.
**Palate:** Enveloping and warm. Velvety. Cream fudge. A lot of spices. Nutmeg, cinnamon, pepper.
**Finish:** Long-lasting. Warm. Gently vanishing with almonds and nuts.

6½ **Dave: A bit disappointing.**
**Nose:** Cereal with some nutty/toffee notes and baked fruits. Water kills it.
**Palate:** Light-to middle-weight, and though it has quite a 'thick' feel it lacks any complexity. Immature?
**Finish:** Heathery.

### TOMINTOUL 16 YEARS OLD 40%
Single Malt - Speyside

7¾ **Michael: Slightly more grainy and less fruity than I remember.**
**Nose:** Bread fresh out of the oven.
**Palate:** Lean, firm, grainy. Bread with dried fruits, specially candied orange peels. Welsh tea bread.
**Finish:** Sweet. Expressive. Orange flower water.

7¼ **Dave: Very soft. Just lacking a little grip.**
**Nose:** Nutty (hazelnut) with dry bracken/heather and cereal. Water brings out grassiness, a touch of syrup and green fern.
**Palate:** Soft to start. Rounded with butterscotch and nutmeg. Light, dry.
**Finish:** Spicy.

### TOMINTOUL 1966, MACKILLOP'S CHOICE 46.5%
Single Malt - Speyside

7¾ **Michael: Delicate, and definitely Speyside, but not quite as elegant as some expressions I have tasted.**
**Nose:** Meadow flowers. Clover. Wild herbs. Sweet.
**Palate:** Creamy. Textured. Cereal grain. Crushed barley. Oatmeal.
**Finish:** Distinctly nutty. Hazelnuts. Faint, toasty, hint of peat.

7½ **Dave: Delicate, light and simple.**
**Nose:** Delicate. Nuts, sultana, honey. Hint of linoleum and oily rag.
**Palate:** Gently pleasant. A chewy mid-palate, with a little liquorice bitterness.
**Finish:** Banana, toffee. Short.

### TOMINTOUL 1975 30 YEARS OLD, DEWAR RATTRAY 48.5%
Single Malt - Speyside

7¼ **Dave: Slightly angular. Not a lot seems to have happened.**
**Nose:** Toasted. Cigar wrapper, hard toffee. Oily and juicy with some orange zest. Fairly boisterous.
**Palate:** Dry oak, blonde tobacco, cigarette ash. Cereal, slight mint. Not knitted. Doesn't cope with water.
**Finish:** Dry. Short.

7¾ **Arthur: Subtle and delicate, perhaps a little too much so.**
**Nose:** Ripe melon, guava and a general perfumed fruitiness. Blackcurrant yoghurt. Warm lemon sponge cake, and perhaps a distant, background smoke.
**Palate:** Baked fruit, and a little waxiness, with a complex, aged woodiness.
**Finish:** Lightly medicinal.

### TOMINTOUL 27 YEARS OLD 40%
Single Malt - Speyside

8 **Michael: Normally thought of as a light malt but this is a rich, viscous expression.**
**Nose:** Fresh bread with butter and salad leaves. A picnic in a field of daisies.
**Palate:** Fresh, doughy bread with lashings of real butter.
**Finish:** Lemon marmalade, with bittersweet peel.

7¾ **Dave: An extra layer of maturity. Sweet and ripe but holding age pretty well.**
**Nose:** A dusty start (sacking/cigar ash) with a hint of putty, then mellows into rum-soaked dried fruits. Sweet and slightly savoury. Becomes toffee-like.
**Palate:** Surprisingly light, but has creamy softness and firm oakiness. Clean, orange peel, toffee sauce.
**Finish:** Dry, slightly oak.

### TORMORE 1989, SIGNATORY 43%
Single Malt - Speyside

7¾ **Martine: Wood has the word in the finish. An assertive Speysider to enjoy after dinner.**
**Nose:** Beeswax, polished floor. Greengage. A touch of lemon balm.
**Palate:** Full and richly flavoured. Discloses more cereal than on the nose.
**Finish:** Hot and spicy (ginger).

7 **Dave: Inoffensive but not hugely exciting.**
**Nose:** Slightly hard and biscuity. Some bran flakes, a little smoke. Water makes it more fragrant. Not hugely complex.
**Palate:** Dry start. Shuts up shop quickly on the palate. Malt, some spice but it's all straight down the middle.
**Finish:** Some cream and spices again.

### TULLIBARDINE 10 YEARS OLD 40%
Single Malt - Highland

7½ **Michael: A delicate malt, but with some complexity.**
**Nose:** Leafy. Flowery. Buttercups. Lemony.
**Palate:** Silky-smooth. Lightly buttery. Light cobnut. Developing a hint of wineyness.
**Finish:** Decidedly spicy (vanilla pods?).

7¼ **Jim: A pleasant malt but missing the old trade mark creaminess.**
**Nose:** Light and airy with a simple, untaxing maltiness. A few orange notes add a thin extra dimension.
**Palate:** Lusciously sweet at first then a chewy toffee depth.
**Finish:** Light oak and rich malt persist.

### TULLIBARDINE 1973, SIGNATORY 49.6%
Single Malt - Highland

7¾ **Michael: Rounder than a previous Signatory bottling at 1972.**
**Nose:** Fresh, herbal. Clover and honey. Creamy.
**Palate:** Light, clean, grassy. A hint of straw.
**Finish:** Flowery dryness, quite drying.

8½ **Martine: A typical Perthshire-style honey-ball. Perhaps too sweet for some palates but it holds its age brilliantly.**
**Nose:** Floral rather than fruity, there is also a deep sweetness on which the malt hangs.

**Palate:** A momentary dryness is washed away with an incredible wave of honeyed sweetness.
**Finish:** The finish is drier, quite toasty and with a late arrival of slightly burnt honeycomb-chocolate.

## TULLIBARDINE 1993 SAUTERNE WOOD FINISH 46%
Single Malt - Highland

7 1/4 **Dave: There's lots of elements at play here. They're just not playing together.**
*WHISKY Magazine Recommended*
**Nose:** Clootie dumpling [suet, masses of dried peels, allspice]. Little woody with water which also brings out bracken, malt.
**Palate:** Date loaf, light oiliness, bere meal, oaky. Slightly flat.
**Finish:** Sweet fruits.

8 3/4 **Martine: A very appetising dram. More complex than it seems. Needs time to reveal all its richness.**
**Nose:** Intense. Malty and grassy. Dried grass. With an animal touch. Sheepskin maybe. Then shifting to bakery aromas. Almond and pear tart.
**Palate:** Gently flowing. Rich, oily. Sweet luscious bakery flavours.
**Finish:** Fruity (summer fruit).

## TULLIBARDINE 1993, MARSALA WOOD FINISH 46%
Single Malt - Highland

8 1/4 **Martine: A lovely dram. Fresh, natural, cheery. The perfect companion for a cheese party. Preferably undiluted.**
**Nose:** Malty, chestnut flour, muesli. A leafy note. A lovely bouquet of late summer outdoor fragrances. Touch of crème caramel.
**Palate:** Beautifully rounded and silky. The cereal notes mingle with marzipan and vanilla. Rewarding and refreshing.
**Finish:** Dry, leafy. Quite short.

7 1/2 **Ian: Team work results in glimpses of different flavours rather than individual close ups.**
**Nose:** Linseed, Brazil nut and extra-virgin olive oil overture, spicy oak emerges with a hint of crème caramel peeping through.
**Palate:** Laid back and opens slowly to deliver nutty, spicy, dried fruit, chocolate and crème caramel nuances, quite tightly knit, before an oakey garnish joins in.
**Finish:** Creamy, fruity maltiness.

## TULLIBARDINE 1993, PORT WOOD FINISH 46%
Single Malt - Highland

7 1/4 **Michael: Somewhere in the mid palate, there was a momentary hint of malt**
*WHISKY Magazine Recommended*
**whisky. I don't know how that found its way into this obscure liqueur from Heaven.**
**Nose:** Fry's Turkish Delight.
**Palate:** Bakewell tart.
**Finish:** Belgian raspberry beer.

6 **Dave: The feeling here is that the finish is being used to cover something up. It hasn't worked.**
**Nose:** An alarming colour like an angry sunset. Red fruits, rosehip syrup with crisp oak behind. Cooked fruits and dusty/cereal. Splits with water into edgy green spirit with a layer of jam on top.
**Palate:** Numb to begin with. Quite liquorous and sweet with a light cherry character.
**Finish:** Dry.

## TULLIBARDINE 30 YEARS OLD, STILLMAN'S DRAM 45%
Single Malt - Highland

7 3/4 **Michael: Perilously easy to drink. The whisky world's answer to a New World Chardonnay.**
**Nose:** Very flowery indeed. Pollen. Dark liquid honey-very distinct.
**Palate:** Very creamy. Flowery, fruity, sherryish.
**Finish:** Touch of true Chablis stoneyness and dryness.

8 3/4 **Jim: The most stylish, complex and hearty of drams which only underlines the tragedy in the demise of this fine distillery.**
**Nose:** Full, fat and fabulously fruity. Slightly unripe pears mingle deliciously with oak and custard.
**Palate:** Busy arrival on palate: early oak-induced spice tempered by a big demerara-sweet middle.
**Finish:** Pretty long with that intense barley lingering on with a tinge of oak and molassed raisins.

## TULLIBARDINE 35 YEARS OLD, CASK 2112, ADELPHI 54.6%
Single Malt - Highland

7 3/4 **Michael: Tullibardine is a gentle, civilised, malt that seems to live in obscurity. Nice to be reminded of its existence. Could be a golfers dram – the distillery is near Gleneagles.**
**Nose:** Lovely soft peat, rounded with malt.
**Palate:** Medium to full body. Some treacle toffee. Cobnuts. Sherry. Winey. Coffee. Straw.
**Finish:** Woody. Less so with water. Light, dry.

8 **Dave: Has held its character well considering its age.**
**Nose:** Initially perfumed: dried herb, heather honey, dried lavender, mothballs. Followed by a pleasant dunnage warehouse smell: alcohol, earth, mellow wood.
**Palate:** Dry and intensely perfumed honey and spice with fresh malt.
**Finish:** Dry, woody. Fresh herbs, light smokiness.

## VINTAGE MALT WHISKY CO. CLASSIC OF ISLAY CASK STRENGTH SINGLE ISLAY MALT 60.2%
Single Malt - Islay

8 1/2 **Gavin: Powerful, pungent malt with everything an Islay enthusiast would wish for.**
*WHISKY Magazine Recommended*
**Nose:** Peat smoke, wet moss, scorched timber.
**Palate:** Intense peat, seaweed, and dry, sooty oak. Cooked fruits struggling to come through.
**Finish:** Long and smoky.

8 3/4 **Dave: A punchy, deep malt. Good balance.**
**Nose:** Pungent, intense, almost balsamic. Soot/wood embers, canvas, a hint of Arbroath smokie and grassy like a peat bank. Hairy chested.
**Palate:** Rounded with good weight and depth. Seaweedy and lightly medicinal, hint of cattlecake. The firm centre is tempered by cooked orchard fruit.
**Finish:** Sweet and slightly nutty. Smoke. Oatcake.

## WEMYSS VINTAGE MALTS DRIED FRUIT BASKET 46%
Blended Malt - Scotland

7 **Dave: That raw sulphury edge suggests an immature whisky or one where there's been little communication between cask and whisky.**
**Nose:** Initial citrus note (lime) soon give way to bready aromas: wholemeal flour, hot baguette, butter. Sweet with a sulphury underpinning.
**Palate:** Drier notes emerge: malt and a green, unripe quality. Things begin to turn bitter towards the finish...
**Finish:** ...and end up like cabbage.

7 **Arthur: Certainly lively, but a little too astringent.**
**Nose:** Vibrant fruits: Satsuma, lemon pith and Braeburn apples. Sultanas. With water more lime and a slight oiliness and metallic element, like a hot engine.
**Palate:** More cute fruits, with artificial lemon and lime flavours.
**Finish:** Malty toast, made with wholemeal bread.

## WEMYSS VINTAGE MALTS SMOOTH GENTLEMAN 43%
Blended Malt - Scotland

7 1/2 **Dave: It was all going so well...**
**Nose:** Bread dough, yeast with some maturity. Good balance with water which brings out spicy oakiness and a deep slightly nutty centre with raisin and dried flowers, then dry bracken.
**Palate:** Slightly stubborn to open. Solid but in time a zesty note and a contrast with coriander spices and a vanilla-led sweetness.
**Finish:** Sadly this falls apart on the finish.

7 1/2 **Arthur: A mis-nomer?**
**Nose:** Smoked cheese, citronella. Damp earth and wet rock. I was reminded of the inside of a megalithic tomb. Leather and crepe suzette. A light cheesiness again.
**Palate:** Burnt twigs, fruit bonbons and tangy orange marmalade.
**Finish:** Earthy and drying.

## WEMYSS VINTAGE MALTS SPICE KING 43%
Blended Malt - Scotland

**7½ Dave: Best neat.**
**Nose:** Initially there's damp earth in the late summer. Wet cut grass, macadamia, Weetabix sprinkled with sugar, tangerine. Slightly musty.
**Palate:** Ripe/baked summer fruits baked. The oak sits on top of some crispbread, toffee and melting chocolate.
**Finish:** Nutmeg and cinnamon, digestive biscuit and light smoke.

**8½ Arthur: Unusual, and composed of many distinct elements that mesh well.**
**Nose:** Freshly cut apples, white pepper, orange sorbet, blackberry jam, and cold roast lamb.
**Palate:** Berry fruits, dark chocolate sauce and then a dryish harissa spice.
**Finish:** Some spicy woodsmoke.

## WHYTE & MACKAY 12 YEARS OLD 40%
Blended - Scotland

**8 Michael: Do you have a sweet tooth? Verges on the liqueur-ish.**
**Nose:** Rich, sweet, creamy. Clean maltiness.
**Palate:** Firm, smooth, almost slippery. Creamy, fruity (Cherries? Peaches?).
**Finish:** Big, firm, Fruity, peppery.

**9 Dave: An absolute cracker. Taste a whisky as good as this and you'll be instantly converted to blends.**
**Nose:** A lifted spicy nose without water, dipping into lemon sherbet, lime and mandarin with some chocolate, smoky wood and cold tea as well.
**Palate:** Seriously chewy stuff with a layer of almost minty toffee running through it.
**Finish:** Long and rich with dry coconut and spice.

## WHYTE & MACKAY 15 YEARS OLD 40%
Blended - Scotland

**8½ Michael: Still on the sweet side but dexterously balanced. Beautifully rounded flavours.**
**Nose:** Richer aromas. Spicier. Appetising.
**Palate:** Bigger, softer. Again a suggestion of cherries. Rose-hip tea. Spicy balancing dryness.
**Finish:** Smoother. Very long. A fragrant, lightly smoky, hint of peat.

**8 Dave: If this were a person it would be Salma Hayek.**
**Nose:** Unreduced there's some coconut along with meaty notes. When water is added out come toasted nuts, orange blossom, butter and real sexy richness.
**Palate:** A lovely start which builds slowly from digestive biscuit into a soft juicy centre with vanilla, mocha, tobacco and not bracken notes.
**Finish:** Juicy and creamy with good weight.

## WHYTE & MACKAY 15 YEARS OLD, PREMIUM RESERVE 40%
Blended - Scotland

**7½ Martine: Oak is better expressed on the palate than on the nose. Will please sweet tooths. Very drinkable but lacks the distinction of the older expressions.**
**Nose:** Resin. Pine cone. Oak. Forest fragrances. Malt flour. Touch of rancid butter in the back. Raisin buns.
**Palate:** Very round. Sweet. Brown sugar. Red and black fruit. Raspberry. Blackcurrant.
**Finish:** Gentle, minty.

**7¾ Dave: Richer than many and well balanced.**
**Nose:** Fleshy and ripe (crème brûlée, plum, blackbberry tart) then aromatic note of cedar/cigar ash. Dry and sweet in balance.
**Palate:** Sweet hay with a firm structure. Deep and long with an unctuous feel. Stewed fruits, sherry, black cherry, treacle tart, dark chocolate.
**Finish:** Dry, clean.

## WHYTE & MACKAY 18 YEARS OLD 40%
Blended - Scotland

**8½ Michael: More backbone. Slightly haughty, but club-bable.**
**Nose:** Notably sweet, but also tea-like.
**Palate:** Satiny. Starts drier. More tightly combined flavours take longer to unfold. Gradually sweeter and more orangey (or tropical fruit?), but always with burnt-grass peatiness behind. Much more complex.

**Finish:** Very long, soothing, warming.

**8 Dave: Big, sexy and luscious. Sophia Loren (or George Clooney depending on your preference).**
**Nose:** We're in a soft world of fruits: caramel, overripe banana, raspberry, cocoa powder and with water, raisin bread, pulpy fruits and lemon tart.
**Palate:** Soft and chewy with a good elegant grainy platform for some pretty spicy attack.
**Finish:** Silky and soft.

## WHYTE & MACKAY 18 YEARS OLD, FOUNDERS RESERVE 40%
Blended - Scotland

**7¾ Martine: A well balanced dram. Rather shy and restrained at start but with time and a drop of water, becomes more attractive.**
**Nose:** Sweet. Floral. Refreshing. Touch of acacia. Sawdust. Marshmallow. Quite slow to open up.
**Palate:** Smooth and creamy. Nutty. Almond. Raisins. Fudge.
**Finish:** Lingering. Dry, slightly astringent.

**8 Dave: A big broad, spicy number typical of the house style.**
**Nose:** Closed then wine gum, raspberry, briary fruits. Becomes big and generous with coffee, rum and raisin. Mature. Raisin and light smoke.
**Palate:** Grippy, tea-like start then Oloroso sweetness. Teasing smoke, perfumed (lavender bags) then dark dusty black fruits. Good weight.
**Finish:** Ripe. Coconut.

## WHYTE & MACKAY 30 YEARS OLD, RARE RESERVE 43%
Blended - Scotland

**8 Martine: Heavier than the 21 Years Old due to its sweetness. But harmonious and elegant.**
**Nose:** Sweet. Elegant. Bourboney. Buttery. Toffee. Cappuccino. Barley sugar. Lemongrass. Star anise. Forest bouquet. Dried leaves, touch of mushroom.
**Palate:** Round and mellow. Clean and fresh. Candied quince. Honeyed apples. Fruit and nut chocolate.
**Finish:** Lingering on liquorice. Ginger root.

**8 Dave: Like all old whiskies everything is delivered on the nose.**
**Nose:** Unctuous. PX/Bristol milk. Walnut, raisin. Very sweet and soft. Moscatel and heathery smoke.
**Palate:** Mouth coating and soft then the grip of oak. Has a mature character giving it an extra dimension.
**Finish:** The dry oak lessens and out comes rich sherried flavours.

## WHYTE & MACKAY SPECIAL RESERVE, 21 YEARS OLD, SHERRY WOOD FINISH 40%
Blended - Scotland

**8¾ Martine: Well-balanced and luscious. Keeps talking if you let it breathe. A blend of distinction.**
**Nose:** Resiny at start. Old furniture. Beeswax. Floral. Pear drop with a hint of nail polish.
**Palate:** Smooth, velvety. Sherried. Fruit. Stewed plums. Marmalade. A touch of milk chocolate.
**Finish:** Long and delicate, full of charm with a lively fresh oak touch. Appetising gingery dryness.

**8¼ Dave: One for people who like 'em big boned.**
**Nose:** Liquorous. Peach syrup, butterscotch. Liqueur chocolate, orange chocolate truffle. Lingering and rich with notes of black forest gateau.
**Palate:** Very full and thick. Covers the tongue. Pastille like black fruits. Liquorous. Raisin, sticky toffee pudding, molasses, demerara sugar. Mellow.
**Finish:** Rich, raisined fruits. The chocolate.

## WILD SCOTSMAN 46%
Blended - Scotland

**6¾ Arthur: Didn't do enough. A badly named whisky if you ask me … I've met wilder Scotsmen at a Morningside tea party.**
**Nose:** Yeast, graininess, lemon biscuits and gravel.
**Palate:** Light in body, but sweet, hot and citric.
**Finish:** A mumbled murmour of peat.

**6 Owen: Easily drinkable, but I fear it will be insufficiently challenging for the enthusiast.**

**Nose:** Flat dusty caramel, punctuated by acetic spirity. After time develops some citric notes, especially lime. Youthful.
**Palate:** Creamy and minty up front, but lacks development.
**Finish:** Modest; faintly linctus-like taint right at the end.

## WILD SCOTSMAN 15 YEARS OLD 46%
Blended - Scotland

**7¾ Martine: A comforting dram, cheery, brings in visions of a warm summer day in the country.**
**Nose:** Earthy, wet moss, turf. Fruity as well. Juicy pears. Cereal notes rise up in a fragrant spiral of honey and ripe hay. Appetising.
**Palate:** Malty sweetness teased by a spicy edge. The cereal is dominant. Muesli. Rich, fulfilled.
**Finish:** Long, balanced with a wave of liquorice. A hint of smoked wood.

**7¾ Dave: Very well balanced and with immediate appeal, exactly what you want from a vatted malt.**
**Nose:** Robust, autumnal: raked leaves and toasted chestnut. Some dried pear and a syrupy sweetness. Water brings bran flakes then peanut.
**Palate:** Soft, slow and slightly creamy. Picks up from mid palate onwards. Silky and deep.
**Finish:** Great length.

## WILLIAM GRANT'S 15 YEARS OLD 40%
Blended - Scotland

**7¾ Martine: Quite an assertive blend. The nose delivers to the palate but it tastes older than 15 years.**
**Nose:** Rich and sherried. antique shop. Cigar box. Meaty. Oxtail. Bacon. Cedar. Tarte Tatin.
**Palate:** Syrupy. Mouth-coating. A beautiful harmony between oak and fruit. Praline. Baked apple in maple syrup. Sweetness prevails.
**Finish:** Sweet. oak, spices try to calm it down.

**9 Dave: This is great blending. Top flight stuff.**
**Nose:** Clover honey, vanilla, cooked pear moving into caramelised fruits and peat smoke balanced by toasty oak. There's some very old whiskies in here.
**Palate:** Sweet and "sherried", but with good grip. Ripe. Balanced between sweetness, richness, oak, fruit and spice.
**Finish:** Long and ripe.

## WILLIAM GRANT'S 15 YEARS OLD 43%
Blended - Scotland

**7¾ Michael: A dessert malt? Remarkably sweet and chocolately until water is added.**
**Nose:** Sweet. Fudge. White chocolate. Oranges.
**Palate:** Syrupy. Creamy. White chocolate. Sweet.
**Finish:** Honeycomb. Crisp caramel wafers. Slightly toasty, burnt, dryness.

**8 Dave: If this was an actor it would be Cary Grant.**
**Nose:** The nose is fragrant and juicy with toffee honey, mint, kumquat, but the smoke is a little more obvious than on Robbie Dhu and there's a teasing dry heather, coconut/gorse edge.
**Palate:** A lovely soft start. Fruity and soft with a good crisp/cracked pepper bite.
**Finish:** Spicy with a touch of smoke.

## WILLIAM GRANT'S 18 YEARS OLD 40%
Blended - Scotland

**7¼ Martine: The nose lets us expect some exotic promises. Did too much dilution blow all that galore off? Disappointing.**
**Nose:** Floral. Fading roses. Almond. Sandalwood. Touch of curry – reminded me of opening the door of an Indian restaurant. Distant echo of smoke.
**Palate:** Soft. Watery. Light oak and not much more.
**Finish:** Not so short though. Slightly oaky. Drying on soft spices.

**8 Dave: Firmer and smokier than the 15.**
**Nose:** Heavy and concentrated with layers of aroma. Sherry (raisin, Dundee cake) and smoke, but also a moist coconutty edge. Cooked black fruits. Rich.
**Palate:** Drier than you expect with plenty of peat. Leather, burning heather, antique shop. Old style.
**Finish:** Dried fruits.

## WILLIAM GRANT'S 18 YEARS OLD, DELUXE BLEND 40%
Blended - Scotland

**8¼ Michael: Leans toward peat-smoke, but beautifully composed. Luxurious. With a cigar?**
*WHISKY Magazine Recommended*
**Nose:** Clean, fresh, earthiness. Soft nuttiness. Slight peaty dryness.
**Palate:** Honeyed but lively. Sweet sherry. Rich maltiness but also well-intergrated peat-smoke dryness.
**Finish:** Restrained. Gentle. Gradually warming. Long. Lingering smokiness.

**9 Dave: So thick and honeyed you could paint it on your lover's body. A true star.**
**Nose:** A lusciously rich, complex nose with heather bell, lemon, honey, spicy sandalwood and an intriguing winey note.
**Palate:** Very sweet to start and holds beautifully in the mouth. Ripe and rich with a lovely mix of vanilla, heather honey and spice.
**Finish:** Long, rich and elegant.

## WILLIAM GRANT'S 25 YEARS OLD 43%
Blended - Scotland

**8¼ Michael: A long maturation for a blend, but this has emerged with confidence, style and sophistication.**
*WHISKY Magazine Recommended*
**Nose:** Oak. Slight char. Beeswax. More flowery (peach blossom) and leafy when water is added.
**Palate:** Surprisingly fresh. Mint toffee. Sweet tobacco.
**Finish:** Dusty spices. Cinnamon. Ginger. Quite sweet.

**8¾ Dave: Bosky, ancient.**
**Nose:** The impression is of great age. Big, mature truffley aromas: lilies tobacco, honeycomb/wax, black walnut, rancio, oak. Complex and dense.
**Palate:** Very soft and heavy. Honey, beeswax, beech woods, russet apple. In time a lighter nuttier side emerges. Chewy and weighty.
**Finish:** Dry and lightly perfumed. Heather.

## WILLIAM GRANT'S ALE CASK RESERVE 40%
Blended - Scotland

**8½ Michael: Fresh and seductively drinkable. I'm astonished how well this innovation worked. The ale was brewed especially to add much more malty sweetness than hop.**
**Nose:** Tropical fruit. Paw-paw? Lemon grass.
**Palate:** Lightly nectar-like. Soft and soothing. A very unusual texture. Creamy when water is added. Peachy. Slightly syrupy. Malty. Clean and smooth.
**Finish:** Sweet orange peel. A suggestion of steamed pudding. Sticky toffee? Slightly smoky.

**7 Dave: Good fun and well-made but will this just open another can of worms? Lager finish anyone?**
**Nose:** Scented aromas: cereal, apple, banana, mixed fruit jam and a hint of the beer cellar/warehouse.
**Palate:** Soft and creamy with silky texture. Light smoke.
**Finish:** Slightly dull and flat.

## WILLIAM GRANT'S SHERRY CASK 40%
Blended - Scotland

**8 Michael: Masculine. Rather austere, aloof.**
**Nose:** Soft oak. Earthy. Truffle-like. Smoky.
**Palate:** Slightly slippery. Slips down. Medium dry. Cedary, some steely notes, and some smoke.
**Finish:** Very lively flavour development. Grassy, peaty, smoky. Drier with water.

**8 Dave: Attractive and well-balanced. Not as heavily sherried as you might expect.**
**Nose:** Attractive with soft, cakey aromas that mix nut and honey with a hint of smoke and a slightly rubbery note.
**Palate:** Clean and not overly sweet. Almond cooked fruits, chocolate, smoke.
**Finish:** Soft, then nutty wood.

## WILLIAM GRANT'S THE FAMILY RESERVE 40%
Blended - Scotland

**7½ Michael:** I have always felt this blend to lack dimension but, as it warmed in the glass, more flavours emerged, especially heathery-peaty elements. Also a more honeyed, malty fullness.
**Nose:** Light peat. Heather-honey. Orange blossom.
**Palate:** Delicate. Camomile. Apples, pears. A hint of oatmeal. Grainy.
**Finish:** Burnt grass. Dry.

**8 Paul:** This blend has stayed at a very high level for the decade I've been sampling it. This time around I noticed the Balvenie presence more than in the past. Very nice job here.
**Nose:** I've always admired this biscuity, cake batter, honeyed, grainy bouquet.
**Palate:** Another blend with the word Speyside branded into it, especially in the feline dry, and smooth-as-glass palate entry. Toasted cereal, sweet malt, light caramel, vanilla extract, and almonds abound. Medium-bodied.
**Finish:** It excels in the aftertaste where the silky toasted cereal taste turns a bit fiery (love that), resin-like, and oily in the throat.

## WILSON & MORGAN MACDUFF 1989 PORT FINISH 46%
Single Malt - Speyside

**7½ Michael:** My guess is that the whisky was initially less rich and malty than the "official" Glen Deveron bottlings. The port finish adds some roundness and interest.
**Nose:** Sand dunes. Gorse in blossom. Clean, fresh, very dry, fudge. Or perhaps Scottish tablet.
**Palate:** Creamy, oaty, becoming grainy. Cereal grain. Slightly vegetal flavours. Scotch broth?
**Finish:** Some grainy astringency.

**6¾ Dave:** Inoffensive, but what's the point?
**Nose:** Quite light, delicate and fruit: raspberry is the main note along with very light malty notes.
**Palate:** Sweet all the way through from start to finish. Some boiled sweet, marzipan; winey rather than malty.
**Finish:** Very light. Rose wine (Tavel).

**Above:** The view from Jura across to Islay
**Main:** Strathisla Distillery in Speyside makes for a picture perfect location to make whisky

# Medals

## GOLD WHISKIES

A comprehensive list of the *Whisky Magazine* medal winners from the last 10 years

### AMERICAN WHISKIES
BERNHEIM ORIGINAL STRAIGHT
WHEAT WHISKEY 45%
CADENHEAD'S 10 Years Old,
Bourbon 45%
ELMER T. LEE 45%
EVAN WILLIAMS 23 Years Old Kentucky
Straight Bourbon Whiskey 53.5%
OLD RIP VAN WINKLE'S 15 Years Old,
Family Reserve 53.5%
SAZERAC 18 Years Old Straight Rye 45%
TWO BOBS KENTUCKY BOURBON 1994
Cask No. 65 63.7%
VAN WINKLE 13 Years Old,
Family Reserve Rye 47.8%
WILD TURKEY 17 Years Old 50.5%
WILD TURKEY 8 Years Old, 101 50.5%
WILD TURKEY Rare Breed 54.2%

### CANADIAN WHISKIES
CROWN ROYAL Special Reserve 40%
FORTY CREEK Barrel Select 40%
GIBSON'S FINEST 18 Years Old 40%

### IRISH WHISKIES
BUSHMILLS 12 Years Old
'Distillery Reserve' 40%
BUSHMILLS 21 Years Old
Madeira Finish 40%
JAMESON 18 Years Old
Master Selection 40%
REDBREAST 12 Years Old 40%

### JAPANESE WHISKIES
HIBIKI 17 Years Old 43%
HIBIKI 505 17 Years Old,
Non chill filtered 50.5%
ICHIRO'S MALT 1988
King of Diamonds 56%
ICHIRO'S MALT King of Spades,
21 Years Old 57%
YAMAZAKI 1979, Japanese Oak Cask,
119.2, Scotch Malt Whisky Society 57.4%
YOICHI 10 Years Old, Single Cask 59.9%
YOICHI 116.1, Scotch Malt Whisky
Society 56.6%
YOICHI 116.4, Scotch Malt Whisky
Society 64.9%

### REST OF WORLD WHISKIES
PENDERYN Grand Slam 46%

### SCOTCH WHISKIES
ABERLOUR 30 Years Old 43%
ARDBEG 10 Years Old 46%

ARDBEG 1974,
Connoisseur's Choice 43%
ARDBEG 1977 46%
ARDBEG 1992 12 Years Old, Rum Finish,
Park Avenue Liquors, Douglas Laing 50%
ARDBEG Provenance, 1974,
bottled 1998, 24 Years Old 55.6%
ARDBEG Uigeadail 54.2%
AUCHENTOSHAN 1966,
31 Years Old 45.8%
BALBLAIR 1973, Private Collection 45%
BALBLAIR 38 Years Old 44%
BALBLAIR 40 Years Old,
The Whisky Exchange 47.2%
THE BALVENIE 1970 Vintage Cask 44.6%
THE BALVENIE 1972 Vintage Cask 49.4%
THE BALVENIE PortWood
21 Years Old 40%
THE BALVENIE PortWood
21 Years Old 40%
THE BALVENIE Rumwood
14 Years Old 47.1%
THE BALVENIE Vintage Cask 1967 40%
THE BALVENIE Vintage Cask 1972 47.3%
BENRIACH 21 Years Old 56.7%
BENRIACH 21 Years Old,
The Whisky Exchange 56.7%
BENRIACH 30 Years Old 50%
BOWMORE 14 Years Old,
Dewar Rattray 57.8%
BOWMORE 1968 43.4%
BOWMORE Voyage 56%
BRORA 18 Years Old, Old Malt Cask 50%
BRORA 21 Years Old, Rare Malts 56.9%
BRORA 30 Years Old 52.4%
BRORA 30 Years Old,
Limited Edition 55.7%
BRUICHLADDICH 1991, 12 Years Old,
Dewar Rattray 60%
BRUICHLADDICH 20 Years Old 46%
BUNNAHABHAIN 1968 Auld
Aquaintance, Hogmanay Edition 43.8%
CAOL ILA 12 Years Old 43%
CAOL ILA 12 Years Old,
The Wee Dram 40%
CAOL ILA 13 Years Old,
Bottle for the Whisky Fair 54.2%
CAOL ILA 1990 Port Wood Finish,
Private Collection 40%
CELTIQUE CONNEXION Vin de Paille du
Jura Wood Finish 1994 43%
CHIVAS REGAL 18 Years Old 40%
COMPASS BOX Eleuthera 46%
COMPASS BOX The Peat Monster 46%
COMPASS BOX The Peat Monster 46%

CRAGGANMORE 12 Years Old 40%
CRAGGANMORE 12 Years Old 40%
DALLAS DHU 23 Years Old,
Cadenhead's 60.8%
GLEN GARIOCH 1988, 16 Years Old,
Duncan Taylor 56.1%
GLEN GARIOCH 1988,
Duncan Taylor 54.6%
GLEN MORAY 1962, Ed Dodson's Last
Manager's Choice 51%
GLEN SCOTIA 1974 30 Years Old,
CHIEFTAIN'S Choice 42.2%
GLENCADAM 1975 30 Years Old,
Dewar Rattray 54.4%
GLENFIDDICH 1965
Vintage Reserve 47.8%
GLENFIDDICH 1991 Vintage Reserve 40%
GLENFIDDICH 40 Years Old 43.6%
GLENFIDDICH 40 Years Old,
Rare Collection 44%
GLENGOYNE 32 Years Old,
Single Cask 48.7%
THE GLENLIVET 15 Years Old
French Oak Reserve 40%
THE GLENLIVET 16 Years Old,
Cask Strength 56.6%
THE GLENLIVET 1959
Cellar Collection 41.7%
THE GLENLIVET 1974,
Murray McDavid Mission 46%
GLENMORANGIE Original 43%
GLENMORANGIE Tain L'Hermitage 46%
THE GLENROTHES 1991 43%
HIGHLAND PARK 17 Years Old,
Cask 2903, Adelphi 55.3%
HIGHLAND PARK 18 Years Old 43%
HIGHLAND PARK 1988, Signatory 46%
HIGHLAND PARK 29 Years Old 1978,
Old & Rare 56.7%
HIGHLAND PARK 8 Years Old,
MacPhail's Collection 40%
JOHNNIE WALKER Black Label 40%
JOHNNIE WALKER Black Label 40%
JOHNNIE WALKER Blue Label 40%
THE MACALLAN 15 Years Old,
Fine Oak
THE MACALLAN 17 Years Old,
Dewar Rattray 58.4%
THE MACALLAN 1937,
37 Years Old, Vintage 43%
THE MACALLAN 1948
Select Reserve 43%
THE MACALLAN 1949,
50 Years Old, Millennium 46%
THE MACALLAN 1961 Vintage 54.7%

THE MACALLAN 1970,
32 Years Old, Vintage 54.9%
THE MACALLAN 1979
18 Years Old, Gran Reserva 40%
THE MACALLAN 1981,
Unfiltered Cask Strength 57%
THE MACALLAN Thirties 40%
LAGAVULIN 12 Years Old 57.8%
LAGAVULIN 16 Years Old 43%
LAGAVULIN Distillers Edition,
Pedro Ximenez Finish 43%
LAPHROAIG 17 Years Old,
Feis Ile 2004, Cask Strength 55.2%
LAPHROAIG 1988 Unchillfiltered,
Signatory 46%
LAPHROAIG Quarter Cask 48%
LINKWOOD 17 Years Old, Adelphi 64.2%
LONGMORN 15 Years Old 45%
MONKEY SHOULDER Batch 27 40%
MORTLACH 1938, 60 Years Old,
Gordon & MacPhail 40%
PORT ELLEN 1978 Port Wood,
Signatory 58%
PORT ELLEN 20 Years Old,
Rare Malts 60.9%
PORT ELLEN 24 Years Old,
Chieftain's Choice 59.4%
PORT ELLEN 25 Years Old,
Special Release 2005 57.4%
ROSEBANK 1989, 9 Years Old,
Cadenhead's 43%
ROSEBANK 1990,
Berry's Own Selection 46%
ROSEBANK 20 Years Old,
Rare Malts 62.3%
ROYAL MILE WHISKIES BOWMORE 1999,
Young Peaty Islay 61.5%
ROYAL SALUTE 21 Years Old 40%
ROYAL SALUTE 50 Years Old 40%
SPRINGBANK 12 Years Old,
Rum Cask 54.6%
SPRINGBANK 1975
Limburg Whisky Fair 49.2%
SPRINGBANK 1989, Limited Edition
Limburg Festival Bottling 55.8%
TALISKER 10 Years Old 45.8%
TALISKER 18 Years Old 45.8%
TALISKER 1975, 25 Years Old,
Cask Strength 59.9%
TALISKER 1982, 20 Years Old 58.8%
TALISKER 25 Years Old 56.9%
TALISKER 28 Years Old 43.3%
TEACHER'S HIGHLAND CREAM 43%
TEANINICH 31 Years Old,
Adelphi 57.8%

## SILVER WHISKIES

### AMERICAN WHISKIES
BLANTON'S 46.5%
BLANTON'S Original Bourbon 49.5%
BOOKER'S 6 to 8 Years Old 62.5%
BOOKER'S 6 Years Old 63.25%
ELIJAH CRAIG 12 Years Old 47% •
EVAN WILLIAMS 1990,
Single Barrel 43.3%
EVAN WILLIAMS 1993,
Single Barrel 43.3%
EVAN WILLIAMS
Single Barrel Bourbon,
1994 45%
GEORGE T. STAGG 71.35%
OLD FITZGERALD Very Special 45%
PAPPY VAN WINKLE 15 Years Old,
Family Reserve 53.5%
PAPPY VAN WINKLE 20 Years Old,
Family Reserve 45.2%
PARKER HERITAGE COLLECTION 1996
Cask Strength Small Batch
Bourbon 61.3%
ROCK HILL FARM Single Cask
Bourbon 50%

TWO BOBS KENTUCKY BOURBON 1994
Cask No. 66 63.7%
W.L. WELLER 60.95%
W.L. WELLER 12 Years Old 45%
WILD TURKEY 10 Years Old,
Russell's Reserve 50.5%
WOODFORD RESERVE Kentucky
Straight Bourbon Whiskey 45.2%
WOODFORD RESERVE Kentucky
Straight Bourbon Whiskey 45.2%

### IRISH WHISKIES
BLACK BUSH 43%
BUSHMILLS 16 Years Old 40%
BUSHMILLS 1608 Reserve 40%
BUSHMILLS 21 Years Old 40%
BUSHMILLS Black Bush 40%
BUSHMILLS Millennium 40%
CONNEMARA Single Malt
Irish Whiskey 40%
JAMESON 12 Years Old 43%
JAMESON Gold 40%
JAMESON Limited Edition,
15 Years Old 40%

MICHAEL COLLINS Blend 40%
MIDLETON Very Rare 40%
MIDLETON Very Rare 40%
TYRCONNELL Madeira Finish
10 Years Old 46%

### JAPANESE WHISKIES
HAKUSHU 12 Years Old Pure Malt 43%
ICHIRO'S MALT 1988
Single Malt Vintage 56%
ICHIRO'S MALT Ace of Hearts,
22 Years Old 56%
ICHIRO'S MALT Two of Clubs 57%
KARUIZAWA 1988 59.3%
KIRIN 18 Years Old, Fuji-Sanroku 43%
YAMAZAKI 18 Years Old 43%
YAMAZAKI 1980
Japanese White Oak Cask 58%
YAMAZAKI 1980 Vintage Malt 56%
YAMAZAKI 10 Years Old, 119.3,
Scotch Malt Whisky Society 56.2%
YOICHI 10 Years Old 43%
YOICHI 12 Years Old,
Peaty and Salty 55%

YOICHI 12 Years Old,
Woody and Vanillic 55%
YOICHI 15 Years Old 45%
YOICHI 1991, Cask No 129504 64%

### SCOTCH WHISKIES
ABERLOUR 15 Years Old,
Sherry Wood 40%
ABERLOUR a'bunadh 59.6%
ABERLOUR a'bunadh,
Limited Edition 59.6%
ARDBEG 15 Years Old,
Old Malt Cask 50%
ARDBEG 17 Years Old 40%
ARDBEG 1976,
Distillery Manager's Choice 56%
ARDBEG 1976,
Single Cask Committee bottling 51%
ARDBEG Oloroso Finish, Cask 4704 47.2%
ARDBEG 28 Years Old,
The Ardbeggeddon 1972, Sherry Cask,
Old Malt Cask 48.4%
ARDBEG Airigh Nam Beist 1990
16 Years Old 46%

## SILVER WHISKIES CONTINUED

ARDBEG Almost There 54%
ARDBEG Lord of the Isles,
25 Years Old 46%
ARDBEG Lord of the Isles,
25 Years Old 46%
ARDBEG Oloroso Finish,
Cask 4704 47.2%
AUCHENTOSHAN 10 Years Old 40%
AUCHENTOSHAN 17 Years Old,
Bordeaux Wine 51%
AUCHENTOSHAN 1978,
18 Years Old 58.8%
AUCHENTOSHAN 21 Years Old 43%
AUCHENTOSHAN Three Wood 43%
BAILLIE NICOL JARVIE 40%
BALBLAIR 1969 Vintage 45%
BALBLAIR 1979 Vintage 43%
BALBLAIR 1997 Vintage 43%
BALBLAIR 40 Years Old,
Single Malts of Scotland 42.8%
BALLANTINE'S LIMITED 43%
THE BALVENIE 10 Years Old,
Founder's Reserve 43%
THE BALVENIE 12 Years Old,
Double Wood 43%
THE BALVENIE 12 Years Old,
Double Wood 43%
THE BALVENIE 1968 50.8%
THE BALVENIE 21 Years Old
PortWood 40%
THE BALVENIE Islay Cask,
17 Years Old 43%
THE BALVENIE Roasted malt
Aged 14 Years 47.1%
BEN NEVIS 12 Years Old,
Glenkeir Treasures 40%
BENRIACH 25 Years Old 50%
BENRIACH Authenticus
Peated Single Malt 21 Years Old 46%
BENRIACH Madeira wood finish 46%
BENROMACH Sassicaia Wood Finish,
Gordon & MacPhail 45%
BENROMACH Traditional,
Gordon & MacPhail 40%
BERRY'S Best Orkney, 14 Years Old 43%
BLACK BOTTLE 10 Years Old 40%
BLUE HANGER 25 Years Old,
Second Release 45.6%
BOWMORE 12 Years Old 40%
BOWMORE 1990, 15 Years Old,
Dewar Rattray 55.7%
BOWMORE 1990, 16 Years Old,
Dewar Rattray 54%
BOWMORE 20 Years Old,
Douglas Laing 50%
BOWMORE Claret
BOWMORE Darkest 43%
BOWMORE Dusk 50%
BRORA 1977, 21 Years Old,
Rare Malts 56.9%
BRORA 1982, 20 Years Old,
Rare Malts 58.1%
BRORA 24 Years Old,
Chieftain's Choice 46%
BRORA 30 Years Old 55.7%
BRUICHLADDICH 1969, 33 Years Old
Duncan Taylor 48.7%
BRUICHLADDICH Celtic Nations 46%
BRUICHLADDICH Infinity
Second Edition 52.5%
BRUICHLADDICH Second Edition 15
Years Old 46%
BRUICHLADDICH XVII, 17 Years Old 46%
BUNNAHABHAIN 27 Years Old,
Dewar Rattray 49.9%
BUNNAHABHAIN 35 Years Old,
Limited Edition 44.9%
CAMPBELTOWN 1970,
The Almond Tree 46%
CAOL ILA 10 Years Old, Rare Cask,
Queen of the Moorlands 46%
CAOL ILA 13 Years Old,
Chieftain's Choice 46%

CAOL ILA 15 Years Old,
Dewar Rattray 56%
CAOL ILA 16 Years Old,
The Whisky Exchange 57.9%
CAOL ILA 1969, Private Collection 45%
CAOL ILA 1979 26 Years Old,
The Whisky Fair, Douglas Laing 57.2%
CAOL ILA 1988 Cognac Finish,
Private Collection 40%
CAOL ILA 1991, 15 Years Old,
Dewar Rattray 56.7%
CAOL ILA 1991, Gordon & MacPhail 57.4%
CAOL ILA 1992, 13 Years Old,
Cooper's Choice 46%
CAOL ILA 25 Years Old,
Special Release 58.4%
CAOL ILA Cask Strength 55%
CELTIQUE CONNEXION 1993
Monbazillac Wood Finish 43%
CELTIQUE CONNEXION Cadillac
Wood Finish 1990 43%
CHIVAS REGAL 18 Years Old 40%
CLAN DENNY Lochside 1963,
Great Single Grain 50.2%
CLYNELISH 10 Years Old 59.8%
CLYNELISH 23 Years Old,
Old Malt Cask 50%
COMPASS BOX Flaming Heart 48.9%
COMPASS BOX Oak Cross 43%
COOPER'S CHOICE Glenlivet 1991 43%
COOPER'S CHOICE Mortlach 1990,
Sherry Cask 46%
CRAGGANMORE 17 Years Old 55.5%
CRAGGANMORE 1984 Distillers Edition,
Ruby Port Finish, 12 Years Old 40%
CRAGGANMORE 29 Years Old 52.5%
CUTTY SARK 25 Years Old 45.7%
DAILUAINE 1985,
Berry's Own Selection 46%
DAILUAINE 21 Years Old,
Cask 4150, Adelphi 56.1%
DALLAS DHU 1970, 32 Years Old,
Cooper's Choice 46%
THE DALMORE 1991,
Madeira Finish 60%
THE DALMORE 21 Years Old 43%
THE DALMORE 30 Years Old,
Gonzalez Bypass 42%
DUMBARTON (Inverleven Stills)
18 Years Old, Cadenhead's 57.9%
DUN BHEAGAN Lowland
8 Years Old 43%
FAMOUS GROUSE 1987
Vintage Malt Whisky 40%
FAMOUS GROUSE 1989
Vintage Malt 40%
FAMOUS GROUSE Scottish Oak 45%
GIRVAN 15 Years Old, Cask 110636,
Old Masters 60.4%
GIRVAN 1989, Berry's Own Selection 46%
GLEN ELGIN 19 Years Old,
Centenary Bottling 60%
GLEN ELGIN 1975,
Berry's Own Selection 46%
GLEN ELGIN 32 Years Old 58.3%
GLEN GARIOCH 1968,
29 Years Old 56.3%
GLEN GARIOCH 35 Years Old,
Old & Rare Platinum 56%
GLEN GRANT 1948,
Gordon & MacPhail 40%
GLEN GRANT 1968,
Gordon & MacPhail 40%
GLEN GRANT 1969, Adelphi 52.9%
GLEN GRANT 1970, Speyside Region
Selection No 2, Duncan Taylor 51.7%
GLEN GRANT 1976, Signatory 58.2%
GLEN GRANT 1977 27 Years Old,
Sherry Cask, Cooper's Choice 46%
GLEN GRANT 1985 19 Years Old,
Dewar Rattray 58.4%
THE GLENLIVET 1967
Cellar Collection 46%

THE GLENLIVET 1967 Vintage 53.32%
THE GLENLIVET 1970 Vintage 56.58%
THE GLENLIVET 25 Years Old 43%
GLEN MORAY 1971 Vintage 43%
Glen Ord 30 Years Old,
Special Reserve 58.7%
GLENALLACHIE 15 Years Old,
Cask Strength Edition,
Chivas Brothers 58%
GLENCADAM 1985, 16 Years Old,
CHIEFTAIN'S Choice 43%
GLENDRONACH 33 Years Old 40%
GLENDULLAN 1978 26 Years Old,
Rare Malts 56.5%
GLENFARCLAS 15 Years Old 46%
GLENFARCLAS 17 Years Old 43%
GLENFARCLAS 1955 44.6%
GLENFARCLAS 21 Years Old 43%
GLENFARCLAS 40 Years Old,
Millennium Edition 54.7%
GLENFIDDICH 15 Years Old,
Solera Reserve 40%
GLENFIDDICH 1973 Vintage 48.1%
GLENFIDDICH 1973
Vintage Reserve 49.5%
GLENFIDDICH 1974 50th Anniversary
of the Queen's Coronation,
The Whisky Exchange 48.9%
GLENFIDDICH 21 Years Old,
Gran Reserva 40%
GLENGOYNE 2000 AD 43%
GLENLIVET 1972,
Berry's Own Selection 46%
GLENMORANGIE 12 Years Old,
Millennium Malt 43%
GLENMORANGIE 1995
Artisan Cask 45%
GLENMORANGIE 30 Years Old 44.3%
GLENMORANGIE Artisan 46%
GLENMORANGIE Burr Oak 56.3%
GLENMORANGIE Côte de Beaune 46%
GLENMORANGIE Fino Sherry
Wood Finish
GLENMORANGIE Madeira Finish
GLENMORANGIE Madeira
Matured 56.6%
GLENMORANGIE Malaga Wood Finish,
25 Years Old 43%
GLENMORANGIE Original 43%
GLENMORANGIE Truffle Oak 60.5%
GLEN ORD 30 Years Old,
Special Reserve 58.7%
THE GLENROTHES 1971 43%
THE GLENROTHES 1985,
Berry Bros. & Rudd 43%
GLENTURRET 14 Years Old 59.7%
GLENTURRET 1980
Limited Edition 55.2%
GLENTURRET 21 Years Old 40%
GLENTURRET 29 Years Old 55.6%
HIGHLAND PARK 12 Years Old
HIGHLAND PARK 16 Years Old,
Douglas Laing 50%
HIGHLAND PARK 1970, 4.73,
Scotch Malt Whisky Society 52.5%
HIGHLAND PARK 1970, Rare Old 40%
HIGHLAND PARK 1979,
Murray McDavid 46%
HIGHLAND PARK 25 Years Old
Single Cask, Dewar Rattray 52.3%
HIGHLAND PARK 25 Years Old
HIGHLAND PARK 30 Years Old,
MacPhail's Collection 43%
HIGHLAND PARK 36 Years Old,
Cask 10252, The Whisky Exchange 49.7%
INCHGOWER 1974,
Berry's Own Selection 46%
INCHGOWER 1980,
Berry's Own Selection 46%
INVERGORDON 1964,
Dewar Rattray 52.1%
INVERGORDON 40 Years Old,
Dewar Rattray 48.1%

INVERGORDON 40 Years Old,
Duncan Taylor 50.3%
INVERLEVEN 26 Years Old, Cask 1873,
Duncan Taylor 50.1%
ISLAY MIST 17 Years Old 40%
ISLAY MIST Blended Scotch Whisky 40%
ISLE OF JURA 1999, 5 Years Old,
The Whisky Exchange 63%
JAMES MACARTHUR 14 Years Old
Islay Blended Malt 58.3%
JOHNNIE WALKER Gold Label 40%
KINGSBURY ISLAY 1973,
27 Years Old 47.4%
LAGAVULIN 12 Years Old 57.7%
LAGAVULIN 1979 Distillers Edition,
Pedro Ximenez Finish 43%
LAPHROAIG 10 Years Old 43%
LAPHROAIG 15 Years Old 43%
LAPHROAIG 15 Years Old, 1987,
Douglas Laing 50%
LAPHROAIG 16 Years Old,
Limburg Whisky Fair Bottling,
Douglas Laing 56.1%
LAPHROAIG Rare Cask,
Queen of the Moorlands 54.7%
LEAPFROG 1987, Murray McDavid 40%
LINKWOOD 1973,
Murray McDavid Mission II 46%
LITTLEMILL 21 Years Old,
Sherry finish, Dun Bheagan 46%
LOCHSIDE 1991,
Berry's Own Selection 40%
LONGMORN 15 Years Old 45%
LONGMORN 16 Years Old 45%
LONGMORN 1990,
Berry's Own Selection 46%
LONGMORN 31 Years Old
Bottle for the Whisky Fair 49.8%
LONGROW 10 Years Old 46%
LONGROW 10 Years Old,
Sherrywood 46%
THE MACALLAN 10 Years Old 40%
THE MACALLAN 12 Years Old 40%
THE MACALLAN 18 Years Old 40%
THE MACALLAN 1926, 60 Years Old
THE MACALLAN 1937, 36 Years Old 43%
THE MACALLAN 1940, 35 Years Old
THE MACALLAN 1946, 52 Years Old
THE MACALLAN 1951 Vintage 49.6%
THE MACALLAN 1977, 25 Years Old,
Christopher's Queen's Jubilee Magnum
THE MACALLAN 1989,
Exceptional Cask V 59.2%
THE MACALLAN 21 Years Old, Fine Oak
THE MACALLAN 30 Years Old, Fine Oak
THE MACALLAN 50 Years Old,
Millennium Decanter
THE MACALLAN Exceptional Cask IV 57.4%
THE MACALLAN Fifties 40%
THE MACALLAN Forties 40%
THE MACALLAN Replica 1874
THE MACALLAN Replica 1841 41.7%
THE MACALLAN Special Reserve
THE MACALLAN Twenties 40%
THE MACALLAN 28 Years Old,
Old & Rare Platinum 48.2%
MILLBURN 1969 35 Years Old,
Rare Malts 51.2%
MILLBURN 31 Years Old,
Cadenhead's 52.3%
MORTLACH 15 Years Old,
Dewar Rattray 55.44%
MORTLACH 1989 Unchillfiltered,
Signatory 54%
MORTLACH 1990 16 Years Old,
Sherry Cask, Cooper's Choice 46%
OBAN DISTILLERS EDITION
Montilla 43%
OLD MALT CASK Director's Tactical
Selection, 18 Years Old 50%
OLD PULTENEY 12 Years Old 40%
OLD PULTENEY 15 Years Old,
Cask Strength 57.8%

# Medals & Producers

OLD PULTENEY 17 Years Old 46%
PORT DUNDAS 34 Years Old 57.9%
PORT ELLEN 1978 20 Years Old,
Rare Malts 60.9%
PORT ELLEN 1978, Signatory 59%
PORT ELLEN 24 Years Old 57.3%
PORT ELLEN 24 Years Old,
Burgundy finish, Signatory Straight
from the Cask 58.8%
PORT ELLEN 25 Years Old,
Douglas Laing 50%

PORT ELLEN 6th Release 54.2%
ROYAL SALUTE 21 Years Old 40%
ROYAL SALUTE 21 Years Old 43%
SCAPA 12 Years Old 43%
SCOTCH MALT WHISKY SOCIETY
9 Years Old Millennium Malt 58.1%
SMOKEHEAD 43%
SPEYBURN 21 Years Old 58.5%
SPRINGBANK 10 Years Old 40%
SPRINGBANK 1965,
Murray McDavid 43%

ST MAGDALENE 1975,
Gordon & MacPhail 43%
TALISKER 1986,
The Distiller's Edition 45.8%
TALISKER 25 Years Old 57.8%
TALISKER 25 Years Old,
Special Release 2005  57.2%
TALISKER The Distiller's Edition
Amoroso Sherry
TULLIBARDINE 1993
Sauterne wood finish 46%

TULLIBARDINE 1993
Port Wood Finish 46%
VINTAGE MALT WHISKY CO.
Classic of Islay Cask Strength
Single Islay Malt 60.2%
WHYTE & MACKAY
Special Reserve, 21 Years Old,
Sherry Wood Finish 40%
WILLIAM GRANT'S 18 Years Old,
Deluxe Blend 40%
WILLIAM GRANT'S 25 Years Old 43%

## PRODUCERS
### The whisky companies and distilleries that feature in this guide

ABERFELDY DISTILLERY
www.dewarswow.com
ABERLOUR DISTILLERY
www.aberlour.co.uk
ADELPHI DISTILLERY LTD
www.adelphidistillery.com
AMRUT DISTILLERIES LTD
www.amrut.com
ANGUS DUNDEE
www.angusdundee.co.uk
ARDBEG DISTILLERY
www.ardbeg.com
AUCHENTOSHAN DISTILLERY
www.morrisonbowmore.co.uk
www.malts.com
AULTMORE DISTILLERY
www.dewars.com
BAKERY HILL DISTILLERY
www.bakeryhilldistillery.com.au
BALBLAIR DISTILLERY
www.inverhouse.com
BALVENIE DISTILLERY
www.balvenie.com
BARTON BRANDS LTD
www.bartoninc.com
BARTON DISTILLERY
www.bartoninc.com
BEAM GLOBAL SPIRITS & WINE, INC
www.jimbeam.com
BEN NEVIS DISTILLERY
www.bennevisdistillery.com
BENNACHIE WHISKY COMPANY
www.unitedbrands.co.uk/whiskey_ben
nachie
BENRIACH DISTILLERY
www.benriachdistillery.co.uk
BENROMACH DISTILLERY
www.benromach.com
BERNHEIM DISTILLERY
www.heaven-hill.com
BERRY BROS. & RUDD
www.bbr.com
BLACKADDER INTERNATIONAL
www.blackadder.com
BLADNOCH DISTILLERY
www.bladnoch.co.uk
BLAIR ATHOL DISTILLERY
www.malts.com
BOWMORE DISTILLERY
www.morrisonbowmore.co.uk
BROWN-FORMAN BEVERAGES
WORLDWIDE
www.brown-forman.com
BRUICHLADDICH DISTILLERY
www.bruichladdich.com
BUFFALO TRACE DISTILLERY
www.buffalotrace.com
BUNNAHABHAIN DISTILLERY
www.Bunnahabhain.com
BURN STEWART DISTILLERS PLC
www.burnstewartdistillers.com
CADENHEAD'S WHISKY SHOP
www.wmcadenhead.com
CANADIAN CLUB DISTILLERY
www.canadianclubwhisky.com
CANADIAN MIST DISTILLERS LTD.
www.canadianmist.com

CAOL ILA DISTILLERY
www.malts.com
CARDHU DISTILLERY
www.malts.com
CASCADE DISTILLERY
www.dickel.com
CELTIC WHISKY COMPAGNIE
www.celtic-whisky.com
CHIVAS BROTHERS
www.chivas.com
CLEAR CREEK DISTILLERY
www.clearcreekdistillery.com
CLYNELISH DISTILLERY
www.malts.com
COCK O' THE NORTH LTD
www.cockothenorth.com
COMPASS BOX DELICIOUS WHISKY LTD
www.compassboxwhisky.com
COOLEY DISTILLERY PLC
www.cooleywhiskey.com
CORBY DISTILLERIES LTD
www.corby.ca
CRAGGANMORE DISTILLERY
www.malts.com
CRAIGELLACHIE DISTILLERY
www.dewars.com
CRAIGELLACHIE HOTEL
www.craigellachie.com
THE CREATIVE WHISKY CO LTD
www.creativewhisky.com
DAILUAINE DISTILLERY
www.malts.com
DALMORE DISTILLERY
www.thedalmore.com
DALWHINNIE DISTILLERY
www.malts.com
DEANSTON DISTILLERY
www.burnstewartdistillers.com
DEWAR RATTRAY LIMITED
www.dewarrattray.com
DIAGEO
www.diageo.com
DISTELL GROUP LTD
www.distell.co.za
DISTILLERIE WARENGHAM
www.distillerie-warenghem.com
DOUGLAS LAING & CO.
www.douglaslaing.com
DRAMBUIE
www.drambuie.com
DUFFTOWN DISTILLERY
www.malts.com
DUNCAN TAYLOR & COMPANY
www.dtcscotch.com
EARLY TIMES DISTILLERY
www.earlytimes.com
EASY DRINKING WHISKY COMPANY
www.johnmarkandrobbo.com
EDRADOUR DISTILLERY
www.edradour.co.uk
THE EDRINGTON GROUP
www.edringtongroup.com
THE FAMOUS GROUSE EXPERIENCE
www.famousgrouseexperience.com
FOUR ROSES DISTILLERY
www.fourroses.us
GEORGE A. DICKEL & COMPANY
www.dickel.com

GLEN DEVERON DISTILLERY
www.dewars.com
GLEN ELGIN DISTILLERY
www.malts.com
GLEN GARIOCH DISTILLERY
www.morrisonbowmore.co.uk
GLEN GRANT DISTILLERY
www.chivas.com
GLEN MORAY DISTILLERY
www.glenmoray.com
GLEN ORD DISTILLERY
www.malts.com
GLEN SPEY DISTILLERY
www.diageo.com
GLENCADAM DISTILLERY
www.angusdundee.com
GLENDRONACH DISTILLERY
www.chivas.com
GLENDULLAN DISTILLERY
www.diageo.com
GLENFARCLAS DISTILLERY
www.glenfarclas.co.uk
GLENFIDDICH DISTILLERY
www.glenfiddich.com
GLENGOYNE DISTILLERIES
www.glengoyne.com
GLENKEIR WHISKIES LTD
www.whiskyshop.com
GLENKINCHIE DISTILLERY
www.malts.com
GLENLIVET DISTILLERY
www.glenlivet.com
GLENLOSSIE DISTILLERY
www.diageo.com
GLENMORANGIE DISTILLERY
www.glenmorangie.com
THE GLENMORANGIE COMPANY
www.glenmorangieplc.com
GLENROTHES DISTILLERY
www.glenrotheswhisky.com
GLENTURRET DISTILLERY
www.famousgrouse.com
GORDON & MACPHAIL
www.gordonandmacphail.com
HAKUSHU HIGASHI DISTILLERY
www.suntory.com
THE HARRIS WHISKY CO.
www.harriswhisky.com
HART BROTHERS
www.hartbrothers.co.uk
HEAVEN HILL DISTILLERIES, INC.
www.heaven-hill.com
HIGHLAND PARK DISTILLERY
www.highlandpark.co.uk
HIGHWOOD DISTILLERY
www.highwood-distillers.com
HOT IRISHMAN LTD
www.hotirishman.com
IAN MACLEOD DISTILLERS LTD
www.ianmacleod.com
INCHGOWER DISTILLERY
www.diageo.com
INVER HOUSE DISTILLERS LTD
www.inverhouse.com
IRISH DISTILLERS GROUP
www.irishdistillers.com
ISLE OF ARRAN DISTILLERIES
www.arranwhisky.com

ISLE OF ARRAN DISTILLERY
www.arranwhisky.com
ISLE OF JURA DISTILLERY
www.isleofjura.com
J & A MITCHELL & CO
www.springbankdistillers.com
J & G GRANT
www.glenfarclas.co.uk
J & W HARDIE LIMITED
www.jwhardie.com
JACK DANIEL DISTILLERY
www.jackdaniels.com
JAMES MACARTHUR & CO.
www.james-macarthur.co.uk
JOHN DEWAR & SONS
www.dewars.com
KARUIZAWA DISTILLERY
www.mercian.co.jp
KIRIN BREWERY CO. LIMITED
www.kirin-seagram.co.jp
KITTLING RIDGE DISTILLERY
www.kittlingridge.com
KNOCKANDO DISTILLERY
www.malts.com
KNOCKDHU DISTILLERY
www.inverhouse.com
LABROT & GRAHAM DISTILLERY
www.J-g.com
LAGAVULIN DISTILLERY
www.malts.com
LAPHROAIG DISTILLERY
www.laphroaig.com
LINKWOOD DISTILLERY
www.diageo.com
LOCH FYNE WHISKIES
www.lfw.co.uk
LOCH LOMOND DISTILLERY
www.lochlomonddistillery.com
LOCKE'S DISTILLERY
www.iol.ie/wmeathtc/lockes
LOMBARD SCOTCH WHISKY
www.lombardscotchwhisky.com
LONGMORN DISTILLERY
www.chivas.com
MACALLAN DISTILLERY
www.themacallan.com
MACDUFF INTERNATIONAL
www.macduffint.co.uk
MACKMYRA SWEDISH WHISKY
www.mackmyra.se
MAJESTIC DISTILLING CO. INC
www.majesticdistilling.com
MAKER'S MARK DISTILLERY
www.makersmark.com
MANNOCHMORE DISTILLERY
www.malts.com
MATISSE WHISKY
www.matissewhisky.com
MCDOWELL & COMPANY
www.clubmcdowell.com
MCLAIN & KYNE DISTILLERY
www.mclainandkyne.com
MERCIAN CORPORATION
www.mercian.co.jp
MORRISON BOWMORE DISTILLERS
www.morrisonbowmore.co.uk
MORTLACH DISTILLERY
www.malts.com

## PRODUCERS CONTINUED

MURRAY MCDAVID
www.murray-mcdavid.com
NIKKA WHISKY DISTILLING COMPANY
www.nikkawhisky.co.jp
OBAN DISTILLERY
www.malts.com
OLD BUSHMILLS DISTILLERY
www.bushmills.com
OLD COURSE HOTEL GOLF RESORT & SPA
www.oldcoursehotel.co.uk
OLD JAMESON DISTILLERY
www.jameson.ie
OLD MIDLETON DISTILLERY
www.jamesonwhiskey.com
OLD PULTENEY DISTILLERY
www.oldpulteney.com
OLD RIP VAN WINKLE DISTILLERY
www.oldripvanwinkle.com
PERNOD RICARD USA
www.pernod-ricard-usa.com
PITTYVAICH DISTILLERY
www.diageo.com
POGUE DISTILLERY
www.oldpogue.com
PORT ELLEN DISTILLERY
www.malts.com
PRESTON ASSOCIATES
www.milfordwhisky.co.nz
THE QUEEN OF THE MOORLANDS
WHISKY COMPANY
www.wineandwhisky.com

ROSEBANK DISTILLERY
www.malts.com
ROYAL BRACKLA DISTILLERY
www.dewars.com
ROYAL LOCHNAGAR DISTILLERY
www.malts.com
ROYAL MILE WHISKIES
www.royalmilewhiskies.com
SAZERAC COMPANY INC
www.sazerac.com
SCAPA DISTILLERY
www.scapamalt.com
SCOTCH MALT WHISKY SOCIETY
www.smws.com
SENDAI DISTILLERY
www.nikkawhisky.co.jp
SIGNATORY VINTAGE SCOTCH WHISKY
CO LTD
www.edradour.co.uk
SINGLETON DISTILLERY
www.diageo.com
SMALL BATCH DISTILLERY
www.smallbatch.com
SOUTHERN DISTILLING COMPANY LTD
www.hokonuiwhiskey.com
SPECIALITY DRINKS LTD
www.thewhiskyexchange.com
SPEYBURN DISTILLERY
www.inverhouse.com
SPEYSIDE DISTILLERS
www.speysidedistillery.co.uk

SPRINGBANK DISTILLERY
www.springbankdistillers.com
SQUARE BARREL
www.squarebarrelwhisky.com
ST. GEORGES SPIRITS
www.stgeorgespirits.com
STRATHISLA DISTILLERY
www.chivas.com
STRATHMILL DISTILLERY
www.malts.com
SUNTORY
www.suntory.com
TALISKER DISTILLERY
www.malts.com
TAMNAVULIN DISTILLERY
www.whyteandmackay.co.uk
TASMANIA DISTILLERY
www.tasmaniadistillery.com
TEANINICH DISTILLERY
www.malts.com
TOBERMORY DISTILLERY
www.burnstewartdistillers.com/toberm
orydistillery.htm
TOMATIN DISTILLERY
www.tomatin.com
TOMINTOUL SPEYSIDE DISTILLERY
www.tomintouldistillery.co.uk
TULLAMORE DEW HERITAGE CENTRE
www.tullamore-dew.org
TULLIBARDINE DISTILLERY
www.tullibardine.com

VINTAGE MALT WHISKY COMPANY
www.vintagemaltwhisky.com
WEE DRAM
www.weedram.co.uk
WELSH WHISKY COMPANY
www.welsh-whisky.co.uk
WEMYSS VINTAGE MALTS LTD
www.v-v-m.com/wvm/Home.html
WHISKY EXCHANGE
www.thewhiskyexchange.com
THE WHISKY FAIR
www.festival.whiskyfair.com
WHYTE & MACKAY LIMITED
www.whyteandmackay.co.uk
WILD SCOTSMAN WHISKY AND SPIRITS
LIMITED
www.wildscotsman.com
WILD TURKEY DISTILLERY
www.wildturkeybourbon.com
WILLIAM CADENHEAD LTD
www.wmcadenhead.com
WILLIAM GRANT & SONS
www.williamgrant.com
WILSON & MORGAN
www.wilsonandmorgan.com
THE WINE SHOP
www.wineandwhisky.com
YAMAZAKI DISTILLERY
www.suntory.com
YOICHI DISTILLERY
www.nikka.com

## RETAILERS

### A selection of the world's leading whisky retailers

**ANDORRA**
CAVA BENITO | *Escaldes-Engordany*
www.cavabenitowhisky.com

**AUSTRIA**
POT STILL | *Vienna*
www.potstill.org
WEINTURM LINZ | *4040 Linz*
www.winturm.at

**BELGIUM**
WHISKY HOUSE | *Essene*
www.thewhiskyhouse.com
CORMAN-COLLINS | *Battice*
www.corman-collins.be
WHISKYCORNER | *Houthalen*
www.whiskycorner.be

**CANADA**
ALBERTA GAMING AND LIQUOR
COMMISSION | *St. Albert*
www.aglc.gov.ab.ca
BRITISH COLUMBIA LIQUOR
DISTRIBUTION BRANCH | *Vancouver*
www.bcliquorstores.com
HIGHLANDER WINE & SPIRITS | *Calgary*
www.highlanderwine.com
LIQUOR CONTROL BOARD OF ONTARIO
*Toronto*
www.lcbo.ca
MANITOBA LIQUOR CONTROL
COMMISSION | *Winnipeg*
www.mlcc.mb.ca
NEW BRUNSWICK LIQUOR
CORPORATION (NBLC) | *Fredericton*
www.nbliquor.com
NEWFOUNDLAND LIQUOR
CORPORATION | *St. John`s*
www.nlc.nfld.com
NOVA SCOTIA LIQUOR CORPORATION
(NSLC) | *Halifax*
www.nsliquor.ns.ca
PEI LIQUOR CONTROL COMMISSION
*Charlottetown*
www.peilcc.ca
SASKATCHEWAN LIQUOR AND
GAMING AUTHORITY | *Regina*
www.gov.sk.ca/govt/lga/

SOCIÉTÉ DES ALCOOLS DU QUÉBEC
*Montréal*
www.saq.com
WILLOW PARK LIQUOR | *Calgary*
www.willowpark.net
YUKON LIQUOR CORPORATION
*Whitehorse*
www.ylc.yk.ca

**CZECH REPUBLIC**
KRATOCHVÍLOVCI SPOL | *Prague*
www.kratochvilovci.cz

**DENMARK**
CADENHEAD'S WHISKY & LIFESTYLE
*Odense*
www.whiskyandlifestyle.com
ERIC SORENSENS WINE SHOP | *Kokkedal*
www.es-vin.dk
JUUL'S VIN & SPIRITUS | *Copenhagen*
www.juuls.dk
MAC Y AS | *Karup J*
www.macy.dk
SINGLEMALT-SHOP.DK | *København*
www.singlemalt-shop.dk

**ENGLAND**
ARKWRIGHTS | *Highworth*
www.whiskyandwines.com
BERRY BROS. & RUDD | *London*
www.bbr.com
CADENHEAD'S COVENT GARDEN
WHISKY SHOP | *London*
www.coventgardenwhiskyshop.co.uk
CLANARK TARTAN WHISKY
*Stockton-on-Tees*
www.clanarkwhisky.co.uk
JEROBOAMS GROUP | *London*
www.jeroboams.co.uk
JUST MINIATURES LTD | *Hadleigh*
www.justminiatures.co.uk
JUSTERINI & BROOKS | *London*
www.justerinis.com
LA ZOUCH CELLARS
*Ashby-de-la-Zouch*
www.lazouch.co.uk
LINCOLN WHISKY SHOP | *Lincoln*
www.lincolnwhiskyshop.co.uk

MAINLY MALTS | *Doncaster*
www.whisky-malts-shop.com
MILROY'S OF SOHO | *London*
www.milroys.co.uk
NICKOLLS AND PERKS | *Birmingham*
www.nickollsandperks.co.uk
ODDBINS | *London*
www.oddbins.com
ROYAL MILE WHISKIES | *London*
www.royalmilewhiskies.com
S.H. JONES | *Banbury*
www.shjones.com
TANNERS OF SHREWSBURY
*Shrewsbury*
www.tanners-wines.co.uk
THE DRAM ROOM | *Newbury*
www.thedramroom.co.uk
THE DRAM SHOP | *Sheffield*
No web site available
THE WEE DRAM | *Bakewell*
www.weedram.co.uk
THE WINE SHOP | *Leek*
www.wineandwhisky.com
VINOLOGY WINE & SPIRIT MERCHANTS
*Stratford-upon-Avon*
www.vinology.co.uk
VINTAGE HOUSE | *London*
www.vintagehouse.co.uk
WHISKY EXCHANGE | *London*
www.thewhiskyexchange.com
WHISKY-ONLINE.COM | *Blackpool*
www.whisky-online.com
WINDERMERE WINES STORES
*Windermere*
www.maltlounge.co.uk
WINE LODGE | *York*
www.whiskys.co.uk
WORCESTER WINE COMPANY | *Worcester*
www.worcesterwineco.com
WORLD DUTY FREE EUROPE | *Egham*
www.worlddutyfree.com
WRIGHT WINE & WHISKY COMPANY
*Skipton*
www.wineandwhisky.co.uk

**FRANCE**
LA MAISON DU WHISKY | *Paris*
www.whisky.fr

LA MAISON DU WHISKY | *La Reunion*
www.whisky.fr
WHISKY LODGE | *Lyon*
No web site available

**GERMANY**
CADENHEAD'S WHISKY MARKET
*Cologne*
www.cadenhead.de
CADENHEAD'S WHISKY MARKET | *Berlin*
www.cadenhead-berlin.de
CELTIC WHISKY | *Nuernberg*
www.celticwhisky.de/www.whisky.de
DUDELSACK | *Aschaffenburg*
www.dudelsack.com
FINLAYS WHISKY SHOP | *Wehrheim*
www.finlayswhiskyshop.de
GETRAENKEWELT-WEISER | *Heppenheim*
www.thewhiskytrader.de
GRADLS WHISKYFAESSLA | *Nurnberg*
http://web.whiskyfaessla.de
GRANDWHISKY | *Muhlheim*
www.grandwhisky.de
HOUSE OF WHISKY | *Obernkirchen*
www.houseofwhisky.de
KRUGERS WHISKY GALERIE | *Rendsburg*
www.whiskyauction.com
LIQUIDS | *Kerpen-Bruggen*
www.liquids-and-more.de
MACHA WEINE & FEINES | *Heidelberg*
www.macha-weine.de
MALTS AND MORE | *Wedel*
www.maltsandmore.de
MARA MALT RARITIES | *Limburg*
www.maltwhisky-mara.de
SCOMA | *Jever*
www.scoma.de
TAIBER SPIRITUOSENGROSSHANDEL
*Pentling*
www.spirituosen-superbillig.de
WEIN AND WHISKY | *Berlin*
www.world-wide-whisky.de
WEINKELLEREI KLEEFISCH | *Cologne*
www.weinkellerei-kleefisch.de
WEINQUELLE LUHMANN | *Hamburg*
www.weinquelle.com
WHISKY & CIGARS | *Berlin-Mitte*
www.whisky-cigars.de

WHISKY DEPOT | Hamburg
www.whiskydepot.com
WHISKY EMPORIUM | Markt Schwaben
www.whisky-emporium.com
WHISKY RARITAETEN | Wallrabenstein
www.whiskyraritaeten-langer.de
WHISKY SHOP TARA | Munich
www.whiskyversand.de
WHISKY SPIRITS | Frankfurt
www.whiskyspirits.de
WHISKY STORE | Seeshaupt
www.thewhiskystore.de
WHISKY WAGNER | Hohentengen
www.whisky-wagner.de
WHISKY-CORNER | Illschwang
www.whisky-corner.de
WHISKYMAX-GROSSHANDEL
Aschaffenburg
www.whiskymax.com
WHISKYSCHEUNE | Usingen
www.whiskyscheune.de
WHISKY-VERSANDHANDEL | Stuttgart
www.whisky-versandhandel.de
WHISKIWIZARD.DE | Neunkirchen
www.whiskywizard.de
WHISKYWORLD E.K
Grafenau/Haus im Wald
www.whiskyworld.de
WHISKYLADEN.DE | Witten
www.whiskyladen.de

## GREECE
VINTAGE WHISKY SHOP | Thessaloniki
No web site available

## IRELAND
MITCHELL & SON WINE MERCHANTS
Dublin
www.mitchellandson.com

## ISLE OF MAN
WHISKY SHACK | Ramsey
www.whiskyshack.com

## ITALY
BAR METRO | Milano
www.collectorsencyclopedia.com
KIK BAR "THE WHISKY HOUSE"
Bologna
www.thewhiskyhouse.it
OLD WHISKY DI SERAFINI ANNAMARIA
Piacenza
www.oldwhisky.net
WHISKY PARADISE | Bologna
www.whiskyparadise.com

## JAPAN
ASUKA MEISHU HANBAI | Kumamoto
www.asuka-meisyu.com
BIG TSUKIJI | Tokyo
www.bigtsukiji.com
KAGAYA | Tokyo
www.kagaya-smokeweb.com
KAMEYA-YAZAKI SHOTEN | Tokyo
www.kameya.jp
KOROSUE SHOTEN | Hyogo
www.korosue.com
LA MAISON DU WHISKY JAPON
Yokohama
www.rakuten.co.jp/whisky-jp
LIBERTY | Shizuoka
No web site available
LIQOURS & TOBACCO SHOP MOMOYA
Sapporo
www.susukino.gr.jp/others/momoya
LIQUOR SHOP TSUZAKI | Oita
www.bottles.jp
LIQUOR VILLA AIZAWA | Tokyo
www.aizawa-web.com
LIQUORS HASEGAWA | Tokyo
www.liquors-hasegawa.com
MAC CORPORATION | Saitama
www.yamaichi-mac.com

MEJIRO TANAKAYA | Tokyo
No web site available
MILLECOTE | Osaka
www.bonili.com
MISAWAYA SHOTEN | Niigata
www9.ocn.ne.jp
MITSUKURA PRICE CLUB | Hyogo
www.price-club.co.jp
MIYUKIYA | Yamanashi
www.miyukiya.com
MURAKOSHI SAKETEN | Tokyo
No web site available
NEMOTO SAKETEN | Gunma
No web site available
NERO DAIKOKUYA | Aichi-ken
www.rakuten.co.jp/nero
OSAKE NO OGATA SENMON TEN
KAWACHIYA - KASAI | Tokyo
www.rakuten.co.jp/kawachi
SAKE MAX | Oita
www.sake-max.com
SAKE SHOP SATO | Osaka
www.sakeshop-sato.com
SAKE YOSHIDA | Aichi-ken
www.yoshidaya.co.jp
SAMWOOD CO.LTD | Osaka
www.samwood.co.jp
SEIJOISHII CO.LTD | Tokyo
www.seijoishii.co.jp
SHINANOYA SHOKUHIN | Tokyo
www.rakuten.co.jp/shinanoya
WINE GARALLY HIROSE | Wakayama-shi
www.wine-hirose.ne.jp
WORLD LIQUOR BRUTUS | Osaka
www.sake-brutus.com
YAMATAKE SAKETEN | Saitama
www.e-yoshinoya.co.jp
YAMAZAKI SAKETEN | Tokyo
http://homepage2.nifty.com/ysake/

## NETHERLANDS
CADENHEAD'S SPECIALIST WHISKIES
Amsterdam
www.cadenhead.nl
VAN WEES WHISKY WORLD | Amersfoot
www.whiskyworld.nl
WHISKY-EN WUNHANDEL VERHAAR
Bilthoven
www.whiskyshop.nl
WHISKYSLITERIJ DE KONING
Hertogenbosch
www.whiskykoning.nl
WUNHANDEL VAN ZUYLEN | Den Haag
www.whiskyvanzuylen.nl
WUNWINKEL-SLIJTERIJ | Amsterdam
www.tonovermars.nl

## NEW ZEALAND
MALTS OF DISTINCTION | Remuera
www.malts-of-distinction.co.nz
THE WHISKY GALORE SHOP
Christchurch
www.whiskygalore.co.nz

## NORTHERN IRELAND
CLASSICWHISKEY.COM | Greyabbey
www.classicwhiskey.com

## PORTUGAL
WHISKY & CO. | Lisbon
No web site available

## REPUBLIC OF IRELAND
CELTIC WHISKEY SHOP | Dublin
www.celticwhiskeyshop.com

## RUSSIA
THE COLLECTION OF WINES | Moscow
www.vine.ru
UNITED LUXURY SPIRITS | Moscow
www.unitedluxury.ru
VELD 21 | Moscow
www.veld21.ru

## SCOTLAND
ANGELS' SHARE WHISKY | Stirling
www.angelsshare-whisky.com
CADENHEAD'S CAMPBELTOWN
WHISKY SHOP
Campbelltown
http://argyll.wmcadenhead.com
CADENHEAD'S WHISKY SHOP
Edinburgh
http://edinburgh.wmcadenhead.com
DRINKON.COM | St Andrews
www.drinkon.com
GLOBAL WHISKY SHOP.COM LTD
Glasgow
www.globalwhiskyshop.com
GORDON & MACPHAIL | Elgin
www.gordonandmacphail.com
GREEN WELLY STOP | Crianlarich
www.thegreenwellystop.co.uk
J. A. MACKAY | Thurso
www.getwhisky.com
JOHN SCOTT & MILLER LTD | Kirkwall
www.jsmorkney.co.uk
LOCH FYNE WHISKIES | Inveraray
www.lfw.co.uk
LUVIANS BOTTLE SHOP | Cupar
www.luvians.com
LUVIANS BOTTLE SHOP | St Andrews
www.luvians.com
MALTWHISKYONLINE.COM | Peterhead
www.maltwhiskyonline.com
PARKERS WHISKY | Banff
www.parkerswhisky.co.uk
ROBBIE'S DRAMS | Ayr
www.robbiesdrams.co.uk
ROBERT GRAHAM LTD | Edinburgh
www.whisky-cigars.com
ROBERTSON'S OF PITLOCHRY | Pitlochry
No web site available
ROYAL MILE WHISKIES | Edinburgh
www.royalmilewhiskies.com
S.R & E. BARRON (DYCE) LTD | Aberdeen
www.maltman.co.uk
SINGLE MALTS DIRECT | Aberdeen
www.singlemaltsdirect.com
SPECIAL SCOTCH WHISKY | Edinburgh
www.specialscotchwhisky.co.uk
TB WATSON | Dumfries
www.tbwatson.co.uk
THE ISLAY WHISKY SHOP | Bowmore
www.islaywhiskyshop.com
THE WHISKY CONNOISSEUR | Biggar
www.whiskyconnoisseur.co.uk
THE WHISKY SHOP / GLENKEIR
Glasgow
www.whiskyshop.com
VILLENEUVE WINES | Peebles
www.villeneuvewines.com
WEESPEYDRAM | Grantown-on-Spey
www.weespeydram.co.uk
WHISKIES OF SCOTLAND | Huntly
www.dtcscotch.com
WHISKY CASTLE | Tomintoul
www.whiskycastle.com
WHISKY NET | Elgin
www.whiskynet.co.uk
WHISKY SHOP OF DUFFTOWN
Dufftown
www.whiskyshopdufftown.co.uk

## SINGAPORE
LA MAISON DU WHISKY PTE LTD
Singapore
www.whisky.sg

## SOUTH AFRICA
NORMAN GOODFELLOWS
Johannseburg
www.normangoodfellows.co.za
PICARDI REBEL | Cape Town
www.picardirebel.co.za
SPAR SA LTD | Pinetown
www.spar.co.za

## SPAIN
WKYREGAL S.L. | Barcelona
No web site available

## SWITZERLAND
ANGELS SHARE SHOP | Zürich
www.scotandscotch.ch
EDDIE'S WHISKIES | Horgen
www.eddies.ch
GLEN FAHRN GMBH | Morschwil
www.glenfahrn.com
MONNIER | Studen
www.whiskytime.ch
SCOT & SCOTCH | CH-8001 Zürich
www.scotandscotch.ch
VINOTHEK AND MALT-WHISKY
SHOP OF CHUR
Chur
www.malt-whisky.ch

## USA
BELTRAMO'S FINE WINE & SPIRITS
Menlo Park
www.beltramos.com
BEVERAGES AND MORE | Concord
www.bevmo.com
BINNY'S BEVERAGE DEPOT | Chicago
www.binnys.com
CENTRAL LIQUORS | Washington DC
www.centralliquors.com
D & M WINES & LIQUORS
San Francisco
www.dandm.com
FEDERAL WINE AND SPIRITS | Boston
www.federalwine.com
GARNET WINES & LIQUORS INC.
New York
www.garnetwine.com
GRAPE VINE MARKET | Austin
www.grapevinemarket.com
JOHN WALKER & CO. | San Francisco
www.johnwalker.com
KENWIN LIQUOR STORE | Snyder
No web site available
LENELL'S LTD | New York
www.lenells.com
LOVESCOTCH.COM | Los Angeles
www.lovescotch.com
MORRELL | New York
www.morrellwine.com
PARK AVENUE LIQUOR SHOP | New York
www.parkaveliquor.com
PEARSON'S WINE | Atlanta
www.pearsonswine.net
PEARSON'S WINE & LIQUOR
Washington
www.pearsonswine.com
SAM'S WINE & SPIRITS | Chicago
www.samswine.com
SHERRY-LEHMANN | New York
www.sherry-lehmann.com
SHOPPERS VINEYARD | Clifton
www.shoppersvineyard.com
SIGEL'S LIQUORS | Dallas
www.sigels.com
SOUTH EGREMONT SPIRIT SHOPPE
South Egremont
www.spiritshoppe.com
SPEC'S LIQUOR WAREHOUSE | Houston
www.specsonline.com
SPORTSMAN'S FINE WINES AND SPIRITS
Phoenix
www.spiritshoppe.com
TODDY'S LIQUORS | Bardstown
No web site available
TOWN WINE & SPIRITS | East Providence
www.townwineandspirits.com
WALLY'S WINE SHOP | Los Angeles
www.wallywine.com
WINE & LIQUOR DEPOT | Van Cuys
www.wineandliquordepot.com
WINE SPECIALIST | Washington
www.winespecialist.com